Promoting polyarchy examines the apparent change in US foreign policy from supporting dictatorships to an "open" promotion of "democratic" regimes. William I. Robinson argues that behind the facade of "democracy promotion," the policy has been designed more to retain the elite-based and undemocratic *status quo* of Third World countries than to encourage mass aspirations for democratization. Contrary to received opinion, he shows how poverty amidst plenty and global social apartheid characterize the new world order. While US policy is more ideologically appealing under the title of "democracy promotion," it does nothing to reverse the growth of inequality and the undemocratic nature of global decision-making. This challenging argument is supported by a wealth of information garnered from field-work and hitherto unpublished government documents, and assembled in case studies of the Philippines, Chile, Nicaragua, Haiti, South Africa, and the former Soviet bloc. With its combination of theoretical and historical analysis, empirical argument, and bold claims, *Promoting polyarchy* is an essential book for anyone concerned with democracy, globalization, and international affairs.

CAMBRIDGE STUDIES IN INTERNATIONAL RELATIONS: 48

Promoting polyarchy

Cambridge Studies in International Relations is a joint initiative of Cambridge University Press and the British International Studies Association (BISA). The series will include a wide range of material, from undergraduate textbooks and surveys to research-based monographs and collaborative volumes. The aim of the series is to publish the best new scholarship in International Studies from Europe, North America, and the rest of the world.

CAMBRIDGE STUDIES IN INTERNATIONAL RELATIONS

Series list continues after index

Promoting polyarchy
Globalization, US intervention, and hegemony

William I. Robinson

The University of Tennessee

CAMBRIDGE
UNIVERSITY PRESS

Published by the Press Syndicate of the University of Cambridge
The Pitt Building, Trumpington Street, Cambridge CB2 1RP
40 West 20th Street, New York, NY 10011–4211, USA
10 Stamford Road, Oakleigh, Melbourne 3166, Australia

First published 1996

Printed in Great Britain at the University Press, Cambridge

A catalogue record for this book is available from the British Library

Library of Congress cataloguing in publication data
Robinson, William I.
Promoting polyarchy: Globalization, US intervention, and hegemony
/ William I. Robinson.
        p.   cm. – (Cambridge Studies in International Relations: 48)
Includes bibliographical references and index.
ISBN 0 521 56203 1 (hc) – ISBN 0 521 56691 6 (pb)
1. United States – Foreign relations – 1981–1989.
2. United States – Foreign relations – 1989–
3. Democracy – History – 20th century.
4. Democracy – United States – History – 20th century.
5. World politics –1985–1995.
I. Title.   II. Series.
E876.R63   1996
327.73 – dc20   95–52083   CIP

ISBN 0 521 56203 1 hardback
ISBN 0 521 56691 6 paperback

CE

Truth is always revolutionary
Antonio Gramsci

To Amaru and Tamara:
question *everything*,
seek out the truth,
and *live* that truth.

Contents

Acknowledgments

Intellectual production as a form of social action is a collective process. No book is authored by a single individual, no matter whose name appears on a cover. It is impossible here to list all those people who contributed in a myraid of ways, ranging from critical commentary, intellectual insights and scholarly interest, to editorial assistance, material support, interest, personal encouragement, and time invested in mundane tasks, to making this book possible.

The first order of thanks is to those who have contributed to my own intellectual, professional, political, and personal development over the years. A full list of such people would comprise a book in itself, but several stand out. One is my lifelong friend, colleague, and intellectual comrade, Kent Norsworthy, who has selflessly contributed to the present work in every imaginable way, starting with our collective political-intellectual awakening many years ago, and involving the most solid friendship a person could provide through good and difficult times, including through a dream deferred – for the two of us and millions more – in one little corner of this world. Another is Kevin Robinson, whose encouragement in the most difficult moments of the present work helped see me to its completion. Apart from their enthusiasm and other forms of support for this project, both provided invaluable, chapter-by-chapter editorial and content suggestions. A third is Felipe Gonzales, former professor and now friend and colleague, who provided editorial recommendations, encouragement, and other magnanimous assistance in critical moments. Many thanks also to William Stanley for his critical feedback on much of the manuscript, and for many a stimulating intellectual exchange, on the present study and related matters.

The Interhemispheric Resource Center, a private non-profit research and policy institute located in Albuquerque, New Mexico – and in particular, Tom Barry and Beth Sims – made available to me for research purposes the extensive archive it has accumulated as part of its ongoing "US Government Democratization Programs and Other Democratization Issues" project. I have made use of several dozen documents obtained by the Center (referred to subsequently in this volume as The Resource Center) through periodic Freedom of Information Act (FOIA) requests it files with the National Endowment for Democracy and other agencies. How I have chosen to make use of these documents is my sole responsibility and this study does not reflect in any way the work or positions of The Resource Center. Robert Sandels and Robert Fiala gave critical comments on several journal articles dealing with the themes of this book that later gave me some important insights and correctives for the manuscript. Thanks also to Nelson Valdes, David Dye, Wilmar Cuarezma, Worth Cooley-Prost, and Martin Vega, and to Alejandro Bendaña of the Center for International Studies (CEI) of the Central American University in Managua, for varied contributions. Craig Murphy showed a much appreciated interest in my work, and provided encouragement and crucial editorial suggestions in the final phases of the manuscript. His work, involving a research agenda closely related to my own, has been a source of intellectual inspiration, as have been the works of other scholars from the "Italian School" in international relations, and from the cutting edge of development, comparative, and globalization studies in sociology, whom I have not yet had the opportunity to meet or correspond with but whose imprint should be unmistakable in the text. Thanks are also in order to anonymous Cambridge University Press readers. Finally, I am also grateful to the Press's amicable social science commissioning editor, John Haslam, for his professional concern and attentiveness for the manuscript, as well as his patience with the whims of at least one fussy author, and with whom it has been a pleasure to work. And an apology to those I might have unintentionally forgotten to acknowledge. The content of this book, and all the inevitable shortcomings therein, are my sole responsibility.

There is a final and very special acknowledgment, to Gioconda, my *compañera de lucha*, and to my children, Amaru and Tamara, to whom this book is dedicated. As tender young representatives of a new generation, they symbolize my hope and faith in humanity, no matter how grim our plight may seem to me in these trying times.

Acronyms and abbreviations

AAFLI	Asian-American Free Labor Institute (US)
AALC	African American Labor Council (US)
AD	Democratic Alliance of Chile
ADF	America's Development Foundation (US)
AFL-CIO	American Federation of Labor-Congress of Industrial Organizations (US)
AFP	Armed Forces of the Philippines
AID	Agency for International Development (US)
AIFLD	American Institute for Free Labor Development (US)
ANC	African National Congress (South Africa)
APF	American Political Foundation (US)
APN	National Popular Assembly (Haiti)
ASEAN	Association of Southeast Asian Nations
AVEC	Neighborhood and Community Action (Chile)
BAYAN	New Patriotic Federation (Philippines)
CAD	Corporation for Community Action (Chile)
CAD	Center For Democratic Consultation (Nicaragua)
CATH	Autonomous Federation of Haitian Workers
CBI	Caribbean Basin Initiative
CDJ	Center for Youth Development (Chile)
CDRH	Human Resources Development Center (Haiti)
CDT	Democratic Workers Federation (Chile)
CEFOJ	Center for Youth Development (Nicaragua)
CEL	Committee for Free Elections (Chile)
CEP	Center for Public Studies (Chile)
CFD	Center for Democracy (US)
CGT	General Federation of Workers (Haiti)
CHADEL	Haitian Center for Human Rights

CIA	Central Intelligence Agency (US)
CINCO	Central American Research and Information Center
CIPE	Center for International Private Enterprise (US)
CLED	Center for Free Enterprise and Democracy (Haiti)
CNT	National Workers Command (Chile)
CODESA	Convention for a Democratic South Africa
COSEP	Superior Council of Private Enterprise (Nicaragua)
CPT	Permanent Congress of Workers (Nicaragua)
CSIS	Center for Strategic and International Studies (US)
CUT	Unified Workers Federation (Chile)
CUT	United Workers Central (Chile)
DIA	Defense Intelligence Agency (US)
DPI	Democratic Pluralism Initiative (US)
FAO	Broad Opposition Front (Nicaragua)
FBIS	Foreign Broadcast Information Service (US)
FNDC	National Front for Democracy and Change (Haiti)
FOIA	Freedom of Information Act (US)
FOS	Federation of Unionized Workers (Haiti)
FRAP	Popular Action Front (Chile)
FRAPH	Front for the Advancement and Progress of Haiti
FSLN	Sandinista National Liberation Front (Nicaragua)
FTUI	Free Trade Union Institute (US)
GABRIELA	Assembly Binding Women for Reforms, Integrity, Equality, Leadership, and Action (Philippines)
GAO	General Accounting Office (US)
ICFTU	International Confederation of Free Trade Unions
IDASA	Institute for a Democratic Alternative in South Africa
IDB	Interamerican Development Bank
IFES	International Foundation for Electoral Assistance (US)
IHRED	Haitian Institute for Research and Development
ILO	International Labor Organization
IM	International Monetary Fund
INSI	Institute for North South Issues (US)
IPCE	Institute for Electoral Promotion and Training (Nicaragua)
IRG	Inter-Regional Deputies Group (Soviet Union)
IRI	International Republican Institute (US – same as NRI)
ISTRA	Institute for the Transition (Chile)
IU	United Left (Chile)

KABATID	Women's Movement for the Nurturing of Democracy (Philippines)
KMU	May First Movement (Philippines)
KONAKOM	National Congress of Democratic Movements (Haiti)
MAPU	Movement of United Popular Action (Chile)
MDP	Popular Democratic Movement (Chile)
MIDH	Movement to Install Democracy in Haiti
MMN	Nicaraguan Women's Movement
MPP	Papaye Peasant Movement (Haiti)
NAFP	New Armed Forces of the Philippines
NAMFREL	National Movement for Free Elections (Philippines)
NCFO	National Congress of Farmers Organizations (Philippines)
NDF	National Democratic Front (Philippines)
NDI	National Democratic Institute for International Affairs (US)
NED	National Endowment for Democracy (US)
NGO	non-governmental organization
NIEO	New International Economic Order
NPA	New People's Army (Philippines)
NRI	National Republican Institute for International Affairs (US)
NRIIA	*See* NRI
NSC	National Security Council (US)
NSDD	National Security Decision Directive
OAS	Organization of American States
ODI	Office of Democratic Initiatives (US)
OECD	Organization for Economic Cooperation and Development
OFITH	Independent General Organization of Haitian Workers
OPD	Office of Public Diplomacy (US)
PARTICIPA	Crusade for Citizen Participation (Chile)
PCCI	Philippine Chamber of Commerce and Industry
PDC	Christian Democratic Party (Chile)
PIRED	Integral Project for the Reinforcement of Democracy in Haiti
PPD	Pro-Democracy Party (Chile)
PSYOPS	psychological operations
PVO	private voluntary organization
SIN	National Intelligence Service (Haiti)

STR	scientific and technological revolution
TUCP	Trade Union Congress of the Philippines
UDF	United Democratic Front (South Africa)
UDI	Independent Democratic Union (Chile)
UDT	Democratic Workers Union (Chile)
UN	United Nations
UNO	Nicaraguan Opposition Union
UP	Popular Unity (Chile)
USAID	*See* AID
USIA	United States Information Agency
WSF	Worker–Student Forum (Philippines)
YOU	Young Officers Union (Philippines)

Introduction
From East–West to North–South: US intervention in the "new world order"

> In any society the dominant groups are the ones with the most to hide about the way society works. Very often therefore truthful analyses are bound to have a critical ring, to seem like exposures rather than objective statements... For all students of human society sympathy with the victims of historical processes and skepticism about the victors' claims provide essential safeguards against being taken in by the dominant mythology. A scholar who tries to be objective needs these feelings as part of his working equipment.
>
> Barrington Moore[1]

"We have 50 percent of the world's wealth, but only 6.3 percent of its population... In this situation we cannot fail to be the object of envy and resentment," noted George Kennan in 1948. "Our real task in the coming period is to devise a pattern of relationships which will allow us to maintain this position of disparity," said the then Director of Policy Planning of the Department of State. "We should cease to talk about the raising of the living standards, human rights, and democratization. The day is not far off when we are going to have to deal in straight power concepts. The less we are then hampered by idealistic slogans, the better."[2]

Kennan's candid statement emphasizes that the strategic objective of US foreign policy during the Cold War was less battling a "communist menace" than defending the tremendous privilege and power this global disparity of wealth brought it as the dominant world power, and suggests that democracy abroad was not a major consideration for the United States in the formative years of the post-World War II order.

In contrast, four decades later, Carl Gershman, the president of the National Endowment for Democracy (NED), a new US foreign policy

1

agency created in 1983, admonished: "In a world of advanced communication and exploding knowledge, it is no longer possible to rely solely on force to promote stability and defend the national security. Persuasion is increasingly important, and the United States must enhance its capacity to persuade by developing techniques for reaching people at many different levels." Gershman went on to stress that "democracy" abroad, should be a major consideration for the United States, in its effort to "enhance its capacity to persuade" around the world.[3]

The East–West prism in which Kennan and his generation had cast the North–South divide evaporated with the end of the Cold War. Yet, as Gershman's statement suggests, the fundamental objective of defense of privilege in an unjust international system did not change with the collapse of the Soviet system. What *has* changed are the strategies for securing this objective. What I term the "new political intervention," and the ideological dimensions it entails, has been developed as an effective instrument of "persuasion," in contrast to (or more often, alongside) force, to assure "patterns of relationships" that protect US interests.

The shift from "straight power concepts" to "persuasion" has been predicated on a new component in US foreign policy: what policy-makers call the "promotion of democracy." The end of the Cold War has opened up new possibilities. Mass movements striving for democratization and social change have proliferated at this time of momentous political changes, accompanying disruption, restructuring and even the complete collapse of national and regional economies. From Nicaragua to the Philippines, from Haiti to Eastern Europe, Southern Africa, and the Middle East, diverse forces battle to reshape political and economic structures as a "new world order" emerges. Under the rubric of "promoting democracy," the United States has intervened in the crises, transitions and power vacuums resulting from the breakup of the old order to try to gain influence over their outcome. These interventions are those newfound "techniques for reaching people at many different levels" to which Gershman refers.

Origins and scope of this study

This book analyzes "democracy promotion" in relation to hegemony and the intersection of politics and economics in the emergent global society and twenty-first-century world order.[4] It grew out of an earlier

2

study of the massive, largely covert US program of intervention in the 1990 Nicaraguan elections.[5] Several years of investigative research convinced me that what had taken place in Nicaragua was a blueprint of worldwide patterns and much broader changes in US foreign policy. Over the course of the investigation, I turned from the empirical evidence to theorization, weaving together several bodies of literature – among them, studies in foreign policy and democratization literature (mostly from political science), the sociology of development (particularly, world-system/dependency and modernization schools), and the multidisciplinary field of international relations – and some central concerns of political sociology, among them, the state, social class, power, and ideology. The disciplinary tool which underlies and connects these disparate strands is the application of political economy to sociological phenomena, and the meta-theoretical framework, historical materialism, which remains, in my view, the most fundamental instrument of social science research, unsurpassed in its explanatory and predictive powers, in its ability to generate "conceptual leaps" and to recombine elements of the social universe into a dialectic, holistic, and coherent picture.

We are living in a time of transition from one major epoch to another; we stand at a great historic crossroad, the fourth in modern world history. The first epoch opened in 1492, when the "modern world system" was born, along with the division of the globe into haves and have nots. What was "discovered" in that year was not the Americas, but universal human history and the world as one totality. The second was ushered in with the great bourgeois revolutions of the eighteenth century. The third began with the Soviet revolution of 1917, which triggered a set of global tensions that dominated much of the twentieth century. What was defeated with the collapse of the Soviet system was not socialism as an ideal-type of society, or as a human aspiration, but one particular model and the first experiment. We are now at the threshold of a new era. A transition implies that things are changing fundamentally. Yet the direction of that change, as well as the outcome of the transition, is still in dispute. And it is certainly not "the end of history." The end of the twentieth and the beginning of the twenty-first century is a particularly strategic moment for humankind; the profound changes now underway, and the correlation of forces that emerges in this period, will determine the contours of the emergent twenty-first-century global society.

There are two interrelated, defining features of our epoch: the shift in

3

the locus of world tensions from East–West to North–South, and the emergence of a truly global economy. The emergence of a global economy brings with it the material basis for the emergence of a single global society, including the transnationalization of civil society and of political processes. The old units of analysis – nation-states – are increasingly inappropriate for understanding the dynamics of our epoch, not only in terms of economic processes, but also social relations and political systems. Much has been written on the global economy, yet research into the transnationalization of political processes and of civil society has lagged behind. Among several notable exceptions are the pathbreaking works of Robert Cox, Stephen Gill and other scholars who have begun to develop a Gramscian model for analyzing international relations in the age of globalization, and whose contributions I have drawn from and build on in this study.

Within this framework, this study has a dual purpose. The first is to analyze and explain a specific phenomenon – "democracy promotion" in US foreign policy. The second is to show how this phenomenon is linked to the process of globalization and to explore crucial political dimensions of globalization. I see "democracy promotion" as inextricably linked to globalization. "Democracy promotion" in US foreign policy can only be understood as part of a broader process of the exercise of hegemony within and between countries in the context of transnationalization. Polyarchy, or what I alternatively refer to as "low-intensity democracy," is a structural feature of the new world order: it is a global political system corresponding to a global economy under the hegemony of a transnational elite which is the agent of transnational capital. My objective is to document the specific phenomenon of "democracy promotion" as a US policy change that emerged in the 1980s, and to give that change a novel theoretical explanation.

US policymakers have characterized "democracy promotion" as the new "cornerstone" in foreign policy. As such, this policy merits serious analytical and theoretical attention by scholars. However, the existing literature is remarkably inadequate. There is a huge (and still growing) body of literature on democratization in the Third World, but the focus here is on endogenous political processes, not US interaction with those processes. Most of the literature that does exist on the US policy of "democracy promotion" has come from the policymaking community.[6] A handful of academic volumes have reviewed dimensions of "democracy promotion" with little, if any, *theorization* on the nature of the shift in policy or the actual policy practice. This literature finds its

4

implicit theoretical grounding in structural-functionalist models of pluralism.[7] Much of this literature is value-laden, and steeped in implicit assumptions. Whether any social science is value-free (I tend to think not) is open to debate. It is the implicit assumptions that are unacceptable, and which I attempt to uncover.

Most explanations attribute this new policy to the evolution of normative or of practical-conjunctural considerations among policy-makers: US policymakers have gone through a "learning process" in selecting the most appropriate policies; with the collapse of the old Soviet bloc, the United States can now afford to implement its policies with "softer tools"; the "ideal" of liberal capitalism has reached its apogee (this argument finds its ultimate expression in Fukuyama's Hegelian "end of history"), and so on.[8] While these behavioralist arguments merit attention, none of them link, through theoretical discourse, the practical-conjunctural considerations on the part of policymakers to broader historical processes, social structure, or political economy, which inform foreign policy. Events and outcomes in the social universe cannot be explained by the intentions of individual actors or decisions taken on the basis of role perception. Policymakers are not independent actors. As I discuss in chapter 1, US foreign policy is not explained by specific policy views of individuals, much less by policy pronouncements by political leaders taken at face value. Besides, US foreign policy is not to be analyzed on the basis of what policymakers *say* they do, but on what they actually *do*.

Ultimately, to analyze or theorize US foreign policy on the basis of practical-conjunctural considerations weighed by policymakers is to assume that social behavior flows from pre-given subjectivities. To be sure, analysis of what takes place internal to the immediate policy-making community within a state apparatus is important, and I operate at that level of analysis throughout much of this study. However, just as individual existence is grounded in sets of social relations and material conditions, and these in turn drive political life, so too, foreign policy flows from the historical and the structural conditions under which individual policymakers and governments operate. The whole point of theory, of social science, is to uncover the forces and processes at work in the social universe which lie beneath – indeed, epistemologically speaking, out of the range of – sensory perceptions. This is the starting point of analysis and of theorization on "democracy promotion" in US foreign policy. Behavioral changes transpire within structural contexts which shape behavioral responses.

5

Behavioral analysis is therefore structurally contingent and must be grounded in structural analysis. Below I expound on how these different levels of analysis are applied and on the methodological framework through which my alternative argument is developed. First, however, let me summarize that argument.

Summary of the argument

All over the world, the United States is now promoting its version of "democracy" as a way to relieve pressure from subordinate groups for more fundamental political, social and economic change. The impulse to "promote democracy" is the rearrangement of political systems in the peripheral and semi-peripheral zones of the "world system" so as to secure the underlying objective of maintaining essentially undemocratic societies inserted into an unjust international system. The promotion of "low-intensity democracy" is aimed not only at mitigating the social and political tensions produced by elite-based and undemocratic status quos, but also at suppressing popular and mass aspirations for more thoroughgoing democratization of social life in the twenty-first-century international order. Polyarchy is a structural feature of the emergent global society. Just as "client regimes" and right-wing dictatorships installed into power or supported by the United States were characteristic of a whole era of US foreign policy and intervention abroad in the post-World War II period, promoting "low-intensity democracies" in the Third World is emerging as a cornerstone of a new era in US foreign policy.

Stated theoretically:

The emergence of a global economy in the past few decades presupposes, and provides the material basis for, the emergence of a global civil and political society. The Gramscian concept of hegemony as "consensual domination" exercised in civil and political society at the level of the individual nation (or national society) may be extended/applied to the emergent global civil and political society. In the context of asymmetries in the international political economy, the United States has exercised its domination in the periphery in the post-World War II years chiefly through coercive domination, or the promotion of authoritarian arrangements in the Third World. The emergence of "democracy promotion" as a new instrument and orientation in US foreign policy in the 1980s represented the beginnings of a shift – still underway – in the method through which the core regions of the capitalist world system exercise their domination over peripheral and semi-peripheral regions, from coercive to consensual mechanisms, in the context of emergent transnational configurations. What is emerging is a new political model of North–South relations for the twenty-first century.

My approach to this issue involves bold claims which run contrary to conventional wisdom and mainstream thinking. However, in the pages that follow, my argument is presented theoretically and then supported empirically (including by reference to hitherto unpublished US government documentation obtained through the Freedom of Information Act). It is my hope that this study not only generates debate, but also contributes to the current voluminous research into globalization by providing elements for an ongoing research agenda on the crucial political dimensions of globalization. In my view, scholars have yet to recognize the truly systemic nature of the changes involved in globalization. One of the objectives of this book is to sound an alarm on the need to modify all existing paradigms in light of globalization, to put out a call for imaginative and forward-looking "new thinking." Indeed, I am arguing that only through such fresh, imaginative thinking on globalization and its systemic implications can "democracy promotion" be properly understood.

Organization and methodology

This book's structure reflects its dual objective: a thorough explanation of "democracy promotion" in US foreign policy and at the same time, an open-ended inquiry into larger theoretical issues in which "democracy promotion" is rooted. The study links five "conceptual arenas," integrating the empirical, the analytical, and the theoretical, and proceeding from greater to lesser levels of abstraction: (1) the world system or world order, as the "meta-theoretical framework" in which patterned social relations are conceived (2) the global economy, as the current stage in the world system (3) an emergent global polity and civil society, as concomitants of the global economy (4) changes in US foreign policy, as shifts in the modalities of domination in an asymmetric international order, in concurrence with the changes in the world system and the emergence of the global economy (5) the specific processes and mechanisms in which this shift is unfolding (for instance, "democracy promotion" operations conducted through new US foreign-policy instruments, debates and perceptions among policymakers, and so on). Levels of abstraction 1–3 are structural contexts which require structural analysis. Level 4 straddles structural and behavioral analysis, and level 5 is generally behavioral analysis.

The methodological model is one of *multicausality* and the variables brought into the analysis explain the social phenomena under observation in a highly *interactive* (rather than additive) way. In terms of conceptual method, the relationship between the specific phenomenon of "democracy promotion" and the more general process of globalization is *recursive*. There is a "doubling-back" quality between the phenomenon to be explained ("democracy promotion") and the process in which it is embedded (globalization), whereby the result of a process affects the process that caused it. The etiology of "democracy promotion" is the historic process of globalization, yet at the same time it is a transnational practice which helps shape and facilitate globalization, particularly crucial political dimensions of the process, such as transnational class formation, the externalization of peripheral states, and new forms of articulation between the political and the economic in a global environment. It is these political dimensions of globalization, less recognized than economic globalization, that I wish to call attention to, and "democracy promotion" is a phenomenon (one among many) that signals globalization at the level of political processes. Such a multicausal model is very different from non-recursive models, the latter exhibiting clear distinctions between "dependent" and "independent" variables. Ultimately, my "independent" variable is economic globalization, or the emergence of the global economy. But the specific phenomenon of "democracy promotion" should not be narrowly conceived as the "dependent variable." In more traditional language, there is a "base–superstructure" relation at play. The "base" is the world system, which has entered into a qualitatively new phase, that of the global economy, in which all national economies are becoming integrated. The "superstructure" is the transnationalization of political processes and systems, involving changes in world politics and international relations. "Democracy promotion" as a new US policy has emerged as one such reflection of this superstructural movement. However, caution should be taken in positing base–superstructure models since they can easily lend themselves to mechanical analyses which oversimplify complex interactive relationships among variables.

The book is divided into three sections. The first, chapters 1 and 2, presents a theoretical exposition of the underp[...] political intervention and an analytical framewor[...] how it operates, respectively. Chapter 1 introduce[...] work for analyzing international relations, takes [...] globalization, shows how "democracy promo[...] sively to globalization, and then concludes w[...] explanation of "democracy promotion." Chapter [...] emergence of "democracy promotion" in US foreign policy a[...] focuses on changes in the US state apparatus to conduct "democracy promotion."

The next section, chapters 3 through 6, comprises individual case studies on the Philippines, Chile, Nicaragua, and Haiti, which operationalize the theoretical propositions and analytical precepts and show how "democracy promotion" actually works in practice. In each of these cases, the United States undertook to "promote democracy" in the context of larger foreign policy operations. The studies show how, both covertly and overtly, the United States intervened in mass movements for democracy and endogenous democratization processes. This intervention, through a multiplicity of political, economic, military, diplomatic, and ideological channels, has helped to shape the contours of these processes, to bring them under US influence, and to determine outcomes. The level of analysis here is largely practical-conjunctural, although I demonstrate how events in each country are related to the broader theoretical issues of globalization.

As the text progresses, the analytical and theoretical "density" increases from one case study to the next. This is an intentional "building-block" procedure, so to say. I start by testing the most basic and broadest of the analytical-theoretical propositions in the first case study, and progress in subsequent case studies to expand the scope, exchanging, in effect, the proportion of empirical evidence for analytical-theoretical reflection on the central tenets of the study, in what can be seen as ever-closer approximations. Thus the first case study, the Philippines, is highly descriptive, whereas that on Haiti is as much theoretical as empirical in content.

The Haiti case study thus provides the logical stepping-stone to the concluding chapter, which is the final section. Beyond summing up the central findings, this chapter offers some comparative conclusions and discusses implications of this new intervention for social change in the Third World and for efforts to build a more democratic international order. I also look briefly at US "democracy promotion" activities in the

Soviet bloc and South Africa for the purpose of strengthening
eralizing conclusions. With the benefit of the hindsight provided by
e empirical studies, I retake some of the theoretical issues alluded to
in chapter 1. These include a reexamination of the historical relationship between capitalism and democracy and a new theoretical interpretation of this relationship in light of globalization, the presentation
of a novel Gramscian approach to the issue of "regime transitions,"
discussion of the composition of an emergent transnational hegemonic
configuration, and an examination of the prospects for world order
and for counter-hegemonic blocs in the twenty-first century.

In brief, I have chosen a comparative historical method which is
macro-structural in approach and case study in design. This is a
macro-sociological study, but with a distinct interdisciplinary character. I view theory as a heuristic instrument that may best be
utilized in an interdisciplinary setting, and that multidisciplinary,
holistic reconstruction is essential in reaching theoretical conclusions
on such a broad subject as global civil society. However, theoretical
propositions must be verified in concrete events and circumstances
temporally, spatially, and longitudinally, just as all good theory must
be able to move down to concrete application and back to theoretical
abstraction. In this process, there are three levels of analysis at which
I operate and which I term the *structural*, the *structural-conjunctural*,
and the *practical-conjunctural*. A fuller explanation of these three
levels and how they interact is provided in chapter 1. The point I
wish to emphasize here is that the "macro-structural-historical"
framework introduced at the onset in chapter 1 flows into a
structural-conjunctural and practical-conjunctural analysis in subsequent sections and chapters, *in which structural factors structure a
situation, and conjunctural factors condition the concrete outcomes*. I strive
to avoid the twin traps of structural determinism (à la Althusser)
and of behavioralism, or motivational subjectivism (à la Habermas or
Laclau), and try to focus instead on the dialectical tension between
structure and agency and, whenever possible, to identify mediating
links.

Caveats

Several caveats are in order. First, the critics who may be tempted to
dismiss the arguments in this book with the normative claim that it is
preferable to have "democracy," however so defined by US policy-

makers, than authoritarianism and dictatorship, are missing the point. Whether "democracy" is preferable, in a normative sense, to dictatorship, is not under debate. To place the issue in this light is tantamount to claiming that the juridical equality which African Americans enjoy in the late twentieth century is preferable to the juridical discrimination of earlier times (it *is*, of course, preferable), and that this alone is grounds to dismiss a political or theoretical discussion of contemporary racism in US society.

Second, this book does *not* argue that democratization movements around the world are products of US intervention. To the contrary, I am arguing that they are endogenous developments springing, on the one hand, from deep and age-old aspirations of broad majorities, and on the other hand, from the structural, cultural, and ideological transformations wrought by the global economy. What I am concerned with is the new methods developed by the United States to interact with these movements, methods which form part of new modalities of domination.

Third, I do not pretend to analyze the complexities and nuances of democratization movements in each country examined in the book. Despite the process of globalization, each nation's entry into global society is predicated on its own national history, and researchers need to be deeply attuned to the history, culture, idiosyncrasies, and particular circumstances of each nation and people. I can only claim, to evoke Weber's phrase slightly out of context, such an "empathetic understanding" for my own country of origin, the United States, and for Nicaragua, which has been my home for many years. There is a risk of simplification of complex phenomena. Relations between indigenous elites and the United States are multifarious and checkered with contradictions and conflicts. Also, popular movements operated under complex internal dynamics, political alignments, and shifting strategies. I do not attempt to analyze the heterogeneity and complexities of the popular and elite forces, or national democratization movements. My purpose is to examine how US policy intersects with these in pursuit of an agenda of an emergent transnational elite. Through a comparative study of several "democracy promotion" operations, general patterns and tendencies in US conduct become clear.

Fourth, there are issues raised in chapter 1 which beckon elaboration, and may even appear contradictory. For instance, I simultaneously analyze "democracy promotion" as a *United States* policy intended to secure *US* interests *and* argue that this policy responds to an agenda of

11

a *transnational* elite. This indeed appears at first blush to be a contra-dictory proposition. My reasoning is that on the eve of the twenty-first century the United States (more precisely, dominant groups in the United States) is assuming a leadership role on behalf of a transnational hegemonic configuration. Similarly, I argue, contrary to mainstream notions (particularly among realists and world-system analysts) that the historical pattern of successive "hegemons" has come to an end, and that the hegemonic baton will not be passed from the United States to a new hegemonic nation-state, or even to a "regional bloc." "*Pax Americana*" was the "final frontier" of the old nation-state system and hegemons therein. Instead, the baton will be passed in the twenty-first century to a transnational configuration. These issues are mentioned, but not taken up in any detail, in chapters 1 and 2. This is intentional; a reflection of the inductive origins of the study and a consequence of the organizational structure I have chosen. The purpose of the first two chapters is to lay out just enough theoretical propositions to analyze "democracy promotion" in the context of globalization. The broader theoretical issues are then retaken in the concluding chapter as exploratory ideas to be developed more fully in future research. In other words, there are questions raised but not fully answered and certain limits to this study. This leads to a final caveat:

We should remember that we tend to adopt analytical constructs that best lend themselves to making sense of the social phenomena under study. But these social phenomena are always, and inevitably, many times more complex than our explanations. Our analytical constructs are simplifications of reality that facilitate our cognitive understanding and guide our social action. Good social science can do no more.

1 From "straight power concepts" to "persuasion" in US foreign policy

> In all societies... two classes of people appear – a class that rules and a class that is ruled... The first class, always the less numerous, performs all political functions, monopolizes power and enjoys the advantages that power brings, whereas the second, the more numerous class, is directed and controlled by the first, in a manner that is now more or less legal, now more or less arbitrary and violent.
>
> Gaetano Mosca[1]

> There has been an explosion of human interaction and correlatively a tremendous increase of social pressure. The social texture of human life has become more complex and its management more difficult. Dispersion, fragmentation, and simple ranking have been replaced by concentration, interdependence, and a complex texture... Because of the basic importance of the contemporary complex social texture, its management has a crucial importance, which raises the problem of social control over the individual... Because they (citizens) press for more action to meet the problems they have to face, they require more social control. At the same time they resist any kind of social control that is associated with the hierarchical values they have learned to discard and reject. The problem may be worldwide.
>
> *The Crisis of Democracy* (1975 Trilateral Commission Report)[2]

How are we to understand our world? Our everyday experiences are played out in milieus. These milieus are linked to institutions that organize our lives and bind us to a great many people. Varied and encompassing combinations of institutions and their interrelations form social structures. History, or how social structures have changed over time, tells us where we came from, how we have arrived at the present, and where we are headed. To see our own personal existence as bound up with history and social structure is to acquire what the

13

great modern sociologist C. Wright Mills called the sociological imagination, "the most fruitful form of self consciousness." Democracy, or
the ability to exercise a measure of control over the vital affairs of our
lives as they are played out in personal milieus connected to historical
processes and social structures, is, I believe, the great problem of our
age. Humanity's fate is now so collectively linked that the most
intimate personal milieu and the broadest global social structure are
one. In this chapter, we begin the inquiry into democracy with the
historic juncture that opened up after World War II and concluded at
the dawn of the current age of globalization, and which saw the United
States as the dominant world power. We will end the inquiry by
returning, in the final chapter, to democracy as the most pressing
problem of the human condition and the key to our collective survival.

The Cold War and US interventionism

The United States emerged from the ashes of World War II as the
dominant world power. The postwar global order was designed by top
US policymakers during a six-year period, 1939–1945, and then implemented in the immediate postwar years. The plan called for the
establishment of a "Grand Area" of US influence in Latin America,
Asia, and Africa, the reconstruction and integration of Europe and
Japan into a new world order under US domination, and the creation
of international institutions to stabilize this new order. Creating *Pax
Americana* involved filling the vacuum left by the collapse of the old
colonial empires by deploying its military forces and political agents
worldwide. From World War II to the end of the Cold War, the United
States employed military force across its borders more than 200 times,
became embroiled in large-scale wars in Korea and Indochina, and in
"small wars," counterinsurgency campaigns, and covert operations
throughout Latin America, Africa, the Middle East, and Europe.
Military and economic programs were developed to consolidate the
emergent order, and billions of dollars in investment and finance
capital flowed where US intervention assured a stable environment.
Global *interventionism* became a structural feature of the post-World
War II US empire.[3]

Much postwar literature on US foreign policy has erroneously
interpreted this interventionism as having been driven by Cold War
considerations. Perceived competition from the former Soviet Union
was an important factor, but it was *not* the driving force behind foreign

policy. The driving force was defense of a budding post-colonial international capitalism under US domination. Behind the "communist threat" there has always been another, more fundamental threat: any challenge to "patterns of relationships" which underpinned US domination and prerogative derived from its privileged position in an asymmetric international order. National Security Council (NSC) Memorandum NSC-68, one of the key foreign policy documents of the post-World War II era, stated, for instance, that postwar policy embraced "two subsidiary policies." One was to foster "a world environment in which the American system can survive and flourish"; the other was "containment of the Soviet Union," which "seeks to foster the seeds of destruction within the Soviet system." The Memorandum went on: "Even if there was no Soviet Union we would face the great problem" of achieving "order and security" for US global interests. It concluded by calling for "a rapid buildup of [US] political, economic, and military strength" around the world.[4] And the whole focus of President Roosevelt's Advisory Committee on Postwar Foreign Policy was not a "communist threat" but control over the world's resources, and in particular, securing US access to the raw materials, markets, and labor power of the Third World. *Behind East–West relations, therefore, North–South relations were always intrinsic and central to the whole Cold War era.*

Although democracy often entered the foreign policymaking vocabulary, it was *not* the dominant form in which the United States exercised its domination, especially in the post-World War II years. As the historical record shows, the principal form was the development of strategic alliances with authoritarian and dictatorial regimes. The outcome of intervention, whether intentional or as a by-product, was the establishment and defense of authoritarian political and social arrangements in the Third World as a support for the maintenance of international order and stability. The United States promoted and supported a global political network of civilian-military regimes and outright dictatorships in Latin America, white minority and one-party dictatorships in Africa, and repressive states in Asia. Authoritarian arrangements were judged to be the most expedient means of assuring stability and social control in the Third World.

But by the 1970s, mass popular movements were spreading against repressive political systems and exploitative socioeconomic orders established during the years of the Cold War. The structures of authoritarianism and dictatorship began to crumble, above all, in US client regimes, and a general crisis of elite rule began to develop in the South.[5] As the "elective affinity" between authoritarianism and US domination unravelled, "democracy promotion" substituted "national security" in the US vernacular. A "democracy promotion" apparatus was created in the policymaking establishment, including new governmental and quasi-governmental agencies and bureaus, studies and conferences by policy-planning institutes, and government agencies to draft and implement "democracy promotion" programs. Where it had earlier supported dictatorship, such as in Chile, Nicaragua, Haiti, the Philippines, Panama, Southern Africa, and elsewhere, the United States now began to "promote democracy." By the mid-1980s, the intellectual community had joined the fray. University presses churned out a whole new class of "democratization" literature and democratization courses sprang up on campuses.

"Democracy promotion" has a crucial ideological dimension, given that democracy is a universal aspiration and the claim to promote it has mass appeal. Under the rubric of "democracy," new policies set out not to promote, but to *curtail*, democratization. Democratization struggles around the world are profound threats to US privilege and to the dominance of core regions in the world system under overall US leadership. If the objective of US interventionism in the post-World War II years was control of the world's resources, labor, and surpluses, then logically the end of the Cold War should not eliminate interventionism. But the policies pursued during the Cold War years to confront challenges to domination have proved increasingly ineffective. This has led policymakers to a shift in the dominant form through which the United States seeks to assure stability under the hegemony of an emergent transnational elite, from promoting authoritarian to promoting "democratic" political and social arrangements in Third World countries. Behind this shift in favor of ostensibly democratic arrangements is the replacement of coercive means of social control with consensual ones.

This chapter is divided into two parts. In the first, I combine world system theory and a Gramscian model in international relations into a framework for understanding the new political intervention. In the second, I explore the relation between intellectual production and US foreign policy, discuss democracy as an essentially contested concept, and provide a theoretical explanation for the shift to promoting polyarchy.

16

The world system and a Gramscian model of international relations

The foreign policy of nations and the world system

Much foreign-policy literature is based on the realist axiom that the foreign policy of nations is designed to secure the perceived interests of the states from which that policy emanates. But the axiom raises a host of questions: What *are* US interests, and how (and by whom) are they defined? What is the relation between interests and policies? Is there (or under what conditions does there exist) a convergence, or a clash, of interests between the United States and nations which become the target of US foreign-policy operations? Are nations, in fact, the appropriate units of analysis in looking for convergence and clashes of interests? Or are social groups and classes across national boundaries the more appropriate focus?

Much of the contemporary literature affirms that the search for *stability* drives US policy.[6] This emphasis on stability fails to raise a question crucial to understanding policy: the stability of *what*? US foreign policy is aimed at assuring the stability of a given set of economic, social and political arrangements *within* each country in which the US intervenes, *and* in the international system as a whole. The stability of arrangements and relations which girder an international system in which the United States has enjoyed a dominant position is seen as essential to US interests, or "national security." When these arrangements are threatened US policy attempts to undercut the threat. And when these arrangements are *altered* in ways that are perceived as detrimental, the United States attempts not to pursue stability, but to *destabilize*. In the Western Hemisphere alone the United States pursued destabilization rather than stability in Guatemala (1954), Chile (1970–1973), Grenada (1979–1983), Jamaica (1977–1980), Cuba (1959–present), Panama (1988–1989), and Nicaragua (1979–1990), among others.[7] In identifying US interests abroad, analysts often focus on a linear relation between specific interests (an economic investment in one country, a fear of "communism" in

17

another, an anti-drug campaign in a third, geo-strategic considerations in a fourth, and so on) and resulting policies. This disaggregation of interests and consequent policies conceals the greater sum in an analysis of its component parts. Historian Lloyd C. Gardner identifies an *interventionist impulse* as a constant in US policy abroad.[8] The term "interventionist" refers to involvement abroad – military, economic, political, or otherwise – pursuant of interests, and "impulse" connotes precisely that enmeshing of economic, political and strategic factors that drives foreign policy. This aggregation of distinct *policy considerations* into a *policy impulse* that drives US policy is important but not in itself enough to explain policy.

There is both a *foreground* and a *background* to policy. The foreground is the aggregate of considerations weighed by a policymaking community. Many foreign-policy analysts, particularly those from pluralist and realist paradigms, limit their work to an exploration of this territory, thus conflating human perceptions and public discourse, which are not causal explanations of policy but structurally contingent variables. The background is an international political economy and a world system in which nations and social groups interact, and which constitutes the structural underpinning of policymakers' perceptions and policies, and their evolution. The critical linkage between the background and the foreground are *asymmetries and inequalities in the international political economy* and *cross-national relations of power and domination*. Both realists and Marxists identify an organic and symbiotic relation between the *wealth of nations* and the *power of nations*, and great disparities in power and wealth among nations. This asymmetry is the bedrock upon which international relations unfold. For Marxists (in distinction to realists), asymmetric relationships are *both between nations* and *between social classes and groups within nations and across national boundaries*, although it is more accurate to speak of relations of *asymmetric interdependence* than of dependency. More insightful studies on international political economy focus neither on the internal nor on the external dimensions, but on the *interaction* between internal and external, between social groups within *and* among nations.

A thorough discussion on international political economy, world system and related theories is beyond the scope of this study.[9] In sum, a world system came into being in the past 500 years as a consequence of the genesis and expansion of the capitalist mode of production, which gradually linked the whole world into a single system. The linkage of social formations on a global scale brought with it an international division of labor. The central dynamic of the "modern world system" is a process of global capital accumulation, the benefits of which accrue unequally among nations and among social groups within and between nations. The formation of a world system has brought about a division of the world into "center" (or "core") and "periphery," (or satellite and metropolis, or developed and under-developed), despite considerable diversity and a process of uneven development. The production, circulation and appropriation of surplus on a global scale are central to understanding world-historic dynamics. Superimposed upon the process of surplus extraction (the appropria-tion of wealth) from certain social groups or classes to others is a process of surplus extraction from one nation or region to another, or from peripheral to core regions within a single world economy. Social struggles over the control of wealth, therefore, take place within nations and across national boundaries, and national struggles over the circulation and appropriation of surpluses take place in the context of a transnational environment and the dynamic of international relations.

World system theory, in particular its theoretical proposition that the development of international society is constituted by the spread of a social system at the international level, forms a powerful macro-structural framework for analyzing world events, including US foreign policy and "democracy promotion." There are three general assump-tions which I posit on the basis of world system theory and which are later woven into the analysis. First, political systems in the periphery have, seen through the long-historic lens of the modern era, been penetrated and influenced, if not entirely imposed, by the core. Changes in general core–periphery relations have consequences for peripheral political systems. Modern colonialism created political systems outright or transformed existing ones, which then gained new-found autonomy following decolonization. The relationship between changes in general core–periphery relations and changes in peripheral political systems should be viewed as a legitimate unit of social scientific inquiry. The global economy is fundamentally redefining North–South general relations, economic as well as political. Second, globalization is a new phase of capitalism which involves a transition to a *qualitatively* new stage in the world system. My application of the world system framework differs from the more orthodox approach advanced by sociologist Immanuel Wallerstein in historical period-ization, in the Weberian definition of capitalism as a market rather than a production relation, and in the view of the state and its relation to nations and social groups. The assumption here, regarding period-ization and production relations, is that the modern world system was characterized in an earlier period by a dominant capitalist mode, headquartered in the core, which articulated itself with distinct semi- or pre-capitalist modes in peripheral regions. Under globalization, capitalist production relations are displacing, rather than merely becoming articulated with, all residual pre-capitalist relations. Re-garding the state, the assumption is that globalization is separating the state, conceived as a theoretical abstraction, from the nation-state as a concrete sovereign territorial unit. Third, a key disjuncture in the globalization process is the internationalization of productive forces within an institutional system still centered around the nation-state. This contradiction helps explain why outdated nation-state-centered approaches persist among scholars whose objects of inquiry are transnational phenomena. The increasing separation of classes from territoriality and class power from state power involves a dispersal of global decision-making away from specific core states, even though transnational groups continue to filter policies through existing state apparatuses. In elaborating a policy of "democracy promotion," the United States is not acting on behalf of a "US" elite, but playing a leadership role on behalf of an emergent transnational elite.

Asymmetry in international relations and hegemony

There are three dimensions, or levels, in analyzing policy development. One is intentional human agency, intersubjectivities clustered in a polity – a community which makes foreign policy. Social scientific analysis which operates at this level is *practical-conjunctural*, or alter-natively, *behavioral*. At this level, it is important to draw the distinction in policy between means (which are policies) and ends (which are interests), and to recognize the tactical nature of many disputes within policymaking communities and view them as debates over the most effective means of achieving ends. The second level is the underlying global structure in which states and groups engage with the broader world system. Analysis at this level is *structural* analysis. Structure frames and conditions events and activities in the behavioral realm, often independently of intentionality. Intersubjective perceptions are structurally contingent and the two levels cannot be homogenized.

20

Rather, we need to develop conceptual methodologies which problematize boundaries. Identifying a third mediating level of analysis contributes to methodological clarity and cognition of the phenomena under observation. This is the *structural-conjunctural*. It refers to processes in the social universe which do not lend themselves to easy cognition either at the structural or at the practical-conjunctural levels, but straddle the two and involve a mix of agency and structure. Structural analysis frames practical-conjunctural analysis, while structural-conjunctural analysis interfaces "backwards" and "forwards" with both and allows us to identify "feedback mechanisms" that keep in check functionalist teleology. Much literature on policy, international relations and world events tends to operate at *either* the structural or the behavioral level. A more useful approach, and one which I believe essential to properly understand the subject of this book, is a combination of both with the third, mediating level.

If world system theory provides a framework for a structural analysis of the background to US foreign policy, and aggregates of policymakers' considerations, for a behavioral analysis of the foreground, a Gramscian model of international relations provides a theoretical nexus between the background and the foreground. Gramscian concepts, particularly of *hegemony* and the *extended state*, help link propositions drawn from structural and behavioral levels of analysis.

The concept of hegemony is not generally used in the social sciences, including in most world system and Marxist models, in the Gramscian sense. The commonplace usage refers broadly to domination, rooted in the original Greek meaning of hegemony as predominance of one nation over another. The United States exercised global "hegemony" in the post-World War II era, or Great Britain was the "hegemonic" world power in the nineteenth century. Gramsci's notion of hegemony is more circumscribed, positing distinct *forms*, or relations, of domination, in brief: *coercive domination* and *consensual domination*. Hegemony in the Gramscian sense may be defined roughly as a relation between classes in which one class or fraction of a class exercises leadership over other classes and strata by gaining their *active consent*.[10] A Gramscian hegemony involves the internalization on the part of subordinate classes of the moral and cultural values, the codes of practical conduct, and the worldview of the dominant classes or groups – in sum, the internalization of the *social logic* of the system of domination itself. This *logic* is imbedded in ideology, which acts as a cohesive force in social unification (in Gramsci's phrase, "cement").

But hegemony is more than ideology, and is not reducible to Marx's "false consciousness." Hegemony is a social relation which binds together a "bloc" of diverse classes and groups under circumstances of consensual domination, such that subordinate groups give their "spontaneous consent" to "the direction imposed on social life" by the dominant groups.

A social order in which hegemony has been achieved is one which takes the form of consensual ("democratic") arrangements in the political system and in society. These arrangements are characterized by a given set of juridical relations as the arbiter of social relations and procedural mechanisms for the resolution of group and class conflict. Hegemony mediates relations between dominant and subordinate groups, and *also* relations among dominant groups. The same consensual processes for the reproduction of a given constellation of dominant social forces also involve mechanisms for consensus among dominant groups themselves through *consensus-creating processes*. Stated in admittedly simplified terms, dictatorship or authoritarianism may be conceived as the exercise of coercive domination and hegemony refers to consensual domination. However, it should be stressed that hegemonic (consensual) domination does not mean the absence of coercion, much less the absence of conflict in a social formation, whether conceived as national or transnational. It is better conceived as the reproduction of social order through the salience of consensual means of social control. As Gramsci put it, hegemony is consensus protected by the "armor of coercion," and the political superstructures of a coherent social order (whether authoritarian or "democratic") always combine both coercive-based and consensual-based elements. These two forms are (in Gramsci's Hegelian language) distinct "moments" in the social relations of domination, separable only in theoretical abstraction for methodological purposes.

A critical element in the Gramscian construct is the distinction and unity of political and civil society. *Social control* takes place on two levels: in civil society and through the state (political society), which are fused in Gramsci's *extended state*. "These two levels correspond on the one hand to the function of hegemony which the dominant group exercises throughout society and on the other hand to that of 'direct domination' or command exercised through the State and 'juridical' government."[11] The hegemony of a ruling class or fraction is exercised in civil society, as distinct from its coercive power exercised through the state. Civil society is the arena of those social relationships which are based on consent – political parties, trade unions, civic (voluntary) associations, the family, and so forth.

Gramsci originally developed the concept of hegemony in its application to relations among classes and social groups within a nation. But the premise can be applied to international relations, as has been advanced elsewhere in recent international relations and development literature, and an "Italian school" has begun to emerge. However, a Gramscian theory of international relations remains sparsely developed, and most work has emphasized intra-elite relations over those between elites and subordinate classes, and has focused on intra-core and not on core–periphery relations.[12] In contrast, I wish to highlight hegemonic relations between dominant and subordinate classes in the core–periphery context. This emergent "Italian school" is heterogeneous in interpretations of Gramsci and in application of his concepts to international phenomena, but here is not the place to take up debates on Gramsci.

My application is as follows. Hegemony is exercised in relations among nations and among classes or groups in a transnational setting. The structures of asymmetry in the international political economy are sustained and international relations of power and domination exercised through variants of coercive or consensual mechanisms of transnational social control. Hegemony applied to international relations is not synonymous with the application of power by one nation over others; this is domination, or, as specifically concerns core–periphery relations, *imperialism*, understood as the transfer of surpluses from one country or region to another and the military, political, and ideological mechanisms which facilitate such transfer. Such power may be gauged as the *relative* ability to influence events and their outcomes in a transnational arena. Cross-national relations of domination express given correlations of international force. A critical mass of asymmetrical power in international relations may be applied in a myriad of ways that create or sustain asymmetries, such as colonial conquest and direct military intervention. During its "American century," the United States applied such a critical mass of power, both direct (political-military) and indirect (economic), flowing from its location in the world system, to construct global empire and to exercise worldwide domination, just as Great Britain did in the nineteenth century. Relative power may be exercised in numerous ways, and the means with which it is applied can become as important as the degree of such power. A more effective means may require less application of power, or offset an absolute or relative decline. More importantly, changes in the nature of power itself may necessitate changes in the form in which it is exercised.

Hegemony is one *form* in which nations or groups in a transnational setting may exercise their domination in the international arena. The foreign policy of core states may be conceived, in the broadest sense, as international engagement by groups operating through states to maintain or extend the advantages accrued from a dominant location in an asymmetrical international order, including the supression of groups that challenge those advantages. Mass movements for the democratization of social life are *threats* to dominant groups in a transnational setting. Yet the earlier authoritarian arrangements are increasingly unable to manage such threats. New modalities of intervention have emerged to face more complex threats. Transnational dominant classes and groups and the state apparatuses which they manage may sustain core–periphery relations of domination through coercion ("straight power concepts"), such as direct colonial control, an invasion, or a CIA-orchestrated *coup d'état*, and more characteristically, through the promotion of dictatorial or authoritarian social arrangements. Or, transnational social control may be achieved through foreign-policy undertakings intended to bring about spontaneous consent through the political and ideological incorporation of subordinate groups.

A Gramscian construct allows us to synthesize the structural and the behavioral levels of analysis. Hegemony is not simply something which happens, a mere superstructural derivative of economic structures. It is, in large part, the result of a permanent and persuasive *effort*, conducted through a multiplicity of "superstructural" agencies and instances. However, the possibility of hegemonic order is conditioned by the structure of production and social relations that flow from political economy. Therefore, policy ultimately flows from the dialectic of agency and structure, but analysis requires a methodological distinction.

Regarding first the behavioral level of analysis, the US policymaking community has analyzed the dramatic changes in the international correlation of forces between the early 1970s and the early 1990s, and in the domestic political landscape in which foreign policy is constructed, which provided the basis for a reformulation of US policies and helped to consolidate the shift towards "democracy promotion." State managers have perceived that absolute power has declined, and have sought to adjust policies, even if they are not cognizant of the underlying structural and historical processes at work which account for this decline. Greater cognizance on the part of policymakers of the need to develop policies calibrated to actual power and potential, as well as the perception of decline in absolute US power, conceived in nation-state terms, has been an important part of the thinking among those who have developed "democracy promotion." However, international asymmetries no longer correlate to nation-states and their relative power, although the disjuncture between transnationalization and an institutional system still centered around the nation-state can produce seemingly contradictory phenomena, and even illusions among state managers, most of whom do not theorize on Gramscian concepts.

Regarding now the structural level of analysis, the decline in the relative power of the US nation-state and other core states in recent decades, the gradual separation of class power and state power (or the structural power of capital and the direct power of states), the disbursal of global power to geographically diffuse classes and groups operating in a transnational environment, and the requirement of democratic legitimation are all factors accounting for the decreased effectiveness of traditional military power and the absolute coercive capacity of the core in the world system. Debate over whether the United States is losing or merely reconfiguring its position as the dominant world power reflects an outdated state-centered approach which fails to appreciate changes in the nature of power under globalization, and which therefore obscures our understanding of the relation between economic and political change in global society.

How is US foreign policy made? The state, civil society and power

Great power in America is concentrated in a tiny handful of people. A few thousand individuals out of 238 million Americans decide about war and peace, wages and prices, consumption and investment, employment and production, law and justice, taxes and benefits, education and learning, health and welfare, advertising and communication, life and leisure.

Thomas R. Dye, *Who's Running America?*[13]

To understand US foreign policy we must analyze the nature of foreign policymaking and draw out the linkage between politics and power

25

and between state and society as central concerns of political sociology.[14] Pluralist (liberal) interpretations, rooted theoretically in Durkheimian-Parsonian structural-functionalism, maintain that power is diffused throughout society and the state is a neutral arena or arbiter whose policies are determined by competition among multiple "interest groups," or Toquevillian "voluntary associations." Accordingly, foreign policy reflects the interests of pluralist majorities. Most realists share with pluralists the dichotomy between state and society. But the state is less an institution instrumentalized by pluralist majorities than a corporate entity independent of society – a "state-in-itself" or a "state-for-itself" – a view drawn from Weberian and managerial models of political sociology.[15] Foreign policy is managed by state actors who, operating independently of backward linkage to society, face a competitive state system in an anarchic world.

However, the empirical evidence weighs heavily in favor of elitist and class models of political power. These models, whether they lean towards the "instrumentalist" or the "structuralist" side in theoretical conceptualization of how the state performs the functions that it does, or whether power rests in control over institutions or over the means of production, share the view that the state serves the interests of those groups and classes which are dominant in society.[16] The state is conceived as institutionalized social relations, not as an independent unit linked externally to society through its functions but as an *organic* expression of the social structure itself. Many well-documented studies, among them C. Wright Mills's classic *The Power Elite*, Ralph Miliband's *The State in Capitalist Society*, and more recent works by sociologist G. William Domhoff and political scientist Thomas R. Dye, have shown that the foreign policymaking process is tightly controlled by an inner circle of political, business, and intellectual elites, scattered throughout the organs of the US state, the corporate echelons, and a handful of elite policy planning institutes.[17] Dye summarizes this as an oligarchical model of power. Foreign policy reflects the interests of a small elite, which also controls the domestic political economy, and which is generally not accountable to mass constituencies and their interests. States do possess varying degrees of autonomy in policymaking. However, foreign policy is in large measure the outcome of the conflicts among dominant groups within each society, and dominant classes utilize foreign policy in their interests. There are no such things as US "national security" or "national interests." There are interests and security considerations (albeit shifting and conflicting) among dominant classes and groups, distinguishable from those of other classes and groups. These dominant groups exercise inordinate influence over the instruments of foreign policy in pursuit not of "national" but of class or group interests. This does not preclude circumstantial convergence of interests among different classes or groups, or foreign-policy development that is influenced, although not determined, by subordinate classes and groups.

State policy is developed in broader linkage to society and political economy. The linkage of the state, from where policy is actually managed, to society is crucial. Most pluralist/liberal and managerial/realist analyses of foreign policy assume that society and the state form a unitary entity and that foreign policy is determined by an objective national interest. Policies are attributed simply to the perceptions and decisions of those who actually occupy government posts: government officials or policymakers-proper, whose activities attract the attention of analysts and who *appear* to be the makers of policy. Dye refers to these government officials as "proximate policymakers" that constitute only the *final phase* of a complex policymaking process largely determined by forces in civil society. These forces structure the options available for the formal law-making institutions through which formal policymakers operate.[18] G. W. Domhoff dissects the mechanisms and processes by which dominant forces in civil society (at whose apex are the agents of corporate capital) come to utilize the state and policymakers in their own interests. Domhoff identifies a core of policy specialists which extends beyond the proximate policymakers themselves. These specialists, operating out of policy groups, foundations, think-tanks, university research institutes, and government agencies, bring long-range political considerations and issues concerning social stability to the attention of the dominant classes and their inner core in the corporate community.[19] This group of private and public "specialists," including but not limited to "proximate policymakers" operating within formal government structures, forms what I refer to as the *extended* policymaking community and constitutes the crucial mediating link between agency and structure in the development of policy and the construction of hegemony.

An "immediate policymaking community" is comprised of state managers and government agencies, and is often referred to as an "administration" – a particular and temporary group of elected officials and their appointees. Much policy analysis tends to focus on this immediate community, yet policy is best analyzed as it flows from

27

the extended policymaking community. This community extends backwards into civil society, goes well beyond specific elected administrations, spans the panoply of institutions in which power is exercised, and brings together the formal state apparatus with the network of universities, think-tanks, corporate groups, and so forth. It conducts ongoing and regenerative processes of policy formation and implementation over extended periods. This extended policymaking community is the appropriate locus of behavioral analysis of foreign policy.

Gramsci's concept of the extended state clarifies the intricate interpenetration of state and society and overcomes dualist notions of the two. Hegemony is exercised in civil society itself, and power is exercised through the state only on the basis of a given constellation of forces in civil society. In turn, as Karl Marx noted in 1859, "the anatomy of civil society is to be sought in political economy."[20] Once a given "historic bloc" (a constellation of social forces with a hegemonic class or class fraction in the leadership) has achieved hegemonic order, those classes or groups who have achieved hegemony in civil society effectively exercise state power, whether directly or indirectly. The correlation of forces in civil society is at least as important as who actually holds state power, maybe more so. Gramsci's distinction between civil society and the state is purely methodological; the state and civil society are fused, or "intertwined," as are the mechanisms of consent and coercion for the purpose of rule. Gramsci's extended state is thus "political society plus civil society." Political society corresponds to the *formal* state apparatus, which is what most literature refers to when it discusses "the state."[21] The rise of civil society, once the capitalist mode of production has become consolidated, is at the core of the historic process. The complex of "private" but national (social) organizations, such as mass political parties, trade unions, mass media, and civic associations, integrates subordinate classes and groups into the capitalist society. The state is the means through which the dominant class "not only justifies and maintains its dominance, but manages to win the active consent of those over whom it rules."[22] The state is not simply "negative and repressive," but also "positive and educative," encompassing repressive organs such as the military and police, but also legislatures and educational systems. The state unites with the "trenches of civil society" to organize and structure interests in accordance with the preservation of the social order.

This is relevant to "democracy promotion" on two accounts. First, as I shall draw out below, the understanding on the part of US policymakers that power ultimately rests in civil society, and that state power is intimately linked to a given correlation of forces in civil society, has helped shape the contours of the new political intervention. Unlike earlier US interventionism, the new intervention focuses much more intensely on civil society itself, in contrast to formal government structures, in intervened countries. The purpose of "democracy promotion" is not to suppress but to penetrate and conquer civil society in intervened countries, that is, the complex of "private" organizations such as political parties, trade unions, the media, and so forth, and *from therein*, integrate subordinate classes and national groups into a hegemonic transnational social order. Since social groups vie for control over the levers of state power (and to put their agents into positions of proximate policymakers), and since the strength of social groups in civil society is a determining factor in this struggle for control, it is not surprising that the new political intervention emphasizes building up the forces in the civil society of intervened countries which are allied with dominant groups in the United States and the core regions of the world system. This function of civil society as an arena for exercising domination runs counter to conventional (particularly pluralist) thinking on the matter, which holds that civil society is a buffer between state domination and groups in society, and that class and group domination is diluted as civil society develops.

Second, viewing power through the lens both of the state apparatus and formal policymakers *and* the correlations of force in civil society further clarifies a complex new convergence of interests between certain groups in countries where the United States has intervened to "promote democracy" and those who exercise effective power in the United States. Insofar as we are dealing with democratization around the world, there has been circumstantial convergence of interests between dominant US groups and majoritarian groups in some Third World countries (including elites and popular sectors) around the strategy of "democracy promotion," such as in Chile and the Philippines. In other instances, the convergence is not between US policy and majority groups, but a conspiratorial convergence against majorities, as in Nicaragua and Haiti. Under "democracy promotion," US foreign policy links up with specific groups in other countries. The location of these groups in the state apparatus and in the civil societies is of prime importance. These transnational political processes involve a complex matrix of relations between social groups, classes, and institutions *within* nations and *between* nations.

Gramsci analyzed "historic blocs" in *individual societies*, within a specific constellation of class and social forces, whose "glue," or binding element, is ideological hegemony. With the shift from coercive to consensual forms of social control, the importance of ideology in maintaining social order increases dramatically. Coercion is the glue that sustains and reinforces social control and oppressive social relations in a dictatorship, and ideology is reduced to crude rationalization of repression. Ideology constitutes the glue that sustains social control under consensual arrangements.[23] Ideology is more than an anthropological belief system and is not equivalent to mere illusion. It is a *material force* insofar as it orients and sets limits on human action by establishing generalized codes of conduct which organize entire populations.[24] Consciousness is the medium between structure and agency, mediating between objective conditions and social action as subjective response to those conditions. Dominant ideologies therefore tend to set circumscribed frames of reference in which subordinate groups politically challenge the dominant. Under a hegemonic social order, embedded in ideology are definitions of key political, economic and philosophical concepts and the ideological framework establishes the legitimacy or illegitimacy of the demands placed on the social order. I argue later that one particular definition of the key political/philosophical concept of democracy, the polyarchic definition, has become hegemonic, and that this serves hegemony by filtering out as illegitimate demands that actually call into question the social order itself.

Hegemony in the world system is transnational consensual domination in a structural situation of international asymmetries in which neither power and wealth, nor politics and economics, are separable or dichotomous. Gill characterizes hegemony at the transnational level as the fusion of ideological dominance by class or group fractions with structural dominance in the international political economy. In the world system perspective, the center countries enjoy structural dominance in the international political economy. My notion of international hegemony is distinct from most world system theorists, for whom it is equated with structural domination alone. However, it also differs from Gill, Cox, Augelli and Murphy, and others from the "Italian school," who focus on ideological consensus *within* dominant groups across nations, or transnational *intra*-elite consensus. I suggest that transnational domination, in order to be hegemonic, requires the ideological incorporation of both dominant and subordinate groups in the center and periphery. Prior to globalization leadership in the world system shifted from one core power to another over time, a process involving periodic swings between conflict and consensus among core powers and a fairly constant relation of coercive domination of the periphery. A hegemonic world social order has only become possible for the first time in human history in the current age of globalization. Elaboration rests on a structural analysis of globalization.

Global economy, global society and transnational political processes

The shift from authoritarian to consensual mechanisms of social control corresponds to the emergence of a global economy since the 1970s and constitutes a political exigency of macro-economic restructuring on a world scale.[25] Globalization comprises two interwoven processes. First is the culmination of the process begun several centuries ago, in which capitalist production relations are undermining and supplanting all pre-capitalist relations across the globe, in those areas specializing in manufacturing or services and those in primary production. Second is the transition over the past several decades from the linkage of nations via commodity exchange and capital flows in an integrated international market, in which different modes of production coexisted within broader social formations and national and regional economies enjoyed autonomy despite external linkages, to *the globalization of the process of production itself*. This involves the restructuring of the international division of labor and the reorganization of productive structures in each nation. It has major consequences for the social and political texture of every society and for the world polity.

The general international division of labor was based in earlier periods on the production of manufactured goods in the centers of world capitalism and primary goods in the peripheral areas, often under semi- or pre-capitalist relations. This "colonial" division of labor has been transformed with the appearance of the multinational corporation as the principal agent of international economic activity and several consecutive waves in the scientific and technological revolution (STR). The first STR began during or soon after World War II and focused on capital-intensive technologies (nuclear energy, new automation techniques, synthetics, computers and electronics, etc.). The second STR began in the late 1960s and includes a second generation of computerization, electronics, and synthetics, and new communications technologies. The first constituted a shift from labor-intensive industrial production to capital-intensive production as the core of accumulation on a world scale; the second from capital-intensive to technology- (and knowledge)-intensive. Several clusters of completely new industries based on high technology and scientific content – advanced electronics and computerization, telecommunications, robotics, cybernetics, aerospace science, biotechnology, and so forth – are coming to dominate in the North.

These profound transformations in the technological and material structure of human society facilitate global economic restructuring, transforming the very nature of the industrial production process and, along with it, the role of human labor. It has allowed for the decentralization across the globe of complex production processes simultaneous with the centralization of decision-making and management of global production; the complete separation of the site of management from the site of production and the geographic fragmentation of production and of capital. This new ability to set up what Barnet and Muller describe as the "global factory" has allowed capital to realize across the globe what, at one time, it had to restrict to national borders: total mobility in the search for the cheapest labor and the most congenial conditions for the different circuits of production and distribution, without regard for national borders. The rich countries of the North are increasingly based on control of technology, information and services (including finances), whereas the labor-intensive phase of international production, and in some cases whole manufacturing processes, shift to the South through the "comparative advantage" of abundant, cheap labor.

The globalization of production involves a hitherto unseen integration of national economies and brings with it a tendency towards uniformity, not just in the conditions of production, but in the civil and political superstructure in which social relations of production unfold. A new "social structure of accumulation" is emerging which is for the first time *global*. A social structure of accumulation refers to a set of mutually reinforcing social, economic and political institutions and cultural and ideological norms which fuse with, and facilitate, a successful pattern of capital accumulation over specific historic periods. A new global social structure of accumulation is becoming superimposed on, and is transforming, all existing national social structures of accumulation. The agent of the global economy is transnational capital, organized institutionally in global corporations, in supranational economic planning agencies and political forums, and managed by a class-conscious transnational elite based in the core of the world system. In his analysis of the structural changes in the international political economy from the late 1960s to the late 1980s, Gill argues that the international economic turmoil of that twenty-year period was not, in fact, reflective of the breakdown of world capitalism nor of the accelerated division of the centers of world capitalism (Western Europe, North America and Japan) into competing trade and financial blocs. Rather, it was precisely the rough bumps of the emergence of transnationalized capital, concentrated in international finance capital, as the hegemonic fraction of capital at a world level.[26]

The concentration of capital and economic power around this transnational elite in core countries has a transformative effect on arrangements between social groups, class constellations, and political systems in every country of the world system. Political and economic power tends to gravitate towards new groups linked to the global economy, either directly or through reorganized local state apparatuses which function as "transmission belts" for transnational interests. In every region of the world, in both North and South, from Eastern Europe to Latin America, states, economies, and political processes are becoming transnationalized and integrated under the guidance of this new elite. Barnet and Muller have shown how transnational capital integrates local elite groups in the centers of the world economy into "transnational circuits."[27] Cox identifies transnational class fractions which coalesce out of specific national class fractions exhibiting a strong congruence in a cross-national setting. The internationalization of production involves the transition from nationally defined class structures to a global class structure "alongside or superimposed upon national class structures," in which "class action penetrates countries through the process of the internationalization of the state." Transnational fractions of capital have become dominant in center countries, and a "transnational managerial class" appears at the apex of the global class structure.[28]

This transnational elite has its exact counterpart in each nation of the South, in a new breed of "technocratic" elite in Latin America, Africa and Asia – what economists Osvaldo Sunkel and Edmundo F. Fuenzalida have called "transnational kernels" in peripheral countries.[29] These elites in the South, the local counterparts to the global elite, are overseeing sweeping processes of social and economic restructuring. However, analysis of transnational kernels in the periphery has lagged

33

behind analyses of the emergence of a transnational Northern-based elite. Domhoff has analyzed the ties that bind dominant elites in advanced capitalist societies, in which ideological affinities and social cohesion is developed through formal and informal socialization processes and institutional interlocks in "private" institutions, the economy, and the state.[30] Gill, in his analysis of the Trilateral Commission, elevates the binding process to a transnational setting as regards class fractions drawn from the United States, Western Europe and Japan.[31] Writing from the perspective of dependency theory, sociologist Peter Evans explores "problems of integration" and identifies some of the concrete mechanisms by which local (Southern or peripheral) and multinational (Northern or core) capital has become interdependent and interpenetrated in the accumulation process.[32]

I wish to take the analysis of global class formation a step further. Relations of dependency and asymmetry are not superseded by globalization. Control over the accumulation process increasingly rests on technology and its diffusion, on decision-making in a worldwide (spatial) distribution of productive resources, and the global (as distinct from local) management of these resources, which remains in general a monopoly of core country elites. And the most dynamic centers of capital accumulation on a world scale – technology, management, finances, and knowledge-intensive services – remain concentrated generally in core regions. However, I submit that the transnationalization of civil and political society is performing an integrative function in cohering a dominant transnational social group that is linked in overlapping North–North and North–South class constellations. Evans analyzes a contradiction between "national rationalities" of Southern elites whose interests lie in *national* accumulation processes and the "global rationality" of multinational capital. But the global economy provides the material basis for the supersession of this contradiction. The logics of local and global accumulation increasingly coincide. The central concern of this study is to show how new instruments of political intervention, originally developed in the United States and then applied around the world in the name of "democracy promotion," are aimed at suppressing the demands of popular sectors in the South. However, it will become clear through the empirical evidence presented, and class analysis applied, in the case studies that these same instruments are also integrative mechanisms which forge North–South social and political cohesion among elites operating in the new global environment. These instruments help bridge the gap between

the logic of local and of global accumulation by cultivating transnationalized kernels in each intervened country, helping place these local
class fractions into direct state power, and linking them to the transnational elite under a single global logic.

By a "transnational elite," therefore, I refer to class fractions drawn
around the world that are integrated into fully transnationalized
circuits of production, and whose outlook and political behavior is
guided by the logic of global rather than local accumulation. However,
relations of asymmetry and dependency are not superseded by globalization, such that the transnational elite brings together "junior partners" in the South who are involved in local decisions and the local
management of global capital and "senior partners" in the North who
are involved in global decisions and global management. Southern
contingents of the transnational elite are agents, in their respective
countries and regions, of the interests of hegemonic transnational
capital. These southern contingents are "technocratic" elites because
they apply, through both the formal state and "private" institutions,
the technical criteria of capitalist production efficiency in managing the
operations of transnational capital, in distinction to earlier "crony
elites," leaders of populist projects in the Third World, and other
competing elites whose criteria and outlook tend to differ from that of
transnational capital.

The transnational elite has an economic project and a political
counterpart to that project. The economic project is neo-liberalism, a
model which seeks to achieve conditions for the total mobility of
capital. This model includes the elimination of state intervention in the
economy and of the regulation by individual nation-states of the
activity of capital in their territories. Neo-liberal structural adjustment
programs sweeping the South seek macro-economic stability (price
and exchange-rate stability, etc.) as an essential requisite for the activity
of transnational capital, which must harmonize a wide range of fiscal,
monetary, and industrial policies among multiple nations if it is to be
able to function simultaneously, and often instantaneously, across
numerous national borders.

Globalization upsets the ability of individual states (in both North
and South) to regulate economic activity within national borders, to
capture and redistribute surpluses, to harmonize conflicting social
interests, and to realize their historic function of sustaining the internal
unity of a nationally conceived social formation. Globalization reduces
the need capital has for each individual state to serve the accumulation

process. The result is a dramatic intensification of what Barnet and Muller called the "managerial dilemma of the state," or what James O'Connor, with more precision, referred to as "the fiscal crisis of the state." According to O'Connor, the capitalist state has dual and ultimately contradictory functions: that of providing the conditions for capital accumulation (its class function), and that of legitimating the social order by representing the nation (its general function) and thus assuring social harmony and a reconciliation of class interests. The globalization process triggers, in particular, spiralling crises of legitimacy.[33] Transnational capital requires that states perform three functions: (1) adopt fiscal and monetary policies which assure macroeconomic stability (2) provide the basic infrastructure necessary for global economic activity (air and sea ports, communications networks, educational systems which impart the specific skills among labor which capital requires in different spatial locations, etc.), and (3) provide social order, that is, stability, which requires sustaining instruments of direct coercion and ideological apparatuses. In a nutshell, we are not witnessing "the death of the nation-state" but their transformation into *neo-liberal states*. The "commanding heights" of state decision-making are shifting to supranational institutions, such as the IMF, the World Trade Organization, and the Trilateral Commission. Gill and Law refer to the imposition of the "structural power" of transnational capital over the "direct power" of the state,[34] which redefines the historic relation between the power of nation-states and the power of formerly nation-based classes. The result is a changing correlation of forces at the international level *not* correlative to changes in the relative power of nation-states.

The economic and political planks of the the transnational elite project are reciprocal. Neo-liberal restructuring makes more porous national borders and deepens the subordination of each nation's internal productive process to external economies. It modernizes capital accumulation by creating conditions under which the capitalist production process can take place in the global economy (hence neo-liberal restructuring is often called "modernization"). This restructuring is "efficient" to the extent that it regenerates the circuit of capital accumulation in the new global environment. The adjustment process facilitates a simultaneous contraction in overall demand and a transfer of income and resources from workers and small-scale producers to large producers and bureaucratic personnel who are subordinate to transnational capital. Restructuring brings about a regressive redistribution of income and a concentration of productive resources in the hands of smaller groups. Absolute and relative poverty has escalated and real wages have plummeted in the South (and much of the North) *simultaneously* with increased growth and increased external debt.[35] There is no objective correlation between economic growth and living conditions and the two are distinct variables. The opening of Third World economies facilitates the transfer of resources from the domestic to the external sector within national economies, and from these to the exterior, strengthening in the process transnational pools in each nation. Thus any effort at a more equitable distribution of political power through democratization runs up against the further concentration of economic power. Shifts in the relative economic weight and power of groups bear directly on the capacity of different sectors to intervene in political processes. By deepening asymmetries between the North and the South and social and economic inequalities within Third World nations, neo-liberal restructuring also redistributes political power locally and globally.

In close correlation to neo-liberalism, the political project of the transnational elite is the consolidation of political systems that function through consensual mechanisms of social control. The new elites in the South have entered into alliances to "promote democracy," or to develop "democratic" consensual forms of social control in their countries in contrast to the earlier forms of authoritarian or dictatorial control. But why consensual over coercive control? Authoritarianism and dictatorship had become a fetter to the emergent patterns of international capital accumulation corresponding to the global economy. Globalizing forces have been disintegrating previously embedded forms of political authority. As Gill points out, the "globalizing thrust of internationally mobile capital [contradicts] the more territorially bounded nature of political authority in the late 20th century."[36] Transnational capital has become sufficiently disruptive and intrusive as to break down barriers that earlier separated and compartmentalized groups in and between societies, while mass communications are integrating what were once secluded social and cultural experiences of different peoples within the world system. The communications revolution has penetrated even the most remote and isolated regions of the world and linked them with an increasingly global civilization. On the one hand, even the most isolated communities are broken up and their members dispersed. The old bonds of social cohesion dissolve and individuals are reintegrated into new national spaces. In turn, mass communications combine with generalized social dislocations to create new intersubjectivities and link national to international spaces. This globalization of social life has brought with it new social movements and revolutions in civil society around the world. In short, people have been pushed by the global economy into new roles as economic and social protagonists, and in this process, have been demanding from below the democratization of social life.

This is what the Trilateral Commission, in its 1975 report *The Crisis of Democracy*, referred to as "the explosion of social interaction, and correlatively a tremendous increase of social pressure." Social and economic developments in the world over the past several decades "have made it possible for a great many more groups and interests to coalesce... the information explosion has made it difficult if not impossible to maintain the traditional distance that was deemed necessary to govern."[37] The report noted that "democratic ethos make it difficult to prevent access and restrict information, while the persistence of the bureaucratic processes which have been associated with the traditional governing systems makes it impossible to handle them at a low enough level." Authoritarian political systems are unable to manage the expansive social intercourse associated with the global economy. Social interaction and economic integration on a world scale are obstructed by authoritarian or dictatorial political arrangements; under the hegemony of transitional capital, they require *consensual* arrangements and their mechanisms of ideological hegemony. It should be recalled that the Trilateral Commission brings together the highest echelons of the corporate, government and intellectual elite in the developed capitalist countries, and represents the thoroughly transnationalized fraction of capital which has become hegemonic on a world scale.

The emergence of a global economy provides the material basis for a *global civil society*. Gramsci noted that the consolidation of the capitalist mode of production in the center countries in the nineteenth century shifted the locus of power firmly and fully into a rising civil society. Similarly, the emergence and consolidation of the global capitalist economy signals the rise of global civil society as the locus of global power and the dispute for hegemony in a transnational setting. According to Cox, power at the global level should be gauged by "state–civil society complexes" not in any one nation, but in an international correlation of force in which Great Powers have the maximum degree of external autonomy, whereas the subordinate powers are penetrated by the former. "The hegemonic concept of world order is founded not only upon the regulation of inter-state conflict but also upon a globally conceived civil society, i.e. a mode of production of global extent which brings about links among social classes encompassed by it."[38] Democratization movements around the world thus develop within the context of transnational political processes and an extended civil society which transcends national bounds.

The globalization of civil society provides the basis for the first time in human history for a global order based on hegemony or consensual domination. Gramsci saw the mechanisms of hegemony tied to consolidation of capitalist production relations, which separates political and civil society into distinct spheres of the social totality. Both Karl Polanyi and Nicos Poulantzas elevated this observation to theoretical status with their respective analyses of the formal (apparent) separation of the political and the economic under capitalism.[39] With the transnationalization of capitalist production and the extension of commodification to the most dispersed and remote communities around the globe civil society emerges on a global scale. Hegemony is a form of domination exercised through civil society. Only in the age of a global civil society can we speak of a global hegemonic social order. Until globalization, transnational hegemony was limited to relations between nations and their complexes of the state and civil society among the industrialized capitalist countries. Cox argues that the liberal world order under *Pax Britannica* achieved world hegemony, since Great Britain had the coercive capacity to enforce obedience and thus achieved global consent to its rules of free trade, the Gold Standard, etc.[40] But this hegemony was among the Great Powers of the center of the world system, whereas the relations that mediated center and periphery – colonial and neo-colonial – were ones of coercive domination. While subordinate classes in the center were drawn into consensual domination, the colonized populations of the peripheral regions, drawn into the world system by European and US powers, never gave their "spontaneous and active consent" to imperial domination.[41] In contrast, in the current epoch, globalizing processes affect all elements (dominant and subordinate groups), directly and indirectly, of each society inserted into the global system, through labor markets, socializing agencies, the mass media, and other institutions. Emergent transnational pools in the South liaise in diverse ways, "inwards," with national and local populations, and "outwards," with their senior Northern counterparts. These pools are therefore transmission belts, located on the boundaries of the national and the transnational, for the penetration of global society and hegemonic incorporation of world majorities.

With the externalization and transnationalization of civil societies, correlations of force at the international level are gauged as much by the power of states and wealth of nations as by power exercised in an increasingly global civil society. Globalization also tends to transnationalize and to integrate national political processes. Prior to globalization, the civil societies and political systems of specific nations could enjoy varying degrees of autonomy, so long as linkage to the world system was through the state and the main actors in the international arena were, in fact, states. In other words, the existence of an authoritarian political system in one country and a "democratic" system in another was not consequential to the linkage of these two countries via trade and financial flows, in distinction to an *organic* linkage via the integration of production systems. Just as earlier in history it was not possible to have two separate political systems and civil societies within the boundaries of a single, integrated national economy, globalizing pressures break down national autonomies and make it increasingly impossible to sustain distinct political systems in an integrated global economy. Economic globalization generates pressures for integration into a single "political regime." Polyarchy is the emergent global political superstructure of the emergent global economy.

Promoting polyarchy should be situated within the model of "transnational practices" (TNPs) proposed by sociologist Leslie Sklair in *Sociology of the Global System*. Sklair argues that the global system as the starting point "is increasingly necessary for the analysis of a growing number of rapidly changing phenomena" and may provide a way out of the impasse into which, in his view, globalizing processes have led international relations and development studies. Sklair's model involves TNPs at three levels: the economic, whose agent is transnational capital; the political, whose agent is a transnational capitalist class; and the cultural, involving a "culture-ideology of consumerism":

> The global system is made up of economic transnational practices and at the highest level of abstraction these are the building blocks of the system. The political practices are the principles of organization of the system. They have to work with the materials on hand, but by manipulating the design of the system they can build variations into it. The cultural-ideological practices are the nuts and bolts and the glue that hold the system together.[42]

But Sklair limits exploration of "transnational political practices" largely to instrumental political pressures exerted by corporate agents, such that transnational corporations and their activity are seen as representing a new political order. What must be problematized is the relation between economic globalization and political processes and systems as linkages which mediate structure and agency. The new US political intervention can be conceived, in the broadest sense, as a transnational political practice by dominant sectors in the United States, acting as the political leadership of an increasingly cohesive transnational elite, for the purpose of installing and stabilizing polyarchic political systems in the South.

US foreign policy and intellectual production: competing definitions of democracy, democratization theory, and reconstituting "democracy" for transnational hegemony

Organic intellectuals: the link between academia and US foreign policy

Whether it is possible for intellectuals to remain above the social conflicts which engulf society, or whether any intellectual activity is neutral in status, is highly questionable. Karl Marx argued that intellectual production cannot be separated from the social relations under which it is produced, and that thought itself flows from the material conditions of life. Karl Mannheim went further: an element of social conflict is that people "think with or against one another." Mannheim claimed that the "intelligentsia" are not a class, have no common interests and are incapable of common and concerted action. They are, he insisted, *ideologues* of one or another class but never speak for "themselves."[43] It is Gramsci's concept of organic intellectuals that does the most to clarify the relationship between US foreign policy and mainstream US academia. This concept is multidimensional and open to distinct interpretations. It concerns the relation of intellectuals to the dominant classes and also their relation to subordinate classes. My concern here is with the former, and in particular with the role of the intellectual strata in developing a relatively coherent worldview rooted in philosophy, science, sociological theory, law, and so forth, in the function of domination.

A class or class fraction that makes a bid for hegemony must acquire *intellectual* and *moral* leadership. Gramsci described organic intellectuals as "experts in legitimization" who do the political and theoretical thinking of the dominant groups, thereby constructing the ideological conditions for hegemony. But organic intellectuals also make essential practical and technical contributions to social order. They theorize on the conditions of existence of a social order as a whole, suggest policies and their justifications, and even participate in their application. The activity of organic intellectuals constitutes a key element of mediation between the structural and the behavioral levels of analysis (and analysis of intellectual production may be seen as structural-conjunctural analysis). The Trilateral Commission report, for instance, is properly seen as reflection by organic intellectuals upon structure in order to orient policy. Organic intellectuals provide the theoretical understanding of historical processes and of structure necessary for dominant groups to engage in the social practice of domination, and for the construction of hegemony as a fit between power, ideas, and institutions.[44] The *immediate* policymaking community has demonstrated a cognizance and intentionality in policy formation without necessarily theorizing on the social activity in which they are involved and the structures with which they interact. However, "backward linkage" between this community and the scholarly community is realized in the intellectual activity of mainstream US academia, where such theorization does take place.

There has been a close "fit" in the post-World War II period between US foreign policy and the mainstream academic community. In particular, modernization and political culture/development theorists provided intellectual guidelines and legitimization for foreign policy, and also contributed important theoretical and practical elements – including developing a new generation of democratization theory – to the development of the new political intervention. These theories should be seen as intellectual movement parallel to and deeply interpenetrated with US policy. In a scientific sense, this intellectual activity is deceptive insofar as (a) value-laden intellectual production steeped in assumptions is presented as objective, scientific and value-free, and (b) there are antinomies internal to these theories which can be exposed and positively associated with real social and political contradictions.

The relation between the scholarly community and the action of dominant groups in US and other state apparatuses, and in supranational institutions, is not merely one of theoretical abstraction. There are organic ties which subordinate intellectuals to dominant groups, ultimately on the basis of the latter's control over the material life of society. Dye documents the role of universities and intellectuals in the policymaking process. "While university intellectuals working independently occasionally have an impact on the policy-making process, on the whole intellectuals who would be heard must respond to policy directions set by the foundations, corporations, and government agencies that underwrite the costs of research" and set overall academic and public agendas.[45] It is worth quoting Cox at some length in this same regard:

> Intellectual production is now organized like the production of goods or of other services. The material basis of networks is provided by formal (usually nongovernmental) organizations as mobilizing and coordinating agencies with research directors and funds (from sources sometimes more, sometimes less visible) for commissioning studies, financing conferences, and symposia or informal luncheon discussions... The material basis of networks allows for a selection of participants which guarantees a certain homogeneity around a basic core of orthodoxy. However, since the object of the exercise is consensus-building, narrow orthodoxy or exclusiveness would be a self-defeating criterion, and the activators of each network extend their search to those whose ideas reach the outer boundaries of what might ultimately be acceptable. Above and beyond material support, the organized network holds out to the intellectual the prospect of political influence, of being listened to by top decision-makers and even of becoming part of the decision-making team.[46]

Ideology and its production are generally spontaneous (intellectually reflexive) and should not be confused with deliberate falsehood. It is not necessary to assume a conspiracy among scholars in the service of hegemony. Such intellectuals need not be conscious of their role in relation to ideology and the structures of domination. Some intellectuals are indeed quite conscious of their role as ideologues and their participation in the structure of power, and they routinely alternate between academia and positions in the formal state apparatus. However, what is pertinent is not the subjective status or conscious intent of intellectuals but the objective significance of the scholarship in question, independent of its agents, in the ideological rationalization of the new political intervention as the "promotion of democracy" and in the provision of technical solutions for effectively carrying out this intervention. Insofar as hegemony is problematic and not given it is constructed and must constantly be reconstructed. The evolution of modernization and political development theory into the new democratization literature parallels the reconfiguration of US–Third World and North–South relations over the past few decades.

From modernization and political development to democratization: theoretical development in the function of policy development

The shift from supporting authoritarian regimes to promoting polyarchy led many intellectuals and academicians who had previously distanced themselves from policies seen as hypocritical or morally objectionable into an enthusiastic embrace of the new modalities of intervention. At the same time as "a democratic miracle sweeping the world" became standard phraseology in US foreign policymaking circles, "democratization" became a veritable boom industry on US campuses and for academic publishers. By the early 1990s, a whole new body of literature on "transitions" and on US "democracy promotion" had become established in government circles, policy planning institutions and mainstream academia.[47] Much of this literature is value-laden and steeped in implicit analytical and theoretical assumptions in such a way that the distinction between those who are writing from the outlook of a policymaker or power-holder, and those who are writing from the viewpoint of social science inquiry, often becomes confused.[48] A critique of "democratization" literature, particularly those works which interface closely with the policymaking community, sheds important light on theoretical and practical aspects of the new political intervention, and also demonstrates how ideology and political practices become rationalized in intellectual activity, which in turns forms the basis for developing the ideological dimensions of hegemony.

There is an underlying continuity between modernization and political culture/political development theories of the 1950s and 1960s, and democratization theories of the 1980s and 1990s. The former constitute the theoretical forerunners of the latter and the development of both has involved a close association between the US state and US academia. Links include generous government funding for research projects, conferences which bring policymakers and intellectuals face-to-face, and studies which either originate in universities and become standard materials used by policymakers, or which originate in policy planning institutes tied to the policymaking process and become standard materials used in universities. This is the case, for example, with two of the most widely cited and circulated volumes: *Transitions from Authoritarian Rule: Prospects for Democracy*, a four-volume collection, edited by Guillermo O'Donnell, Philip C. Schmitter, and Laurence Whitehead, and *Democracy in Developing Countries*, another four-volume series, edited by Larry Diamond, Juan J. Linz, and Seymour Martin Lipset. Both were commissioned with the intent of informing US policy and policymakers, and are considered standard references in government and academia on "transition to democracy."[49] There are direct and indirect mechanisms which mediate the relations between organic intellectuals and state policies, including, but not limited to, a revolving door between posts in universities, posts in the US government, and posts in government-linked but nominally private policy planning institutes, similar to (and overlapping with) the corporate–government revolving door. In turn, literature originating in the government–university nexus has a natural advantage in establishing dominance and authority in the field. It sets the frame of reference for general treatment of the issue, defines the parameters of debate and circumscribes research agendas. In this way, it achieves a certain *intellectual hegemony*.[50]

It was no coincidence that John W. Burgess, founder of the first department of political science in the United States, explained in 1890, at the beginning of a decade which began extra-territorial US expansion, that the new discipline of political science would help "the civilized states" to "undertake the work of state organization" for the populations of the colonial and semi-colonial regions who were "in a state of barbarism or semi-barbarism."[51] The "manifest destiny" and the "civilizing mission" to which Burgess referred reflected racial and colonial theories that provided crude justification for the imperial policies of the United States and the other Great Powers in the era of modern colonialism, from late last century through to the World War II. But the relation between intellectual labor and policy development became considerably more sophisticated after the War. Modernization theories that emanated out of the US social sciences were closely associated with the rise of the United States as the dominant world power and with the emergence of "Third World" protagonists on the world stage, involving simultaneous processes of decolonization and of the reconstruction of world order after the War.

Modernization theory, and its twin cousins, political culture and political development theories, were grounded in the structural-functionalism of sociologist Talcott Parsons and political scientist David Easton that dominated the US social sciences in the postwar years, with its embedded system-maintenance and social order biases.[52] Modernization theory argued that all societies were moving along a continuum from "traditional" to "modern," and "development" meant the process of movement down this continuum. The more developed countries were seen as further advanced along the road, while the underdeveloped countries were "late comers" who were behind but on the same path as the developed countries. The sharp inequalities between nations in an asymmetric international order were to be explained by factors internal to each country and region, particularly to the "traditions," the "anti-modern" attitudes and other impediments located in the cultures of the backward regions, while the colonial experience was not of consequence. Third World countries would be helped along the felicitous path of capitalist economic development with US (and other Western) aid and investment.

Political development and political culture, as concomitants of economic modernization, were seen as two sides of the same coin. The first was the ensemble of political roles, institutions, and actions, and the second, the attendant values, beliefs, and attitudes that underlie political behavior. Modernization would bring about a change in the "political culture" of the developing population, defined along the lines of Parsons's "pattern variables," away from "traditional" values which impede progress and towards "modern" values which facilitate development. As agents of "modern" values, a "modernizing elite" would steer countries down the road to development. This "enlightened" elite, by definition, would need to hold power and be insulated from any popular pressures from below. "The need for elite power requires that the ordinary citizen be relatively passive, uninvolved, and deferential to elites," explained political scientists Gabriel Almond and Sydney Verba in *The Civic Culture*.[53] And just as a country modernizes economically by moving through a continuum of economic stages, it would move through a continuum of political stages which the developed capitalist countries had already passed through, in the build-up of political structures, particularly of state structures.

46

An analysis of the political development literature reveals that the emphasis, at times explicit, at times implicit, was on *order*, and on the capacity of political institutions to perform the function of the maintenance of order. David Easton's "input–output" model constituted the basis for political development theory: inputs are demands and supports for the political structure and the social system, and outputs are the consequent system performance (taxes, legislation, etc.).[54] In the middle there are Easton's "capabilities" and "conversion process" and Parsons's "maintenance" and "adaptive" functions of the political system. The goal is to develop the capacity for the political system to absorb demands, prop up supports, and augment "output." This is to be based on two "developmental processes" – structural/role differentiation and the secularization of values. The normative end goal is to maximize the capacity for system maintenance (social order). The political system has the function of compelling compliance in a social order, and political science assumes as its primary problem the establishment and maintenance of political structures capable of assuring the stability of a social order. The questions addressed in Easton's construct are: How might the political system, the instrument which compels compliance, survive? How might it fulfill its function most effectively? How might the political system absorb "stress" from the larger "social system" in such a way that social order is not threatened? Political development becomes the study of how to manage or change the political system in such a way as to maximize the ability of the state to reproduce the social order and the relations of domination therein.

The political development literature sought to dissect how political systems in the Third World could be constructed which would most effectively perform the role of shielding the prevailing social order from demands that could not be met from within that order.[55] This involved "state-building," "nation-building," "institution-building," "bureaucracy-building," and so forth. Subordinate groups who challenged elites were responsible for disorder. But if the goal of political development was to achieve stability, the concept of social order was not neutral. Social orders involve winners and losers. Stability is not necessarily a condition in the general welfare; it places a normative premium not on order *per se*, but on maintenance of the prevailing social order. Strong governments and political institutions, which were the objective of political development, were not just better able to create declared "public interests," but also to thwart, or deny, collective interests of popular classes.[56] Political development theories

47

approximate Mannheim's notion of "bureaucratic conservatism," whereby specific social interests are attained through forms of political organization, yet these interests are concealed under the implicit assumption that *a specific order is equivalent to order in general.*

Modernization theories guided the thinking of policymakers at the State Department's Agency for International Development (AID) and the non-military aspects of such US undertakings as the Alliance for Progress and economic development programs in Vietnam, in which economic development through US aid and investment was to have removed the political basis for radical movements and for more fundamental changes. Political development theory also became incorporated into foreign policy through development programs in the Third World. "Political development is anti-Communist, pro-American political stability," explained an AID official.[57] The assumptions of modernization theory continue to provide theoretical guidance for, and legitimization of, the economic dimensions of US foreign policy, and particularly the neo-liberal model and its notion that the unfettered operation of transnational capital will bring about development. However, political development theories have undergone major modifications which have helped to theoretically inform the shift to "democracy promotion." The problem with the earlier political development strategizing was that it focused almost exclusively on the state as the locus of social power and the arena for the reproduction of the relations of domination. Gradually, in the social sciences, the focus began to shift to civil society as the principal site of social control. This new focus was congruent with the shift in US policy towards the new political intervention. I return to this point later.

From power of the people to polyarchy

Definitions of concepts are not theoretically neutral and are not simply the result of individual taste or preference of the writer... Definitions of concepts are also mandated by the dominant usages in a group or society, made authoritative by dictionaries, by sanctions against the "wrong" usage. And definitions are also part of the hegemony of language itself, the "deep structure" of meanings buried in the foundations of social order. To broaden the classic statement of Marx, the ruling ideas of an age are not only the ideology of its ruling class but also the vocabulary of dominant elites.

Robert Alford and Roger Friedland[58]

Democracy means only that the people have the opportunity of accepting or refusing the men who are to rule them.

Joseph Schumpeter[59]

Democracy is what philosopher W. B. Gallie terms an *essentially contested concept.*[60] This refers to a concept in which different and competing definitions exist, such that terms themselves are problematic since they are not reducible to "primitives." Each definition yields different interpretations of social reality. In and of themselves, these terms are hollow and their meaning is only discernible from the vantage point of the social and theoretical context of their usage. By their nature, these terms involve implicit assumptions, are enveloped in ideology, and are therefore subsets of broader discourse which sets the framework of the social-political or theoretical agenda in question. Each essentially contested concept comes to have multiple and internally contradictory meanings which are given to it by specific class and group interests with a stake in its definition. Ideological positions, or more precisely, the intersubjective expression of vested class and group interests, are often ensconced in what is presented as scientific, objective discussion of democracy. Analysis should thus uncover these assumptions and their relation to interests.

What US policymakers mean by "democracy promotion" is the promotion of *polyarchy*, a concept which developed in US academic circles closely tied to the policymaking community in the United States in the post-World War II years (the word was first coined by Robert Dahl[61]). Polyarchy refers to a system in which a small group actually rules and mass participation in decision-making is confined to leadership choice in elections carefully managed by competing elites. The pluralist assumption is that elites will respond to the general interests of majorities, through polyarchy's "twin dimensions" of "political contestation" and "political inclusiveness," as a result of the need of those who govern to win a majority of votes. It is theoretically grounded in structural-functionalism – and behind it, the positivist focus on the separate aspects and the external relations of things – in which the different spheres of the social totality are independent, each performing systems maintenance functions and externally related to each other in a larger Parsonian "social system." Democracy is limited to the political sphere, and revolves around process, method and procedure in the selection of "leaders." This is an *institutional* definition of democracy. Political scientist Samuel Huntington notes that the

[handwritten margin note: gov't is supreme]

49

classic definition of democracy as *power/rule by the people* – rooted in the original Greek, power or rule (*cratos*) of the people (*demos*) – and "its derivatives and applications over the ages" have "sharply declined, at least in the American scholarly discussions, and have been replaced by efforts to understand the nature of democratic institutions." Huntington concludes: "Democracy has a useful meaning only when it is defined in institutional terms. The key institution of democracy is the selection of leaders through competitive elections."[62] In turn, polyarchy has been conflated to the staple definition of democracy in both "democratization" and "democracy promotion" literature.[63]

The concept of polyarchy is an outgrowth of late nineteenth and early twentieth-century elite theories developed by Italian social scientists Gaetano Mosca and Vilfredo Pareto. On the one hand, these theories were developed to legitimize the rapid increase in the concentration of wealth and political power among dominant elites, and their ever-greater control over social life, with the rise of corporate capitalism. On the other hand, democracy, by the late nineteenth century, had ceased being an instrument of this industrial elite against the old feudal oligarchy and was instead becoming a vehicle for the demands of those it dominated. In the latter part of their careers, Mosca went on to argue that "democratic" rather than fascist methods are best suited to defend the ruling class and preserve the social order, whereas Pareto went on to embrace fascism as the best method. This split, on the basis of a shared commitment to preserving the social order, constitutes an historical analogy to the debate in US foreign policymaking circles over whether "democracy" or authoritarianism in the Third World is actually the best method of preserving international order. "In perceiving the insight underlying the apparent paradox that democratic methods prudently used can enhance the strength and stability of a ruling class, Mosca solved his problem," notes political scientist Peter Bachrach. "But before his theory could be successfully integrated within the context of modern democratic theory, the theory of democracy itself required a radical revision."[64] That radical revision took place in US academia in the post-World War II years.

The institutional definition embodied in polyarchy came to substitute, at the level of mainstream Western social science, the classic definition of democracy. Despite the emergence of the earlier elite theories, the classic definition had been fairly well established until the post-World War II period. This redefinition thus coincided with a worldwide upsurge of democratic aspirations and movements in the wake of the defeat of fascism and the breakup of the old colonial system. Behind the birth of dozens of newly independent nations, the spread of democratic and national liberation movements, and several successful Third World revolutions were struggles over what new social and political systems would replace the crumbling colonial order. The redefinition of democracy also took place alongside the postwar construction of a new international system and the emergence of the United States as the undisputed world power. It began with Joseph Schumpeter's 1942 study, *Capitalism, Socialism and Democracy*, in which he rejected the "classical theory of democracy" defined in terms of "the will of the people" and "the common good." Instead, Schumpeter advanced "another theory" of democracy: "institutional arrangements for arriving at political decisions in which individuals acquire the power to decide by means of a competitive struggle for the people's vote."[65] This redefinition gave "democratic" content to the anti-democratic essence of Mosca's and Pareto's earlier elitism theories, thus providing for their legitimization. According to Huntington, the debate between the institutional and the classical definition of democracy went on for several decades after World War II, and was concluded with the publication of Robert Dahl's *Polyarchy* in 1971.

In its Parsonian-Schumpeterian version, the polyarchic definition of democracy is equated with the stability of the capitalist social order. By definitional fiat, power is exercised in the general welfare and any attempt to change the social order is a pathological challenge to democracy. "The maintenance of democratic politics and the reconstruction of the social order are fundamentally incompatible," states Huntington.[66] There is no contradiction in this model in affirming that "democracy" exists and also acknowledging massive inequalities in wealth and social privilege. The problem is posed as to how these inequalities might negatively affect the maintenance of "democracy." Therefore, the notion that there may be a veritable contradiction in terms between elite or class rule, on the one hand, and democracy, on the other, does not enter – by theoretical-definitional fiat – into the polyarchic definition. At best, the polyarchic conception leaves open the possibility as to whether "political democracy" may or may not facilitate "social and economic democracy." In contrast, I am arguing that polyarchy as a distinct form of elite rule performs the function of legitimating existing inequalities, and does so more effectively than authoritarianism.

Historian Raymond Williams holds that a class perspective on the politics of language is necessary, since "many crucial meanings have been shaped by a dominant class."[67] Sociologists Robert Alford and Roger Friedland argue that "concepts come to be part of dominant or subordinate paradigms. Clusters of terms come to control discourse when a particular school of thought dominates a university department, a professional association, or a government agency." As such, "paradigms of inquiry become part of the substructure of meanings, which may disappear into the underpinnings of a discipline as its ideology."[68] The polyarchic definition of democracy, which is only one variant of an essentially contested concept, has come to enjoy hegemony, in the Gramscian sense, in social scientific, political, and mass public discourse.

Separating the political system from the socieconomic order: promoting polyarchy and promoting free markets

Ideological development is a process in which ideological positions are constantly modified in an effort to render them internally logical and self-consistent in the face of logical inconsistencies and contradictions in material reality (empirical fact). The labor of organic intellectuals involves resolving logical inconsistencies and offering solutions to real social contradictions. Uncovering the inner ideological core of intellectual production is not achieved by focusing on the reasoned forms of this thought, but rather on the unreasoned assumptions and preconceptions that underlie – and belie – its own external (surface) logics.

Creating an institutional theory of democracy was an intellectual and ideological attempt to resolve once and for all the intrinsically contradictory nature of democratic thought under capitalism, in which one side stresses the sanctity of private property, and therefore legitimizes social and economic inequalities and privileges which rest on the monopolization by minorities of society's material resources, while the other side stresses popular sovereignty and human equality. A similar effort to resolve ideological contradictions springing from real social contradictions took place in the evolution of modernization and political development theory into democratization theory. This intellectual movement paralleled change in policy, from promoting dictatorship to promoting polyarchy, as a response to the real material contradiction of the crisis of elite rule in the Third World. But democratization theory exhibits manifold logical and empirical inconsistencies which become glaring once we study each of its component parts in their interconnections and uncover its *antinomious essence*. In this way we are able to demonstrate the relation between democratization theory, the promotion of polyarchy, globalization, and real social contradictions in emergent global society.

The antinomy in democratization theory is located in its theoretical construct, in Alford and Friedland's "superstructure of meaning," but not in substructure of meaning. The antinomy disappears once we uncover the ideological discourse concealed in the construct or in the political practice which it legitimizes. For example, Adam Przeworski describes democracy as "a particular system of processing and terminating intergroup conflicts." Democracy "thus constitutes an organization of political power... as a system, it determines the capacity of particular groups to realize their specific interests." He separates the political from the socioeconomic system by positing the former as a neutral forum theoretically capable of pendular swings between antagonistic social and economic interests. "The distribution of the probability of realizing group-specific interests – which is nothing less than political power – is determined jointly by the distribution of resources that participants bring into conflicts and by specific institutional arrangements."[69] The political system and the state become chameleons, or clothes that fit any class or group which tries them on. Society is multi-class but power is determined in a "classless democracy" as process: political power is deposited in a democratic state through which classes and groups may withdraw or utilize their share of power in accordance with their resources and their organizational capacity. But the distribution of material resources is determined in the socioeconomic sphere, and the particular distribution will determine the relative strength of groups and group access to political power. The extent of democracy should therefore directly correlate to the extent in which material resources are distributed in an egalitarian fashion, but this proposition is excluded by definition from the construct.

Przeworski acknowledges that democracy is a means for securing ends, an organizational form of the dispute for power as the ability to realize social and economic interests. What makes this "democracy" is that intergroup conflict is processed and terminated by established rules of procedure and a juridical structure. Internal coherence would require the construct to demonstrate how procedure and juridical structure are in the first place established, since these are not pre-given. Such established rules and procedures are, in the Gramscian explanation, those which the dominant classes are able to impose once they have achieved hegemony. Having achieved this hegemony, consensual arrangements are at play for the resolution of conflict without transgressing a given social order. To demonstrate a fit between internal logic and empirical reality, and therefore achieve consistency, Przeworski's construct would have to problematize how the distribution of material resources and the arrangements for the resolution of intergroup conflict are derived. This remains theoretically external to the construct itself and its implicit consensus theory. Its substructure, hence, legitimizes as "democratic" immanent inequalities in the social order.

The antinomy in democratization theory is the separation of the political system from the social order, in turn justified by the institutional definition of democracy and theoretically grounded in structural-functionalism, which separates the "internal" from the "external," and the political from the social and economic spheres of society, conferring a functional autonomy to each subsphere. For instance, Diamond, Linz, and Lipset affirm that democracy "signif[ies] a political system, separate and apart from the economic and social system... Indeed, a distinctive aspect of our approach is to insist that issues of so-called economic and social democracy be separated from the question of governmental structure."[70] An antinomious argument is one in which its inconsistencies or contradictions become apparent only when conclusions are drawn from the synthesis of two propositions which are reasonable in isolation from one another. The separation of the political from the socioeconomic allows for apparently reasonable propositions regarding either sphere; the inconsistencies in *both* only become apparent in the synthesis.

Central to democratization theory is an inconsistent argument: first, it separates the social and the economic from the political sphere, and then it turns around and connects the two by claiming an affinity between democracy and free-market capitalism! Huntington argues, for example:

> The exit from power of rulers who lose elections means that limits must exist on what is at stake in controlling government. If winning or losing was an all-or-nothing affair, those in power would have overpowering incentives to suppress opposition, to rig elections, and to resort to coercion to remain in power if it appeared they had lost an

election. Hence government cannot be the only or even the principal source of status, prestige, wealth, and power. Some dispersion of control over these goods – what Dahl calls "dispersed inequalities" – is necessary. The most important issue here concerns economic power... In all democracies, private ownership of property remains the basic norm in theory and in fact... The existence of such private power is essential to the existence of democracy... Political democracy is clearly compatible with inequality in both wealth and income, and, in some measure, it may be dependent upon such inequality... Defining democracy in terms of goals such as economic well-being, social justice, and overall socioeconomic equity is not, we have argued, very useful.[71]

Huntington unambiguously connects the economic and the political spheres: dispersed inequalities, private property, a free market, etc., are required for the maintanence of a "democratic" political system. Despite his claim to do so, he does not, therefore, limit democracy to the government structure, or to process centered around competitive elections! Neither does Przeworski. And Diamond, Linz, and Lipset, despite their stated definition of democracy as "a political system separate and apart from the economic and social system," similarly assert that "democracy" requires capitalist free markets.[72]

All theory, to acquire social scientific status, must demonstrate logical consistency and empirical verification. Democratization theory fails on both accounts. It argues against any linkage between the political and the socioeconomic system, but then validates itself by making just such a linkage. This is its logical inconsistency. The very theoretical construct precludes from the empirical terrain on which the theory is based the relation between wealth and power, and therefore precludes either empirical verification or falsification of the pluralist assumption on power by examining this relation. Empirical evidence demonstrates that those who hold wealth in society exercise political power directly, through their inordinate influence over (or direct participation in) the state apparatus, and indirectly, through their dominant position in economic institutions and the organs of civil society. This is its failure of empirical verification.

Having exposed the antinomious essence of democratization theory, what concerns us now is its connection to hegemony, which resides in the relation of intellectual thought to the transnational elite project. Promoting polyarchy and promoting neo-liberal restructuring has become a singular process in US foreign policy. The AID explains that promoting polyarchy in the latter part of the twentieth century "is complementary to and supportive of the transition to market-oriented economies."[73] (Since the promotion of capitalism and of polyarchy are seen as symbiotic in US policy, it is therefore more precise to qualify the policy as promoting *capitalist polyarchy*.) If democracy is only "a system of government, separate and apart from the economic and social system," as democratization theory maintains, yet policymakers assert that promoting polyarchy and promoting free markets are inseparable, there is an evident disjuncture between this theory and actual US policy. The discrepancy is an extension of the contradictions already identified in democratization theory and reflects its legitimating function. It is not dispersed inequalities, free markets, the exclusion (from democracy) of economic well-being, social justice, socioeconomic equity, and so on, which enhance democracy, as the theory suggests. Rather, the polyarchic concept of democracy which the United States promotes is an effective political arrangement for legitimizing and sustaining inequalities within and between nations, which, we have seen, are deepening under global capitalism, and therefore of utility to dominant groups in an asymmetric international order.

If the political sphere is separated from the socioeconomic and democracy limited to the former then these inequalities and international asymmetries are of little concern to democratization in the Third World (or only of concern insofar as they threaten the stability of the social order). If democracy is limited to "a system of government," then enormous concentrations of wealth and power in "private" institutions such as transnational corporations are not relevant to "democracy." Discussions of democratization are extraneous to those of transnational power relations, elite domination, hegemony, international asymmetries, and US interventionism. Beyond its legitimating function, mainstream democratization theory, as we shall see below and in the following chapter, also provides technical solutions to practical problems of domination in global society by contributing intellectual precepts to the policy of promoting polyarchy. Its legitimating function is made easier owing to the hegemonic status of the polyarchic definition of democracy. But polyarchy competes with alternative definitions.

Polyarchy versus popular democracy

As an essentially contested concept, polyarchy competes with concepts of *popular democracy*. Although, in distinction to polyarchy, there is no fully elaborated *theory* of popular democracy (a situation which strengthens the hegemonic status of the polyarchic definition), an abundance of literature is available on the subject and on the debate over democracy.[74] The various concepts and views on popular democracy are traceable to the literal, classical Greek definition of democracy as the rule, or power (*cratos*), of the people (*demos*), and rooted in Rousseauian-Marxist traditions. They posit a dispersal throughout society of political power through the participation of broad majorities in decision-making. The model conjoins representative government to forms of participatory democracy that hold states accountable beyond the indirect mechanism of periodic elections. Popular democracy is seen as an emancipatory project of both form and content that links the distinct spheres of the social totality, in which the construction of a democratic political order enjoys a theoretically internal relation to the construction of a democratic socioeconomic order. Democratic participation, in order to be truly effective, requires that democracy be a tool for changing unjust social and economic structures, national as well as international.

In sharp contrast to polyarchy, popular democracy is concerned with *both process and outcome* (although a fully elaborated theory of popular democracy would have to address such issues as the institutional structures of popular democracy and the relation between process and outcome). Popular democracy is thus distinghished from the polyarchic focus on process only, and from the focus of the statist models of the former Soviet bloc on outcome only (and the concept of popular democracy should not be confused with the types of political system that developed under the former Soviet bloc). Elitism theories claim that democracy rests exclusively on process, so that there is no contradiction between a "democratic" process and an anti-democratic social order punctuated by sharp social inequalities and minority monopolization of society's material and cultural resources. Under the polyarchic definition, a system can acquire a democratic form without a democratic content. Popular democracy, in contrast, posits democracy as both a process and a means to an end – a tool for change, for the resolution of such material problems as housing, health, education, access to land, cultural development, and so forth. This entails a dispersal of political power formerly concentrated in the hands of elite minorities, the redistribution of wealth, the breaking down of the structures of highly concentrated property ownership, and the democratizing of access to social and cultural opportunities by severing the link between access and the possession of wealth. It includes acknowledging the public (social) character of "private" institutions in civil society such as universities, cultural establishments, and transnational corporations, holding them accountable, and thoroughly democratizing their operation. Democracy begins with respect for human rights, civil liberties, the rule of law, and elections, and includes the outlawing of racial, ethnic, gender, and other forms of discrimination. These should be seen in the model of popular democracy, not as democracy in itself, but as "pre-conditions" for processes of democratization, which unfold to the extent that structures are developed which allow for participatory democracy, for the direct participation of majorities in their own vital affairs, "upwards" from the local, grassroots level. It is what Carl Cohen refers to as the "breadth, depth, range" of democracy.[75]

The locus of power in both models is civil society: formal political structures regulate the instruments of the state, and democracy (however so defined) limits the powers of the state *vis-à-vis* civil society, in distinction to authoritarian coercive domination, and to statist models of the former Soviet bloc. Relations between the state and civil society theoretically take on the same form under both polyarchy and popular democracy – power flows "upwards" to the state. This is why state managers and organic intellectuals who have developed "democracy promotion" argue that the powers of the state should be limited *vis-à-vis* civil society in intervened countries, and why they emphasize developing the organs of civil society in these countries. The contradiction between polyarchy and popular democracy is not expressed in the degree to which the organs of civil society are able to influence local and national affairs, but in whether elite or popular sectors have achieved hegemony in civil society, and in the degree to which these organs are themselves democratic institutions that popular majorities are able to utilize in their own interests. In polyarchy, the state is the domain of the dominant classes, while the popular classes are incorporated into civil society under the hegemony of the elite – which is the formula for the exercise of consensual domination. Popular democracy involves participatory mechanisms for popular sectors to subordinate and utilize the state in pursuit of their interests, with mobilization in civil society as the principal form in which political power is exercised.

Elections are meaningful components of popular democratization to the extent that mechanisms of participatory democracy linked to formal representative structures allow for accountability and control by the population over those elected. Under polyarchy, "political inclusiveness" (polyarchy's "first dimension") is limited to the right to vote, and mass constituencies have no institutional mechanisms for holding elected officials accountable to them and to the platforms upon which they are elected. Polyarchy theory claims that democracy requires that those elected be insulated, once they take office, from popular pressures, so that they may "effectively govern." If rulers deviate from the "course of action preferred by the citizenry," according to this reasoning, they are to be held accountable by being voted out of office in subsequent elections, since accountability is defined as nothing more than the holding of elections.[76] Polyarchy not only limits democratic participation to voting in elections, but focuses exclusively on *form* in elections. The polyarchic definition of "free and fair" elections are those which are procedurally correct and not fraudulent. Equality of conditions for electoral participation is not relevant to whether elections are "free and fair." These conditions are decidedly unequal under capitalism owing to the unequal distribution of material and cultural resources among classes and groups, and to the use of economic power to determine political outcomes. But economic considerations are excluded by definition from the polyarchic conception, in which "political contestation" (polyarchy's "second dimension") means the juridical right, not the material ability, to become a candidate and vie for power in elections. Equality of influence, as Miliband has noted, "is in fact an illusion. The act of voting is part of a much larger political process, characterized... by marked *inequality of influence*. Concentration on the act of voting itself, in which formal equality does prevail, helps to obscure the inequality, and serves a crucially important legitimating function" (emphasis in original).[77] This legitimating function accounts for polyarchy's *electoral fixation*.

Behind essentially contested concepts are *contested social orders*. Popular democracy and polyarchy rest on antagonistic notions of what a democratic society resembles. In popular democracy, ultimately, a society is democratic to the extent that popular majorities are able to impose their sovereignty – popular sovereignty properly conceived does not refer to a "general interest" but to the interests of popular classes – that society is governed by the "logic of the majority." Under polyarchy it is the inverse: sovereignty is exercised by dominant minorities, but under conditions of hegemony (consensual domination). Terms vary: in mainstream social science consensual domination is "liberal democracy," while critics have coined such phrases as "limited democracy," "restricted democracy," "controlled democracy," or "low-intensity democracy." Class (or popular versus elite) sovereignties are at the heart of worldwide social struggles unfolding under globalization. As is illustrated in the case studies, broad popular movements tended to put forward the model of popular democracy in their demands and in their alternative visions for organizing post-authoritarian societies. In contrast, elites sought capitalist polyarchy as the goal of anti-dictatorial struggles.

An exploration of the contradiction between polyarchy and popular democracy raises two questions. First, to what extent do processes of popular democratization run up against constraints inherent in the capitalist mode of production? Private appropriation of the social product is in the last instance the social relation which underpins the separation of real from formal power, and democratic form from democratic content. Without doubt, implementation of the full model of popular democracy requires the supersession of capitalism, and I return briefly to this issue in the conclusion. But the question may be a relative one: just how much popular democratization is possible within the limits imposed by capitalism is not clear. However, it is not theoretical reflection that motivates masses of people to demand the democratization of their life conditions. Perceptions of individual and collective interests and the dynamics of mass consciousness are as important in this regard as structural analysis of political economy. Democratization struggles are played out at the level of intersubjectivities not as contradictions between modes of production or social orders, but as concrete struggles for practical change in daily life. Democratization struggles take on a dynamic which is autonomous of historic contradictions between modes of production. The global economy generates pressures under which subordinate groups mobilize and dominant groups tend to shift from coercive to consensual forms of domination. But the outcome to societal struggles against authoritarianism in peripheral and semi-peripheral regions of the world system is not predetermined.

The second question raised is to what extent does a polyarchic political system itself constrain popular democratization? Polyarchic political systems tend to set boundaries in which social struggles unfold whose parameters do not transgress the social order. Polyarchy plays a legitimating function for an increasingly cohesive transnational elite that seeks to legitimate its rule by establishing formal democratic institutions. And ideology as a material force establishes patterns of conduct which fix limits on social action. But the problem is not just ideological. Polyarchy also place enormous *institutional* constraints on popular democratization. Polyarchy as the political institutionalization of social relations of power limits state accountability to periodic elections. Between elections groups who control the state are free to pursue their agenda without any accountability and insulated from popular pressure. The polyarchic state may legitimately employ repression against popular sectors that transgress legality when the demands they place on the state are not met (they usually are not). Thus while authoritarianism insulates but does not legitimate elite rule, polyarchy performs both functions. Attempts to challenge elites within the bounds of polyarchic legality run up against the vastly superior resources of the elite. The structural power of transnational capital in the global economy gives political and ideological power to elites tied directly and indirectly to transnational capital, and also gives the transnational elite "veto power" over local states which by chance of circumstances are captured by popular sectors. This structural power combines with the institutions of polyarchy and provides an immanent class advantage to those who command superior resources. These ideological, institutional and structural constraints to the democratization of social life under global capitalism are mutually reinforcing. They lend themselves to non-coercive mechanisms of social control and, therefore, to elite hegemony. The case studies tend to support these propositions.

The notion of national sovereignty requires theoretical rethinking in light of globalization. In an interdependent world economy, in which autarky, besides being undesirable in terms of restricting development possibilities, is not possible, the issue is not "economic independence." Rather, it is how popular majorities whose locus of political life is still the nation-state may take advantage of economic interdependence to develop autonomous economic spaces. Popular democratization ultimately depends on international conditions which are beyond the control of individual nations. However, the conjoining of formal political (state) sovereignty and popular sovereignty in society, springing from internal popular democratization, constitutes the terms under which majoritarian social groups organized in nations and groups of nations may struggle for greater equity in the international order. The utilization of political sovereignty to secure greater equity between nations and greater control over national resources involves struggles over redirecting surpluses and stemming the outward drainage of wealth towards the centers of an asymmetric world economy. Shifts in the correlation of forces towards the popular classes within nations and regions, conjointly at the level of state and civil society, have deep repercussions for international relations and changes in world order. This is what Gramsci meant when he wrote: "Do international relations precede or follow (logically) fundamental social relations? Any organic innovation in the social structure... modifies organically absolute and relative relations in the international field too."[78] Modifications in the international political economy, including the creation of more symmetric relations among peoples and regions, begin with basic changes in social relations of the type envisioned by popular democracy.

Despite the open-endedness of these issues, the implications of substituting this literal or classic definition of democracy with the institutional definition embodied in polyarchy are vast. By limiting the focus to political contestation among elites through procedurally free elections, the question of who controls the material and cultural resources of society, as well as asymmetries and inequalities, among groups within a single nation and among nations within the international order, becomes extraneous to the discussion of democracy. It should be clear that promoting popular democracy constitutes a profound threat to the interests of dominant classes in the United States and the centers of the world system and their junior counterparts in the South. When US policymakers and organic intellectuals speak of "promoting democracy," they do not, as a matter of course, mean promoting popular democracy. But more than this, they mean the *suppression* of popular democracy, in theory and in practice.

Controlling (and limiting) democratization during "transitions": "trade-offs" and elections

Successful politics is always "the art of the possible". It is no less true, however, that the possible is often achieved only by reaching out towards the impossible which lies beyond it.

Max Weber[79]

What happens in other forms of government – namely, that an organized minority imposes its will on the disorganized majority –

happens also and to perfection, whatever the appearance to the contrary, under the representative system. When we say that the voters "choose" their representative, we are using a language that is very inexact. The truth is that the representative *has himself elected by the voters*. [Emphasis in original.]

Gaetano Mosca[80]

Struggles for democracy go beyond class lines. Democratization movements may ultimately be pro- or anti-systemic, and usually incorporate aspects of both.[81] However, these movements are not separable from class struggle. Under dictatorship, struggles for democracy often become multi-class and majoritarian. But the further majorities push in these movements for outcomes of popular democratization, the more dominant classes either withdraw from these movements (or revert to supporting authoritarianism), or alternatively try to gain control over and contain society-wide mobilization. Where enough social forces accumulate to create a polar situation between authoritarianism/ dictatorship and social majorities – such as in Chile, the Philippines, Nicaragua, and Haiti – the underlying struggle shifts from democracy versus dictatorship to the terms and reach of the democratization process. Under the policy of promoting polyarchy, the United States converges with broad majorities in the dictatorship-versus-democracy divide. But in the underlying struggle, the convergence is between the United States and local elites around a program whose objective is to suppress popular democracy. Controlling and limiting popular democratization during transitions becomes the goal of US intervention.

As mass popular pressures grow for an end to dictatorship, a quick return to elite civilian rule becomes a means for defusing a popular or revolutionary outcome to the demise of authoritarianism. In such situations, notes Gramsci, "various strata of the population are not all capable of orienting themselves equally swiftly, or of reorganizing with the same rhythm. The traditional ruling class, which has numerous trained cadres, changes men and programmes and, with greater speed than is achieved by the subordinate classes, reabsorbs the control that was slipping from its grasp."[82] These are controlled transitions. Dominant social classes that were direct governing classes prior to dictatorship, and had lost direct political power, turn – in competition with popular sectors – to recovering that power. Their high-risk gamble is to assure the transfer of power to their hands from authoritarian regimes *and* simultaneously to keep under careful control the mobilization of the masses and limit their agenda of social

63

emancipation. This is why, in instances such as Marcos's Philippines, Pinochet's Chile, and Duvalier's Haiti, the United States stepped in just as mass, society-wide mobilization in favor of democratization was reaching a peak, and began to "promote democracy" where it had formerly supported dictatorship, as we shall see.

This is rationalized in democratization theory with the argument that the only way to assure "democracy" is to accept the boundaries of the possible, and "the possible" is a functional capitalist polyarchy.[83] Popular forces have to be restrained in order to assure a stable transition, and are held responsible for jeopardizing "democracy" by inducing with their social demands a resurgence of authoritarianism. Democratization theorists such as O'Donnell and Schmitter argue prescriptively that demands which go beyond the acceptable boundaries of capitalist polyarchy should be deferred as "trade-offs" necessary to assure the end of authoritarianism. One is the "equity trade off," or the deferral of social justice and economic equality under the supposition that deprived majorities will at some future point win justice and equality through the "freedoms" afforded by "liberal democracy." But the consolidation of polyarchy and its legitimizing rules and institutions systematically constrain social change in the post-transition period, as we shall see in the case studies. Another "trade-off" is concessions to the military, including preservation of existing military structures and promises not to prosecute militaries for human rights violations committed during dictatorships. Hegemony is "consensus armored by coercion." What takes place in transitions to polyarchy is a shift from coercive to consensual mechanisms in the practice of domination, but not the elimination of a coercive apparatus which, in the last instance, girds the social order. In the practice, preservation of the military (and even a legal impunity often built into post-transition juridical structures) in transitions to polyarchy in the 1980s and early 1990s kept in place formal apparatuses of coercion that acted to thwart – by the threat of repression or by actually repressing, legally or extra-legally – any challenges to the social order, or even those popular demands which do not transgress the social order itself but are deemed unacceptable. Latent coercive force thus circumscribes the decisions of groups and the actions they take in the exercise of formal legal rights. The preservation of the coercive apparatus during transitions guards against demands for popular democracy in the post-transition period.

"Trade-offs," therefore, are not merely "transitional" concessions of a tactical character; they become a structural feature of the post-authoritarian political landscape, as the case studies illustrate. What is at stake with the end of authoritarianism is the political and socio-economic project that will replace it. So-called "trade-offs" facilitate the hegemony over transitions by polyarchic elites, often called the "moderates" or the "center" in democratization literature. These promoters of polyarchy strive to assure that in recovering power from authoritarian regimes, the relations of class domination themselves are not jeopardized. The process of regime transition should not get out of hand, such that a greater quota of political power passes from the authoritarian regime directly to the popular classes.

Electoral processes, when properly controlled, can contribute to this elite effort. Elections serve a legitimacy function, provide an immanent advantage to those who command superior resources, and, when isolated from other aspects of popular democratization, provide a key mechanism for intra-elite compromise and accommodation, and therefore stability. For these and other reasons, electoral processes are often pivotal in transitions to capitalist polyarchy and figure prominently in both democratization theory and in the actual US policy of promoting polyarchy. "For a transition to political democracy to be viable in the long-run, founding elections must be freely conducted, honestly tabulated, and openly contested, yet their results *cannot be too accurate or representative of the actual distribution of voter preference* [emphasis mine]," argue O'Donnell and Schmitter. "Put in a nutshell, parties of the Right-Center and Right must be 'helped' to do well, and parties to the Left-Center and Left should not win by an overwhelming majority."[84] Elections play a key role in channeling mass protest and social demands into controllable processes and non-threatening outcomes. When electoral processes controlled from above substitute society-wide mobilization for democratization, it is easy to steer "transitions," or the breakup up of authoritarianism, into clearly delineated parameters with attendant constraints on current outcomes and on future possibilities. And we shall see that the United States *does*, in fact, "help" right-center and right parties to do well.

Controlling transitions also involves *controlled* demilitarization. The effort to demilitarize Latin America and other regions on the part of local civilian elites and US policymakers in the wake of "transitions to democracy" should not be confused with an intent to eliminate the coercive capacity of the new neo-liberal states. The new elites of the global economy did not perceive the old-style militaries as capable of providing conditions propitious to transnational models of capital accumulation and long-term political stability. Corrupt militaries seeking their own corporate privileges were a fetter to capitalist modernization, an unproductive drain on resources, necessary only insofar as social control requires a coercive component, and dangerous to the consolidation of polyarchy. For economic, social and political reasons, controlled demilitarization is a requirement for the success of the transnational elite agenda. *Controlled* demilitarization as a component of *controlled* "democratization" sought to make military authority subordinate to civilian elites, but *not* to do away with a repressive military apparatus, and its ideal type, for US policymakers and local elites, is the "Panama model," imposed on that country following the 1989 US invasion. In this model, armed forces are "professionalized," purged of both nationalist tendencies and the most unruly and ambitious authoritarian elements, and reduced to constabularies able to suppress popular demands and protests against neo-liberalism, while the United States retains the role of international policeman, responsible for regional and global "security," fighting drug-trafficking, terrorism, and other "threats."[85]

Reconstituting "democracy": the shift in social control from political to civil society

In the distinction between means (policies) and ends (interests) in US foreign policy, the imperative for polyarchy lies in the view that "democracy" is the most effective means of assuring stability, the former seen as but a mechanism for the latter. This is in contrast to prior periods in US foreign-policy history – and correlatedly, to the historic norm in center–periphery relations predicated on coercive modes of social control, such as in the colonial era – when military dictatorships or authoritarian client regimes (and before them, colonial states) were seen as the best guarantors of social control and stability. The intent behind promoting polyarchy is to relieve domestic pressure on the state from subordinate classes for more fundamental change in emergent global society. Military regimes and highly unpopular dictatorships, such as Somoza in Nicaragua, the Shah in Iran, Marcos in the Philippines, the Duvaliers in Haiti, and Pinochet in Chile, defended US and local elite interests. But they also engendered mass-based opposition movements that sought outcomes, beyond the mere removal of dictatorships, of popular democratization. These movements became transnational in their significance as globalization proceeded and threatened core and local elite interests. The old authoritarian arrangements were no longer guarantors of social control and stability. On the one hand, says Gershman, "traditional autocrats... simply cannot adapt to the pace of change and conflicting political pressures of the modern world." On the other is "the declining utility of conventional military force in the contemporary world." In this context, "competition is likely to continue to shift from the military to the political realm, and it will become increasingly important for the West to develop a sophisticated and long-term strategy for democratic political assistance."[86] Several events in the late 1970s brought home this lesson to US policymakers. One was the successful transitions in Southern Europe, particularly Portugal, from authoritarianism to polyarchy as a result of decisive Western European support for polyarchic elites as a strategy of containing socialist movements. Another, more compelling for US policymakers, was the Iranian revolution, followed shortly afterwards by the Nicaraguan in July 1979. "The Nicaraguan experience shattered both sides of the argument over US attitudes towards friendly Third World autocrats," explained Gershman:

> On one hand, the conservative view that such regimes are a bulwark against communism seemed a good deal less compelling after the Sandinistas took over from Somoza. The Nicaraguan events seemed to bear out a different analysis, namely, that right-wing authoritarianism is fertile soil for the growth of Marxist-Leninist organizations... On the other hand, the liberal side of the argument – that policy sufficed in simply seeking the removal of authoritarian dictatorships, as communist movements could be defeated by denying them this easy target – fared no better. As long as the Communists were the most determined alternative to Somoza, the downfall of the dictatorship would enable them to take power. Thus in the wake of Nicaragua both conservatives and liberals needed a fresh approach to the question of defending democracy in the Third World... Shirley Christian said in the epilogue of her study of the Nicaraguan revolution: "Only by promoting democratic political development on a long-term basis can the United States hope to avoid the hard choices between sending troops and accepting a regime that overtly opposes its interests." Promoting democracy, in other words, is... a matter of national security.[87]

In the past, the US state promoted authoritarianism as the political system judged most appropriate for the free operation of international capital, and in this way functioned as what sociologists James Petras and Morris Morley refer to as the "imperial state," promoting and protecting the expansion of capital across state boundaries by the multinational corporate community.[88] Under globalization the "imperial state" still plays the same role of promoting and protecting the activity of transnational capital, but globalizing pressures have inverted the positive correlation between the investment climate and authoritarianism. Now, a country's investment climate is positively related to the maintenance of a "democratic" order, and the "imperial state" promotes polyarchy in place of authoritarianism. But this shift required a corresponding reconceptualization of the principal target in intervened countries, from political to civil society, as the site of social control.

There is a critical link in this regard between the "breakdown of democracy" referred to in the 1975 Trilateral Commission report, *The Crisis of Democracy*, and the subsequent development of "democracy promotion" in foreign policy. The "breakdown of democracy" was seen as generated by the uncontrolled demands of popular sectors and oppressed groups in societies where formal political democracy allowed these groups to mobilize and press their demands. This was described in the report as "intrinsic challenges to the viability of democratic government which grow directly out of the functioning of democracy," and an example of "the dysfunctions of democracy."[89] This seminal report was not, in fact, really about the "breakdown" of democracy; it was about the *breakdown of social control*. It argued that an "excess of democracy" was a "threat" to the social order and established authority. Huntington, one of the authors of the report, stated that the danger

> comes not primarily from external threats, though such threats are real, nor from internal subversion from the left or the right, although both possibilities could exist, but rather from the internal dynamics of democracy itself in a highly educated, mobilized and participant society... there are also potentially desirable limits to the indefinite extension of political democracy.[90]

This concern with how too much "uncontrolled" democracy can threaten the existing social order materialized in Chile. There, a self-declared socialist came to power and proposed to implement a project of sweeping, popular socioeconomic transformation for which he was elected, utilizing the constitutional instruments of formal democracy. Henry Kissinger called this a "fluke of the Chilean political system."[91]

Allende's government challenged the existing social order from within its own legitimizing institutions (see chapter 4). With the Chilean experience in mind, among others, the Trilateral Commission report stressed the need to "reconstitute democracy" in order to assure that "democracy" does not generate its own instability, both within states and in the international system.[92] Another of the report's authors, Michel Crozier, emphasized the need to "carry through a basic mutation in [the] mode of social control," to "experiment with more flexible models that could produce more social control with less coercive pressure."[93]

US "democracy promotion," as it actually functions, sets about not just to secure and stabilize elite-based polyarchic systems but to have the United States and local elites thoroughly penetrate civil society, and *from therein* assure control over popular mobilization and mass movements (that is, correct the "flukes," or "dysfunctions," of democracy). This is in distinction to earlier strategies to contain social and political mobilization through a focus on control of the state and governmental apparatus. Stephen Gill, in analyzing the Trilateral Commission report and the thinking at the highest echelons of the US foreign-policy establishment, notes that the emergent model of "reconstituted democracy" corresponds "to the concept of civil society, and indicate[s] its centrality in the making of state policy."[94] Philip Schmitter and Terry Lynn Karl note: "At its best, civil society provides an intermediate layer of governance [read: control] between the individual and the state that is capable of resolving conflicts and controlling the behavior of members without public coercion."[95] US strategists have shifted attention from the state and governmental apparatus of other countries to forces in civil society as a key locus of power and control. The composition and balance of power in civil society in a given Third World country is now just as important to US and transnational interests as who controls the governments of those countries. This is a shift from social control "from above" to social control "from below" (and within), for the purpose of managing change and reform so as to preempt any elemental challenge to the social order. This explains why the new political intervention does not target governments *per se*, but groups in civil society itself – trade unions, political parties, the mass media, peasant associations, women's, youth, and other mass organizations.

This shift concurs with critiques made from within the policymaking establishment and its organic intellectuals of earlier theories of modernization in the Third World. These theories argued that Third World countries would be helped along the felicitous path of capitalist economic development with US (and other Western) aid and investment, and that stable polyarchic democracy would naturally flow from economic modernization. However, modernization theories came under criticism as political unrest in the Third World increased during the 1960s despite US aid and investment programs and registered growth in GNPs. As a result, a new body of literature emerged: *political development*. Most notable is Huntington's 1968 classic, *Political Order in Changing Societies*, which argued that the political and civil institutions in the Third World (i.e., political parties, trade unions, civic groups, governmental structures) were not sufficiently developed to absorb the tensions and dislocations associated with modernization. US policy, therefore, had to look beyond merely assuring a friendly government and promoting economic growth; it had to focus on the development of political and civic institutions as it became involved in the Third World. After arguing in the Trilateral Commission report that "excessive democracy" was a "threat," Huntington updated the thinking developed there in an oft-cited 1984 article, "Will More Countries Become Democratic?" linking it more explicitly to the emergent transnational agenda by positing a close relation between unfettered free-market capitalism (neo-liberalism) and democracy (polyarchy). Reiterating that "democracy" could best absorb the social and political tensions associated with global restructuring, he argued that the prospects for "democracy" in the 1980s and beyond would require, in addition to implementing neo-liberalism, building autonomous institutions in civil society, and particularly a bourgeoisie autonomous of the state and of state economic intervention. Huntington added that "democracy" could be further enhanced "as a result of direct efforts by the American government to affect political processes in other societies."[96] Through "democracy promotion," the United States seeks to build up in other countries the political and civic infrastructure that Huntington stressed was insufficient to absorb tensions and thereby to assure stability.

Promoting polyarchy to suppress popular democracy and construct transnational hegemony

Formal democratic structures are seen as more disposed to diffusing the sharpest social tensions and to incorporating sufficient social bases with which to sustain stable environments under the conflict-ridden and fluid conditions of emergent global society. Under a hegemonic social order, that is, under consensual domination, the state is still the site of the "processing" of demands and the reproduction of the relations of domination, yet the "input" side of the Eastonian equation is altered, since many an "input" is "resolved" within civil society, before it ever reaches the state. Hegemonic ideologies contain key political and socioeconomic concepts which establish the legitimacy or illegitimacy of the demands placed on the social order. The "political system" remains the institutionalized arena for processing these demands, yet a hegemonic social order implies a more expansive political system incorporating, or fusing, the state and civil society. All demands are not processed in the same way. Those that serve to reproduce the social order (and thereby benefit the long-term interests of the dominant groups) are legitimized in civil society and filtered *upwards* to the state. Those that challenge the social order itself are delegitimized and filtered *out* of the very legitimizing parameters of that order.[97] Polyarchy, as a form of elite rule distinct from authoritarianism and dictatorship, is better equipped under the conditions of social dislocation and political reorganization that accompany each nation's entrance into the global economy to confront, or at least control, popular sectors and their demands. Polyarchic political systems lend themselves to more durable forms of social control, and therefore to stability.

But trappings of democratic procedure in a polyarchic political system do not mean that the lives of those in nations where the United States is "promoting democracy" become filled with authentic or meaningful democratic content, much less that social justice or greater economic equality is achieved. Seen in the light of popular democracy, US "democracy" and "democratization," have nothing to do with meeting the authentic aspirations of repressed and marginalized majorities for political participation and for greater socioeconomic justice. Nevertheless, the new political intervention is complex and cannot be reduced to simplistic scenarios or conspiratorial plots in which elite, polyarchic players A, B, and C in the intervened countries are supported by Washington, and popular democratic leaders D, E, and F are suppressed (even though, ironically, this *is* what sometimes takes place). Even as alternative concepts of democracy compete, the aspirations for democratization strike deep chords among broad sectors of the population, and calls for democracy in historically anti-democratic systems find resonance throughout civil and political society. Democratization movements are therefore almost always majoritarian social struggles. This study requires assimilating a level of analytical abstraction in which the focus is on the intersection of US policy with the aims and objectives of multiple and competing groups who are involved in majoritarian struggles for democracy.

In synopsis, the extended policymaking community has developed a theoretical awareness and a practical attunement to what is required for the maintenance of social control in twenty-first-century global society. The community analyzed the dramatic changes in the international correlation of forces between the 1960s and the 1990s which occurred simultaneously with new challenges raised by subordinate groups in the world system for a redistribution of resources and the democratization of social life. This community also perceived the increasing structural power of transnational capital and the emergence of transnational forces in the wake of globalization, including reconfigured transnational blocs, and explored the prospects for new forms of transnational political organization. Its awareness and attunement (the behavioral level) developed on the basis of the theoretical and intellectual reflection (the structural-conjunctural level) that took place among organic intellectuals linked directly and indirectly to the state, and on the heels of the general crisis of elite rule in the South. Authoritarianism increasingly proved to be an untenable mode of domination and an unpredictable means of preserving asymmetries within and among nations as globalizing processes began to assert themselves (the structural level). As argued by its promoters, polyarchy should prove to be more resilient in constructing and maintaining global order. But the shift is in the means, not the ends, of US policy. It involves a change in methods, in formal political-institutional arrangements, and in cultural and ideological discourse. The ends are defense of the privileges of Northern elites and their Southern counterparts in a highly stratified world system. Promoting polyarchy is an attempt to develop a transnational Gramscian hegemony in emergent global society. These are the theoretical underpinnings of the new political intervention.

2 Political operations in US foreign policy

> A US stance in favor of democracy helps get the Congress, the bureaucracy, the media, the public, and elite opinion to back US policy. It helps ameliorate the domestic debate, disarms critics (who could be against democracy?), provides a basis for reconciliation between "realists" and "idealists"... The democracy agenda enables us, additionally, to merge and fudge over some issues that would otherwise be troublesome. It helps bridge the gap between our fundamental geopolitical and strategic interests... and our need to clothe those security concerns in moralistic language... The democracy agenda, in short, is a kind of legitimacy cover for our more basic strategic objectives.
>
> Howard Wiarda[1]

> Support for democracy... is becoming the new organizing principle for American foreign-policy.
>
> State Department policy document, 1987[2]

The policy shift from promoting authoritarianism to promoting polyarchy was a lengthy process drawn out over several decades, and reflected in the mainstream social sciences in debates over modernization, economic development, political development, democracy, and so on. It involved the gradual emergence of a working consensus in the foreign-policy establishment in support of the new political intervention. As well, it involved the development of new modalities, instruments, and agencies for actually accomplishing the transition, in intervened countries in the Third World, from authoritarianism to polyarchy. This reorientation entailed, in particular, the expansion of what is known as *political operations* in US foreign policy. This included a new foreign-policy instrument, *political aid*, which has come to supplement the two main tools of US foreign policy since World War

II, military and economic aid programs. These are the issues explored in this chapter.

Reconstructing foreign-policy in a new world order

The United States rode on the crest of global power in the decades following World War II. With its overwhelming military superiority, economic power, and political influence, Washington had little difficulty imposing its will on the Third World through "straight power relations." Given its critical mass of both direct (military-political) and structural (economic) power, such a strategy was highly effective. But the global US empire was shaken in the 1960s and 1970s by nationalist revolutions in the Third World, culminating in the US defeat in Indochina. That defeat eroded the US capacity to shape events abroad, threw into disarray traditional strategies towards the Third World, and shattered the post-World War II foreign policy consensus at home. As US influence continued to wane, two subsequent events demonstrated the vulnerability of authoritarian regimes and underscored to policy-makers the imperative of reconstructing foreign policy: the collapse of the Shah's client regime in Iran in early 1979 and the inability of the United States to control subsequent developments there, followed just months later by the Nicaraguan revolution.

For a brief period in the late 1970s, policy was thrown into confusion and paralysis, as the foreign-policy community groped for an effective and coherent new formula for coming to terms with a waning *Pax Americana*. What was taking place at a structural level was the transition to the global economy, the emergence of transnational capital as the hegemonic fraction of capital on a world scale, and the dissolution of an international system whose stability had rested on competing nation-states with a dominant center (a "hegemon"). But a disjuncture appeared between this level and that of the practical-conjunctural, in which the policymaking community perceives world events, conducts often acrimonious internal debates, and develops and implements policies.

By the end of the 1970s, a consensus was emerging around the broad contours – but not the concrete policies – of the transnational agenda among the dominant classes in the United States. These classes are correlated to the policymaking community, but are not synonymous with it *per se* nor with the specific governing bureaucracy, that is, with those groups who exercise the formal powers of state.[3] That consensus revolved around the notion that the United States, playing a leadership role for the transnational elite, had to develop policies to reconstruct the international order, and to move from the defensive to the offensive as a first step. This would include broad new political, military, and economic programs to place revolutionary and nationalist forces in the Third World, as well as the Soviet Union, on the defensive, and to help adjust the United States to the reality of the emergent global economy and society. There was a perceived need for a new reassertionism," a term which entered the lexicon of the foreign-policymaking community at this time (although "reassertionism has been identified with Reagan, it was first launched by the Carter administration, whose cabinet was drawn almost entirely from the Trilateral Commission and represented the transnational fraction). The consensus also included the fiscal and monetary policies of "Reaganomics," which sought to attune US economic policies to changes in global capital accumulation and in the role of the state.

These policies were articulated by the transnationalized fraction of the US elite as the agent that gradually forged consensus. The semi-private institutions which are at the very core of the transnationalized fraction, the Council on Foreign Relations and the Trilateral Commission – through which it debates and elaborates strategies, develops cohesion and outward projection – sponsored studies in the late 1970s to design a new world order. These included the Council's "1980s Project" and the Commission's study, "Towards a Renovated International System."[4] The Council is broadly "bipartisan" and its general policy directives normally represent consensus positions reached among dominant groups in the United States. It is the single most powerful and influential elite policy planning group, and has been largely responsible for the overall direction of US foreign policy since World War II. In turn, the Council on Foreign Relations is closely tied to the Trilateral Commission, which is the quintessential political forum of the transnational elite, the "transnational managerial class" which stands at the apex of the global class structure. The conclusions of the two projects were broadly congruent. They called for a "moderate international order," which meant a world economic environment in which barriers to the free movement of capital, goods, and technology would be dismantled, and a new international division of labor in which labor-intensive phases of production would be transferred to the South, and they reiterated the Trilateral Commission's earlier call for reconstituted "democracy." In addition, the "1980s Project" called for a military build-up and the redeployment of US forces around the globe.

The notion of consensus here corresponds to the Gramscian concept of positions advanced by hegemonic fractions within classes and groups, and not to perfect agreement, to a congruence of interests, or to the absence of conflict. One expression of the disjuncture mentioned above between structural and conjunctural levels of policy was the neo-conservative movement that came to exercise formal state power with the election of Ronald Reagan to the presidency in 1980. In a phenomenon that confused analysts of foreign-policy, the direct agents of US "reassertionism" and "Reaganomics" became this highly vocal neo-conservative movement, concentrated in a new right-wing within the Republican Party. The neo-conservatives renewed the Cold War with a vengeance and launched a worldwide counteroffensive against liberation movements and nationalist Third World governments, involving dozens of interventionist campaigns.[5] Its discourse was extremist: "War, not peace, is the norm in international affairs," proclaimed the Santa Fe document, drafted in 1980 by Reagan officials as a blueprint for a new US foreign policy. "Detente is dead. Survival demands a new US foreign policy. America must seize the initiative or perish."[6] The "Reagan Doctrine" of aggressive support for counterrevolutionary insurgencies and heightened confrontation with the Soviet Union was backed by the biggest peacetime military build-up in US history and a redeployment of US military, paramilitary, intelligence, and political forces around the globe.

While some neo-conservative policies coincided with the transnational agenda, such as a deepening of "reassertionism" and the military build-up, certain policies diverged, including a tendency towards protectionism (reflecting the interests of regional and national capitalist fractions that formed part of the neo-conservative political base). But what is of particular importance to this study is that original officials in the first Reagan administration, such as Jeanne Kirkpatrick and Alexander Haig, favored uncritical support for traditional client regimes and pro-United States dictatorships. The effect of failing to support allies such as Somoza is that "everywhere our friends will have noted that the United States cannot be counted on in times of difficulty and our enemies will have observed that American support provides no security against the forward march of history," reasoned

Kirkpatrick, in her oft-cited article "Dictators and Double Standards."[7] In fact, Kirkpatrick argued that the United States should *strengthen* its reliance on authoritarianism to defend US interests.

This disjuncture is a complexity grounded in issues of political sociology, among them conflict between competing class fractions, the relative autonomy of the state, the divergence between the public discourse of "proximate policymakers" and strategic discourse private to members of dominant groups, and strategies of developing and appropriating legitimizing symbols and ideology. Besides, the disjuncture should not be exaggerated. In analyzing the reconstruction of US world supremacy under the Reagan administration, Augelli and Murphy point out that Reagan appealed to what Gramsci referred to as the "common sense" (contradictory consciousness) of significant portions of the US mass public.[8] But Augelli and Murphy overstate the discrepancy between the Reaganites and the "world management oriented" (transnational) fractions. When closely scrutinized, the Reagan program served the interests of transnational capital on the eve of globalization – a shift in wealth from labor to capital, dismantling the Keynesian state, and deregulating capital at home and pursuing liberalization and reassertionism abroad. Ideological mass appeal to the emotive and psychological chords of "common sense" played an important role in relegitimating US and world order and thus helped surmount the post-Vietnam War, post-Watergate "crisis of governability" which had led to an incipient breakdown of hegemony. In this sense, Reaganism laid the ideological terrain for the agenda of the transnational elite in the 1980s, in a way not dissimilar to the Gingrich phenomenon in the 1990s.

The point to stress here is that the right-wing insurgency in US policy associated with the rise of the the neo-conservatives in the early 1980s actually masked a broad consensus then emergent in the strategic centers of US power and in the foreign-policy establishment around the transnational agenda. In Gill's analysis, the transnational fraction of capital had unequivocally established its hegemony by the mid-1980s and was able to fully impose its policies on the US state. Gill identifies the second Reagan presidency, beginning in 1984, as the turning point. From that point on, core economic and foreign policy responded to the agenda of the transnational elite, even though the neo-conservatives of the Republican right-wing retained prerogative over domestic social and other secondary policies. Debates in Washington after the early 1980s were less over content than over form –

over the wisdom of the fanaticism, the military dimensions, and reckless aspects of the Reagan Doctrine, a debate most clearly reflected in the controversial Contra policy towards Nicaragua and the conflicting postures adopted towards Soviet–US negotiations.

The radical rhetoric of such highly visible figures as Haig and Kirkpatrick, as well as President Reagan himself and other high-profile Reaganites, concealed the adoption and implementation of the transnational agenda within the apparatus of state. Above all, behind the debates that continued in the mid-1980s was a very broad liberal and conservative confluence around the new methods of political intervention and the shift to promoting polyarchy. "Much of the Washington foreign-policy establishment, and by no means only the Reaganites, had come to the conclusion that the United States now needed to take the political and ideological offensive," noted one counselor to Project Democracy, a government program to develop "democracy promotion" strategies (see below). "Of course, many within the foreign-policy establishment had reservations about one or another of these activities... But by the late 1970s–early 1980s, something of a bipartisan consensus had begun to emerge [around promoting polyarchy]."[9]

Political operations

Reassertionism and the shift from backing authoritarianism to promoting polyarchy involved a thoroughgoing refurbishing and fine-tuning of the instruments and ideology of foreign policy. This took place over an extended period, from the Vietnam War to the late 1980s. The crucial link between what might appear as contrary processes – the resurgence of US aggressive intervention abroad in the 1980s, and the emergence of a "softer" "democracy promotion" in foreign-policy – is the concept and function of *political operations* (the more benign term used by the foreign-policy establishment is "political development"), and what has been described as its "handmaid," *psychological operations* (similarly referred to in more benign language as "communications programs").

As conceived by policymakers, political operations fall into three broad categories: *political action*, described by US strategists as "A full range of activities including certain kinds of multilateral diplomacy, support for foreign political parties or forces, and support for or work with international associations of various kinds"; *coercive diplomacy* – "Diplomacy presupposing the use or threatened use of military force

78

to achieve political objectives"; *covert political warfare* – "The covert aspects of active measures, [including] support for insurgencies, operations against enemy alliances, influence operations, and black propaganda."[10] For its part, psychological warfare, as described by one Reagan NSC official, is the "handmaid" of political warfare, "the planned use of communications to influence human attitudes and behavior. It consists of political, military, and ideological actions conducted to create in target groups behavior, emotions, and attitudes that support the attainment of national objectives... [PSYOPS] will usually be carried out under the broader umbrella of US national policy."[11]

Political operations are broad and inclusive. Rather than being viewed as any specific program, policy, or practice, it should be more accurately conceived of as a general framework for interaction in the international arena. One specialist explained that "politics is the marshaling of human beings to support or oppose causes... Such marshaling must be the objective of all international action, from the delivery of public speeches to the dropping of bombs." As such, political operations is in a sense coextensive with all international action and "is not confined to the tools [specifically] associated with political warfare" operations, and may be overt or covert.[12] When divested of the rhetoric, the "democracy promotion" programs in the Philippines, Chile, Nicaragua, Haiti, and elsewhere were, in fact, large-scale political operations in foreign policy, involving heavy doses of political action, coercive diplomacy, covert political warfare, and psychological operations.

Throughout the 1970s and early 1980s, as US strategists revamped foreign policy, they developed a critique of the reasons for the decline in US influence. This rethinking was neither a uniform nor a conspiratorial process, and these policymakers were scattered throughout the extended policymaking community. Different vantage points offered different views. However, within the foreign-policy establishment as a whole a consensus was developing on the need to inject foreign policy with broader political and psychological operations. The conclusion was that foreign policy had faltered at the political-psychological level of engagement, and that political operations should be broadly introduced. The "failure to identify and assimilate the lessons of the chief defeats the United States has suffered internationally in the post War [World War II] period [and] above all, the Vietnam War," pointed out a member of the NSC in the early 1980s, reflects great US weaknesses "at the psychological-political level of conflict."[13] Starting in the early 1980s, the United States began reorganizing the apparatus of state and the instruments of foreign policy, in order to enhance the capacity for sustained political operations.

The two main tools of US foreign policy since World War II have been military (or security) and economic aid programs, integrated into overall foreign-policy endeavors. Between World War II and 1990, the United States spent some $400 billion in such foreign "aid" (over a trillion dollars at 1990 values).[14] The purpose of military aid was to bolster local repressive forces (at times, proxies) which could suppress dissent and maintain social control. As well, military aid created bridges between local forces and the US military and established the prerequisite conditions for military, intelligence, and covert intervention where required. For their part, economic aid programs helped facilitate US political influence, and more importantly, were intended to integrate the economies of recipient countries into the international corporate political economy – by opening up markets, securing access to resources, building the infrastructure necessary for the operations of international capital, and shaping the process of local capital accumulation so that it was synchronized and subordinated to the centers of the world economy.[15] These two instruments – military and economic aid programs – were used efficaciously in the post-World War II years to reshape the global order and to thrust the United States into the affairs of the majority of nations around the globe. As part of the process of revitalizing foreign policy in the post-Vietnam period, policymakers gave considerable thought to how these two tools of intervention might be fine-tuned and given a more explicitly "political focus."

Those policymakers who saw things through the lens of the military establishment found that traditional military interventions were often counterproductive. They began developing the concept of low-intensity warfare, which entered into the US foreign-policy vocabulary as a term for new modalities of engagement against nationalist and revolutionary movements and governments in the 1980s.[16] This new doctrine placed primary emphasis on the political dimensions of conflict and on the coordination of military activities with economic programs, diplomatic initiatives, and psychological warfare. Strategists of low-intensity warfare argued that while the US had concentrated on preparing for conventional or nuclear war with the Soviet Union in Europe, the vast majority of the conflicts in which the US had engaged since World War II were unconventional encounters with "Soviet proxies" in the Third

World. In conventional warfare, superior military resources predominate. But in unconventional conflicts of the types generated by the "position of disparity" in the world order that Kennan mentioned, such resources in themselves are *not* the deciding factor. They concluded that the US had failed because it had not recognized that unconventional war is often more a political than a military undertaking.

In Vietnam the United States enjoyed vast conventional military superiority and won most of the battles but lost the war precisely because its outcome was determined by imperfectly understood political variables. Conventional military supremacy can alter those variables, but the military apparatus is only a means to achieve political ends. US military strategists rediscovered, as they do periodically, the famed nineteenth-century Prussian military theorist Carl von Clausewitz, and his axiom that "war is the extension of politics by other means." The strategists drew several essential conclusions regarding future US participation in unconventional conflicts (with or without a military component), and then applied these conclusions in Third World conflict situations. These conclusions were: first, the target of such campaigns must be the population itself, the minds of the people rather than the enemy's military forces; second, in this undertaking, policymakers had to take into account the specific culture, sensibilities, and history of the target population, as well as the capabilities of the adversaries. Campaigns against other countries would be tailor-made to suit the particular circumstances of each foreign-policy operation. Third, it is not enough to try to destroy the organized forces of adversaries (be they revolutionary or nationalist forces or otherwise); a movement or group responsive to US interests had to be created, legitimated and presented to the target population as a viable alternative to the government to be overthrown or replaced or the movement to be defeated. Fourth, new forms of political and military organization had to be developed. (This conclusion helped lead to the formation of the NED and other "democracy promotion" agencies.) Fifth, interventionist projects can only be sustained if there are strong US constituencies who support the effort. These, too, have to be garnered, mobilized, and legitimized. These "lessons" of Vietnam led to a simple yet fundamental premise: the ultimate objective of unconventional engagements is to achieve the political, not the military, defeat of adversaries. Crucial here is the shift from military to political competition as the core of US undertakings abroad, even when the military dimensions of these undertakings appear as the most salient.

In the 1980s, these lessons were applied to numerous low-intensity conflict situations, such as in Central America and Southern Africa, and in many countries and regions which were to undergo transitions to polyarchy. Starting in the early 1980s, the United States began to reorganize the military establishment to conduct low-intensity warfare campaigns. The Joint Chiefs of Staff formed special low-intensity conflict divisions within the Department of Defense and within each military service, and also reintroduced political and psychological warfare branches. The Pentagon even drafted a PSYOPS "master plan" at the behest of a Presidential Directive, and the National Security Council set up a top-level "board for low intensity conflict."[17] The shift in the military establishment towards a capacity for flexible, unconventional engagements in the Third World accelerated in the early 1990s with the end of the Cold War.[18]

For their part, economic policymakers began developing new ideas, such as humanitarian resource use and an expansion of traditional development aid to incorporate "institution-building." One member of Reagan's National Security Council noted that "international aid and humanitarian affairs," including "foreign economic and development aid, food aid, humanitarian assistance (rescue operations, disaster relief, famine relief, and the like), and technical assistance of various kinds," are crucial components of political operations in foreign policy. "Although these functions are bureaucratically scattered and very largely autonomous, they have a very important psychological-political component. Whether intentionally or otherwise, they serve as significant instruments of US foreign policy and national strategy."[19] In 1966 Congress had passed the Title IX addition to the US Foreign Assistance Act, which called for a specifically "political focus" to traditional US-funded development programs.[20] As a development growing out of Title IX, the AID created an Office of Democratic Initiatives in 1984 and launched numerous "political development" and "institution-building" programs during the 1980s. In addition, economic assistance programs in the 1980s and 1990s, both bilateral and multilateral, became effective precision instruments in promoting the neo-liberal economic model in the Third World. One analyst has appropriately termed this function of "economic aid" in the late twentieth century as "financial low intensity warfare."[21]

Political aid as political operations

Programs to strengthen friendly political movements in other countries are one of the foreign-policy arms of a modern great power.
Until this century, there were three instruments for such efforts:
diplomacy, economic, and military. This triad retains its primacy
today, but it has been supplemented by two additional instruments.
One is propaganda... The other new policy instrument – aid to
friendly political organizations abroad – ... helps build up political
actors in other polities, rather than merely seeking to influence
existing ones. In international affairs, organization is now as important as issues, just as has always been the case in domestic politics.

Michael A. Samuels and William A. Douglas (Project Democracy
consultants)[22]

The new political intervention did not eclipse the two traditional
foreign-policy instruments; to the contrary, they were refurbished and
widely deployed. However, the key ingredient was still missing. The
third instrument, "political aid," had remained sporadic and underdeveloped. It was the introduction of this third category which would
play a centripetal role in facilitating the shift in policy and bringing
about consensus around promoting polyarchy. As Allen Weinstein, the
first president of NED, put it: "A number of separate strands...
converged in the 1981–82 period to produce a critical mass of public
attention" on the issue of "democracy promotion" as a component of
overall foreign policy.[23]

The intellectual underpinning of "political aid" was the argument
contained in the political development literature that the United States
must build up the institutions of political and civil society of intervened
countries in order to develop structures capable of absorbing tensions,
maintaining social control, and steering societies in directions responsive to US and transnational interests. Those arguing for the introduction of political aid, including a commission supervised by the
National Security Council to create the NED, made broad reference to
the conclusions of a 1972 book by William A. Douglas, *Developing
Democracy*.[24]

In his study, Douglas reviewed the modernization and political
development literature and the debates over whether authoritarianism
or "democracy" is best suited to meet US interests. Douglas coined the
term *regimented democracy* to describe the type of political system the
US should promote in place of authoritarianism. Comparing the

populations of developing nations with "children," and asserting that underdevelopment was the result of their "traditional attitudes," Douglas argued that the peoples of the Third World required "tutelage," "regimentation," and "social control," but that "democracy" could achieve these goals more effectively than authoritarianism:

> That a firm hand is needed is undeniable. However, it is harder to accept the claim that only dictatorship can provide the sufficient degree of firmness. First, in regard to keeping order, what is involved is basically effective police work, and there is no reason why democratic regimes cannot have well-trained riot squads... democratic governments may be able to do the same things as dictatorship to overcome centripetal social forces: use police to stop riots, strike bargains with the various groups to keep them reasonably satisfied, and call out the army when peaceful means fail... There is no denying the need for organization structures by which the modernized elite can exercise tutelage. However... it is common experience that in obtaining the desired behaviour from a balky mule, a balky child, or a balky peasant, the real key is to find just the right balance between carrot and stick... Democracy can provide a sufficient degree of regimentation, if it can build up the mass organizations needed to reach the bulk of the people on a daily basis. Dictatorship has no monopoly on the tutelage principle.[25]

After making the case for "democracy" over authoritarianism, Douglas went on to develop detailed recommendations on how "political aid" programs should be introduced. Just as economic aid addressed economic underdevelopment, reasoned Douglas, political aid "should address political underdevelopment." Third World nations "need assistance in politics just as much as in building infrastructure, industry, or institutions such as universities, cooperatives, and trade unions," he argued. "Without political aid, their political systems may lag behind development in the economic and institutional sectors, with the resulting political instability... we should undertake an active policy of political aid, for both developmental and security reasons." The trick, said Douglas, was to devise the correct "transplanting mechanisms" for establishing polyarchy in the Third World, as well as "insulating devices" which would allow polyarchic systems to incubate, take hold, and stabilize in the intervened societies.[26] Included among the recommendations were: the establishment of a specialized agency (later to become the NED); the participation of the private sector (i.e., the dominant organs of US civil society) in government-supervised "democracy promotion" abroad; and the modification of existing government institutions and programs so as to synchronize overall foreign policy with "political development." Two decades after his study, the "transplanting mechanisms" and "insulating devices" which Douglas called for became embodied in the new "democracy promotion" programs. Douglas himself went on to become a senior consultant to the NSC's Project Democracy (see below), which led to the creation of the NED and other "democracy promotion" organs of the US state.

Although fierce foreign-policy debates continued in the 1980s over the basis on which US influence and world order should be reconstructed, the introduction of "political development" programs garnered a broad consensus. "The Endowment represented an integration of conservative and liberal reactions to the American failure in Vietnam," stated Gershman. "Conservatives, anxious to overcome the Vietnam malaise, welcomed a new effort to reassert American democratic values and to meet the Soviet ideological challenge head on. Liberals, on the other hand, welcomed an approach that offered a political alternative to military competition and a creative means of addressing complex political problems that did not lend themselves to military solutions."[27] Another consultant on political aid noted in the mid 1980s: a "US policy of political aid... is in its incipient state and, in time, may well replace in importance military and economic aid as the principal foreign assistance program."[28]

Political aid has become an efficacious instrument of the United States, in the context of the transnationalization of political processes, in its effort to establish control over transnational politics and to reconfigure a new "historic bloc" over which the transnational elite exercises hegemony. Similarly, the notion of "institution building" in political and civil society in intervened countries as part of political operations abroad, which was first put forward in the political development literature of the 1960s and has now become part of the standard lexicon of "democracy promotion," should be seen theoretically in its relation to hegemony. There is a close relation between institutionalization and hegemony, although the two are by no means identical. As discussed earlier, institutions provide ways of processing conflicts so as to minimize the use of force in domination. In this way, institutions may become what Gramsci called "anchors" for constructing hegemony. The passage from "political development" of the 1960s to "democracy promotion" of the 1980s and 1990s involves an expansion from "institution building" at the level of formal state structures to the level of both state structures and civil society.

The shift from the CIA to the NED

What little political aid the United States has attempted in the past 35 years has been more or less covert, largely financial and most often administered through the CIA. It did not take long for most policymakers to realize that such covert operations were inappropriate, awkward, and embarrassing.

Project Democracy consultant[29]

Political aid programs were sporadic and underdeveloped in the post-World War II period. Those programs that did exist were managed by the CIA. The Truman administration created the CIA out of its World War II precursor, the Office of Strategic Security, as a covert branch of the US state in the Cold War. Since its inception, the CIA has carried out thousands of covert operations; overthrown countless governments; and contributed to the death, directly or indirectly, of millions of people as a result of its actions.[30] Alongside intelligence gathering and paramilitary campaigns, a major component of CIA intervention has been political operations involving the creation, covert funding and guidance of allied political groups and individuals in target countries – media, political parties, trade unions, businesses, and associations.

At the height of the Cold War in the 1950s and 1960s, despite occasional scandals and failures like the Bay of Pigs, the CIA enjoyed the respect of much of the US public, and the full extent of its activities remained hidden from the international community. But during the 1970s, as many of its seamy covert operations became public, it fell into disrepute. In 1974–5, congressional investigations revealed the sordid underworld of CIA covert activity at home and abroad. Top-level CIA officers defected and exposed the history of overseas intrigues, and investigative journalists uncovered unsavory details of US secret activities.[31] After the US defeat in Indochina and the delegitimization of foreign intervention, the CIA by the late 1970s was badly discredited. In the United States, bipartisan and constituent support crumbled. In target countries abroad, association with CIA programs meant instant repudiation. In addition to the stigma, there were other problems. The CIA had proved adept at staging coups, assassinations, and installing dictators. It achieved its stated goal in 1973 in Chile, for instance, when it orchestrated the military overthrow of the democratically elected government of Salvador Allende. In Guatemala, it was impeccably efficient in organizing the removal in 1954 of the elected government of Jacobo Arbenz. The CIA showed similar proficiency in operations in Brazil, Iran, the Congo, the Philippines, Iraq, and dozens of other countries.

Yet there was something clumsy about these operations. The political aftermath of covert operations seemed to create new, more complex problems over the long term. The CIA could destabilize quite well, but, its detractors argued, it was not good at *creating stability*. Nearly four decades after the CIA overthrew the Arbenz government, Guatemala remained a cauldron of guerrilla insurgency, gross human rights violations and social instability. The Pinochet regime lasted sixteen years but was an international pariah. Iran's nationalist prime minister, Mossadegh, was ousted in the CIA-led coup of 1954, which installed the Shah and recovered Iranian oil fields for Western petroleum companies. But, despite twenty years on the throne, the Shah was unable to sustain himself in the face of a rising Islamic fundamentalist movement and popular struggles against his policies. CIA operations seemingly lacked sophistication and long-term vision. The CIA was not able to create stable governments or to mold structures in civil society itself that could provide long-term protection for a core-dominated market economy and a pro-US political program. Here, the capable hands of a political surgeon were needed, not the heavy hand of a paramilitary assassin.

The new, post-Vietnam breed of political professionals lobbied for the transfer of crucial aspects of the CIA's political operations – namely, "political aid" – to a new agency. They lobbied for the establishment of an institution that would use sophisticated techniques, including elections, political aid, and other political operations, to achieve lasting results. Two of the original NED founders noted: "Since the advent of the Cold War, the United States has worked abroad politically, mainly covertly, with direct government action and secret financing of private groups." This US political intervention capacity "is necessary for protecting US security interests," but efforts to date have proven inadequate: "[The] various covert means for filling the political gap in US policy solved some short-term needs, but did not provide effective long-term solutions. Covert political aid provided directly by the US government is limited in its effectiveness."[32]

Thus, while CIA intervention has continued, a more specialized, sophisticated entity with a focus on political operations a long-term vision, and a strategic agenda came into existence with the creation of the NED in 1983. This new entity would not only play the role of skillful political surgeon, but it would overcome the taint associated with the covert political operations that the CIA had been carrying out abroad. Specifically, NED would take over much of the funding and political guidance for political parties, trade unions, business groups, news media, and civic organizations that the CIA had traditionally supplied. The NED is a "combination of Government money, bureaucratic flexibility and anti-Communist commitment... which mixes public funds and private interests," noted the *New York Times* shortly after the Endowment's founding. The NED's work "resembles the aid given by the Central Intelligence Agency in the 1950s, 60s and 70s to bolster pro-American political groups."[33] Former CIA director William Colby commented in regard to the NED program: "It is not necessary to turn to the covert approach. Many of the programs which... were conducted as covert operations [can now be] conducted quite openly, and consequentially, without controversy."[34] The idea was to create a further division of labor within the organs of US foreign policy. The NED would not replace the CIA, whose programs have continued and even expanded in the 1990s.[35] Rather, it would specialize in the overt development through political aid programs of political and civic formations, supplementing CIA covert activities in synchronization with overall US policy towards the country or region in which it operated.

The NED, with its ideological underpinning of "promoting democracy," was well equipped for rebuilding US domestic consensus for political operations abroad. The name National Endowment for Democracy conjures up an apolitical and benevolent image not unlike that of the National Endowment for the Arts or other humanitarian societies. The efforts to project such an image are, in fact, part and parcel of the ideological dimensions of the new intervention, and have been remarkably successful. Standard university texts perpetuate such an uncritical image. "The National Endowment for Democracy, launched by the Reagan administration in 1983, is a recent manifestation of a tradition with a long heritage," states *American Foreign Policy: Pattern and Process*, one of the staple US college texts on foreign policy. "Its purpose is to encourage worldwide the development of autonomous political, economic, social and cultural institutions to serve as the foundations of democracy and the guarantors of individual rights and freedoms."[36] Yet the NED was created in the highest echelons of the US national security state, as part of the same project that led to the illegal operations of the Iran–Contra scandal. It is organically integrated into the overall execution of US national security and foreign policy. In structure, organization, and operation, it is closer to clandestine and national security organs such as the CIA than apolitical or humanitarian endowments as its name would suggest. The NED has operated in tandem with all major interventionist undertakings in the 1980s and 1990s.

The NSC's Project Democracy

Efforts to create "political development" programs date back to the 1950s, at the height of the Cold War, when Congress discussed, but declined to approve, several bills to establish a "Freedom Academy" that would conduct party-building in the Third World. The passage of the Title IX addition to the Foreign Aid Act in 1966 spurred renewed interest in such an agency. The Brookings Institute, one of the most important policy planning institutes, undertook an extensive research program on political development programs in coordination with the AID and other government agencies.[37] In 1967, President Johnson appointed the three-member Katzenback Commission which recommended that the government "promptly develop and establish a public-private mechanism to provide public funds openly for overseas activities of organizations which are adjudged deserving, in the national interest, of public support."[38] A bill was introduced in Congress in 1967 by Rep. Dante Fascell (D.-Fla.) to create an "Institute of International Affairs," but it was not approved.[39] Meanwhile, the public outcry against intervention abroad in the early 1970s as a result of the Indochina war and the revelations of CIA activities, as well as the Watergate scandal, put these initiatives on hold for much of that decade.

Then, in 1979, with reassertionism taking hold, a group of government officials, academicians, and trade union, business, and political leaders connected to the foreign-policy establishment, created the American Political Foundation (APF), with funding from the State Department's United States Information Agency (USIA) and from several private foundations. The APF brought together representatives of all the dominant sectors of US society, including both parties and leaders from labor and business. It also brought together many of the leading figures who had been developing the ideas of the new political intervention, many of them associated with the transnationalized fraction of the US elite.[40] Among those on the APF board were Lane Kirkland of the American Federation of Labor-Congress of Industrial Organizations (AFL-CIO), former Republican National Committee chair William Brock, former Democratic National Committee chair Charles Manatt, international vice-president for the US Chamber of Commerce Michael Samuels, as well as Frank Fahrenkopf, Congressman Dante Fascell, Zbignew Brezezinski, John Richardson, and Henry Kissinger. The APF was chaired by Allen Weinstein, who would later become the first president of the NED. The names of APF activists and the composition of the APF board are revealing. They fall into three categories. One is members of the inner circle of second-generation post-World War II national security and foreign policymakers, such as Kissinger, Brezezinski, and Richard Allen, all former National Security Advisors. Another is top representatives of the four major constituencies that made up the post-World War II foreign-policy coalition – the Democratic and Republican parties, labor and business. The third is operatives from the US intelligence and national security community. These intelligence and security operatives include people associated with the CIA and dozens of front organizations or foundations with which it works, as well as operatives from the USIA.

The prominence of the USIA is significant, since this is an agency with a long track record in political and psychological operations. It was created by the Eisenhower administration in 1953 as an agency within the NSC at the recommendation of a top-secret report issued by the President's Committee on International Information Activities. Its explicit purpose was to conduct propaganda, political and psychological operations abroad in conjunction with CIA activities.[41] A National Security Action Memo in 1962 stipulated coordination among the USIA, the AID, the CIA, the Pentagon, and the State Department in waging political warfare operations, including civic action, economic and military aid programs.[42] Based on research programs it conducts directly or commissions governmental and non-governmental agencies to conduct, the USIA selects propaganda themes, determines target audiences, and develops comprehensive country plans for media manipulation and communications programs. As part of Project Democracy, USIA activities were greatly expanded in the 1980s.[43]

The APF recommended in 1981 that a presidential commission examine "how the US could promote democracy overseas." The White

House approved the recommendation for Project Democracy. At its onset, Project Democracy was attached to the NSC, and supervised by Walter Raymond Jr., a high-ranking CIA propaganda specialist who worked closely with Oliver North, a key player in the Iran–Contra scandal, on covert projects.[44] "Overt political action," explained Raymond, could help achieve foreign-policy objectives by providing "support to various institutions [and]... the development of networks and personal relationships with key people."[45] Raymond explained that the creation of the NED as a "vehicle for quasi-public/private funds" would fill a "key gap" in US foreign-policy – it would be a "new art form."[46] Raymond and his staff at the NSC worked closely with Democratic Congressman Dante Fascell of Florida. Fascell chaired the House Foreign Affairs Committee which would draft the legislation creating the NED and organized support for the project within Congress.[47]

In June 1982, in a speech before the British parliament considered the symbolic inauguration of the new policy, Ronald Reagan announced that the United States would pursue a major new program to help "foster the infrastructure of democracy around the world."[48] A secret White House memo on the minutes of a Cabinet-level planning meeting to discuss Project Democracy held two months later, in August, set the agenda: "We need to examine how law and Executive Order can be made more liberal to permit covert action on a broader scale, as well as what we can do through substantially increased overt political action."[49] Then, in January 1983, Reagan signed National Security Decision Directive 77 (NSDD 77), which laid out a comprehensive framework for employing political operations and psychological warfare in US foreign policy. At least $65 million was allocated by the administration to underwrite the activities and programs contemplated in the NSC directive.[50] NSDD 77 focused on three aspects of Project Democracy.[51] One aspect was dubbed "public diplomacy" – psychological operations aimed at winning support for US foreign policy among the US public and the international community – and involved an expansion of propaganda and informational and psychological operations. The directive defined "public diplomacy" as "those actions of the US Government designed to generate support for our national security objectives." An Office of Public Diplomacy (OPD) operating out of the White House was established.[52] The General Accounting Office ruled OPD an illegal domestic propaganda operation in 1988. Another aspect set out in the NSC directive was an expansion of covert operations. This aspect would develop into the clandestine, illegal government operations later exposed in the hearings on the Iran–Contra scandal of the late 1980s. Parallel to "the public arm of Project Democracy, now known as the National Endowment for Democracy," noted the *New York Times*, "the project's secret arm took an entirely different direction after Lieut.-Col. Oliver I. North, then an obscure National Security Council aide, was appointed to head it."[53]

The final aspect was the creation of a "quasi-governmental institute." This would engage in "political action strategies" abroad, stated NSDD 77.[54] This led to the formal incorporation of the NED by Congress in November 1983. While the CIA and the NSC undertook "covert" operations under Project Democracy, some of which were exposed in the Iran–Contra investigations, the NED and related agencies went on to execute the "overt" side of what the *New York Times* described as "open and secret parts" of Project Democracy, "born as twins" in 1982 with NSDD 77.[55] But while the Iran–Contra covert operations that grew out of Project Democracy were exposed and (assumed to be) terminated, the NED was consolidated and expanded as the decade progressed. With the mechanisms in place by the mid-1980s, the "reassertionists" turned to launching their global "democracy offensive." "The proposed campaign for democracy must be conceived in the broadest terms and must weave together a wide range of superficially disparate aspects of US foreign policy, including the efforts of private groups," noted one Project Democracy consultant. "A democracy campaign should become an increasingly important and highly cost-effective component of ... the defense effort of the United States and its allies."[56] The countries in which the NED became most involved in the 1980s and early 1990s were those set as priorities for US foreign-policy. "Such a worldwide effort [a 'crusade for democracy'] directly or indirectly must strive to achieve three goals," one Project Democracy participant explained. "The preservation of democracies from internal subversion by either the Right or the Left; the establishment of new democracies where feasible; and keeping open the democratic alternative for all nondemocracies. To achieve each of these goals we must struggle militarily, economically, politically and ideologically."[57]

In countries designated as hostile and under Soviet influence, such as Nicaragua and Afghanistan, the United States organized "freedom fighters" (anti-government insurgents) in the framework of low-intensity conflict doctrine, while the NED and related organs introduced complementary political programs. Those countries designated for transition from right-wing military or civilian dictatorships to stable "democratic" governments inside the US orbit, including Chile, Haiti, Paraguay, and the Philippines, received special attention. By the late 1980s and early 1990s, the NED had also launched campaigns in Cuba, Vietnam, and other countries on the US enemy list, and had also become deeply involved in the self-proclaimed socialist countries, including the Soviet Union itself. While these first programs were tied to the 1980s anti-communist crusade, the NED and other "democracy promotion" agencies made an easy transition to the post-Cold War era. As the rubric of anti-communism and national security became out-dated, the rhetoric of "promoting democracy" took on even greater significance. Perestroika and glasnost highlighted authentic democratization as an aspiration of many peoples. But US strategists saw in the collapse of the Soviet system an opportunity to accelerate political intervention under the cover of promoting democracy. In the age of global society, the NED and other "democracy promotion" organs have become sophisticated instruments for penetrating the political systems and civil society in other countries down to the grassroots level.

Structure of the "democracy promotion" apparatus

Constitutive documents describe the NED as an "independent" and "private" organization. "Non-governmental" is its juridical status. In any political or practical sense, such a classification is meaningless; structurally and functionally it operates as a specialized branch of the US government. The NED is wholly funded by Congress with funds channeled through the USIA and the AID, both entities of the Department of State. From its inception in 1983 to its financial year 1992 allocation by Congress, it has received approximately $210 million in monies allocated by Congress.[58] According to the NED's public documentation, these allocations account for some 99 percent of its funding. However, it is clear from the study of its operations abroad that NED spending is so interlocked with other direct and indirect, secret and public US government spending, that talk of fixed budgets is not all that meaningful. All NED grants are submitted to the State Department for approval, and US embassies abroad frequently handle logistics for and coordination of NED programs. The State Department and other executive agencies regularly appoint personnel to participate in NED programs.[59] The decision to make the NED a quasi-private entity was based on several considerations. First, this would make it easier to insulate its operations from public scrutiny and accountability. For instance, the NED would not be subject to congressional oversight, as is the CIA. Second, a "private" organization would not be subject to the same bureaucratic encumbrances as a formal government agency, and therefore would be afforded greater flexibility in its operations. Third, formally separating the NED from the State Department would eliminate apparent or potential conflicts between government-to-government diplomacy and partisan interference in the political systems of other countries.

The NED operates *overtly*, at least on paper, as opposed to the CIA's *covert* activities. Its assistance to groups and individuals in other countries is conducted *publicly* – above board – according to the NED charter. This shift from covert to overt is a product of several practical and ideological concerns held by policymakers. Overt political intervention described as "democratic, nonpartisan assistance" is more difficult to discredit than "CIA bribes," "covert payoffs," or "secret intervention." Similarly, it is easier and more ideologically convincing to sell intervention as "democracy promotion" than as national security, and thus this assists in legitimizing foreign policy. Transferring political intervention from the covert to the overt realm does not change its character, but it does make it easier for policymakers to build domestic and international support for this intervention. It also provides policymakers with greater flexibility and options in pursuing their country-specific objectives. Despite its officially overt character the NED also engages in extensive covert operations. In fact, "overt" appears to be more an aspect of the "democracy" rhetoric than actual NED policy. NED activities are often shrouded in secrecy, and NED officials operate more often in the shadows than in the open, much like an agency dedicated to covert operations. Revealingly, NSC and other governmental documents of the early 1980s spoke almost interchangeably of "political action" and "covert action," and one secret White House planning document on Project Democracy referred to "covert action on a broad scale" to promote public and private "democratic institutions" abroad.[60] Clearly those involved in Project Democracy were not yet clear how covert and overt aspects of the new political intervention would be portioned out.

The NED functions through a complex system of intermediaries in which operative aspects, control relationships, and funding trails are nearly impossible to follow and final recipients are difficult to identify. Most monies originating from the NED are first channeled through US organizations which, in turn, pass them on to foreign counterparts, who are themselves often pass-throughs for final recipients. Dozens of US organizations have acted as conduits for NED funds. Financial accounting becomes nearly impossible, facilitating all sorts of secret funding, laundering operations, and book-keeping cover-ups which allow for unscrutinized transactions. Through the multi-tiered structure of go-betweens, it is difficult to establish the links between US government operations on the one hand, and seemingly independent political activities in other countries on the other. In this Alice's Wonderland of political intervention, things are not what they seem, at first blush, to be.

The first tier in this system of intermediaries consists of what are known as the NED *core groups*. These groups handle the bulk of appropriated NED funds and programs. They are: the National Democratic Institute for International Affairs (NDI) and its counterpart, the National Republican Institute for International Affairs (NRI, whose name was later changed to International Republican Institute, or IRI), which are the "international wings" of the Democratic and Republican parties; the Center for International Private Enterprise (CIPE), a branch of the US Chamber of Commerce; and the Free Trade Union Institute (FTUI), an international branch of the AFL-CIO (the AFL-CIO also operates abroad through three regional organizations, the AALC, for Africa, the AAFLI, for Asia, and the AIFLD, for Latin America). These core groups carry out programs in target countries with those sectors considered strategic pillars of society: labor (FTUI), business (CIPE) and the political parties and organizations (NDI and NRI). A host of other US "private" organizations enmeshed with foreign policy, such as Freedom House, the Council on the Americas, the Center for Democracy, and US universities, foundations, think-tanks, and even the YMCA, handle programs for "civic" sectors. In this structure, the US state foments direct linkages between the organs of US civil society and their counterparts in other countries.

Another characteristic of the NED is its fusion of the public and the private domains in its operations. In "democracy promotion" operations, "congressional testimony, agency budgets, speeches for department heads, planning and programming have been routinely farmed out to private firms rather than done internally by the responsible bureau," candidly explained one Project Democracy counselor. "In some cases, these 'private' agencies are really just fronts for the departments they serve; the agency may prepare a report or a research project that it then gives to the private firm to attach its letterhead to, as if it were really a private activity or initiative."[61] The lines of funding in leadership which originate at the highest levels of the formal state apparatus and filter down through public and "private" networks ostensibly unconnected to the government obscures the linkage between many on-the-ground activities in intervened countries and the US state. Although they are projected as non-governmental organizations (NGOs – or in official AID terminology, private voluntary organizations, or PVOs), the "private" groups which actually manage many "democracy promotion" programs in intervened countries form part of an extended US state apparatus. Obscuring this linkage means that the governmental identity of these groups and the function of their activities in the service of US foreign policy are almost universally unrecognized by US and foreign publics, and may even be unrecognized by other branches of the state apparatus (e.g., members of the US Congress), by many of their own employees, and by governments and publics in intervened countries. (However, the leadership of these quasi-private groups, top-level policymakers and field operatives, quite fully recognize their status as instruments of US foreign policy.) This blurring of "public" and "private" in US foreign policy was exposed in the 1980s during investigations into the Iran–Contra dealings. However, this was mistakenly seen as an aberration limited to that scandal. It is actually a structural feature of foreign policy in the current era. In this process, the US state oversees and guides the application of the overall resources of society to foreign-policy objectives. This means tapping the technological, intellectual and organizational expertise of those not formally in the government in which diverse interests are merged and the distinction between state activity and private activity disappears. For instance, US intervention in the Nicaraguan elections involved the coordinated actions of the White House, the National Security Council, the CIA, the Department of State, the Pentagon, the USIA, the AID, Congress, the Democratic and Republican parties, the AFL-CIO, the US Chamber of Commerce, and dozens of "private groups," ranging from Freedom House and the Cuban American National Foundation, to the National Association of Broadcasters and sectors of the US Catholic Bishops Conference (see chapter 5). In theoretical terms, this should be seen as a feature of transnationalization. The US state acts to combine and fuse the actions and resources of elites operating in synchronization in civil and political society, and then project them into a transnational setting, through which cross-national politics are conducted and efforts are undertaken to construct hegemony.

A striking feature of the NED structure is the system of interlocking directorates. The boards of the "core groups" and the host of other "private" groups in US civil society that participate in "democracy promotion" programs, such as Freedom House, the Council on the Americas, and so on, heavily overlap with government and "private" organization officials who promoted Project Democracy and who sit on the NED board itself.[62] In turn, this is an exact mirror of the institutional structure of power in the United States, in which the top leadership of the corporate world, government, and civic groups is thoroughly interlocking – what Dye has analyzed as the "oligarchic model" of power and national policymaking. This oligarchic model has its flip side in the intervened country, where the United States promotes a string of civic, political, labor, and media organizations whose leadership is remarkably interlocking. Through US intervention programs, this leadership is brought together, trained and groomed by the United States in the art of polyarchic political processes, the ideological and other dimensions of consensual domination, and is expected to cohere into a society-wide elite exercising effective institutional power. This elite becomes responsive to the concerns of their US mentors and to the transnational agenda. The goal is to construct a functioning oligarchic model of power and a polyarchic system which links local elites to the transnational elite.

This interlocked core group of political warfare specialists strategizes on and actually *conducts* these "democracy promotion" projects as agents of the US elite, but does not constitute a unified group in terms of domestic US politics or affiliation. They do not represent any specific sector or ideological strain in mainstream US politics, and include right-wing Republicans and moderate Republicans, liberal Democrats and conservative Democrats and even social democrats, representatives of labor and representatives of business, and so forth. The new political intervention is less a creature of the right-wing Republican presidencies of the 1980s which actually oversaw the shift in policy than of dominant groups in the United States as a whole, and underscores the importance of Project Democracy for the restoration, beyond the specific program of any one administration, of bipartisanship in foreign policy which had collapsed in the aftermath of the Vietnam and Iran debacles. Behind its mere restoration, those who developed the new political intervention sought the *reconstitution* of consensus among the major sectors of US society (political parties, government, labor, and business). "One byproduct" of the creation of the NED "may well be the restoration of bipartisanship to its central place in the American foreign-policy-making process," noted the principal Project Democracy report. "Not since the post-World War II consensus broke down during the debates over American involvement in Vietnam has this missing ingredient – bipartisanship – been present."[63] This bipartisanship represented a *consensus* among the US elite on the political aspect of the transnational agenda (promotion of polyarchy), reflecting the hegemony that the transnationalized fraction had won.

The NED is only one of several new agencies and programs established to undertake "democracy promotion." The Reagan administration reorganized US foreign aid programs in the 1980s to make them more responsive to the needs of the transnational agenda. This reorganization involved establishing four new "pillars," including "private sector initiatives" and "institution building."[64] It led to the establishment by the State Department in 1984 of the Office of Democratic Initiatives (ODI) attached to the AID "to support and strengthen democratic institutions... [in a] capacity complementary to the strengths of other US government and private agencies, and in coordination with them."[65] The ODI originally specialized in financing electoral processes abroad and spent over $25 million between 1984 and 1987.[66] After 1987, the NED assumed some of these operations. In the division of labor, the NED conducts such overtly political activities as "party-building," whereas the ODI manages government-to-government "democracy enhancement" programs, such as sponsoring judicial system reforms, training legislators of national parliaments, and financing electoral tribunals in intervened countries. In financial year 1990 alone, the AID spent over $93 million through the ODI.[67]

Communications are another component in promoting polyarchy. In 1981, the Reagan administration expanded US government capabilities in the area of "international communications." This was described by one NSC member as a "general category... encompassing international information and international educational and cultural affairs."[68] In March 1983, President Reagan signed National Security Decision Directive 130, which stipulated international communications as "an integral part of US national security policy and strategy." The directive called for an expansion of US radio and television broadcasting abroad, the development of a long-term strategy for "communications assistance" to Third World countries, and increased research on foreign public opinion. It also sanctioned an expansion of US military peacetime psychological operations.[69] This communications component pursues the informational dimensions and the ideological discourse of the transnational elite agenda via the web of global communications established through the communications revolution.

The NED is thus only one component of "democracy promotion," and often merely an auxiliary instrument of foreign-policy operations. Its magnitude should not be exaggerated since it is quite small (sometimes dwarfed) relative to other organs and does not engage directly in policy formation. However, it undertook the crucial function in the 1980s as the midwife of the new political intervention, bringing together centrifugal forces in a cohesive new policy orientation, and its importance should be seen in how it symbolizes the new intervention and its strategic insertion into broader intervention undertakings. Moreover, it has come to coordinate a good portion of the intellectual thinking and promote the ideological permeation of the new intervention. This involves funding and coordinating academic research and scholarly exchanges around the world, including the sponsorship and dissemination of studies, conferences, and seminars which bring together people involved in NED programs and representatives of elite sectors in Third World countries. It also involves publication of a pseudo-academic journal, the *Journal of Democracy* (articles are commissioned by the NED staff rather than being submitted, manuscripts are not sent out for peer review and the journal is not attached to any scholarly institution but is run out of the NED's Washington D.C. headquarters by the Endowment staff[70]). The NED acts as a clearinghouse for the exchange of ideas and debate among intellectuals and public and private sector officials around the world. Seminars and conferences, ongoing informal gatherings, the production and circulation of books, journals, and bulletins, and so forth, bring these officials together, integrate them into transnational elite circuits, and help them develop ideological affinities and political cohesion. These circuits put elites in the South in touch with one another and also attune them to the ideology, discourse, and program of the transnational elite. While there are other, more important forums for developed core elite cohesion (such as the Trilateral Commission at the informal level and the Group of Seven at the state level), the NED, in tandem with other

US programs designed for these purposes (e.g., AID-funded programs of study at elite US universities), plays an important integrative function in transnational class formation, and especially in South–North elite linkage.

The shift in US policy from backing authoritarianism to promoting polyarchy, and the development of new policy instruments and agencies it entails, accelerated dramatically in the 1990s. Total federal government spending through the AID, the Departments of State and Defense, the NED, and the USIA under the rank "assistance for democratic development" increased from $682 million in 1991 to $736 million in 1992 and to $900 million in 1993.[71] On assuming office, the Clinton administration defined three overarching priorities in foreign policy: (1) promotion of free trade and international economic integration; (2) preservation and modernization of the US military capacity, and (3) "promotion of defense of democracy and human rights."[72] The new administration increased the 1993 NED budget by nearly 40 percent, from $35 to $48 million and proposed an eventual increase to $100 million annually, announced plans to expand USIA media programs and to introduce "democracy promotion" programs in other branches of the federal government, and replaced the ODI with a new division, the Center for Democracy and Governance, to "centralize and globalize all democratization policies and programs," with a budget of $296 million.[73] It created several new cabinet and sub-cabinet offices in the Departments of State and Defense dedicated specifically to issues of "democracy promotion" and globalization themes. The administration also created an Inter-Agency Working Group on Democracy in the NSC, the nerve center of the US state apparatus.[74] The United States will "take the lead around the world" in the 1990s, declared Assistant Secretary of Defense for Democracy and Peacekeeping, Morton Halperin, not only in assisting, but in "guaranteeing" the results of "free elections" and in defending "constitutional democracies," including through "military action when necessary."[75] Along with the development of low-intensity warfare doctrines and unconventional capabilities, the US military theater shifted from Cold War Europe to the Third World, where new military technologies and highly trained special units would be deployed in place of conventional units. Promoting polyarchy had become a long-term and institutionalized aspect of foreign policy, but one which would be synchronized with, rather than replace, US military intervention.

Modus operandi of the new political intervention

The *modality* of "democracy promotion" is a complex transnational political practice. In the typical operation, the State Department, the NED, or some quasi-private agency funded by the US government will commission reports on local conditions in the target country. Often, teams from the NDI, the NRI, professional consulting agencies, or another branch of the "democracy network" will be sent to the country for on-site research, interviews, and meetings with local leaders, "democratic" political parties, civic groups, and government officials. Assessments are made of each sector and its needs – political parties, trade unions, peasants, youth, women, civic groups, etc. In distinction to the clumsy interventionism of the past, these operations seek flexibility and workable strategies based on a careful analysis of country-specific circumstances and the requirements of developing a polyarchic elite with political action capabilities. The extent to which outside political professionals actually understand the system and the local political figures with whom they deal is often questionable. Outsider accounts are often self-serving and deluded. However, as part of the new techniques, the US teams employ local operatives who can provide a more accurate reading of indigenous conditions. A concrete strategy is drawn up, in synchronization with overall US policy towards the country or region. Later, funding is approved by the NED, the State Department, or other organs, and channels for coordination with the US embassy in the target country are set up. Often a new high-level ambassador is sent in. The core groups and other intermediaries, as well as the recipient groups in the target country, are instructed to draft program proposals and request funding. Then the flow of money and operatives begins. Once the "democracy program" is fully underway, the movement of funds and personnel between Washington and the target country becomes ubiquitous. The case studies confirm this pattern.

Organizing and advising mass political parties ("party-building") is a central component of these programs. The task is usually assigned to political professionals commissioned by the NDI or the NRI. The emphasis is on training leaders, setting up party structures, and devising political and electoral strategies honed to the particular conditions of each intervened country.[76] "Building social and economic institutions without building political parties is like building an automatic factory but omitting the computer," according to Douglas.

"Building mass movements requires trained leaders, skilled organizers, and comprehensive thinkers. Such persons are in short supply [in developing nations]... Even if fitting programs can be devised, the political skills needed to build mass organizations are lacking. Modern political skills obviously cannot be learned in traditional societies, and therefore will be absent unless taught from outside."[77] More to the point theoretically, political parties provide mediating links between the state and civil society and reconcile and aggregate the different interests of dominant class fractions, articulate cross-class aspirations, and incorporate subordinate class demands into larger hegemonic projects. "Precisely because [dominant elites] are not solid, congealed economic and social blocs, they require political formations which reconcile, coordinate and fuse their interests, and which express their common purposes as well as their separate interests," notes Ralph Miliband. "These purposes and interests also require ideological clothing suitable for political competition," clothing which modern political parties are ideally suited to provide.[78] Parties thus create what Talcott Parsons called a "national supra party consensus" based on "higher order solidarity [read: hegemony]."[79] A polyarchic political system, by its nature, requires a functioning political party system. The construction of such a system, or its penetration and transformation where parties already exist, is generally a top priority of political intervention programs.

Labor is another strategic sector because of its economic importance and because of its real and potential political influence.[80] Programs focus on promoting moderate and compliant trade unionism and on assisting allied unions to develop political action capacities in competition with more militant tendencies among workers. Major goals are to control potential worker unrest in response to economic restructuring and to cultivate a trade union movement receptive to US penetration and the activity of transnational capital. Moreover, trade unions are springboards for penetrating wider political sectors. Often, unions are key access points to political parties and social groups and function as "agents of influence" within national labor organizations. "Governments and political parties have used the international labor movement as one of the principal vehicles for their covert interactions with political parties and governments in foreign nations," noted one former AFL-CIO official. "The international trade union movement has been, and continues to be, a vital tool of governments in shaping the political destinies of foreign political parties and states and is an important part of most nations' foreign-policy systems."[81] In their trade union operations, US officials employ a double standard. In those countries where "democracy promotion" programs are designed to stabilize pro-United States regimes, the United States encourages allied unions to practice an apolitical "business" unionism focusing on bread-and-butter issues at the level of individual employers, and to recognize the overall legitimacy of the social order. But in countries targeted for destabilization, such as Nicaragua, Poland, and Panama in the 1980s, allied unions were encouraged to mount explicitly political actions, and to mount them against governments, not business management.

In addition, most "democracy promotion" programs involve penetration of the target country's media, the nurturing of women's and youth movements, and, in agrarian countries, peasant organizations.[82] Each of these sectors, for one or another reason, has been identified by US specialists as exhibiting specific sectoral characteristics and social linkages that require addressing individually within overall interventionist projects. A 1986 CIA report, for instance, noted that the "youth factor" in the Third World is crucial because young people tend to be "receptive to recruitment by extremist politicians." Another specialist argued: "The youth of a growing population may very well play a major role in pressing for change. They are among those who are actually disproportionately disadvantaged; they have less at stake in the existing structure of authority, more idealism, more impatience."[83] And programs targeting the business sector are usually designed to disseminate free-market values and the ideology of neo-liberalism, in synchronization with restructuring. Moreover, these programs seek to assist the technocratic "New Right" business community in intervened countries to become politicized and develop the skills necessary to participate in internal political processes (to develop what is referred to as a "political action capability"), to develop private sector policies, and to have these policies incorporated into government policy.

There is a strong reciprocity between economic globalization pressures and the activities of transnational capital, and the particular character of "democracy promotion" programs that political operations specialists will mount in each of these target sectors. For instance, just as transnational capital has proved deft at appropriating local, often pre-capitalist patriarchial social relations and cultural patterns into its economic activity, "democracy promotion" programs which target women in intervened countries also appropriate and utilize for the purposes of social control existing gender relations. There has been a proliferation of research into the new sexual division of labor being brought about in many countries by the disruption of traditional "female" activities through capitalist penetration and globalization, and the subordinate incorporation of women into new activities linked to the global economy, such as assembly work in *maquilladora* export zones and farm labor in agri-business enterprises.[84] "Democracy promotion" programs targeting women, in turn, attempt to channel and control the diverse forms of political and cultural mobilization that women in the Third World have undertaken, at the level of feminist organizations, trade unions, political parties, and other multi-sectoral organizations. The US effort is not to thwart women's mobilization *per se*, but to counter the popular content of national feminist projects and to bring them under the hegemony of women from the elite and of female representatives of transnational pools in intervened countries. In a similar manner, programs targetting labor will give special emphasis to workers in internationalized manufacturing zones, and programs targetting peasants will concentrate on the agro-export sector.

Media programs are also of special importance. Two Project Democracy consultants noted: "The inventory of US work abroad with the various sectors of democratic pluralist societies reveals that the biggest gap is in party-building and the next obvious lack of effort is in working with news media."[85] The communications revolution reached nearly all parts of the Third World in the 1980s, and has turned radio, television, and print media into crucial instruments for penetrating the "political animal" of a nation. The communications revolution has provided new means of informing and manipulating public opinion, educating a mass public, influencing the culture of a general population and providing various demonstration effects. It thus makes a major contribution to the shifts in power and social relations in an intervened country, to the relationships between leaders and masses, and between parties and social groups, and to the political behaviour in general of the population. In almost every political intervention project, the media has become a key target of US operations. The objective is to place a polyarchic elite cultivated by the United States into a position where it is able to utilize the communications networks so as to exercise its influence and achieve its hegemony over the internal political system.

Such sectorial specialization in political intervention is designed to lead to the creation of a society-wide network of political, social, cultural, business, and civic organizations in the target country – as the counterpart in civil society to elite power in political society – dependent on and responsive to US direction, or at least sympathetic to the concerns of the transnational agenda. The goal is to establish and consolidate the polyarchic model of power in the intervened society, predicated on the view that direct power is deposited in institutions and exercised by those who wield influence in, or control, governmental, political, labor, social, and civic institutions. The aim is to construct in intervened countries an exact replica of the structure of power in the United States. This is done by strengthening existing political parties and other organizations identified as congenial to US interests, or by creating from scratch new organizations where ones do not already exist. With few exceptions, the leaders of these organizations are drawn from the local elite and their efforts are aimed at competing with, or eclipsing, existing broad-based popular organizations and neutralizing efforts by popular sectors to build their own organizations in civil society, as we shall see in detail in the case studies.

At the same time, the shift from promoting authoritarianism to promoting polyarchy often involves a change in Washington's previous political alignments. Promoting authoritarianism usually meant supporting the right; promoting polyarchy often means supporting the center to center-right, or sometimes even the center-left. The strategists of the new political intervention emphasize developing a flexible political center. The recipients of US support are more progressive and enlightened in the target country's political landscape than the earlier autocrats, and may include Christian Democrats, Social Democrats, and even self-proclaimed Socialists. For instance, in Nicaragua's 1990 elections, Washington betrayed the most right-wing elements of the anti-Sandinista opposition, to which it had earlier given steadfast support, and backed the more moderate candidates. In Cuba, as NED-style "democracy promotion" programs got underway in the early 1990s, US backing for the most rabidly right-wing and extremist opponents of the revolutionary government began to wain and support began to shift to more moderate and centrist elements of the Cuban internal and exile forces. For many years these elements had opposed the extremism of the far-right and had advocated – despite US opposition – a more sophisticated strategy for undermining the revolution, not through crude destabilization but by more subtle political, diplomatic, and ideological means. In Chile, given the circumstances in the late 1980s of a right-wing dictatorship and an opposition polarized between centrist and leftist camps, the United States opted to promote a center-left alliance under the hegemony of moderate centrists. In South Africa, Washington chose to support *both* the militant African National Congress and the conservative Inkatha movement.[86]

"Party-building" and other activities for grooming an elite and for organizing the population of a target country into the society-wide networks employ multi-tiered structures and a "multiplier" system of training and control.[87] Top leaders are recruited, trained, advised, and funded by US political professionals (or, as is sometimes the case, by third country activists indigenous to the region who are sent in by US mentors). A pyramid structure is established, in which these top leaders set up offices and a staff with US funds. In turn, the national staff supervise regional offices and staff, which supervise provincial and local leaders the next level down. And so on. In this way, US political operatives, working with the top leadership in the intervened country, are able to foment and control a vertically organized nation-wide structure for political intervention. US influence and lines of patronage gradually ripple out through foreign parties, trade unions, and civic groups.

The actual *content* of programs ranged from education and training to institution-building, social projects, information dissemination and visitor exchanges, and political action. These activities are monitored by ubiquitous US advisors and supervised by US embassy personnel, in close coordination with other aspects of US policy towards the target country, including the judicious use of aid programs, formal diplomacy, military exchanges, "civic action," and so on. These activities groom leaders and supply them with financial and material resources. They are also designed to build up patronage networks around local leaders and institutions. Such programs transmit a generally positive view of US foreign policy, of the world order the United States is promoting, and through such images they shape the general attitude of members of parties, civic organizations, and trade unions towards politics and economics. The FTUI's former director Eugenia Kemble was quite candid in this respect: "The basic point [of US support for foreign unions] is to build interest groups capable of shaping public policy in other countries."[88] Apart from imparting actual skills and material resources for political action, the provision of money itself, in the form of salaries and stipends, provides opportunities for personal income and status unlikely to exist in the target countries. Eventually, the leaders and organizations cultivated by the United States become effective transmission belts for US and transnational interests.

According to former Secretary of State George Shultz, a participant in Project Democracy, the actual content of "democracy promotion" activities involves five closely related and often overlapping areas:[89]

(1) "Leadership training." This involves a wide range of activities to select, groom, and train a broad-based polyarchic leadership in the target country, ranging from in-country party-building seminars to scholarships for special training programs at US universities.

(2) "Education." This means inculcating "the principles and practice of democracy [read: polyarchy] and... the character and values of the United States in the educational systems of other nations." It also involves penetrating the educational and mass media systems in the intervened country.

(3) "Strengthening the institutions of democracy." This is the core category, and involves organizing, funding, and advising parties, unions, the media, business, and civic groups in intervened countries. "Here again, we will rely on American nongovernmental organizations to carry most of the load."

(4) "Conveying ideas and information." This involves the creation of ideological spaces and assistance programs intended to develop the work of organic intellectuals within intervened countries. It has two aspects. One is organizing activities such as publications and forums whose target audience is the elite. The purpose is to facilitate elite cohesion around the broad contours of the transnational agenda but attuned to the specific conditions and requirements of legitimacy in the intervened country. The other is programs aimed at establishing the ideological hegemony of that agenda among the popular classes of the intervened country, including the dissemination of ideas through the media, the educational system, and public cultural activities.

(5) "Development of personal and institutional ties." "Perhaps the most important results of all our programs will be the develop-

ment of lasting ties and working relationships between American individuals and organizations and their foreign counterparts." In the broadest sense, this refers to the trans-nationalization of political structures and civil society, in which local and transnational elites merge their activities in a cross-national setting.

All of these programs areas target two dimensions simultaneously: intra-elite relations, and relations between dominant and subordinate groups. Diverse intellectual and cultural exchanges and the types of linkage that develop among different dominant class fractions and elite clusters are critical components of Gramscian *consensus-building processes* among elites in intervened countries, and are at the same time important mechanisms for constructing elite hegemony, as we shall see.

The role of electoral processes and electoral assistance

Gershman has categorized US political intervention programs into those aimed at securing a "democratic transition," that is a change of regime, and those aimed at "long-term democratic political development."[90] The latter category signifies programs to consolidate poly-archic political systems (and US influence) in societies already considered "democratic" by bolstering elite forces in political and civil society, and by inculcating what the theoreticians of the new political intervention consider to be the "political culture" of polyarchy.

The first of Gershman's categories, "transitions," usually hinges on interference in foreign electoral processes, or *electoral intervention*. Since a transfer of formal state power is at stake in elections, electoral intervention is a pivotal component of the new political intervention. US policymakers identify two types of transitions: from "authoritarian," or right-wing dictatorships, to elitist civilian regimes; and from left-wing, popular, or nationalist regimes considered adversaries, to elitist regimes allied with the United States. Chile and the Philippines were of the first type, Nicaragua of the second. Haiti fell under the first in the effort to remove the Duvalier dictatorship, and then shifted to the second type after Father Jean-Bertrand Aristide won the presidency in 1990. Interference in the electoral processes of other countries is not a new feature of the foreign policy of the United States or other core powers. The United States since World War II has intervened in elections in dozens of countries around the world, from Italy and Greece, to the Congo, Vietnam, Guatemala, Chile, and Jamaica, in support of US foreign-policy goals in the target countries or regions.[91]

The United States, in conjunction with local allies, has grown adroit in staging "demonstration elections," as a mechanism for installing groups Washington deems favorable to its interests, or legitimizing internal social orders and US policies through a "free" vote.[92] This was the case in Vietnam in the 1960s and El Salvador in the 1980s, among other instances. The flip side has been intervention in elections to prevent "adverse" groups from coming to power through the vote. Thus the CIA gave clandestine funding to centrist parties in the Italian elections of 1948, and in the same period it began working to destroy the political left in Greece. When "adversaries" did come to power through elections *despite* US efforts, then the United States turned to withdrawal of support and clandestine destabilization campaigns to remove constitutionally elected governments, as in Guatemala and Chile in 1954 and 1973, respectively, or through outright invasions, as in the Dominican Republic in 1965.

However, the new electoral intervention is more sophisticated. In the post-Cold War reconstruction of world order, the role of the electoral processes in US foreign policy has changed. The process tends to be less a crude product exported from Washington than a careful blend of indigenous political factors with US policies. Washington became encouraged by the prospects for such a convergence after repressive military regimes in several Latin American countries (Argentina, Uruguay, and Brazil) turned over power to elected civilian governments. The key distinction between the so-called "transitions to democracy" in these Southern Cone countries, and the US-promoted regime changes later in the decade (Philippines, Chile, Panama, Paraguay, etc.) is that in the former US intervention was marginal or even extraneous to endogenous processes, whereas in the latter endogenous developments deeply intersected, or were actually transformed, by external intervention. In such electoral processes, as in the Philippines and Chile, sectors of the local elite joined forces with the United States as a mechanism for transition from military dictatorships to more stable polyarchies.

These became controlled transitions, managed jointly by local elites and US operatives. The key analytical variable in these cases is how endogenous processes and external intervention become *interwoven* in highly complex situations which do not lend themselves to simplification or predetermined outcomes. There is not a crude US imposition of elections. Rather, in interacting with indigenous political processes, the United States penetrates foreign electoral processes in operations that are many times more elaborate and extensive than before. Electoralism in the new political intervention is thus more than mere public relations. Formal electoral processes become what William Douglas referred to as a "transplanting mechanism": they allow for transplanting viable polyarchic political systems into intervened societies, that is, stable, electorally legitimized institutions that at least resemble US or Western analogies, which are apparently national but are pliable to US and transnational direction and control. In the US construct, these should be the characteristics that define (and circumscribe) all, or almost all, the competing groups in a pluralist political system. Moreover, controlled electoral processes provide the United States with the opportunity to permeate the institutions of civil society and the political structures of the target country, and to try, from that vantage point, to bring about long-term stability around free-market economies and social orders tied to transnational interests.

To undertake this new form of electoral intervention, the United States has created an elaborate machinery for "electoral assistance": "get out the vote" drives, ballot box watching, poll taking, parallel vote counts, civic training, and so on. In this new elections industry, the United States despatches specialized teams to carry out everything from "party-building seminars" to "civic training" and "international monitoring," and employs the tools of mass psychological manipulation and the new means of communications developed over the past fifty years. In these undertakings, the US teams attempt to shape and manage (and, under certain circumstances, to *hijack*) indigenous political processes and to latch them on to transnational political processes. The substitution of the NED for the CIA and the introduction of overt "political aid" has helped Washington to legitimize electoral assistance. Said one Project Democracy counselor:

> In most countries, foreign financing of campaign activities is viewed as an extreme form of interference in internal affairs. Neither the donors nor the recipient groups want the existence of the funding known. Typically, the funds flow through the intelligence agencies of foreign governments... Ironically, it is often more politically effective to provide the money openly. The most obvious advantage to overt transactions is that if one is not hiding anything, one is not subject to

exposure... [P]rocedural secrecy [should be] maintained only to protect recipients working clandestinely.[93]

Despite all the rhetoric on "electoral democracy" and emphasis on "free and fair elections," the United States is only concerned with assuring procedurally clean elections when the circumstances or results favor US interests. In official rhetoric, the United States holds that a country is a democracy when it has a government that comes to power through reasonably free and fair elections, and that a process of democratization in a country is synonymous with organizing a national electoral process. But this rhetoric is easily cast aside. For instance, in Nicaragua, the Sandinista government won, hands down, the 1984 elections, which were judged by the international community to be free and fair yet the United States continued to claim that the Sandinista government was undemocratic and pressed ahead with its war against Nicaragua. Similarly, when United States-backed candidates lost hands down in free and fair elections in Angola in 1992, Washington refused to recognize the winning Popular Movement for the Liberation of Angola, which had been the target of US destabilization campaigns since the mid-1970s, and instead pressed the electoral victors to negotiate "power sharing" with the losers and to convene a new vote.[94] On the other hand, governments came to power in Latin America and elsewhere in the 1980s and 1990s through elections that were marred by fraud, such as the 1984 elections in Panama, the 1988 and other elections in Mexico, numerous elections in El Salvador, and the 1994 elections in the Dominican Republic. Yet the United States recognized these governments as "democratic." The United States thus held a country to be democratic either when *US allies came to power* through reasonably free and fair elections, or when US allies came to power in elections which were *not* free and fair, but which *nonetheless* required recognition because of broader policy concerns.

In sum, US policymakers claim that they are interested in *process* (free and fair elections) and not *outcome* (the results of these elections); in reality, the principal concern is outcome. The objective of political intervention is *not* to organize or impose free and fair elections on a nation (in which the left, or traditional autocrats, might win) but rather, to organize an elite and to impose it on the intervened country through controlled electoral processes. The mistake in merely promoting free and fair elections regardless of the outcome, pointed out former CIA Director William E. Colby, a strong advocate of the new intervention, is:

> It assumes that, if the revolutionary forces were to join the elections and win them, the outcome would be quite satisfactory. It also ignores the prospect that the most oligarchic and brutal forces may win elections, even free ones. The first outcome gives power to those hostile to the United States. The second ensures repudiation by American public opinion. The United States must have a better choice than a brutal dictator or a hostile terrorist. The missing dimension must be vigorous support of decent, responsible, centrist leadership and political forces in these countries... rather than pretending neutrality among the potential winners of free elections.[95]

Electoral intervention as one component of "democracy promotion," and "democracy promotion" as one component of overall foreign policy

To recapitulate: exercising influence, and even gaining control, over foreign electoral processes is an increasingly important component of the new political intervention, although the objectives might vary from changing a regime considered undesirable ("electoral coups" or electoral destabilization), to installing a regime considered more favorable or stable, to simply heightening the presence and strength of transnational pools and other allied constituencies in political and civil society. However, the new intervention is not limited to electoral involvement, and takes place before, after, and often irrespective of, elections. This intervention functions in coordination with overall US policy, and that NED activity is coordinated with the full panoply of US policy instruments. Specific foreign-policy operations can only be understood in the context of US policy as it has evolved towards specific countries and regions over a period of years and decades. In other words, electoral intervention is only one component of the new political intervention, and "democracy promotion" is only one component of overall, multidimensional US foreign-policy undertakings.

A caveat must be stressed. US preference for polyarchy is a general guideline of post-Cold War foreign policy and not a universal prescription. Policymakers often assess that authoritarian arrangements are best left in place in instances where the establishment of polyarchic systems is an unrealistic, high-risk, or unnecessary undertaking.

"Authoritarian regimes are not all the same," noted Howard \
"Some are of such overwhelming strategic importance (for ex\
Saudi Arabia) that we are probably best advised not to tampe\
their internal political structure."[96] Washington continues tacitly to
support authoritarian regimes even when they remain in power by
obstructing electoral processes or breaking with polyarchic procedure,
if a withdrawal of support is seen as running too much of a risk by
opening space for popular or other forces opposed to the transnational
agenda or generating unmanageable instability. This was the case, for
instance, with continued tacit US support for authoritarian regimes in
Kenya and Algeria following fraudulent elections in 1992, Nigeria in
1993, and several Middle Eastern and Asian countries in the early
1990s. As a general rule, authoritarian regimes are supported *until* or
unless a polyarchic alterantive is viable and in place. This makes perfect
sense, once it is understood that the US objective is to promote
polyarchy and oppose authoritarianism only when doing so does not
unacceptably jeopardize elite rule itself.

The case studies to follow all show how the typology of the new
political intervention laid out in this chapter is actually operationa-
lized. In both the Philippines and Chile, the goal was to remove US
allies, brought to or maintained in power by earlier US interventions,
whose continuation in office no longer served US or transnational
interests. The US effort in these two countries intersected with indigenous and broadly based movements against dictatorial governments. In Nicaragua, the goal was to remove a designated enemy, the
Sandinista government, and restore elite rule. In Haiti, as in the
Philippines and Chile, a dictator supported for decades by the United
States had generated a mass popular ferment and therefore came to
represent a threat to US interests. In distinction, however, the United
States was unable to control a transition in Haiti despite massive
political intervention. Haiti was thus a unique case where the United
States succeeded in imposing the process, but lost control over the
outcome. In the former Soviet bloc, the objective was not specifically to
bring about the demise of communist regimes (that was a goal actively
pursued on all fronts since 1917). Rather, it was to accelerate that
demise and, more significantly, to assure, in elections and in subsequent programs, that those forces most closely identified with the
interests of the transnational elite came to power in place of discredited
communist parties, or that those forces, at the minimum, spread their
influence and positioned themselves strategically in the emerging

societies of the former Soviet bloc. In South Africa, the goal was to bring under control and maintain within limits the struggle against apartheid so as to prevent a popular outcome, substituting, in effect, white minority rule by inter-racial polyarchic minority rule.

Case study selection was based on several considerations. First, the four countries underwent high-profile "transitions" in which the United States was heavily involved. They thus provide a wealth of empirical data in which to examine the new policy of the promotion of polyarchy. Second, the "transitions" in all four were touted by policymakers, and praised by journalists, supportive scholars, and public commentators, as "success stories" in which the United States broke sharply with earlier support for authoritarianism and dictatorship and contributed in a positive way to "democracy," and therefore as "models" for future US interventions of this type. Third, as becomes clear in the narrative, the temporal dimensions of these four cases paint a cogent portrait of how the new political intervention and its instruments emerged in the early 1980s and had become consolidated by the early 1990s. The Philippines was the first high-profile "success story." Chile was the second, and so on. It becomes clear that in each subsequent case, policymakers incorporated the lessons from, and modified techniques developed in, the preceding cases. Fourth, these four cases provide sufficient diversity with which to draw some comparative conclusions whose generalizability is strengthened by the examinations of the former Soviet bloc and South Africa. In the Philippines and Chile, the "transitions" were from right-wing dictatorships to elite civilian regimes. In Nicaragua, it was from a revolutionary left-wing regime to a conservative elite regime. In Haiti, it was a combination of both within a brief six-year period. "Democracy promotion" programs unfolded in these four countries in the context of overall US policy which differed sharply in each country. For example, intervention in Nicaragua combined counterrevolutionary military actions with political actions. In the Philippines it combined counterinsurgency military actions with political actions. In Chile the "transition" involved heavy doses of coercive diplomacy but not US military operations, and in Haiti it involved all aspects, culminating in a full-scale US invasion and occupation. Since the circumstances in each country and of US intervention in each were quite distinct, a comparative summation of these cases allows us to identify general patterns and tendencies not particular to the specific national circumstances of intervened countries. The combination of this particular set

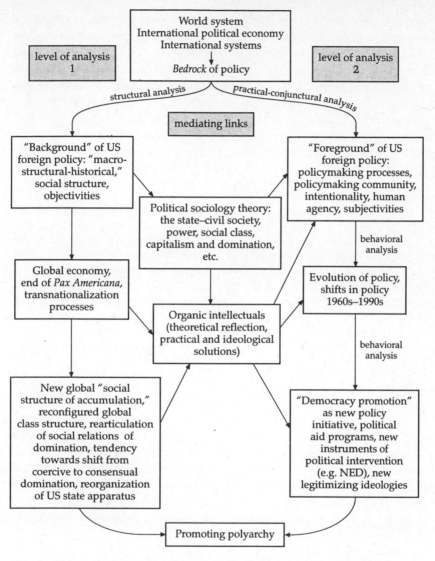

Note: Social forces and class struggle are fields that imbue and undergird all levels of the model.

Fig. 1. Conceptual-methodological model of the promotion of polyarchy in US foreign policy.

of case studies, combined with the two briefer studies, provides a comparative perspective with which to critique implicit and explicit assumptions regarding "democracy promotion." Among other things, a comparative perspective reveals not a sharp discontinuity in US policy towards these countries but a remarkable historical continuity in underlying policy along with modifications in accordance with changing circumstances.

3   The Philippines: "Molded in the image of American democracy"

I walked the floor of the White House night after night until midnight; and I am not ashamed to tell you, gentlemen, that I went down on my knees and prayed Almighty God for light and guidance more than one night. And one night late it came to me this way – I don't know how it was, but it came: (1) that we could not give them back to Spain – that would be cowardly and dishonorable; (2) that we could not turn them over to France and Germany – our commercial rivals in the Orient – that would be bad business and discreditable; (3) that we could not leave them to themselves – they were unfit for self-government – and they would soon have anarchy and misrule over there worse than Spain's was; and (4) that there was nothing left for us to do but to take them all, and to educate the Filipinos, and uplift and civilize and Christianize them, and by God's grace, do the very best we could by them, as our fellow-men for whom Christ also died.

William McKinley, President of the United States, 1899[1]

From a colony to a dependent nation in the periphery of the world system

It was with great irony that Ronald Reagan, after making his famed June 1982 speech before the British parliament at Westminster on a "worldwide campaign for democracy," traveled on to the Philippine capital of Manila, where he announced in a public homage to the dictator, Ferdinand Marcos, that "the Philippines has been molded in the image of American democracy."[2]

The US conquest of the Philippines, an aftermath of the 1898 Spanish–American War, took place at a moment when the United States was emerging as a modern imperial power. The United States, driven by Manifest Destiny, spent much of the nineteenth century in western territorial acquisition, involving the annexation of one-half of Mexico and the systematic extermination of the indigenous populations of North America. In 1892, the Census Bureau declared the "Indian wars" over. The severe economic depression that began in 1893 convinced US rulers that the problem which they had identified as overproduction at home could only be resolved with the conquest of markets overseas, to be opened by military force. The passage to empire required promoting political stability and a military presence in those areas where the United States had established commercial interests. With attention turned from westward expansion to overseas intervention, the possessions of a feeble and declining rival, Spain, became the most suitable new acquisitions. Spain's remaining colonial possessions in Latin America, Cuba and Puerto Rico, became important platforms for expansion in the Western Hemisphere, the US traditional "sphere of influence." On the other hand, the conquest of the Philippines established the United States as an Asian power for the first time. The Philippines became the springboard for expansion throughout Asia via the Pacific, and particularly, to the vast and lucrative Chinese market.

After enduring 300 years of Spanish colonialism, Filipino nationalists were at the point of defeating Spanish forces and had already proclaimed their own sovereign republic when the US navy, as part of the 1898 Spanish–American War, defeated Spain's flotilla in Manila harbor. The US forces then proceeded to turn their guns on the Filipino nationalists, with the objective of transferring the country from Spanish to US colonial control. The ensuing war of conquest, from 1899 to 1902, known as the Philippine–American War, was a protracted and bloody exercise in colonial conquest involving over 70,000 US troops.[3] "It may be necessary to kill half of the Filipinos in order that the remaining half of the population may be advanced to a higher plane of life than their present semi-barbarous state affords," explained one US commanding officer, General Shafter.[4] In the end, up to one million Filipinos lost their lives.

The conquest and subsequent colonization established a pattern of US intervention in the country's affairs. The US colonial administration cultivated an upper-class elite of wealthy landowners, exporters, administrators, and later, commercial and industrial groups – the same elite, known as the *ilustrados*, that had been the junior partners of the Spanish colonialists in an earlier era. This Filipino oligarchy readily collaborated with the Japanese occupation force during World War II, and were then restored to power by the United States following liberation. Brought up under colonial tutelage, this elite was handed the reins of power in 1946, when the US conferred formal independence on the Philippines and the country moved from a colony to a neo-colony.

Over the following decades, a series of elite civilian regimes ruled the Philippines through a vice-ridden political culture of corrupt party machines, back-room deals and competition over the economic largesse that came with political office. Elections were held on a regular basis, checkered by routine vote-buying, fraud, and violence by the private armies of the elite. The fragile post-colonial political system rested on enough of an inter-elite consensus for functional civic competition between ruling groups and effective control over the popular sectors – a protopolyarchic political system which was ill-equipped to deal with the pressures of the early neo-colonial period. Contending elite factions from the two major parties, indistinguishable in terms of ideology, the Nacionalista and the Liberal, rotated in and out of office. "The firmly established two party system is a strong asset," noted with satisfaction one CIA report in 1965. "The similarity of the parties, while depriving the voter of clear choices between programs, nevertheless encourages moderation, readiness to compromise, and lack of dogmatism in the political elite."[5]

The basis of a tenuous Philippine stability during the 1950s and 1960s was the alliance between this elite and the United States, which exercised external domination through a myriad of informal mechanisms, ranging from military aid and counterinsurgency programs to economic aid programs, covert CIA operations, and outright political imposition. The Philippines became a key client regime in the post-World War II US empire. Washington set up the Clark Air Base and the Subtic Naval Base, which became the largest US military facilities outside the US mainland, and were key staging points for US military interventions in the Pacific. The Pentagon also created, supplied, and trained the Philippine military as a repressive guarantor of "internal security," under the direct supervision of a permanent US military advisor group. The US military advisors and the CIA designed and led the bloody suppression of the nationalist Hukbalahap (or "Huk") uprising in the 1950s.[6]

Notwithstanding Cold War ideological musings, the real threat to US and elite interests in the Philippines in this period was not external aggression but the demands of the impoverished Filipino masses for social change and democratization of Filipino society, as one secret 1950 NSC assessment openly acknowledged:

> External threats to the Philippines appear to be relatively remote... a sound Philippine military policy justifies maximum emphasis on effective forces required for internal security and, under existing conditions, minimum expenditure for defense against external invaders... The United States has as its objectives in the Philippines the establishment and maintenance of: a) An effective government which will preserve and strengthen the pro-US orientation of its people. b) A Philippine military capability [*sic*] of restoring and maintaining internal security. c) A stable and self-supporting economy.[7]

Meanwhile, the Philippines became an appendage of the US economy under trade agreements and economic aid programs imposed by Washington. The United States demanded, and was granted, trade treaties providing it with "equal access" with Filipinos to Philippine natural resources and utilities, and "parity," or unrestricted entry to Filipino markets. In accepting US aid packages, explained Secretary of State Dean Acheson, the Philippines "will accept American advisers throughout their Government. We will come up to Congress with an aid program, which will be modest in dimensions but which lays the foundation for American technicians and American advisers all through their Government."[8] Military and economic aid were thus used quite effectively, and they remained key elements of US policy in the 1980s and 1990s. Political aid was still handled by the CIA, which conducted widespread covert operations, among them, stage-managed elections to assure the preferred US outcome, payoffs to government officials, financing for favored business and civic groups, pro-US propaganda campaigns among the population, the supply of intelligence on dissidents to the Filipino security forces, and so on.[9]

As United States and other foreign investment poured in, the economy grew to the benefit of US capital and the Philippine elite simultaneously with the increasing impoverishment of the majority and deep social polarization. In 1974, the International Labor Organization reported that the country's development model "nurtures and sustains trends in the structure of earnings that result in steadily increasing inequality [and] cannot expect to continue for very long."[10] By the early 1970s a popular movement was snowballing, based in trade unions, peasant groups, students, grassroots neighborhood organizations in the cities, and the clergy. Nationalism and radicalism spread throughout the country. The desperate social and economic conditions also spawned a growing insurgency, led by the New People's Army (NPA), the military arm of the Communist Party of the Philippines. Repression, mass jailings, systematic human rights violations, street conflict and rural insurgency became the order of the day. Ferdinand Marcos, who had assumed the presidency in 1965 in questionable elections and was then "reelected" in 1969, declared martial law in September 1972. Although martial law was also a means for Marcos to perpetuate his personal hold on power (new elections were scheduled for 1973), it was foremost a means for the Philippine elite and the United States to face the crisis-level challenge of a popular rebellion against the status quo.

Shortly before he imposed martial law, Marcos met secretly with US Ambassador Henry Byroade to seek endorsement of "stronger measures" to deal with the unrest sweeping the country. Byroade delivered to Marcos a confidential State Department message promising US support.[11] A 1972 US Senate report on the declaration of martial law noted that the United States was "altogether uncritical of what occurred in the Philippines." It continued:

> We found few, if any, Americans who took the position that the demise of individual rights and democratic institutions would adversely affect U.S. interests. In the first place, these democratic institutions were considered to be severely deficient. In the second place, whatever U.S. interests were – or are – they apparently are not thought to be related to the preservation of the democratic process... U.S. officials appear prepared to accept that the strengthening of presidential authority will... enable President Marcos to introduce needed stability; that these objectives are in our interests; and that military bases and a familiar government in the Philippines are more important than the preservation of democratic institutions.[12]

The report went on to note that Marcos was drafting a new constitution which Washington considered to be highly favorable to foreign investors, and that US business welcomed martial law prohibitions on strikes and lockouts, the lifting of work restrictions on Sundays and holidays, and other presidential decrees favorable to foreign capital. At the time, *Business International* reported that "the overwhelming consensus of the foreign business community in the Philippines was that martial rule under President Marcos was the best thing that ever happened to the country."[13]

As the tenuous post-colonial order thus crumbled, the United States sustained its support for Marcos and authoritarianism as the preferred instrument of social control. As with such strongman and dictatorial regimes in other countries, the US relationship with Marcos was a two-way street. Marcos proved adept at manipulating Washington for his own ends as much as Washington utilized the dictatorship as an instrument in its policy (just as the Philippine elite utilized the dictatorship to preserve its interests and in turn granted special privilege and authority to the dictator's inner circle). But the two found a symbiotic meeting place in the preservation of the social order. Although President Jimmy Carter had declared human rights the centerpiece of his foreign policy, his administration provided the Marcos regime with nearly half a billion dollars in economic and military aid, and when Marcos lifted martial law Carter advised the Philippine opposition to accept Marcos's action as a "generous offer" and to forswear violence.[14] The incoming Reagan administration applied the same kind of "quiet diplomacy" it had developed towards the Latin American Southern Cone dictatorships to the Philippines, expanding support for the Marcos regime. President-elect Ronald Reagan personally received Marcos's wife, Imelda, on the eve of his inauguration, and advised against a too-hasty lifting of martial law. Six months later, in August 1981, Vice-President George Bush raised a toast to Marcos during his visit to Manila, declaring "We love your adherence to democratic principle and to the democratic process."[15]

Nonetheless, enthusiasm among the Philippine elite and the United States for the crackdown gradually tapered, as Marcos converted his rule into the most vulgar form of "crony capitalism," similar to that of the Somozas in Nicaragua or the Duvaliers in Haiti. Corruption and the spoils of state, which in an earlier period had been "equitably" distributed among the upper and middle classes through the competition of different factions and rotation in office, now became monopolized by Marcos and his own family and clique. Beyond being a political liability, "crony capitalism," by disturbing free markets, eventually became a hindrance to transnational capital and neo-liberal restructuring in the Philippines as the global economy emerged. Far from resolving the crisis of elite rule, authoritarian political structures ended up rupturing minimal inter-elite consensus and accommodation necessary for stability. Meanwhile, the crackdown, rather than suppressing the popular movement, gave further impetus to it. The NPA, a minor force in 1972, grew rapidly after the imposition of martial law. The National Democratic Front, formed in April 1973, brought together the Communist Party, the urban poor, radical youth, and clergy influenced by liberation theology. By the early 1980s, observers began to speak of the coming Philippine revolution.

A key turning point came in August 1983 with the assassination by Marcos henchmen of the most prominent leader of the elite opposition, former senator Benigno Aquino Jr. For over a decade, the poor and the popular sectors had been fighting the dictatorship. Now, the Aquino murder had galvanized the non-Marcos elite – the business community, the Catholic Church hierarchy, the politicians, and the middle classes – into active opposition. By rendering the inter-elite split irreversible, the Aquino murder marked the beginning of the end for Marcos. The middle classes soon joined the popular sectors in massive street demonstrations and a burgeoning nationwide movement for democracy ensued. A convergence between a radicalized elite opposition and a radicalized popular opposition became a real possibility. The Aquino murder also hastened debate in Washington over support for Marcos. Behind this debate loomed the larger issue of the merits of authoritarian versus polyarchic methods of transnational social control, as analyzed earlier.

In theoretical perspective, developments from Philippine independence after World War II to the early 1980s reflected a gradual process of transition from a formal colonial relationship with the United States to a country's entrance into the emergent global economy as a dependent and peripheral country, with concomitant social and political repercussions. From a mere narrow appendage of the US economy, the Philippines was becoming a haven for transnational corporate capital which poured into the country from the 1960s on. The earlier colonial relationship was based, for the most part, on feudal and semi-feudal production relations in much of the Philippines, and on the provision on the part of the Philippines of raw materials for the US metropolitan power. In the theoretical discourse of world system and dependency theory, a largely pre-capitalist social formation in the periphery was articulated to a capitalist social formation in the core. The penetration of transnational capital, starting in the 1960s, disrupted rural communities, forged new solidarities, and led to mobilization among subordinate classes in these communities and in expanding urban communities.[16] The internal political structure of authoritarianism, and the "crony capitalism" tendencies which authoritarianism tends to generate, had served the purpose of social control in the first few decades of this process. But as this process unfolded, authoritarianism proved unable to respond to the twin challenges of containing popular pressures from below generated by capitalist penetration and of providing mechanisms for intra-elite accommodation.

Shifting from this structural analysis to behavioral analysis, US policymakers were witness to a dual crisis in the making in the early 1980s: an irreconcilable inter-elite split alongside a burgeoning mass popular movement and armed insurgency. It was the same type of pre-revolutionary situation that had developed in Nicaragua and led to the Sandinista triumph in 1979. As US policy began to shift in the first half of the 1980s, Washington's challenge became: (1) to transfer support from Marcos to the anti-Marcos elite (2) to assure that the anti-Marcos elite would gain hegemony over the anti-dictatorial struggle, and (3) to reconstruct consensual, polyarchic behavior among the elite as a whole.

Managing the transition

The shift in policy was checkered by a fierce debate and infighting among policymakers. This reflected a surface split between "hard-liners" who argued for staying the course and "pragmatists" who argued for active intervention in the Philippines to redirect the anti-dictatorial struggle, and behind it, the deeper debate between author-itarianism and polyarchy in the Third World. US policy became ambivalent and contradictory from 1983 to 1985, as this debate was played out.[17] However, sufficient consensus emerged following the Aquino assassination that continued economic and military aid should be made conditional on steps by Marcos towards reform. Thus, while military involvement in the counterinsurgency campaign escalated, overall policy shifted from unqualified support for the dictatorship to active and critical intervention in the country's political affairs. At this point, explained Ambassador Stephen Bosworth in a 1984 speech to the Philippine Rotary Club, "it is not a question of how to avoid change; it is rather a question of how change can best be managed."[18] By 1985, US state managers had entered a stage of managing a high-risk transition from dictatorship to polyarchy.

In November 1984, a secret NSC Study Directive made the call for a concerted US intervention in the Philippines to facilitate a transition. "The United States has extremely important interests in the Philip-pines... Political and economic developments in the Philippines

124

threaten these interests," stated the directive. "The US does not want to remove Marcos from power to destabilize the GOP [Government of the Philippines]. Rather, we are urging revitalization of democratic institutions, dismantling 'crony' monopoly capitalism and allowing the economy to respond to free market forces, and restoring professional, apolitical leadership to the Philippine military to deal with the growing communist insurgency." "These efforts," it went on, "are meant to stabilize [the country] while strengthening institutions which will eventually provide for a peaceful transition." The directive concluded by recommending "an occasional presidential letter, regular visits by administration officials, close Embassy contact, and regular one-on-one meetings between President Marcos and Ambassador Bosworth."[19] In particular, the directive proposed the visit of a high-level US emissary and a presidential letter.

These recommendations were implemented. In May 1985, CIA director William Casey visited Marcos in Manila's Malacañang Palace, the presidential residence, to press for an early presidential election. Five months later, in October, Reagan dispatched his close friend, Senator Paul Laxalt, to Marcos with the same request, and in addition to deliver a personal letter from the US president. A fanfare of publicity accompanied Laxalt's mission in order to maximize public perceptions in the Philippines and in the United States of an imminent change in US policy.[20] Following the Laxalt visit, Marcos called for "snap" elections, to be held in February 1986. During this same period, in a track parallel to the pressures on Marcos, the United States began to develop broad contacts with the elite political and military opposition as a counterweight to the popular sectors, a strategy detailed in the 1984 NSC directive. In July 1985, the CIA, DIA, and the State Department prepared a joint study on the situation in the Philippines. It predicted a growth in the left-wing military insurgency over the following eighteen months, but, more significantly, it estimated that left-wing and popular *political* influence and sentiment among the masses would spread if the dictatorship remained in place until the scheduled presidential elections of 1987 (these elections were subsequently moved up when Marcos called "snap elections"). Washington turned to facilitating Marcos's removal under circumstances which it could control.

The opposition forces were diverse and well organized, ranging from the NPA insurgency, to the mass, left-of-center civic movement BAYAN (New Patriotic Federation, which went by its acronym in

Tagalog), which brought together millions of Philippine citizens, to numerous parties and groups of the center, center-right and right. Perhaps the weakest among the opposition were the center and conservative sectors which, as in Nicaragua and other authoritarian Third World regimes, had vacillated during many years between support for, and opposition to, the dictatorship. It was precisely these sectors that the United States had set about to develop in the mid-1980s through new political aid programs targeting civil society. Between 1984 and 1990, Philippine organizations received at least $9 million from the NED and other US sources. These included: the Philippine Chamber of Commerce and Industry (PCCI), which mobilized the business community against Marcos; the Trade Union Congress of the Philippines (TUCP), a minority, conservative union federation affiliated with the International Confederation of Free Trade Unions (ICFTU) and which competed with more radical and left-leaning labor organizations; Philippine "youth clubs" established under the guidance of US organizers to mobilize Philippine youth; the KABATID Philippine women's organization (KABATID is the Tagalog acronym for Women's Movement for the Nurturing of Democracy), also established under the guidance of US organizers; and the National Movement for Free Elections (NAMFREL).[21] I analyze below the significance of this political aid, both before and after the transition.

Washington was becoming increasingly concerned over the prospects for the coalescence of a nationalist and independent-minded bloc within the moderate opposition. In late 1984, at a meeting in the home of Corazon Aquino, the wife of the assassinated Benigno, a declaration that became known as the Convenors' Statement was drafted and signed by twelve of the most important leaders of the opposition to Marcos, among them prominent business executives and nationalist politicians, most of whom were regarded as possible presidential candidates in a future election. The document spelled out a nationalist-oriented program of social reform and development and also called for the removal of US military bases from the Philippines.[22]

As the "snap" elections approached, Cory Aquino and Salvador "Doy" Laurel emerged as the two favorites in the field of opposition candidates. Both were members of the Philippine elite. Aquino, from a wealthy landholding family, also enjoyed genuine popularity as an anti-Marcos symbol. The leader of the right-wing opposition was Salvador "Doy" Laurel, a long-time Marcos loyalist who finally broke with the strongman in 1980. He maintained close contacts with the US embassy, and had refused to sign the 1984 Convenors' Statement. As the head of the opposition UNIDO party, he had a well-oiled political machine at his service. On the other hand, Aquino had won the backing of many in the center-to-left opposition, who were exercising important influence in her coalition. Fearing the possible emergence of a left–center popular alliance, Washington thus set about to forge a center–right alliance and to minimize popular and leftist influence in the anti-Marcos ticket. The State Department despatched a team of officials to Manila to meet with Aquino and Laurel and convince them to run under a united ticket that would stress anti-communism and refrain from opposing US bases in the Philippines (Laurel subsequently became Aquino's running-mate as candidate for vice-president). US Embassy Chargé d'Affaires Philip Kaplan began assembling key leaders of the anti-Marcos political parties and, according to a confidential embassy cable, "emphasized the need for the [US assembled] opposition to get its act together given the limited time left before a campaign starts."[23]

In the weeks leading up to the elections, on voting day and in the days that followed, the Philippines were swept by what became known as "people power." The Philippine people voted *en masse* for Aquino and then launched a popular insurrection when, in the face of widespread fraud, Marcos declared himself the winner. "People power," it should be stressed, was not a creation of US political intervention; to the contrary, it was what Washington had hoped to avoid. However, faced with the inevitability of a mass, popular uprising, US actions sought at all times to control its development and minimize its effects, and to bolster simultaneously the positions of those institutions and leaders most allied to US interests. The State Department sent at-large ambassador Philip Habib to Manila to urge Aquino to keep her followers off the streets and to convince Marcos to step down. In the weeks before the elections, reported the *Far Eastern Economic Review*, "the US Embassy, which had been augmented by dozens of officers with some Philippine expertise, was engaged in intense secret contacts with the opposition, Marcos' ruling party, and the military in an effort to bring about a reconciliation of the two political groups, without Marcos."[24]

At the same time, Washington sought to assure an important role for the Armed Forces of the Philippines (AFP), having developed extensive contacts with key AFP officers and supporting a loosely organized reform movement within the AFP that had been established in

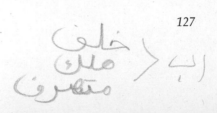

February 1985. The goals of this reform movement were not to democratize the Philippines but to "professionalize" the armed forces, improve the counterinsurgency campaign, and preserve the institutional integrity of the military in the face of the crisis of the dictatorship. The reform movement secured the support in mid-1985 of the Defense Minister, General Juan Ponce Enrile, and the acting Chief of Staff, General Fidel Ramos, both right-wing and long-time Marcos loyalists who switched sides in the dictator's final hour. Enrile and Ramos led a military reformers' revolt against Marcos's attempt to steal the elections, an event which was crucial in convincing Marcos, on February 23, to step down and leave the country.

Although the military revolt against Marcos was clearly crucial in the dictator's overthrow, it was also crucial to the US strategy for managing the transition and preserving the social order in the post-Marcos period. In the days following the vote, Aquino had announced a campaign to protest Marcos's efforts to steal the elections, which included an economic boycott and a general strike. Such actions would have greatly enhanced the labor movement, with its militant base and left-wing tendencies, in both removing Marcos and in shaping the post-Marcos government and policies. The military revolt not only assured the preservation of the repressive AFP in the post-Marcos period, but left Aquino more indebted to, and dependent on, the conservative military than to the labor movement. US military aid and involvement in the counterinsurgency expanded dramatically in the Aquino period and the military gained major influence in the new government. The preservation of the coercive apparatus and military impunity and the active role played by the "armor of coercion" during and after the transition placed clear limits on social transformation and demands for equity in the post-Marcos period.

Meanwhile, the Philippine left and sectors of the mass, popular movement made a serious tactical mistake in boycotting the elections, with the reasoning that Marcos would steal them anyway and then legitimize his dictatorship. However, the population overwhelmingly wanted to partake in these elections as an act of rejection of Marcos and an expression of its desire for democratic change. The left boycott thus facilitated the concentration of both popular and elite support around Aquino and helped the United States push through its own agenda.

In backing Aquino, the United States latched on to her popularity and posited itself as the firm champion of a new "democratic" government in the Philippines. Although the US claimed for itself a pivotal role in organizing the Aquino victory, it is difficult, in the general context of Philippine politics and the special circumstances attending to the demise of a moribund dictatorship, to measure the influence of US intervention in the Philippine political process on the outcome of the anti-dictatorial movement. This became a hotly debated issue in both Washington and Manila. But whether or not US intervention was itself the determining factor in the overthrow of Marcos obscured a much more significant issue: *US intervention was decisive in shaping the contours of the anti-Marcos movement and in establishing the terms and conditions under which Philippine social and political struggles would unfold in the post-Marcos period.*

By 1983 it had become clear that the dictatorship's days were numbered; from that point on, for all actors involved, including those seeking a polyarchic outcome and preservation of the social order and those seeking a project of popular democracy and basic change in the social order, the underlying issue was not whether Marcos would go but what would take the dictatorship's place. The underlying struggle shifted from democracy versus dictatorship to the terms and outcome of the anti-dictatorial movement and the reach of the Philippine democratization process. US intervention in the transition was crucial in limiting the extent of popular democratization in the post-Marcos era. By accelerating the removal of Marcos before further polarization could take place, by helping to supplant popular with elite leadership in the anti-Marcos movement, by preserving the integrity of the armed forces, by bolstering those constituencies responsive to elite and US interests, and so on, the United States was able to channel the anti-Marcos movement into a less threatening outcome, and then to win more favorable circumstances for shaping the post-Marcos period. This new period involved heightened US political and military intervention aimed at diminishing left and popular influence in the new government, reconstructing consensus within the dominant groups around a polyarchic political system, and building up allied constituencies in Philippine civil and political society.

The role of "political aid"

Political aid and the new modalities of intervention analyzed in chapter 2 began to play an important role in US policy towards the Philippines from 1984. After helping to bring to power "a government

129

with legitimacy and democratic commitment," the NED and other US agencies set about, following Aquino's election, to "build and consolidate a new democratic system."[25]

The United States gained important experience in electoral intervention in the 1986 Philippine elections, particularly in giving the character of a plebiscite to elections, in which political forces are polarized into two camps, a "democratic opposition" (which US aid and advisors ensure will be dominated by moderate, pro-United States elites) and dictatorship. This tactic of turning elections into a polarized referendum was subsequently developed and adroitly applied in Chile and Nicaragua. In particular, the creation of an observer apparatus for the 1986 election, and for subsequent ones, gave US officials important experience in the use of electoral observation as part of overall policy. In 1951, the NAMFREL was set up by a former civic affairs director of the Philippine army with the help of US government funds and officials. This "good government" organization played an important role in the political-electoral aspects of the massive counterinsurgency underway at that time against the Huks. In particular, NAMFREL became the vehicle for building a political machine that could deliver the 1953 electoral victory of the CIA-backed candidate, Ramon Magsaysay.[26]

In 1984, the NED renewed US funding for the NAMFREL, which then played an important role in denouncing Marcos's attempted fraud. Money for the TUCP also went to finance the participation of some 7,000 TUCP members in NAMFREL's observer program. In addition, the NED funded a joint delegation from the NDI and the NRI, which also denounced the attempted fraud. On the eve of the election, President Reagan appointed Senator Richard Lugar to lead a congressional team to monitor the vote. Lugar then commissioned Allen Weinstein, head of the Center for Democracy (CFD), to organize the delegation. Weinstein was one of the original organizers of Project Democracy, which led to the formation of the NED, and was the Endowment's first president, a post from which he resigned after setting up the CFD in 1984. His observer delegation played an important role, upon its return from Manila, in advising US policymakers on how to proceed in the tense days of the transition from Marcos to Aquino.

International electoral observation is not equivalent to foreign intervention in a nation's internal political process, and such observation may play an important role in democratization processes. However, the United States has developed international observation into an instrument for achieving its objectives in each target country, in close synchronization with US policy and political intervention programs. First, electoral observance places the United States in a position to decide when an election is "free and fair" and who the victor is. Second, with the broad publicity they achieve, electoral observer groups financed and organized by the US government are in a position to set the international public relations agenda in accordance with overall US goals. Third, in distinction to neutral or impartial observation, the new political intervention has utilized electoral observation as an instrument for penetrating foreign electoral processes and manipulating them. Under the guise of "observation," US operatives become deeply involved in the activities of the groups and candidates being promoted by the United States. In the case of the 1986 Philippine elections, US and other observer delegations did contribute to exposing and denouncing Marcos's attempt to steal the election. Although this coincided with the Philippine people's efforts to defeat Marcos, the US denunciation was intended to serve not the aspirations of Filipinos but concrete US policy objectives. Following the Philippine experience, electoral observation became an important component of political intervention projects in Chile, Nicaragua, Haiti, and elsewhere.

Similarly, the NED set up an assistance program for the PCCI, channeled through the CIPE. "The overall goal is to support the restoration of private enterprise values in place of the 'crony capitalism' system as a key element in the overall transition to democracy," stated a NED report.[27] Funds went for the PCCI to build a nationwide business federation, with local chambers all over the country, to "assist in generating active programs to reach local businessmen and opinion leaders." The purpose of this program was to cultivate consensus within the Philippine private sector, and elites in general, around the project of neo-liberalism, and to provide transnational kernels within the Philippine elite with a capacity for developing concrete neo-liberal policy reform proposals and interacting with the Philippine government so as to have these proposals adopted.

Washington also funded and promoted the creation of a new women's organization, the KABATID. Funds went to pay for a headquarters in Manila, regional offices and equipment, the publication of a monthly magazine (*KABATID Express*), and salaries for paid staff, among other items. Why would Washington create an entirely new women's movement in the Philippines, a country that could boast by the early 1980s of having the broadest and most vibrant feminist movement in Asia? Women form a significant portion of the 20 million Filipino workers. Women became highly active in the trade union movement and constituted a major force in the anti-Marcos and democratization struggles. In the late 1970s, women's organizations proliferated. In 1984, many of these groups came together in a coalition, the General Assembly Binding Women for Reforms, Integrity, Equality, Leadership, and Action (GABRIELA). GABRIELA brought together poor women workers with middle-class professionals, and also attracted the support of some women from the elite. The organization enunciated four objectives: the restoration of democracy; the attainment of a genuinely sovereign and independent Philippines, "where women will be full and equal partners of men in developing and preserving national patrimony"; support for "the struggles of women workers, peasants, and urban poor settlers to attain their economic well-being"; and "women's liberation" as an integral component of "national liberation."[28]

The existing women's movement thus put forth a program of popular democracy that threatened the transnational agenda for the post-Marcos period – an agenda which the KABATID would promote.[29] The purpose of the NED program was not to help poor Filipino women to democratize their society; if this were the intent there already existed dozens of active women's groups which Washington could have supported. Instead, KABATID was to *compete* with the existing women's movement, undercut its progressive tendencies and popular leadership, and at the same time organize women from the elite around the efforts to stabilize a polyarchic political system. The KABATID, as is the case with similar civic groups created and/or funded by the United States abroad, did not envision itself as a mass women's movement. US funds, provided in relatively small doses, were intended not to finance a large-scale operation, but to deliver the resources necessary for a small group of women from the country's elite to network and become mobilized. The KABATID was to be a club to groom women leaders well placed in the country's civil and political society. The KABATID's newsletter, for instance, was not published for mass distribution or for news-stand sales, but for exclusive circulation to "KABATID members, the Executive and Legislative Branches of government, major media outlets, and other non-governmental organizations."[30] The magazine was intended to link, organize, and provide strategy guidelines to core constituencies

132

around the US-transnational agenda, including neo-liberal restructuring, the continued presence of US military bases (for which the
KABATID lobbied unsuccessfully), and opposition to legalization of
the Communist Party and to negotiations with the insurgency, and to
"counteract the powerful propaganda machine of the Left forces."[31] A
glance at the KABATID trustees indicates that the organization was led
by middle- and upper-class professionals, business women, and government officials from state agencies, the private sector, and the
educational system, and that all were drawn from the transnationalized fraction of the elite.[32] Four of its five top officers were also
NAMFREL leaders. The KABATID's chairperson was Dette Pascual,
who also served on the board of NAMFREL and was that organization's director for external affairs until she resigned to head the
KABATID.

In turn, the KABATID was to gain hegemony – in the Gramscian
sense, not of *domination*, but of *leadership* – over the mass women's
movement and help influence the contours of post-Marcos society
along the agenda of the transnational elite. One KABATID document
warned that the economic crisis in the post-Marcos period "makes the
lower income masses susceptible to ideological solutions," and that,
therefore, the organization should "develop a core of women citizen-
leaders who can respond effectively to the needs of their community...
Since women are the traditional nurturers and transmitters of family
traditions and values, KABATID members will be catalysts in their
community, and [will] sustain an effective middle force group that will
serve as role models to the young and impressionable."[33] The idea was
to cultivate core constituencies of leaders which could become public
opinion makers, simultaneously competing with popular sectors and
inculcating in the elite as a whole the virtues of consensus-building
and polyarchic procedure. This was part of the broader efforts to
cohere a "political center" and have it exercise hegemony in the organs
of civil society and the internal political system. The KABATID documents stressed "the creation of a visible middle force," the "bonding
together of women" around "a visibly moderate force," the creation of
"circles of influence" around the country, training for KABATID
members in "leadership skills and value orientation," and exercising a
"catalyst function" in the formation of public opinion over national
issues.[34] The core of "women citizen-leaders" cultivated by the
KABATID was expected to reach out to women in the TUCP trade
unions, the Philippine "youth clubs," business groups, and elsewhere,

in tandem with US political aid programs in those areas. In this way, the leaders of the NAMFREL, the TUCP, and the KABATID sat on each other's boards and came to constitute a national network, with interlocking directorates as discussed in chapter 2. The KABATID also used the "multiplier effect" analyzed in chapter 2 to set up regional offices and local leadership structures.[35]

Seen from a more structural level, the penetration of the global economy from the 1960s and on had thoroughly disrupted the traditional sexual division of labor, had thrust millions of women into the capitalist sector of the economy, particularly in to the external sector tied to transnational capital. The peculiar gender dimensions of the shift in the labor-intensive phases of international production to the South are the concentration of female labor in these externally linked sectors, and notorious export-assembly platforms (*maquilladoras*), where labor is largely female, although management remains male. This new sexual division of labor – springing from pre-capitalist divisions and patriarchal social relations and cultural patterns – provides advantages to transnational capital in the form of wage differentials between male and female workers, an alleged "docile" and "dexterous" workforce, and the creation of new hierarchies among oppressed strata that deflect challenges to exploitation. But the disruption of traditional gender roles, the new experiences of capitalist exploitation superimposed on gender oppression, and the subjective experience of broader gender, group, and class solidarities which develop, often catalyze and politicize women to challenge their exploitation as laborers *and* to challenge residual and new types of patriarchal relations. US political aid programs, such as those in the Philippines, were designed precisely to contain mass mobilization among women displaced from traditional roles and to utilize, and even strengthen, patriarchal social relations, as part of the broader strategy. In this way, transnational political and economic practices conjoin to sustain relations of class domination in a process properly conceived as the reproduction of social order during the integration of national societies into an emergent global social formation.

Philippine youth were also identified as a key sector, given young people's rapid politicization and radicalization in the anti-Marcos struggle, especially those in the militant high-school and university student movement. In 1986, the NED began its Youth Democracy Project in the Philippines, channeling funds through the International Division of the YMCA for "seminars on democratic procedures" with

134

thousands of high-school students around the country.[36] Also in 1986, the NED provided the NDI and the NRI with funds to conduct "training courses" for Philippine congress members.[37] US officials conducted the courses with the Evelio B. Javier Foundation, a Philippine think-tank whose trustees included many leaders of the KABATID, the TUCP and the PCCI.

Probably the most important plank in the political aid program was support for the conservative TUCP. Post-World War II industrialization generated a 20-million-strong urban workforce by the late 1970s, and labor had become a central component of the democratization movement by the end of the decade. In an effort to curtail labor militancy, the Marcos regime, with the assistance of the AAFLI, set up the TUCP in 1977, under the operating principle of tripartite cooperation among labor, management, and government. Established when the country was under martial law, it was the only legally recognized union during the Marcos years. Right up to his downfall, the TUCP maintained friendly relations with the dictator, who, until 1984, was the regular featured speaker at the TUCP's annual May Day Breakfast.[38]

Meanwhile, eight union federations dating back to the previous two decades, disenchanted with the TUCP's pro-government program, had set up the Kilusang Mayo Uno (May First Movement), or KMU, in 1981. The KMU spread throughout Manila and other urban centers and became the largest anti-Marcos union center. Branded as "communist" by US officials, the KMU was, in fact, a multi-tendency labor federation, uniting workers of communist, Christian, social democratic and other political persuasions, and controlled by its membership, not by any outside organization, whether of the left or the right. Following the overthrow of Marcos, the KMU continued to grow. It became the largest labor federation in the country, and one of the most dynamic in the world. The KMU waged campaigns in the late 1980s for national control over natural resources, the removal of all US military bases, a comprehensive agrarian reform (the TUCP supported the Aquino program – see below), for worker participation and improvements in wages and benefits. The real threat to US interests posed by the KMU was clearly its program of nationalist political demands and popular democratization.[39]

In 1984, the NED took over funding for the TUCP and supplied neaerly $7 million between 1984 and 1991, channeled through the FTUI to AAFLI field offices in the Philippines.[40] "A major effort to strengthen democratic unions is being undertaken in the Philippines, where democratic forces have been stymied by martial law, the turbulence following the Aquino assassination and the growth of Marxist-oriented organizations," explained the NED, in inaugurating its Philippine program in 1984.[41] US policymakers were particularly concerned about the dramatic decline in worker support for the TUCP, whose ranks had dropped from 2 million when it was formed to 1.2 million workers in 1985.[42] The NED report made clear that the main objective of the program was not to bring down the Marcos dictatorship, but to counter left-wing unionism. The purpose of the TUCP funding is to "strengthen pro-democratic unions in the Philippines so that they will become the preeminent representatives of workers under the umbrella of the TUCP," according to the NED. Funds went for the purchase of office and press equipment, staff salaries, the maintenance of regional offices, "training in democratic ideology" and in "technical organizational skills," and a "media relations and communications program" to "counteract left-wing propaganda."[43] With the massive infusion of funds, the TUCP was able to set up a nationwide patronage network. "Some of the regional [labor leaders receiving AAFLI money] are becoming powerful politically," explained Bud Phillips, AAFLI's administrator in the Philippines. "Imagine if you have $100,000 to give out to families in $500 chunks: Your stock goes way up, faster than the stock of any of the militant labor groups" (at the time, per capita annual income was $790). Phillips went on to explain: "If people hadn't had immediate assistance then, the success of the political left in the trade unions would have been phenomenal. It would have been a Waterloo. Our help saved the free trade union movement here."[44]

One of the reasons for such emphasis on Philippine labor was the challenge from the militant KMU and the importance of labor in national political struggles. However, another reason was that, with its already-existing infrastructure and leadership, the TUCP was in a good position to develop what NED documents described as "sectoral linkages" with women, youth, political parties, religious, and civic groups, and thus act as the centripetal nucleus for the cultivation of a nationwide network of "agents of influence" endowed through US assistance with a "political action capacity," that is, with the skills and resources to mobilize distinct constituencies.[45] Thus, the FTUI funded specific programs designed to "strengthen organizational relations" between the TUCP and the women's, youth and church groups and to eclipse popular leadership in all areas. "Such relationships serve to establish bulwarks against Communist front groups," explained a FTUI document. In addition, AAFLI funds went to NAMFREL programs, including the training of thousands of TUCP members to staff NAMFREL offices and conduct poll-watching.[46] Ernesto Herrera, TUCP's Secretary-General, was also a member of the Executive Council of the NAMFREL. Similarly, NED funds, passed through FTUI, on to the AAFLI, and from there to the TUCP, were used in 1988 to establish the Workers–Student Forum (WSF) as "a counterweight" to the left-leaning Filipino Federation of Students and League of Filipino Students.[47]

Between 1984 and 1990, the TUCP became the second largest recipient of FTUI funds worldwide, surpassed only by Poland's Solidarity. The objective became an all-out war against the KMU. The primary goal of the KMU, warned one FTUI document, was not "to bargain with employers or work through the country's fragile democratic institutions," but to "radically change the country's entire political system." It explained: "A variety of approaches will be used to reach disparate groups of workers. These efforts will directly address KMU attempts to bring workers in specific industries in key economic sectors under their control [*sic*] ... [and] will allow the TUCP to supplant the KMU as the spokesman [*sic*] for working men and women in the Philippines."[48] The NED also funded a TUCP think-tank, the Center for Social Policy and National Issues.[49] AAFLI officials working at this center helped the TUCP to "develop a formal capability to lobby the Philippine Congress" and ran "training and education projects designed to provide every union with political action capabilities."[50] The center endorsed Aquino's conservative agrarian reform and advocated approval of a referendum to endorse the continuation of US military bases in the country (see below).

Through these efforts, the TUCP garnered a working-class base of support in urban areas for a gradual realignment of the Aquino coalition from the center-left towards the center-right. The TUCP leadership established close working relations with Vice-President Laurel and the right wing of the Aquino administration. US funding also went to the TUCP's affiliated rural unions, grouped into the National Congress of Farmers Organizations (NCFO). The NCFO, in its competition with militant groups from the National Peasant Union (KMP), which was founded in June 1985, lent support to the traditional rural oligarchy and agri-business in their efforts to reestablish authority in the countryside following the turbulence of the mid-1980s. Most chilling was TUCP and NCFO collaboration with landowners who had begun organizing politically and militarily, forming private armies and "vigilante groups" (death squads) with official government sanction.[51]

US allied groups and "agents of influence" cultivated with political aid pushed the US post-Marcos agenda. Apart from the general program of polyarchy and neo-liberalism, the specific points on this agenda of concern to US policymakers included the renewal of the 1947 Military Bases Agreement, which was set to expire in 1991. The TUCP, the KABATID women's organization, the PCCI, and other US-funded groups all endorsed a renewal of the lease.[52] Despite the efforts of constituencies cultivated through US economic and political aid programs, mass sentiment, expressed in a 1992 referendum, opposed the bases and the treaty was allowed to expire. While the loss of the Philippine bases was a setback for US geo-political concerns, policymakers were able to link the base closings to the transnational agenda for the Philippines: the AID designed and financed a program for the conversion of the Philippine military bases into a duty-free *zona franca* for transnational corporate investment, as part of the country's neo-liberal program.

Conclusion: Consolidating polyarchy and neo-liberalism in the Philippines

Although Filipinos were genuinely elated by the overthrow of the dictatorship, different political projects had been masked by broad national and international convergence around the removal of Marcos and under the generic term "democracy." These now became manifest in new conflicts as the country entered a highly fluid political situation.[53] Mass constituencies pushing diverse programs of popular democratization contended with the efforts by the United States and much of the elite to achieve a conservative stabilization. Aquino's assumption to the presidency was followed by institutionalization of the post-Marcos order. A new constitution was approved in a February 1987 plebiscite by over 75 percent of those voting. Legislative elections in May 1987 and local elections in January 1988 consummated the efforts to legitimize the new regime.

After six years in power, amidst a precarious period of mass mobilization, attempted coups, and the ebb and flow of insurgency and counterinsurgency, Aquino left office in 1992 in national elections which brought General Fidel Ramos to the presidency. The 1986 "revolution" had been effectively divested of its popular promises and polyarchy seemingly institutionalized. On the one hand, there was electoral competition and constitutional rule, including a separation of powers, formal respect for civil and political liberties, and so on. Although still factionalized, the elite had apparently reached consensus on the rules of polyarchic competition, which became quite intense, with a thriving press and a plethora of political parties. On the other hand, after six years, social and economic structures remained frozen and the formal political system continued to be a domain of the rich and powerful, as closed as ever to meaningful popular participation. A series of studies conducted by Philippine and foreign scholars in different rural and urban locations around the Philippines in the late 1980s on the actual extent of social, economic, and political change since 1986 concluded: "The overwhelming evidence shows that what was achieved by Aquino replacing Marcos is much more modest than what is suggested by the notion of 'a transition from authoritarianism to democracy'... no decisive reform of iniquitous social structures has taken place."[54]

As noted earlier, the unfolding of events in the Philippines before, during, and after the Marcos–Aquino transition cannot be reduced to the results of US policy. Rather, US policy interacted with distinct Philippine sectors in seeking preferred US outcomes. These sectors included the Philippine military, civilian elites, and the left. One State Department official commented several weeks after Aquino's inauguration: "Our objective was to capture... to encourage the democratic forces of the center, then consolidate control by the middle and also win away the soft support of the NPA. So far, so good."[55] US objectives in the new period were to marginalize the Philippine left, consolidate and gain leverage over a center-right alliance, and "professionalize" the military, which meant achieving its subordination to civilian elites (an "apolitical" military leadership) but also preserving its repressive capacity. Political aid was not a crucial determinant, but one of several factors, affecting the outcome of the anti-Marcos movement. Along with economic and military aid, it played an important role in the consolidation. Gradually, a transnational kernel was gaining control over the state and positioning itself to exercise hegemony in civil society, in consort with US economic, political, and military aid programs, and in consort with transnational capital and international financial agencies.

Shortly after Aquino's inauguration, the US Congress approved the Assistance for Democracy Act of 1986, and several supplemental appropriations, involving some $700 million in economic and military aid for the Philippines for 1986–7. The objectives were to keep the Philippine economy open and closely tied to foreign capital, promote free-trade and neo-liberal reform programs along the lines of the export-oriented development model, and also to keep US military facilities open.[56] "Crony capitalism" was not to be replaced by any popular economic program but by free-market reforms and deeper integration of the Philippine economy into the global economy. Also, high in the minds of foreign creditors was assuring that the Philippines would continue to repay its $30 billion foreign debt. "[An] important test for the government is its ability to pre-empt the insurgents' promises of nationalized industry and radical redistribution of land and wealth, which have fallen on fertile ground, especially in the rural areas where 70 percent of Filipinos live," warned Sandra Burton, a fellow at the US Council on Foreign Relations.[57] US officials organized the Multilateral Assistance Initiative consultative group, which brought together international financial agencies, private banks, government donors, and the AID. The group conditioned the flow of several billion dollars in external resources in the late 1980s on privatization, deregulation, currency devaluations, the lifting of trade barriers and restrictions on foreign capital, and so on. In this way, the AID, a US government agency, acted on behalf of transnational capital and its interests in the Philippines.

Of particular concern was promoting to positions of authority local Philippine counterparts of the transnational elite. Between 1986 and 1989, cabinet positions and economic policy were arenas of struggle in Manila among diverse fractions. "There are powerful dissenters, vocal elements in the democratically-elected Congress vociferously oppose key elements [of the neo-liberal reform program], and the 1992 elections loom over the entire process," cautioned an AID document. The US "role is to mobilize its resources to support, encourage, leverage, and assist, where possible and as most likely to ensure success, in this absolutely vital undertaking" of continued reform.[58] By 1990, the job was accomplished with the "purging" of "leftists" and "protectionists" from the cabinet, and the appointment of the technocratic finance minister Jesus Estanislao to head the government's economic team. Under Estanislao's New Economic Program, sweeping neo-liberal restructuring was launched. The transition to polyarchy involved the ascent to internal leadership of a transnationalized fraction of the Philippine elite over the elite as a whole, and the ideological and political incorporation, or at least neutralization, of enough of the popular sectors to restore social order in the wake of the Marcos crisis. The ascent of the transnationalized kernel, linked organically to the transnational elite, tied internal hegemonic order in the Philippines to emergent transnational hegemony.

Following the ouster of Marcos, Washington lifted the ban on military aid to Manila applied in 1985, and allocated $50 million in fresh military aid, to what was now known as the New Armed Forces of the Philippines (NAFP). Although Washington opposed any new military takeover, it adopted a strategy of penetrating and gaining leverage over the military. The NAFP had an important role to play in creating a new post-Marcos environment. Philippine specialists Walden Bello and John Gershman described this new environment as "politically sanitized – in which anti-elite candidates with radical political programs have been driven from the electoral arena by the threat of force – so that even intense electoral competition would not be too destabilizing."[59] Between 1986 and 1991, factions within the NAFP launched six coup attempts. Although all were put down (the one in November 1989 by US air force jets and the threat of direct US military intervention), each plot helped expand the military's autonomy and influence. The military won not only a blank check to conduct the counterinsurgency unscrutinized and as it saw fit, but also power of veto over vital areas of national policy. The coup attempts forged an accommodation between the civilian and military elite, and more importantly, imposed a consensus among the elite that any substantial social or economic reform was outside the accepted parameters of the new "democracy." While the spate of abortive coups had provided Washington with greater leverage over Aquino (who survived the military revolts thanks to US support), it also gave Washington influence over the NAFP.

Containment of the insurgency remained a key US goal in the post-Marcos period. The Pentagon expanded a large-scale training program that it had first introduced in 1982, and used its influence in the NAFP to isolate reformist and populist currents in the military. These elements had grouped together into the Young Officers Union (YOU). "YOU's leaders look towards a 'coup cum revolution,' meaning a military seizure of power associated with a 'people's uprising',"
cautioned political scientist Carl H. Landé in the NED's *Journal of*

Democracy. "Critical of the present political system, they hope to replace it with a reformist military regime. Thus YOU, like the NPA, represents a populist reaction to the elite-dominated democracy now presided over by Corazon Aquino. Were YOU and the NPA ever to join forces, they would become a formidable threat to the state."[60] By the early 1990s, the Pentagon and the CIA were assuming an ever-deeper role in the design and command of counterinsurgency. Following the ouster of Marcos, US officials set about to transform the NAFP into an effective counterinsurgency force that would integrate military, political, economic, and social initiatives, including broad "civic action" campaigns, psychological operations, military aid and training, and so on. In the 1980s and early 1990s, the Philippines became a key staging ground of low-intensity warfare.[61]

This effort involved pressuring Aquino to back down from her policy of "reconciliation" with the NPA, and the left in general, similarly to US pressuring of the Chamorro government in Nicaragua and other post-authoritarian elite regimes in the 1980s and 1990s to marginalize popular and left participation in new polyarchic political systems.[62] Policymakers did not want to see a radical left integrated into the country's political and civic structures, pushing a program of popular reform. Upon coming to office, Aquino released political prisoners from jails, and in September 1986, after a month of negotiations, the government signed a temporary truce with the guerrillas. But under intense pressures from Washington, the military, and the rural oligarchy, peace talks broke down in November. A month later, Assistant Secretary of Defense Richard Armitage publicly lashed out at Manila for pursuing reconciliation. Aquino apparently got the message; shortly afterwards, she declared in a speech at the Philippine Military Academy that "the answer to the terrorism of the left and the right is not social and economic reform but police and military action."[63]

The struggle over agrarian reform is a clear example of how US intervention intersected with complex local struggles with the aim of controlling social change, as James Putzel documents in his study on the subject.[64] The Philippines is the fourteenth-largest food producer in the world, yet hunger and poverty are endemic in the countryside. In the mid-1980s, a mere 20 percent of the population owned 80 percent of the land. The remaining 80 percent either worked as landless laborers or subsisted on tiny plots, often rented at exorbitant prices in usury arrangements with landlords.[65] Behind this system was an alliance between Philippine landowners and foreign agri-business, based on lucrative cash crops for export and a ready pool of cheap rural labor. At the time of her 1986 victory, Aquino made agrarian reform the centerpiece of her promise of broad social and economic change, and the new constitution specified that ownership of land should be transferred to those who tilled it.

Following the ouster of Marcos, a coalition of popular organizations, the Congress of Peoples' Agrarian Reform (CPAR), was formed with the aim of mobilizing for a comprehensive agrarian reform. The CPAR included the KMU trade union federation and its rural counterpart, the KMP peasant association, numerous civic organizations, political parties, and a plethora of clerical groups. It called for the abolition of absentee landownership, the redistribution of lands usurped during the Marcos years, and the legalization of landholdings by peasants who actually tilled the land. At the other end of the spectrum, the US-backed TUCP and the NCFO, which had publicly endorsed what Aquino described as the hub of her economic program, a "partnership between labor and capital," drafted their own position on land tenure under a US-funded and advised program.[66] Between 1986 and 1990 diverse groups struggled in civil and political society to shape the contours of an agrarian reform. The AID set up its own agrarian reform office, working out of the TUCP's Manila offices. The AID's objective was to design an agrarian reform that would not disrupt the agro-export sector and that could be synchronized with the counter-insurgency program and could diffuse peasant unrest.[67]

With the help of the AID, the endorsement of the TUCP, and the backing of a Congress dominated by large landowners and business interests, Aquino drafted a bill, approved in 1988, which was blatantly biased in favor of the traditional, politically powerful families, agri-business corporations and large landowners (for instance, 75 percent of all lands remained exempt from reform). In the first three years of the law, only 7 percent of the total land area which the legislation was intended to cover had actually been distributed to farmers. The agrarian reform subsequently sputtered to a standstill.[68] In addition to resistance from traditional landowners, the exporting commercial elite, transnational agri-business and multilateral lending agencies did not want to see a disruption of the country's agro-export sector, which, along with *zona franca* labor-intensive manufacturing, linked the Philippines to the global economy. Blocking authentic agrarian reform resulted in heightened social polarization, which fueled rural unrest, the simmering NPA guerrilla movement, counterinsurgency and militarization of the countryside. As a result, the human rights situation, after having shown an improvement in the first few years of civilian government, dramatically deteriorated. By the early 1990s, international human rights groups were once again documenting widespread and systematic human rights violations and government repression.[69]

To be sure, US policymakers *did* want to see a social reform process in the Philippines. But it had to be a process which could be carefully managed, and under elite hegemony. For instance, Washington, along with the international financial agencies, expressed support for their own version of an agrarian reform, one that would preserve and expand the capitalist agricultural export sector and also divert the assets of landlords into urban, export-oriented industry, as had taken place earlier in Japan, Taiwan, and South Korea. However, such a scheme was simply not applicable to the particular social, political, and economic conditions of the Philippines. And when push came to shove, the first priority was to avert *fundamental* transformation of the social order. Moreover, political intervention specialists viewed consolidation of "democracy" in the Philippines not in terms of socio-economic reform but of strengthening polyarchic political culture and institutions.[70] In 1991, Washington allocated $12 million in new "democracy enhancement" funds, via the State Department's ODI and the NED, not for social reform but explicitly for "democratic institution building [in conjunction with] a strong free-market private-sector orientation."[71]

The left, seemingly unable to adapt to the post-Marcos circumstances, contributed to US endeavors.[72] The boycott of the 1986 elections allowed the centrist elements to seize the political initiative from the left. Ambivalence towards electoral participation persisted in subsequent elections, which contributed to isolating the left from mass constituencies that viewed electoral politics as a legitimate arena of political struggle. The armed and unarmed left remained a vital – even ascendant – force in the national equation. Yet it seemed unable to find a formula for operating effectively in the new political-ideological terrain – a challenge posed for much of the left internationally in the post-Cold War world and which is closely related to the lack of any viable programmatic alternative to integration into global capitalism. However, it should be pointed out that serious attempts by the left groups, such as the Partido ng Bayan (People's Party), to run candidates in elections ran up against repression and the vastly superior resources of the elite. One specialist writing in the NED's *Journal of Democracy* acknowledged, for instance, that in the 1992 elections "it cost $25 to $50 million to run for president, $1 to $5 million to run for senator, and anywhere from several hundred thousand to $1 million to run for the House," a barrier "which narrowed the field to people from (or supported by) the middle and upper classes."[73]

The democratic aspirations of the masses of Filipinos might have been further away than ever from fulfillment, but, in the view of the State Department, the Philippine government since 1986 had "brought about fundamental political change," involving "a strong free-market, private-sector orientation," and "human rights" and "social justice."[74] Washington assessed that the Philippine political system was consolidated enough by the 1990s to stand on its own and that the 1992 elections posed little threat to transnational interests. In April 1992, a month before the vote, US ambassador Frank Wisner told a group of business leaders that the United States expected the vote to be "decisive and not contested, and that you can get on [with] the job of governance... [the US] took an active role in putting [*sic*] a return of an election process in 1986... what matters to us is that there is a democratic system in place."[75]

In summary, the mid-1980s Philippine "transition to democracy" gave a crucial impetus to the new political intervention. The successful outcome of the crisis of dictatorial rule there, and the contribution made by novel US political operations to that outcome, proved decisive in consolidating consensus in Washington around the new strategy. Thus, as crisis brewed in Chile, there was little debate in Washington, as well as valuable accumulated experience, on the course of action to be taken by the United States.

4   Chile: Ironing out "a fluke of the political system"

Mr. Minister, you come here speaking of Latin America, but this is not important. Nothing important can come from the South. History has never been produced in the South. The axis of history starts in Moscow, goes to Bonn, crosses over to Washington, and then goes to Tokyo. What happens in the South is of no importance. You're wasting your time.

Henry Kissinger, speaking to Chilean Foreign Minister
Gabriel Valdes, June 1969[1]

From dictatorship to "redemocratization" and the US role

"I don't see why we need to stand by and watch a country go communist because of the irresponsibility of its own people," declared National Security Advisor Henry Kissinger in June 1970.[2] Kissinger was referring to the election that year of Salvador Allende as president of Chile. For Kissinger, the election of a self-declared socialist "represented a break with Chile's long democratic history," the result of "a fluke of the Chilean political system."[3] What followed was one of the darkest chapters in inter-American relations: a massive US destabilization campaign against the Allende government, culminating in the bloody 1973 military coup. For fifteen years, successive US administrations propped up the dictatorship of General Augusto Pinochet. Then, in the mid-1980s, on the heels of the "success" in the Philippines, policymakers switched tracks and began to "promote democracy" in Chile.

The coup in Chile was part of a general pattern in Latin America of military takeovers in the 1960s and 1970s, in the face of mass struggles against ubiquitous social and economic inequalities and highly restricted "democracies." Similarly, the "return to democracy" in Chile in the late 1980s was part of a hemispheric pattern, referred to in US academic literature as "redemocratization." There is more than semantics behind this term. Underlying specific terminology is the debate over a contested concept. If democracy is considered power of the people, then there is little basis, intellectually and theoretically, to speak of "redemocratization," whereby, in regular cycles, power is held, then lost, then held again by the people. If, however, democracy is limited to its institutional definition, then the formal structures of polyarchy – civilian government, elections, etc. – can, in fact, be established, dismantled, and established again in regular cycles. When scholars speak of the "breakdown of democracy" and a "redemocratization," they are therefore utilizing the hegemonic version of an essentially contested concept, and what they really mean are cycles in the breakdown and restoration of consensual mechanisms of domination.

US policy towards Chile from the 1960s to the 1990s involved four successive stages: (1) covert support for centrist and rightist groups against the Chilean left in the 1960s (2) destabilization of the left once it came to power through free elections (3) support for military dictatorship until the mid-1980s, including its program of decimation of the left and economic restructuring (4) intervention in the anti-dictatorial movement from the mid-1980s to bring about a transition to polyarchy. The United States had spent millions of dollars in the 1960s in Chile in covert intervention to marginalize the left and bolster its favored parties,[4] particularly the Christian Democratic Party (PDC), which was headed by Patricio Aylwin. Two decades later, Aylwin and his party again became the recipient of US assistance, this time channeled through the NED and the AID, which would help Aylwin become the Chilean president. It was with telling irony that the return to power in early 1990 of the same Aylwin and the PDC that openly participated in the 1973 military coup was projected around the world as the culmination of a "democratic revolution" that swept Latin America.

United States–Chile relations must be seen in the context of the evolution of post-World War II US policy towards Latin America, from open support for dictatorship, to a period of "rethinking" and then to "democracy promotion." Washington launched a hemispheric campaign to isolate the left following the declaration in 1947 of the Truman Doctrine, which initiated the Cold War. This included the development of close ties between the United States and Latin American militaries, and the supply of $1.4 billion between 1950 and 1969 in military assistance.[5] The Cuban revolution in 1959 constituted a dangerous rupture in traditional inter-American relations and a hemispheric threat to US domination. The Kennedy administration's Alliance for Progress aimed to prevent repeats through a combination of United States-led counterinsurgency and reform efforts.[6] The breakdown of that effort led the Nixon administration to commission the Rockefeller Report of 1969.[7] This blueprint for Nixon–Ford policy towards Latin America claimed that the "new militaries" – armed forces and security apparatuses that had been "modernized" through US military and security assistance and training programs – were the "last best choice" for preserving social order and traditional inter-American relations, and coincided with the turn to military dictatorship in many Latin American countries. The Rockefeller Report was followed by the Trilateral Commission's report *The Crisis of Democracy*, which argued that "democracy" had to be reconstituted to assure that it did not generate its own instability, both within states and in the international system.[8] A year later, the Linowitz Report, which provided guidelines for Carter administration policies, highlighted the conclusions of the Trilateral Commission and stressed that military dictatorship and human rights violations threatened to destabilize capitalism itself and undermine US interests.[9] It also recommended a US policy thrust of "redemocratization" in order to avoid crises and preserve the hemispheric order. The triumph of the Nicaraguan revolution in 1979 demonstrated to US policymakers the need for such an undertaking. The 1984 Kissinger Commission report stated that promotion of civilian regimes was an essential requisite of US policy and should be coupled with greater linkage of the Latin American economies to the world market as well as with a political, military, and ideological offensive against leftist forces in the region.[10]

Transnational economics, transnational politics, and military rule in Latin America

South American politics changed from the 1960s to the 1990s concurrently with the emergence of the global economy. In theoretical abstraction, we see most clearly in South America how movement in the "base" (globalization) intersected in a highly interactive and complex manner with movement in the "superstructure" (political and social changes). During the 1960s and 1970s repressive military regimes took over in Brazil, Argentina, Chile, Uruguay, and elsewhere. Authoritarianism was an instrument of local elites, acting in conjunction with the United States, for suppressing an upsurge of nationalist, popular, and leftist challenges to the status quo. There was an "elective affinity" between these authoritarian regimes and US domination in the hemisphere, corresponding to the exercise of domination through coercive mechanisms in the inter-American arena. The relation between the military and the social order is complex. Mechanical reduction of the military regimes to "guardians of imperialism" denies any autonomy to politics and institutions and to endogenous national dynamics. However, the argument common to much mainstream "democratization" literature that the military was an independent institution merely seeking to preserve its own "institutional interests and prerogatives" in the face of social turbulence is equally fallacious and particularly misleading.[11] It theoretically separates a coercive apparatus from the function of coercion in reproducing a social order, and hence extricates the military from its structural location in the socioeconomic organization of society and from the broader international setting. This separation is grounded in structural-functionalism, with its functional separation of the different spheres of the social totality and their respective institutions, and an internal logic assigned to each institution such that movement may occur independent of the totality. The following discussion is intended to provide the historical background and a theoretical framework for the Chile case. But beyond that, it is also an attempt, in contradistinction to the structural-functional approach associated with "democratization" theory, to substantiate essential theoretical issues raised in chapter 1, including how politics and economics intersect and evolve over time and how they correlate to globalization.

The military coups of the 1960s and 1970s responded to threats to social orders resulting from the breakdown of the prevailing model of dependent capitalist development, known as import-substitution industrialization, or ISI.[12] This model provided the economic basis for populist political projects that prevailed throughout much of Latin America in the post-World War II period. Populist projects were multi-class alliances under the dominance of local elites and foreign capital that undertook state-sponsored income redistribution, social welfare, and the promotion of local capital accumulation. The ISI model and the populist program were the form that Keynesian capitalism took in the periphery and semi-periphery. Taking place prior to globalization, it subordinated national economies in the periphery to the core, but hinged on local accumulation processes at a time when these economies enjoyed a measure of autonomy and "inward-oriented" development programs were viable. Populist programs were often led by national elites whose interests lay in local accumulation and who often clashed with foreign capital and core country elites. But globalization, by undermining the ability of any nation to pursue an autonomous development path, led to the breakdown of the ISI model by the 1970s, which in turn undermined the economic basis for populist programs. Chronic inflation and macro-economic instability, a decline in local and foreign investment, and the fiscal crisis of the state made it increasingly impossible to sustain these programs. Economic crisis thus begat political crisis as the social structure of accumulation unravelled. Leftist alternatives and mass movements clamoring for more fundamental social change threatened local elites and US interests. In Chile, there was even more at stake: an avowedly socialist coalition had actually assumed the reins of government.

The military takeovers had dual objectives: (1) to crush popular and revolutionary movements through mass repression and institutionalized terror, and (2) to launch processes of economic adjustment and deeper integration into the world market in response to the exhaustion of the ISI model and in concurrence with the emergence of the global economy. The military regime's economic model – a regional prototype of the full-blown neo-liberalism of the 1980s and 1990s – was anti-popular, involving a compression of real wages, the opening of markets, lifting state regulations, price and exchange controls, reallocating resources towards middle and higher income groups in the external sector, and deepening ties with transnational capital. These tasks could not be carried through under formal "political democracy," which became, in effect, a fetter to the restoration of capital accumulation under globalization. Military dictatorship provided the political conditions for economic restructuring, bringing about an entirely new correlation of national and regional forces in South America. By the 1980s, the militaries, having launched restructuring and having accomplished the destruction of popular and leftist movements, could "safely" withdraw.

"Redemocratization" must thus be seen in light of globalization. The military regimes provided the political conditions for initiating the restructuring of social classes and of productive processes reciprocal to the changes taking place in the world political economy. Restructuring generated new economic and political protagonists with distinct interests. A critical variable in this conjuncture was the debt crisis. Latin America's foreign debt went from some $50 billion in 1974 to over $300 billion in 1981 and over $410 billion in 1987. This massive borrowing spree responded in immediate terms to chronic balance-of-payments crises associated with the exhaustion of the ISI model. But structurally it was rooted in long-term movements in the world economy, particularly the emergence of transnational finance capital as the hegemonic fraction in the global economy.[13] The massive infusion of capital into Latin America in the 1970s, linked to the concentration of economic power in transnationalized finance capital in the center countries, had profound effects on existing groups and class constellations. This point is crucial: the need to earn foreign exchange to pay back the debt requires that nations restructure their economies towards the production of exports ("tradables" in official neo-liberal jargon) in accordance with the changing structure of demand on the world market.[14] Debt leads to the reinsertion of these countries' economies into a reorganized world market. Over an extended period, debt contraction and subsequent reservicing has the consequence of strengthening those sectors with external linkage, redistributing quotas of accumulated political and economic power towards new fractions linked to transnational finance capital. Two new social agents appear: a transnationalized fraction of the bourgeoisie tied to external sectors; and regrouped popular sectors displaced from traditional peasant and industrial production. Each agent becomes politically active and articulates its own project: the former, a return to polyarchy and the consolidation of neo-liberalism; the latter, projects of popular democratization pushed through "new social movements." Each agent, for its own reason, mounted opposition to the military regimes and this opposition coalesced into national democratization movements.

During the 1980s, the transnationalized fractions of the bourgeoisie (the "New Right") came to the fore and achieved hegemony within their class. Sociologist Ronaldo Munck has documented the emergence of "a lucid bourgeois technocracy, based on the internationalized sectors of the capitalist class with the strong backing of global capitalist agencies such as the International Monetary Fund." There was "a felicitous blend between global economic transformations – the era of finance capital hegemony was arriving – and the international class struggle which had thrown up a decisive bourgeois leadership committed to ending the populist cycles and reasserting a new order."[15] In other studies, political scientists Eduardo Silva and Alex Fernandez Jilberto show how new capitalist coalitions emerged in Chile between 1973 and 1988 dominated at all times by transnationalized fractions, drawn from financial, extractive export, internationally competitive industrial, and commercial sectors, all linked to the global economy, and how these fractions linked with the military regime and shaped state policies.[16] After the military dictatorships created conditions for its emergence, this New Right swept to power in the 1980s and early 1990s in virtually every country in Latin America, especially through electoral processes in "transitions to democracy." In power, it set about to deepen neo-liberal restructuring and to stabilize new patterns of accumulation linked to hegemonic transnational capital.

In sum, by the 1960s the ISI model and populism had lost their dynamism simultaneously with increased political activation among popular sectors. The social order faced a crisis of accumulation and of political legitimacy. The military regimes sought to resolve both the economic impasse and the political challenge. The authoritarian form of the political system achieved these objectives, yet resulted by the 1980s in a situation of disjuncture between the economic and political spheres of the social order, whereby the economic rearticulation of society had proceeded more rapidly than the political. A synchronization of the two was required. "The State is the instrument for conforming civil society to the economic structure, but it is necessary for the State to 'be willing' to do this," states Gramsci, "i.e., for the representatives of the change that has taken place in the economic structure to be in control of the State."[17] The New Right had to retake formal control of the state as an economic and a political requirement. In the civilian government to dictatorship to "redemocratization" cycle, new transnational fractions among the dominant classes entered the political stage and vied for hegemony, calling for "democratization" so as to regain direct political power, carry forward neo-liberalism, and create the "democratic" mechanisms for managing the conflicts associated with restructuring.

Ironically, in the ten to twenty years from the turn to dictatorship and the return to "democracy," polyarchy started out as a fetter to new patterns of capital accumulation, only to later become a necessity for continuing neo-liberal restructuring. This is because, on the one hand, the dictatorships were blocking the further development, both political and economic, of the new fractions among the bourgeoisie linked to transnational capital accumulation. On the other hand, they had engendered anti-dictatorial social movements by the 1980s that threatened to burgeon out of control and pose an alternative of popular democratization. The relative autonomy dominant classes granted military regimes was based on their fear of the threat from below. When the dominant groups felt they could work within civil society, they began to feel constrained by the shackles of an all-powerful military state. A reactivated civil society played a major role in the rearticulation of the state and the dominant classes.

The military regimes preserved the capitalist social order. But they could never achieve legitimation or a political-juridical formula for consensus in the exercise of power. The dictatorships could not establish institutional mechanisms for harmonizing the interests of dominant classes under the hegemony of the newly emerging transnationalized fraction. The establishment of legitimation through the return to polyarchy became a necessity for the reproduction of capitalism. However, "redemocratization" provided all social classes with access to the political arena. Fractions within dominant groups competed with each other as well as with other social groups. In Chile, "redemocratization" became not the struggle of any one class but a majoritarian social struggle, in which the primary contradiction shifted from society versus military dictatorship to which social classes would lead the democratization process.

Chile: a "long tradition" of polyarchy

Sealed off from the rest of the South American mainland by the Andean cordillera, Chile was a secondary center for the Spanish empire, valued largely as a backwater producing agricultural and mineral goods for neighboring colonies and the metropolis. As in much of Latin America, with independence from Spain in 1818, an oligarchy of landlords and a small class of urban aristocrats seized control of the new nation. The government apparatus was controlled by an indigenous elite which coalesced through the nineteenth and twentieth centuries, made up of the landed oligarchy, mine-owners, merchants and nascent manufacturers. Unlike the case in neighboring countries, this elite, whose members overlapped extensively through family and commercial ties, developed a high level of cohesion. This allowed for relative stability and intra-elite consensus, notwithstanding

153

brief civil wars in 1859 and 1891.[18] The early formation of a polyarchic system among the elite was a central factor in the country's subsequent social and political development, and would lead US and Chilean political observers to extol Chile's "long democratic tradition." What these observers fail to mention is that this "democracy" was the exclusive reserve of a tiny elite, an imprimatur on the feudal *hacendado* system in the countryside that kept the mestizo-Indian majority in virtual peonage and disenfranchised the vast majority of the population until the second half of the twentieth century. What these analysts are really applauding is not democracy but the viability and stability of elite consensus and cooperation in ruling Chile. In reality, Chilean "democracy" developed much like US polyarchy – restricted exclusively to the elite until well into the twentieth century, when mass pressures gradually opened up the formal political system. By enfranchising only literate, male property-owners, the political system successfully prevented the overwhelming majority of Chileans from participating.

In the 1840s, only 2 percent of the nation's one million citizens were allowed to vote. The figure rose to about 5 percent late in the nineteenth century, and to only 14 percent in the 1940s. A repressive patronage system prevailed in the countryside, where 40 percent of the population resided at mid twentieth century. Instead of providing peasants with ballots, the government authorized rural landowners to "collect" the votes from their *inquilinos* (serfs or squatters), thus assuring political control by the landed oligarchy. In 1958, women were enfranchised, but the illiterate were still barred from voting, so that in national elections that year only 20 percent of the adult population could actually cast a ballot. With gross socioeconomic inequalities and limited educational opportunities, especially in the countryside, the natural functioning of this electoral system was enough in itself to assure the elite's political power. It was not until the 1964 national elections that the *inquilinos* were allowed to vote freely, and not until the 1970 elections that illiterates were finally granted voting rights.[19]

Because of the relative unity of the Chilean elite, an established polyarchic system, and the growth of a militant working class, Chilean social conflict was characterized from the outset less by the intra-elite feuding that predominated in much of Latin America than by class conflict and demands from subordinate groups, first for integration into the political system, and later for fundamental change in the entire social order. By the early twentieth century, workers in the mining enclave, railroads, ports, and manufacturing had begun to organize. The growth of labor strength worried the oligarchy and the emergent middle sectors, which responded in the early decades of the twentieth century with a combination of systematic repression, economic concessions, and the gradual integration of urban workers through suffrage into the formal political system. Anarcho-syndicalist movements gave way to two organized left parties, the Communist, founded in 1921, and the Socialist, formed in 1933, and popular support for the left rose. Chile entered a period of equilibrium, or relative stalemate, among social classes in the post-World War II period, against the backdrop of industrialization and development, a dynamic political party system, and growing conflict between popular sectors, on the one hand, and a complex convergence of local elites and foreign interests, on the other. This laid the basis for a strong tradition of populist programs and fierce party politics.

The major political parties in this period were: the traditional Conservatives and Liberals dating back to independence (which merged into the National Party in 1966), representing the right and the traditional oligarchy; the Radical Party (which dated back to 1863) and the PDC, representing the center and anchored in urban middle sectors; and the Communists and Socialists, representing the left, the working classes and the poor. This three-way division of political forces lent itself to an unusual and highly unstable situation of a strong right, a strong left and a strong center, without any decisive hegemony among them. The three-way left–right–center balance resulted in a political equilibrium for several decades, but also constituted a cleavage which later opened space for popular classes to utilize politics to challenge elite hegemony.

US penetration of the Chilean economy and political system

Great Britain, as the premier imperial power of the nineteenth century, had eclipsed the Spanish crown as the foreign "hegemon" after Chilean independence. Foreign, mostly British, capital came to control some two-thirds of Chile's nitrate, silver and copper mining concerns, the lifeblood of the nineteenth-century economy. But in the final decades of the nineteenth century, US capital also steadily penetrated the Chilean economy as part of the broader process of the displacement of other imperial powers by the United States and the definitive establishment of US domination over the Americas as its "natural" sphere of influence. "The United States is practically sovereign in this continent and its fiat is law upon the subjects to which it confines its interpositions," declared Secretary of State Richard Olney in 1896.[20]

In the early 1900s, US capital quickly came to dominate the Chilean economy. By the 1920s, the mining industry was dominated by three US companies: Anaconda's Andes Copper and Chile Exploration Company, and the Kennecott Corporation's Braden Copper.[21] US banks, utility companies, and industrial concerns also poured in. US domination of the mining industry, which in turn dominated the Chilean economy, had major ramifications for Chilean society and laid the basis for US–Chilean relations. Following World War II, copper came to dominate the economy, accounting for over half the country's exports, and taxes on the US companies' profits yielded one-fifth of the government's entire revenue. Resentment over US domination and intervention grew throughout the twentieth century. US domination over Chile intermeshed with and helped shape the local social structure. The rural sector contained a traditional landowning elite, a peasantry tied by labor obligations to the estate where they lived, and a small but mobile workforce that provided wage labor for the large commercial estates which produced for the foreign, principally US, market. There was a mining, industrial, and commercial elite, many of whose members had kinship ties to the landed oligarchy, and which became thoroughly subordinated to US capital that dominated these sectors of the economy. There was also a relatively large middle class and urban working class.

As US economic interests in Chile grew, so did its political involvement. As in the Philippines, Washington used a judicious combination of military and economic aid, and it also introduced large-scale, covert "political aid" programs as early as 1953, including founding and funding "friendly" media outlets, intellectual and political figures, under the aegis of the CIA, the AID, the USIA, and various non-governmental organizations.[22] Meanwhile, the left grew in strength in the 1950s and 1960s. In the 1958 elections, Allende, running as the candidate for an alliance of Socialists and Communists under the Popular Action Front (FRAP), won 28.9 percent of the vote. A FRAP triumph appeared likely until a defrocked radical priest, Antonio Zamorano, encouraged by the US embassy and by reported CIA payments, entered into the presidential campaign. The former cleric siphoned enough votes from Allende to allow the conservative Jorge Alessandri to win a narrow victory.[23] As the 1964 elections approached, US officials and corporations with large investments in Chile became increasingly concerned over a possible move to the left. The Kennedy administration set up a secret Chile electoral committee in 1961, operating out of the White House and composed of top-level State Department, White House and CIA officials.[24] As many as a hundred CIA agents and other US operatives were covertly despatched to Santiago to carry out the program, whose purpose, according to a US Senate investigation committee, was to establish "operational relationships with key political parties and [create] propaganda and organizational mechanisms capable of influencing key sectors of the population." Projects were undertaken "to help train and organize 'anti-communists'" among peasants, slum-dwellers, organized labor, students, and the media, "disinformation and black propaganda" campaigns were conducted, and so on.[25]

Three candidates eventually entered the 1964 race: Allende for the FRAP alliance, Eduardo Frei of the PDC as the centrist candidate, and Julio Duran representing a right-wing coalition. Pre-electoral polls indicated an even split between Frei and Duran, with the FRAP winning by a small but significant margin. Washington thus pressured for a united center-right ticket, and this included channeling funds directly to Duran's coalition for him to withdraw from the race and unite under the Frei ticket.[26] The task was made easier by the Chilean elite's own recognition of the threat from below, including the rapid rise in support among the rural population for the left, following the dissolution of the traditional patronage networks among landlords and peasants. Some $20 million were then spent in US covert assistance for Frei's 1964 presidential campaign, which amounted to over $8 per voter and constituted 50 percent of Frei's total campaign expenses.[27] These US political operations were crucial in influencing the elite as well as the general electorate. Allende won 39 percent of the popular vote, but lost to the center-right alliance, which together pooled 56 percent of the vote.

Once in office, Frei's government was selected by Washington to be a model for the Alliance for Progress. Alliance objectives were to bolster political centers and promote limited reforms in Latin America in order to undercut radical change and stabilize the hemispheric status quo. "In supporting the Alliance, members of the traditional ruling class will have nothing to fear," explained Kennedy official Teodoro Moscoso.[28] Frei's government received over $1.3 billion from US government agencies and private creditors during its six-year tenure (1964–1969), as well as several billion more from other foreign and multilateral sources – by far the largest per capita US aid program in Latin America.[29] Parallel to this overt assistance from Washington, the Christian Democrats and other center and right groups were recipients of massive covert funding and advisement aimed at helping them to challenge the left at every level in civil and political society, including battles for control over unions, student associations, cooperatives, professional groups, and so forth. The Senate committee listed some of the specific projects:

> Wresting control of Chilean university student organization from the communists;
> Supporting a women's group active in Chilean political and intellectual life;
> Combatting the communist-dominated *Central Unica de Trajabadores* (CUTCh) and supporting democratic labor groups; and,
> Exploiting a civic action front group to combat communist influence within cultural and intellectual circles.[30]

Although the Christian Democrats developed a significant support base, their reform program was unable to resolve the plight of an impoverished majority. Only 28,000 families benefitted from their agrarian reform and income inequality continued to grow. By 1968, 2 percent of the population still controlled 45.9 percent of the national income, at least half of all Chileans were considered malnourished, and half of all workers earned wages below the subsistence level.[31] The failure of the reform program had the effect of radicalizing popular sectors and weakening the Christian Democratic center. In 1969, leftist dissidents representing some 30 percent of the PDC membership, based in the trade union and youth wings, broke off from the party, formed the Movement of United Popular Action (MAPU), and announced their intention to seek an alliance of all popular forces. Both the left and political polarization grew.

The extent of US business involvement was a constant debate in Chile, and had become a critical political issue by the late 1960s, pitting the right, with its support for US (and their own) profit-taking, against the left, which organized increasingly fractious labor strikes and public demonstrations against US firms. On the eve of Allende's victory, foreign, mostly US, corporations controlled virtually every sector of the economy, including the mines, where US corporations controlled 80 percent of copper production and 100 percent of processing. Foreign capital also controlled machinery and equipment (50 percent); iron, steel, and metal products (60 percent); petroleum products and distribution (over 50 percent); industrial and other chemicals (60 percent); automotive assemblage (100 percent); tobacco (100 percent); office equipment (nearly 100 percent); and advertising (90 percent). US direct private investment in 1970 stood at $1.1 billion, out of total foreign investment of $1.7 billion.[32] Profits for US firms were enormous: during the 1960s Anaconda earned $500 million on its investments in Chile, whose value the company had estimated at only $300 million, yet it reinvested back into Chile only some $50 million.[33]

As the 1970 elections approached, the US NSC's "Forty Committee," an interagency group set up to oversee all US covert operations abroad, supervised a full range of intervention activities. But the right, having lost confidence in the Christian Democrats, ran its own candidate this time, Jorge Alessandri. With the split in the elite, Allende, running on the Popular Unity (UP) coalition ticket, won the September 1970 election with 36.3 percent of the vote.

Allende ran on a platform of popular democratization and radical socioeconomic changes, including nationalization of key areas of the economy (especially the mines), a far-reaching agrarian reform, redistribution of income, judicial reform, direct popular participation in government structures, and worker participation in management. The UP program aimed to create conditions for a transition to socialism while respecting Chile's constitution. The economic plan was for a mixed economy, rather than a statist model, involving a public sector, a private sector, and a mixed sector.[34] The fear in Washington was that for the first time in Latin American and world history, a declared Marxist assumed the reigns of government within the established constitutional process to initiate a transition in Chile from polyarchy to popular democracy.

From covert operations to all-out destabilization

The US destabilization campaign against the Allende government and its contribution to the 1973 coup has been amply documented.[35] It was in this campaign that the word "destabilization" entered world currency for the first time. Coined by then-CIA director William Colby, it means studying the myriad of factors that constitute the basis of a society's cohesion and then using that knowledge to literally undo the fabric of society and bring about internal collapse, through overt programs of socioeconomic and diplomatic harassment and covert programs of political, psychological, and paramilitary terror.

In the weeks leading up to the October 1970 ratification by the Chilean Congress of Allende's appointment, Washington scrambled to prevent him from taking office through a host of covert operations, including unsuccessful attempts to have him assassinated, to organize a pre-inaugural military putsch, and, by lobbying in the Chilean Congress, to have it veto Allende's investiture.[36] After Allende's inauguration, the destabilization program moved into high gear. Kissinger himself chaired weekly interagency meetings on Chile in the White House, attended by high-level officials from State, Treasury, the Pentagon and the CIA. The leaders of US businesses in Chile, among them ITT, PepsiCo, the mining companies, W. R. Grace Co., Bank of America, and Pfizer Chemical, worked closely with the US government in destabilizing the Allende government. Under the aegis of ITT, US corporations formed an Ad Hoc Committee on Chile to urge on the US government in its campaign.[37]

The program included an "invisible blockade." National Security Council Memorandum 93 was issued prohibiting economic aid to Chile.[38] As US ambassador to Chile Edward Korry put it, "not a nut or bolt [will] reach Chile under Allende... We shall do all within our power to condemn Chile and the Chileans to utmost deprivation and poverty."[39] To this was added a myriad of economic sabotage activities and training and support for the paramilitary terrorist activities of the ultra-right Patria y Libertad organization. The high levels of dependency on the United States, including direct corporate investment, reliance on US financing, and a huge debt owed to US creditors, left the Chilean government extremely vulnerable to US economic sanctions. As they sought to do later in Nicaragua, US strategists set about to finance and mobilize those sectors in Chile most adversely affected by the hardships created by US economic sanctions, and then to channel their political energies against the popular government.

The CIA penetrated *all* major political parties, supplying funds to organize and sustain every major anti-government strike, demonstration and boycott between October 1971 and the September 1973 coup. Among recipients were the Christian Democrats, headed by Aylwin, who represented the conservative wing of the PDC. The PDC leadership participated actively in the destabilization efforts. Aylwin himself, as head of the Chilean Senate during Allende's administration, urged continued armed repression of the militant, but peaceful, popular mobilization that escalated under the UP government, and all but called publicly for a military coup. He was the architect of what became known as the "white *coup d'état*" strategy, which called for placing increasingly broad sectors of public administration under military control and the progressive militarization of government and society to put the brakes on the UP program.[40]

Another program conducted by the CIA and the DIA was penetrating and courting the Chilean military. The difficulty in gaining influence over the military was described by the CIA as a problem of overcoming "the apolitical, constitutional-oriented inertia of the Chilean military."[41] In a secret memorandum early in 1971, US ambassador Nathaniel Davis emphasized that a military coup would only occur when public opposition to the Allende government became "so overwhelming and discontent, so great that military intervention is overwhelmingly invited."[42] The economic sanctions and political intervention created internal conditions propitious to a coup. US penetration of the military prompted it to go forward.

While economic aid was cut off, Washington actually increased its military assistance to the Chilean armed forces and training for select military personnel in the United States and Panama. Military aid, after dropping to less than $1 million in 1970, reached an all-time high of $15 million in 1973.[43] A flood of US military advisors poured into Chile, and a long list of "intelligence assets" in the three branches of the military was drawn up. Following the September 11 coup, intelligence information collected by the CIA's Santiago station such as "arrest lists, key civilian installations and personnel that needed protection, key government installations that would need to be taken over, and government contingency plans which would be used in case of a military uprising," according to the US Senate report, guided Pinochet and his cohorts in their takeover.[44]

The overall US response to the Allende government was twofold, note James Petras and Morris Morley:

> A combination of severe economic pressures whose cumulative impact would result in internal economic chaos and a policy of disaggregating the Chilean state through creating ties with specific critical sectors (the military, political parties, etc.) and supporting

their efforts at weakening the capacity of the state to realize a nationalist development project. This sustained policy of direct and indirect intervention culminated in a general societal crisis, a coup, and a military government.[45]

The US-instigated coup was the bloodiest in Latin American history. At least 20,000 people were killed in the first few months of the military takeover.[46] This was a veritable totalitarian regime, one of the most vicious in twentieth-century history, and one that was warmly embraced by the United States. A year later, President Gerald Ford declared that what the United States had done in Chile was "in the best interests of the people of Chile and certainly in our own best interests."[47]

Defending "our own best interests" in Chile was *not* seen by US policymakers as a Cold War fight against Soviet influence. State Department analysts assessed that "Soviet overtures to Allende [were] characterized by caution and restraint... [the] Soviets desire to avoid" another Cuba-type commitment.[48] A CIA study three days after Allende's electoral victory concluded that "the US has no vital national interests within Chile, the world military balance of power would not be significantly altered by an Allende regime, and an Allende victory in Chile would not pose any likely threat to peace in the region." The study made clear what was under threat in Chile: the Allende triumph would fragment "hemispheric cohesion [and] create considerable political and psychological problems" for the United States in Latin America.[49] Petras and Morley note: "The changes envisioned by the Allende government not only restricted the capacity of US capital to expand in Chile but threatened to disarticulate the economic and trade patterns within the region. Changes in Chile potentially laid the basis for modifying and redefining Latin America's external economic relations."[50] The only threat of the Allende government was as a potential challenge to international assymetries by modifying Chile's internal system through popular democratization, as discussed in chapter 1. In the wake of the coup, one US official declared: "We are now in a position to take a much tougher position toward other [Latin American] countries now that we have eliminated a major problem."[51]

US intervention in Chile does not provide a total explanation of events in that country, neither before, nor during, nor after the Allende period. US destabilization of the Allende government played a crucial role in its overthrow. But it was only effective in conjunction with a host of internal factors, including the local elite's determination to preserve its own historic privileges, as well as the grievous miscalculations, failures, and fierce infighting in the UP government, which should not be downplayed, and which US strategists were able adroitly to exploit.[52] In jeopardy in Chile was the ability of the dominant groups to preserve the social order under a polyarchic system. This threat firmly united Washington and the Chilean elite, above and beyond any differences within the local elite or between it and Washington.

The Christian Democrats had signed a formal unity pact with the right-wing National Party against the Allende government and in favor of the destabilization program, and Frei, Aylwin and other PDC leaders voiced their unqualified support for the coup.[53] Given that the Christian Democrats, under Aylwin's personal leadership, would later be projected as the bulwark of the "democratic forces" in Chile and the steward of the anti-Pinochet democratization movement, it is important to recall the party's long history of linkages to US political, security, and intelligence organs and its alliance with the Chilean military during the Allende government *and* after the coup. It was only in 1977, when it became clear that the military was not a mere caretaker government that would shortly hand over power to the Christian Democrats – as the military had promised to Frei and Aylwin before the coup – that the PDC moved into full opposition.[54]

From counterrevolution to restoration of polyarchy

The Chilean case provides for rich theoretical abstraction regarding relations between states, political systems, and social classes. On the heels of a century and a half of polyarchic tradition, the UP government proposed to implement the project of popular democratization for which it was elected within the legal, constitutional framework, that is, to put "liberal democracy" to a test of *its own* rules. Allende was overthrown when his coalition attempted to use the legal and constitutional instruments of polyarchy itself to transform the socioeconomic structure of society.

This seems to confirm the thesis which Nora Hamilton developed on the basis of her study of post-revolutionary Mexico of "the limits to state autonomy." Hamilton shows how the Mexican state exhibited the maximum degree of autonomy which states may enjoy, but that such autonomy falls short of the ability of states to actually realize a revolutionary transformation of the social order. Such a transformation would signify a "structural autonomy" of the state, which it does not possess. This transformation would have to come from within the womb of the social order itself, beyond the boundaries of the state power and the state itself (hence the "limits" of state autonomy).[55] As regards Chile, the UP government, having captured a portion of the state on behalf of the subordinate classes, attempted to carry through what Hamilton referred to as "structural autonomy," to utilize the state to actually transcend capitalism. This experiment ran up against the "structural boundaries" of the social order. Previously fragmented interests and segments among the dominant classes quickly achieved internal unity, coherence, and class consciousness. The "structural relations" between the legislative, judicial, and military apparatus were such that they became organs penetrated and influenced by the dominant classes, and at the same time both the Chilean state and the dominant classes became closely linked to internationalized organs of the US "imperial state." At the same time, the formal rules and the legitimizing boundaries of polyarchy placed institutional constraints on any UP effort to transcend the social order, while the world economy placed structural constraints on that effort. We will see a similar pattern in Nicaragua and Haiti.

In Chile, polyarchy was ruptured by authoritarianism in order to preserve the social order. Allende's UP moved to challenge capitalism *utilizing the very procedures and institutions (i.e., the political-juridical superstructure) of its legitimacy.* This situation placed Chile apart from other revolutionary ruptures with existing social orders, whether in the United States (1776), France (1789), the USSR (1917), or Nicaragua (1979), which challenged social orders from outside of their own legitimizing institutionality and created their own, new legitimacy. When a self-declared socialist government came to power, the dominant classes – conceived here as a convergence of dominant groups in Chile and in the United States – were forced to stave off the challenge to their domination from within their own institutions of legitimacy; their only alternative was a rupture with legitimacy in order to preserve the capitalist social order. The Pinochet regime rescued the social order at the cost of legitimacy. Restoration of such legitimacy required reorganizing the political system and restabilizing class domination prior to "redemocratization." The restoration of polyarchy involved a three-step process: first, the brutal destruction of the popular movement and the left; second, the complete restructuring of political economy; third, a tightly controlled "transition to democracy," under a new correlation of political, social, and economic forces that would assure a polyarchic, rather than popular, outcome to the anti-dictatorial movement.

The first step, the suppression of the left and the mass social movements and the reversal of the popular structural transformations of the late 1960s to 1973, was swift and brutal. In addition to the reign of terror, expropriated properties were returned to their former owners or auctioned off (all US corporations reclaimed their investments, with the exception of the copper companies, which were paid compensation), peasants who benefitted from the agrarian reform were thrown off their land, trade unions were abolished by junta decree, popular organizations and the UP parties were outlawed (all other parties were placed in temporary "recess"), twenty-six newspapers and magazines were closed, and society became militarized at every level.

"Conditions in Santiago's slums had deteriorated markedly since the military coup, with a reappearance of delinquency, heavy liquor traffic, and disease," reported *Le Monde* newspaper in January 1974. "Left-wing leaders who helped organize the shantytowns, eliminating crime and improving health and housing conditions, have either disappeared or been arrested or killed since the coup," continued the report. "Local clinics have been dismantled, leading to a reappearance of diarrhea in infants, and the price of public housing has been raised so high that members of the shantytowns could no longer afford it."[56] Workers organized into trade unions dropped from over 40 percent of the workforce before the 1973 coup to about 10 percent in the late 1980s. One observer points out: "The smashing of Chilean democracy by the military in 1973 carried with it – not a byproduct of the coup but as a strategic objective – the destruction of organized labor and the imprisonment, torture, exile and murder of thousands of union activists."[57] Some one million opponents of the regime were sent into exile, and tens of thousands murdered or imprisoned.

Only after this first step was completed – the destruction of the popular movement, the decimation of the left, and thus the achievement of a completely new correlation of forces favoring elite hegemony and dominant foreign interests – was the next step undertaken. Structural adjustment began with the "Chicago Boys" team, a group of Chilean New Right technocrats provided with scholarships by the AID to be schooled in the free-market ideology of neo-liberalism. At least 150 Chileans, drawn from the upper class and recruited mostly from the conservative Catholic University of Santiago, were sent to the

165

University of Chicago to study economics under Milton Friedman and Arnold Hargberger before returning to Chile to take the reins of the economy and become the technocratic interlocutors between the military dictatorship and international finance capital.[58] In this process new class fractions and social groups came into being with political interests that eventually crystallized around a return to polyarchy. Valenzuela points to the emergence of "a powerful new breed of dynamic business leaders who flourished with the opening of Chile's economy to the world market."[59]

The third and final phase was restoring legitimacy via a return to polyarchy – but now under the new conditions of globalization. The dictatorship turned over the government to a civilian regime only *after* that task of anti-popular economic restructuring had been accomplished and only *after* the left and the popular sectors had been decimated.

In all three phases, the United States was intimately involved, playing a key role as the dominant power under which Chilean classes and groups fought with each other and political and socioeconomic processes unfolded.

Although the new military regime became an international pariah, Washington established cordial relations with the junta. US corporations with interests in Chile and the CIA drafted blueprints for dismantling the social transformations of the Allende period.[60] In the two years following the coup, US economic aid, systematically denied to Allende, cascaded into Chile. Washington provided Santiago with $324 million in direct aid and assisted the junta in securing an additional $300 million through multilateral sources. Chile received almost half the foodstuffs authorized by the Food for Peace program for Latin America. The United States also increased aid to the military to an all-time annual high of $18.5 million in 1974, and the CIA provided technical assistance to the newly formed secret police, the National Directorate of Intelligence.[61] This aid was crucial in restabilizing the Chilean economy and putting into motion a long-term, neoliberal program. "The disparity between state and corporate involvement is evident in post-coup Chile," note Petras and Morley. "Heavy imperial state involvement is *not* matched by the multinationals: for the immediate foreseeable future, the imperial state and its financial network is the major political-economic prop for the junta. Only after a substantial and prolonged commitment by the state can we expect the insertion of private capital, despite the junta's policies of 'opening' the country to unrestrained foreign exploitation."[62]

By 1976, these conditions had been achieved, and foreign private capital substituted US bilateral aid. From 1975 to 1978, nearly $3 billion in foreign private capital flowed in, while US government aid dropped to $25 million.[63] Military aid remained at record high levels – $107 million from 1973 to 1977, and then another $20 million from 1978 to 1982, despite the Carter administration's professed human rights policy. And the Carter White House provided Pinochet with $114 million in loans, grants, and donations, and also approved further lending by the international agencies.[64] Jimmy Carter himself, following Nixon's and Ford's lead, refused to acknowledge any US complicity in Allende's overthrow.[65] After several years of massive economic aid to reorganize and reactivate the economy, Washington thus used military aid to preserve the junta's repressive capacity, which secured conditions congenial to the operation of transnational capital in Chile.

From the mid-1970s to the early 1980s, "political aid" programs in Chile were phased out, partly because of the scandal over CIA involvement against Allende and the shift underway in Washington to Project Democracy and the NED, but mostly because such aid, covert or overt, was neither necessary nor appropriate for US objectives in that period. On the one hand, the dictatorship was effectively using direct mass repression against the popular sectors and their organizations, and on the other hand, traditional civil and political society had been dramatically disarticulated and was still in an early process of reconstitution. This would change in the mid-1980s.

Washington turns to "democracy promotion" in Chile

We believe that a restoration of democracy is the best way of assuring Chile's political, social and economic stability. Terrorism, human and civil rights violations, a substantial Communist party committed to the violent overthrow of the government, the national debt crisis, are only a few of the current obstacles to be overcome in achieving genuine political stability. Perhaps the most difficult challenge of all is forging a broad consensus on the institutional means of rebuilding a stable democracy.

US Senate resolution on Chile, 1985[66]

By 1985, given the demise of military regimes in other Southern

Cone countries and mounting unrest inside Chile, the Reagan administration had concluded it was time to phase out the Pinochet regime.
Between 1985 and 1988, the United States shifted its support from the
dictatorship to the elite opposition.[67] The shift came quite abruptly.
Between 1981 and 1985, the Reagan administration strengthened relations with the dictatorship under the policy of "quiet diplomacy"
towards the South American military regimes. Then, in November
1985, Washington sent to Santiago a new ambassador, Harry Barnes,
to replace James Theberge, a one-time CIA consultant whom the
Chilean opposition had nicknamed the military junta's "fifth man."
Barnes's instructions were twofold: to signal to Pinochet that the
United States was shifting tracks; and to develop ties with the elite
opposition that was to replace the dictatorship.[68] A month later,
Undersecretary of State for Inter-American Affairs Elliot Abrams
articulated the shift: "The policy of the United States government
toward Chile is direct and unequivocal: we will cultivate the transition
toward democracy."[69]

Apart from the general shift to promoting polyarchy, there was a
specific Chilean imperative behind the sudden shift: a mass protest
movement against the dictatorship had emerged and was gathering
steam, encompassing a broad spectrum of groups whose confidence
and militancy steadily grew from 1983 to 1987. During this period,
leadership of the anti-dictatorial struggle was disputed between
popular groups and the elite opposition. If it did not intervene in
support of the latter, Washington risked opening space for a popular
or leftist outcome to the anti-Pinochet movement, as had happened a
decade earlier in Nicaragua. "The challenge is how to support democratic change," said Abrams. "This challenge creates a genuine
dilemma because change in friendly countries may, in the short run,
entail some risks... But we know that the risks will become larger –
unacceptably large, in the long-run – if there is no opening toward a
democratic political order." For Abrams, the risk was that "Chile
remains a special target for foreign Marxist-Leninists"[70] (read: the left
is strong in Chile).

Despite the harsh repression, by the late 1970s there had been a
gradual recovery within the popular movement, particularly among
the *pobladores*, or residents of poor neighborhoods, and the trade
unions, which had been two of the most active sectors before the coup.
In mid-1983, the popular opposition initiated a series of *jornadas de
protesta* (days of protest) across the country. The protest movement,

although it enjoyed the active support of the Communists, Socialists, and other organized left groups, was initiated not by political parties but by the labor unions and the community-based grassroots popular movement. It caught the elite and US policymakers by surprise as much as it did the dictatorship. The regime, badly shaken, responded by declaring a state of siege and unleashing a wave of repression. Political arrests, which had subsided to an annual number of fewer than 1,000 between 1976 and 1982, climbed to 5,000 by 1984.[71] The protests stirred concern in Washington that the dictatorship was becoming vulnerable and that events might slip out of US control.

Two positions emerged between 1983 and 1987, the years in which the direction of the democratization movement hung in the balance. The left and the grassroots popular movement took the lead, arguing for mass mobilizations to bring down the dictatorship. In October 1984, these sectors called a successful national protest strike based on the slogan "Without protest there is no change." As protests increased, so too did the strength of the movement. In March 1986, a new umbrella group, the Civil Assembly (Asemblea de la Civilidad), emerged, encompassing 300 organizations ranging from labor unions, to student, women's, professional, and civic organizations, community groups in the *poblaciones*, and political parties. Events were snowballing towards an uprising in civil society *under popular forces*.

The political parties, and particularly the traditional center and right groups, passive and disorganized, were marginal to the rapidly developing movement. A prime objective of US political intervention became to reactivate and unify the traditional political parties, and simultaneously to bolster, or help organize from scratch, moderate groups in civil society to compete for leadership with the popular forces. Once the elite opposition organized, it began its own mobilization and set about to try to gain control of the burgeoning opposition movement. Its strategy, designed in collaboration with US policymakers, was to eschew mass mobilization and instead open a process of direct negotiation with the dictator and seek a pact – behind the back and to the exclusion of the popular movement – for a transition to civilian rule. The popular sectors, in the elite scenario, would constitute "bargaining chips," called upon for disciplined and controlled actions to apply pressure on the regime at key moments in the negotiations.[72]

Between 1983 and 1985, there was a flurry of low-profile diplomatic activity between Washington and Santiago, as US emissaries tried to open a quiet dialog between Pinochet and the elite. In late 1984, US officials conducted a month-long inter-agency policy review. As a result of the review, said one official, Washington decided to "increase high-level contacts with Chileans in the government and in the opposition to try and bring about a compromise." The US goal was "to get the military and the civilians to realize that the growing split only helps the radical left," and could make Chile "another Nicaragua," said the official.[73] However, these efforts amounted to little, because mass popular opposition had seized the initiative and because the elite opposition itself was highly divided; desirous on the one hand to regain direct political power, yet fearful, on the other, of putting too much pressure on Pinochet lest a weakened dictatorship open further space for the popular sectors. These fears were shared by Washington, and the State Department maintained a strict policy of not pressuring the regime publicly and not vetoing any of its loan applications.[74]

After a new wave of mass protests broke out in November 1984, US officials began to implement the "democracy promotion" program announced by Abrams, which, as we shall see, proved to be a crucial factor in the direction the democratization movement would take. Following the 1985 shift, Washington applied the same combination of coercive diplomacy and carrot-and-stick pressures toward Pinochet as it had done so skillfully toward Marcos. For instance, in June 1985, Washington blocked a $2 billion loan package from the World Bank that Chile had requested. Secretary of State George Shultz stated that the purpose was to demonstrate US "concern" over Chile's domestic situation. If Santiago wanted the loans, it would have to meet certain "conditions" which the State Department had relayed to Pinochet, among them, a lifting of the state of siege so that the elite opposition could mobilize. Two days later, Pinochet lifted the state of siege and the World Bank approved the loan.[75] Then, in December 1987, Washington abstained from supporting – *rather than vetoing* – a new World Bank loan to Chile. "Many argued that the Pinochet regime would collapse if Washington vetoed these loans," one observer noted. "The White House, however, did not want Pinochet to fall unless a moderate democratic government took his place."[76]

Massive external financing for the regime was not suspended, but *sustained* by Washington during the entire transition, parallel to the introduction of political aid for the elite opposition. The economic aid was used to keep the regime afloat at the same time as Pinochet was being prodded by a combination of internal and external pressures. In contrast, one month before the $2 billion was released for the Chilean dictatorship, in May 1985, Washington imposed a full economic embargo on Nicaragua, simultaneously with an increase in political and military aid to the anti-Sandinista opposition. The comparison is important: in Chile, the United States wanted the dictatorship to *survive*, as a bulwark against popular forces, while it carefully nudged power from its hands to the civilian elite; in Nicaragua, the United States wanted to *destroy* the revolutionary government by any means possible and transfer power to the elite opposition.

Meanwhile, encouraged by the grassroots upsurge, political parties by the mid-1980s had become reactivated and two major contending coalitions were formed, one of the left and the other of the center. One, the Popular Democratic Movement (MDP), was led by the Communist Party and included the main Socialist faction (the Socialist Party, having never recovered from the 1973 coup, had splintered into several factions) and several other left groups. It was promptly banned by the regime. The second was the Democratic Alliance (AD), headed by the Christian Democrats. While the MDP joined the burgeoning protest movement (as did much of the AD rank and file), the AD leadership sought to open a "gentlemen's" dialog with the regime.[77]

A querulous hodgepodge of new parties and party factions also sprang up, as part of a continuous, and confusing, process of opposition regroupment during the mid-1980s.[78] One of these was the Humanist Party, formed in 1985 and attracting urban middle-class youth, another was a Green Party, and a third was the Pro-Democracy Party (PPD), founded in late 1987 out of the second main Socialist faction headed by Ricardo Nuñez and Ricardo Lagos. These middle-of-the-road groups, espcially the PPD, which attracted middle classes and a portion of the popular sectors, were important in the subsequent formation of a centrist bloc under Christian Democratic hegemony (see below) and in helping shift the correlation of forces in the period 1987–1989 towards a unitary center. With the "democracy program" now underway, Washington's objective became twofold: first, to transfer leadership of the democratization process from the mass movement to the political parties; and second, to isolate the left within the cluster of political parties, bolster the center, and wean the right away from support for the dictatorship.

The shift in policy in Washington was little understood by the Chilean left and the popular sectors, which assumed that the United States would continue unswerving support for the dictatorship. The new US strategy thus contributed to popular disorientation. At the same time, the left seemed unable to find an effective formula for translating the social mobilizations into a viable political strategy. One left faction tied to the Communist Party formed the Manuel Rodríguez Patriotic Front (FPMR) as an underground guerrilla wing (the Communists, after fifty-eight years of peaceful, legal struggle, had endorsed armed struggle as legitimate in 1980). This development caused considerable tactical debate and division within the left.[79] In September 1986, an FPMR commando ambushed Pinochet's motorcade, but the General emerged unharmed and promptly reinstated the state of siege that had been lifted a year earlier. The action (or rather, its failure) quieted mass protests and strengthened the moderate opposition's alternative strategy.

The divisive debate over anti-dictatorial tactics also led to the dissolution of the MDP in June 1987. Shortly afterwards, the Communist Party renounced the armed struggle strategy (the FPMR broke away and become an independent group). The left parties regrouped into a new coalition, the United Left (IU). Although the United Left brought together many of the old UP groups – the MAPU, the Christian Left, Communists, Socialists, a sector of the Radical Party, the MIR, and so on – it clearly represented a waning of leftist influence in the democratization movement and enhanced conditions for the elite to vie for the initiative. Following the abortive ambush on Pinochet, the Christian Democrats declared that, because of the Communists' support for violence, any joint action with them was incompatible with a struggle for democracy – quite a hypocritical position, given that the Christian Democrats had championed the violent overthrow of the Allende government after they could not attain their goals through peaceful means. With the active backing of Washington, they set about to shape an opposition that excluded the left.

Meanwhile, the junta had drawn up a new constitution – approved in 1980 in a national plebiscite widely viewed as fraudulent – that laid out an ambiguous program for a return to civilian rule. It called for a plebiscite to be held in 1988, in which voters could simply confirm or reject a candidate put forward by the armed forces. According to the plan, if the military candidate was rejected, power would be turned over to the winner of competitive elections by March 1990. At first, the IU and sectors within the AD advocated a boycott of the plebiscite, fearful that Pinochet would resort to fraud and legitimize his rule. Other groups in the AD, including Christian Democratic factions, argued that, if conducted skillfully, a combination pact–plebiscite strategy could provide for a "safe" transition. These sectors argued that exhaustion and disillusionment had been gradually setting in among the popular sectors, which could be harnessed and channeled into a pact–electoral formula. US funds and policymakers were deeply involved, behind the scenes, in ongoing discussion and analysis with the elite on the most promising "democratization" formula (see below). In November 1987, the IU groups and the Civic Assembly organizations, with the support of many AD sectors, joined together for massive street demonstrations against the Pinochet plebiscite. At this point Washington intervened decisively to press an increasingly united opposition not to oppose the plebiscite, but rather to participate massively in it. The strategy in Washington was to combine its own tough coercive diplomacy toward Pinochet with massive intervention to organize and advise an elite-led opposition to defeat Pinochet in the plebiscite, and then to proceed, on the basis of more political intervention, to guide subsequent national elections.[80]

In December 1987, the State Department released an unusually strongly worded statement calling for a fair plebiscite followed by a "legitimate electoral process."[81] For its part, the conservative but influential Roman Catholic Bishops' Conference, which had supported the 1973 coup and for many years had provided ideological and symbolic legitimization for the dictatorship, came out vocally against the regime when the elite opposition began to mobilize. By the 1980s it was leading the cause of human rights. In contrast to the increasingly radicalized grassroots base of clergy and lay workers within the Church, the hierarchy established close ties both with US policymakers and with the elite opposition. Archbishop Francisco Fresno of Santiago worked with US emissaries in brokering a dialog between the elite and the regime.[82] In April 1987 Pope John Paul II made a visit to Chile during which he both rebuffed Pinochet and called for "constraint" and "nonconfrontation" among the population, making clear the Church's preference for an elite-led return to civilian rule. Several months later, the Chilean Bishops' Conference called publicly for the plebiscite to proceed under fair conditions, a call which was particularly persuasive with the Christian Democrats.

The combination of US pressures (on both the regime and the opposition), the Church's influential position, and changes in the balance of forces between 1983 and 1987, eventually brought the opposition into a united front to participate in the plebiscite. This same combination of pressures led the regime to agree to lift the "recess" on moderate opposition parties ("Marxist" parties remained outlawed), end the state of emergency, allow exiled opposition leaders to return, establish electoral registries, and provide the opposition with access to the communications media. Genaro Arriagada, a top PDC leader, noted that "the political situation had undergone a change by 1987," such that "the notion had taken hold that the decisive confrontation between Pinochet and the democratic opposition would be an electoral contest. The theme of free elections now began to dominate the debate."[83] The conditions were propitious for a broad national anti-dictatorial front, which crystallized in late 1987 in an agreement to organize a "no" vote in the plebiscite and under the banner of a coalition known as the "Command for the NO." Pre-plebiscite polls funded by the NED and supervised by the NRI indicated that 70 percent of Chileans wanted an end to the regime, but nearly 60 percent were convinced that, through fraud, opposition errors or a new coup, the military would manage to stay in power.[84] The goal thus became to build public confidence in the plebiscite and to channel mass energies into the electoral-institutional process.

The baton had passed fully to the elite. By then, the PPD had attracted members of the right-wing Republican Party, the Radical Party, factions of the MAPU and individual Communists, as well as a number of Chilean celebrity figures (artists, singers, and actors). It became an odd grouping, embracing factions from the center-left to the center-right, solidly subordinated to an emergent bloc under Christian Democratic hegemony. By 1988, the entire "democratic" opposition and a significant portion of the left in Chile had united under the hegemony of the Christian Democrats to square off against the dictatorship. This was not a predetermined outcome. The Christian Democrats emerged as the hegemonic party of the opposition only after the crucial 1983–1987 period, and taking into account that the left, already decimated politically and militarily after fourteen years of military rule, continued to suffer intense repression. Apart from generalized repression against the popular sectors, the Communist Party, most Socialist factions, and other left groups remained illegal throughout this period, under a law banning "the advocacy of Marxism." PDC leader Genaro Arriagada noted frankly that, during the long years of dictatorship, the Christian Democrats had the advantage of "less risk of violent repression" than the Communists or the Socialists. "The greatest personal risk for Christian Democrats was exile, while for the communists, it was death."[85] The decline of left and

174

popular hegemony was due to a synchronization of three factors: US political intervention activities, now conducted under the rubric of "promoting democracy"; the regime's repression; and, just as during the Allende period, the left's own sectarian infighting and inability to develop an effective alternative strategy.

This combination of factors laid the basis for the gradual transfer of hegemony over the anti-dictatorial struggle from the left to the center-right. However, the elite opposition was also quite fractious, and US political intervention played an important role in instilling discipline and unity in its ranks. Strengthened by NED funds, political advisors, organizers, and other forms of US support that began to pour in, the elite would take the reins of a tightly controlled transition that would preclude popular democratization from the national agenda.

Ironing out the political system through political operations

Between 1984 and 1991, Washington allocated at least $6.2 million through the NED, and another $1.2 million through the AID's ODI for an array of programs in support of moderate political parties, labor unions, and women's, youth, business, academic, and civic groups. These same groups were also incorporated into regional US programs involving another $5 million.[86] Given the long history of CIA and other forms of intervention in Chile's political process, US officials were able to rely on an infrastructure and a broad network which were already established. This US political intervention performed three closely related tasks: (1) reconstituting elite consensus (2) unifying and organizing the elite opposition on the basis of this reconstituted consensus, and (3) competing with the popular sectors at the grassroots level.

Step I: Reconstituting elite consensus

The first step involved cultivating ties with moderate and conservative political, civic, and business leaders and tapping the talents and knowledge of leading intellectuals. It involved funding several elite think-tanks in Chile to recruit and train these leaders and intellectuals, and draw upon their resources and constituencies. One was the Center for Development Studies, a center-right policy planning institute focusing on political issues. Its director was Edgardo Boeninger, a PDC leader who had been a cabinet minister in the Frei government and had participated actively in the 1970–1973 anti-Allende campaign.[87] Boeninger lobbied heavily within the PDC against the social mobilization line, and in 1986 he personally drafted the blueprint for the alternative pact–plebiscite strategy. The PDC was seriously split from 1983 to 1987. The progressive wing supported the social mobilization line in alliance with left and popular forces. The conservative wing, led by Aylwin, Boeninger, and Arriagada, supported the pact–plebiscite line. In this intra-party struggle, US backing for the conservative faction assured its predominance. The strategy sought to win over the middle and upper classes from support for Pinochet, and to demobilize the poor and leave them with no other option than the pact–plebiscite line under elite leadership. (Other NED programs at the grassroots, discussed below, targeted the poor and workers for this purpose.)[88] Another think-tank was the Center for Public Studies, run by businessmen and women and focusing on economic affairs. The NED also gave monies for research projects to the Chilean branch of the Latin American Social Sciences Faculty (FLACSO).[89] As part of these programs, analysts from NED core groups, the AID, the Department of State, US think-tanks, and universities were sent to Chile to participate and, reciprocally, Chileans from the think-tanks were brought to the United States. These programs included diverse intellectual and cultural exchanges, seminars, training courses, research projects, and so forth.

The objective was to investigate the social and political conditions in Chile under which the democratization process was unfolding and with which US political intervention programs could intersect, and to undertake *consensus-building* processes around a transnational strategy and on the transnational agenda for Chile in the post-transition period. Collecting precise information on the specific social, political, and cultural conditions in target countries has become a standard feature of these programs. Academic studies in the service of "democracy promotion" may be objective, and often recruit reputable and virtuous intellectuals. However, these academic undertakings enlist Gramscian organic intellectuals to do political and theoretical thinking for dominant groups. As became quite clear in Chile, where many of those who prepared reports through the think-tanks were simultaneously key political actors in the transition, such organic intellectuals are tied directly to contending groups in social struggles and serve key intellectual-ideological functions in those struggles. Information produced through "academic" investigations conducted under "democracy promotion" programs serves to guide US policymakers and their local allies. Chilean and US organic intellectuals and policymakers worked together closely in devising and then implementing an elite transition. The Council on Foreign Relations, for instance, established a special Chile Study Group in 1987. This group brought together representatives from the State Department, the NED groups, private US corporations with major interests in Chile, and key Chilean politicians and academicians involved in the US "democracy promotion" program. Study group participants included Georgetown University professor Arturo Valen-zuela (who in 1993 became a high-level Clinton official for Latin American policy), Gershman, Ambassador Barnes, William Doherty of the AIFLD, Edgardo Boeninger and other PDC leaders, leaders from other Chilean political parties, and so forth.[90]

In Chile, these projects helped to strengthen local elite consensus, cohesion, and unity of purpose, and to orient the elite democratization strategy. The goal, according to a NED document, was "to collect objective empirical data on the political attitudes and behavior of Chileans to serve as a basis for the formulation of a more realistic and consensual set of political strategies of a transition to democracy." Another NED document explained that activities by these policy planning and research centers sought "to conduct an open, pluralistic project of study and dissemination of the basic values of democratic theory to different organized social groups, such as unions and profes-sional associations, and create objective conditions for dialogue among individuals and institutions of diverse democratic political leanings, with democratic theory as the field of analysis."[91] Conferences, semi-nars, and studies conducted by the think-tanks were followed by "outreach activities," including "lectures, conferences, publications, [and] radio programs," to disseminate the results in order to "inform political elites, social and civic leaders as well as the public-at-large."[92]

The NED also developed exchanges between the Catholic University in Chile and US academic institutions, particularly the conservative Georgetown University. The Catholic University was a major base for the Christian Democrats in the 1960s and a key organizing center for opposition to Allende. Campus-based student and professional groups received AID and CIA funds as part of the destabilization program.[93] One NED-sponsored symposium on "problems of democracy" held at the Catholic University brought US academics and policymakers together with their Chilean counterparts, and was "a major step in an ongoing effort to foster dialogue among individuals and institutions of diverse democratic political orientations within Chile."[94] Subsequently, the Catholic University sponsored a slew of meetings and forums of the elite opposition and became a clearing-house and organizing headquarters for its political activities.

The US organization Freedom House was given several hundred thousand dollars for the Editorial Andante publishing house in Santiago. Freedom House, a Washington-based clearing-house on foreign policy issues, has been closely tied since its inception in 1941 to the US national security and intelligence apparatus. Its principal officers sit on numerous boards of the interlocking political intervention network.[95] It specializes in informational and communications aspects of political intervention, such as the circulation of "democratic theory" literature, funding international speaking tours of NED recipients in intervened countries, and funding media outlets in target countries. The Andante program included "the production of books that promote the spread of democratic values... and the best methods for producing a stable democratic future for this country."[96] Representatives of five political parties were chosen to participate in the project: one from the right-wing and four from the center.[97] Andante, although it was technically a publishing house, functioned throughout the transition period as a policy planning institute and as a clearing-house for disseminating information to public opinion makers in the news media, political parties, and civic groups.

The importance of these "academic" undertakings in Chile in building a Gramscian consensus and in devising technical solutions as the basis for a hegemonic project should not be underestimated. Out of the think-tanks, research centers, and US–Chilean political and academic exchanges came a steady flow of policy planning and academic literature analyzing the strategies and tactics of a "democratic transition" and providing an intellectual and ideological compass for reconstituting elite consensus. They set the discourse of the democratization agenda and the tone and parameters of public debate. They also contributed to the development of a network of prominent political and civic leaders with a public projection and a political action capacity. "Experts" from these same Chilean think-tanks and research centers were recruited by the NED groups to assist the opposition political parties – together with teams of US advisors – in the plebiscite and elections of 1988 and 1989.[98] And after Aylwin came to power in 1990, these policy planning institutes had already drafted concrete

social and economic programs for the new government and provided a
ready pool of organic intellectuals and technocrats to fill cabinet posts.
These NED programs thus helped groom the leadership of a broad and
interlocking civic opposition network in Chile of US-allied parties,
labor, youth, academic, and neighborhood organizations, and the
communications media (see below).

The overall conclusions that emerged from this US-sponsored
research was that the popular classes had earlier been able to challenge
elite hegemony from within the framework of constitutional legitimacy
as a result of a poorly structured polyarchic system. A weakened
center and heightened divisions between the center and the right had
paved the way for the ascent of the left. If properly organized, a
polyarchic system involves a series of functional mechanisms and
organizational forms for structuring politics in such a way as to assure
precisely that social and political struggles are resolved or defused
without any challenge to hegemony itself. Valenzuela, in a NED-
funded study, went to great pains to show that a better mechanistic
and institutional organization of the political system in Chile would
have prevented subordinate groups from utilizing the state for their
own project. Such a better organized polyarchic system would include
more parliamentary power *vis-à-vis* the executive, a less fractious
center and right party structure, and stronger institutional links
between the state and civil society (with less autonomy for popular
sectors operating in civil society).[99] This conclusion is echoed in the
reports that came out of the US-funded think-tanks.[100] Constant
themes in the conferences and studies funded by the NED were "the
relationship between institutional forms of governance and democratic
stability in Chile," "party building for political leaders of the democratic center and center-right," and "strengthen[ing] the Congress'
policy-making role in a democratic Chile."[101]

In sum, the "flukes of the Chilean political system" referred to by
Kissinger, which had facilitated a legal and constitutional opening for a
project of popular democratization, had to be ironed out. This ironing-
out required reshaping the political landscape so as to achieve a strong
center, a strong right and a weak left. The tripolar historic left–right–
center stalemate had to be replaced by a bipolar system and a greater
fusion of right and center in a stable and solid hegemonic bloc, under
centrist leadership. The US objective in Chile was to bolster the center
forces – primarily a renovated Christian Democracy – to strengthen a
"democratic" right under centrist hegemony, and to wean away the

most "moderate" element of the left and subordinate it to the center. As we shall see below, Christian Democratic leaders were placed at the head of every organization and project supported by the NED. The goal was not just to manage the transition from dictatorship to polyarchy, but also to assure that there would be no future "flukes" in the Chilean political system. One 1990 NED document, reflecting back on the successful "democracy promotion" program in Chile, noted:

> With their victory [the PDC electoral triumph], it is clear that the Christian Democrats have a key role to play in the transition process that will unfold over the next four years... it is crucial that the Christian Democratic party be able to maintain itself as a buffer between the newly elected president, Pinochet, and pressures from the left. The next four years are very important for Chile's democratic future, because after this transition period, new elections will take place. A repeat of 1973 [*sic*: the document probably meant 1970] where three distinct political positions emerged – the right, a weak center, and the left, creating a polarized society between two extremes – would have drastic consequences. There are many barriers to be overcome before Chile's democracy is firmly installed but the first steps have been taken to launch the country in that direction.[102]

Step II: Unifying and organizing the elite

Endowment programs helped reactivate political parties, forge a bloc with the center-right at its helm, and have this bloc gain leadership of the democratization movement. Abrams and others in Washington had stressed marginalizing the left and the groups from Allende's Popular Unity coalition in a post-dictatorial period. The NDI and the NRI received some $2 million to work with the Chilean parties between 1984 and 1990.[103]

Chilean opposition leaders were brought to Venezuela in 1985 to hold meetings with US organizers at the School for Democracy that the NED had set up there in 1984. This "School" was intended to replace an "Institute for Political Education" that the CIA had secretly established in San Jose, Costa Rica in 1960. The purpose of this institute had been to recruit peasant, labor, and political leaders from Latin America and turn them into "assets." The institute was closed after its CIA links were exposed. But the idea was revived as part of Project Democracy, and then reactivated as the School for Democracy in Caracas, now under the auspices of the NED rather than the CIA.[104]

Also in 1985, the NDI brought leaders of Chile's centrist and right-wing parties to a conference in Washington on "Democracy in South

180

America."[105] The conference, declared NDI vice-president Ken Wallock, was "pivotal in promoting unity within the Chilean opposition." On the heels of the conference, the NDI, working in tandem with the Catholic Bishops' Conference in Chile, and particularly with Archbishop Francisco Fresno of Santiago, brokered an agreement among eleven of Chile's moderate political parties on working collectively for a "democratic transition." The agreement, known as the National Accord for the Transition to Democracy, called for constitutional reforms and elections, and explicitly excluded the Chilean left, as did the conference in Washington.[106]

Pinochet's negotiator with the elite opposition, Interior Minister Sergio Onofre Jarpa, gave his blessing to the accord when it was first signed since it explicitly excluded the left and because, in his view, it provided a good strategy for diffusing the groundswell of popular protest.[107] That groundswell, however, did not dissipate, and in the face of continued mass protests, the accord quickly crumbled. The right pulled out over fear that its participation would help fuel the anti-Pinochet ferment beyond elite control, since in 1985 the left still had the initiative. In addition, the Pinochet regime did have a significant support base beyond an inner circle of cronies, including sectors of the technocratic business community that had flourished under neoliberal restructuring and sectors of the traditional political right that felt more secure under authoritarian rule than in risking any popular resurgence in an uncertain transition.

It became a top priority of US strategists to convince these sectors to cast their lot not with the dictatorship but with a return to polyarchy.[108] For this purpose, the NRI and the CIPE conducted programs with respective right-wing political and business constituencies in Chile. The big-business community and the traditional right were represented politically in two major parties, the National and the National Renovation parties. The NRI worked with "conservative and moderate political parties... [which] have traditionally suffered from a sense of isolation, and in local political battles they have regularly faced well-financed leftist and totalitarian forces," stated one NED report.[109] Meetings and forums conducted by the NRI focused "on those institutions and actors who are not currently as active as they could be in the difficult politics of opposition to the military government."[110]

The CIPE was put in charge of programs with the pro-Pinochet business community, with the goal of bringing it into the democratization movement and simultaneously imbuing the overall movement with the neo-liberal free-market ideology. The democratization program would thus be committed to free-market neo-liberalism, and in turn the business community would be committed to the democratization program. One CIPE program, conducted through the Chilean businessmen's think-tank, the Center for Public Studies, for instance, involved "a series of seminars on privatization for academics, journalists, government leaders, and the business community... By building support for a competitive private enterprise economy, CEP seeks to enhance the economic role of the individual and encourage the inclusion of private enterprise principles in the democratic transition process."[111] Another CIPE program in 1989, conducted through the Catholic University's Foundation of Economics and Administration, focused on educating the public "on the importance of a free enterprise system in fostering economic growth and supporting stable democracies." The program included designing "courses on free market economics" which were imparted to the leadership of the NED-funded parties, trade unions, and youth, neighborhood, and other civic groups.[112] Subsequent activities conducted by both the NRI and the CIPE included the preparation of economic policy documents and their distribution among the political parties and the entire overlapping network of national political, business, and civic leaders being cultivated by Washington.[113]

The efforts of the NRI and CIPE were largely successful. Although they did not actually join a unitary opposition, much of the business community and the political right did eventually come out in favor of a restoration of polyarchy and of the post-Pinochet political order under construction. Thus the right became, in the words of US officials, a "democratic right." Seen theoretically, the objective – successfully achieved – was gradually to forge a transnational nucleus made up of political, civic, and business elites, and later, to have this nucleus fuse with state managers through a transition from the military to a civilian regime. The new polyarchic state would advance the economic aspect of the transnational agenda, neo-liberalism, through a polyarchic political system, in contrast to the military regime's implementation of neo-liberalism through authoritarianism, which generated too many cleavages to achieve elite consensus and too much social conflict to bring about hegemonic social control. Forging a Gramscian consensus among the elite around neo-liberalism and polyarchy in this way involved three dimensions: converting sectors of the elite formerly committed to ISI inward-oriented and statist development to neo-liberalism; converting the new business elite tied to the global economy to polyarchy; and bringing the two together around the transnational agenda for Chile.

For its part, the NDI took responsibility for encouraging a solid center-left to center-right anti-Pinochet coalition among a broad range of political parties, under the hegemony of the Christian Democrats, and for supervising its campaign activities. It sponsored a follow-up meeting of Chilean parties in 1986 in Venezuela,[114] and then transferred activities to inside Chile. US assistance was made conditional on opposition unity. In 1987, as the opposition was beginning to form a single bloc, the NED provided the NDI with several grants to form the Committee for Free Elections as a formal coalition of opposition parties.[115] The NDI described the Committee as a "non-partisan and independent group of prominent Chileans,"[116] but the Committee was a virtual front, in fact, for the top PDC leadership. Its head was Sergio Molina, a PDC leader, former government minister in the Frei administration, and a confidant of Patricio Aylwin. Aylwin himself became the Committee's official spokesperson. The Committee's second-in-charge was Genaro Arriagada, a member of the PDC Central Board who became the Executive Secretary of the Command for the NO. Arriagada was also head of the Christian Democrats' Radio Cooperativa, one of the most important media outlets in the country and a mouthpiece for the elite strategy. The Committee's fourteen-member board was dominated by PDC leaders and, in fact, brought together much of the top leadership of the "civic opposition front" that US political operatives were weaving together. Among them were Christian Democrats Eduardo Frei (son of the former president and the winner of the 1993 presidential elections), Monica Jimenez, who helped run the Catholic University programs and also directed another NED program known as Participa, and Oscar Godoy, Director of the Institute of Political Science at the Catholic University.[117]

In 1988, the NDI sent a team of specialists to Chile to work directly with the political parties. Under the watchful eyes of the ubiquitous US advisors, sixteen opposition parties, including those that had originally signed the National Accord and the newly created Pro-Democracy Party, formed the Command for the NO. Simultaneous to NDI's work with the opposition coalition, both it and the NRI spent over half a million dollars conducting a series of nationwide public opinion surveys from 1987 to 1989, in conjunction with the think-tanks and research institutes.[118] The surveys were judiciously used to design campaign themes and strategies and to guide the coalition's activities. "The findings [of the surveys and polls]," explained the NED, "clearly achieved their objective of guiding democratic leaders in planning their strategies for attaining widespread public support."[119] For instance, an early poll indicated a split three ways in the plebiscite, with one-third undecided.[120] "The undecided vote became the key," said one NDI polling analyst. "They had ambiguous feelings about the policies and plans of the opposition." On the basis of this poll, NDI media consultant Frank Greer drew up a Madison Avenue-style media blitz for the Command for the NO, specifically targeting the undecided.

Another NED program conducted in tandem with the work of the NDI and the NRI was known as Crusade for Citizen Participation, or simply as Participa. Headed by well-known PDC leader Monica Jimenez, Participa carried out a variety of projects intended to cohere the different political parties through consensus-building activities among the elite. These activities included convening several seminars among political parties, government officials, policy planners, and the media on future social policies in the country, as well as conducting a series of broadly publicized "debates" among political party leaders, and designing specific activities to target women. In these activities, Participa was guided by full-time US "trainers," and the materials for its programs were sent to Chile from the United States through Partners of the Americas (which ran NED-funded US–Chilean exchange programs), the NDI, and the Delphi organization, another US-based conduit for NED funds.[121]

Through Delphi, the NED provided support to *La Epoca*, a newspaper launched by the Christian Democrats in 1987 which quickly became one of the country's main dailies. *La Epoca* proved to be a refreshing alternative to the tightly censored media outlets that functioned under the dictatorship, including *El Mercurio*. The latter had been a major recipient of CIA funds in the 1960s and had played a key role, through its psychological operations, in the anti-Allende destabilization activities,[122] but after the coup it refused to switch loyalties from Pinochet to the opposition. *La Epoca* provided a broad outlet for the opposition's public projection and for fostering discussions conducive to consensus-building and unity around the centrist bloc under formation.[123]

US intervention in Chile's internal political process reached a pinnacle in 1988, the year of the plebiscite. Washington allocated approximately $4 million through the NED and through the AID's

ODI to organize and guide the Command for the NO.[124] The AID granted $1.2 million to the Costa Rican-based Center for Electoral Assistance and Promotion (CAPEL), an organization formed in 1982 at the behest of US policymakers as a conduit for US political operations in Latin America, and whose board members were drawn from the same sources as the interlocking directorates of the other NED groups.[125] The CAPEL sent a team to Chile to work with the Catholic Church-sponsored Fundacion Civitas and with Participa for "voter education" campaigns.

In the division of labor, the NDI guided the political parties in the campaign, while CAPEL supervised such activities as highly successful voter registration drives, door-to-door canvassing, distribution of electoral paraphernalia, and poll monitoring. A US trainer was selected to prepare step-by-step manuals and other materials for Chilean organizers, and other US advisors managed the "national forums" that Participa and the Fundacion Civitas conducted.[126] Meanwhile, NDI advisors designed the coalition's campaign and even produced its media advertisements, exporting US campaign techniques, particularly those which took full advantage of new communications technology and the use of television. "In Chile, we went in very early," said one consultant sent down by NED. "We literally organized Chile as we organize elections in precincts anywhere in the United States."[127] And as in the Philippines, US pressures on Pinochet, along with the presence of some 6,000 foreign electoral observers and quick-count tallies on voting night conducted by US advisors, were crucial in preventing fraud and assuring that the dictator would respect the outcome of the vote.

Following the plebiscite, the Command was transformed into a coalition of seventeen political parties, known as the Concertacion, which nominated Aylwin as its presidential candidate. Aylwin was more concerned during the brief campaign with containing popular enthusiasm for change than with squaring off against his electoral opponents. The NO victory generated "enormous expectations among the common people," he said during a campaign interview. "These sectors will press for popular demonstrations and protests. The biggest challenge that we political leaders face is controlling such pressures."[128] Pinochet's followers nominated Hernan Buchi to the pro-military Independent Democratic Union (UDI) ticket. The traditional right decided to run its own candidate, Francisco Havier Errazuriz, a prominent businessman from the National Renovation Party. Aylwin's coalition, with more NED support, won the December 1989 election with 55 percent of the vote (the two right-wing candidates garnered 45 percent of the vote between them).[129] This was the first election in modern Chilean history in which the left had no candidate of its own and no conspicuous or autonomous participation in the political process. US efforts had largely succeeded in completely reconfiguring the Chilean political landscape, and in particular, in restructuring three blocs (left, center, right) into two blocs, the center (with left and right elements at its fringe) and the right. By the late 1980s, even before the 1990 transfer of government to Aylwin, US political operatives were referring with great satisfaction to "two major political currents" in Chile, the center and the right.[130] This new political configuration appeared to have stabilized in the early 1990s. The 1993 national elections were a contest between two presidential candidates, Arturo Alessandri, candidate for a coalition of rightist parties, and Christian Democrat Eduardo Frei, candidate for the Concertacion coalition – both sons of former right and center presidents in the pre-Allende period.

Step III: Suppressing popular mobilization

If step I was defining the contours of a controlled transition and step II was unifying and organizing the elite, the third step was competing with, and displacing, existing popular leadership and initiative at the grassroots level. There were two priority target sectors: the *poblaciones* and labor. The sprawling *poblaciones* had historically been hotbeds of radical political activism, and were bastions of support for the Allende government. Following the 1973 coup, the junta made an unsuccessful effort to pacify the *poblaciones* by replacing leftist community leaders with junta supporters, in many cases Christian Democrats.[131]

In mid-1985, the NED planned a program for funding and advising the Neighborhood and Community Action (AVEC) group, a civic organization that targeted *poblaciones* in Santiago and other major Chilean cities. A NED summary document in May 1985, titled "Democratic Action in Slum Areas," stated:

> The political, social and economic crisis inside Chile is being used by the Communist party to penetrate the "poblaciones" through an effective campaign to incorporate the poor into their ranks. Moreover, the restrictions and prohibitions imposed by the military regime on democratic political parties have smoothed the way for the Communist party, accustomed as it is to working under clandestine condi-

tions... In an effort to counter the predominance of the Communist party in the "poblaciones"... [the AVEC project] is designed to support the activities of the avowedly democratic organizations, focusing on the country's most densely populated areas; in order to counter the Marxists' intensive activities in these areas, the proposed program... would initiate professional training and indoctrination programs particularly for Chilean women and youth. (Courses would include sewing, children's fashions, hairdressing, knitting, cooking, first aid and arts and crafts.) Democratic education would place great emphasis on the value of representative democracy, and would stress the proposers' [sic] opposition to the popular democracies advocated by Marxism.[132]

The AVEC program was administered by the Delphi International Group, a self-described multinational consulting and management firm. Since the early 1980s, Delphi had functioned as a large-scale contractor for the USIA and the AID. With the NED's creation in 1984, Delphi became one of the principal contractors for its projects in Latin America, especially those involving the communications media, and women, youth, and community groups. In late 1987, Delphi assigned its staff member Henry "Hank" Quintero to coordinate its Chile programs.[133] Quintero was an intelligence community veteran who, together with Richard Miller and Carl "Spitz" Channel, had run the Institute of North–South Issues, which was exposed in the Iran–Contra scandal as an Oliver North front group.[134]

The AVEC was actually founded in 1964 under the auspices of the Santiago archdiocese as a "self-help" charity-oriented program. It was run by Christian Democrats, with US support, as one of their "commu-nitarian" projects in the 1960s campaigns to develop a social base and counter the left. In the late 1970s, Christian Democratic organizers reactivated AVEC. Its president was Sergio Wilson Petit, a PDC leader and a lawyer involved in the early and mid-1980s negotiations between the elite opposition and the dictatorship. Another AVEC leader was Hernol Flores, also a PDC leader. In 1973, Flores had come out vocally in support of the coup.[135] Not surprisingly, simultaneously with his leadership in the AVEC and militancy in the PDC, Flores was also the Secretary-General of a US-funded trade union federation (see below).

Using the "multiplier effect" method, and manuals, audiovisual, and other materials supplied by Delphi, the AVEC conducted leadership training seminars for several thousand local leaders, who then spread out and organized the *poblaciones* zone by zone. Activities focused on weaning the poor neighborhoods away from leftist influence and radical sympathies, and channeling political energies into the plebiscite, and later into the 1989 presidential elections. "These programs were active in organizing residents in their communities to either challenge established leaders or assume the presently unoccupied role of community leaders," reported Delphi. "Discussions [in NED-AVEC seminars] held in the *poblaciones* centered on the concept of heritage and the concept of rights residing with the individual and not with the state."[136] Another document cautioned: "the urban slums and shantytowns are centers of acute social conflict... due to the permanent non-satisfaction of their demands, it is urgent to address this situation and incorporate them into the redemocratization process." There is "intense opposition in the *poblaciones* to the regime," it warned: "This intense social mobilization has generated repression [from the regime] and has also opened up new space for some of the historic political parties of the center to restructure their work" in the poor neighborhoods. It then listed the specific objectives of the NED-AVEC program: "mount a democratic alternative that undercuts the process of communist and fascist penetration of the marginal sectors in our country"; and "conduct intense promotional work so as to penetrate the organizations that currently exist, and to incorporate these actively into the objectives of this project."[137] A NED report on the program stated that "the project with AVEC directly filled a void within poor community organizations in Chile. AVEC is one of the few Chilean organizations working with the poor to enhance both socio-economic well-being and political and social awareness."[138] In reality, there was no such void in the *poblaciones* – both the organized left parties and the communities themselves were *highly* organized, and politically and socially aware. The objective was not to fill a void but to compete with existing organizational forms and to try and displace their leaders.

An important aspect of the AVEC, and all NED and AID "democracy" programs in Chile and elsewhere, is the propagation of specific ideological messages associated with capitalist polyarchy and consensual domination, including a highly individualist and atomized conception of "individual rights and responsibilities," in contradistinction to competing concepts of collective mobilization, demands, and rights. The objective is to *defuse* and *destructure* autonomous mass constituencies. "AVEC's civic education programs were closely linked to the socio-political situation in the targeted communities and were aimed at supporting momentum for the return to democracy," explained the

NED. "[NED] grants enabled AVEC, during a critical juncture in Chilean politics, namely the pre- and post-Plebiscite periods, to provide a viable alternative." Through the NED program, "AVEC has gained the loyalties of its constituencies, and has effectively encouraged a self-help approach in the targeted organizations."[139] At a time when mass mobilization was sweeping the *poblaciones*, placing collective *political* demands on the dictatorship for democratization and also collective *socioeconomic* demands for public resources for food, housing, and employment, the AVEC propagated its alternative approach of community "self-help" and "individual participation" in the political process. Explained another NED report: "At the communal level, AVEC's main area of emphasis, civic education efforts, continued to address the individual's rights, obligations, and participation in a democracy."[140]

The NED program targeting the second priority sector, labor, was conducted by the FTUI.[141] As in the Philippines, the United States backed a minority labor federation with the aim, not of defending workers, but of tempering the revival of labor militancy. In 1983, in the heat of the renewed protest movement, a broad new labor federation was formed, the National Workers Command (CNT), described by one informed observer as "the most representative labor coalition since the United Workers Central (CUT) was abolished by the military in 1973."[142] Chile's trade unions have a long history of militancy and of genuine pluralism in their own ranks.[143] Before the coup, over a million workers in some 10,000 workplaces – more than 40 percent of Chile's workforce – belonged to the CUT. Labeled by Washington as a "communist front," the CUT, formed in 1953 out of diverse federations, brought together trade unionists of differing ideologies and political affiliations, including Christian Democrats, Socialists, Communists and Radicals, into a single body, and was perhaps unique in Latin America in its commitment to labor unity.[144] Now, once again, in 1983, the CNT mushroomed into the largest and most representative federation. Its leadership included Communists, Socialists, Christian Democrats, and others under a program of broad labor unity and militant opposition to the dictatorship.

In 1984, a year after the CNT was formed, the FTUI began funding a small grouping, the Democratic Workers Union (UDT). The UDT had grown out of the "Group of Ten," a small club of trade union leaders led by Christian Democrats from the right-wing of the PDC and financed by the AFL-CIO since 1976.[145] As in the Philippines, the

"Group of Ten" was for the most part unmolested by the dictatorship and even collaborated openly in the mid-1970s with the junta, which continued to brutally repress unionists from the banned CUT.[146] According to the NED, the UDT received support because its "development has been severely curbed by government restrictions and threatened by communist-subsidized rivals."[147] Briefly, in 1983, the UDT joined the CNT, but in 1984, the same year that it began receiving NED funds, it broke off, and subsequently renamed itself the Democratic Workers Confederation (CDT). US funds enabled the CDT "to establish youth and community services, to distribute an information bulletin and to conduct a media outreach campaign," explained a NED report. "Regional offices have been established and seminars have been held" by FTUI specialists to train local leaders. The NED also financed a CDT campaign to garner workers' support for the abortive National Accord signed by the moderate parties in 1985.[148]

Thus, between 1984 and 1988, the crucial period in which the leadership and direction of the democratization movement was being fought out, there were two principal labor organizations, the pluralist and militant CNT, which advocated continued social mobilization against the dictatorship, and the minority CDT, which called for an "orderly return to democracy" and the exclusion of Communists, Socialists and other left groupings from the labor movement.[149] But pressures were mounting in Chile for a unitary labor federation. A convention was planned for late 1988 to form a new labor central out of the CNT and other groupings, to be called the *Unified* Workers Central (CUT, with the slight change of name meant to get around the regime's ban of the defunct *United* Workers Central). The US-sponsored CDT had remained a minority grouping, but clusters from its rank and file had steadily broken off to join the CNT under the banner of labor unity. In that year, the NED described the minority group as "the embattled Chilean trade union federation," meaning that it was losing ground to the CNT. Thus, in 1988, US strategy shifted from trying to bolster the parallel unionism of the CDT to trying to gain as much influence as possible within the soon-to-be-formed CUT, eclipse leftist influence and counter the social mobilization line. The NED continued funding its parallel federation, but at the same time advised the group to join the new CUT as a constituent member. Then, starting in 1989, the NED simultaneously funded the CDT and began to penetrate and fund the CUT. As with the political parties, the strategy was to try and achieve the overall hegemony of pliant, moderate and pro-US forces within the national democratization movement. This dual funding – for the CDT as a small, constituent member of the CUT, and for the CUT overall – continued into the 1990s.[150]

The CDT, affiliated to the ICFTU, became the Chilean representative to that body. CDT Secretary-General Hernol Flores, a Christian Democrat and also an AVEC leader (the CDT central offices in Santiago also housed the AVEC national headquarters) endorsed Aylwin early on and campaigned actively for labor support for the Aylwin ticket. In addition Hernol Flores was interviewed regularly in the television programs sponsored by the Catholic University, in *La Epoca*, and in the other public forums and media outlets of the US-promoted civic opposition front, as "the representative of labor."

In targeting labor, the FTUI sent in several dozen AIFLD field organizers to train top-level Chilean union leaders, who then, through the multiplier effect, branched around the country with the dual agenda of organizing labor into the anti-Pinochet, pro-centrist bloc then under formation, and competing with more radical and leftist labor tendencies.[151] Following Aylwin's inauguration, funds went for CDT recruitment drives and stepped-up activities to counter leftist opponents. "The democratic sector of CUT needs reinforcement in several important provinces of the country, as the antidemocratic sectors of the organization have mounted vigorous recruitment campaigns among workers in these areas."[152] Beyond seeking to marginalize militant tendencies, US activities also sought to garner workers' support for the neo-liberal program. NED funds sponsored the drafting by the CDT of a forty-point program for labor–management relations (the program was presented to, and adopted by, Aylwin's administration), and a series of forums to promote "dialogue and cooperation" between labor and the business sector.[153]

A third sector targeted by US operatives was Chilean youth. "Political education has been tragically neglected in Chile during the past fourteen years, weakening the ability of centrist forces to consolidate popular support and posing a serious obstacle to the reemergence of a stable democracy," warned a 1987 NED document. "Given the dearth of democratic education, youth, in particular, are highly susceptible to the 'idealistic' rhetoric of Chile's Marxist parties."[154] Delphi took charge of a program with the Institute for the Transition (ISTRA), which subsequently changed its name to the Center for Youth Development (CDJ). Another NED document noted: "The US Embassy in Santiago reports that ISTRA is the moderate wing of the Christian

Democratic Party's youth organization... ISTRA is described as markedly pro-US and dominated by moderates."[155] Under Delphi advisors, Miguel Salazar was named CDJ president. Salazar at the same time held the post of PDC National Advisor. Another top CDJ leader was Sergio Molina, also a Christian Democratic activist and a personal advisor to Aylwin.

Young people were considered a strategic sector because the anti-Pinochet strategy devised by Chilean activists and US advisors was based on registering a vast bloc of the population to vote. Through a voter registration campaign, they hoped not only to assure a high turnout and an electoral victory, but also to reach a major portion of the population with the elite political message. "Among the nearly 5 million citizens who have not registered" of an estimated 8 million eligible voters in Chile, noted a 1988 NED document, "the CDJ estimates that sixty-five percent are between the ages of eighteen and twenty-eight, mostly from the poorer sectors of the population."[156] Thus a huge proportion of the electorate had reached maturity under the dictatorship, when politics was illegal and civil society suppressed. According to CDJ president Salazar, "we must do something to orient and channel the conduct and attitudes" of this youth generation. "The idea is to be able to make this new line of work [among youth] complementary to our other work in the doctrinaire and political areas."[157] The youth program implemented the multiplier method: 2,500 university, labor, peasant, and community youth leaders were trained by US advisors. "Each individual trained will reach an additional 15–30 young people over a two-year period," explained the NED.[158] The youth leaders were oriented, following their training, to liaison with the political parties that had signed the US-brokered National Accord.[159] The CDJ also established an "academic committee" to liaise with the political parties and the think-tanks being funded by Washington. The flood of literature and paraphernalia from the think-tanks, research centers, and publishing outlets thus supplied the US-funded civic groups with political orientation and materials to conduct their work.

The new modalities of US political intervention in Chile did not cease with "redemocratization" but shifted focus, from guiding a transition to further penetrating Chilean political and civil society and consolidating an emergent polyarchic system and elite hegemony. The same groups funded during the transition, many of them now in government, continued to receive political aid from Washington, and new programs focused on fine-tuning the mechanisms and institutions of Chilean polyarchy. As PDC leader Sergio Molina stated in a late 1989 report to the NED: "Now that the elections are over, what is needed is to provide for administrative functioning under the new institutionality, as regards the process of decision making and the system of relations between state powers, especially executive–legislative, and between the state and the social organizations and private entrepreneurs."[160] New programs in the early 1990s focused on strengthening the center and the right, fostering polyarchic political culture in the parties and civic groups, and maintaining consensus for the neo-liberal program.[161]

Conclusion: Neo-liberalism and polyarchy: the dialectics of transnational economics, politics, and social order

The changes in work patterns [resulting from economic restructuring] have had a significant impact on social relations... The fragmentation of the social relations of the workplace has obscured the sense of collective fate and identity among Chile's working class. The transformation of the workplace has been complemented by the transformation of the political system... The fragmentation of opposition communities has accomplished what brute military repression could not. It has transformed Chile, both culturally and politically, from a country of active, participatory grassroots communities, to a land of disconnected, apolitical individuals. The cumulative impact of this change is such that we are unlikely to see any concerted challenge to the current ideology in the near future.

Cathy Schneider, scholar on Chile[162]

As in the Philippines, Chileans were genuinely elated over the opportunity to rid themselves of a dictatorship. Participation in the NO campaign and the 1989 elections as a means of removing Pinochet was genuine and mass-based. But there are important differences between the two countries' democratization movements. By 1988 the anti-Pinochet forces were well organized, the hegemony of the elite opposition over the anti-dictatorial movement was already achieved, and the transition from authoritarianism to polyarchy was proceeding considerably more smoothly than in the Philippines. Yet in both countries there was a convergence between popular sectors, the left, the elite opposition, and US interests in getting rid of dictatorships, and simultaneously a contention between popular and elite alternatives to the authoritarian regime.

Through its ubiquitous and multi-layered intervention in Chilean society, ranging from influence over international lending agencies to state-to-state relations with the Pinochet regime, Ambassador Barnes's influential diplomatic activities inside Chile, political assistance and advisement of the opposition parties, and grassroots intervention in civil society, the United States was able to foster a well-oiled "democratization" machine that latched on to the Chilean masses' authentic democratic aspirations and helped to channel the entire process into an elite outcome. Protagonists of the new political intervention could boast of consecutive "success stories" in the Philippines and Chile. US intervention synchronized with internal Chilean factors and the macro-structural context described at the outset of this chapter to determine the outcome. US intervention in the transition must be seen as part of an uninterrupted process of intervention in Chile's internal political process over some twenty-five years that was crucial in shaping the dynamic of "democratization." Following the transition a torrent of academic works published in the United States on this "democratic miracle" argued that "democracy" had been successfully "restored" to Chile and that the United States played a remarkably constructive role – a position which has uncritically been taken for granted, indeed, a position which has achieved intellectual hegemony.[163]

Just as in the Philippines, the reach of the democratization process in Chile became severely curtailed, and was contained comfortably within the prevailing social order, as a result of the manner in which the anti-dictatorial movement unfolded. But unlike the Philippines, where left and popular sectors enjoyed sufficient strength and autonomy in the climax of the anti-Marcos movement and the first part of the Aquino administration to force the government to launch an authentic reform program (which was subsequently undermined), the new Chilean rulers were explicit in stating that there would be no fundamental changes in the socioeconomic order. The entire Chilean elite, historically divided over development models, had achieved consensus during the twenty-year overhaul of the Chilean economy and society in the context of globalization.

And as in the Philippines, the preservation of the repressive military apparatus and its impunity remained an instrument of blackmail against popular claims for deeper social transformations. Virtually all military institutions remained intact, Pinochet himself was scheduled

194

to remain the head of the armed forces until 1998, the constitution stipulated that the military appoint eight non-elected representatives to the Senate, and the Supreme Court upheld an amnesty for human rights violators decreed in 1978. Edgardo Boeninger, who helped design the elite democratization strategy through the NED-funded think-tanks and went on to become Aylwin's chief of staff, made clear: "Should a government attempt to make drastic changes in the socio-economic system – as was the case of Chile under Allende – the threatened sectors [that is: the dominant minority] will decide that democracy is no longer able to protect their basic values and interests. A 'coup mentality' is the likely result."[164] Such reasoning was shared by the entire coalition that backed Aylwin. Socialist deputy Camilo Escalona asserted: "We think... that the greatest threat to the democratic process isn't Pinochet. The greatest threat is that the people will not see its demands satisfied, that the people will be disenchanted with democracy, that millions of persons will turn their backs on the democratic process because it is not capable of responding to their enormous demands."[165] The "threat" to Chile's new "democracy" thus became, not the specter of a new coup by a privileged military caste, but potential demands by an impoverished majority for changes in the socioeconomic system that might improve their lot.

In his first year in office, Aylwin increased the military budget. In November 1990, the Bush administration lifted an earlier ban on the sale of military equipment to the Chilean armed forces and resumed military aid. An intact and autonomous military and security apparatus functioned to keep the left and popular forces in fear and in check in the post-transition period and to further circumscribe democratic participation. Human rights organizations reported a spate of continued violations despite the end of systematic repression.[166] As part of the "negotiated transition," the military and the incoming civilian government agreed that the military budget could not fall below the 1989 level of $1.4 billion out of a total of $7.7 billion. In 1989, the military budget was $432 million *higher* than the housing, health, and education budgets taken together.[167] By guaranteeing the military such huge resources, there was little surplus to attend to the pressing needs of the impoverished majority. Thus, even if the new government had the will to undertake basic social and economic reforms affecting wages, housing, health, and education, it could not do so without challenging the military's preeminent role in political life. Why the new civilian government remained so beholden to the military, beyond the latter's own threats, is explained by the dynamics of polyarchy and neo-liberalism.

Chile provides a clear example of the fusion of "promoting democracy" and promoting free markets in US foreign policy. Chile has been held up to the world as a model of "successful redemocratization" *and* as an "economic miracle" which demonstrates the virtues of global capitalism, from which other Third World countries should take inspiration. In this view, uncritically adopted by a host of academics, journalists, and policymakers, Pinochet is criticized for his authoritarianism but credited as a hero for the "economic success story," and "redemocratization," as a matter of course, meant a return to civilian rule without any change in the socioeconomic order. Alejandro Foxley, a leader of the elite opposition to Pinochet, declared following his appointment by Aylwin as the new finance minister: "A country shows maturity when it is capable of taking advantage of the positive experiences which others have implemented, even when one doesn't like the government which implemented these measures. I respect technically and professionally those who were in the previous government."[168]

However, a cursory empirical glance at the actual structure and performance of Chile's economy reveals the real "miracle" was (and continues to be) a "success story" for a minority of the Chilean upper and middle classes together with transnational capital operating in Chile's free-market environment, but a burden for the broad Chilean majority. The mass of Chileans have sunk into ever deeper impoverishment. What took place between 1973 and 1993 was a severe, and still continuing, *regression* in democratization of the economy and in the well-being of the mass of Chileans. During the military regime, poverty levels *increased by 100 percent*, and by 1990, 45 percent of the population were living in poverty.[169]

Petras and Vieux show that in four key areas touted as "success stories" – poverty management, growth, privatization, and debt management – Chile's performance under the dictatorship does not stand up to an empirical test. As for what neo-liberal jargon calls "poverty management," what took place in Chile was just that: *the management, not the decrease or elimination, of poverty*. As wealth continued to concentrate in the 1970s and 1980s, overall poverty levels increased. Real wages fell 40 percent during the first decade of military rule. By 1987, GDP per capita barely equaled that of 1970, while per capita consumption was actually 11 percent lower than the 1970 level.[170]

Contagious diseases spread as health expenditures fell from $29 per capita in 1973 to $11 in 1988. Typhoid cases, for instance, more than doubled between 1970 and 1983, and in the 1980s, Chile accounted for 20 percent of all reported cases of typhoid in Latin America. While 45 percent of the population dropped below the poverty line, nearly one million families were homeless out of a population of some twelve million people.[171] Modern shopping malls rivalling the most luxurious found in the developed countries sprang up in Santiago's plush upper-class neighborhoods in the 1980s and 1990s, at the same time as shantytowns spread like wildfire in the outskirts of the capital and other Chilean cities, fed by the growing army of those marginalized and excluded from the "miracle."

As for growth, GDP grew by an average of 3.9 percent in the period 1950–1972, dropped to 1.4 percent from 1974 to 1983, and averaged only 1.2 percent during the 1980s, the years of the alleged "miracle."[172] Moreover, given the cyclic nature of this growth, it being interrupted by several economic crashes, including a 1982 collapse which brought unemployment to over 30 percent and shrank the GDP by an incredible 14 percent, "these rates didn't contribute to growth at all, properly speaking, but to the recovery of previously achieved levels."[173] In another study, Chilean economist Pedro Vuskovic points out that economic growth rates between 1974 and 1989 were considerably below the overall Latin American average of 4 percent for this same period.[174] "Far from advancing," he notes, "Chile receded with respect to Latin America as a whole." Even if one were to disaggregate growth rates and point to high rates from the mid-1980s into the early 1990s, the more important question is not whether total output has increased, but what impact an increase in the total production of wealth has meant for the Chilean majority. Increased wealth has *not* meant an improvement in the living conditions for the majority – it has meant "poverty amidst plenty," has brought a concomitant increase in the drainage of wealth out of Chile, and a concentration of that wealth remaining in Chile into the hands of a minority.

Pinochet's regime's alleged dexterous "debt management" is based on its successful renegotiations in the late 1980s and on its perfect debt-servicing record. Chile's perfect record in its foreign debt-service payments is without doubt a "success story" for the international banks, which recover loans and earn interest, as is privatization for local investors and transnational capital. But the regime was forced to manage a debt which *it* accumulated in the first place, mostly to increase imports of consumer goods destined for luxury consumption under the neo-liberal lifting of trade controls, and which totalled $20 billion by late 1987, the *highest* per capita level in the world. Renegotiations amounted mostly to exchanging bilateral debts with commercial banks for new debt with multilateral lending institutions. Most important, debt-servicing has meant a permanent drainage from the country of whatever increased wealth was actually produced. In the late 1980s debt-servicing consumed a full 5 percent of the country's annual economic output. Compared with average annual growth in this period of 1.2 percent, we are left with a dramatic net outflow of wealth, well beyond new growth, as a result of debt-servicing.[175] Privatization has brought the government temporary and non-sustainable revenues, used mostly for debt-servicing, and at the same time has resulted in a dramatic concentration of capital and the transfer of a huge portion of the Chilean economy from local hands to transnational capital. The much-touted inflow of foreign investment in the 1980s did not constitute, in its majority, new productive investments, but foreign purchases of existing Chilean assets through debt conversion programs.[176] The bulk of productive foreign investment which did enter the country was in the form of agri-business, which accelerated a process of proletarianization of the Chilean peasantry and increased urban and rural unemployment.[177]

The "miracle" involved the successful rearticulation of Chile to the world market, and a dramatic expansion of exports, at a time when the global economy was emerging. Exports as a proportion of GDP soared from 19 to 32 percent from 1984 to 1988,[178] due to a pattern of dynamic growth confined to a narrow range of "non-traditional" primary goods exports, particularly seafoods, timber, and fruits, which, together with the traditional mining sector, accounted for nearly 90 percent of exports.[179] Historic dependence on primary exports has dramatically increased in an entirely unsustainable model. Overexploitation of maritime resources, which are expected to be depleted by the next century, has already led to the extinction of several marine species. As timber reserves become depleted, overexploitation has triggered an ecological disaster – rapid soil depletion, a decrease in precipitation, and an incipient process of desertification. Moreover, given heavy foreign participation, much of the wealth produced in these dynamic export sectors is sent abroad through profit remittance. By way of example, two-thirds of the increase in export earnings produced in 1990 was transferred abroad (of that remaining in Chile, 85 percent corresponded to capital profits and only 15 percent to that retained by the wage sector).[180]

This is a general Latin American pattern – a crucial point simply ignored by the proponents of neo-liberalism, yet one which belies the very basis for legitimizing the model. Both the volume and the value of Latin American exports grew in the 1980s and early 1990s – a central goal of restructuring – yet these "gains" merely resulted in net capital transfers abroad in the form of debt servicing and profit remittances. Benefits from the generation of greater surplus as a result of increased production for export are canceled out by the permanent drainage of surplus from Latin America. Pointing to increased export-oriented production as an isolated variable therefore conceals the reproduction, and *intensification*, of relations of dependence and domination and of real social inequalities. The Chilean "success story" also includes macro-economic equilibrium (low inflation, balanced budgets, stable and "realistic" exchange rates, etc.) – another factor which, when seen as a variable isolated from a larger totality, serves to mystify real relations of domination and inequalities. The importance of equilibrium is contingent and relative to concrete interests. It is a "success" to the extent that it provides transnational capital with the stability required for its incessant and diverse operations within and between nations, and thus helps reproduce and stabilize patterns of capital accumulation whose immanent outcome is the polarization and concentration of wealth and of political power that wealth yields. Macro-economic stability, in itself, tells us nothing about the actual well-being of the broad majorities in Chile and in the Third World. In short, success and failure are not mutually exclusive; some have benefitted and many have lost out from Chile's neo-liberal program.

Chile's new polyarchic rulers were, if anything, more committed than their authoritarian predecessors to neo-liberalism. The new regime declared that its mission was to continue neo-liberal restructuring under "democratic" managers. "The main economic challenge facing Chile is to consolidate and expand its integration into the world economy," explained Boeninger.[181] Social unrest is the objective consequence of the anti-popular character of the model. Thus there is more behind the new civilian regime's relation to the military than a delicate effort to consolidate the "transition to democracy." As Petras and Vieux note: "Managing the model also means taking political responsibility for defending it with the armed power of the state. This is a task the Aylwin government has equipped itself to face, in part by increasing the Carabineros [militarized police] by 4,400 slots... It also reflected a long term commitment by the Aylwin government to expand the size and better equip the national and political police, who were also carefully nurtured during the dictatorship."[182] By the early 1990s, Aylwin's honeymoon was over and a new cycle of strikes, popular protests and government repression had set in – hegemony remained consensus protected by the "armor of coercion."

Transnational economics and transnational politics converged as a new hegemonic bloc was forged in Chile through a "transition to democracy." The achievement of center and right consensus around a free-market economy overcame the historic split in the dominant groups between two alternative strategies, one of free-market, externally linked development (the right's historic program), and the other of nationally oriented dependent capitalist development with a measure of state intervention (the centrists' historic program). These different strategies had, in the past, resulted in different political programs and in elite splits that opened space for the left. The unification of elite criteria over the country's economic model, linked to the global economy and the reconfiguration of Chile's dominant groups, thus also resolved the political stumbling bloc, or "fluke," of the Chilean political system. The neo-liberal model of structural adjustment as the "grease" for the operation of the global economy leaves little room for maneuver or for minor alterations. The constraints it has imposed on Chile, with its concomitant implications for the political system, go beyond the control of local Chilean sectors, whether dominant or subordinate. What is required is the development of strategic alternatives in the interests of, and implemented by, broad majorities who have gained hegemony in a transnational setting.

5　Nicaragua: From low-intensity warfare to low-intensity democracy

> Preventive diplomacy and preemptive reform can reduce the risks of extremist political infection and radical contamination. When confronted with such situations, the United States must define its interests early on and then develop strategies in cooperation with regional friends that will promote the likelihood of peaceful change and successor governments compatible with our own.
>
> Henry Kissinger and Cyrus Vance[1]

> Washington believes that Nicaragua must serve as a warning to the rest of Central America to never again challenge US hegemony, because of the enormous economic and political costs. It's too bad that the [Nicaraguan] poor must suffer, but historically the poor have always suffered. Nicaragua must be a lesson to others.
>
> Richard John Neuhaus[2]

Preventative diplomacy and preemptive reform

In May 1989, on the eve of the opening of the Nicaraguan electoral process, one of President Bush's national security advisors observed: "Since Manila, the United States has gotten into this; we have been brandishing this new tool of giving support to electoral processes. The Plebiscite in Chile was analogous, where we saw we could shake an entrenched regime by [getting involved in] elections... We are learning these techniques, and they should be applied to Nicaragua."[3]

In the Philippines and Chile, the United States applied "preventive diplomacy and preemptive reform" as part of shifts in policy to "democracy promotion." The shift and the concomitant introduction of new forms of political intervention came precisely when society-wide anti-dictatorial movements were reaching a critical mass under the leadership of *popular* forces. The objective of US intervention moved from trying to shore up these crumbling dictatorships to seizing the initiative from popular leadership and aiding the local elite in an effort to redirect anti-dictatorial movements.

As in the Philippines and Chile, the United States had exercised its domination over Nicaragua through authoritarian arrangements for nearly half a century. The Somoza dictatorship was the amalgamated product of US domination and the structure of social classes and elite rule since that country's independence from Spain in 1821. As in the Philippines and Chile, Washington undertook preventative diplomacy and preemptive reform in Nicaragua as the Somoza dictatorship crumbled in the late 1970s. Here, however, the effort failed and popular forces seized and retained leadership of the anti-dictatorial movement. The triumph of a popular revolution in 1979 led the United States to launch its "undeclared" war against Nicaragua in an effort to destabilize the new government and restore the old elite to power.

US strategy towards Nicaragua from the 1970s into the 1990s can be divided into several successive phases: (1) efforts throughout the 1970s to prop up the Somoza dictatorship via military, economic, diplomatic, and other forms of support (2) an unsuccessful undertaking, after the dictatorship had entered into an irreversible crisis, in preventative diplomacy and preemptive reform (3) a strategy of destabilization following the 1979 revolution, culminating in political intervention in the 1988–1990 electoral process under the banner of "democracy promotion," and (4) consolidating a transition from popular democratization to polyarchy and neo-liberalism following the 1990 electoral defeat of the Sandinistas.

All four of these phases are linked to each other in a process that flowed from policy reorientations underway in Washington in the wake of the US defeat in Indochina. The "democracy promotion" programs were not a departure from, but an integral part of, the war launched in 1980. This demonstrates that "democracy promotion" and other less "benign" forms of US intervention, such as military aggression, are not exclusive; they are complementary and mutually reinforcing. If the destabilization campaign was intended to destroy the Sandinista experiment in popular democracy, electoral intervention from 1988 to 1990 was designed to facilitate a transition to a regime of "low-intensity democracy." Both were phases in a single strategy, involving the defeat at the polls of the Sandinista National Liberation Front (FSLN) in February 1990 and subsequent undertakings to construct a neo-liberal state and reconstitute an elite social order. US involvement in Nicaragua in the 1970s and 1980s was crucial in shaping the transnational shift from authoritarian to polyarchic systems of social control. Nicaragua has been and remains a laboratory for the new political intervention and a battleground in the struggle for hegemony, and thus sheds a great deal of light on the theoretical issues at hand.

From US filibusters and marine occupations to the Somoza dynasty: Nicaragua's strategic importance

When the Monroe Doctrine staked out the US claim to the Western Hemisphere in 1823, top in the minds of statesmen was the strategic importance of the Caribbean Basin for eventual empire-building. With its system of rivers and inland lakes, only twelve miles of land in Nicaragua separate the Atlantic and Pacific oceans. The country was therefore strategically located for an inter-oceanic canal. By linking the two oceans, such a canal would provide a crucial worldwide commercial advantage to that capitalist power that controlled Nicaragua. Christopher Columbus, it should be recalled, had set out from Spain not to "discover" the New World but to find a passage from the West to the Orient. On his last voyage, he spent three weeks exploring the Atlantic coast of Nicaragua. He was followed by the *conquistador* Gil Gonzáles de Dávila, whose forces killed thousands of Indians in pacification and colonization campaigns in Nicaragua and sent another 500,000 to other parts of the Spanish empire as slaves.[4]

Under colonial rule, Nicaragua became a stagnant tributary of Spanish mercantilism, based on the *encomienda* system, in which land and Indian labor were parceled out to the *conquistadores*. The history of Nicaragua from independence in 1821 to the 1930s is a story of endless feuds, intrigues, civil wars, temporary truces, and pacts, between the two rival groups that took over from Spanish administrators, Liberals and Conservatives. This conflict originated less in strategic or ideological differences than in rivalries among networks of extended oligarchic families, descendants of the original *conquistadores*, and their tussle for control of a central government and the spoils that this provided.[5] This endemic infighting made impossible in Nicaragua the development of a viable polyarchic system among the ruling class, such as had developed in Chile on the basis of a more united post-independence creole elite. The weakness of Nicaragua's post-independence ruling class lent itself to manipulations and rivalry by Great Powers. Reciprocally, elements of the Nicaraguan elite were eager to seek the intervention of outside agents, mostly from the United States, to shift the balance of power within Nicaragua. Louis Napoleon once claimed Nicaragua for the construction of a French canal,[6] but it was Britain and the United States that competed for domination over the country. With the US annexation of the northern half of Mexico in 1848, expansion westward was now contained by the Pacific Ocean, and increasing commercial interest in Asia made the construction of an inter-oceanic canal in Central America a US imperative.

Cornelius Vanderbilt, one of the richest men in the United States, had set up the Nicaragua Transit Company to shuttle California gold-rushers from the US East Coast to the West Coast via Nicaragua, and simultaneously to explore the possibilities of constructing a canal. In 1855, the US filibuster William Walker, bankrolled by Vanderbilt's Transit Company and invited by Nicaraguan Liberals in their latest civil war with the Conservatives, landed on Nicaraguan shores at the head of a mercenary army. Over the next two years, Walker and his mercenary forces, supported by the southern slave aristocracy as well as northern merchants and admiring politicians in the United States, turned against both Liberals and Conservatives to conquer the country. Walker had himself "elected" President of Nicaragua, declared English an official language, reinstituted slavery, and took measures to expropriate and transfer to US planters and settlers large portions of Nicaraguan land. Almost overnight, Walker became the agent of Manifest Destiny in the region. His regime was recognized by the administration of President Franklin Pierce. And when the mercenary was finally rooted from the country by a combined Central American patriotic army (at the cost of 20,000 Central American lives), he was rescued by the US Navy, given a hero's welcome upon his arrival in New York, idolized by the press, and then received at the White House by President James Buchanan.

Meanwhile, the completion of the transcontinental railway in 1869 ended interest in overland passenger transit through Nicaragua. But plans for a canal were resumed in the aftermath of the US Civil War. With rapid industrialization, the growth of global commerce, and large-scale penetration of the Caribbean by US capital, the main interest of the post-Civil War class of wealthy US merchants, industrialists, and reborn planters lay in the competitive advantage that a base in the Caribbean would provide. The centerpiece of a new expansionist foreign policy was the construction of a canal across the Isthmus. The canal was eventually constructed in Panama, a shift due in large part to the maneuvering by the pro-Panama lobby among business and political interests in Washington. But it also had to do with Great Power rivalry, and with the rise in Nicaragua of a nationalist regime, headed by Liberal president José Santos Zelaya, who sought a greater measure of sovereignty and modernization for the country in the face of foreign domination. Zelaya took measures to bring Nicaragua into the modern capitalist era, including curbing clericalism, expanding public education and opening it to the lower classes for the first time, modernizing and professionalizing public administration and the military, and improving infrastructure. Most importantly, he wrested from the British dominion over the Atlantic coast region, in this way unifying the country for the first time since independence and also, as an unintentional side-effect, putting an end to US–British rivalry and sealing US domination. Zelaya was no radical; these measures spurred on a nascent process of proletarianization and capitalist production relations, benefitting Nicaraguan as well as foreign capital, which was now pouring into the country as part of the large-scale export of US capital into the Caribbean.[7]

Zelaya, however, went too far in asserting Nicaraguan sovereignty and nationalist interests over US prerogative. "Nothing effective... can be accomplished in accordance with our policy of friendly guidance of the Central American Republics as long as Zelaya remains in absolute power," wrote US minister to Nicaragua John Coolidge to President Roosevelt in 1908, adding that the ouster of Zelaya would also have a "salutary effect" on the isthmanian countries in demonstrating US resolve.[8] In his correspondence, Coolidge said that Zelaya's plans, such as establishing a chemical laboratory to analyze and regulate imported US foodstuffs and medicines, imposing tariffs on US and other foreign imports, contracting with a German company to build an Atlantic–Pacific railway line, and the rumored offering of canal concessions to Britain and Japan, all violated the Monroe Doctrine. A year later, Conservative leaders, bankrolled by US companies in Nicaragua, aided by foreign, mostly US, mercenaries, and enjoying the tacit support of the incoming Taft administration, launched an armed revolt against Zelaya. The two leaders of the Conservative uprising were Emiliano Chamorro and Adolfo Díaz, both members of powerful oligarchic families and agents for leading US firms in the country. In December

1909, US Secretary of State Philader Chase Knox, who held shares in several of these firms, sent a letter to Zelaya, known as the Knox Note, which severed diplomatic relations with Nicargua and called on Zelaya to resign. Although Zelaya bowed to this US hostility, marines nevertheless landed in the country under order to oppose any attempts by Zelaya loyalists to resist. With that, the Zelaya forces relinquished the presidency to Adolfo Díaz, and Nicaragua was plunged into another round of debilitating Liberal–Conservative civil wars.

The overthrow of Zelaya strengthened an internal social and class structure propitious to US penetration and domination, yet highly detrimental to Nicaragua's own national development. The Zelaya era represented a belated attempt at nation-building, including the beginning of a modern, national consciousness that included both elites and the Indian and mestizo masses. By stifling a nationalist-oriented bourgeoisie and fomenting for its own purposes the divisions that had plagued the dominant groups since independence, Washington contibuted in a decisive manner to a truncated elite and to a process of dependent capitalist development in Nicaragua. Both the Walker affair and Zelaya's overthrow underscored the essential dynamics in US–Nicaraguan relations. The fragmentation and weakness of the elite in Nicaragua called forth US intervention as much as the US intervention – serving the immediate interests of sectors of the dominant classes in both countries – aggravated this fragmentation and weakness.

The Conservative oligarchs that replaced Zelaya achieved recognition from Washington in exchange for the dismantling of many of Zelaya's nationalist reforms, including the promulgation of a new constitution that "guaranteed the legitimate rights of foreigners," the placing of Nicaragua's customs in US receivership, and the turning-over of Nicaragua's central bank, railroads and steamships to US corporations. In 1917, a High Commission was established, composed of one Nicaraguan and two US citizens appointed by the Secretary of State, to supervise the entire financial life of the republic and arbitrate in all political matters. While Nicaraguan presidents rotated in and out of office, this High Commission virtually governed the country until the mid-1920s.

Meanwhile, US marines returned in 1912, and stayed on as an occupation force almost continuously for the next two decades. No fewer than ten uprisings were suppressed by the marines between 1912 and 1924, and Nicaragua remained under martial law for virtually this entire period. The country's first modern labor unions also emerged, and strike activity spread on US-owned mining, lumbering, and banana operations. Inter-elite feuding gradually give way to mass agitation against US domination and the wholesale giveaway of the country. Both Washington and the Liberal and Conservative oligarchs began, for the first time, to feel the heat of nationalist popular sentiment and social stirrings from below.

The backdrop to the US marines' occupation was the importance of the Caribbean Basin as the most proximate overseas market and outlet for surplus US capital. Opening up the "Yankee lake" required direct military interventions, including a series of expeditions by marines in Nicaragua, the Dominican Republic, Haiti, Cuba, Panama, Honduras, Puerto Rico, Mexico, and elsewhere. This, President Teddy Roosevelt's doctrine of the "Big Stick," was followed by President William Taft's doctrine of "Dollar Diplomacy." Expanding US interests and establishing protectorates required political stability in its "strategic backyard," which was to be achieved through President Woodrow Wilson's "civilizing mission." This early twentieth-century attempt to construct quasi-polyarchic political systems in the region via elite pacts aimed to achieve political stability can be considered an historical predecessor to "democracy promotion." However, these earlier efforts focused exclusively on achieving accommodation among elites in political society, while masses were either ignored or repressed outright by occupying US marines. In contrast, the current strategy focuses on achieving – parallel to elite accommodation – the organization of the popular sectors in civil society and their incorporation into hegemonic blocs.

Wilson dispatched US envoys who, with military and financial muscle firmly behind them, "offered" their good offices to mediate disputes, arrange truces, forge pacts, and hammer together elite coalitions around US-managed elections. It was in this context that Washington organized a spate of "elections" in Nicaragua over the next few years, which rotated rival Liberal and Conservative factions in and out of power, all under marine occupation and the supervision of US ministers. These elections were not intended as exercises in democracy. In the 1913 balloting, for instance, which placed Adolfo Díaz in the presidency after marines had crushed an anti-United States rebellion, all those who supported the uprising were disenfranchised, US marines manned polling places and counted the votes, and there was but one candidate – Díaz himself. All told, only 3–4,000 people were allowed to vote, yet Secretary of State Knox immediately recognized the results and expressed US satisfaction. The purpose of these charades was strictly to hammer out accommodations among the elite factions and to simultaneously legitimize rapidly expanding US control over the country. The US occupation forces organized subsequent elections in 1916, 1920, 1924, 1928, and 1932.[9]

From the Sandino rebellion to the Somoza dictatorship

In early 1926, Liberal–Conservative feuding broke out into civil war again, prompting a new US military intervention and another round of Liberal–Conservative mediation, this time by President Calvin Coolidge's special envoy, Henry Stimpson. In 1927, Stimpson organized a pact between the two bands, according to which the rebellious Liberals would surrender their weapons to US forces and partake with Conservatives in new elections in 1928. The only Liberal general to reject the pact was Agusto César Sandino, who declared that his troops would continue to fight until the marines were expelled and US interference in the country brought to an end. In this way, Sandino converted what started out as just one more feud among the ruling cliques into a national rebellion against US domination, in defiance of both the local elite and Washington.[10] Sandino's struggle inspired, and was supported by, many members of the lower classes, whose fight became a popular national movement incorporating peasants, miners, workers, and artisans. Over the following six years, Sandino waged a guerrilla resistance movement against US marines, who launched Washington's first counterinsurgency war in the Hemisphere.

In 1929, Sandino publicized a peace proposal, in which the Sandinistas promised to lay down their weapons and recognize the government installed by Stimpson and the marines in 1928 in exchange for a series of social reforms, including measures to favor small peasants, an eight-hour work day for all workers, abolition of wage payments in scrip, equal pay for equal work for women, the regulation of child labor, and the recognition of workers' rights to organize. "Only the workers and peasants will go all the way, only their organized force will attain victory," concluded the declaration. The entire focus in Nicaragua had shifted from the search for forumulas to end intra-elite conflict to a contest between the elite and the country's emergent popular sectors. US Chargé Willard Beaulac cabled to Washington his "fear that the movement has attained a revolutionary character."[11]

Sandino's movement never managed to change the social system, but it did force the marines to withdraw in 1933. In their place, they left behind a new Nicaraguan military force, the National Guard, which was first set up in 1927 under the command of US officers. The newly created National Guard went on to become an effective instrument for safeguarding the elite social order in Nicaragua, and the represssive and despised mainstay of the Somoza dictatorship.[12] Anastasio Somoza Garcia, who had been the personal interpreter for several US envoys, maneuvered his way into the position of Guard commander. From his new position, Somoza personally ordered the execution in early 1934 of Sandino, who had come to Managua for further peace talks, in a crime which might have involved the US embassy.[13] Two years later, Somoza overthrew the civilian government and then had himself elected "president" in a fraudulent vote – one of a spate of such electoral farces conducted over the next forty-five years. Neither the coup nor the fraudulent elections produced many objections in Good Neighbor Washington. The dictator was recognized by President Franklin Roosevelt, who received Somoza personally in a pompous state visit in 1939. The dynasty continued to rule for nearly half a century, with US support, until it was overthrown in 1979 by the Sandinista movement.[14]

The collapse of the Wilsonian project in Nicaragua is particularly important because it came through a mass, popular rebellion from below. Sandino's rebellion was largely responsible for an entire rethinking of US policy in Latin America. Sandino's threat from below demonstrated to Nicaragua's dominant groups that the very survival of elite rule depended on a united effort to subdue the popular classes. It thus forged a collective class consciousness among the elite for the first time, demonstrating vividly how class formation and historical outcomes are as much a result of class conflict between subordinate and dominant classes as they are of intra-elite conflict among dominant classes. After a century of internecine feuding, the dominant groups finally subordinated their squabbles to their common self-interests in the face of the poor and newly awakened majority, and entrusted the Somoza dictatorship and the National Guard with safeguarding the social order as a whole. This intra-elite accommodation converged remarkably with conclusions being reached at the time by Washington. In a 1930 report summarizing policy options for Nicaragua, the State

Department concluded that a dictatorship would be the most expedient means of securing the long-sought stability: "The third alternative [that which was adopted among several policy options] is a policy whereby the United States would merely guarantee stability in Nicaragua, regardless of whether this involved the maintenance of unrepresentative or dictatorial government... This policy would have the merit of simplicity – it would be the easiest policy for the United States to apply."[15]

Over the next half-century, Washington shored up the Somoza family dictatorship through military and economic aid and a close diplomatic alliance. Nicaragua became the bastion of US domination throughout the Caribbean Basin. The country was a launching pad for the 1954 CIA-organized *coup d'état* in Guatemala and for the aborted 1961 Bay of Pigs invasion of Cuba. Despite the democratic rhetoric of the Alliance for Progress, Somoza enjoyed the support of the Kennedy White House, which provided $30 million in Alliance economic funds and military aid while counseling the dictator to "legitimize his government by receiving a clear popular mandate" through another round of fraudulent elections, held in 1962.[16] Between 1946 and 1978, Nicaragua received $23.6 million in military aid for the National Guard and thousands of Guardsmen passed through US military training programs. No other country in Latin America had so many of its troops trained by the Pentagon.[17]

The Somoza family dictatorship created a hospitable environment for the Nicaraguan elite and for foreign capital, while US policymakers found an ideal ally in the dictatorship. Just as with Marcos, this was a fractious three-way marriage of convenience. Much of the elite shunned the dictatorship but was indebted to it for its containment of the popular threat. The Somozas and Washington policymakers manipulated each other at different moments and for each one's convenience. Yet all three – dictatorship, the elite, and Washington – found a common meeting ground in defense of the social order. The historical function of the dictatorship was the exercise of local state power on behalf of the alliance between the dominant groups in Nicaragua and the United States.

During the post-World War II years, the large-scale penetration of US capital firmly tied Nicaragua's economy, along with the rest of Central America, into the US economy as an appendage based on agro-exports, and it led to massive displacement of the peasantry and local artisanal production.[18] The inflow of foreign capital to Central America accelerated in the 1960s and 1970s, integrating the region into the emergent global economy and laying the structural basis for the social upheavals that shook the Isthmus. The stimulation of agro-exports by the United States produced in Nicaragua one of the most extreme concentrations of land and wealth in the world. In 1978, some 50 percent of all arable land was owned by just 0.7 percent of the population, while more than half of the rural population was crammed onto just 2.1 percent of the land. Per capita income was less than $805 for 80 percent of the population. For two-thirds of these, it was a mere $286.[19] Gross inequalities, poverty, and political repression spawned a growing popular movement in the 1960s and 1970s. In 1961, several survivors of Sandino's army and a younger generation of Somoza opponents had formed the FSLN, which conducted sporadic guerrilla actions in the 1960s but was largely contained with the help of US counterinsurgency assistance. But by the early 1970s, a restive population began to turn to the Sandinistas for alternatives, as the FSLN stepped up its rural and urban organizing.

The failure of preventative diplomacy and preemptive reform in Nicaragua

[What is] at stake is not just the formula for Nicaragua, but a more basic matter, namely whether in the wake of our own decision not to intervene in Latin American politics, there will not develop a vacuum... In other words, we have to demonstrate that we are still the decisive force in determining the political outcomes in Central America...

Zbigniew Brzezinski, addressing an emergency 1979 NSC meeting on an imminent Sandinista victory[20]

The Christmas Eve earthquake that leveled Managua in 1972 marked the beginning of the end of the dictatorship. It simultaneously shattered elite consensus around the dictatorship and accelerated the process of social polarization and political radicalization among the popular sectors. Following the earthquake the Somoza clique, through its control of the state and the National Guard, monopolized the massive reconstruction assistance that poured in from abroad. With its rampant corruption and patronage networks, the dynasty implemented the same brand of "crony capitalism" that Marcos had practiced in the Philippines, locking much of the capitalist class out of the reconstruction bonanza and unraveling the basis of accommodation among the dominant groups. At the same time, the earthquake considerably heightened the hardships endured by the poor majority. The FSLN grew from a sporadic insurgency to a national force, and Somoza responded with a wave of repression, imposing a state of siege, rounding up hundreds of opponents, and launching new counterinsurgency campaigns. International human rights groups, US congressional committees, and religious representatives in Nicaragua denounced before the world systematic and widespread tortures, rapes, and disappearances. The crisis of the dictatorship had become irreversible, but it was not until 1977 that Washington ceased to view authoritarianism and its agent in Nicaragua – the Somozas – as the best instrument of US domination. This led to an initial schism between a growing anti-Somoza faction of the elite and the United States. The lack of support from Washington for the anti-Somoza elite paved the way for an incipient alliance between the Nicaraguan elite and the popular forces, led by the Sandinistas, in a situation remarkably similar to the Philippines in the early 1980s. On this basis, a sector of the elite acknowledged Sandinista legitimacy (and even leadership), thus helping to undercut the effort, when it was finally launched by Washington, at preventative diplomacy and preemptive reform.

The elite found itself caught between a mass movement that was threatening the entire structure of domination and a dictatorship which was no longer capable either of representing its interests or of holding back the popular upsurge.[21] The anti-Somoza elite turned to political organizing, forming several new business, civic, and political associations. "The dominant classes," wrote FSLN leader Jaime Wheelock in 1983, "began the task of seeking a substitute, [which] appeared as a struggle against Somocismo when in reality it was an effort to sustain Somocismo without Somoza."[22] Thus throughout the 1970s, two anti-Somoza blocs coalesced: one was the conservative opposition; the other was the popular movement, led by the FSLN and by trade union, peasant, and other grassroot organizations. In October 1977 the FSLN launched its general offensive, with widespread popular backing. It became clear that Somoza's ouster was only a matter of time; in dispute was who would hold the reins of the anti-dictatorial movement and what would follow the fall of the regime. This struggle was fought out during 1978.[23] In January of that year, Pedro Joaquín Chamorro, the most prominent member of the elite opposition, was gunned down by Somoza henchmen as he drove to work. Just as with the Aquino murder in the Philippines five years later, the Chamorro assassination galvanized the non-Somoza political and economic elite. But in distinction to the Philippines, the poor and popular sectors, considerably unified around the FSLN, held the initiative. By 1978, these events prompted US policymakers to switch policies, to a strategy of encouraging a dialog between Somoza and the conservative opposition as the first step in its effort to mediate a gradual transfer of power from Somoza to his elite opponents, and to preserve the National Guard as an institution so as to prevent a popular Sandinista victory.

In February 1978, the business community called its own general strike, hedging its bets on the judicious use of carefully controlled mass mobilization. The strike was broadly supported by workers (managers even payed their wages during the strike) as part of their own anti-Somoza struggle. But Somoza refused to budge. In May, the Carter administration released $12 million in economic aid to Somoza as a carrot, simultaneously urging the dictator to negotiate with his elite opponents. In August 1978, Assistant Secretary of State Vyron Vaky recommended, in the first meeting of a special interagency group set up in the NSC to address the mounting Nicaraguan crisis, that the United States assemble a coalition government in Nicaragua. Vaky feared that "otherwise, the situation would polarize even further, increasing the probability of a Marxist victory."[24] Just days later, a Sandinista command dressed in National Guard uniforms seized the National Palace in downtown Managua and took Assembly members hostage. With world attention riveted on Nicaragua, Somoza was forced to cede to the insurgents' demands, including a release of political prisoners and safe passage out of the country for the command. The daring action sparked nationwide protests. Opposition leaders declared a national strike, and spontaneous insurrections erupted throughout the country. These events proved the decisive point at which the anti-dictatorial movement passed fully under the leadership of the FSLN.

With Nicaragua in insurrection, Congress approved $3.1 million in new military aid to Somoza. Although this and subsequent military aid was conditioned on an improvement in the human rights situation in Nicaragua, the military pipeline from Washington stayed open from then until Somoza's final days.[25] Behind this seemingly incoherent US policy was a touch-and-go game. Washington needed to maintain the National Guard to prevent a Sandinista victory, yet also needed to place enough pressure on Somoza to force him to relinquish power to the elite opposition. With the September insurrection suppressed, Carter's special envoy to Nicaragua, William Bowdler, arrived in Managua in October under instructions to facilitate a transition that would preserve the National Guard. In a remarkable replay of Stimson's mission fifty years earlier, Bowdler was sent to defuse a popular rebellion and organize an elite pact. "If the Guard collapsed as a result of US pressure, the United States would be responsible for eliminating the only barrier to a Sandinista military victory, or it would have to intervene militarily to prevent that," explained Robert Pastor, a member of the special NSC group. The administration "emphasized again that the unity of the Guard was an important objective for US policy. There was no disagreement [in Washington] on this latter point as everyone recognized that a post-Somoza government that lacked a firm military base could be overrun by the FSLN."[26]

Working now in day-by-day coordination, Washington and the elite tried desperately to regain the initiative, but ultimately failed. In February 1979, the elite called another general strike, intended specifically to pressure Somoza to resign. Its failure led to a last-ditch effort to prevent a revolutionary triumph through closed-door US-brokered negotiations between elite opposition leaders and Somoza over the dictator's departure. As an incentive, US officials approved, in May 1979, a $65.6 million emergency IMF loan to the disintegrating regime.[27] Carter's NSC group also drew up a series of contingency plans, including an attempt to have the OAS endorse a US-led military intervention, all to no avail. In June the FSLN, which had now achieved a true Gramscian hegemony among the Nicaraguan population in their anti-dictatorial struggle and recognition in the international community as the legitimate alternative to Somoza, launched the "final insurrection" against the dictatorship. The US-brokered negotiations between Somoza and the elite collapsed and most of the elite watched the final act of the liberation war from the sidelines – from Miami, Caracas, and other Latin American capitals.

All these Carter administration efforts to maintain a "Somocismo without Somoza" and to preserve the brutal National Guard appear on the surface as contradictory to Carter's stated "human rights policy." But they should be seen as part of a logical and consistent strategy of preventative diplomacy and preemptive reform. It was clear that Carter's "human rights policy" was a precursor to the full-blown "democracy promotion" strategy that emerged a decade later. The policy sought to regenerate ideologically US interventionism (albeit in new forms) following its post-Vietnam delegitimation and to imbue the embryotic transnational elite agenda with moral purpose. Much later, in early 1994, US Assistant Secretary of State Alexander Watson, explained: "Human rights was the big task of the 1970s, elections was the task of the 1980s, and in the 1990s the big task is... making democracy work."[28]

Why, then, did the administration's efforts to effect a transition fail? They failed, in part, for historic reasons – the deep historical weakness of the elite, its half-century-long reliance on dictatorship, and the hegemony won by the FSLN through its own deft revolutionary strategy. But they also failed because they were based on traditional interventionist tactics, principally state-to-state diplomacy, military and economic aid as carrots and sticks, and *repression*, rather than *incorporation*, of the mass of the population. The Nicaraguan revolution began to brew a decade before the change in Washington from promoting authoritarianism to promoting polyarchy, and before the machinery and institutions of the new political intervention could actually have been mobilized to facilitate a transition. The ingredient that led to success in the 1980s in the Philippines and Chile, but which was lacking in Nicaragua in the 1970s, was a sophisticated program of political aid and intervention that could have cultivated a polyarchic alternative to the Somoza regime and incorporated the popular sectors under the hegemony of this alternative. The option of a non-Somocista "Third Force" strong enough to achieve hegemony over a transition prrocess was simply non-existent. This weapon of political intervention was missing from the US arsenal, and together with the general post-Vietnam weakness of US interventionism, created sufficient space for the Sandinista victory – a momentary political "opening" in the world system for the Nicaraguan revolutionaries.

From Somoza to the Sandinistas: low-intensity warfare against high-intensity democracy

The Sandinista revolution ushered in a socialist-oriented program along the lines of the model of popular democracy and the "logic of the poor majority." The redistribution of economic and political power challenged not only the legitimacy of the old elite but of US domination in the region. The structure of property ownership was radically democratized in favor of poor peasants in the countryside and the urban poor.[29] The Sandinista experiment in "high-intensity democracy" combined representative with participatory democracy, and was as different from polyarchy as it was from Soviet-style bureaucratic "socialism."[30] The constitution drafted in the mid-1980s provided traditional political rights and civil liberties, such as freedom of speech, assembly, and movement, and the right to due process. It legally proscribed racial, ethnic, religious, and sexual discrimination, established the traditional separation of powers in a presidential system, and mandated national elections every six years, thus establishing the alternatability of power. But it also included economic, social, and cultural rights – e.g., health care, education, agrarian reform, decent housing, women's emancipation, a healthy environment – as constitutional rights in themselves, restricted only by the material limits of society. The document stated that "the basic needs of the poor have a prior claim on scarce resources in relation to the wants of those whose basic needs are already satisfied." It enshrined the structures of participatory democracy alongside representative democracy, mandating that the population has the right, and the duty, to participate in decision-making at all levels of society. At the theoretical level, this model overcame the "liberty versus equality" divide by institutionalizing the structures of representative democracy *alongside* those of participatory democracy. In contrast to other revolutionary parties that came to power through arms, the FSLN institutionalized the election of national authorities in multi-party, periodic, secret elections. The first of these competitive elections was held in 1984, with the participation of seven parties from the left, center, and right, and the next one was scheduled for 1990. The 1984 elections were won by the FSLN and judged to be free and fair by the international community, despite Washington's decision to encourage a boycott among its Nicaraguan allies and not to recognize the results.[31]

With the revolution, the Nicaraguan majority became organized, from civil society, in mass organizations, trade unions, and peasant, women, student, and neighborhood associations of all kinds. The "subaltern classes" began to participate in local and state decision-making through numerous formal and informal mechanisms and structures, in a manner envisioned by Gramsci, and in conjunction with the structural transformations of the state, the political system, and the economy. Nicaraguans for the first time began to gain some real control over their lives and their destiny, a sensation probably not

216

that different to what traditional ruling classes are accustomed to feeling. "Despite the poverty of democratic examples in both the capitalist West and socialist East, Nicaragua had set about the process of constructing real democracy within a socialist state," note political scientists Harry Vanden and Gary Prevost. "The Sandinista revolution had rediscovered Nicaragua's popular history and thus its popular consciousness; it had indeed unleashed the power of the masses. Unlike other revolutionary experiences, there was enough understanding among the Sandinistas, members of the popular church, Nicaraguan and internationalist youth, and others involved with the revolutionary process to set up institutional structures that included and channeled mass participation."[32]

To be sure, there were limitations in democratization and legitimate grievances under the revolutionary government, and the Sandinistas committed numerous mistakes while in power. As in the Philippines and Chile, left and popular forces in Nicaragua faced contradictions in their project and weaknesses internal to their own logic. In implementing the popular program, the Sandinistas turned to control over the state apparatus and "top-down" political verticalism ("vanguardism"). The Sandinistas also faced problems of bureaucratism and arrogance in the use (or abuse) of power. While the population engaged for the first time in direct grassroots decision-making, inside the FSLN party structure, decision-making became concentrated in the top leadership echelons, and this leadership increasingly utilized the state to implement decisions in a way that retarded the bottom-up influence of civil society that flourished in the early years of the revolution.

Vanden and Prevost describe three types of democratic political practice under the Sandinistas: at the level of the state (formal representative); at the level of society and the grassroots (participatory); and at the level of the FSLN party structures ("Leninist vanguardism"). They argue that the overwhelming pressures imposed on the country by the US war and the economic crisis, combined with the legacy of an authoritarian political culture, "vanguardism," and the excessive emphasis on the formal, representative structures of democracy, in which the old elite could regain institutional leverage, acted to gradually dilute popular power in the mass organizations and weaken the participatory side of the model.[33] Operationalizing my discussion in chapter 1 that polyarchy acts to institutionally constrain popular sectors, they show that the Sandinistas' drive to construct the formal, representative side of the model gradually constricted participatory democracy. But there are deeper theoretical issues. First, the structural power of transnational capital obliges states and political forces to seek survival within the parameters of a global system and its external dictates. Linking to the global economy in order to survive implies the penetration of free-market forces into the internal system with definite social consequences, and international legitimacy made contingent on the establishment of polyarchic political institutions. The contradiction between representative and participatory democracy identified by Vanden and Prevost was less internal to Nicaragua – that is, a consequence of "options" selected by the Sandinistas – than a result of contradictions located in the global system. This point is often lost upon those who inflate the real power of states under globalization and harshly criticize the Sandinistas for their policies of seeking alliances with "patriotic" factions of the propertied classes and of implementing in the late 1980s anti-popular economic adjustment policies.[34] Second, Vanden and Prevost theoretically limit democracy to the political sphere and describe polyarchy as "Western democracy," a variant – or in their words, a "style" or "preference" – of democracy alongside the variant, or "style/preference," of participatory democracy. In contrast, I argue that "Western democracy" is not "democracy" but a political system corresponding to the capitalist mode of production and distinct from authoritarianism insofar as it rests on social control of subordinate groups through consensual mechanisms.

Despite the Sandinistas' own deficiencies and the contradictions internal to their model, the proposition that Nicaragua under the Sandinistas was undemocratic was little more than a convenient ideological prop for US policy. The US objective in Nicaragua was to *subvert* the Sandinista experiment in popular democracy, to prevent any transition to a democratic form of socialism, and to restore the old elite to power. The campaign against Allende in Chile was conducted under the banner of anti-communism, but the real motive was the threat to US domination in Latin America that a socialist Chile posed. Similarly, the real threat from a Sandinista Nicaragua was less "Soviet penetration" than the threat of an independent and nationalist-minded regime in the Caribbean Basin and the potential success of an alternative model of political and economic development in the Third World. The revolution empowered dispossessed majorities that, in neighboring countries closely allied with the United States, remained locked out of political power. A more equitable redistribution of wealth, agrarian and urban reform, and broad programs to favor the poor, violated individual property rights and free-market principles. The burgeoning of mass organizations among women, youth and students, small farmers, and others, was a dangerous threat to US domination and the traditional elite.

The United States responded to this threat by launching a destabilization campaign against Nicaragua that was even more extensive than the campaign against Chile, and constituted the most far-reaching intervention abroad since the Indochina war.[35] Carter's initial "neutralization" strategy, which sought to bolster the conservative political and business groups that had worked desperately with the United States to prevent the revolutionary triumph, gave way to Reagan's full-blown destabilization campaign. Its centerpiece was the Contra army, initially drawn from the remnants of the National Guard. Between 1981 and 1990, the United States spent $447.69 million in official aid for the Contras, although estimates approach $2 billion if unofficial and informal transfers, donations from "private" US groups, and other forms of logistical support are included.[36] By 1986, the Contras had become a powerful armed force, more numerous and with better weapons and training than the National Guard had enjoyed under Somoza. US forces trained and advised the Contras, and played a more direct role in key logistical and intelligence operations and, on several occasions, in the execution of attacks, such as the mining of Nicaragua's harbors in 1984, carried out by US Navy SEAL special forces units. These US forces also conducted countless covert and paramilitary operations, ranging from organizing internal military fronts in Nicaragua's cities to such bizarre incidents as an attempted poisoning of Nicaragua's foreign minister, Father Miguel D'Escoto.[37]

The original Reagan plan sought a quick military victory over the Sandinistas. However, these plans changed in conjunction with the development of low-intensity warfare doctrines in Washington and the gradual shift to "democracy promotion." By late 1983 the US aim was no longer the military overthrow but the *political defeat* of the Sandinistas through a complex *war of attrition* – a campaign of low-intensity warfare tailor-made to Nicaraguan conditions. This strategy sought to impose on Nicaragua a process of attrition using multiple, well-synchronized military, economic, political, diplomatic, psychological, and ideological pressures against the revolution. The Contras ground away at economic and social infrastructures and paralyzed production in the countryside. Washington imposed an economic embargo and blocked multilateral financing. The constant threat of a direct US invasion was effectively used to force Nicaragua to maintain high levels of defense mobilization and expenditure, to impose a war psychosis on the population, and to modify the behavior of different actors – the Nicaraguan government and population, the international community, the US public – in ways conducive to the continuation of the attrition process. The war of attrition adroitly exploited mistakes made by the Sandinista government and the weaknesses and objective limitations in the revolutionary model, manipulated raised expectations, and capitalized on legitimate grievances to generate and mobilize anti-Sandinista constituencies. It aimed to isolate, delegitimize, and suffocate the revolution to the point where it was no longer considered a viable political option in the eyes of the population, or of other populations that might take inspiration from it. The goal was to *undermine the hegemony of the new historic bloc* that had been galvanized in the war against Somoza and consolidated, under Sandinista leadership, in the years immediately following the revolution.

Years of low-intensity warfare shattered the economy and tore the social fabric, leaving 50,000 casualties and $12 billion in damages in a society of barely 3.5 million people and with an annual GNP of some $2 billion. These direct and indirect losses to the economy represented 4,400 percent of annual export earnings and 600 percent of GNP. Proportionally equalvalent figures for US society would be approximately 5 million casualties and economic losses of $25 trillion.[38] The crux of the strategy for breaking Sandinista hegemony was to foment an economic crisis through the hemorrhaging of the country's productive infrastructure, to convert this economic crisis into a social crisis, and in turn, convert a social crisis, through complex new forms of US political intervention, including "democracy promotion" programs, into a political crisis in which the Sandinistas lost their legitimacy and were displaced from power.

With the old order shattered, much of Nicaragua's traditional elite, both agents and beneficiaries of the US destabilization campaign, turned to the task of regaining political power under the guidance of US war stategists. The elite divided, roughly, into two camps. (Apart from these two camps, a significant minority of the old elite chose to forsake their historic privileges and support the revolution.) One group went into exile, where its members often became leaders, political spokespeople, and financial supporters of the armed counterrevolution.

Another group chose to remain inside the country, where they formed a legal right-wing opposition to the Sandinistas. Within a calculated division of labor, the purpose of this internal opposition was to act in tandem with the overall US destabilization campaign as a sort of "fifth column," complementing the military, economic, diplomatic, and other operations.[39]

A series of events led the war of attrition to take an increasing "democracy promotion" focus from the mid-1980s and on, in the context of the broader changes underway in US foreign policy at this time. These events included the controversy over military support for the Contras, the International Court of Justice's 1986 ruling that US policy towards Nicaragua was in violation of international law (the ruling was ignored by Washington), the Iran–Contra scandal, and the signing by the Central American countries of a regional peace accord in 1987 which called for electoral and democratization procresses and an end to all insurgencies in the area, including the Contras. Thus, while the attrition process against Nicaragua continued year after year, by the late 1980s strategy began to shift from the Contras and a siege waged from abroad, to the internal "civic opposition" and deep penetration of Nicaragua's civil society and political system. This shift meant deploying against Nicaragua, on a hitherto unseen scale, the newly formed apparatus of political and electoral intervention which was simultaneously proving so dexterous in the Philippines and Chile. It required transforming CIA, NED and other "political aid" programs directed toward the internal civic groups from an adjunct of the Contra effort to the very centerpiece of a redefined anti-Sandinista strategy.

The overall goal became to create in Nicaraguan civil society a *counterhegemonic bloc*, in the Gramscian sense, to the hegemony won by Sandinismo in the anti-dictatorial struggle. The war of attrition was a powerful, ongoing weapon of *destruction*. It was not enough to destroy the revolution; a viable alternative had to be *constructed*. The new forms of internal political intervention brandished by US operatives would develop just such an alternative. Between 1987 and 1990, the crucial battle for hegemony was waged in Nicaraguan civil society between the Sandinistas and a transnational alliance led by the United States and a reorganized Nicaraguan elite. This battle climaxed in the electoral defeat of the Sandinistas as the culmination of the war of attrition. As the 1990 elections approached, the goal was to "harvest" ten years of attrition into an anti-Sandinista vote. The process of attrition laid the groundwork for the *electoral intervention project*, which was itself a complex and multi-dimensional undertaking in political warfare.

The anti-Sandinista elite and the role of US political aid[40]

Following the Sandinista triumph, the CIA continued a program of covert assistance to conservative anti-Somoza elements that it had begun in 1978.[41] Six months after the triumph, Carter signed a top-secret presidential Finding authorizing an expansion of this covert funding, including funds for Violeta Chamorro's conservative newspaper, *La Prensa*, anti-Sandinista political parties, trade unions, business groups, and the conservative Roman Catholic Church hierarchy, "intended to build ties for the agency [CIA]... to keep an opposition alive and insure that the agency would have contacts and friends among the leaders of a [post-Sandinista] government."[42] This CIA funding expanded under the Reagan administration, and helped piece together an alliance of political parties, minority trade unions, and the big-business umbrella group, the Superior Council of Private Enterprise (COSEP).[43] With the formation of the NED in 1984, much of this funding for the internal opposition was gradually transferred from the CIA to the Endowment. The NED became the principal US agency that managed the 1988–1990 electoral intervention project. The NED spent some $16 million between 1984 and 1992, of which some $1.5 million were spent from 1984 to 1987, when internal political intervention took a back-stage to the Contra military effort. This spending swelled to an imposing $13 million during the 1988–1990 electoral period.[44]

Given their history of infighting and factionalism, the traditional elite, including the exiled and internal wings, spent as much time in the wake of the 1979 revolution squabbling among themselves over petty issues and personal rivalries as they had spent engaged in anti-Sandinista activities. The US largesse exacerbated divisions because money was made available for any professed opposition group, and it became quite profitable to set up one's own party, no matter how tiny or uninfluential. By 1989 there were no fewer than twenty-one different opposition political parties and several additional factions. The anti-Sandinista forces were "centrifugal in dynamic, fratricidal in outlook," bemoaned one report by US consultants sent to Nicaragua in 1987 to begin organizing the internal opposition. Another observed that the opposition was "bureacratic, static, atomized, with low credibility in the population."[45] Overcoming the truncation and underdevelopment of the Nicaraguan elite would not be an easy task. The US plan called for mobilizing two main bodies: a political coalition to oppose the Sandinistas, and a network of mass civic organizations, or what US strategists referred to as a "civic opposition front," and it also called for the large-scale use of transnational communications.

Step I: Creating and funding a political opposition coalition

Forging the first body, the political coalition that eventually became the Nicaraguan Opposition Union (UNO), began in 1987 with formalized and systematic contacts between US organizers and the opposition. The NDI and the NRI organized a spate of seminars with opposition leaders in Managua and abroad to "provide training in how to formulate organizational strategy and tactical planning to the civic opposition... [the seminars] were designed around three core themes: party planning and organizational strategies, constituency building, and coalition formation." The training efforts also stressed "recruitment and development of resources, constituency support... and the development and delivery of a coherent message. These sessions [were to] focus on methods for identifying and expanding a base of support and on communication techniques which are compatible with the political culture."[46] The NDI and the NRI also sent US consultants and "international experts" to Nicaragua to analyze the opposition's strengths, weaknesses, and needs. Reports were produced which laid out a concrete, multi-thematic agenda for the US organizers. The workshops and inflow of funds and advisors succeeded in bringing together top-level and mid-level leaders from more than a dozen political parties. Bickering and rivalries continued, but US political tutelage put into motion centripetal forces. In late 1987, two multi-party coalitions formed, and in 1988, the NDI and the NRI encouraged the two groupings to come together as the Group of Fourteen (fourteen parties in all were involved), which later coalesced into the UNO coalition.[47]

In mid-summer 1988, officials from the State Department, the White House, the NED and its core groups met in Washington to evaluate the initial efforts and to map out a more comprehensive course of action. The anti-Sandinista forces "need political and financial support from multiple sources" and "should be encouraged to mobilize and channel popular discontent" inside Nicaragua, argued one NED official, pointing out that, according to polls, a majority of the Nicaraguan electorate was undecided. An abstention from this undecided bloc would favor the FSLN. So US strategy should be to provide would-be abstainers with incentives for casting their lot with the opposition.[48] Following the meeting, the NED contracted the Delphi International Group, which was already involved in Chile and elsewhere, to merge different opposition factions under a larger opposition umbrella. Delphi's report on the program noted that the group "has been able to implement its principal objective of... promoting cooperation and dialogue leading to a broader-based united civic opposition. The organization [Delphi] is now involved in getting the 14 political parties and the various private sector organizations to come together."[49] In February 1989, a NED team headed by Gershman arrived in Managua. In a strategy session at the US Embassy, Gershman and US Chargé d'Affaires John Leonard spoke of creating a formal electoral coalition: "What should the procedure be to organize the opposition around a single candidate? It should include as many parties as possible, COSEP and the labor movement, women and youth." The opposition, they agreed, would have to be instructed "to postpone any announcement of a presidential candidate. To do so now would provoke divisions in the fledgling movement. First [we must] successfully negotiate [with the Sandinistas] the conditions for the elections, the rules, and then they can squabble amongst themselves over the candidates."[50]

US officials inundated Managua over the next several months. These visitors, according to another NED document, brought one overriding message: "It is essential that the opposition understand that failure to unify jeopardizes external assistance."[51] In May, US officials convened two plenary meetings at the US Embassy compound with the opposition leadership. An assembly was scheduled for July to bring the UNO into formal existence. This July assembly was attended by NED and US Embassy officials and analysts and consultants whom NDI and NRI brought in from around the Americas to offer concrete advice on how to mount the electoral campaign. Several of these "experts" had previous experience in US political intervention programs, including the Panamanian opposition leader Plutarco Arrocha and the coordinator of the anti-Pinochet coalition that the NED had brought together in Chile, Genaro Arriagada.[52]

Following the formation of the UNO, Washington acted as the power-broker to diffuse sharp disputes in the UNO over candidate selection that nearly split the fragile coalition. Under heavy pressure from US officials, the opposition chose Violeta Chamorro as its presidential candidate, and Virgilio Godoy, president of the Independent Liberal Party, as her running mate. The sixty-year-old housewife from the traditional aristocracy had little personal experience in politics, and was not knowledgeable on domestic or international affairs. She was chosen to head the UNO ticket as a figurehead, a symbolic "unity candidate" who could attract the votes of would-be abstainers.[53] She was the widow of the martyr Pedro Joaquin Chamorro, and respect for his memory would maintain opposition unity and win popular support. Chamorro's US and Nicaraguan campaign strategists leaned heavily on psychological images of motherhood, Christian devoutness, unity, and so on, in synchronization with the main themes of the UNO campaign. Religious symbolism was particularly important in this devoutly Catholic country. Chamorro had long maintained a close relationship with conservative Catholic leaders, particularly Cardinal Miguel Obando y Bravo, the archbishop of Managua and the premier anti-Sandinista symbol. The Cardinal had received millions of dollars from the AID and private US religious and conservative groups in the 1980s,[54] and the AID gave his archdiocese another \$4.166 million during the electoral campaign.[55]

The US strategists propagated a parallel with Aquino, whose husband was also a martyr. The White House arranged for a state visit to Washington by Aquino to coincide with a visit by Chamorro and for a photo-opportunity of the two together. Creating Chamorro's international image did not stop with the Aquino parallel. Washington planned flashy meetings between Chamorro and other world leaders, including Pope John Paul II, British prime minister Margaret Thatcher and other European leaders, and President Bush.[56] The purpose of these visits, in which photo-opportunities were stressed and statements kept to a minimum, was to have the *image* of Chamorro beside world leaders reverberate in the minds of the Nicaraguan electorate. What was important was that Chamorro be seen as capable of securing the political and economic support of the developed capitalist world at a time of severe crisis in Nicaragua and diminishing options for its resolution. The photos were splashed across *La Prensa* and repeated each night in the UNO media outlets.

Having achieved the paramount goal of political unity, US officials provided this unified political bloc with the financial and material resources necessary to organize and sustain a nationwide electoral campaign. In addition to "private" and secret funding, the Bush administration made a massive "overt" investment in the opposition using NED and AID as the conduits. In October 1989, Congress approved a $9 million "electoral appropriation" for Nicaragua, which allocated $5 million for the UNO and other anti-Sandinista groups, $2.9 million for discretionary NED spending, and $1 million for observer groups, including Jimmy Carter's organization, and the CFD, which had observed the Philippine vote.[57] Publicly, the United States spent $12.5 million through NED on the elections. Washington also spent at least $11 million in two CIA authorizations, one in April 1989 involving $5 million in UNO "housekeeping expenses," and a second in October 1989 involving $6 million for "regional programming" for the oppositon.[58] If we add circuitous spending, the figure approaches $30 million, or some $20 per voter.[59] In contrast, George Bush spent less than $4 per voter in his own 1988 campaign.[60]

Since the NED charter technically prohibited direct campaign support for the UNO, US strategists set up a conduit for the coalition, the Institute for Electoral Promotion and Training (IPCE). Instead of providing funds directly to the UNO, the NED channeled them through the IPCE as "non-partisan" spending on a "multipartisan organization." However, IPCE's five-member board of directors were all top UNO leaders: Alfredo César was Chamorro's chief campaign advisor; Luis Sánchez was the UNO's official spokesperson; Guillermo Potoy was a leader of the UNO-affiliated Social Democratic Party; Silviano Matamoros led a faction of the Conservative Party belonging to the UNO; and Adán Fletes was a leader of the Democratic Party of National Confidence, also a member of the UNO coalition. In fact, the record shows that the IPCE was conceived entirely in Washington by US officials who hand-picked its five-member board and brought them to Washington to set up its structures and arrange funding.[61]

Step II: Consolidating a "civic opposition front"

Unifying and organizing the political parties was a staging point for a broader effort to penetrate (or create from scratch) the institutions of Nicaraguan civil society and to orient their activities. Washington had already been supporting a host of such institutions. As the US strategy shifted from the Contra to the electoral phase in the war of attrition, the effort was vastly expanded and the second body, the "civic opposition front," was assembled. "The topic of the form a united civic opposition should take in the upcoming pre-electoral period received considerable discussion," the Delphi International Group reported after a meeting its officials held with anti-Sandinista leaders in Managua in March 1989. "The idea discussed included a movement that was coordinated by a commission of political party, private sector, and labor union representatives... It also was determined that it would be important to have the youth organizations represented, as well as the women's movement."[62]

According to the US strategy, labor was particularly crucial because the Sandinistas enjoyed strong support among workers and this had to be eroded. Exploiting economic hardship was critical to anti-Sandinista organizing. In distinction to the youth and women's sectors, where the NED organizers had virtually to start from scratch, the United States had a long history of trying to create a pliant trade union movement in Nicaragua, as in the Philippines and Chile, and since 1979, Washington had been actively promoting anti-Sandinista trade unions. The NED channeled support to the opposition trade unions through the FTUI, which in turn operated through the AIFLD. The FTUI relied on a complex of third country mechanisms for sending human resources to the opposition unions. NED and the AIFLD created a Nicaraguan Labor Solidarity Office in Costa Rica and funded a group in that country, the Center for Democratic Consultation, known by its Spanish acronym, CAD, whose tasks included sending Latino union organizers into Nicaragua. In addition, they brought in a team of twenty organizers from the AIFLD-funded Venezuelan Federation of Workers.[63] With these international structures in place, US officials worked inside Nicaragua for labor unity in the opposition. Embassy officials held a series of meetings with anti-Sandinista trade union leaders in 1988, urging them to work at unifying all the unions in order to confront the government under one banner. Later in 1988, the FTUI sponsored several trade union seminars in Managua, from which emerged the Permanent Congress of Workers (CPT) umbrella organization. By the time the electoral process began, the CPT was working as an homogeneous entity, the trade union parallel of the UNO.[64]

An August 1989 FTUI document described plans to spend another $1 million, recently approved as part of Congress's special appropriations, for the electoral mobilization of workers and their families. The plan involved the "multiplier" system to organize 4,200 activists. After being trained and put on FTUI salary, each activist operated in one of the 4,200 administrative zones in Nicaragua where voting boards were set up. These activists were "to mount an effective nation-wide effort

227

to register workers and their families and then see that they vote." The FTUI needed to "motivate these activists for their roles," as well as "provide transportation and communications support" for the network, stated the document.[65] A trained Managua headquarters staff supervised an elaborate network reaching down to ten-member voter teams in towns and villages. The national headquarters was staffed with Venezuelan and Costa Rican teams and top CPT leaders under the supervision of FTUI officials. At the next level down, provincial organizers were sent out to each of the country's sixteen provinces. Directly under their supervision, were a hundred district organizers, "whose first responsibility was to recruit and train about 400 labor activists for the next level down."[66] And so on. In this way, the NED created and controlled a vertically organized nationwide structure for intervention in the political system and the electoral process via the trade union sector. Between August and December 1989, FTUI held a total of 130 local training seminars, sixteen departmental and one national, with the NED funds. The newly trained activists were sent around the country with NED salaries and per diems.[67]

Youth was also considered a strategic sector. Demographically, Nicaragua is a youthful society. Some 50 percent of the population is under thirty years of age, and the voting age was set at sixteen years. Youth was the core of the revolutionary energy that overthrew the Somoza dictatorship. On the basis of the Nicaraguan experience some social scientists even developed new theories of youth as a third revolutionary sector, after workers and peasants.[68] Delphi was assigned to launch the youth project, and, with NED funds, created and advised the Centro de Formación Juvenil (CEFOJ) as a new "civic youth organization."[69] Seminars were held throughout 1988 to train and organize a core group of salaried youth leaders from opposition political parties. This group formed a national leadership paid from NED funds. In turn, they were to select regional leaders who would oversee local activists working in secondary schools, communities, and recreational centers to organize an anti-Sandinista political youth movement.[70]

Women were identified as another special sector. Many women had become empowered through the revolutionary process, particularly by their participation in mass organizations such as the women's associations, neighborhood groups and trade unions. US organizers concluded that women as a group needed to be separated from Sandinismo, were susceptible to US psychological pressures through the manipulation of traditional gender roles and of motherhood, and could play a critical role in the electoral intervention project. Targeting women, the backbone of most Nicaraguan families, would be a way to penetrate the very nucleus of society – the family. The draft of young men – itself a measure enacted as a defensive response to US military aggression – was particularly unpopular among mothers as heads of households, who saw their sons shipped off to war fronts and often returned maimed or dead. The traditional sexual division of labor meant that women predominated in the informal economy, including market networks and household economies. Sandinista economic policies in favor of formal sector labor, producers and consumers, rather than traders and others in the informal sector, had a positive effect on the poor overall, but they antagonized the "market women" and others in the informal sector who made up sizeable constituencies. And those women who were homemakers bore the brunt of food shortages and other economic hardships.

While this reflects, in part, a carry over of pre-revolutionary gender relations, and in part, Sandinista weaknesses in incorporating gender issues into overall programs, US operatives were keen on exploiting factors that made women susceptible. Delphi designed a "women's project" focusing on organizing efforts in the market-place and in households. The NED provided Delphi with a grant to form the Nicaraguan Women's Movement (MMN) in April 1989 by bringing together female leaders from several UNO parties and creating a board of directors.[71] "Nicaraguan women have begun to speak of the decisive role they must play in organizing rallies and protests," explained one document, which prescribed "seminars and workshops tailored to train 'multipliers' to train and motivate their peers to participate."[72] Another Delphi document explained: "Women... see themselves as victims of the state's exploitation, having suffered from the lack of food and poor education. They now realize that it is in their obligation to help liberate the country through civic opposition." The document concluded: "As the [Delphi] program advances, women will play a significant role in the electoral process as never before seen in the history of Nicaragua. As they transform absenteeism into participation and negative votes into positive ones, they will have the potential to attract more votes and will be seen as a decisive force in the electoral process."[73]

By mid-1989, the opposition had become unified and was developing a national profile. NED officials analyzed overall progress:

> There are three main centers of activity in this election. One is the political parties grouped in UNO. Another is the labor group in CPT. Each of these has come together fairly well and there is a good working relationship between them... The third group is a civic group which has yet to solidify. Conceptually, this is a vital part of the democratic process... The civic group needs to be independent and non-partisan, but it should also coordinate with the other two main groups and avoid duplication of effort.[74]

Shortly afterwards, the NDI sponsored a seminar in Managua between US organizers and opposition representatives to set up this "civic component," and then to "arrive at an agreed-upon division of labor among the three components."[75]

Among those attending this Managua meeting was Henry Quintero, the intelligence operative who had managed several programs in Chile and had also helped run Delphi programs in Nicaragua. This time he was representing yet another US-based organization, the International Federation for Electoral Systems (IFES). This group, formed just months before the Nicaraguan electoral process opened in order to "support and improve the process and management of free elections in emerging democracies throughout the world," was put in charge of running a Via Cívica program. Its board of directors heavily inter-locked with the other NED groups.[76] At a press conference after the meeting "civic leaders" announced the formation of Via Cívica. This new organization, they proclaimed, was "a non-partisan grouping of notables" which would press its cause "through ballots, not bullets." Via Cívica, without any interest in promoting one or another political position, would merely help register the voting age population and promote civic values. "Just think of it as a League of Women Voters," was how Quintero put it.[77] However, all ten directors of this new group were prominent UNO activists. Three were leaders from UNO political parties, five were COSEP leaders, and two represented the CPT unions. With Via Cívica established, the three separate components of the US program were in place, and were expected "to function during the election as a single unit," one NED document concluded.[78]

The broader strategy behind the trade union, women's, youth, and Via Cívica projects was to face the Sandinistas at every level of society – social, political, and cultural – where Sandinismo held influence. US funds, political training, and guidance were instruments to erode Sandinista hegemony and construct an opposition hegemonic bloc.

230

What US rhetoric referred to as "building the institutions of democracy" in Nicaragua meant creating or strengthening a series of parallel pro-US groups led by representatives of the traditional elite, achieving vertical and horizontal linkages among them, and providing them with an effective political action capacity to compete with mass organizations in which Sandinismo held sway.

Step III: Utilizing transnational communications

US policymakers targeted the communications media as another critical element in the strategy. An examination of this program provides a case study in the use of transnational communications in "democracy promotion" programs. Symbolic manipulation was meant to influence the US public (creating a domestic constituency for the war), the international community (mobilizing transnational resources against the Sandinistas and isolating Nicaragua internationally), and inundating the Nicaraguan population with a host of messages conducive to the overall objectives of the war. Several US agencies became deeply involved in the communications and propaganda efforts, among them the CIA, the NED, the State Department, the Office of Public Diplomacy, and the USIA.[79]

Covert and psychological operations aimed at influencing the coverage of Nicaragua in the US and international media involved calculated "leaks," manipulating and even paying off journalists, planting disinformation and black propaganda, and designing public relations blitzkriegs. This "war of images" was complex and multidimensional. It sought to "demonize the Sandinista government," as one US official admitted, in order to "turn it into a real enemy and threat" in the eyes of the US public and international community.[80] The themes of a lack of democracy in Nicaragua, political repression, persecution of the church, economic disaster, militarization, the export of revolution, and so on, were projected on a daily basis during the course of a decade. The flip side of the strategy was to inculcate the image of the Contras, and even more so, of the internal opposition, as the democratic alternative.

Another part of the propaganda campaign was actually creating communications media for the anti-Sandinista forces. The USIA and the CIA set up several radio stations in neighboring countries that transmitted into Nicaragua sophisticated anti-Sandinista messages.[81] The USIA also expanded Voice of America transmitters in the Caribbean Basin region so as to inundate Nicaraguan airwaves. The

Contras also had several shortwave radio stations targeting specific Nicaraguan communities, and in addition published propaganda newsletters and magazines, assisted by the USIA and funded out of general budgets provided by the CIA.[82] The NED also financed anti-Sandinista publications published outside of Nicaragua. The group that managed most of these programs was Freedom House, which also participated in the Contras' public relations efforts.[83] With approximately one million dollars in NED funding, Freedom House created an anti-Sandinista publishing house, a think-tank, and a scholarly quarterly journal in San José, Costa Rica, run by prominent personalities and intellectuals from the Nicaraguan elite.[84]

Of the internal opposition media outlets, the most important was *La Prensa*, which became a leading symbol of the anti-Sandinista campaign. Although the United States projected an image of *La Prensa* as a struggling "independent" news outlet, it was funded by the United States and functioned as an important outlet inside Nicaragua for the US war and the unofficial organ of the internal opposition. *La Prensa* began to receive covert CIA subsidies (through third-party "cutouts") as early as 1979 to enable it to play a counterrevolutionary role, particularly through psychological warfare, just as *El Murcurio* had done in Chile under Allende.[85] In addition to covert funding, the NED began overt funding for the newspaper in 1984, and in 1986 placed the *La Prensa* operation under Delphi supervision. With the shift from the military to the internal political track, the United States bolstered the media outlets of the internal opposition. The NED launched a Nicaraguan Independent Media Program under Delphi supervision, involving a huge expansion of both funding and direct political guidance for the creation and expansion of the opposition media, including *La Prensa* and several radio stations. In 1988, Delphi initiated an Independent Radios Project with the objective of equipping and advising opposition radio. The program funded four radio stations during the campaign, including training radio journalists and programmers, and coordinating opposition radio programming with the UNO and the youth, women's, civic, and other groups.[86]

Washington also sent in experts in video and image propaganda to guide and fund UNO's television media strategy. US media and public relations experts were contracted to manage a fully equipped production facility which the NED and USIA officials opened in Managua to prepare a half-hour programs, a "fast-paced, entertaining and aggressive show that could be a hybrid between a regular newscast and a news magazine." The slick UNO television segments and vignettes began airing in September 1989. The segments were highly professional, and played heavily on a mixture of sound, image, and core themes to which the Nicaraguan population would be sensitive – religious sentiment, childhood, contrast between misery in the present and hope for the future, and so on – themes which reinforced the psychological content of the US intervention strategy. NDI consultant Peter Fenn designed a television vignette that showed the Berlin Wall falling and Solidarity head Lech Walesa. "Now Nicaragua has the opportunity to choose democracy," it concluded.[87] Other television spots juxtaposed scenes of economic and social misery with a bright UNO future, with a backdrop of heavy religious symbolism. The "civic opposition front" worked in close conjunction with UNO/US media strategy. Via Cívica, the CEFOJ, and the MMN plastered advertisements each day in the US-funded media outlets.

Another aspect of the communications program was polling. Polls and pollsters have become a methodological and systematic component of political and electoral processes. Surveys on voter behavior and political preferences serve both to guide parties and candidates, and to shape public opinion itself. Images of the strength, weakness, and prospects of candidates can be projected and reinforced through the dissemination of survey results. Beyond its own political system, the US has developed the use of polls as instruments in its machinery for political intervention abroad. The NDI and the NRI, for instance, relied on polling extensively as part of the NED programs in the Chilean elections. Polls are easily manipulated for the political motives of pollsters, and were used by both sides in the Nicaraguan elections as part of broader campaign strategies. Some dozen Nicaraguan and foreign organizations – pro-Sandinista, pro-UNO, and neutral – conducted voter surveys during the electoral process. Independent polls conducted in the final weeks of the campaign, among others the ABC–Washington Post, showed the Sandinistas winning by a significant majority. Polls conducted by several regional pollsters contracted by UNO, showed UNO winning by margins similar to the actual voting results. Given the highly polarized and politicized environment of a country torn by war, as well as the methodological difficulties that abound in Nicaragua, it was no wonder that analysts were often unable to interpret contradictory survey results. Nevertheless, polls taken in the pre-campaign period agreed on the existence of a core of FSLN supporters (some 25–30

233

percent) and a committed anti-Sandinista opposition (some 20–25 percent), with the majority, probably 40 percent or more, being undecided and potential abstainers.[88]

Political opinion polling served two essential, yet contradictory, purposes in US-UNO strategy. The first was propagandistic. The polls became an important instrument in Washington's international campaign to cast doubts upon the electoral process, tarnish the Sandinistas' image, apply pressures on the Nicaraguan government, and influence the electorate. Polls showing the UNO way ahead and the Sandinistas trailing by wide margins would reinforce arguments that the only way the FSLN could win would be through a fraudulent election, and give UNO an image of strength in the eyes of Nicaraguan voters. Second, polling became an important medium for assessing the extent to which the attrition process had advanced over the years. US strategists used internal polls as a guide in assessing the direction of the undecided majority and the real prospects for converting would-be abstainers into opposition votes. Thus, polling was an instrument to obtain information necessary for US operatives to carry out more effectively and precisely their work among the Nicaraguan electorate.

In conjunction with media manipulation, international observation has become an instrument for penetrating and manipulating foreign electoral processes, obscuring in the process the distinction between neutral or impartial observation and partisan intervention, as discussed in the Philippines chapter. The 1990 Nicaraguan elections were probably the most closely scrutinized by observers in world history, observed by thousands of representatives from the UN, the OAS, the European Parliament, countless governments, and human rights, political, and religious groups. Many of the groups had a presence in Nicaragua for the duration of the campaign period. Washington saw both problems and opportunities in this flood of observers. Should the Sandinistas win under the watchful eyes of the international community, the US would find it difficult to discredit the voting or to deny legitimacy to the Sandinistas. On the other hand, the window of international observation provided US operatives with numerous opportunities for manipulating the electoral process and influencing observer views and conduct.

Most of the groups from the electoral intervention network sent US-funded "observer" teams. These included the AIFLD, which was advising the UNO trade unions, the CAD from Costa Rica, the NDI and the NRI, and Freedom House. US "electoral observers" were a way for Washington to set itself up as sole judge and arbiter of the electoral process. Had the Sandinistas won the elections, many of these partisan observer groups would have been in a position to issue reports questioning the results and influencing international opinion. Another US-funded observer team was sent by the CFD, an organization which had been involved in anti-Sandinista activities throughout the 1980s, including awarding its annual "Sentinel of Freedom" award to Violeta Chamorro in 1987.[89] With \$325,000 granted to it by Congress and the NED, the CFD was sent to "observe" the Nicaraguan elections. With these funds, the CFD conducted a host of questionable activities, ranging from distributing paraphernalia resembling the UNO logotype, to carrying out its own "get out the vote drives" as if it were a Nicaraguan civic organization, preparing "press packets" on the elections for distribution to other observer groups in Managua, and proposing that the Contras, who were still active militarily, remain armed until after the elections so as to see if the vote was "really fair."[90]

Electoral *coup d'état*: the making of a Faustian bargain

Along with coercive diplomacy, the United States skillfully wove military aggression and economic sanctions into the project. In April 1989, Congress approved a new aid package of nearly \$67 million for the Contras, intended, in Secretary of State James Baker's own words, to "keep the Contras alive, intact and in existence throughout the electoral process." Baker stated that by keeping the Contras intact, the United States would have "an insurance policy until after the February elections are certified as free and fair" so that the Contras would be available "for their possible or potential use further down the road."[91] This aid allowed the Contras to remain mobilized and active for the duration of the electoral campaign. This was particularly significant, since in the year leading up to the electoral campaign, the military war had wound down considerably as a result of the Central American peace accords and international mediation efforts, and there was a general mood throughout much of the country that real peace was not too far off. With fresh US funds, Contra officers were given a course in Honduras to help them strengthen their military structure.[92] At least \$4.5 million was spent on electoral propaganda training, including "courses in civic action, in basic democratic processes, forms of government and Nicaraguan history and geography," said one State Department report.[93] One Contra participant said the courses taught the virtues of UNO and how Contra electoral campaign activities in the rural areas could contribute to the "civic defeat" of the Sandinistas.[94]

In August 1989, the month in which the electoral campaign officially opened, the Contras began a redeployment into Nicaragua of 8,000 to 12,000 troops that had been inactive, stationed in Honduran base camps. The US aid program had permitted a quick deployment. Contra actions, which averaged about fifty per month in 1988, increased in the first half of 1989 to about one hundred, and then, following the August redeployment, jumped to an average of three hundred per month, a rate sustained right through to the voting. The Contras took up the task of armed propaganda and intimidation in favor of the opposition, becoming in effect an armed wing of the UNO. Contra armed propaganda teams distributed huge quantities of pro-UNO leaflets. "Our infiltration into Nicaragua has nothing to do with combat," explained one Contra commander of a twenty-person "electoral unit." "Our only goal is to maintain a presence in our fatherland and alert the people about the elections and who they can vote for."[95] The Contras also carried out a highly selective campaign of terror against Sandinista campaign workers and designated rural communities known for their Sandinista sympathies. No fewer than fifty FSLN rural campaign activists were assassinated. Several large-scale massacres of civilians and hundreds of incidents of military harassment were reported. This Contra military activity underscored the fact that the electoral process unfolded in the midst of war. Voting was literally under the gun. Some 42 percent of the electorate resided in rural areas, and of these, over 50 percent directly in the zones of military conflict. In other words, approximately 25 percent of the electorate were *directly* affected by Contra military activity.[96]

The objective of the Contra redeployment was much more than electoral propaganda or garnering UNO votes among peasant communities. It was the cornerstone of a sophisticated psychological warfare operation aimed at sending a powerful message to the entire electorate: the Sandinistas are not capable of ending the war. By reinfiltrating the Contras and having them engage in enough visible activity so as to make their presence an issue in the media, and thus have the image of ongoing Contra activity reach the entire population, it was possible to prevent the Sandinistas from claiming to be able to bring peace to Nicaragua. The electorate as a whole had to contemplate the conse- quences of their vote. The message was simple: because the Contras support the UNO, and because the United States sponsors both UNO and the Contras, an electoral victory for UNO will mean an end to the war, and therefore a vote for UNO is a vote for peace. The use and the threat of the use of military aggression were thus employed as political trump cards. "When we examine coercive diplomacy and limited military actions as forms of psychological warfare," said one US strategist, "we should bear in mind that [their] effectiveness depends on our enemy's perception of what will happen to him if he fails to do as we wish."[97]

As noted earlier, ten years of US war had shattered the fragile Nicaraguan economy. The war forced Nicaragua to transfer huge quantities of material, financial, and human resources from production to defense. Between 1979 and 1981, defense accounted for 15 percent of the national budget. By 1985 the defense effort was consuming 60 percent of the budget, 40 percent of material output, 25 percent of the GNP and 20 percent of the economically active population.[98] The Nicaraguan revolution won international awards for its literacy cam- paign and broad praise for its great strides in improving the basic health and living conditions of the people. However, the war gradually eroded the government's capacity to finance these programs – exactly what the attrition process was intended to do. The grueling economic crisis included a 33,000 percent inflation rate in 1988, a fall in the GNP for every year from 1984, and damages as a result of the war exceeding $12 billion.

Policymakers sought to assure that the hardships would continue and there would be no tangible improvement in the economy during the electoral campaign. Preventing any shift from defense to social spending by keeping the Contras mobilized became a top priority. "The economic situation in Nicaragua is very bad, and the resistance forces remain an element in the equation," said Luigi Einaudi, the US Ambassador to the OAS. "So there are reasons for which to believe that the Sandinistas [can be removed]. That is our operating assump- tion. That is the situation we are trying to induce."[99] In addition Bush renewed the trade embargo twice during the electoral process, first in May 1989 and then again on October 25, at the height of the campaign. In November, Chamorro was brought to the White House for a well- publicized photo session with Bush, after which the US president released a statement, reproduced under splashy headlines in *La Prensa* and in the other UNO media outlets, declaring that if Chamorro was elected, the US would lift the embargo.[100]

US officials also blocked international assistance for Nicaragua. In 1988, Nicaraguan authorities requested that the World Bank send a team to explore renewed lending to Managua, cut off in 1982. The Bank agreed. However, Baker sent a letter to Bank president Barber Conable, voicing US opposition to any attempt to mend relations with Managua.[101] Bank authorities eventually succumbed to the pressure, reversing their decision to send the team, "due definitely to very strong pressure" from the United States, according to a senior Bank official. In May 1989, President Ortega made a three-week tour of Western Europe in search of emergency economic assistance. The tour culminated in an international donors' conference in Stockholm which the Swedish government sponsored in order to explore ways to secure international aid. The Bush administration pressured the World Bank, the IMF, and the IDB not to send delegates to the meeting. At the time of the conference, Baker was in Europe, making phone calls to European government officials in last-minute attempts to dissuade them from participating, or from providing Nicaragua with assistance.[102]

As with the Contra military activity, sustaining the economic crisis sent a clear psychological message: a vote for the FSLN means the United States will continue economic destabilization, and is thus a self-punishing vote for continued economic hardship. A vote cast for UNO will lift the economic sanctions, open the spigot of international aid, and bring economic respite. Surveys conducted one month before the vote revealed that the economy was the most important issue for 52 percent of the electorate, and the Contra war was the most important for 37 percent; 87 percent of all voters identified the war and economic crisis as the paramount issues in their voting decision – issues in which the United States exercised the decisive levers.[103] Equally as revealing was a post-election survey: presented with the statement, "If the Sandinistas had won, the war would never have ended," 75.6 percent of those surveyed agreed, and this percentage included 91.8 percent of those who voted for the UNO.[104]

Essential to the US strategy was converting the vote into a referendum, a simple plebiscite-type decision by the people: "war – yes," or "war – no." A vote for the Sandinistas meant a continuation of hostility from the US, and thus continued poverty, hardship, war, and isolation.

A vote for UNO, to the contrary, would bring respite, an immediate end to the US aggression, a definitive cessation of military hostilities, and millions of dollars in foreign aid. The US electoral intervention project can only be understood when seen in its entirety: the skillful combination of military aggression, economic blackmail, CIA propaganda, NED political interference, coercive diplomacy, and international pressures, into a coherent single strategy. And then, the project can only be appreciated as the culmination of ten years of war. The entire population had become *exhausted* from war and economic crisis. The US strategy was precisely to "harvest" this exhaustion through the elections. This "Faustian bargain" hijacked the vote into an *electoral coup d'état*.

Historical outcomes, in Nicaragua and elsewhere, are not reducible to US intervention alone, and the conceptual focal point of this Faustain bargain is neither Nicaragua's internal process nor US intervention but how the two became interwoven. The incomplete fulfillment of the promises of the revolution, which ultimately eroded its legitimacy and undermined its hegemony, was a consequence of internal and external and subjective and objective factors that must be seen in their dialectic relation, in which interactive variables unfold under a macro-structural-historical framework. US intervention radically altered the political system in Nicaragua and was crucial in determining the conditions, as well as constraints, under which the electoral process, and the revolution as a whole, unfolded.

US intervention after the Sandinistas: constructing polyarchy and a neo-liberal state

— In has been two years since I was last in Nicaragua and I am taken aback by the tremendous increase in indigence. For example, there is an army of children living in the streets, naked and begging. You had promised to resolve the economic crisis. How do you propose to do this when poverty is increasing month by month?
— Look, my dear, here people are used to going naked in the streets because of the heat. It is true that children go about like that in the streets, that they go around begging. But it is because their mothers send them out to beg due to a lack of good manners.

Violeta Chamorro, 1993 interview with a foreign journalist[105]

The electoral results were a stunning success for low-intensity warfare and the new political intervention. But US intervention did not end there; it entered a new stage.[106] The goals became (1) to dismantle the revolution (2) to reconstitute an elitist social order under the leadership of "technocrats" and a "New Right" attuned to the transnational agenda, and (3) to deepen the process of penetrating Nicaraguan civil society and constructing a counter- (and counter-revolutionary) hegemony therein. One side of the post-electoral strategy was to neutralize the influence of Sandinismo at every level – political, ideological, economic, and military – and to reverse the socioeconomic transformations achieved over a decade of radical change. The flip-side was the consolidation of an anti-Sandinista alternative. Ten years of revolution did not make the Nicaraguan bourgeoisie disappear, but it did further disfigure a class which, as a result of external dependency and decades of dictatorship had never fully developed. Washington set about, through the judicious use of economic and political aid allocations in the years proceding the 1990 elections, to reconstitute a propertied class and a political elite tied to the emergent global order.

The Sandinistas surrendered the formal executive apparatus. But this transition unfolded within a constitutional framework developed under the revolution, whose social, economic, and political structures remained in place. The electoral defeat plunged the Sandinista party, its social basis and legitimacy already seriously eroded during the long years of war, into a sharp internal crisis over programs, ideological orientation, and strategy. But the FSLN in 1990 was still the largest and best organized party in the country. The popular sectors remained politicized and mobilized in the old mass organizations and, even more so, in new social movements and specific interest groups which flourished after the elections.[107] The vote for the UNO was *not* a vote of support for its anti-popular program. Nicaragua was very different from Chile, where the left had been virtually decimated and the popular sectors demobilized and largely pacified. The situation in Nicaragua was closer to that of the Philippines, where consolidation of a polyarchic political system and the neo-liberal project proved difficult after a successful "transition." Yet the Philippines never underwent an experiment in popular democracy that radically altered the country's social, economic, and political structures. Most importantly, neither old and new factions of the Nicaraguan elite nor the United States could count, in 1990, on a repressive military apparatus to impose their agenda, since the Sandinista People's Army (EPS) remained largely intact following the change in government. The new Minister of the

Presidency, Antonio Lacayo, was forced to recognize that "what happened in Nicaragua was not a social revolution, but an electoral victory within the legal order."[108]

The difficulties in the US/elite project became evident in the months following Chamorro's April 1990 inauguration. The new government announced sweeping neo-liberal measures, including massive public sector layoffs, privatizations, rate increases in transportation, utilities, and other services, a sharp reduction in social spending, and the elimination of subsidies on basic consumption. The measures triggered two consecutive national strikes, in May and in July, both of which paralyzed the country and demonstrated the popular classes' willingness and ability to mount resistance. The new government was forced to compromise. Clearly, the anti-popular program would have to be implemented gradually, through a strategy of "slow-motion counterrevolution." Nicaragua entered a period of endemic social conflict, in which cycles of standoff, negotiation, and compromise alternated with peaceful or violent strikes, demonstrations, and clashes in the countryside and the cities. Chronic instability and social conflict provided the backdrop to ongoing realignments of the country's political forces and a "creeping" implementation of the neo-liberal program.

US officials were aware of the enormous challenge they and their Nicaraguan allies faced. After a year-long study, the newly opened AID mission in Nicaragua (the AID had withdrawn altogether from the country in 1981) stated in a report laying out overall US policy for 1991 to 1996, the year in which the next elections were scheduled: "The strategy presented in this document is an extremely ambitious one. It is difficult to overemphasize the degree of change in the Nicaraguan economy and Nicaraguan society which it envisions."[109] This Strategy Statement, a remarkable blueprint for the construction of a neo-liberal republic, laid out a comprehensive program for restructuring every aspect of Nicaraguan society on the basis of the economic power the United States would be able to wield over the shattered country.

Dismantling the revolution and restructuring Nicaraguan society involved "counter-reform" in every institutional and policy arena: reform of the state, sweeping economic policy reforms, reforms to the constitution, reforms in the police, educational reform, social policy reform, recomposition of the hegemony of private capital, accelerated market liberalization, and so on. Such massive economic and institutional restructuring would logically lead to a change in the correlation of internal political and social forces and thus provide a solid material basis for the more gradual, yet crucial, cultural and ideological dimensions of "slow-motion counterrevolution."

Following the elections, Washington approved a two-year $541 million assistance package for Nicaragua, including at least $10 million in political aid channeled through the ODI and $3 million in new NED funding.[110] The AID program in Nicaragua became the largest in the world, and the embassy became the most heavily staffed in Central America. Personnel increased from 78 accredited diplomats in 1989 to over 300 by mid-1990.[111] Washington appointed as its new ambassador Harry Shlauderman, a veteran diplomat who had a history of involvement in US-guided interventionist efforts in Latin America, including being Deputy Chief of Mission in Chile before and after the 1973 military coup, where he played a pivotal role in CIA covert operations against the Allende government as the in-country counterpart to Kissinger's Committee of forty at the NSC.[112]

Post-electoral political aid

Formal state power passed from the Sandinistas to pro-US representatives of the elite. But this elite did not enjoy hegemony in civil society. Rooting out any vestige of Sandinista influence and incorporating into an emergent transnational historic bloc the Nicaraguan masses, whose consciousness and "daily practices" had been transformed in ten years of revolution, would therefore be a long-term process. As Nicaraguan sociologist Oscar René Vargas noted, revival of a latent fatalism and submissiveness of the popular classes would have to rely heavily on cultural and ideological mechanisms.[113] Political aid played the main role in this endeavor. Following the election, the AID immediately sent a team of international legal advisors to the Chamorro transition team and provided the CFD with funds to set up a permanent office in Managua to advise and train UNO legislators.[114] The ODI sent advisors and funds: to the National Assembly, "to improve its internal operations in resolving conflict and forging consensus on national policy" and to implement "constitutional reforms"; to the Electoral Commission, "to prepare for and monitor the 1996 national elections"; to judicial institutions and to the Comptroller-General, "to install financial controls in government institutions"; and to municipal governments, to help in "implementing overall [US] strategy."[115]

In the view of US officials, the development of a polyarchic political culture among the elite and the legitimization of a neo-liberal social order among the population was the crucial counterpart to eroding the revolution's value system. "As the Mission has considered how best to promote democracy in Nicaragua, it has carefully reviewed a broad range of potential interventions," noted the AID report, and concluded that "transformation of the political culture is essential."[116] The manipulation of religious values, patriarchial and traditional cultural patterns, and economic insecurities was central to this political-ideological endeavor. One of the first steps was the penetration and restructuring of the educational system as a key institution of ideological reproduction. The ODI allocated $12.5 million to replace textbooks used in public schools that were developed under the Sandinista government. The old texts were ordered burned by the new Minister of Education, Humberto Belli. The new "depoliticized" textbooks began with the "Ten Commandments of God's Law," referred to divorce as a "disgrace" and to abortion as "murder," and stressed the importance of "order in the family," as well as "obedience to parents and legitimate authorities." Augusto Sandino was removed from the chapter on national heroes. Catholicism was defined in the geography textbook as the world's dominant religion, "based on the preaching of Our Lord Jesus Christ." The world history text asserted that all US interventions were carried out to bring "peace and stability" to countries around the world. The AID's director in Nicaragua, Janet Ballantyne, stated that the textbooks would help "reestablish the civics and morals lacking in the last eleven years."[117]

While the ODI focused on government-to-government programs, the NED continued earlier programs and also introduced new ones to consolidate constituencies built up during the electoral process. One of these programs was ongoing allocations for the CPT trade unions: "[This program is] aimed at countering antidemocratic trade union destabilization during the transition period," stated one NED document. "After having suppressed strikes for years, some Sandinista trade unionists now threaten mass political strikes to 'protect the gains of the revolution.' A successful organizing drive by independent trade unions, aimed at creating a visible democratic presence in communities and industries throughout Nicaragua, is crucial to maintaining a stable transition period."[118] The AID Strategy Statement was even more to the point: "Free democratic unions can offer alternatives to radicalized Sandinista unions."[119] The CAD program also continued, including new "training and civic education" programs among "youth, women, teachers, professionals, cooperatives and community development organizations."[120] Delphi was given nearly $1 million to continue the media program, including start-up funds for a new television station run by private businessmen.[121] "The Sandinista controlled media has contributed to a generalized atmosphere of uncertainty and anxiety by constantly emphasizing the problems which lie ahead, and fomenting distrust of the new government's future economic, political and social policies among the peasants, government employees, and the general public," stated one Delphi document.[122] In 1991, the MMN changed in name to the Nicaraguan Women of Conciencia (MNC), making it a Nicaraguan branch of the Latin American network of Conciencia organizations of women from the elite set up by the NED. According to the new MNC director Francis Blandon, with US funding the MNC would be able to "rescue religion and the family from the libertine philosophy of the Sandinistas." The MNC would help women overcome misfortunes they suffered as a result of the Sandinistas – such as "abandonment by men, battery, sexual laxity, and lesbianism" – and their "contempt for Christian morals."[123] Similarly, the CEFOJ youth organization's post-electoral work focused on "the transmission of a moral and Christian orientation" to overcome the "great decadence in values" brought on by the Sandinista revolution.[124]

Post-electoral economic aid

The Nicaraguan case demonstrates the enormous constraints imposed by the global economy on peripheral countries. Despite systematic popular resistance to the full restoration of capitalist property relations and measures to open up the country to the unfettered operation of transnational capital, Nicaragua's desperate economic situation and extreme dependence on external financing gave the United States and international financial institutions enormous leverage. "The capitalist sectors that govern want to internationalize the country to the core, and in that option there's no space for national producers or for small and medium-sized growers or for a peasant economy or for anything else on that order," pointed out Nicaraguan economist Angel Saldomando. "The government has hedged all its bets on international accords and commitments that give it the correlation of forces abroad that it doesn't have domestically. This government has permanently held the conditions of AID, the IMF and the World Bank over people's heads like an axe: if we don't do this, the foreign resources won't come, we won't have money, there's no choice but to comply."[125] In Nicaragua, the standard neo-liberal program was particularly abrasive because it involved not just free-market reform, but the reversal of prior popular and revolutionary changes.

Economic aid went to bolster the debilitated private sector, for balance-of-payments assistance, and to pay debt arrears to the World Bank and the IMF. The AID made disbursal of all assistance contingent on stringent conditions on to the Chamorro government's social and economic policies. The AID's Strategy Statement stipulated across-the-board conditionality. US assistance was aimed at "returning the country to a market economy," an AID official said. "What we are looking for is the standard orthodox stuff"[126] – the privatization of industry, agriculture, and services, elimination of domestic subsidies, lifting market regulations, eliminating conditions on foreign investment, financial and trade liberalization, and a domestic austerity program. The largest portion of US aid went to pay the country's arrears to private foreign lenders and international agencies (and thus never even entered the country), which reestablished the country's credit standing and opened the spigot for new lending from the World Bank and the IMF. World Bank and IMF representatives, together with AID officials, designed a comprehensive neo-liberal structural adjustment program and made all credits, disbursements, and debt restructuring contingent on compliance with this program. After 1992, Washington began to phase out bilateral US aid and replace it with funding from the international agencies.[127] US aid was a transitional mechanism for Nicaragua's insertion into international financial structures representing transnational capital.

Foreign aid inserted Nicaragua inexorably into the global economy. By 1992, Nicaragua's foreign debt stood at nearly $11 billion, one of the highest per capita debts in the world. Nicaragua paid out $495 million in that year *in interest alone* on this debt, and, according to government projections, was scheduled to pay $508 million in 1993, $629.8 million in 1994, $654 million in 1995, and $733 million in 1996. (In comparison, export earnings stood at $217 million in 1991.)[128] Debt-servicing would clearly be a powerful mechanism for many years to come in compelling a thorough restructuring of Nicaragua's productive structure in accordance with a changing world market and the new international division of labor. Of a total of $1.2 billion in foreign aid allocated for the country in 1991, over $500 million – or 43 percent – went for debt-servicing. Another 26 percent went for imports, mostly of consumer goods. Figures for 1992 and 1993 showed an almost identical pattern. In 1991, public consumption dropped 35 percent and private consumption rose 33 percent, indicating a converse relation between the drop in government spending on social services for the popular sectors and an increase in private consumption among the tiny upper and middle classes. As a result of the sudden opening of the market to imports, Nicaragua experienced an import boom that forced thousands of small-scale industrial and agricultural producers into bankruptcy. The majority of new imports were not inputs for production but consumer goods, especially luxury items, benefitting a new high-income sector, as well as large-scale importers who began to use newly accumulated capital to purchase properties and establish financial concerns, thus contributing to the process of a reconcentration of wealth and a restoration of pre-revolutionary property relations.[129]

Commercial reactivation through non-productive imports was a calculated element in US strategy, conducted through a Commodity Import Program (CIP) whose stated purpose was to strengthen the private sector.[130] The CIP was tied to a program to create ten private banks, for which purpose the AID spent $60 million in 1991 and 1992 alone in capitalization funds and in commodity imports by large-scale private importers financed by these private financial institutions (the importers and the members of the new banks' boards of directors often overlapped, encouraging the development of powerful new economic groups).[131] In this way, private banks rather than the Nicaraguan state channeled external resources, including balance-of-payments support that flowed into the private banks from the AID and the IMF.[132] A private banking system was to act as a direct link between emergent Nicaraguan entrepreneurs and transnational finance capital. The AID Strategy Statement stated that a key purpose of these banks would be to mobilize internal resources for the activities of domestic and foreign investors. Another purpose was to transfer the money supply, credits, credit policy-setting, and financial levers of the economy from the state to the private sector, thereby giving a powerful boost to the reconstitution of a hegemonic propertied class linked to transnational capital and with the capacity and resources to develop a new economic model for Nicaragua (see below).

The international economic straitjacket imposed on Nicaragua was accomplishing what direct repression had accomplished in Chile. For instance, the AID's "agricultural reform" did not propose the forcible return of lands to their prior owners. Rather, it called for privatization of the economy, the promotion of agro-exports, and the determination of property relations by free-market forces. Purely "economic" considerations applied under the banner of "efficiency" and fiscal and monetary policies to achieve macro-economic stability acted as non-coercive mechanisms that alienated peasant smallholders, undermined the peasantry as a class, reconcentrated land, and fomented a new, modernized capitalist agri-business sector. Macro-economic stability mandated a drastic reduction in bank credit to smallholders and the elimination of government price guarantees for the peasant sector. Deprived of credits, peasants were forced to sell their land. The promotion of large-scale export agriculture over food production for internal consumption also undermined the peasantry, since peasant producers accounted for nearly 100 percent of domestic food production, while export crop production was mostly in the hands of large landholders and agri-business. The credit structure and fiscal and monetary policies designed by AID and the international agencies benefitted a reorganized domestic propertied class that set about to reinsert Nicaragua into the international market. In 1993, for instance, 28,000 small farmers received no credit whatsoever, while just nine newly consolidated capitalist agri-business and export groups monopolized over 30 percent of all credits.[133] This same credit structure and related adjustment policies also undermined urban workers and smallholders. US and international aid, for instance, was made conditional on the speedy privatization of 400 state enterprises, representing 40 percent of the GNP. Militant labor struggles to have public enterprises turned over to workers' collectives led to the creation of a new trade-union owned "Area of Workers Property," comprising some 25 percent of privatized firms. But the same mechanism of credit allocation began to undermine the viability of these worker-run enterprises. Privatization thus became synonymous with a reconcentration of property.

This financial structure is an example of how, in the era of the global economy, transnational capital comes to penetrate, disrupt, and incorporate into its structures sectors previously outside of (or enjoying a certain autonomy *vis-à-vis*) the global economy. Land reconcentration meant immiseration for the expanding ranks of the newly dispossessed peasantry. Simultaneously, in the first year of the adjustment program alone, nearly 20 percent of the country's salaried workers lost their jobs as a result of mass dismissals of civil servants *and* of workers in productive public enterprises.[134] Some 70 percent of the economically active population was underemployed or unemployed by 1991.[135] Yet, in the larger scheme of things, the alienation of smallholders, property reconcentration, and the contraction of public sector employment helped facilitate conditions for the new economic model for Nicaragua envisioned by transnational capital and its local representatives. In this model, Nicaragua's reinsertion into the global economy was to be based on a modernized agro-export sector emphasizing "non-traditional" exports and on *maquilladora* assembling activities in urban-based duty-free export zones, as part of Central America's position as the southern rump of the emergent North American free-trade zone.[136] In 1990, the government set up in the outskirts of Managua the first of what was to be a series of tax-free *zonas francas* for transnational companies. By 1993, some dozen companies were operating mostly textile plants, paying wages of $30 a month to mostly female workers under state regulations prohibiting unionization.[137] Export-oriented agri-business and *maquilladora* assemblage required abundant cheap labor drawn from a huge pool of propertyless laborers and the unemployed, alongside a reserve army of the unemployed keeping wages down. The neo-liberal program was creating just such a labor force through the reconcentration of rural and urban property-holdings and massive layoffs in the public sector.

These programs were part of the far-reaching process of class restructuring, including atomization of the formerly well-organized working class, proletarianization of the peasantry, and the development of a New Right elite comprising a modernized private sector and administrative technocrats. In this process, economic and social policies were reciprocal. Cheap and unskilled labor does not require advanced education, but a workforce composed of a docile majority with minimal literacy and numeracy skills, and a small group of skilled technicians and managers. It was perfectly logical that the neo-liberal project involved drastic cutbacks in the educational budget (in the first year of the new government alone, the budget was cut by 44 percent),[138] the privatization of most secondary schools, and the introduction of tuition into previously free public schools. Once again education was becoming a privilege of the wealthy. US aid was used to finance several elite universities and technical institutes, including a new AID $3.1 million program in the Central American Institute of Business Administration (INCAE) to "train consultants" and place them in different government ministries as "technical and economic advisors."[139] The neo-liberal program, with its distinct class bias, placed the burden of adjustment on public and formal sector wage-earners and the domestic market and favored exporters, large-scale producers, and commercial and financial conglomerates tied to transnational capital. The transnational agenda advanced through US economic and political aid programs could not be realized without national actors strong enough to act as mediators and attuned to the transnational strategy, in which the relation is less that of complete subordination than of broad common interests and understanding. National histories and actors do exist in autonomy from the external milieu, but the latter imposes structures and circumstances which condition the contours and behavior of the former.

Direct US support for a reorganized private sector through the CIP, the private banks, the privatization process, and so forth, had the intent of building up a "modernizing" elite with the capacity to (1) influence state policies (2) influence civil society through predominance in the economy (3) serve as local links to transnational capital, and (4) develop its own economic power and give it the ability to promote and manage capital accumulation within the new economic model. US programs intended to build ties to local elites and challenge popular sectors sought to penetrate the state and civil society, to form a network of institutions in civil society as structures parallel to the state and able to instrumentalize the state, and to develop a nexus of state–civil society linkages displaying an interpenetration of interests and personnel between the government and "private" spheres. These linkages were developed through close coordination among, and institutional interpenetration between, the government (managing the state) and a private-sector elite hegemonic in civil society. Although the appointment of numerous US advisors in key economic, social and policy planning ministries was a requirement of US aid disbursals in the first years after the elections,[140] a more important activity funded by the United States was the creation of a core of New Right "technocrats" thoroughly trained and ideologically steeped in the worldview and logic of the transnational elite – people who, in the long-term US strategy, would go on to assume the reins of the Nicaraguan state.

While economic and political aid poured into the country, military aid to the EPS was out of the question. The preservation of a popular army born out of revolution deprived the Nicaraguan propertied classes of a repressive instrument. "The military and the police currently are dominated by Sandinista supporters," stated the AID Strategy Statement. "Loyalty of these institutions and its members to the current government is questionable and their actions in response to public disturbances over the last year have raised doubts about whether they respond to the dictates of the party or the mandate of the government." It concluded: "these institutions must be 'professionalized' so they can perform their proper function in society as guarantors of security and justice."[141] The Bush and the Clinton administrations applied enormous pressure in the years following the elections, including diplomatic threats and freezing US aid disbursements on several occasions, to purge the EPS leadership and to "de-Sandinisitize" both the army and the police, as part of broader pressures to push forward slow-motion counterrevolution.[142]

By late 1993, these pressures had registered some success. A combination of defunding, restructuring and the recruitment of new police officers from the ranks of the former Contras and right-wing political activists had gone a long way toward turning the police into a typical Latin American repressive force, routinely breaking up strikes, dispersing popular protests, and so forth. More importantly, the EPS leadership came to develop a corporate identity of its own once it was no longer tied to a revolutionary state. The EPS leadership came to view the army's institutional integrity as dependent on achieving legitimacy in the eyes of the local elite, Washington, and the international community. Achieving legitimacy meant adopting a doctrine of "constitutionality" and demonstrating its ability to repress protests by popular sectors when such protests transgressed legal or institutional channels.[143] In the 1990 general strikes, the EPS ignored government orders to violently repress the protesters, arguing that its constitutional mandate was limited to defending the country's sovereignty from foreign aggression, not to use force in internal political events. But over the next several years, the EPS began more and more to violently dislodge peasants who had taken over land in the countryside, to attack striking workers who occupied factories or government offices, and to break up often peaceful street demonstrations. Low-intensity democracy acts as a centripetal force in conforming distinct political and institutional forces to the parameters of its own legitimizing logic. The fact that neo-liberalism could be implemented despite the existence of the EPS demonstrated the power of the global economy to impose its agenda through economic power, irrespective of the balance of military force itself.

250

Conclusion: Intent is not ability: the contradictions between polyarchy, neo-liberalism, and social stability

Exuberant over the success of the electoral intervention project, US officials originally expected post-electoral strategy to fall smoothly into place. The AID Strategy Statement stated:

> Over the course of the [1991–1996] period, we anticipate a major transformation of the Nicaraguan economy and society. By the end of this period, the economy will be dominated by the private sector, traditional exports will be growing rapidly, and a variety of non-traditional agricultural exports will be well-established. By 1996, enclave manufacturing will have moved beyond an initial concentration in textiles into a wide variety of manufacturing operations. The United States will once again become Nicaragua's principal trading partner... Civic education efforts and the spread of a wide range of ideas through the media will have helped achieve general acceptance of democratic ideas, attitudes and values.[144]

But reality has proven to be less rosy than US forecasts. Social inequalities and consumption differentials, the concentration of wealth and income, and widespread impoverishment, a result of unbridled free-market forces released under the neo-liberal program, advanced at an alarming rate in the early 1990s. An austerity program had been in effect since the early years of the Contra war, and in 1988 the Sandinistas took a series of stabilization measures which proved highly controversial.[145] However, there were important differences between the Sandinistas' stabilization measures and the orthodox neo-liberal program introduced by the UNO government. The Sandinista program – whose frame of reference was a mixed and not a free-market economy – did not eliminate the "social wage" that protected the most vulnerable sectors and distributed the burden of austerity, and which included hefty education and health budgets and subsidies on essential consumption. Although the Sandinistas also sought to stimulate exports, they simultaneously pursued policies such as low-cost credit, guaranteed prices, etc., and retained an important role for the state, which allowed domestic-market producers to survive.

Relative poverty for much of the population under the Sandinistas became absolute poverty under the new government. Real wages dropped 50 percent in the first year of the new government, 69 percent of the population lived in poverty in 1992, and per capita food consumption fell by 31 percent between 1990 and 1992.[146] The health, educational, and other social gains of the revolution, although they deteriorated in the late 1980s as a result of the war, suffered a dramatic reversal with the change of government and the application of the neo-liberal program. In 1988 the government made an annual per capita investment in health of $57.10. This had dropped by 1993 to just $16.92. Vaccination coverage of children under five years old, which was 20 percent in 1980 and had reached 80 percent in 1990, fell in 1991 to about 60 percent (only 80 percent coverage or higher can guarantee the prevention of epidemics).[147] During the 1980s, cholera, malaria, measles, and other diseases had been eradicated or nearly eradicated. Between 1990 and 1993 these diseases reappeared and reached epidemic proportions. The infant mortality rate, brought to under 50 per 1,000 births in the 1980s, rose to 71 per 1,000 in 1991, and to 83 per 1,000 in 1992.[148]

Widespread rural immiseration and the government's policies of squeezing the peasantry fueled renewed military conflict in the countryside. The Contra rank and file, of poor peasant extraction, had been demobilized and promised land and credit following the change of government. Similar promises were made to thousands of demobilized Sandinista troops, also drawn from the ranks of the peasantry. By 1991, many of these demobilized peasant-fighters had taken up arms again. Although the old Sandinista–Contra antagonisms played a part, the new rural conflict, including land invasions, spontaneous violent clashes, and even organized warfare in some areas, reflected the emergence of class polarization and class-based conflict in the countryside. Adding fuel to the fire was opulence amidst mass poverty that did not exist under the Sandinistas, generating a sociological relative deprivation and further heightening social conflict.

The UNO, a fragile coalition united only in its opposition to the Sandinistas and held together by US money and pressures, disintegrated in the years following the elections into numerous competing factions, as much in conflict among themselves over sectoral and personal interests as with the FSLN. At the risk of simplifying highly complex phenomena, in the post-electoral period the Nicaraguan elite divided roughly into two groups. The first was attuned to the transnational agenda of polyarchy and neo-liberalism, with a more long-term vision of capitalist modernization based on the model mentioned above. This group was clustered in the executive inner circle, in key ministries such as Finance and the Central Bank, and in the new universities, think-tanks and financial concerns set up with US assistance. The other was grounded in the old agro-export oligarchy, in the traditional politics of partisan corruption and patronage, and inclined to restore a Somocista-style authoritarian order. The struggle between and within these two groups often took the form of highly visible political infighting and personal interests. In part, this was a result of the political culture rooted in Nicaragua's history, but it also reflected a more fundamental conflict over class formation and fractional interests therein, intermeshed with the penetration and germination of the transnational project for Nicaragua.

Washington opted, in the first few years after the elections, to support *both* sectors against the Sandinistas and the popular organizations in its zeal to eclipse the FSLN and to resubordinate the popular classes. The intelligence of US officials should not be overestimated: the strategy of political intervention was adroit in undermining the revolution and restoring power to the elite. But gut-level anti-Sandinismo in Washington led to short-term measures that acted against the long-term project of consolidating a polyarchic political system and a neo-liberal social order. Ultra-right forces, such as Managua mayor Arnoldo Alemán and Alfredo César, whose personal ambitions and agenda were closer to a restored authoritarianism and "crony capitalism" than to a modernized polyarchy, received substantial support for no other reason than their anti-Sandinista credentials. Given their self-serving agenda, Alemán, Cesár, and others became as much opponents of the executive and the New Right technocrats as of the Sandinistas; their activities might have helped to further erode Sandinista influence but they also disrupted the development of a polyarchic political culture among the elite. Success of the transnational project for Nicaragua required ensuring a cohesive elite. Yet US intervention in Nicaragua, from the Walker affair, to Zelaya's overthrow, the establishment of the Somoza dynasty, and the installation of the Chamorro government, had not resolved, but only suppressed, the historical conflict of a fractured elite.

The FSLN was a party in crisis in the early 1990s, with fierce and unresolved debates over a viable popular and revolutionary program for Nicaragua and the tactics and strategy to achieve such a program. Attempting to undertake the transformation from a party that had emerged from guerrilla clandestinity directly into state power to a legal opposition party operating within the legitimizing parameters of formal democracy proved difficult. The inability to articulate a coherent alternative to neo-liberalism meant political vulnerability, lack of definition, and incoherence in its own conduct. The Sandinistas wavered between providing critical support for the government in the name of national stability and reconstruction (in turn, such support for the government eroded the FSLN's authority among the popular classes), and opposing the government without providing an alternative program or decisive leadership to protesting popular sectors. The crisis of the FSLN reflected the challenge of the left and popular forces worldwide in the post-Cold War era: what type of a program and strategy is viable and realistic for a small, peripheral nation, given global forces which are too powerful to confront head on, the impossibility of withdrawal from the international system, and well-known limits to social change in any one country.[149] Space constraints limit discussion, but it is worth noting that, apart from personal ambitions and opportunism among Sandinista leaders, the objective conditions of free-market capitalism and the legitimizing logic of polyarchy laid the basis for coopting a sector of Sandinismo into a reconstituted Nicaraguan elite whose interests lay in the transnational bloc under the domestic hegemony of the emergent New Right and the overall hegemony of the transnational elite. Further research should explore theoretical implications from the Sandinista post-electoral experience.

As noted in chapter 1, the neo-liberal state has three functions: assuring macro-economic stability and juridical conditions (including the guarantee of property rights) for the operation of capital; providing the human and physical infrastructure necessary for capital accumulation; and maintaining social order. Only the first of these goals was met in Nicaragua in the early 1990s. The AID Strategy Statement warned:

> Investors will be looking for clear indications that political turmoil will be contained and for evidence of progress toward the establishment of a free-market economy... the government will need to demonstrate that it has developed a working legal and regulatory structure such that it can guarantee contracts, establish property rights, resolve disputes, and enforce laws which govern business and investment. It must also be able to demonstrate that law enforcement entities have the capability to maintain order in accordance with government directives and policy.[150]

Nicaragua, seen from the logic of the neo-liberal project, was in a vicious circle. Structural adjustment was to have provided the macro-economic stability for private capital to enter and operate freely.

Private foreign investment was to bring about growth and development. Growth and development was to bring about social peace and political stability. But the popular classes would not allow an anti-popular project to stabilize, and thus the economy continued to sink. Although Washington and the Nicaraguan elite were fond of blaming "Sandinista destabilization" for the permanent and myraid protests of the poor majority, the truth is that, by 1994, the Sandinistas no longer exercised much control over popular sectors, which demonstrated an increasing autonomy of action. Transnational capital, literally with "the world to exploit," would hardly choose Nicaragua to invest, given the belligerence and organization of the popular classes and the inability of the dominant groups to achieve hegemony.

In comparative perspective: the United States was able to facilitate a transition from authoritarianism to polyarchy in the Philippines and Chile as a result of the conditions particular to these countries, an astute reading among US policymakers of these conditions, and the existence in Washington of an emergent apparatus for carrying out the new political intervention. Conditions in the late 1970s did not allow the United States to facilitate such a transition in Nicaragua, and so, following the revolution, the United States launched a massive destabilization campaign, including political operations conducted under the rubric of "democracy promotion." The objective of the campaign was to make it impossible to implement popular democracy, break revolutionary hegemony, regroup the old elite forces, and restore them to power. Yet the possibility of consolidating a polyarchic political system and elite social order and renewing externally oriented capital accumulation seemed bleak in 1994. The popular classes resisted being drawn into a renewed elite hegemony and became increasingly restive, putting aside political allegiances as the entire country became polarized into an impoverished mass and an affluent minority. These difficulties in Nicaragua underscore the contradictions internal to global capitalism and the transnational elite's project of "market democracy." Nicaragua demonstrated the gap between goals and outcome, between intent and ability. Nowhere was this gap more evident than in Haiti.

6   Haiti: The "practically insolvable problem" of establishing consensual domination

The experience of Liberia and Haiti shows that the African race are [*sic*] devoid of any capacity for political organization and lack genius for government. Unquestionably there is in them an inherent tendency to revert to savagery and to cast aside the shackles of civilization which are irksome to their physical nature. Of course there are many exceptions to this racial weakness, but it is true of the mass, as we know from experience in this country. It is that which makes the negro problem practically insolvable.

US Secretary of State Robert Lansing, 1918[1]

Cité Soleil (Sun City) is a name filled with bitter sarcasm. It refers to the vast shantytown slum just north of Port-au-Prince. Poverty here reaches absolute bottom, below which can only be death. Barefoot children play on banks of muddy streams of raw sewerage or amidst toxic waste spills. A crippled man hasn't been able to get enough to eat for two days. A mother can't treat her baby's serious injury because of the cost of medical care. Despite these conditions, the most striking thing about Cité Soleil is not its desperate poverty. Rather it is the hope that is surging here with the growth of the Lavalas mass movement and the election of radical priest Jean-Bertrand Aristide.

US visitor reporting from Cité Soleil, March 1991[2]

As in the Philippines, Chile, and Nicaragua, the United States sustained an alliance in Haiti with a dictatorial regime, the Duvalier family dynasty, during much of the post-World War II period. By the early 1980s, the dictatorship was beginning to crumble under pressure from a burgeoning popular movement. Washington intervened to bring about a "transition to democracy." The first step, "preventative diplomacy," proved highly successful: Duvalier was removed from power in early 1986, in the face of a mass uprising, yet the Haitian state and, in particular, its coercive apparatus, the army, remained intact,

256

and the elite order largely unaltered. But the second step, cohering elements of the Haitian elite around the transnational agenda and placing this elite in power through free elections, proved hopelessly elusive. The project fell completely out of Washington's control: it *backfired*, bringing to the Haitian presidency, through elections in 1990 organized and financed by Washington, the representative of the highly mobilized and belligerent popular classes, Father Jean-Bertrand Aristide. "Preventative diplomacy" averted a revolutionary insurrection, but ironically the installation of a popular government and the initiation of a program of socioeconomic transformation was achieved through the very "democracy promotion" structures set up by Washington.

The military *coup d'état* against Aristide in September 1991 represented a regression to outright dictatorship. For the Haitian majority, this military dictatorship represented a return to the suffering and tribulation endured throughout the nation's history. For the United States and the Haitian elite, it was a mixed outcome. On the one hand, the dictatorship was an embarrassing and destabilizing anomaly in an emergent transnational political system whose legitimization lay in polyarchy, and its coming to power; created a foreign-policy crisis for Washington. On the other hand, the new military dictatorship, not unlike Pinochet in Chile, showed an uncanny proficiency in cutting short the embryonic project of popular democracy and in demobilizing and resubordinating the popular classes. The September 1994 US invasion, conducted under the banner of restoring Aristide to power and democracy to the country, was the complex and paradoxical result of the failure of the project to modernize the traditional structures of power in Haiti and to stabilize elite domination. The goal of the invasion, despite appearances to the contrary, was to place back on track that project *contra* Aristide and the popular classes.

The attempt to facilitate a "transition to democracy" in Haiti is illuminating on several accounts. First, it took place after the Cold War, and after the string of transitions in the 1980s, demonstrating that the reorientation of US policy has been less a conjunctural response to events in that decade than a long-term transformation. Second, as analyzed below, it brings home the point made by Gramsci that effective hegemony (as distinct from mere domination) is exercised in both civil and political society (in "state and society"); achieving superordination in only one is insufficient, either for the popular sectors or for dominant minorities. Third, it lays bare the deep contradictions internal to the project of the transnational elite, a theoretical and practical issue which I take up in the concluding chapter.

Saint-Domingue: paradise and hell[3]

In 1492, Columbus landed on the northwestern coast of the island of Hispaniola, in what is now Haiti. The place he described as a lush tropical "paradise" was inhabited by up to three million Taino-Arawak Indians. The indigenous population were soon put to work as slaves, and within two generations the Taino-Arawak people had become extinct, the victims of massacres, overwork, European diseases, and despair. Diego Columbus, who was given abundant lands and Indian slaves by his brother Christopher, set up the first sugar plantation in Haiti. Diego Columbus not only introduced "King Sugar" into the Caribbean Basin, which soon became the principal world supplier of the sweet substance that tied the region into the emergent world system, but also first imported African slaves into Hispaniola when the supply of Indian labor became exhausted. Spanish colonial development was concentrated in the eastern two-thirds of the island, which would eventually become the Dominican Republic. The relative neglect of the western portion, now Haiti, made it possible for French competitors to establish influence. At the end of the seventeenth century Spain ceded to France, engaged in intense commercial rivalry with other expanding European powers, the western portion of the island, which was renamed Saint-Domingue by France. The colony soon became France's richest and the envy of other European powers.

With its fertile soils and the thousands of sugar, coffee, cotton, and indigo plantations set up by French settlers and administrators of the French monarchy, Saint-Domingue furnished two-thirds of France's overseas trade, employing one thousand ships and fifteen thousand French sailors. In addition, the colony, which came to be known as *La Petite France* (Little France), supplied half of Europe's consumption of tropical produce. The 800 sugar plantations in the *Grande Ile à Sucre* (the Great Sugar Island) produced more than all the English Caribbean islands put together and the colony's overall trade is said to have outstripped that of the thirteen North American colonies.[4] This colonial paradise, however, was sustained by the most brutal slavery in recorded human history. French planters calculated that replenishing slaves with new ones after several years brought in more profit than making outlays to keep slaves alive. At the height of its productivity, from the early to the late eighteenth century, slavery killed some one million Africans, and Saint-Domingue became one of the world's greatest markets for the African slave trade. By the 1780s, 40,000 French whites ruled over 700,000 slaves and 28,000 mulattos who were technically free but enjoyed limited rights.[5]

In 1791, Haitian slaves launched a revolt against French plantation owners, led by the famed Toussaint L'Ouverture. The revolutionaries had to face successive onslaughts not only from Napoleonic France, but from Spanish and British forces – reflecting the magnitude of the interests involved, and fierce European commercial rivalries. All were defeated at the hands of the Haitians. The only successful slave revolt in modern history led to the proclamation of the Haitian republic in 1804. Jean-Jacques Dessalines, who became the revolutionary leader after Toussaint was captured and died in a French dungeon in 1802, adopted the ancient Taino-Arawak Indian name of Haiti, meaning "land of mountains," for the newly independent country. The establishment of the second independent republic in the New World and the first "Black Republic" had profound international repercussions. It inspired independence movements in Spanish America (Haiti, in fact, provided crucial support to Simón Bolívar), slave revolts throughout the Caribbean and the southern United States, and it decisively shifted the balance of power among European commercial rivals. The masses *do*, in fact, make history: the revolution led to the withdrawal of French ambitions in the New World, symbolized by the sale, shortly after losing Haiti, of the Louisiana territory to the United States, thus shoring up Britain and the United States as dominant powers in this period of capitalist world history.[6]

Independence, however, saw the replacement of the French elite with a new local elite, and led to chronic political instability, changes in government from one elite civilian or military clique to another through *coups d'état*, palace revolutions, and armed revolts, and deep and violent racial tensions. Beneath the post-independence turmoil lay the failure of a century-long attempt at nation-building, a result of contradictions internal to the new republic and of continued outside intervention. This century-long period culminated in 1915 with the invasion by US marines and a subsequent nineteen-year occupation which would lay the basis for the ascension of the Duvalier dictatorship.

Haiti's complex historical experience has been little understood by outside commentators, whose simplistic and Eurocentric observations, usually tinged by (if not steeped in) racism, have led to notions that Haitians are somehow inherently prone to violence, corruption, authoritarianism, disorder, and disaster. The country's tragic history of perpetual misery and crisis is attributed to an unexplainable and ingrained inability of the Haitians to organize their affairs successfully. As late as 1957, for instance, *New York Times*, in an article commenting on the first few months of the Duvalier regime, explained: "With only a few exceptions, Haiti has been unfortunate in her political leadership... This was inevitable in a country with an illiteracy rate of over 90 percent. The highly emotional people, who have little but tribal rule and superstition to guide their thinking, have been notoriously susceptible to demagogic political appeal. The political leaders by and large have approached their tasks with the utmost cynicism."[7] These images of Haiti persisted in the 1990s, with the Haitian people projected internationally as an "AIDS-infested" population, a "boat people" fleeing (not analyzed and not understood) misery, a people living on "international handouts," and a "basketcase" in efforts at nation-building and development.

Haiti's troubled past can only be grasped in its historical and structural context through an analysis of the colonial state of Saint-Domingue, the circumstances in which the Haitian state came into being, the conditions under which it had to survive, and the resultant class and socioeconomic structure. Several factors stand out: the peculiar class and racial composition of the dominant groups; the complete fusion of elite rule with the state and the absence of any organized civil society; an entrenched culture of authoritarianism, corruption, and violence bequeathed by the Spanish, the French, and the Northamericans; and most of all, the crippling limits imposed on Haitians' ability to determine their own national conditions by the country's subordinate position in the world system. An analysis of Haiti belies "political culture" theories, which hold that a people's cultural patterns determine historic socioeconomic outcomes. To the contrary, Haiti is a striking demonstration that historic socioeconomic structures, production and class relations foment certain political cultures, not the reverse.

Slaves in Haiti were kept down by perhaps the most extreme and arbitrary terror known in modern history, which left deep roots for a culture of violence, a political culture which became self-perpetuating after independence with the need for the tiny elite to resort to permanent repression to sustain its rule in the face of enormous inequalities. The incredible wealth produced in, and syphoned out of, Saint-Domingue led to an extremely pronounced system of corruption. As one study by the London-based Latin America Bureau notes, the colony of Saint-Domingue was a volcano of irreconcilable conflicts and racial hatreds. "The economic system which reigned in Saint-Domingue was a predatory one based on an enslaved labour force and unequal trade relations. To keep the conflicts in check and ensure that the process of extracting wealth continued to function, a militarized and authoritarian state was developed, run by the Navy Ministry in France." In turn, French military officers and colonial administrators in charge of towns and districts eagerly took advantage to turn their power into profits and "shamelessly held the island's inhabitants to ransom, exacting tributes far higher than the official taxes." The chief sources of revenue of colonial administrators "were the sale of trading permits, land and decisions on property matters, and involvement in smuggling rackets." The study concludes: "These two features of the colonial system – authoritarian military power and extensive corruption – became so deeply entrenched in the colony that they survived through the following 200 years as permanent and essential features of Haitian life."[8]

Another key factor in explaining post-independence Haitian history was the virtual lack of any continuity between the old colonial economy, based on linkage to the world market through capital accumulation on slave plantations, and the post-independence economy, based on subsistence peasant production.[9] The plantation system was broken up and lands parceled out to peasant smallholders, who over the generations further sub-divided plots among offspring. A process of capital accumulation internal to Haiti never really developed after the revolution. The elite did not engage directly in production but rather acquired wealth through international marketing of peasant production and usurious relations with peasants and small craft producers. As a consequence, rather than the production process, it was the Haitian state, extracting tribute from the peasantry from taxes, duties, and outright thuggery, that became the principal, and virtually only, source of wealth and power for the tiny Haitian bureaucratic and commercial elite. This explains the long-standing practice of ruling cliques to regard the state and government as their personal property, as well as the seemingly endless feuds and intrigues among the elites in and out of the army over which clique would hold the reins of the state – what Haitian anthropologist Michel-Rolph Trouillot refers to as "state fetishism," and what an Althusserian structuralist might refer to as the "overdetermination" of the state in the Haitian social formation. The lack of a process of internal capital accumulation laid the material basis for a disjuncture between civil and political society and created a structural situation highly inpropitious to any variant of consensual domination.

Moreover, the threat of an independent Black Republic at a time when slavery still flourished in the Caribbean, the United States, and much of the eastern seaboard of Latin America, and when Africa was just being conquered and colonized, led the Great Powers that controlled world trade to castigate and isolate Haiti, for whom recognition was a precondition for entry into the world market. Not until 1825 did France recognize Haitian independence, and even then only on extremely onerous terms, requiring an indemnity of 150 million French francs – perhaps the only case in history in which the victor was forced to pay reparations to the vanquished. This "independence debt" placed a heavy burden on the Haitian economy, forced the country into mortgaging arrangements with French, and later US, banks, and was not repaid until 1922.[10] The Vatican withheld recognition until 1860. The United States maintained a century-long *de facto* commercial embargo, refused to recognize Haiti until 1862, and did not establish diplomatic relations until 1886.[11]

The dynamics of race (or color) and class in Haiti is a further crucial historical factor. The mulattos, although they suffered discrimination under the white planters, also acted as a buffer between the French and the African slaves, and were able to acquire education, property, professional titles, and administrative experience. A substantial minority of their ranks even became slave and property owners themselves. Following the revolution, the white colonial elite was virtually banished from the country. In much of Latin America the "creole bourgeoisie," or the colonial elite, assumed the reins of power with independence, and in Africa and Asia post-colonial ruling elites' power had deep historical roots in their native lands and cultures. In Haiti, however, there was no indigenous ruling elite at the time of independence. Class and nation formation proceeded on the most fragmentary basis possible. The mulatto population became a privileged stratum, a new bureaucratic and merchant elite dominating commerce and government. The legacy of French colonialism was thus a deep class divide expressed in ethnic terms between a mulatto elite and a mass of impoverished ex-slaves, along with a tiny black elite that came into existence with independence (the categories of "black" and "mulatto" should be seen sociologically as social constructs particular to Haitian society).

Finally, owing to the fusion between the Haitian elite and the state and the localized, subsistence nature of much of the economy, civil society remained underdeveloped – indeed, virtually non-existent – in Haiti. The elite exercised power through control of the state and through coercion, and thus never developed their own organs in civil society. It was not until the large-scale penetration of transnational capital began in the 1960s and 1970s that localized communities were sufficiently disrupted and integrated into a national formation that the masses began their own organizing in civil society beyond the local level. Indeed, the state was the impenetrable domain of the elite, and civil society that of the popular classes. Thus the struggle of the popular majority against the dominant groups took on the perfect expression of a struggle of civil society against the state, or as Trouillot puts it, "the state against the nation," rooted in the historica; disjuncture between civil and political society which reached its peak under Duvalierism. This also meant that when Washington stepped in in the 1980s to try and implement "democracy promotion" programs, US organizers discovered a civil society already densely organized by the popular classes and under the hegemony of these classes.

Haiti provides graphic empirical support for Andre Gunder Frank's thesis that those regions most intensively exploited during the formative years of the "modern world system" would later, owing to the very intensity of that exploitation and the structures it left behind, become the most backward, marginalized, and impoverished areas.[12] From the wealthiest of all of Europe's overseas colonies, Haiti became, and has remained, the poorest country in the Western Hemisphere and one of the poorest in the world. In 1982, the country exported a mere $197 millions worth of goods, per capita income was $315, life expectancy stood at 48 years, infant mortality at 130 per 1,000, illiteracy at about 80 percent, malnutrition and undernourishment were endemic, and 74 percent of the nation's 6 million people remained in the agricultural sector. A full 74 percent of the rural population, and 55 percent of urban dwellers, were considered by the World Bank to live at or below the *absolute* poverty level. In that same year, 1 percent of the GNP went to public education and 0.9 percent to health, while the military consumed 8.3 percent of the GNP.[13] The Haitian blood plasma scandal of the 1970s was a grizzly expression of how the powers that be in the world system have – literally – sucked the life-blood of the Haitian people. Such is the level of poverty that Haitians blood develops much higher levels of antibodies than most societies in the world, making it highly valued on the world market. In the 1970s, Haitian businessmen, in cooperation with transnational pharmaceutical and chemical firms, among them Armour Pharmaceutical, Cutter Laboratories, and Dow Chemicals, set up a thriving business by indiscriminately extracting blood plasma from poor Haitian donors for $3 a pint and reselling it abroad at $35 a pint.[14]

From the US marine occupation to the Duvalier dictatorship

Dear me, think of it! Niggers speaking French.
US Secretary of State William Jennings Bryan, after receiving a
briefing on Haiti, 1912[15]

The first republic in the New World, the United States, showed only contempt for the Black Republic. The Haitian revolution had inspired Gabriel Prosser's slave uprising in Virginia in 1800, and the Denmark Vesey uprising in 1822. The white government in Washington, which maintained the US slave system for nearly sixty years more, responded to the newborn Haitian republic with a policy of isolation and nonrecognition. When official relations were finally established in 1886, the black diplomat sent by Port-au-Prince was deemed socially unacceptable and instructed by the US government to remain in New York rather than Washington, D.C.[16] Over the next few decades Haiti would acquire strategic importance for the nascent US empire because of the Windward Passage, a waterway shared with Cuba and considered vital to Caribbean and eastern US sea-lanes. Between 1857 and 1913 US Navy ships entered Haitian ports nineteen times to "protect American lives and property."[17] The Spanish-American War was fought by the United States in part to gain control over the vital waterway.

Over 3,000 Haitians died fighting US marines who invaded the country in 1915 and stayed on for nineteen years.[18] The marines were in Haiti as part of the Wilsonian project to install and stabilize elite regimes in the heyday of the young empire's effort to secure domination over the Caribbean Basin, considered the geopolitical springboard for worldwide expansion. In Haiti, however, the United States sent in a

High Commissioner to directly rule the country, which became not a mere protectorate, but an outright colony. "The Haitians are negro for the most part, and, barring a very few highly educated politicians, are almost in a state of savagery and complete ignorance," wrote a State Department official in 1921. Therefore, "in Haiti it is necessary to have as complete a rule within a rule by Americans as possible."[19] Nine years later, in 1930, the US chargé in Haiti reported: "In general, while the Anglo-Saxon has a... profound conviction of the value of democratic government," the Haitians were unsuitable for democracy because they were, "in common with the Latin in general... in the main directed by emotion rather than by reason" and is therefore "apt to scorn democracy."[20]

Operating with a vicious racism not felt in the country since the defeat of Napoleon's army, and with little understanding of the nation's peculiar history and social complexion, the white occupation force assembled political structures responsive to outside interests that only complicated endogenous political development. As noted above, by the 1820s, less than two decades after Haiti's independence, the mulatto and formally free elite, which represented 5 percent of the population, had come to control the reins of government and most of the nation's wealth. Thus began a century of conflict and accommodation between the mulatto elite and the small black upper and middle classes. *La politique de doublure*, or "the politics of the understudy," took root in the final decades of the nineteenth century, in which a black president, responsive to the mulatto elite structure, often occupied the presidential palace and satisfied his own personal constituency through graft. But as the nation's indebtedness and impoverishment increased, lower class unrest and elite infighting began to undo the *politique de doublure*, which had provided a modicum of stability. Between 1911 and 1915, seven presidents were overthrown. The unrest gave Washington the pretext it needed to intervene. The US occupation authorities further aggravated the racial and class divide by excluding all blacks from public life, placing the mulatto elite in power (the US High Commissioner installed four successive mulatto client-presidents), and transferring the economy to near total external control.

The occupation force established a customs receivership, took control of the nation's finances and of every ministry except justice and education, and rewrote the constitution to permit foreign ownership of property, long prohibited by the independent Haitians, who feared a return to complete foreign economic domination. The US official charged with drafting this constitution was Assistant Secretary of the Navy Franklin Delano Roosevelt, who at the time was pursuing numerous private investment schemes in Haiti.[21] One of the US companies that set up operations was the Haitian American Sugar Company (HASCO). HASCO ran a large sugar estate and the country's one giant mechanized sugar mill. The country's sole railway connected the HASCO sugar mill to the port capital, Port-au-Prince, and was also in the hands of US investors. The principal shareholder and financial underwriter of this railway was the National City Bank of New York, which took over Haiti's Banque Nationale. Roger L. Farnham, the bank's vice-president, became the State Department's principal advisor on Haitian affairs during the early years of the occupation. General Smedley D. Butler, who had in 1909 led US forces in the intervention in Nicaragua, would later charge that the marines invaded Haiti as a bill collector for the National City Bank.[22] With the occupation, the United States displaced its French and German rivals and became the principal external power, reorienting the Haitian economy towards dependence on the US market.

"The Marines perform a double function," explained a report by one US commission sent to investigate conditions in Haiti in 1926. "First, they protect the President from assassination; and second, they enable the American High Commissioner, Brigadier General Russell, to give the President authoritative advice."[23] The occupation force instituted forced public labor to construct military roads and other works. Blacks were manacled like slaves, compelled to work for weeks with little or no pay and inadequate food and shot down if they attempted to escape.[24] The US High Commissioner instituted severe press censorship (one proclamation forbad articles or speeches "reflecting adversely upon the American forces in Haiti") and detention without trial of dissidents, declared martial law for much of the occupation, militarized the entire country (US marine officers were appointed as administrators in every province and district and given near-dictatorial powers), and arbitrarily dissolved two rubber-stamp Haitian National Assemblies when deputies refused to carry out Washington's dictates.[25] The occupation force – exclusively white – introduced strict Jim Crow racial segregation in the country. No fewer than 147 brothels, hitherto unknown in Haiti, sprang up to cater for the decadent marines. The absolutely authoritarian and violent character of the occupation exacerbated the adverse local political culture.

The US marines disbanded the army and created a local *gendarmerie* staffed exclusively by mulatto junior officers under the command of US senior officers.[26] The occupation force departed in 1934, and the Haitian army they left behind became the repressive and corrupt regulator of power and guardian of elite interests inside Haiti, while the country remained firmly under US domination. US interests were transmitted via the US ambassador to the mulatto elite which remained in office for another twelve years, until President Elie Lescot was deposed by a military coup. Lescot was replaced by a black president, Dumarsais Estimé, but the army remained the backbone of real power, and overthrew him with US support. His military replacement, Colonel Paul Magloire, was thrown out of office in late 1956, leading to nine months of political chaos which saw five provisional governments and a one-day civil war that left several dozen dead. Thus the US occupation, far from resolving the crisis of elite rule, had aggravated it. This post-occupation instability laid the basis for the advent of Duvalierism, or what Trouillot refers to as a transition from authoritarianism to totalitarianism in response to the crisis of elite domination. Trouillot uses the term totalitarian as defined by Nicos Poulantzas, whereby dominant classes face a deep structural crisis, are unable to organize themselves politically, and face either the immediate threat of, or complete absence of, subordinate classes organizing and contesting political power. In distinction to mainstream political science notions of anti-democratic capitalist regimes as "authoritarian" and former Soviet-bloc regimes as "totalitarian," the term totalitarian is derived from "total" in the original sense meant by Mussolinists, whereby coercive domination pervades every aspect of social relations.

François ("Papa Doc") Duvalier, through a cunning manipulation of the inauspicious blend of local politics and US power, had been quietly working his way into the power structure with the departure of the marines. The black Duvalier appealed to the "politics of the understudy" to win support from the mulatto elite. At the same time, he built support among blacks, who made up 95 percent of the population, through manipulation of the Noirist backlash that spread after the marines departed. Noirism, a form of cultural nationalism, was an ideology of the black middle and upper classes, denied participation in leadership, that stressed racial pride, African cultural revival, and black political rule, yet did not question basic elite structures.[27] In this way, Duvalier squeezed an opening for a black elite and paved the way for a tenuous elite consensus that bridged the racial divide at the level of the dominant groups. Papa Doc was eventually elected president in 1957, with the backing of the army and with secret US support, in elections organized in the chaotic aftermath of Magloire's departure and mired in fraud and intrigue.[28] Rather than facing a second election, Duvalier declared himself President for Life in 1964, promising a stable, long-term alliance between the black and the mulatto elite and foreign (US) interests. "It was a mutually satisfactory relationship," noted one observer, "they [the local elite and the United States] profited from his power, and he became more powerful from their profits."[29] Just like Somoza, Duvalier thus achieved *stable*, although not consensual, domination.

If a modicum of elite consensus and US support was one girder of Duvalierism, its other was a combination of limited cooptation and a new black upward mobility for a chosen few, and the systematic, mass repression of the popular majority. Within days of assuming power, the first Duvalier initiated a wave of terror with few parallels in modern history, and which soon became permanent and institutionalized. At least 50,000 people are reported to have been executed by the Duvalierist regime between 1957 and 1985, hundreds of thousands were detained and tortured or disappeared, and another 1.5 million were driven into voluntary or forced exile.[30] Duvalier used the 1957 election campaign to establish a patronage network, recruited directly from the lower classes, the *chefs de section* (a national network of rural sheriffs), and the *houngans*, or *vodoun* priests, based on personal loyalty, cronyism, extortion, and intimidation of opponents.[31] The original members of this patronage network provided the basis for building the Volunteers of National Security (VSN), known throughout Haiti and the world as the Tonton Macoutes, the notorious paramilitary goon squads that terrorized the population.

Always the Machiavelli, Duvalier formed the Macoutes both as a counterweight to the army – as an insurance policy against a possible putsch to oust him – and as a highly efficient, if brutal and merciless, instrument of mass repression. The Macoutes reached into every layer and niche of society. Armed Macoutes were said to have outnumbered the army by two to one, while card-carrying VSN members numbered up to 300,000. "Duvalier's genius lay in how he designed their hierarchial structure, chose their social origins, and encouraged their recruitment in numbers so vast, they enabled him to survive every obstacle," noted one analyst. "The hierarchy was simple, a giant-bottomed pyramid with most Macoutes at the bottom and a few

Duvalier fanatics as commanders. At the pinnacle, in absolute control was Duvalier himself. Socially, the Macoutes came from the most disadvantaged classes and regarded the VSN as their sole escape from the relentless misery and hard work that inevitably awaited them."[32] The virtually all-black VSN thus insulated the Duvalier dynasty from the popular masses and also from any destabilizing elite intrigues, and at the same time provided the Duvaliers with a minimal social base; Macoutes could, and did, terrorize, extort money from, and just plain rob, any and every citizen, and thus the survival of 300,000 VSN members and their families in the lower classes came to depend on the survival of the Duvaliers.

As with Somocismo, Duvalierism was sustained by naked repression and a triple – if always tension-ridden – alliance between Duvalierist cronies, the Haitian elite, and the United States. To be sure, relations between the Duvaliers and Washington became highly strained at certain moments, particularly in the early years of Kennedy's Alliance for Progress and under Jimmy Carter's "human rights" policy, when dictatorships blemished stated foreign-policy projects. In 1962, the CIA attempted unsuccessfully to organize a *coup d'état* against Papa Doc similar to that which was successfully staged against the Dominican dictator Rafael Trujillo.[33] Although the incident led to a temporary suspension of economic (but not military) aid, shortly afterwards Washington saw the wisdom in long-term accommodation to Duvalier. US economic aid became the mainstay of the regime, while US military advisors providing training and weaponry for the army, the Tonton Macoutes, and later the counterinsurgency Leopard forces.[34] These military forces successfully suppressed scattered guerrilla movements in the 1960s and 1970s, sometimes with direct US participation.[35] When the ailing Duvalier's hand-chosen successor, his nineteen-year-old son Jean-Claude ("Baby Doc"), was sworn in upon his father's death in 1971 and appointed as the second "President for Life," the US ambassador, Clinton Knox, the only diplomat present at the ceremony, greeted the new unelected head of state by calling for an increase in aid to Haiti, while two US Navy warships stood offshore from Port-au-Prince to assure an orderly transfer of power.[36] US economic and military aid continued throughout the duration of the regime, including under the Carter administration notwithstanding its human rights policy.[37]

Foreign capital had first entered Haiti in the late nineteenth century, when French, German, and US business began to invest in commerce, public utilities, and some agricultural concerns, but this investment was small-scale and sporadic. It was not until the 1960s and 1970s that the complete exhaustion of peasant holdings, the large-scale penetration of transnational capital, and the bounding of the country more closely to the international financial system, led to the gradual breakup of the peasant economy. The continuous subdivision of land, one of the most severe ecological crises in the world (due to deforestation), the theft and concentration of lands by Duvalierists and agro-exporting fractions of the elite, and the arrival of foreign agri-business in the 1960s and 1970s, led to massive urban migration and the semi-proletarianization of those remaining in the countryside.[38] In turn, in the 1970s, Haiti was selected by the AID and the international financial agencies as a test-site in the Caribbean Basin for enclave manufacturing and industrial free-trade zones that signalled the beginnings of globalization (in 1981, the Reagan administration's Caribbean Basin Initiative, or CBI, would extend to the entire region the experiment set up a decade earlier in Haiti).[39]

Taking advantage of Haiti's abundant supply of cheap labor, some 240 transnational corporations poured into Port-au-Prince's free-trade zone in the 1970s and early 1980s, employing 60,000, mostly female, workers for a government-set wage of $2.70 a day. By the late 1970s, enclave manufacturing, almost exclusively of baseballs, lingerie, and electronic parts, came to account for about half the country's exports.[40] The Duvalier regime provided the transnational corporations with a tax holiday of ten years, no restrictions on profit repatriations, and the suppression of all trade union activity. Haiti "has an authoritarian style of government," explained the founder of the Haitian American Chamber of Commerce, Stanley Urban, "but there are more freedoms and opportunities in private enterprise than in many Western-style democracies."[41] While this type of assembly production contributed only marginally to government revenue and the number of jobs it created was insignificant in relation to the extent of unemployment and poverty in the country, the Duvalier regime boasted that Haiti was the coming "Taiwan of the Caribbean." A 1982 AID report asserted that it was "a real possibility" that Haiti would soon become developed through enclave industry assembling, and that the final goal was "a historic change to a greater commercial interdependence with the USA."[42]

US economic aid, directed toward bringing about the infrastructural and the technical-administrative changes necessary for assembly production, increased every year in the early 1970s, and quadrupled between 1975 and 1976 alone, reaching nearly $150 million in the latter year.[43] Other "development programs" sponsored by the AID and the international financial agencies accelerated this restructuring of the Haitian economy. These included programs to shift agriculture from subsistence food to agri-business export production, a goal achieved, in part, by dumping surplus food on the Haitian market under the CBI's self-proclaimed "food security" program, which further undercut peasant production. Under these programs, 30 percent of cultivated land shifted from food production for local consumption to export crops. A 1985 World Bank report stated that domestic consumption had to be "markedly restrained in order to shift the required share of output increases into exports... [emphasis should be placed on] the expansion of private enterprises... Private projects with high economic returns should be strongly supported [over] public expenditures in the social sectors [and] less emphasis should be placed on social objectives which increase consumption." An AID report was candid: "AID anticipates that such a drastic reorientation of agriculture will cause a decline in income and nutritional status, especially for small farmers and peasants... Even if transition to export agriculture is successful, AID anticipates a 'massive' displacement of peasant farmers and migration to urban centers."[44]

The CBI in the early 1980s and other "development programs" accelerated this structural process, along with its social repercussions and political consequences for the elite and for the masses. As part of these changes, corresponding to Haiti's insertion into the emergent global economy, Washington and the international financial agencies pressured Baby Doc into adopting a "liberalization" and "modernization" program involving an easing of political repression and greater fiscal and accounting responsibility. The Haitian elite became the local agents and managers of the transnational companies, signalling the alliance, *still under authoritarian arrangements*, of local and transnational elites.[45] In particular, that fraction of the elite tied to transnational capital assumed greater importance within the dominant groups. The complete exhaustion of the peasant economy and the nascent process of capital accumulation and proletarianization provided the structural context for a growing popular movement against the dictatorship. Between the 1970s and the 1980s, absolute poverty in Haiti is estimated to have increased from 50 percent to 80 percent of the population.[46] While the masses began to organize and demand popular democratization, new fractions of the elite tied to assembling and other external-sector activities began to feel the need for a new political structure – elections, an efficient government, and so forth.

✳The Haiti case demonstrates the dialectic between globalization and social, cultural, and political variables. Transnational capital, helped along by its institutional agents (in this case, the AID and the World Bank), penetrates and disrupts local communities. The autonomy and cohesion of even the most remote or autonomous communities are undermined, dispersing populations into new roles connected to a national formation and international relations. Simultaneously, the communications revolution brings together these dispersed populations and creates intersubjectivities who push for social change and democratization. Trouillot documents the change in collective behavior among disrupted peasant communities and new urban clusters which became aware of the decadent opulence of the urban-based elite only after their seclusion had been eroded. Even the poorest and most remote of Haitian communities came to witness – and resent – the ostentation of the elite, whose wild parties and extravagant consumption, broadcast on Port-au-Prince television and "society" communications outlets for the purpose of elite families trying to impress and outdo one another, acquired a national projection through expanded communications. "With the new national roads and major improvements in telecommunications [required by transnational capital], Haiti had become a truly 'national space'," Trouillot points out. "Words and images meant to impress certain segments of the population now reached unintended audiences. In the streets of the provincial towns, despair turned into anger, and anger into defiance... [popular sector leadership] undertook a systematic if modest politicization of the populace, infusing a civil discourse within the 'national space' newly created by increased centralization and improvements in transportation and telecommunications."[47] What Trouillot should add is that this new *national* space was, in turn, linked to emergent *transnational* space.

The Haitian case also demonstrates how an authoritarian political system is unsuitable, on two accounts, for the global economy. On the one hand, the corruption and cronyism of traditional authoritarianism impedes the efficient and modernized technical-rational administration required for the operation of transnational capital. Every effort in the 1970s to "modernize" Haiti ran up, under Duvalierism, against the ingrained system of graft and corruption (to complicate matters, Haiti under Baby Doc became a major drug trafficking center). On the other hand, populations such as the Haitian peasantry, disrupted by capitalist penetration and incorporated into broader structures, begin to mobilize beyond their local concerns and demand democratization. Infrastructural and other projects under which capital accumulation takes place require not just the technical participation, but also the political and social incorporation, of elites, professional strata, and popular sectors.[48] Washington attempted in Haiti, in the 1970s and early 1980s, to "liberalize" and "modernize" the regime without replacing the authoritarian system itself. Only when it became clear that this system could not resolve the two contradictions mentioned above did the United States turn to "democracy promotion." By that time, however, it was too late in Haiti for a smooth "transition to democracy."

Preventative diplomacy in Haiti: removing Duvalier from power

Washington maintained cordial relations with the Duvalier dictatorship in the early 1980s, while simultaneously trying to clean up the regime and continue the free-market policies begun the previous decade. During this time mass popular unrest was increasingly *in the face of* US support for dictatorship. The "modernization" and "liberalization" measures had led, by the early 1980s, to several attempts by a handful of elite opponents of the regime, many of whom were former Duvalierists themselves, to organize small political parties and other opposition groups, among them the tiny but vocal Social Christian and Christian Democratic parties. However, much of the anti-Duvalier movement was led not by traditional political parties, much less by that tiny fraction of the elite opposed in principle to authoritarianism, but by the popular sectors which had begun in the late 1970s a feverish organization at the grassroots level, often under the loose leadership of grassroots clergy and laypeople from the Catholic Church despite strong support from the church hierarchy and the papal nuncio for Duvalier. Among this grassroots Catholic leadership, Father Jean-Bertrand Aristide, the Salesian priest who had been excommunicated from the Catholic Church for his outspoken opposition to Duvalier, criticism of US policy, and promotion of liberation theology, was quietly becoming one of the leading voices of the downtrodden Haitians.

In 1985 localized protests which had been steadily expanding in frequency and scope erupted into nationwide demonstrations. The Haitian masses, from that moment on, began a virtually permanent yet largely uncoordinated uprising that would culminate with the ouster of Duvalier in February 1986. A reassessment in Washington, and concomitant shift in US policy to "preventative diplomacy," took place in 1985. In that year, economic aid was reduced and Washington's public stance on human rights in Haiti suddenly changed. The State Department quietly informed Duvalier officials that Washington expected "free elections, a free press, and genuine improvements in human rights observance" before former aid levels could be restored.[49]

When Duvalier made clear that he would not step down voluntarily, Washington turned to orchestrating his removal. US embassy officials contacted army Chief of Staff Lt.-Gen. Henri Namphy.[50] In turn, Namphy recruited Col. Williams Regala, inspector of the armed forces. The two, in consonance with US embassy activities, began garnering support among key members of the elite in and out of the security forces and important Tonton Macoutes. Wrote one insider sympathetic to the elite–US machination:

> The conspiracy that took shape... was predicated on the inescapable realization that Jean-Claude Duvalier had to go. But after Duvalier, who would rule Haiti, and how? The key issues related to the conditions of Duvalier's replacement... Namphy and Regala, with their military and civilian allies and the American officials who encouraged them, all agreed in principle that no new dictator would replace the old one and that democratic elections would be held as soon as possible. In the interim a provisional government would oversee the difficult period of transition... None of those who led it [the conspiracy] were revolutionaries, or even interested in profound social change... Friendly Americans, including Ambassador Clinton McManaway, Jr., gave them that reassurance [that Washington supported the putsch] and went even further. The US could also be counted on to help them in the ouster and its aftermath... The conspiracy to force Duvalier out was given impetus by surging popular protests, as throughout Haiti oppressed people rose up against Jean-Claude, his government, and the very nature of their daily existence under Duvalierism.[51]

A key turning point came when the powerful Haitian Industrialists Association (ADIH) issued a statement in January 1986 calling on Duvalier to step down and for "democratic structures" to replace him, citing popular unrest as a grave danger to "chances for attracting future investment."[52] The ADIH represented that fraction of the elite tied to the transnational economic concerns that had poured in in the previous two decades, and which was now deeply concerned that the popular-sector uprising could bring down the whole social order. Its break with Duvalier represented the irreversible separation of the elite, except for the Duvalierist inner circle of cronies, from the dictatorship. The ADIH statement coincided with the announcement by the State Department that $26 million in undisbursed economic aid was to be immediately suspended.[53] The conspirators and US officials were in near round-the-clock contact, including regular meetings between Namphy and Ambassador McManaway, who also sustained continual telephone communication with Duvalier himself over the terms of his departure from the country.[54] By this time, all of Haiti was in mass insurrection. Hundreds of thousands of people were attacking Macoute and army posts all over the country, sacking businesses, taking over towns, controlling roads, and nearly paralyzing the capital. In January 1986, US warships were stationed near Port-au-Prince and military planes and other reinforcements were placed on alert on the US mainland:[55] an integral element of coercive diplomacy is the use or threatened use of military force to back up diplomatic posturing. As with Marcos one year earlier, it finally became clear to Duvalier that his only choice was to step down. In the pre-dawn hours of February 7, the Duvalier entourage was accompanied to the airport under a US-French diplomatic escort and flown into exile in France on a US Air Force jet.

While the army and Macoutes carried out numerous massacres, in the final months of the insurrection key army commanders involved in the plan of "preventative diplomacy" ordered soldiers not to fire on demonstrators, in a tactical maneuver meant to place pressure on Duvalier to step down. For a brief period, the army as an institution was tactically aligned with the popular majority against the dictatorship, as part of the anti-dictatorial polarization and convergence of diverse sectors, a situation which, not unlike the Philippines, gave the appearance that the army was an ally of the democratic aspirations of the poor majority. This was one key distinction between Haiti in early 1986 and Nicaragua in the final months of its 1979 revolutionary insurrection: in Nicaragua the National Guard remained loyal to Somoza to the very end, and thus the coercive apparatus of the state disintegrated with the demise of the dictatorship (in addition, the Haitian insurrection was a largely unarmed insurrection). In Haiti, the

✗separation of this apparatus from the dictatorship meant its preservation. Another key distinction, owing to Haiti's distinct history and circumstances, was that the Haitian masses lacked an organized and unified political leadership (whether popular or elitist) ready to seize state power itself. The anti-Duvalier role of the army explains why, in the early morning hours of February 7, when hundreds of thousands of Haitians took to the streets in jubilation over Jean-Claude's pre-dawn departure, they hoisted many a Haitian soldier on their shoulders and shouted such slogans as "long live the army."

But beyond this tactical convergence, the army's strategic objective as an institution was that of preserving the social order. The honeymoon between the army and the people would be extremely short-lived. Six hours after its installation, the new military junta issued its first decree, imposing an immediate and unlimited curfew, and detained hundreds of people – the junta's response to the jubilation that had broken out at once throughout the country.[56] Almost immediately after the dictator's departure, mass protests began against Duvalierism without Duvalier. Over the next five years, Haiti experienced a national power vacuum and became immersed in a cauldron of turmoil – workers' strikes, demonstrations and conventions of opposition groups, shifts in the government, arrests and shootings, mass protests and massacres – as contending interests fought it out and political constellations took shape.

From Duvalier to Aristide: the aborted transition to polyarchy

Elites in the state versus popular classes in civil society

The removal of Duvalier was one phase in a Haitian "transition." The second phase involved two simultaneous processes: one was the cultivation of a modernized Haitian elite with its own political parties and civic groups; the other was countering and neutralizing the influence of the mass and popular organizations that were already flourishing in civil society. Accomplishing this second phase would be extremely difficult. The Haitian elite had a scant presence of its own in civil society, lacked internal cohesion, and demonstrated little interest in forsaking the politics of power plays and patronage for polyarchic competition in its own ranks, much less traditional graft for a process of "honest" capital accumulation in which its relation to a free market,

276

rather than extortion, would be its source of privilege, as called for by the transnational elite agenda.

An even greater challenge was to wrest influence from popular sectors. The correlation of forces favored popular hegemony in civil society by the time the "transition to democracy" began, even though the state remained a bastion of the dominant groups, firmly under elite–US control. The post-Duvalier struggle of the popular classes against the elite took the near-perfect form of a struggle of civil society against the state, or what Trouillot calls "state against nation." This unique situation was explained by factors particular to Haiti's own "deep" structural history: the character of the dominant and subordinate groups, the state, the economy, and so on. But it was also due to the more recent history of the Duvalierist "totalitarian" period: by eliminating political parties, trade unions, media, the rule of law, and every arena of "private" initiatives and activities which Gramsci considered to be the pillars of civil society, Duvalierism eliminated virtually all state–civil society linkages (this was not, it should be noted, the case in the Philippines, Chile, or Nicaragua). This led the popular sectors to seek out new forms of organization based on loosely organized popular and civic groups operating largely outside of the traditional political arena. In particular, neither the elite nor left and popular forces had significantly developed political parties as mediating links between the state and civil society. The anti-dictatorial uprising was not under any unified or coherent leadership or organized national movement of *any* political stripe.

Each side, therefore, faced enormous challenges. For the United States and the Haitian elite, particularly its transnational kernel organized in the ADIH, tied to the international financial institutions and/or to the network of US "democracy promotion" agencies that streamed into the country after Duvalier's departure, the challenge was how to simultaneously cultivate elite constituencies that would forsake the old authoritarian patterns for the culture of polyarchy *and* neutralize the influence of the popular classes. But which representatives of the elite were not tinged by Duvalierism and corruption? And how could Washington juggle its requirement for the army to assure internal order in the face of a growing mass movement for popular change with the need to overcome Duvalierist authoritarianism? Clearly, the process would be gradual, incremental, and long-term, and would be accomplished through political and ideological competition with popular groups as well as through direct state repression. For this purpose, the United States broadly employed economic, military, and political aid in the post-Duvalier period.

For the popular majority, the challenge was how to dismantle the deeply entrenched structures of Duvalierism, resist the ferocious repression that was unleashed within days of Duvalier's departure, and forge a viable popular project in a chaotic and uncertain milieu. "What Haiti represented in the aftermath of Duvalier's flight," noted Latinamericanist scholar James Ferguson in 1987, "is not a post- but a pre-revolutionary society." He continued: "Already, the slum-dwellers of Port-au-Prince, Cap Haitien and Gonaives have organized their own committees and action groups. Already, too, the peasantry of every department are beginning to forge links around common problems of rural underdevelopment and exploitation, thus breaking down the traditional obstacle of regional parochialism."[57] The depth, breadth, and scope of this grassroots activity between Duvalier's ouster and the 1991 *coup d'état* was truly astonishing. A vibrant popular democracy was being constructed at the local level, a spontaneous process of bottom-up democratic development, what Gramsci called "expansive hegemony." One first-hand report by an international delegation noted:

> Until the September 1991 coup, Haiti boasted an abundance of peasant associations, grass-roots development projects, trade unions, student organizations, church groups and independent radio stations... Known broadly as "popular organizations," the members of these groups came mostly from the country's vast poor majority... While many international observers of Haiti bemoan its lack of economic development, its civil society was remarkably advanced. In contrast to many other countries emerging from dictatorial rule, where pluralism among political parties was not matched by social and ideological diversity, political parties in Haiti were among the least developed parts of civil society. Rather, the strength of Haitian civil society lay in its breadth and diversity outside the narrow realm of electoral politics. This development allowed Haitians a considerable voice in local affairs, even as their ability to influence national politics was limited by an unrepentant army intent on preserving the spoils of power.[58]

Thus the elite remained in control of the state and nominally in charge of the country, but the popular majority came to occupy and control civil society. Preventative diplomacy had succeeded in preserving the formal structures of power, but this majority was developing a sense of its own power, irrespective of the eventual outcome of any election.

278

Duvalierism without Duvalier; popular democracy without the state

Baby Doc's departure left intact many of the structures of the dictatorship, including the hated Tonton Macoutes and the army. In fact, as one insider to the "preventative diplomacy" plan noted: "An integral part of the plan was for the post-Duvalier government to protect the Macoutes in return for their cooperation [in removing Duvalier], exempting them from judicial prosecution for crimes committed under Duvalier and guarding their physical safety as much as possible."[59] Following Duvalier's departure, the army, although it formally disbanded the Macoutes, began a process of integrating Macoutes into the armed forces and also allowing them to regroup and resurface, while the junta, led by Namphy, blocked all but a handful of attempts to bring Duvalierists to trial (after the 1991 coup, those few who had been tried and imprisoned were released).[60]

This Duvalierism without Duvalier was sustained by the United States as Washington set about to guide a "transition to democracy." Economic assistance to Haiti jumped from $55.6 million in 1985 to $77.7 million in 1986 and $101.1 million in 1987,[61] while the NED and the AID launched "democracy promotion" and "electoral assistance" programs to mount electoral machinery and develop elite civilian constituencies inside Haiti. Most importantly, the Defense Department and the CIA sustained the military forces of Duvalierism with a security assistance program. Within two weeks of Duvalier's exit, the United States gave the military government $500,000 in anti-riot gear.[62] In July 1986, the US Congress approved $4 million dollars in "non-lethal" military aid to the Haitian army.[63] In early 1987, the Pentagon sent in twenty military advisors.[64] Simultaneously, the CIA set up and funded a National Intelligence Service (SIN) in the Haitian military. When this covert program was revealed several years later, in 1993, CIA officials claimed the unit was intended to fight narcotics trafficking. Yet narcotics trafficking, which had become rampant under Jean-Claude, was run mostly by the military itself and leaders of the unit were also central figures in the drug trade. In practice, the unit had little to do with drug interdiction, and instead acted as an instrument of political repression and as a channel for establishing contacts between Washington and key military and political figures in the post-Duvalier political landscape. These same figures would emerge as important leaders and supporters of the 1991 coup.[65]

Among those on the CIA payroll was Lieut.-Gen. Raoul Cédras, who led the 1991 coup, and other key members of the junta that took over after Aristide. During the 1986–1991 period the CIA-created SIN unit "produced little narcotics intelligence," but, stated one US intelligence officer, its members "committed acts of political terror against Aristide supporters, including interrogations and torture" (among courses taught to SIN trainees were "The Theology of Liberation" and "Animation and Mobilization").[66]

Meanwhile, the Haitian masses, emboldened by their victory over Duvalier and new-found sense of power, demonstrated a burst of creativity and grassroots activity. Thousands of popular community councils sprung up in slums throughout Port-au-Prince and other cities. They engaged in political mobilization, human rights activities, literacy and adult education programs, improvement and self-help projects. In the countryside, peasant leagues, which had been organizing since the 1970s, now burgeoned, demanding land, credits, the removal of local bosses, and so forth. The process of exorcizing Duvalierism became known as *dechoukaj*, meaning "uprooting" in Creole, or, as the slogan went, "we cut down the tree, but we haven't got rid of the roots." The process, portrayed abroad as lawless Haitian mobs obstructing the construction of democracy, was actually a highly selective targeting of those individuals who had committed the worst atrocities and whom the government refused to prosecute.[67] Alongside uprooting the old, new social relations flowered in civil society, based on a new-found sense of hope, community, and collective identity.

This loss of fear on the part of the popular sectors, the sense of self-confidence and hope in place of desperation and passivity, instilled a deep trepidation in the elite and their US backers. Yet US officials pinned their hopes – indeed, displayed an almost blind faith – in a successful electoral process and on repression in the interim to hold back the popular avalanche. With their eyes on elections scheduled by the junta for November 1987, well-known opponents and supporters of Duvalier from the elite set up their own parties. With few exceptions, traditional political parties, when they existed at all, were barely more than arrangements of convenience among a self-aggrandizing leader, his clients, and followers. Some 200 such parties were formed in 1987, either by old-guard politicians and "former" Duvalierists or by the new technocrats and career politicians that had emerged during the "liberalization" and "modernization" period and were being groomed by US political aid programs (see below). None of these parties had ties to the grassroots popular movement, which continued to distrust the formal political arena. Some two dozen of these parties named candidates as the elections approached.[68]

The November 22, 1987 elections, however, were canceled by Namphy's junta on election-day morning, after the army opened fire on civilians at polling stations, killing at least thirty-four and wounding hundreds more. The election-day massacre was not an attempt to prevent a popular electoral victory – neither Aristide nor any other prominent figure from the grassroots popular movement were candidates. Rather, it was an outcome of the lack of consensus among the elite, the fear among the army and the still prevalent Duvalierists of any change that could come through elections, and the extreme difficulty of any orderly transition to polyarchy in Haiti's environment. After the bloody massacre, Washington formally suspended military aid, but the covert CIA assistance to the security forces did not stop.[69] In fact, Washington continued to work closely with the military government. Repression by the new military junta once again became systematic and institutionalized. The strength of authoritarian forces, and of authoritarianism ingrained in the state itself, begat a series of coups and counter-coups over the next few years, against the backdrop of chronic elite infighting and state repression of the popular movement. The Namphy regime and those which succeeded it through the 1991 inauguration of Aristide were responsible for more civilian deaths than Baby Doc managed in fifteen years.[70] Yet US officials downplayed or entirely ignored the systematic violation of human rights that continued, and escalated, under the post-Duvalier regimes. Asked by human rights organizations shortly before the 1987 elections about reports of routine abuses, US ambassador Brunson McKinely said, "I don't see any evidence of a policy against human rights." True, he said, there was violence, but it was just "part of the political culture."[71]

Between 1987 and 1990, three coups took place and another scheduled election was canceled. Namphy was followed in early 1988 by Leslie Manigat who became president in unconstitutional elections boycotted by over 90 percent of the population. When Manigat made preliminary moves to loosen military control over the presidency, he was promptly sent into exile by Namphy, who took over the presidency for himself in June 1988, only to be overthrown by General Prosper Avril in a bloodless coup three months later. In November 1989, newly appointed US ambassador Alvin P. Adams, Jr., arrived in Port-au-Prince. Adams, a former USIA officer in Vietnam and member of the NSC under Kissinger, soon became a familiar face in Port-au-Prince, shuffling from one meeting with Haitian factions to another, conducting political and electoral negotiations, and reminding the military regime that its relations with Washington depended on it carrying through the "transition."[72] When it appeared that Avril might waver in a resumption of the electoral process, it was Adams who personally convinced him in March 1990 to step down.[73] Avril was replaced in the presidency by Supreme court Justice Ertha Pascal Trouillot. Behind the scenes, the US Embassy placed additional pressure on the military to allow new elections, which were subsequently scheduled for December 1990.

As the 1990 elections approached, the grassroots movement burgeoned into a popular revolt against the traditional structures of power and corruption. The issue of electoral participation became a point of contention. Many organizations, especially the grassroots church groups, argued that the establishment of local councils, local empowerment, and regional structures of participatory democracy was more important than national elections and the formal political process. In 1986, dozens of organizations close to the grassroots church groups formed the Liaison of Democratic Forces. In 1987, these and other groups expanded into a loose coalition known as the Democratic Movement. Shortly afterwards, a total of 284 national and local grassroots organizations came together to form the National Congress of Democratic Movements (KONAKOM). Two other multi-sectoral coalitions were formed in 1987, the Group of 57 and the National Popular Assembly (APN).[74] The grassroots base of the Catholic Church, and particularly the Ti Legliz (literally, the "Little Church," or Christian Base Communities), played a major role in the popular movement, providing loose organizational structures and networks and the broad ideological umbrella of liberation theology's "preferential option for the poor" – an ecclesiastical enunciation of popular democracy.

Most towns and cities boasted umbrella organizations which brought together hundreds, and sometimes thousands, of individual community councils. In turn, most of these urban, district, and provincial groups banded together into loosely structured national federations, such as the National Alliance of Popular Organizations. In the rural areas, the poor peasantry was becoming an organized social force with its own identity for the first time in Haitian history. Peasant leagues that had sprung up locally joined together into decentralized regional federations, and then, in 1991, into a loose national coalition, known as the National Peasant Movement of the Papaye Congress, which brought together the powerful Tet Kole movement of the northwest, the Papaye Peasant Movement of the central plateau, the Trou de Nord Peasant Organization of the northeast, and the Sunrise Peasant Movement of the southeastern provinces, among others.[75] These peasant leagues, in turn, joined forces with local development groups in rural social, development, and empowerment projects.

One important link between the urban and rural groups was the Autonomous Federation of Haitian Workers (CATH), which had sprung up in the 1970s among workers in the industrial-free trade zone, led by the veteran trade unionist and anti-Duvalier militant Yves Richards. The CATH had been banned by Duvalier in 1980 but reemerged publicly in 1986. It practiced an activist and community-based trade unionism, bringing together some forty workers' unions with some two dozen urban neighborhood committee federations and twelve peasant associations. Importantly, therefore, Haiti's poor peasant majority allied with other popular sectors in a broad national front for popular democratization, thus avoiding what anthropologist Eric Wolf has identified in other studies of peasant revolts as rural parochialism or manipulation by outside elite interests.[76]

In turn, specific sectoral organizations, including women's, youth, and student groups, proliferated. The Haitian Women's Solidarity (SOFA) formed itself in 1986, with branches throughout the country, for the advocacy of equal rights and social justice for women. Regional women's groups, such as the Determined Women collective in Jacmel, which organized collective boutiques, literacy instruction for women, and meetings to discuss issues of politics and gender equality, also flourished. Youth, which had been most active in the anti-Duvalier uprising, and later in the transition period, formed the Youth Coordinating Committee, tied to Christian Base Communities, and other national, regional, and local groups. Then there was the militant National Federation of Haitian Students, bringing together university and vocational school students, and the Students' Concerns organization, which brought together high-school students nationwide.

A remarkable transfer of the functions of the state from the government to the organized population began to take place: self-governing committees and action groups in urban and rural areas functioned outside formal state structures. Many were identified with the Ti Legliz and others with the CATH, but even more were local and autonomous, creating their own forms of representative leadership and laying the groundwork for radical social transformation. They set up clinics and schools, dug irrigation ditches, constructed silos for grain storage and opened roads connecting agricultural communities to previously inaccessible markets, eliminating the role of exploiting middlemen and a source of urban elite profits. These peasant groups established agricultural cooperatives and collective labor teams, occupied state lands, redistributed private properties and refused to pay rent to large landowners whose land they worked – all of this while state power remained firmly in the hands of the elite and their United States backers.

The outspoken and charismatic Aristide had emerged as the leading voice for change and the unifying symbol of the popular mass movement. Consequently, he was targeted for repeated assassination attempts, including the September 1988 attack on his church, which was burned to the ground by Tonton Macoutes as army units sat by idly watching. Twelve parishioners were killed and seventy-eight wounded. Aristide escaped unharmed and was forced underground. A year later, when Aristide was expelled from the Salesian order, he opened and ran an orphanage in Cité Soleil, a sprawling Port-au-Prince slum. US officials showed nothing but contempt for Aristide during the 1986–1990 period. The US Embassy monitored his every movement and US diplomats portrayed him as a dangerous demagogue and an "extremist" bent on opposing the democratic process.[77]

By 1990, groups from the KONAKOM, the Group of 57, the APN, and other coalitions had effectively joined forces, forming what became known as the Lavalas movement, literally meaning "avalanche" or "flood," or more figuratively, "the cleansing flood." The Lavalas movement was not a political party. Nor was it an organized leftist movement. It was a semi-spontaneous and loosely organized *popular* "civic uprising" from within civil society. It brought together hundreds of thousands, and later millions, of poor Haitians from the teeming slums of Port-au-Prince and other cities together with the impoverished rural population. Lavalas became the political and electoral expression of all Haitians who aspired for a fundamental break with the old order. Aristide had by now become the leader of Lavalas and the most popular figure in Haiti. "Aristide and the poor are one," became the slogan. One would have expected any outside power truly interested in promoting democracy in Haiti to have given technical or organizational support to this highly representative force as a most authentic expression of "people's (*demos*) power (*cratos*)."

284

However, the United States was out to promote *polyarchy* in Haiti, not popular democracy. This meant cultivating elite constituencies (described by the United States as "the moderates," or the "center") and training them in the art of formal democratic procedure. So, as the US funded and guided the development of electoral structures, it simultaneously bypassed the popular democracy movement and instead built up the civic and political organizations of the Haitian elite.

US political aid programs between 1986 and 1990

The NED initiated activities in Haiti in 1985 with a program handled by the CIPE to strengthen the technocratic sectors of the elite tied to transnational capital and organized in the ADIH. After Duvalier's ouster political aid programs were expanded dramatically. The NED spent several million dollars between 1986 and 1990 to organize and fund a series of political parties, trade unions, professional associations, human rights groups, and elite clearing-houses. These included: the Haitian International Institute for Research and Development (IHRED); the Human Resources Development Center (CDRH); the Haitian Center for Human Rights (CHADEL); the Association of Journalists; the mostly conservative Catholic Church hierarchy; Celebration 2004; and two conservative trade union federations.[78]

The IHRED and the CDRH functioned as clearing-houses for efforts to coalesce an elite that could promote the transnational project, establish its own civic organizations, and penetrate civil society. The IHRED became active in Port-au-Prince and other cities, while the CDRH focused on the rural areas. Established by an AID grant in 1985, the CDRH operated a full-time staff of about forty people in Haiti, and, according to one AID document, focused on influencing grassroots groups and on organizing "rural professionals and the elite."[79] The methods used were similar to those documented in the chapter on Nicaragua: identifying potential leaders among the elite; organizing them institutionally around US-funded groups with interlocking boards; imparting training sessions in "democratic" and free-market ideology; utilizing the multiplier effect to recruit and train mid-level and local leaders; and providing these interconnected networks with a political action capacity, communications skills, and the material resources to develop a social base.

The IHRED was created in 1986 at the behest of the USIA and directed by Leopold Berlanger, a conservative Haitian technocrat and well-known figure from the mulatto upper class.[80] Its Board of Directors and its larger Advisory Council brought together many of the prominent leaders of the business and political technocratic elite who had begun to organize in the late 1970s and early 1980s period of "liberalization" and "modernization." Over the next few years, the IHRED fostered a loose formation known as the "Democratic Center," which incorporated the leaders and cadres of the string of NED-funded groups and other elite organizations then under development, and set about to counter Lavalas influence. The IHRED sponsored seminars and colloquia, research activities, and communications and media programs, facilitated the creation of "local leadership councils," and conducted training workshops for professionals and elite leaders, acting as a centripetal think-tank and clearing-house in an effort to bring together a network of political and civic leaders from outside of the Lavalas movement and tied to the elite.[81] The IHRED also participated in intensive "party-building" and "civic education" campaigns in the 1987–1990 period, which were financed with approximately $2 million from the NED and the AID and supervised by the NDI and the NRI, as well as by the ADF and the IFES (the latter groups had also administered US programs in Nicaragua).[82] In these "party-building" activities, leaders from US-sponsored "democracy" programs in the Philippines, Chile, Nicaragua, and elsewhere were brought into Haiti to impart advice and share experiences, demonstrating again how US "democracy promotion," as an expression of transnationalized politics, acts as an "integrating mechanism" for cross-national elite blocs in the South. The NDI and the NRI brought together ten political leaders from the elite, who became known as the Group of Ten. "Haitian participants [in NDI-sponsored party-building seminars] included representatives from 'The Group of Ten,' a centrist grouping that meets periodically under the auspices of the Haitian International Institute for Research and Development," explained one NED document.[83] A US Embassy document advising the NED on which political leaders to select for "party-building" seminars cautioned that Yves Richards, the leader of the militant CATH, "is a Marxist extremist; anti-US," and should be excluded.[84]

The Group of Ten included Leslie Manigat, Louis Dejoie Fils, Gregoire Eugene, Colonel Octave Gayard, Hubert Deronceray, Rockefeller Guerre, and Marc Bazin, among others, all well-known conservative political figures from the elite and most of them tainted by former association with the Duvalier regime, yet touted by Washington as "the leaders of the post-Duvalier democratic movement."[85] Most of these people proved to be more interested in personal ambition that in a coherent political program, and went on to become presidential candidates in the aborted 1987 elections. As the 1990 elections approached, the NRI and the NDI funded a total of sixteen political parties, most formed in Baby Doc's "modernization" and "liberalization" period or through the NED programs in the post-Duvalier period, and none of them from the Lavalas movement. "What unites these disparate parties is a common belief in private enterprise, fiscal responsibility and economic reform as well as a detailed plan for how to bring it all about," explained the NRI.[86] Of these parties, ten fielded candidates, most of which garnered less than 1 percent of the votes in the 1990 elections (see below).[87] The coalition that ran Aristide as its candidate and won nearly 70 percent of the vote, the National Front For Democracy and Change (FNDC), did not receive any funding from the NED.

Among the organizations to emerge from the party-building efforts was the Movement to Install Democracy in Haiti (MIDH), which was headed by Bazin. Bazin was the quintessential representative of the New Right technocrats of the new mold promoted by the NED, the AID, and other institutions of the transnational elite. A World Bank official, Bazin had served briefly as Jean-Claude Duvalier's finance minister in 1981, sent in by the international financial agencies as part of the process of "liberalization" and "modernization." Bazin was to oversee fiscal and monetary reforms and clean up the country's accounting. He resigned after serving only five months and returned to the World Bank, finding it impossible to push through economic reforms in the quagmire of corruption, and he thus enjoyed respectability among the Haitian public.[88] Bazin, a colleague of Berlanger and a member of the IHRED Advisory Council, was back in Haiti after Duvalier's departure, and soon became Washington's preferred candidate for the December 1990 elections.[89] As the IHRED helped cultivate his base, other organizations funded by the NED and the AID cultivated constituencies for his presidential bid. According to one US businessman tending to his investments in Haiti during this time, "US neutrality in the electoral process was only theoretical." Bazin was "adequately financed by the US embassy in Port-au-Prince to build a political machine." He was provided by Washington with the funds and guidance "to campaign throughout most of Haiti's 19 political departments... His campaign included US-style advertising – posters plastered on walls in most towns and the capital, plus radio speeches and television time."[90]

The NED-funded human rights organization CHADEL was headed by Jean-Jacques Honorat, a former minister of tourism under Duvalier. Following the September 1991 *coup d'état*, Honorat was chosen as figurehead prime minister by the military, while the CHADEL released a torrent of criticism of Aristide's human rights performance to justify the military takeover. Honorat himself said the Aristide government was responsible for its own overthrow. "The coup was provoked by the comportment of those in power, " he said. "It was a reaction by the social body politic, and force had to be exerted by the only part of the social body with arms: the army."[91] (After Honorat resigned as figure-head prime minister in June 1992 the regime appointed Bazin to the post.) Washington had selected CHADEL for support despite the fact that several prestigious and internationally prominent human rights organizations already existed in Haiti. These included the League of Former Haitian Political Prisoners, the François LaFontant Human Rights Committee, and the Platform of Haitian Human Rights Organi-zations, a national coalition of local and regional groups, among others, all of which were bypassed in the US funding because of their links to the popular movement and the difficulty in manipulating them from the outside.[92]

The Association of Haitian Journalists was founded in 1955 and maintained a close association with the USIA. It brought together journalists working in the Duvalierist state-run media outlets and was closely associated with the dictatorship.[93] Celebration 2004 (that year will mark the 200th anniversary of Haitian independence) was formed by several Haitian professionals in the diaspora who returned to Haiti following Duvalier's ouster. Between 1986 and 1990, it played a role similar to Via Cívica in Nicaragua – the "civic component" of a national "democracy" network, involving "civic education" programs, "get-out-the-vote" drives and media campaigns. In addition, Celebration 2004 focused on organizing women and youth, given the absence of any elite women's or youth organizations that could operate on their own.[94]

The trade union programs were considered crucial because workers in the enclave assembly industries and rural workers' unions had become among the most militant and an important base of the Lavalas movement. The NED spent some $2 million, via the FTUI, on the Federation of Unionized Workers (FOS), while the AID funneled additional monies through the AIFLD. This was the smallest of three trade union federations in Haiti. It was set up in 1984 with Duvalier's support and funding from the AIFLD, and was the only one which had been allowed to function legally under Baby Doc. Its president was Joseph Senat, who was also a member of the board of the IHRED. The State Department, at the request of several chief executive officers of US-based transnationals operating in Haiti's free-trade industrial zone, had directly requested AIFLD involvement in 1984 "because of the presence of radical labor unions and the high risk that other unions may become radicalized."[95] The "radical labor unions" to which the State Department referred was the CATH, which was tied to the Lavalas movement and had launched a campaign to raise the minimum wage. Yet another NED program went to fund and organize several peasant organizations which set out to compete with the Papaye Movement and other peasant groups.

Apart from these NED programs, the CIA, in addition to the SIN program, conducted other clandestine programs to establish ties with Haitian political and military leaders.[96] In early 1990, the ODI allocated $10 million for the 1990 elections. Some of these funds were channeled through the NED, another portion was given directly to the Provisional Electoral Council, and yet another to several electoral observer groups, including Carter's organization, and NDI-led observer teams.[97] According to the US game plan, by the time the December 1990 vote arrived, the elite should have developed enough to be able to field several credible candidates, articulate a national development program, and attract enough internal support to garner winning candidates that would enjoy a minimum enough social base and enough international recognition to legitimize the new government as the culmination of the "transition to democracy." But this scenario did not unfold. Elite constituencies in civil society remained sparsely developed between 1986 and 1990 – indeed, virtually negligible – and could not fulfill their role in electoral mobilization, much less in holding back the Lavalas tide. The US program, nevertheless, did generate enough interest within the elite for it to support Bazin's candidacy. More importantly, the very organizations and individuals tapped by the 1986–1990 US programs surfaced as the core organized opponents of the Aristide government, and later as important backers of the 1991 coup.

The 1990 elections and the 1991 coup d'état

Distrust of formal political parties and of an electoral process controlled from above – a military junta supported by the United States –

led the popular groundswell to reject over twenty candidates from the elite as the December 1990 elections approached. Instead, several dozen groups associated with the Lavalas movement formed a center-to-left electoral coalition, the FNDC, and asked Aristide to run as its candidate. The Catholic priest at first declined, but in October, just two months before the vote, finally accepted the nomination, under strong pressure from the Lavalas movement organizations. Within days of his nomination, 2 million Haitians, who had earlier shown little interest in the electoral process, rushed to register, bringing the number of registered voters almost overnight from 40 to 90 percent of the voting age population. Despite US support for Bazin and the complete absence of external support for the Lavalas movement, Aristide swept the elections with 67.5 percent of the popular vote. Bazin, who out-spent Aristide 20–1,[98] captured 14.2 percent of the vote. A third candidate, the populist Louis Dejoie, won 4.8 percent (the remainder was shared among another eight parties, seven of them NED-funded).[99]

Taking place in the post-Cold War era, and without formal links to traditional political parties (of the left or otherwise), much less to any foreign powers, the popular revolt in Haiti in the late 1980s constituted a new and innovative form of social mobilization. As the first experiment with meaningful social change and popular democracy after the end of the East–West conflict, the triumph of the Lavalas uprising represented not only a new option for the Haitian majority but also new hope for the Third World – a model in which popular sectors organized in civil society take primacy over the state. In the words of many observers, this was the first political revolution since the end of the Cold War.[100] And it was one whose democratic legitimacy could not possibly be called into question.

The tasks faced by the new government were overwhelming: reorganizing a chaotic and praetorian state, applying sanctions to army officers for past abuses, responding to the demands of the hemisphere's poorest population, and addressing one of the worst ecological crises in the world – the near complete deforestation and soil depletion of the tiny country. At the time of his inauguration, Aristide said, "Our major goal for the coming years and our basic program of action is to go from extreme poverty to a poverty with dignity by empowering our own resources, the participation of the people, and not expecting much from abroad." Aware that his administration had to operate within the constraints of an anti-democratic state and bureaucracy and an *ancien régime* not yet dismantled, Aristide declared: "I will not be president of the government, I am going to be president of the opposition, of the people, even if this means confronting the very government I am creating."[101] The brief period before the new administration's mandate was cut short did not allow for any essential change in the social structure. Among the programs undercut by the coup was a national literacy campaign and an agrarian reform that would have set limits on the size of property holdings, channeled resources to poor peasants and redistributed available lands. A program was in the planning stages to institutionalize participatory structures alongside the formal government apparatus. Although he was making only symbolic gestures, Aristide himself took a salary cut of 60 percent and tried to reduce other top government salaries. He fired and replaced all Duvalierist hold-overs, and rid state enterprises of corruption, which increased state revenues and also reduced the ability of the elite to engage in its time-honored graft. The reform program also called for retaining strategic public enterprises under state control as a source of public income for redistributive measures and raising the minimum wage. A crucial measure Aristide did implement was the elimination of the rural sheriffs (the *chefs de section*), an essential component of the Duvalierist structures and a pillar of traditional power relations in the rural areas.

Under the Aristide government, popular organizations redoubled their activities and attracted new members. After 500 years of oppression, the Haitian people had finally found their voice. For eight fleeting months, Haitians had become the collective subjects of their own social reality. The hegemony won by the popular sectors in civil society in the 1980s was snowballing into a pre-revolutionary situation: representatives from these sectors, as in Chile in 1970–1973, now had one foot in the formal state apparatus. The situation was approximating that of "dual power." Despite the mild reformist character of Aristide's program, all the ingredients for a unique social revolution were present. The elite and the United States acted before those ingredients could brew.

The 1990 elections underscore that the new political intervention enters into play with local forces in intervened countries which are often beyond external control. The new strategy implies risks for the United States, namely, uncertain outcomes and no guarantee of success. The Chilean and the Philippine situations approximated the Haitian, as regards the departure of a dictatorship and US efforts to assure that a pliable centrist alternative replaced the *ancien régime*. In the first two countries, however, the United States was able to interface with local forces in such a way that it obtained the preferred outcome. In Haiti, the United States was *not* able to secure its preferred outcome, owing in large part to Haiti's unique historic conditions and to the structural limits to a polyarchic system presented by the absence of an elite grounded in a process of internal capital accumulation. Until Aristide entered the race, Bazin had been seen as a shoo-in for what was to be an election with a small voter turnout and international certification as "free and fair." Aristide was therefore the unexpected and unwanted outcome of the "transition to democracy" that the United States had so arduously tried to facilitate – an uninvited guest at the table Washington was trying to set. Aristide's rise to power was, to paraphrase Henry Kissinger, a "fluke" in the political system the United States was trying to implant in Haiti.

The US government demonstrated a pattern of increasing hostility and disapproval toward Aristide's government.[102] The Bush administration approved but then withheld the disbursement of $84 million in economic aid because the Aristide government had failed to meet several conditions attached to the aid package, among them, certification by Washington that human rights were being respected (the previous military regimes suffered no such withholding of economic aid despite their gross human rights violations), and Aristide's plan to raise the minimum wage from $3 to $5 a day, criticized by the AID as a measure that would discourage foreign investment and undermine the enclave assembly sector.[103] In addition, US officials launched a campaign to denigrate Aristide's personal integrity and the legitimacy of his government. Alleged human rights violations became the centerpiece of this campaign. Aristide's brief term was "the first time in the post-Duvalier era that the United States government has been so deeply concerned with human rights and the rule of law in Haiti," noted Amy Wilentz, a Haiti specialist. The State Department "circulated a thick notebook filled with alleged human rights violations" under Aristide – "something it had not done under the previous rulers, Duvalierists and military men; they were actually praised by Washington... [which] argued for the reinstatement of aid – including military aid – based on unsubstantiated human rights improvements..."[104] This "thick notebook" was compiled by Jean-Jacques Honorat, whose human rights organizations, CHADEL, was the recipient of massive NED funding.[105]

Cédras and other coup leaders were figureheads for an alliance of old-guard forces in the army and the elite, who, having tolerated Aristide for eight months, feared that any further consolidation of the first democratic regime in the country's history would irreversibly threaten their interests. The Washington Office on Haiti circulated a list of a dozen businessmen said to have spent more than $40 million to back the coup.[106] Haiti is not only one of the poorest countries in the world, but also one which registers some of the sharpest contrasts between wealth and poverty. An estimated 3,000 extended families comprise the Haitian elite, including a reported 200 millionaires. This elite lives in luxury air-conditioned villas in the cool suburbs in the hills above Port-au-Prince, complete with tennis courts, swimming pools, carefully tended gardens and armies of servants. Another 10 percent of the population, the country's middle and professional classes, are reported to earn an average of $90,000 annually. The remaining 90 percent, with a per capita income of a little more than $300, live in conditions of total destitution and squalor. The World Bank reported in 1981 that, of an estimated population of 6 million, just 24,000 people own 40 percent of the nation's wealth, and 1 percent of the population receives 44 percent of national income but pays only 3.5 percent in taxes.[107] Under such conditions, even a minimal plan of social reform – such as was drawn up by the Aristide government – strikes at the very heart of the elite's interests.

Redistributive reforms in themselves were not necessarily a threat to transnational interests. Recall the point made in chapter 1 that tensions and contradictions often checker the relations between dominant groups in intervened countries and the transnational elite operating under Washington's overall leadership. However, the popular social movement which was consolidating and fusing with the state under Aristide's government *was*, in fact, a deep threat, not just to the social order in Haiti, but to a worldwide project whose purpose is to subordinate popular majorities to the "logic of the minority." There was thus a perverted and tension-ridden convergence of interests between the tiny Haitian elite's exaggerated social privileges and the defense of the social order itself. Although some reform measures (such as subordinating the military to civilian authority) are actually part of the transnational agenda in other countries and under other conditions, Aristide's program was rigorously resisted by the Haitian elite and the United States. The difference between these measures in Haiti and similar measures taken with the approval of the transnational elite in other countries is that, in Haiti, their effect was to embolden and hasten the mobilization of the popular majority, which was now seeking a viable formula for becoming a sovereign majority, while in other countries such measures merely make elite political rule and the economy stronger and more efficient. What was at stake for the transnational elite in Haiti was not economic interests (such as those that Allende's government threatened in Chile), but the social mobilization from below and the dangerous "demonstration effects" this could generate in the Caribbean and the Third World in general. In defense of transnational hegemony, the United States was forced to rely on, and ally with, historically underdeveloped and vice-ridden dominant groups in a national formation which lacked the structural basis for a polyarchic political system.

There is no documented evidence of *direct* US involvement in the coup.[108] What the evidence reveals is that those sectors cultivated by US political, economic, and military aid programs from 1986 to 1990 formed the key constituency of the new dictatorial regime – the NED-AID political elite, the commercial and industrial bourgeoisie tied to the assembly sector and other transnational economic activities, and the army and security forces. Moreover, evidence indicates that US officials knew of the coup before it was underway and chose for tactical reasons not to intervene to try to prevent it,[109] and once consummated, the coup was incorporated into the the larger US strategy, as discussed below. There need not be *direct* conspiratorial linkages between Washington and the coup-makers, and empirical evidence of intentionality in US policy regarding the coup is not relevant to the underlying analytical and theoretical issues at hand. First, Haiti's experience bears out Gramsci's argument that hegemony is "consensus backed by armour," such that latent coercion becomes activated when consensual mechanisms of domination either break down or cannot be established. Relations of domination, in Haiti as elsewhere, are, in the last instance, relations of force. Second, given the inability to establish consensual domination, US programs and policies placed great importance on strengthening, and also on emboldening, the coercive apparatus of the Haitian state.[110] The resurgence of authoritarianism in Haiti was a spasm of self-preservation of the social order induced by the very logic of the US-transnational project; the reactionary Caesarist outcome to the dominant groups' crisis of authority.

Beyond the lack of evidence that Washington had a direct role in the coup, some of the evidence suggests, to the contrary, that US policy-makers were developing an alternative three-pronged strategy for undermining popular democracy in Haiti. First, fundamental social transformations would be prevented by withholding US aid, by applying other pressures, and by allowing the global economy and the country's dependence to impose their own constraints. A $26 million AID program to nurture a policy development capacity among the local private sector and its ability to interface with the Aristide government had already been launched.[111] Second, there would be a major expansion of political aid and "democracy promotion" programs, with the aim of gradually accomplishing over a prolonged period what could not be achieved during 1986–1990 – the development of an elite organized around a program of polyarchy and neoliberalism, able to mount its own project in civil society and challenge Lavalas hegemony. Third, the state apparatus itself, particularly such countervailing powers as the legislature, local government councils, and the security forces, would be strengthened and space would be opened up in this way for the elite to exercise influence over both the state and the popular masses.

The clearest indication of this strategy came in May 1991, when the State Department approved a massive $24 million Democracy Enhancement Project program, to be managed by the ODI and designed to hasten the organization, institutional influence, and the communications and political action capacity of elite and anti-Aristide constituencies. Recipients of these funds were the same groups the NED had funded in previous years as well as a host of new groups from those sectors of the Haitian political spectrum where opposition to Aristide could be encouraged. The project included an important legislative and local government component, including advisors and programs to train and guide members of the National Assembly. This component must be understood in the particular Haitian context. The constitution approved in 1987 under which Aristide took power had severely reduced executive strength and given important powers to the legislature. At the time, this was seen by US legal experts who advised the drafters of the constitution as a mechanism best suited for developing polyarchy in Haiti, since it would disperse power among the highly fragmented elite and its numerous ambition-driven leaders, and also curb the tradition of a centralized and all-powerful presidency.[112] The popular movement, with scant enthusiasm in elections except for the vote it gave to Aristide, showed little interest in the legislative elections. As a result, the Assembly remained the domain of the elite after the 1990 vote (anti-Aristide parties won 60 percent of the seats in the Chamber of Deputies and 52 percent in the Senate). Ironically, the legislature, and the constitution itself, became an ideal juridical weapon in limiting the Aristide government's ability to implement its program – a situation remarkably similar to that of Chile under Allende, except under very different international conditions. Strengthening the Assembly under the pretext of "democracy enhancement" became a means of shifting formal institutional power from Aristide's mass constituency to the elite and of blocking implementation of Aristide's program. And after the coup, it allowed the legislature to play a counterrevolutionary role.

"The Democracy Enhancement Project has been designed to strengthen legislative and other constitutional structures, including local governments, as well as independent organizations which foster democratic values and participation in democratic decision-making," stated a highly revealing AID document:

> Pursuit of this [Democracy Enhancement Project] goal is based on three critical assumptions: 1) the democratically elected Government will endure and carry out its mandate according to the terms of the 1987 Constitution; 2) the US Government will have access to and influence with the GOH [Government of Haiti]; and 3) an aggressive project of the kind recommended will make a difference to the durability and effectiveness of the country's evolving democracy... The project has been designed with a built-in flexibility to respond to the changing social, institutional and political context for democracy-enhancement activities... The project constitutes our principal effort to advance the overriding objective of US policy towards Haiti... The design provides for a number of entry points to different institutional "actors" in the democratic scene, with the recognition that some will evolve more quickly than others...
>
> This [the program] must also be accomplished within the atmosphere of strong nationalism, to avoid any sense of a donor or interest group being disruptive of what the rhetoric describes as "the will of the people"... Given current sensitivities, the new relationships must be approached judiciously to mitigate against possible "anti-American" backlash. At the same time, we must not be timid in the pursuit of key foreign policy objectives which our project is designed to serve.[113]

The document went on to note that "the absorptive capacity [of the National Assembly, the electoral council and local government bodies] is in question" – meaning that elite constituencies were not in a strong position to exercise an organized influence in these formal state structures, and that state–civil society linkages needed to be strengthened under the mediation of groups cultivated through the US political aid program. It identified three broad areas for US intervention: (1) "Civil society development, consisting of funding 10 to 15 Haitian independent sector organizations"; (2) "Local government development," consisting of funding "2 to 3 Haitian independent sector organizations and activities to link local government and civil society interest groups"; and (3) "Institutional development, with emphasis on developing plans for participating independent sector organizations to sustain programs." The same recipients of NED funding in the 1986–1990 period were among the specific organizations selected for funding, as well as several new groups, including the Haitian Federation of Aid to Women, the Haitian Lawyers' Committee, the Haitian Bar Association, the Center Petion–Bolívar (a new elite think-tank), and the Integral Project for the Reinforcement of Democracy in Haiti (PIRED). The State Department chose this latter organization, set up entirely with US funds and by US organizers, as an "Umbrella Management Unit" to oversee the entire $24 million program inside Haiti.[114] The AID gave the NDI and the NRI new monies to continue "party-building," and also set up a Consortium for Legislative Development to oversee the work conducted by NED-funded US groups (sub-grantees) with Haitian parties and members of the National Assembly. The AID reported in the wake of the *coup d'état* that it had spent $13 million of the $24 million in the course of Aristide's presidency. The Democracy Enhancement Project was frozen in the aftermath of the coup, and then resumed in late 1992.[115]

The military interlude: the attempted destruction of civil society

The key question following Aristide's ouster was how US policymakers would respond to the coup. Here was a government elected in free and fair elections organized and paid for by the United States and scrutinized by the international community perhaps more meticulously than the Nicaraguan vote of February 1990. Aristide was the unwanted and unexpected outcome of the "transition to democracy" that the US had tried to guide. But formal support for a military coup at a time when Washington was promoting tightly managed "free elections" around the world as the cornerstone of its new political intervention, was simply out of the question. Demonstrating consistency in Haiti was important. Support for the Haitian coup could embolden militaries in Latin America and elsewhere to attempt takeovers, thus undermining the fragile structures of a transnational polyarchic political system then emerging in the Western Hemisphere. The Haitian case became a test for policymakers. Infighting broke out in Washington over post-coup policy. From Aristide's ouster in September 1991 to the September 1994 invasion that restored him to office, Washington became involved in a complex and sometimes contradictory effort to resolve its dilemma in Haiti in a manner compatible with its overall "democracy promotion" strategy.[116]

Washington publicly condemned the coup, declared that it would continue to recognize Aristide, and supported limited economic sanctions imposed by the OAS. At the same time, the Bush administration claimed that the coup-makers had a legitimate grievance in their argument that the Aristide government had violated human rights. Bush officials "have begun to move away from unequivocal support they have voiced for the ousted Haitian President," reported the *New York Times* a week after the coup. "With this shift, the officials, who had said his reinstatement was necessary for the hemisphere's democracies to resist a comeback of military rule, are now hinting that Father Aristide is at least in part to blame for his fall from office."[117] In fact, international human rights monitoring groups had reported that human rights violations in Haiti during Aristide's tenure actually decreased significantly. These groups praised the progress made under Aristide in human rights, noted that *not one* human rights abuse was attributable to the Aristide administration itself, in distinction to the previous regimes, and that most abuses were committed by the security forces which he did not control.[118]

The US concern in Haiti, as elsewhere, was not human rights but how the issue of human rights could be manipulated in diverse manners to further foreign-policy objectives. The unsubstantiated charges were a thinly veiled disinformation campaign aimed at discrediting the Aristide government's international legitimacy and his own integrity – the continuation, in the post-coup period of hostilities toward Aristide dating back to the mid-1980s, and which became, during his brief tenure in office, a campaign to portray his government as repressive, incompetent, and ideologically extreme. Aspects of this disinformation campaign were publicly exposed several years later, in late 1993, when the CIA was forced to admit that it had fabricated and disseminated false reports that Aristide had undergone psychiatric treatment, was "clinically manic-depressive, prone to violence and an unreliable supporter of democratic reform."[119] Such "black propaganda," or "character assassinations," as they are termed in official intelligence jargon, are standard components of destabilization campaigns.

The campaign to blemish Aristide's international stature was one aspect of a broader post-coup US strategy. There were two initial positions in Washington: those arguing for efforts to legitimize an elite civilian alternative to the Aristide government-in-exile, and those favoring the restoration of Aristide. Over the next few years, these two initial positions merged into a more complex, if at times contradictory, strategy of seeking to undermine the possibility of implementing popular democracy in Haiti, yet continuing formal recognition of Aristide as the legitimate head of state. This strategy had two complementary and mutually reinforcing aspects. One was searching for a formula under which Aristide would return as a powerless and largely ceremonial president, under various euphemisms of "power sharing," "reconciliation," and a "consensus government," which would give significant quotas of power to business and political elites who enjoyed no popular mandate yet controlled important levers of the country's economy and the state apparatus. Aristide would thus return with his institutional power so diluted, and the power of the coup-makers and their civilian backers so enhanced, that it would be impossible for his government to fulfill its own political agenda and that of the popular majority. Simultaneously, Washington explored the possibility of installing and legitimizing a new elite civilian regime in Port-au-Prince – a scenario which could be held up as blackmail to the Aristide government-in-exile should it reject the terms imposed on it for its own restitution. The other aspect was the repression and demobilization of the popular classes inside Haiti, a process which the new military regime carried out with brutal efficiency. These two aspects went together like hand and glove: the longer the coup's supporters were in power, the more beaten down and disoriented the population became, the better organized the anti-popular constituencies (both polyarchic and authoritarian) became, and the more elusive the goals of popular democratization and social transformation became. This strategy involved a series of highly duplicitous diplomatic undertakings whose ostensible purpose was to restore Aristide to office, first under OAS-mediated negotiations, then through the UN, and finally under direct State Department mediation. US actions also included a refugee policy broadly condemned as inhumane and illegal, an ineffective and unenforced embargo, the resumption of political aid to anti-Aristide "democratic" constituencies inside Haiti, and the continuation of the CIA campaign to discredit Aristide.

Within days of Aristide's forced exile, the legislature declared his office vacant and named a mulatto old-guard member of the elite, Supreme Court president Joseph Nerette, as interim president, and Jean-Jacques Honorat as provisional prime minister. The OAS opened negotiations between Aristide and Honorat's *de facto* government. Embassy officials in Port-au-Prince drafted a memorandum on the eve of the OAS negotiations, at the request of the junta, which provided guidelines for the *de facto* regime's negotiating team, drawn from anti-Aristide forces in the Haitian legislature. And although the new regime in Port-au-Prince was not officially recognized by Washington, US ambassador Alvin Adams accompanied its delegation to the nego-tiating table as an informal advisor.[120] The embassy document stated:

> other points of the deal should surely include some of the following: that if A [Aristide] returns it would not be until some time later (months away); that he could be impeached and sent back out; that time was permitted to enact new laws limiting some of his outrageous behaviours and that of his followers; that the Prime Minister become the real power of the government; that the Prime Minister be given adequate economic support to secure his position; that no Lavalas people be included in the new Government... If A refuses to deal or refuses what O.A.S. considers a reasonable deal, he is finished... What is needed is a comprehensive, sustained and very discrete approach to US policy-makers and the US media that will balance off and negate the propaganda of the Lavalas organization.[121]

The OAS-mediated talks culminated in an agreement in February 1992 in which Aristide would return in exchange for an amnesty for the coup-makers, recognition of all legislation passed by the Assembly after the coup, and the selection of a new prime minister with legislative approval, instead of one appointed freely by Aristide, as called for by the constitution. The appointment of the prime minister was crucial, because the constitution placed most executive power in the office of the prime minister, not the presidency; the latter's power rested in the president's mandate to appoint a prime minister of his or her choice. Nevertheless, the military and the anti-Aristide legislators reneged on the accord at the last minute, making clear that they considered unacceptable the mere presence of Aristide in Haiti, where, even without much presidential power, he would be the leadership figure around which the Haitian masses could rally. Instead, the parliament approved an alternative plan for a "consensus government" that bypassed Aristide and appointed Bazin as prime minister in June 1992. Washington attempted briefly to legitimize the Bazin regime, threatening to withdraw their recognition of Aristide if he did not negotiate with Bazin.[122] However, Bazin, like Honorat before him, was unable to win enough legitimacy to exclude Aristide from a solution or to move the country towards internal stability.

Intermittent negotiations ensued over the next few years, under the joint auspices of the UN and the State Department. A familiar pattern emerged: demands for new concessions were placed on Aristide in exchange for retaining international recognition. "In two years of negotiations," noted Haiti analyst Kim Ives, "the putschists have given up nothing of their usurped power, and the legitimate government has traded away almost everything."[123] The popular government in exile was caught in a pernicious Catch-22. If it rejected an unfavorable settlement, it faced the loss of international legitimacy. In the new world order, this legitimacy is a prerequisite to any nation's social and economic participation in global society, yet that legitimacy is increasingly conferred by those who control the levers of the global economy, through control over transnational communications media, allocation of resources, and so forth. Sustaining recognition as the legitimate government of Haiti therefore required that Aristide's team play the game of "off-again, on-again" negotiations with the military dictatorship, mediated by international organizations pliant to US manipulations. On the other hand, making continual concessions, each more weakening than the previous, meant forfeiting any chance of bringing about fundamental social change in Haiti, and, for the Aristide government, the loss of its legitimacy and authority within its own mass constituency. The popular movement became increasingly disillusioned with its government-in-exile and frustrated over a negotiations process managed by transnational actors, showing no signs of resolving the situation, and bearing no relation to their daily reality of repression and struggle. The alternatives of sustaining authority among its own mass base by withdrawing from the international negotiations charade, or returning to Haiti under international auspices only to immediately resume the popular project under the status quo ante, could well have led to the loss of all legitimacy internationally under the argument that it was attempting extra-constitutional, extra-institutional forms of social change, and thus a future coup or international sanctions would become "legitimate." Behind the criticism of the Aristide team's strategy are deeper theoretical issues often overlooked by critics of Aristide. The loss of international legitimacy and isolation from world markets that transnational forces are capable of imposing can just as easily suffocate any revolutionary project as could the tenuous strategy that Aristide pursued of trying to walk the tightrope of popular democracy internally and legitimacy internationally. It is not at all clear that the popular struggle in Haiti would have been better off had Aristide simply refused to cooperate in any way with Washington.

As this diplomacy unfolded, at least 3,000 Haitians were executed by the regime in the first few weeks after the coup, and hundreds – or thousands – more over the next several years. Tens of thousands were detained, tortured, and maimed, and several hundred thousand more went into hiding or fled the country. Following the coup, the Macoutes rapidly reorganized and the military government initiated a systematic campaign of repression which human rights groups reported to be worse than at any time since the Duvalier era.[124] The notorious *chefs de section* posts, abolished by Aristide, were reinstated by the military. All but pro-regime media outlets were closed, meetings banned, unions, peasant leagues, and other popular organizations dissolved, leaders "disappeared," and elected representatives in local and regional government structures dismissed and persecuted.

While the diplomatic charade bought time, the military regime was accomplishing precisely what could not be done either with Aristide in power or under any polyarchy regime nominally respecting traditional civil liberties and political rights: the destruction of the organs of the popular classes in civil society and the resubordination of the Haitian masses through the only effective instrument for this purpose under Haitian conditions – direct, widespread, and systematic repression. One international human rights report (echoing many such reports) affirmed that "the goal of the repression is two-fold: first, to destroy the political and social gains made since the downfall of the Duvalier dynasty; and second, to ensure that no matter what Haiti's political future may hold, all structures for duplicating those gains will have been laid waste."[125] While the "ethnic cleansing" that took place in Bosnia in the early 1990s shocked the world, this lesser known but no less brutal process of "class cleansing" of Haitian civil society took place following the coup. This was a process remarkably similar to

Chile under Pinochet and to the other Southern Cone dictatorships, yet with the goal of compacting it into a period of a few short years. Once the popular leadership was decimated, its organizational structures shattered, and the masses sufficiently terrorized, it would be "safe" to dismantle the coup government, with or without Aristide's return.

That the United States did not participate *directly* in this unprecedented wave of repression (for that matter, neither did it participate directly in Marcos's, Pinochet's, or Somoza's repression, and even sometimes criticized that repression) is not relevant to the analytical point. Most of the coup leaders and members of the junta that directly conducted the systematic repression, and the political figures such as Honorat and Bazin that tried to legitimize a post-Aristide order, had long since established extensive relations with Washington through the CIA and the DIA, the NED, and other programs. And Haitian army officers, in fact, continued to receive training *after the coup* in US military facilities.[126] "Virtually all observers agree that all it would take is one phone call from Washington to send the army leadership packing," noted the *New York Times* a year after the coup. But given "Washington's deep-seated ambivalence about a left-ward tilting nationalist... United States diplomats consider it [the army] a vital counterweight to Father Aristide, whose class-struggle rhetoric threatened or antagonized traditional power centers at home and abroad."[127]

The US refugee policy, condemned by human rights organizations and the UN as blatantly racist and a violation of both US and international law, also fed into this strategy. The exodus of refugees out of Haiti under the Duvaliers and subsequent regimes had ground to a halt the moment Aristide was elected, but then recommenced within days of the coup. The Bush administration strengthened a forced US repatriation program in place since 1981, denounced by Aristide as a "floating Berlin wall," and a policy ratified by the Clinton administration. Human rights groups documented a blatant distortion by US officials of evidence that repatriated Haitians suffered persecution, and pointed out that US embassy officials even informed the Haitian army of the whereabouts of those refugees whom it repatriated, thus making them even more susceptible to persecution. A sharp escalation of death squad-style killings coincided with Washington's decision to repatriate Haitians, and those repatriated were subjected to systematic repression.[128]

Right-wing political and paramilitary organizations tied to the army, the *de facto* regime, and US intelligence services, sprang up in the post-coup period. In late 1993, CIA and DIA officials in Haiti encouraged a Haitian official from the SIN (the CIA-run clandestine unit), Emmanuel Constant, to organize these groups into the Front for the Advancement and Progress of Haiti (FRAPH) in order to "balance the Aristide movement" and conduct "intelligence" against it.[129] The FRAPH added a new element to the Haitian political scene that served the anti-popular agenda in the short run but complicated the long-term transnational elite agenda for Haiti. It became a well-organized instrument of repression, operating in a death-squad manner to continue the process of decimating popular sector organization, yet also constituted the political institutionalization of forces bent on preserving an authoritarian political system. FRAPH leaders were not only on the CIA payroll but were also integrated into post-coup, and later post-invasion, US political and economic aid programs.[130]

A concomitant aspect of post-coup US strategy was to provide enough of a lifeline for the military regime to survive. Following the coup, the OAS imposed an economic embargo on Haiti. But the embargo, with numerous loopholes, was largely ineffectual (in sharp contrast to total embargoes against Nicaragua, Chile, Cuba, Panama, Iraq, and elsewhere, which were implemented with devastating effectiveness). Two days after the coup, Washington vetoed the Aristide government's request to have a hearing at the UN security council, arguing instead that the OAS was the appropriate forum to address a matter internal to the Western Hemisphere. As a result, the embargo was hemispheric and not worldwide in scope. The embargo restrictions were breached by exporters and importers not only from Europe, but from the United States and Latin America. Oil tankers and freighters not flying flags from OAS member-states kept Haiti well supplied with petroleum and other goods until the UN finally imposed international sanctions in 1993; even then, the sanctions were limited to oil and arms deliveries.[131] More significantly, in February 1992 the Bush administration unilaterally relaxed the embargo to exclude all goods produced in the free-trade zone, as well as other goods claimed necessary to protect Haitians from losing their jobs. As a result, while the *image* of a US government engaged in active diplomacy to isolate the military dictatorship was propagated, trade between the United States and Haiti actually flourished and registered a sharp increase under the dictatorship. According to US Census Bureau figures, US trade with Haiti jumped from $316.2 million in 1992 to $375.6 million in 1993.[132]

In late 1992, the $24 million Democracy Enhancement Project, which had been suspended following the coup, was resumed. New programs included a resumption of funding for political parties, and a program, jointly managed by the NDI and the NRI, to "promote the consolidation of democracy in Haiti by assisting Haiti's civilian and military leaders to develop mechanisms to integrate the Armed Forces of Haiti in to civilian society." The program "proposes to establish a broad civil–military relations program with senior members of the Haitian government," stated one document.[133] Another NED program, handled by the CFD, was the creation of a new private-sector organization in Haiti, the Center for Free Enterprise and Democracy (CLED). In early 1994, the CLED organized a two-week "strike" of private-sector commercial and industrial enterprises to demand the lifting of the embargo. The CFD also conducted a "legislative development" program to continue training and advising members of the Haitian parliament. Yet another NED program established and funded a group called the Development and Democracy Foundation, which promptly launched a campaign whose slogan was "democracy is discipline." The AID funded a string of newly created community centers known as Centers for Health and Development, headed by the wealthy businessman and Bazin colleague, Reginald Boulos. These Centers were placed in charge of distributing AID-donated food and charitable goods, and were criticized by popular groups as outlets intended to replace the grassroots neighborhood councils and as vehicles for "get-out-the-vote" and other "civic" campaigns in future elections.[134]

The 1994 US invasion: reinforcing political society as an instrument of the elite

In analytical abstraction, what unfolded in Haiti between 1991 and 1994 was an all-sided *war of attrition* against the Haitian people, attuned to the unique context of Haiti. US diplomacy and economic, political, and military aid, the transnational communications media, continued economic activity by transnational capital inside Haiti, the Haitian state, the elite, and the military regime, all converged. The complete dilution of the formal power of the popular Haitian majority within the state (both during Aristide's tenure and after his ouster) was being accompanied by the neutralization through repression of the capacity of this majority to mobilize in civil society in pursuit of its interests. The interim status quo could not be sustained because it failed to meet the two requirements of legitimacy and being a basis for long-term stability. Apart from intentionality on the part of individual actors, public pronouncements made by US officials, and even specific policy actions (none of which should be seen as underlying causal or explanatory factors in historical outcomes), the historical outcome was moving precisely towards that which met the interests of the United States and the Haitian elite: the defeat of a project of popular democracy in Haiti. By mid-1994 either a return of Aristide or his permanent exile looked like creating a no-win situation for popular democracy in Haiti.

The October 1994 invasion was intended to place back on track the decade-long effort to stabilize elite polyarchic rule in Haiti, once the military interlude had thoroughly transfigured the political, social, and economic variables, internally and internationally, to the point where Washington could resume this effort even with Aristide in the presidency.[135] From the coup until mid-1994, US policy failed to persuade the coup-leaders to step down because it was not designed to do so. During this period, US strategists began to fathom just how difficult it would be to carry through the transnational project for Haiti. The undertaking would be very long term and policy goals would have to be gauged over a period of many years. Policymakers set about to devise a *long-term* strategy to achieve lasting results, independent of how the short-term crisis was resolved. "Hope for quick breakthroughs is being revised to consider a longer-term process of institution building," noted one US official in 1993. "This is the central political/ economic context for the US–Haitian relationship in the 1990s. US policy response needs to address both the complexity of the underlying problems and the relatively long time frame for achieving results."[136] In a redefined time-frame, Aristide's return under controlled conditions became a requirement of resuming the overall project. The post-coup strategy was unsuccessful in legitimizing an alternative to Aristide, while the Haitian elite and military rulers proved utterly intransigent regarding his return. The transnational elite had begun to play Aristide's return as their "stability card." "We in the US have misunderstood the Aristide question, which isn't an issue of the evil military versus the good Mr. Aristide," stated the president of the International Industrial Exporters Inc., a major transnational contracting firm operating in Haiti. "Mr. Aristide isn't any more the answer to Haiti's problems than is the military. But his return to power is worth the cost of the US military incursion if it fosters a resumption of free trade and the sale of US goods and services."[137] The road to stability in Haiti necessarily passed through Aristide.

After undertaking a policy reassessment in May 1994, the Clinton administration imposed effective economic sanctions for the first time, which finally squeezed the elite, and utilized the threat of a military action as a high-risk gamble in coercive diplomacy. These measures were intended to apply pressure on the elite to compromise with Aristide in a "power-sharing" arrangement in the short term to get the US policy back on track in the medium and long term. The threat of an invasion was at first intended to be only that – a threat. But once the threat was made without the intended effect on Port-au-Prince, Washington ran the risk of losing credibility if it did not follow through, US options began to dwindle, and a foreign-policy crisis developed. The economic squeeze and diplomatic momentum leading up to the invasion, and the invasion itself, drove a wedge between the elite and the military, and convinced enough of the elite of the need for Aristide's return to establish a solid *elite* base of support for the invasion. As with the military interlude, policymakers incorporated the invasion, once the plans were drawn up, into the larger, long-term strategy as a powerful instrument to further overall goals in Haiti.

True to the original script, Aristide returned as a largely lame-duck president required constitutionally to step down after elections scheduled for December 1995, having spent the vast majority of his presidency in exile. And by having been returned to office by US marines, he was beholden to the very same foreign power that had consistently sought to defuse the popular project he led. The Lavalas movement was forced to accept the piper of US military intervention, thus leaving policymakers in a much stronger position to call the Lavalas movement's – and the country's – political tune. The jubiliation expressed by Haitian masses as they took to the streets to welcome the invading marines reflected a momentary and tactical convergence between Haiti's popular majority and US policymakers almost identical to those between the Haitian army and the people, and the Philippine army and the people, in the immediate aftermath of those dictators' departures. The invasion had the image of a clash between a liberating foreign force and a corrupt local ruling class, but it was the sealing of a long-term pact between that foreign force and the Haitian elite.

At all times, the focus of invasion itself was to *control* the Haitian population during the brief power vacuum following the the departure of the military regime. If the military were to fall before US forces and programs were in place, said one US army psychological operations official, "the people might get the idea that they can do whatever they want."[138] For this purpose, Jimmy Carter led a delegation in advance of the invasion to work out with Cedras what in military parlance is a "permissive entry." The Carter–Cedras deal called for a "peaceful, cooperative entry of international forces into Haiti, with a mutual respect between the American commanders and the Haitian military commanders."[139] The essence of the deal, stated Secretary of State Warren Christopher, was twofold: (1) to keep Cedras in power until October 15, the date Aristide was to return under US military escort, while the US occupation force was "inserted," and (2) to ensure that "a general amnesty will be voted into law by the Haitian Parliament."[140]

The goal was to separate the Aristide government from the popular movement, and to thoroughly penetrate, take control of, and reorganize Haitian political society, and elites operating therein, through massive new US economic, political, and military aid programs that would inundate the country under the canopy of the occupation and the legitimacy afforded to these programs by Aristide's return. "The task," said one AID report, was to "substantially transform the nature of the Haitian state."[141] Post-invasion economic reconstruction aid was a powerful instrument in class restructuring, encouraging the formation and ascendance to internal leadership over the elite of the transnationalized fraction, whittling away at remnants of crony capitalism, and constructing a neo-liberal state. A month before the invasion at a meeting in Paris between the Aristide transition team and representatives from the AID, the World Bank, the IMF, and other mulitlateral, bilateral, and private lenders, a five-year $1.2 billion multilateral and bilateral (mostly US) aid package for Haiti was approved. As in Nicaragua, the vast part of these monies was to go to paying the country's foreign debt arrears, to strengthening the private sector, and financing infrastructure and other amenities for foreign investors. Most of the funds would bypass the Haitian government itself and instead be handled directly by the AID and the private sector.[142]

Conditions for the disbursal of these international resources were many times more stringent than in the pre-coup period, and in the completely redefined environment the Aristide government could not hope to resist outside impositions. It called for across-the-board neo-liberal restructuring, including privatization, trade liberalization, the lifiting of price and other controls, the reduction of public-sector employment by 50 percent, a further contraction of already pitiful social service spending, a commitment not to raise the daily minimum wage, and so forth. The international funders expected to see "a government of reconciliation" [read: power-sharing between Aristide's team and the elite] that could "guarantee stability and a sound economic environment," said one official at the meeting.[143] Even the most mild reforms it had proposed before the coup were absent from the Aristide government's post-invasion social and economic policies. "You have to understand, the world has changed in these three years," said Aristide official Father Antoine Adrien. "What was good in 1991 is not necessarily good in 1994."[144] Adrien was, in effect, acknowledging the tremendous advance made in reinforcing political society as an instrument of the elite as a result of the military interlude, the invasion, and the conditions attendant upon Aristide's return. His comment expressed the Aristide team's decision – taken under overwhelming constraints and limited options – to abandon pre-coup plans to try to transform political society to conform to popular hegemony won by the masses in civil society.

In the weeks following the invasion, personnel from the Pentagon, the AID, the USIA, the Treasury, and other agencies organized into a "Civic Affairs Ministerial Advisory Team," fanned out to virtually all government ministries as "advisers" to the restored government, in an almost instant penetration of the Haitian state for the purpose of, in the words of one US official, achieving "the full merging of their [the ministries'] plans with AID."[145] The invasion itself acted structurally and economically to strengthen the technocratic fraction of the elite. Leaders of the fraction quickly moved into formal institutional positions in the ministries or into the leadership of the countless programs set up by the occupation forces. Held to ransom by the conditions attendant upon his restoration, Aristide turned over key cabinets and areas of the Haitian state to the tiny transnational kernel, including the central bank, the ministries of commerce, public administration, public works, and the treasury, as well as the prime ministership itself, which was given to Smarck Michel, a prominent businessman and leading representative of the fraction.[146] "Businessmen [had] been clamoring for a prime minister able to oversee a new economic plan acceptable to the World Bank, the International Monetary Fund, and top business leaders here," reported the *New York Times* upon Michel's appointment, adding that the program enunciated by Michel "reads like an IMF primer."[147]

Placed into key posts from which it could implement policies formulated in transnational forums abroad and in private-sector policy planning institutes and elite clearing-houses set up inside Haiti by US political aid programs, the embryonic kernel became a transmission belt through which the transnational agenda would be imposed on Haiti via key organs of the Haitian state. All this achieved a hastened externalization of the state and subordinate linkage to emergent transnational state apparatuses – a process which had not been able to go forward, despite US efforts, either under the earlier authoritarian regimes or the pre-coup Aristide tenure. According to this script, the restored government, held ransom by a transnational elite and its structural *and* direct (political-military) power, would bear all the political cost of neo-liberalism and see its own legitimacy eroded, while a transnational kernel would be quietly cultivated under the shield of the popular government itself.

According to the plan, political society would still remain shielded by a coercive apparatus, which was to be *preserved* and reorganized, first through the Carter–Cedras deal and the subsequent amnesty for the military, and second, by submitting the unwieldy Haitian army to the "Panama model." The plan was to reduce the army from 7,000 to 1,500 troops, and to create a civilian police force of about 7,000 officers (many simply transferred from the old army to the new police) to handle internal "law and order." Military "retraining" was launched by the US government's International Criminal Investigations Training and Assistance Program (ICITAP). The ICITAP was created in 1986 "to fortify the development of emerging democracies in the Western Hemisphere," run by the Justice and State Departments, and staffed by the FBI and diverse local and federal US police agencies, as part of the development of a transnationalized "democracy promotion" apparatus within the US state.[148] The new Haitian police force was to be subordinate to elite-US authority, not as prone to indiscriminate violence, and better versed in focused surveillance, selective repression, and more "benign" methods of control over popular mobilization. Aristide himself called for the constitutional elimination of the army, a plan which, at the time of writing (mid-1995) was strongly opposed by the elite and Washington. Even if the army was formally abolished, a "Panama model" police force would be an adequate instrument of coercive social control in defense of a legal order which sanctified and codified the juridical relations of the *existing* social order, including its property relations.

310

New political aid programs were launched almost immediately following the invasion and dwarfed in relative size and scope anything that had been implemented earlier – in Haiti or in any other country of the world. Up to $85 million in "Democracy Enhancement" and "Democratic Governance" programs was allocated to expand earlier NED and AID programs with civic and political groups, to create and support a slew of new groups, to an "Institution-Building Initiative," a "Social Reconciliation and Democratic Development" program, an "Electoral Assistance" project, and so on.[149] While the Aristide government struggled to maintain some influence over the military plank of the US post-invasion plan, it practically gave up any attempt to resist these political intervention programs. "We really can't fight this huge machine," said a transition team member.[150] US Deputy Secretary of State Strobe Talbott was more to the point: "Even after our exit in February 1996 we will remain in charge by means of the USAID and the private sector."[151]

Conclusion: the failure to establish consensual domination in Haiti

No social order can sustain itself indefinitely on the foundation of organized state power. As Gramsci argued, the inclination of dominant groups to revert to repression and violence is a sign not of strength but of *weakness*. Despite the complete penetration and capture of political society it achieved, the US reliance on the military regime for three years to carry forward the project, and the invasion as the US evocation of organized transnational force, were paradoxical signs of the pro-tracted *failure* of the US-transnational project in Haiti.

In the revised "long-haul" strategy, the capture of political society was to provide a trampoline for the gradual and incremental pacifica-tion of civil society through political intervention. The plan called for dividing the Lavalas coalition, according to one AID memo, by weaning away and winning over "responsible elements within the popular movement."[152] The objective was to transform Lavalas from a mass popular-left bloc that united middle and professional strata with the poor majority, into a center-to-left bloc that would incorporate those same middle and professional strata along with a portion of the poor, under the leadership of an embryonic transnational kernel. This new hegemonic bloc would gradually dilute the original Lavalas project of its *popular* content. If enough of the mass base could be coopted into this bloc, then a "center" could cohere, and grassroot leaders unwilling to abandon the project of popular democracy would be marginalized politically and ideologically rather than by repression.

But the Haitian masses remained the wild card in the deck. If US political intervention specialists could not exorcize the culture of authoritarianism and clientelism from the elite, neither could they exorcize what had become a deep-rooted *culture of resistance* among the poor majority. Emboldened by the removal of the military regime, Haitians resumed their struggle for popular democracy following the invasion. Thousands of grassroot leaders came out of hiding, rural and urban networks were rearticulated and reactivated, and civil society again became a beehive of popular organizing, intensely resistant to US-elite penetration and control. Despite the tens of millions of dollars that poured in following the invasion to organize anti-Lavalas constituencies and candidates, Lavalas and independent candidates representing grassroot organizations swept the 1995 parliamentary and local elections, throwing a new monkey wrench into the gears of the US project, to the frustration and chagrin of US officials. Without conquering civil society, the elite project for hegemonic order in Haiti would remain elusive and the crisis of authority would continue.

On the other hand, the popular classes would never be able to realize their own project of popular democracy without conquering and transforming the state. Some in the Lavalas movement criticized Aristide and his administration for confusing the "fluke" of the 1990 electoral victory with the possibility of bringing about fundamental changes in the social order through the elite-oriented political structures set up by the US-sponsored "transition to democracy," and argued that basic social change could only be brought about by the same mass mobilization that brought Duvalier down. "Rather than judging his electoral victory as a fluke, Aristide has tried to universalize the tactic into a political strategy of trying to beat the system at its own game," argued one Haitian analyst. "The question: has the US government lured Aristide into a new, hopelessly rigged game by letting him think he can win again?"[153]

Not surprisingly, the dilemmas faced by the popular sectors following the coup led to increasing infighting and fissures under the Lavalas umbrella and, after the invasion, to formal splits. The middle and professional strata that contributed the core of the institutionalized FNDC leadership and occupied posts in the legislature and the government (what some critics called the "Lavalas bourgeoisie") had begun to operate within the logic of polyarchy and in defense of privilege. Unable or unwilling to commit what Amilcar Cabral referred to as "class suicide," they began to distance themselves from the Lavalas mass base and popular leadership even before the military interlude.[154] Following the invasion, popular sectors created the Lavalas Political Organization (OPL). Instead of joining the OPL, many from the "Lavalas bourgeoisie" chose to remain in the FNDC and the earlier KONAKOM organization, which became formal parties of their own, and even incipient power-bases for ambitious middle-class leaders to participate in polyarchic competition. This gradual fragmentation of Lavalas should be seen within the theoretical argument made in chapter 1 that democratization movements usually become transformed from majoritarian social struggles to class struggles once the polarizing conditions of a disintegrating authoritarianism give way to more complex and multidimensional struggles over the nature and reach of the democratization process. The further popular classes push the process, the more dominant classes, elites, and privileged strata taper off, fall out of the movement, and even become opponents.

The Haiti case demonstrates the contradictions between polyarchy and popular democracy. "In attempting to bring his Lavalas movement into government, Aristide confronted state institutions that had always represented the power of wealth, privilege, and violence," noted Haitian sociologist and Aristide official Jean Casimir, referring to Aristide's pre-coup period in office. "In such an environment, politics was a difficult enterprise... The accountability that the population demands has irritated many elected officials, even some of Aristide's supporters [the "Lavalas bourgeoisie"]... The Haitian parliament represent[ed] a cross section of the intelligentsia, not simply the traditional elites that previously controlled the state machinery... These parliamentary representatives tend[ed] to operate according to the conventions of the formal political system."[155] But when the popular majority used its mobilizing capacity to try to force the state to respond to its interest – in conformity with the model of popular democracy, which posits a state subordinated to and controlled by majorities who have gained hegemony in civil society – then this majority lost its legitimacy (outside of Haiti) because it transgressed the procedures of "representative democracy." In early August 1991, the parliament began to consider a vote of no confidence against Aristide's appointed prime minister, René Preval. Believing that opposition to the prime minister was an attempt to usurp Aristide's mandate, angry Lavalas crowds surrounded the parliament, assaulted two legislators and threatened several others. At the technical level, the legislators, and not Haiti's popular masses, were acting "legally" and "constitutionally." The "harassment" of the parliament by "mobs" was the initial event which precipitated the internal crisis culminating in the *coup d'état*.

A breach in the constitutional procedures of polyarchy in the interests of popular democratization and basic social change required moving beyond the legitimizing parameters of low-intensity democracy. Aristide recognized as much on the eve of his overthrow, declaring: "This is a political revolution, but it's not a social revolution. Now we are trying to achieve a social revolution. If we don't do that, the political revolution will not go anywhere."[156] (For such comments, he would later be accused of bringing on his own downfall.) "It is not really that Aristide advanced too rapidly or not rapidly enough in his reform project," noted Casimir. "Rather, the project itself – built around the enfranchising of the oppressed in Haiti – inevitably produced a reaction."[157] Low-intensity democracy served well as an instrument to contain, within the parameters of the existing social order, the demands of subordinate majorities. The efforts of this popular majority to transform society in its interests, once its representative won the presidency, ran up against polyarchy's "constitutional" limitations. It was no wonder that the Democracy Enhancement Project placed so much emphasis on strengthening legislative and other "constitutional structures." When the Haitian masses attempted to transgress these formal structures, whose levers were still controlled by an elite unresponsive – indeed, antagonistic – to the demands of the majority, their actions were brandished as "anti-democratic" and extra-legal ("mob rule" became the buzzword) – and could be delegitimized, less within Haiti than at the international level. And in the era of the transnationalization of political systems, each nation requires for its survival that its internal political system be legitimized in the international arena (said legitimization deriving from functioning polyarchy).

This, in turn, underscores another theoretical point: effective hegemony is won by a bloc which conquers both civil society and the state. Either control of the state alone, or dominance in civil society alone, is not sufficient to construct a stable hegemonic bloc. As Casimir noted, "Haiti is really the juxtaposition of two societies, one forced to live without the state, even against the state, and one that is associated with the state machinery... This manifestation of anarchism in the proper meaning of the word – a society that previously had not known the state and that suddenly lays its hands upon the state apparatus – has threatened entrenched interests in Haiti and confused other countries in the region."[158] This "confusion" goes a long way in explaining endemic infighting in both the Bush and Clinton administrations over Haiti policy and the see-saw diplomacy of officials from Washington, from other hemispheric governments, and from international organizations, during the 1991–1994 military interlude, as well as the continued feeling of frustration and disorientation experienced by US officials after the invasion. The underlying point is that hegemony, whether it is exercised by dominant minority groups or popular majorities, is not a viable form of rule unless the groups which are to exercise their sovereignty control both the state and civil society. Hegemonic rule is exercised in an *extended state*. Political and civil society are, in Gramsci's Hegelian phrase, "moments" in the same process. Yet in Haiti, the popular sectors could not wrest the state from the elite, and the elite could not wrest civil society from the popular sectors. Neither side could forge a viable hegemonic bloc within the country.[159]

Relatedly, Haiti demonstrates that the transnational elite project of establishing polyarchy and neo-liberalism, under conditions such as those presented in Haiti, runs up against the struggle for popular democratization and fundamental change in the social order. The impossibility of stabilizing the transnational project in Haiti in the short to mid-term forced the US to deny legitimacy to the different post-coup regimes and to continue conferring legitimacy upon Aristide right up until 1995. Moreover, polyarchy, or consensual domination, requires a bourgeoisie that formulates a political discourse on the basis of an economic foundation of capital accumulation. Such accumulation was historically absent among the Haitian "merchant bourgeoisie" and presented a weak, dysfunctional basis upon which to try and implant polyarchy. This, in turn, leads back to the issue raised in chapter 1, and which I touch on in the concluding chapter: the relationship between democracy and capitalism, or democracy and modes of production. Similarly, despite three years of intense repression followed by a dramatic escalation of internal political intervention after the invasion, the popular classes could not be stamped out or coopted. The military interlude and the invasion solidly clenched political society for the transnational elite, but did little to overcome the historic disjuncture between political and civil society. The prospect in 1995 for achieving anything closely resembling a hegemonic bloc in Haiti under a polyarchic elite was close to nil. The Haitian people have proved deftly intelligent in their own collective mass actions, and there is no evidence to conclude they will be pacified into consensual domination. "State against nation" could, at best, lend itself to a highly transient and unstable standoff, and at worst, to new cycles of Caesarism. Thus we see in Haiti contradictions internal to the transnational elite project which the new political intervention, as an instrument to facilitate that project, is unable to overcome. The pro-Aristide slogan which gained popularity after the coup, "democracy or death," was highly instructive: the Haitian downtrodden majority had appropriated the legitimizing symbols and discourse of the transnational elite project. Ongoing crisis is the most likely forecast in the complex Haitian scenario.

7 Conclusions: The future of polyarchy and global society

> Most people in the world put up with very great inequalities, but when these inequalities appear to be increasing without prospect of being reversed and when they mean famine, epidemic, and certain death for millions of people, they cease to be merely aesthetic problems and acquire the status of political crises.
>
> Richard Barnet and Ronald Muller[1]

> The world of humankind constitutes a manifold, a totality of inter-connected processes, and inquiries that disassemble this totality into bits and then fail to reassemble it falsify reality. Concepts like "nation," "society," and "culture" name bits and threaten to turn names into things. Only by understanding these names as bundles of relationships, and by placing them back into the field from which they were abstracted, can we hope to avoid misleading inferences and increase our share of understanding.
>
> Eric Wolf[2]

The present study, as stated in the introduction, has a dual purpose. The first was to analyze and explain the promotion of polyarchy in US foreign policy. The second, more open-ended, was to explore political and social dimensions of globalization. This concluding chapter is divided into two parts. In the first part, I recapitulate my main thesis, take a brief look at "democracy promotion" programs in the former Soviet bloc and South Africa and US activities worldwide so as to strengthen generalizing conclusions, and summarize in comparative perspective the case studies. I then go on to address the relationship between capitalism and democracy in light of globalization, and present a novel Gramscian framework for analyzing this relationship. This discussion forms the backdrop to an analysis of the contradictions internal to the transnational agenda and to an evaluation of the prospects that the promotion of polyarchy will succeed in its objectives.

317

It also forms a logical bridge to the second part of the chapter, an exploration of broader theoretical issues, including the prospects for world order, intended to contribute to current research and debate on emergent global society.

Prospects and contradictions of the transnational agenda: capitalism and democracy in light of globalization

A recapitulation of the central thesis

A significant shift has taken place in US foreign policy, from backing authoritarianism and dictatorships to promoting polyarchic political systems. Behind this shift is a change in the salient form of social control exercised in a transnational setting, from coercive to consensual means of domination within a highly stratified international system, in which the US plays a leadership role as the dominant world power. This policy shift was analyzed through a methodological approach that weaved together practical-conjunctural, or behavioral, analysis with structural analysis (along with a third mediating level, the structural-conjunctural). At the structural level, the shift is grounded in globalization, which occasions highly fluid social relations, "stirs" masses of people to rebel against authoritarian forms of political authority, and thus calls forth new political structures to mediate social relations within and between nations in the world system. Just as polyarchy emerged in the core countries of the world system when capitalism became fully consolidated there, polyarchy is now emerging as the principal political system in the Third World, and increasingly, as a transnational political system corresponding to global capitalist society. At the practical-conjunctural level, the extended policymaking community in the United States developed a theoretical awareness and a practical attunement to changes taking place in the world and to what is required for the maintenance of social control in twenty-first-century global society, which led to the development of new policy instruments, to the reorganization of the foreign-policy apparatus, and to the launching, from the early 1980s and on, of "democracy promotion" operations around the world. The immediate purpose of US intervention in national democratization movements was to gain influence over and to try to shape their outcomes in such a way as to preempt more radical political change, to preserve the social order and international relations of asymmetry. Beyond this immediate purpose, the new political intervention is aimed at advancing the agenda of the transnational elite – consolidation of polyarchic political systems and neo-liberal restructuring. It seeks to develop technocratic elites and transnational kernels in intervened countries who will advance this agenda through the formal state apparatus and through the organs of civil society in their respective countries.

The operating assumption is that these analytical precepts and theoretical propositions should be evaluated by assessing their utility in providing rational explanations congruent with empirical findings. As the case studies make clear, there is a "good fit" between those precepts and propositions and the findings. But to what extent generalizations can be made based on these four case studies alone remains open to question. The particular history and conditions of each country and region determine the circumstances under which it enters global society. Exactly what form US political intervention takes in a specific country (if it even occurs) depends on a host of factors, including the complex of circumstances within the intervened country and its historical relationship with the United States. The countries examined in preceding chapters, while they differed from each other, all shared a long history of US penetration and intervention. The Philippines was an outright colony, Nicaragua and Haiti were near-protectorates, and Chile, although it enjoyed more clout and autonomy *vis-à-vis* the United States, had been under US domination since late last century. It is safe to rule out a "deviant case" argument on the basis of definite patterns identified in four countries. However, on this basis alone it is difficult to draw general conclusions with certainty. Brief overviews of US "democracy promotion" programs in the former Soviet bloc and in South Africa, and a summary of these activities worldwide, allow us to make generalizing claims with much greater certainty and to strengthen the validity of the general thesis.

The Soviet bloc and South Africa: complex convergences of US intervention and globalization pressures

A brief look at the former Soviet-bloc countries and South Africa reveals the same patterns of US conduct apparent in the four case studies, and the intersection of US intervention with endogenous developments and globalization pressures, under circumstances dramatically different from those in the studies. The former Soviet bloc was not a part of the Third World but constituted the "Second World" – powerful contenders in the semi-periphery in the world system framework. South Africa was also a strong semi-peripheral country with a well-developed domestic capitalist class and an advanced process of internal capital accumulation. The United States was not the principal outside power in South Africa, much less in the former Soviet bloc, and relations were never ones of domination and dependency in either case.

The new instruments of political intervention were deployed throughout Eastern Europe starting in the mid-1980s, and later on in the Soviet Union itself. Similarly, the NED and other "democracy promotion" programs were set up in South Africa in the mid-1980s. In neither of these cases did the United States create movements for democratic change – these movements were endogenous developments – but it did set out to gain as much influence as possible over their outcomes. In the former Soviet bloc, the objective was not specifically to bring about the demise of communist regimes; this was a goal already actively pursued on all fronts since 1917. Rather it was to accelerate that demise and, more significantly, to contribute, through elections and in subsequent programs, to strengthening the most pro-capitalist factions with favorable perspectives for developing a "global outlook" and for promoting the agenda of the transnational elite. US intervention helped these factions come to power in place of discredited communist parties, or at the minimum, helped them to spread their influence and position themselves strategically in post-communist societies. In South Africa, the goal was to bring within manageable bounds the struggle against apartheid so as to limit the extent of a popular outcome and to try to substitute white minority rule with inter-racial polyarchic minority rule, as part of a transition from racial to non-racial capitalism.

The Soviet bloc

During the first half of 1982, a five-part [US] strategy emerged that was aimed at bringing about the collapse of the Soviet economy, fraying the ties that bound the USSR to its client states in the Warsaw Pact and forcing reform inside the Soviet empire. Elements of the strategy included: The US defense buildup already under way, aimed at making it too costly for the Soviets to compete militarily with the US... Covert operations aimed at encouraging reform movements in Hungary, Czechoslovakia and Poland; Financial aid to Warsaw Pact nations calibrated to their willingness to... undertake political and free-market reforms; Economic isolation of the Soviet Union and the withholding of Western and Japanese technology... Increased use of Radio Liberty, Voice of America and Radio Free Europe to transmit [US] messages to peoples of Eastern Europe.

Time magazine[3]

In the 1960s and onward, the Soviet-bloc countries became increasingly integrated into the capitalist world market through loans, trade, technology transfers, and even direct foreign investment (a process which, in my view, was inevitable). This integration overlapped with globalization, and had social, political, and ideological ramifications that interacted with, and aggravated, problems internal to the bloc, namely rigid statist models of socialism and highly authoritarian political systems that suppressed popular participation and subordinated civil society to the state. The social response to this process eventually burgeoned into the mass movements for democratic change of the 1980s. A review of these movements prior to the collapse of the bloc in the period 1989–1991 reveals, in highly simplified terms, that two broad strands had developed among the region's political leaders, trade unionists, grassroots activists, and intellectuals who led the revolutions in civil society: those whose vision of change was the creation of societies free from the defects of both capitalism and the existing brand of statist and authoritarian socialism (that is, those who were seeking some type of a democratic socialist renewal along the lines of the model of popular democracy), and those who were more closely tied to the West and who, whether for reasons of personal ambition or of political conviction, sought the creation of capitalist systems modeled after the developed Western countries and managed by polyarchic elites.[4]

It was in this milieu, and alongside the extraordinary structural power which transnational capital could impose on the former Soviet bloc once it had become integrated into the world economy, that the United States introduced massive "political aid" programs into the region. This aid started with support for the Solidarity trade union federation in Poland in the early 1980s and snowballed by the end of the decade into multi-million dollar programs in all the countries of the bloc, in synchronization with the rekindling of the Cold War under the

Reagan presidency and a host of military, economic, political, and ideological activities.[5] Political aid was utilized in a very specific and highly effective manner. Its purpose was to identify and support those groups and individuals within the loose coalitions of political clubs and civic groups in civil society that could gain leadership positions in highly fluid and semi-spontaneous mass movements and steer these movements into outcomes of "free-market democracy."

In 1982, the United States and the Vatican launched a joint secret program, managed largely by the CIA and by the AFL-CIO, to support Solidarity. In 1984, the NED took over much of the US support for Solidarity, which became overt and channeled through the FTUI, in close coordination with the CIA. "Money for the banned union came from CIA funds, the National Endowment for Democracy, secret accounts in the Vatican and Western trade unions," reported *Time* magazine in a 1992 after-the-fact exposé.[6] Solidarity had emerged several years earlier as an authentic movement for democratization incorporating some ten million Polish workers. The covert aid did not create the movement but facilitated US influence over it and helped the more pro-Western elements assume leadership during the course of the 1980s. In 1982, the same year as President Reagan signed the National Security Decision Directive (NSDD) authorizing Project Democracy (see chapter 2) and parallel to the Washington–Vatican program, he also signed NSDD 32, which authorized a vast range of economic, political, diplomatic, military, and psychological operations to destabilize the Soviet bloc. One of the key planks of the regional operation was the use of Solidarity to launch operations throughout the region, often without Solidarity leaders – much less Polish workers at the grassroots – having any knowledge of such external linkages or manipulation for outside purposes. "The Solidarity office in Brussels became an international clearinghouse: for representatives from the Vatican, for CIA operatives, for the AFL-CIO, for representatives of the Socialist International, for the congressionally funded National Endowment for Democracy, which also worked closely with [CIA director William] Casey," reported *Time*.[7]

The assistance for Solidarity provided a precedent and a model for massive overt, as well as covert, political aid programs throughout the decade and into the 1990s. Solidarity was utilized as a point of penetration not only of the Polish state, but of governments and of dissident civic and political groups throughout Eastern Europe and the Soviet Union. In this way, the endogenous and authentic stirrings in civil society in the Soviet bloc were latched on to a US destabilization campaign. It is worth reiterating that the United States did not *create* the democratization movements in the Soviet bloc or the crisis that led to the collapse of Soviet communism, but rather manipulated that crisis and intervened in the mass movements to try to assure an outcome favorable to the interests of the transnational elite. US activity sought to encourage existing discontent and to harness that discontent. Between 1984 and 1992, the NED spent an astonishing $50.5 million in the former Soviet bloc.[8] On the eve of the collapse of the Soviet bloc, Gershman argued:

> [P]iecemeal reforms and greater openness will release pent-up political pressures for change... Indeed, it has now become possible to consider practical measures to support democratic efforts that are already underway in Poland and elsewhere in Eastern Europe, as well as in the Soviet Union itself. The measures will naturally vary, depending on the extent to which democratic movements have developed in different countries... Efforts to assist the emergent pluralism in the Soviet Union and Eastern Europe should have as their overriding objective the growth and eventual empowerment of civil society... As democratic movements in the Soviet bloc take this path, they should receive moral, material, technical and political support from their democratic friends in the West.[9]

One month after the collapse of the Soviet Union, in August 1991, the *Washington Post* reported: "Preparing the ground for last month's triumph was a network of overt operatives who during the last 10 years have quietly been changing the rules of international politics. They have been doing in public what the CIA used to do in private – providing money and moral support for pro-democracy groups, training resistance fighters, working to subvert communist rule."[10] A "strategy paper" drafted a month later, in October 1991, stated that "the Endowment's mission was from the very outset conceived not as anti-communist but as pro-democratic [read: not just to destabilize existing regimes, but to place viable alternatives into power]. Its aim was not only to assist those seeking to bring down dictatorships, but also to support efforts to consolidate new democracies." The document went on to note that NED activities throughout the 1980s involved three essential tasks: "strengthening democratic culture"; "strengthening civil society"; and "strengthening democratic political institutions."[11]

Although a full exploration is not possible here, these programs, in much the same way as programs documented in the case studies, ranged from support for trade unions, to the creation of new business associations, women's, student, and youth organizations, and media outlets, and/or support for existing ones. US officials also convened hundreds of bilateral and multilateral seminars, conferences, and training sessions for the development of political leadership among the civic groups, political clubs, and social movements that sprang up in the bloc. These activities helped to establish a network of individuals and groups throughout the Soviet bloc, to place them in contact with one other, and, with US and other Western backers, to provide them with an effective "political action capacity" and the ability for public projection (thus to creating demonstration effects) through diverse communications technologies. Such financial, technical, and political support allowed these "agents of influence" to assume leadership roles in the uprisings in civil society and was critical in tipping the balance in the string of elections held in the region in 1989–1990. Many of the US organizations that were involved in NED and other "democracy promotion" operations in the Philippines, Chile, Nicaragua, and Haiti also became involved in Eastern Europe and the Soviet Union. Prominent among these was the CFD, which opened a permanent office in Moscow and undertook "a broad program of technical assistance to independent groups and publications."[12]

The case of the Inter-Regional Deputies Group (IRG) in the Soviet Union is a concrete illustration of how strategic doses of US political aid, injected into the complex milieu of a disintegrating communist bloc, proved to be highly effective. The IRG was formed in summer 1989 at a meeting of the Congress of People's Deputies, was led by Andrei Sakharov and Boris Yeltsin, and brought together some 400 members of the Congress, or about 20 percent of the 2,250 seats. The IRG won international attention, but its links to US intervention programs were little known. By the end of 1989, with assistance from the right-wing Free Congress Foundation, the CFD, and other US groups operating with NED and other "private" and public US funds, the IRG had set up a training school for candidates to put forward the IRG program, which called for the restoration of private property, a market economy, and a constitutional system of formal representative (polyarchic) democracy. The IRG provided the institutional basis for Yeltsin's electoral success in securing the leadership of the Russian Soviet Socialist Republic. From that institutional foothold, Yeltsin and the IRG network continued to extend their influence.

The IRG brought together the core group that not only pressed for the demise of the Gorbachev government from within Soviet institutions, but also managed to assume the reins of the state following the abortive 1991 *coup d'état*. Its members most closely approximate those groups within the post-communist elite which are identified with the transnational agenda.[13] The IRG developed enough organizational coherence and a network of strategically placed leaders in the crumbling Soviet government and its different branches to quickly fill the vacuum of power that developed after the abortive coup. The IRG members were not pliant US puppets: US political aid and intervention gave a crucial boost to the IRG by helping its members come together and develop a working network, and create a capacity for communications amongst themselves and before the Soviet public, and for political action from within different institutional bases of the Soviet state. This was achieved on the part of US operatives, apart from the supply of important communications equipment and training programs, through establishing numerous liaison mechanisms with external constituencies, in conjunction with US diplomacy and other components of US policy.[14]

Similarly, throughout Eastern Europe US political intervention played the role of organizing small nuclei that could sweep into vacuums left at the top, once mass pressure from below forced the collapse of the old communist regimes. The Free Congress Foundation and the CFD, for instance, established offices and set up equipment supply, communications, and training programs in Hungary, East Germany, Estonia, Romania, Yugoslavia, Czechoslovakia, and Bulgaria, just as they had done in Moscow with the IRG and other Soviet groups.[15] Reciprocal to Western efforts to seek out potential nuclei, factions in the bloc that identified with the transnational agenda gravitated naturally toward those who managed US political aid programs, knowing that these programs would link them to Western constituencies and resources. In this way, US political aid facilitated East–West elite bonds and shared identities of interest in the heady transition period.

Following the demise of the old communist regimes, the United States played the leadership role on behalf of the transnational elite in a long-term project for integrating the former Soviet bloc fully into the global economy and for promoting the transnational agenda. On the economic side, this involved massive restructuring, including privatization, eliminating trade barriers, creating a new legal framework for private property and the institutions of capitalist economic management, and opening up the region's natural resources and labor force to transnational capital. On the social and political side, this involved attempts to create formal polyarchic structures and to encourage post-communist class formation and the emergence of elites that could promote the transnational agenda within their countries. This included not just bolstering an elite with a transnational outlook, but countering nationalist elements (of the right, in particular) that were exploring inward-looking strategies.

Whether the former "Second World" would move towards the core of the global economy or experience peripheralization was certainly not clear in the 1990s. Nor was it possible to predict whether tenuous polyarchic political systems would stabilize in Russia and Eastern Europe. But the collapse of the Soviet bloc, seen at the structural level and beyond the immediate political unknowns, had the effect of accelerating world economic integration into a single global economy. Economic restructuring went together with the inflow of tens of billions of dollars in external aid, from the G-7 industrialized countries, the IMF, the World Bank, and other multilateral sources, while political aid programs that continued after the 1989–1991 transitions pushed institution-building and class formation.[16]

South Africa

Endowment programs in Africa continued to stress building such pluralist institutions as free trade unions, business associations, a free press, and independent civic organizations as a basis for the eventual development of democratic political institutions. The country of greatest priority for the Endowment in Africa was South Africa... The Endowment has begun programs to develop black consumer groups and cooperatives, support the activities of community groups working to reduce violence and encourage peaceful change, and aid intellectual and informational efforts to promote understanding of democracy and dialogue among anti-apartheid groups seeking alternatives to violence.

NED Annual Report, 1987[17]

US policy toward South Africa was the linchpin of policy toward Black Africa for much of the post-World War II years, and was predicated on support for colonial and racial authoritarian regimes. Successive Democratic and Republican administrations in this period, despite verbal condemnation of white minority regimes, developed strategic alliances with Portuguese colonies and with white minority governments in

South Africa, South-West Africa (now Namibia) and Rhodesia (now Zimbabwe). In 1969, the Nixon administration drafted National Security Study Memorandum 39. This document, which became known as the "Tar Baby Report," concluded that Africa policy should be based on a long-term strategic alliance with the apartheid regime in South Africa.[18] The African National Congress (ANC), the South-West African People's Organization (SWAPO) and the Zimbabwe African National Union (ZANU), all of which went on to win elections and head post-independence and post-apartheid governments, were labelled "terrorist" organizations by the State Department throughout the 1960s, 1970s, and into the 1980s, and the United States provided low-key military assistance, political and diplomatic support, and intelligence information to the white minority regimes. The US alliance with racialized authoritarianism was complementary and subordinate to European imperial powers who pursued similar policies and were historically the dominant outside powers in the region. Support for authoritarianism in southern Africa was not a particularly US policy but a general practice of the core powers in the world system toward this region.

From the 1960s and on, South African capital became thoroughly intermeshed with capital originating in Europe, the United States, and Japan. As globalization advanced, South Africa became a key outpost of transnational capital. South African capitalists had themselves become thoroughly transnationalized (epitomized by the Oppenheimer family and the Anglo-American Corporation, a leading transnational corporation, in the same league as any Northern-based global corporation), and South Africa became the principal staging point for the operations of transnational capital throughout southern and central Africa. In this way, the relations of dependence and the peripheral status in the world system of a good portion of Black Africa "passed through" South Africa itself. On the heels of the mass rebellion that began with the 1976 Soweto uprising, the transnational elite began to push their South African counterparts to search for a political solution that would involve a transition from racial to non-racial capitalism and thus preserve the interests of transnational capital, not just in South Africa but in southern and central Africa as a whole. US calls for such a transition were coordinated with concerted European support for this transition. In was in this context that US policy changed dramatically in the mid-1980s, from support for apartheid to "promoting democracy."[19]

This shift in policy towards southern Africa was part of a broader process of policy reformulation from the 1960s to the 1990s in the face of the mass, popular movements against the repressive political systems and exploitative socioeconomic orders established during the Cold War years. In Africa, this included the collapse of Portuguese colonialism and successful revolutions in Angola and Mozambique in 1975 (these revolutions were subsequently subject to low-intensity warfare campaigns similar to that waged against Nicaragua) and a transition to black majority rule in Zimbabwe in 1980 in the face of an armed insurgency which came close to seizing power. In 1977, the United States, under the Carter administration, publicly called for the first time for majority rule in South Africa. It adopted a policy of applying diplomatic pressure to, but not withdrawing support for, the apartheid regime. At the same time, it sought to identify and support "moderates" among both black and white groups and to isolate the radical elements, including the ANC, which were leading the mass movement against apartheid. The first Reagan administration launched a "constructive engagement" policy similar to its "quiet diplomacy" policy towards the South American dictatorships. This policy was jettisoned in the mid-1980s, however, as mass protests escalated in South Africa and as domestic pressure against apartheid heightened in the United States. The latter included a grassroots anti-apartheid movement and growing consensus among elites that a post-apartheid strategy had to be developed and implemented while events still remained within limits which could be managed by the transnational elite. In 1981, the Foreign Policy Association – a leading private group of the extended US policymaking community tied to the transnationalized fraction – published a 520-page report titled *South Africa: Time Running Out*, or simply the SATRO report. This report was prepared by a special Study Commission on US Policy Toward South Africa set up in the Council on Foreign Relations. It called for a transition to "democracy" and non-racial capitalism.[20]

A key turning point in US policy came in 1985, when Congress imposed limited economic sanctions on South Africa. A year later it enacted the Comprehensive Anti-Apartheid Act, which tightened sanctions, as part of a strategy of pressuring the white regime into negotiations. President Reagan vetoed the Act, but his veto was overridden by a large congressional majority, including a majority of his own Republican Party.[21] Seen in the abstract, the Reagan administration's policies until 1986 reflected the disjuncture analyzed in chapter 2 between the neo-conservatives who held important posts in the formal state apparatus in the first part of the 1980s and the agenda and policies of the transnational elite which had become hegemonic and gradually became official US state policy during the 1980s.

US policy turned to increasing pressure on the apartheid regime and to developing moderate black leaders and organizations in civil society as a counterweight to the militant black movement. This change in policy, synchronized with pressures exerted by the transnationalized capitalist fraction inside South Africa and by other core powers on the state, led the regime to open a reform process. In September 1989, Frederik de Klerk was elected president of South Africa and announced his intention to create a "new [post-apartheid] South Africa." Four months later he released Nelson Mandela from prison and legalized previously banned opposition groups, including the ANC. De Klerk and his cabinet – "proximate policymakers" representing South Africa's transnationalized fraction – faced the dual challenge of negotiating with the black majority and easing the fears of the regime's white base that an end to apartheid would mean radical change in the social order. In 1992 the de Klerk government began negotiations with the ANC and other anti-apartheid groups. In April 1994, Mandela was elected president of South Africa and apartheid came to an official end.

From the mid-1980s and on, the issue for the United States became not whether apartheid would be dismantled, but how South African capitalism and the interests of the transnational elite in the region could be preserved following a transition period. US influence in South Africa should not be exaggerated: intervention in the transition period was only one of many factors shaping the outcome, and events in South Africa consistently overtook US policy. Given the overwhelming support the ANC enjoyed among the black population, and Mandela's tremendous international stature, the US objective was not to disregard the ANC or Mandela, but to check the growing radicalism among the black population by developing counterweights to popular leadership through US political and economic aid programs. One prominent "credible black leader" promoted in this way was Zulu Chief Gatsha Buthelezi, whom President Bush attempted to place, in his public diplomacy toward South Africa, at par with de Klerk and Mandela during the transition period.[22] What concerned the transnational elite most was Mandela's insistence that the dismantling of apartheid should involve not just eliminating racial discrimination from the political sphere but also eliminating inequalities in the socioeconomic order. "As far as the economic policy is concerned, our sole concern is that the inequalities which are to be found in the economy should be addressed," stated Mandela shortly after his release. "We have mentioned state participation in certain specific areas of the economy, like mining, the financial institutions and monopoly industries."[23] Such economic thinking was not only diametrically opposed to the transnational project of neo-liberalism but also went to the "commanding heights" of the powerful (and thoroughly transnationalized) South African economy – mining, finance, and industry. In contrast, Buthelezi argued that "Socialism... has failed miserably... The free enterprise system remains the only system in which wealth can be generated in such a way as to provide the jobs and infrastructure necessary for growth and stability."[24]

In 1985, the NED launched Project South Africa to "identify and assist South African organizations dedicated to a non-violent strategy to eliminate apartheid and to achieve democracy. Among the South African organizations already identified are trade unions, churches and church groups, human rights and voluntary agencies, educational associations and many others. Project South Africa hopes to facilitate direct contact between such groups and Americans dedicated to providing material and moral support to their efforts."[25] Between 1985 and 1992, the NED set up programs with a host of trade unions, community groups, and black business associations. It also set up and funded several clearing-houses whose multiple functions ranged from developing strategies on a transition, coordinating diverse "moderate" political activities, and funding moderate black media outlets and publications. These clearing-houses played a role similar to the think-tanks funded in Chile in that country's transition and to the two clearing-houses of this type funded by the NED and the AID in Haiti.[26]

Alongside NED programs, the AID initiated in the late 1980s a multi-million dollar program, known as Assistance for Disadvantaged South Africans, to fund housing, economic development, and educational programs for black South Africans and provide loans and grants to blacks to set up private businesses. The objective was to open up the economic system to greater black participation without proposing basic restructuring. The program sought "to broaden understanding of the free market system and prepare black business owners, managers, and employees for success in a postapartheid South Africa." Funding went to "strengthen black business associations" and to "training black women to become leaders in the accounting and financial services field and providing credit to small businesses."[27]

These NED and AID programs had several overlapping strategic objectives: (1) identify and support an emergent black middle class of professionals who could be incorporated into a post-apartheid hegemonic bloc (2) develop a nationwide network of grassroots community leaders among the black population that could win leadership positions in diverse organs in civil society and compete with more radical leadership and (3) cultivate a black business class among small and mid-level black-run or mixed enterprises that would have a stake in stable South African capitalism, develop economic power, and view the white transnationalized fraction of South African capital as allies and leaders. Scrutiny of the NED-AID programs reveals that recipients were almost all moderate and conservative groups that competed with the ANC and with the mass popular organizations of the United Democratic Front, a militant national coalition of some 600 affiliated civic associations.[28] For instance, the NED provided funds to the FTUI and the AID provided funds to the AALC in order to support the United Workers Union of South Africa, which was linked to Buthelezi's Inkatha Freedom Council, and the small but influential South African Black Taxi Association, both of which competed with the Congress of South African Trade Unions, the powerful federation, oriented to the social movement, that sympathized with the ANC and organized over one million black workers from the mines, and the industrial, commercial, and civil service sectors. The NED-funded think-tanks and clearing-houses, among them the Get Ahead Foundation and the Institute for a Democratic Alternative in South Africa, organized workshops, seminars, conferences, research programs, and media activities, and set up training programs for black business and community leaders, and for moderate and conservative trade unions, and women's, youth, and church groups. Through these programs, US intervention helped foster a core of grassroots leaders that were strategically placed throughout the organs of an already densely organized civil society comparable to that of Haiti.

Neither Washington nor the apartheid regime had the ability to control the South African mass movement. The counterweights to the ANC and the mass popular movement were not expected to win transitional elections, but rather to continue building constituencies and exerting influence in the post-apartheid period, as part of a long-term project for the construction of a hegemonic post-apartheid social order. The election of Mandela and the end of apartheid was a tremendous victory for democracy worldwide. But it was not clear, given South Africa's thorough integration into the global economy and the strength of transnationalized South African capital and its control over the country's resources, how much structural power Mandela's government would actually be able to exercise in bringing about fundamental transformations in the social order.

US "democracy promotion" operations worldwide

Between 1984 and 1992, the NED and other branches of the US state mounted "democracy promotion" programs in 109 countries around the world, including 30 countries in Africa, 24 countries in Asia, 21 countries in Central and Eastern Europe (including the republics of the former Soviet Union), 8 countries in the Middle East, and 26 countries in Latin America and the Caribbean. In addition, what the NED referred to as "regional programs" (Asia-wide, Africa-wide, Latin America-wide, etc.), and what it referred to as "multiregional programs" (worldwide) involved dozens of other countries.[29] The NED, as discussed in chapter 2, is only one of many policy instruments in "democracy promotion" operations, and is usually not even the principal one. Since it is an adjunct component of US engagement abroad and of the full panoply of foreign-policy instruments, the presence of its activities in a country or region generally indicates that broader and related activities are underway as part of a larger "democracy promotion" undertaking. The operation of the NED in 109 countries in every region of the world underscores that the new political intervention is a worldwide policy.

A review of the NED's Annual Reports from 1984 to 1992 indicates that most of its activities were concentrated in the 1980s in those areas and countries where the United States has traditionally exercised domination, particularly, in Latin America, in key client regimes, such as the Philippines, as well as in crisis situations and in strategic zones and countries, such as Poland throughout the 1980s and the entire former Soviet bloc by the end of that decade. In the early 1990s, NED operations continued in these countries and regions, but also expanded dramatically in Africa, the Middle East and other Asian countries. For instance, the NED reported programs in just two African countries in 1986 but in seventeen in 1992. The new political intervention started in those areas of traditional US influence and then began to spread out

332

around the globe. In an early 1993 meeting of the board of directors, Gershman reported: "the Endowment has taken measures to address... three key elements of its long-term strategy, namely, providing venture capital to advance democratic forces in 'pre-break-through' countries; developing mechanisms to facilitate coordination among its grantees; and increasing its role as a center of democratic thought and activity." He noted that the NED "has begun an active program in the Middle East and increased its efforts in the 'tougher' countries in Africa and Asia."[30]

This expansion of NED activities also reflects the broader issue of the transnationalization of political processes in the age of global society. "Developing mechanisms to facilitate coordination among its grantees," which Gershman identified as one of three key elements in the NED's long-term strategy, implies the development of mechanisms to facilitate coordination among the organs of civil societies [i.e., NED "grantees"] which the United States is promoting around the world – a further sign of the transnationalization of civil society, and relatedly, of the tendency toward a shift in the locus of social control toward civil society. A careful review of the Annual Reports also underscores the tight correlation between the promotion of polyarchy and of neo-liberalism, and efforts to promote political and economic integration of countries and regions into global society. The NED's "regional programs" and "multiregional programs" generally focused on arranging international forums or launching transnational communications projects for the purpose of establishing cross-national South–South and North–South linkages around programs and strategies for promoting polyarchy and neo-liberalism. In turn, individuals and groups drawn into these regional and international forums are the same people involved in NED and other "democracy promotion" programs in their own countries, and represent their country's transnational pools. In this way, we see how "democracy promotion" acts in a recursive manner to facilitate globalization.[31]

The Philippines, Chile, Nicaragua, Haiti, the Soviet bloc, and South Africa in comparative perspective

Each study illustrated, in different manners and on the basis of particular circumstances, the analytical precepts and theoretical propositions advanced in chapters 1 and 2. In all four countries, cross-class majorities had coalesced into national democratization movements against US-backed authoritarian regimes, yet behind these majoritarian movements were distinct visions of what type of social order should follow dictatorship. Opposition elites sought the establishment of polyarchic political systems and free-market capitalism. Popular forces called for fundamental changes along the lines of the model of popular democracy. (The same was true, although in their unique settings, for the Soviet bloc and South Africa.) The strength of the elite versus that of popular sectors and their leaderships varied from case to case. In Nicaragua and Haiti popular sectors were considerably stronger than elites, and in both countries they came to power and attempted to implement projects of popular democracy. In the Philippines, the correlation between popular and elite sectors hung in the balance during a tenuous transition period. In Chile, a combination of circumstances assured a fairly smooth consolidation of elite hegemony over the transition. In all cases, the forces of global capitalism acted to strengthen projects of polyarchy and neo-liberalism and to weaken the projects of popular social change.

The United States intervened when these national democratization movements were reaching crescendos, threatening not just the existing regime but the social order itself. The beneficiaries of this intervention were neither the popular sectors nor the old autocrats, dictators and "crony" elites, but new technocratic sectors tied to the global economy that articulated the transnational agenda. In the Philippines and in Chile, policymakers withdrew support for Marcos, Pinochet and their respective cohorts, and placed support fully behind elite opponents. In Nicaragua, policymakers failed in their attempt to facilitate a transition from Somoza to his elite opposition. By the time they retook the "democracy promotion" effort – in the mid-1980s and as part of a broader war of attrition against the Nicaraguan revolution – they supported not the old Somocistas but new elite groups that went on, following US intervention in the 1990 elections, to assume the reins of the executive. In Haiti, the United States orchestrated the replacement of the Duvaliers with an interim junta but could not place in power a weak and fledgling technocratic elite. After Aristide came to power, support for this elite escalated. How decisive US intervention was as one key variable among many in assuring elite outcomes varied from case to case and depended on the circumstances of each country. However, in all cases, the new political intervention became well synchronized with the complex of factors determining outcomes.

All four cases and the two synopses demonstrated the intersection of globalization and "democracy promotion" and the relationship between polyarchy and neo-liberal restructuring. This included multiple overlaps between the penetration of transnational capital, the reorganization of productive processes, the recomposition of national class structures and the emergence of new political protagonists, external constraints which the global economy placed on internal policy options and socioeconomic transformations, and so on. Transitions to polyarchy coincided with structural adjustment and a deeper insertion into the global economy, and US policymakers intentionally linked the two in the process of policy formation towards each country. In the Philippines, Nicaragua, and Haiti, the increasing penetration of transnational capital starting in 1960s simultaneously spawned popular, mass movements and clashed with local brands of "crony capitalism," making a transition to polyarchy and neo-liberalism necessary for both political and economic reasons (to prevent a popular revolution and to dismantle "crony capitalism" impediments to transnational capital). The transition in the Philippines was followed by a broad neo-liberal program. In Nicaragua, the global economy imposed enormous constraints on the ability of the revolutionary government to effect internal socioeconomic changes in favor of the poor majority. After the 1990 "electoral *coup d'état*," the country's rapid reinsertion into the global economy and free-market mechanisms helped to reverse quickly those transformations that had occurred during the revolution. In Haiti, Aristide's mild reform program was opposed by transnational capital, which helped generate conditions propitious to the 1991 *coup d'état*. In Chile, massive economic restructuring that began under Pinochet corresponded to that country's reinsertion into the world market under new conditions of globalization. This restructuring disaggregated and demobilized popular sectors and facilitated the emergence, and eventual hegemony, of entirely new fractions among dominant Chilean groups tied to transnational capital who became articulate ideologues and promoters of the transnational agenda. The Soviet bloc and South Africa presented more multifarious scenarios, but these same patterns were manifest, including the pressures induced by globalization and the role played by transnational pools as protagonists. Political and economic aid was carefully synchronized in all countries, and these aid flows facilitated the recomposition of internal classes, tied local classes to transnational class structures, and bolstered transnational kernels in each country. Networks were developed that linked the organs of civil society in the United States and in the intervened countries. Penetration of civil societies in the intervened countries by the organs of US civil society, linked in turn to the US state, sought to strengthen elite groups *in order to* compete with and suppress popular organizations and movements and to construct elite hegemony, "bottom-up," from within civil society. Political and economic aid and the policies promoted from within and without the formal state apparatus by these transnational kernels contributed to the construction of neo-liberal states.

The case studies also made evident the contradictions between polyarchy and popular democracy. In the Philippines, for instance, regular elections, a free press, constitutional rule and formal political and civil rights became institutionalized in the post-Marcos period. Yet the elite, through control over the formal legislative process, executive prerogative, and of low-key, but systematic, repression, was able to prevent any significant reform in the social order and to minimize actual mass participation in the formal political process. A similar situation occurred in Chile. In Nicaragua, the Sandinistas' attempt to win international legitimacy led them to expand the institutions of representative democracy (polyarchy) at the expense of the structures of participatory democracy that were established in the early years of the revolution. This process gave the elite increasing institutional leverage and led to a loss of popular support for the revolutionary government – factors which contributed to the subsequent restoration of elite rule. This contradiction became crystal clear in Haiti, where highly organized popular majorities were utterly unable to utilize the formal structures of polyarchy to advance their own interests. These structures acted to institutionally block and to ideologically delegitimize the demands for fundamental change in the social order. All cases show mixed outcomes as regards the stabilization of polyarchic political systems and hegemonic social order. Chile was a tremendous success for the transnational elite (and is touted as such). The Philippines and Nicaragua approximate a situation of highly unstable polyarchies and problems of governability. Haiti was a failure for the US effort to implant a polyarchic political system. The situation in the former Soviet bloc was highly unstable and unpredictable in the early 1990s. The end of apartheid in South Africa is too recent at the time of writing (1995) to venture any predictions.

Comparative conclusions in mainstream social science, whether quantitative or qualitative in approach, are often based on an abstracted empiricism that examines different variables and then measures and correlates the presence or absence of variables (X1, X2, etc.) to distinct outcomes (Y1, Y2, etc.). These relationships are important but must be tempered. In a dialectic model based on the methodology of historical materialism, variables as empirical approximations are recursive, multicausal, and subsumed under holistic reconstruction. The various sequences of historical events are not separate and independent; they are elements of a dialectic process of "social ensembles" in the course of which relations of cause and effect intervene, reverse, and interact. With this caveat in mind , we may note the following: there are clearly certain general conditions propitious to successful transitions to polyarchy and the consolidation of polyarchic political systems. Among these conditions, five stand out: the relative strength of popular versus elite forces; reciprocity of domination in political and civil society; the legacy of authoritarian arrangements and attendant political cultures; the presence and relative strength of transnationalized fractions among dominant groups; and historical timing and conjunctural circumstances during transitions.

A comparative summary reveals a direct correlation between these five factors and outcomes. Popular forces were the strongest in Nicaragua and in Haiti. They were the weakest in Chile. In the Philippines they were on the ascent but faced an elite that had not exhausted its own capacity for political protagonism. Similarly, the transnationalized fraction was the strongest in Chile. It was present and in the process of development in the Philippines, and, to a much lesser extent, in Nicaragua. In Haiti, a technocratic elite was unable to coalesce effectively. Similarly, Haiti, followed by Nicaragua, shows the deepest legacy of authoritarianism and dictatorship, while Chile had a long history of functioning polyarchy prior to dictatorship and globalization. The Philippines also experienced several decades of proto-polyarchy before its lapse into authoritarianism. In Haiti, the correlation of forces favored popular hegemony in civil society even though the state remained a bastion of the dominant groups. State power was seized in Nicaragua by popular classes simultaneously with the development of a Sandinista hegemony in civil society. In the Philippines, hegemony and the state were disputed for several crucial years before the elite consolidated a tenuous hold over the social order. A similar dispute took place in Chile in the Allende period, and then by the time of the late 1980s "transition," the state was returned to the dominant groups simultaneously with the construction by those groups of hegemony in civil society. It is not surprising, therefore, that Chile showed the most developed post-authoritarian hegemonic social order, the Philippines showed a consolidated but somewhat unstable polyarchy, while Nicaragua had a nearly ungovernable polyarchy, and Haiti seemed as far away as ever from hegemonic order. Such "preconditions" for successful transitions to polyarchy can only be gauged by analyzing each country's particular circumstances in historical context, and by factoring in the fifth variable, that of historical timing and conjunctural circumstances, neither of which lend themselves to predictability or facile generalizations.

However, "success" is not measured only by the stabilization of consensual forms of domination. It is also measured by the extent to which projects of popular democracy were suppressed, and to which neo-liberal restructuring has taken place. In this regard, there was remarkable "success" in five of the six cases (South Africa is the unknown) in suppressing popular democracy and in initiating neo-liberal restructuring. The structural power of transnational capital and the impossibility of individual countries and regions remaining outside the global economy makes the imposition of neo-liberal restructuring, as the economic plank of the transnational elite project, considerably easier than the political counterpart of that project, the development of functioning polyarchic systems. Clearly, it is easier to suppress popular democracy than to stabilize its "consensual" antagonist, polyarchic systems, which leaves open the question of a possible general reversion to its "coercive" antagonist, authoritarianism and dictatorship.

Behind the issue of mixed outcomes and the prospects for the consolidation of functioning polyarchies are the contradictions internal to the transnational project. A discussion of these contradictions appropriately rests on a reexamination of the historical relationship between capitalism and democracy. All five variables mentioned above as determinants in outcome are structurally contingent. The structural basis of the variables is the social structure of accumulation: a set of mutually reinforcing social, economic, and political institutions and cultural and ideological norms which fuse with, and facilitate, a successful pattern of capital accumulation over specific historical periods. In turn, examining capital accumulation under distinct institutions and norms brings us to the relationship between capitalism and democracy, which is central to my entire thesis and which allows us to

338

answer the questions: what conditions actually allow for stable polyarchies and what are the prospects that these conditions will be met in
specific regions and in the world as a whole? The reexamination, taken
up in the following section, paves the way for discussion on the
prospects for hegemony and world order in the twenty-first century
and forms a logical bridge between the two parts of this concluding
chapter.

Capitalism and democracy

The contradiction between neo-liberalism and polyarchy

If the promotion of polyarchy is concerned chiefly with social stability,
an assessment of its prospects necessarily begins with an examination
of the causes of social *instability*. Such an examination brings us to the
very heart of the contradiction internal to the transnational project of
neo-liberalism and polyarchy: the dramatic growth under globalization
of socioeconomic inequalities and of human misery in nearly every
country and region of the world, and a frightening increase in the gap
between the haves and the have-nots in the new world order. The
problem of "poverty amidst plenty," a consequence of the unbridled
operation of transnational capital, appears to be worldwide and
generalized. The tendency is for wealth to become concentrated in a
privileged stratum encompassing some 20 percent of humanity, in
which the gap between rich and poor is widening *within* each country,
North and South alike, simultaneously with a sharp increase in the
inequalities *between* the North and the South.

In its widely disseminated report, *Human Development Report 1992*,
the United Nations Development Program (UNDP) provided a frightening global snapshot of this chasm between a shrinking minority of
haves and a vast majority of have-nots. The report provided a
"structural photograph of the planet," which it described as a global
"champagne glass" (see fig. 2). In this champagne glass, 83 percent of
the world's wealth is concentrated in the shallow but ample cup of the
North to the benefit of the 20 percent of the world's population living
there, while 60 percent of the planet's human beings are crammed into
the slender stem and base of the South, which sustains this wealth yet
benefits from only 6 percent of it. The North, noted the report, with
about one-fourth of the world's population, consumes 70 percent of the
world's energy, 75 percent of its metals, 85 percent of its wood and

World's population
classified by income

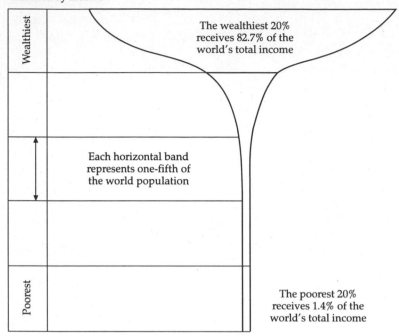

Wealthiest

The wealthiest 20%
receives 82.7% of the
world's total income

Each horizontal band
represents one-fifth of
the world population

Poorest

The poorest 20%
receives 1.4% of the
world's total income

Fig. 2. Distribution of world income.

60 percent of its food. It controls 81 percent of world trade, 95 percent of its loans, and 81 percent of its domestic savings and its investment.[32]

The report noted that the gap between the rich and the poor nations is becoming an abyss. In 1960, the wealthiest 20 pert cent of the world's nations were thirty times richer than the poorest 20 percent. Thirty years later, in 1990, they were sixty times richer. This comparison was based on the distribution between rich and poor *countries*, in which the ratio of inequality went in the thirty-year period from 1:30 to 1:60. However, the report noted: "these figures conceal the true scale of injustice since they are based on comparisons of the average per capita incomes of rich and poor *countries*. In reality, of course, there are wide disparities within each country between rich and poor *people*" (emphasis in original). Adding the maldistribution within countries, the richest 20 percent of the world's *people* got at least 150 times more than the poorest 20 percent.[33] In other words, the ratio of inequality between the global rich and the global poor seen as social groups in a highly stratified world system was 1:150. Broken down into quintiles, global income distribution in 1992, according to the report, was as follows:

World population	*World income* (percent)
Richest 20 percent	82.7
Second 20 percent	11.7
Third 20 percent	2.3
Fourth 20 percent	1.9
Poorest 20 percent	1.4

Source: UNDP, *Human Development Report 1992*. (The UNDP report notes that these statistics hide a part of the picture, because a further breakdown of the distribution of wealth within the top quintile, if one were to generalize from a pattern revealed by forty-one countries for which statistics are available, could be expected to show a very high concentration among the top 1 percent and one-half percent.)

Simultaneous with the widening of the North–South divide, there has been a widening gap between rich and poor in the United States and the other developed countries, along with heightened social polarization and political tensions.[34] Between 1973 and 1990, real wages dropped uniformly for 80 percent of the US population and rose for the remaining 20 percent.[35] The top quintile in the United States had increased its share of income from 41.1 percent in 1973 to 44.2 percent in 1991. The concentration of wealth (which includes income and assets) was even more pronounced. By 1991, the top 0.05 percent of the population owned 45.4 percent of all assets, excluding homes. The top 1 percent owned 53.2 percent of all assets, and the top 10 percent owned 83.2 percent. The United States *belonged* to a tiny minority. In that same year, those living either below the government-established poverty line or below 125 percent of the poverty line represented 34.2 percent of the population of the United States. In other words, 34.2 percent of the US population was "poor" or "very poor," or in more sociologically precise terms, over one-third of the US population lived in absolute or relative poverty. The pattern is similar in other developed countries of the Organization of Economic Cooperation and Development (OECD).

Globalization involves restructuring in both center and periphery, which is resulting in what some have called the "Latinamericaniza-tion" of the United States or the "Third-Worldization" of the First

341

World. The same globalizing forces bringing forth the new international division of labor discussed in chapter 1 are also resulting in a new structure of labor within the developed countries of the North. Labor there is recomposing into three clusters. First, there is that sector "above" traditional industry: those involved in global management, professional services, and high-skill, high-technology production, which constitutes an affluent 20 percent of society in the United States and the other developed countries. Then there is the service sector "below" traditional industry: tens of millions of low-wage, dead-end jobs in diverse local services and assembly line operations which have been subdivided by new technologies to the point at which it has become deskilled work. These jobs often do not even amount to subsistence-level employment. Finally, there is an entirely new group completely marginalized from the production process itself: permanent surplus labor, the "structurally unemployed," or the "supernumeraries" of global capitalism – what mainstream sociology in the North has termed a "permanent underclass." Those in the second and third of these clusters (the tendency is for these two clusters combined to encompass some 80 percent of the population) increasingly approximate, in their life conditions, the vast impoverished majorities of the Third World. This tendency should not be exaggerated. There remain important distinctions between life conditions and opportunities in the underdeveloped and the developed regions. Absolute poverty is becoming generalized in the South; relative poverty is becoming generalized in the North. Nevertheless, the phenomenon further underscores increasing uniformity of social life under global society, and a general worldwide polarization between rich and poor.

There are deep and interwoven racial, ethnic, and gender dimensions to this escalating poverty and inequality in the North, the South, and globally. As transnational capital moves to the South of the world, it does not leave behind homogeneous working classes but historically segmented and racially and ethnically stratified ones. Labor of color, drawn originally, and often by force, from the periphery to the core as menial labor, is disproportionately excluded from strategic economic sectors in the North, relegated to the ranks of the second and third clusters – particularly to the ranks of the supernumeraries – and subject to a rising tide of racism, including repressive state measures against immigrant labor pools.[36] The theoretical root of the historical subordination of women – unequal participation in a sexual division of labor on the basis of the female reproductive function – is exacerbated by globalization, which turns women from reproducers of labor power required by capital into reproducers of supernumeraries for which capital has no use. Female labor is further devalued, and women denigrated, as the function of the domestic (household) economy moves from rearing labor for *incorporation* into capitalist production to rearing supernumeraries. This is one important structural underpinning of the global "feminization of poverty" and is reciprocal to, and mutually reinforces, racial/ethnic dimensions of inequality. It helps explain the movement among Northern elites to dismantle Keynesian welfare benefits in a manner which disproportionately affects women and racially oppressed groups, and the impetuousness with which the neo-liberal model calls for the elimination of even minimal social spending and safety nets that often mean, literally, the difference between life and death.

The socioeconomic portrait of the world makes clear that in the North–South global divide, the "South" refers to the impoverished people of Latin America, Africa, and Asia, and *also* to all the poor and excluded within the rich countries, and the "North" refers to the centers of power that tend to be found in the richest countries of the world and to the rich and powerful in *both* the North and the South who sustain, enjoy, or manage these centers of power. In other words, the geographic fragmentation of production and the separation of production from territoriality is leading to a decrease in the significance of geographic or spatial factors in the division of humanity into haves and have-nots, which requires a rethinking of the whole concept of dominance and spatial organization. Globalization is producing vacuums at national levels, and simultaneously opening up new international spaces, in which the consumption patterns of the top quintile of humanity, through demonstration effects associated with global communications, the marketing strategies of transnational corporations, and the breakdown of cultural barriers in the new "global village," become the standard for generalized emulation and the source of a dramatic rise in global relative deprivation.

The shift in US policy from promoting authoritarianism to promoting polyarchy thus takes place at a time of dramatic increases in global inequalities, in the backdrop of what can only be considered a situation of structural injustice and systemic violence against the world's majority. It is more than a commonsense axiom that deepening socioeconomic inequalities lead to social polarization, and that such polarization leads to social conflict and political instability. The correlation between a deepening of socioeconomic inequality and the breakdown of polyarchy has been fairly well established in the sociological literature. Sociologist Edward Muller, whose research has focused on the relation between income inequality and "democracy," found in a study which analyzed over fifty countries that:

> A very strong inverse association is observed between income inequality and the likelihood of stability versus breakdown of democracy. Democracies... with extremely inegalitarian distributions of income... all experienced a breakdown of democracy (typically due to military *coup d'état*), while a breakdown of democracy occurred in only 30 percent of those with intermediate income inequality. It did not occur at all among democracies with relatively egalitarian distributions of income. This negative effect of income inequality on democratic stability is independent of a country's level of development... Indeed, level of economic development, considered by many scholars to be the predominant cause of variations in the stability of democratic regimes, is found to be an irrelevant variable once income inequality is taken into account.[37]

Because the political system is separated from the socioeconomic basis of society in the polyarchic conception of democracy upon which policymakers and "organic intellectuals" of the extended policymaking community base "democracy promotion," these same intellectuals and policymakers have not concerned themselves with this correlation. Whether this is merely a methodological flaw or a political self-delusion is not relevant to the obvious conclusion: there is a fundamental contradiction between promoting neo-liberalism and promoting polyarchy. By its very nature, the neo-liberal model is designed to prevent any interference with the workings of the free market, including state redistributive policies and such structural transformations as agrarian reform, which could counterbalance the tendency inherent in capitalism toward a concentration of income and productive resources. The neo-liberal model therefore generates the seeds of social instability and conditions propitious to the breakdown of polyarchy. "Democracy promotion" is an attempt at political engineering, at tinkering with the political mechanisms of social control, while simultaneously leaving the socioeconomic basis of political instability intact, and even aggravating that basis through the liberation of capital from any constraints to its operation. This is a contradiction internal to the transnational elite's project.

In a 1990 report assessing the prospects of democratization in the

Third World, the State Department affirmed: "Past failures to establish enduring democratic regimes were the consequence of an inability to meet six critical challenges. To succeed, the peoples and governments of democratic societies must: a) build a national identity; b) foster democratic values and practices; c) build effective democratic institutions; d) guarantee the honesty of government; e) promote democratic competition; and, f) ensure civilian control of the military."[38] What is astonishing is that the State Department did not so much as mention economic inequalities and the lack of social justice as an explanation for the failure of "democracy" in the past or as factors relevant to its prospects in the future. In the view of the State Department, the success of "democracy," even in its polyarchic form, is merely the inculcation of polyarchic political culture and procedures – identity, values, practices, institutions, honesty, competition, and civilian authority over the military.

The global economy is *increasing* what can already be considered a level of generalized immiseration in the South of the planet and relative deprivation in both South and North, and widening the gap between "democratic" political systems and inequalities in the socioeconomic system. A stable polyarchic political system, in which social control is exercised through consensual mechanisms, has historically rested on the material basis of concentric economic development which has brought generally rising standards of living and material well-being. Herein lies the pitfall of the post-World War II modernization and political culture/development theories and their latter-day variants. Ultimately, stability is not grounded in "political culture" but in a socioeconomic system which meets the needs of the majority of society. The possibility of achieving social stability in the South (and of maintaining enough stability to secure the social order in the North) is dependent upon greater socioeconomic equalities within and between nations in the world system, which in turn depends on the extent to which popular democratization advances around the world *against the efforts to curtail popular democracy via the promotion of polyarchy*. Stability in the emergent global society, I submit, enjoys a correlation not with polyarchy but with popular democracy. This poses the need for historical reflection on this relationship between the growing *socioeconomic domination* of a wealthy minority and the ostensible opening of formal political systems through transitions to polyarchy. In turn, such reflection raises important theoretical questions regarding the future of capitalism and democracy in the era of globalization.

Democracy, imperialism and the state

Karl Marx predicted that as capitalism develops, it would polarize society into an ever smaller and richer minority and an impoverished majority. This social contradiction would eventually lead to the breakdown and supersession of the capitalist system. Analyzing the capitalist system before its monopoly stage, there were two factors which Marx did not foresee and which help account for the failure of his prediction to materialize over the past century. The first was the intervention of states to regulate the operation of the free market, to guide accumulation, and to capture and redistribute surpluses. The second was the emergence of modern imperialism to offset the polarizing tendencies inherent in the process of capital accumulation in the core countries of the world system. Both these factors therefore *fettered* the social polarity generated by capitalist production relations, and attenuated contradictions between capitalism and democracy.

The role of states in stabilizing capitalism was already apparent in the late nineteenth and early twentieth centuries in the advanced capitalist countries, with the first social welfare programs, anti-monopoly legislation, and other measures of the "progressive era." John Maynard Keynes raised state intervention to regulate capitalism and offset its internal contradictions to theoretical status, and also developed practical monetary, fiscal, tax, and other policies to achieve this regulation. Keynesianism provided the basis for the "welfare capitalism" or "New Deal capitalism" which prevailed in the core countries of the world system from the Great Depression to the eve of the global economy, and for the various populist models and the "developmentalist states" which prevailed in the peripheral regions.

On the second development, both capitalists such as Cecil Rhodes and socialists such as V. I. Lenin saw eye to eye. Lenin argued that in its monopoly stage, capitalism would incorporate pre-capitalist and peripheral regions via colonization and capital export, which would help offset the social contradictions internal to capitalism in the advanced capitalist countries. Rhodes, a British financial magnate who led colonial expeditions in southern Africa at the turn of the century, wrote in 1895:

> I was in the West End of London yesterday and attended a meeting of the unemployed. I listened to the wild speeches, which were just a cry for "bread!" "bread!" and on my way home I pondered over the scene and I became more than ever convinced of the importance of

346

imperialism... My cherished idea is a solution for the social problem, i.e., in order to save the 40,000,000 inhabitants of the United Kingdom from a bloody civil war, we colonial statesmen must acquire new lands to settle the surplus population, to provide new markets for the goods produced in the factories and mines. The Empire, as I have always said, is a bread and butter question. If you want to avoid civil war, you must become imperialists.[39]

Rhodes had the perspicacity to recognize what social scientists from dependency, world systems and related social science schools of underdevelopment and international political economy would argue decades later: the surpluses syphoned out of the underdeveloped regions and into the centers of the world economy, via direct mechanisms such as colonial plunder and a host of indirect mechanisms such as unequal exchange, would ameliorate in the advanced countries social contradictions germane to capital accumulation. The extraction of surpluses from the peripheral to the center regions of the world system, and the redistribution of these surpluses in the center countries via state policies, led to the emergence of a huge "middle class" in the developed countries (what Lenin termed a "labor aristocracy" and what modernization theorists such as S. M. Lipset assert is essential for "democracy"), averted the civil wars which Marx predicted and Rhodes feared, and provided the social conditions for relatively stable polyarchic political systems. It is not without irony that some baptized as "democratic capitalism" this particular social structure of accumulation that emerged in the center countries on the basis of state intervention in the free market and surplus flows from peripheral to center regions to sustain a high level of development. It was, after all, these two factors that provided the conditions for relatively stable "democracy" in the centers of world capitalism. It is no coincidence that the enfranchisement of the propertyless, the poor, and the illiterate in the centers of world capitalism occurred in the final decades of the nineteenth and the first decades of the twentieth century – precisely as modern colonialism and imperialism were taking hold. The per capita income ratio between rich and poor countries was only 1:2 in the year 1900. Six decades later it was 1:30.[40] Instead of polarization within the nations of the North between a tiny minority of the rich and an overwhelming majority of the impoverished, such a polarization took place on a worldwide level, between the prosperous nations of the capitalist North and the impoverished nations of the newly created Third World – a contradiction which, as I argued at the beginning of this study, always stood behind the East–West conflict. It was therefore no coincidence that formal democratic structures tended to develop in the capitalist North (consensual mechanisms of domination) while authoritarian structures (coercive domination) tended to develop in the South.

By reducing and even eliminating the ability of individual states to regulate capital accumulation and capture surpluses, globalization is now bringing – at a worldwide level – precisely the polarization between a rich minority and a poor majority which Marx predicted. Yet this time there are no "new frontiers," no virgin lands for capitalist colonization and incorporation into the world system which, as Cecil Rhodes argued, could offset the social and political consequences of global polarization. Behind the contradiction between neo-liberalism and polyarchy there is a more fundamental issue, the contradictory relationship between capitalism and democracy.

The relationship in historical perspective

Gaetano Mosca, who most fully developed elitism theories in the late nineteenth and early twentieth centuries, stood on the diametrically opposite side of the social struggles of his time from that of his contemporary and fellow countryman, Antonio Gramsci. Yet they did agree on two points: dominant minorities rule society in their own interests, and they rule by force in the last resort. Generally, a ruling minority succeeds in stabilizing its rule by making it acceptable to the masses. Mosca advanced two intertwined notions of how dominant minorities stabilize their rule. One was a "political formula," or the particular political relations through which the rulers rule, and the other was the "moral principle" which envelops and justifies the particular political formula. He noted that every ruling class constructs a political formula for its rule and then "tends to justify its actual exercise of power by resting it on some universal moral principle."[41] The "political formula" and its "moral principle," although akin to Marx's ruling class ideology, Max Weber's "legitimation" of power, or George Sorel's "myths," is most equivalent to Gramsci's "hegemony." According to Mosca, the "political formula" is not invented and employed "to trick the masses into obedience." It is a "great superstition" or illusion that, at the same time, is a great social force, in the absence of which, maintained Mosca, it is doubtful that societies could exist.[42]

How minorities maintain their control over majorities has constituted the great dilemma of the modern era. Under capitalism, democracy (polyarchy) has been the principal "political formula" for elite rule *in the centers of the world system* ever since the French Revolution, and the "moral principle" of democracy is embodied in the French revolutionary ideals of "liberty, equality, fraternity." Democracy's legitimizing discourse of "liberty, equality, fraternity" stands in stark contrast to the actual reality of deep, structural, and growing *in*equality, increased restrictions and diminished prospects as regards life opportunities rather than more liberties and freedoms in life, and an extremist individualism which breaks down all bonds of human solidarity (fraternity). The legitimizing discourse of the emergent capitalist system became the ideals of the French Revolution – liberty, equality, and fraternity – which in turn embody the contradictory nature of democracy under capitalism, whereby formal juridical equality and political rights exist side by side with gross socioeconomic inequalities and a tendency towards extreme concentrations of wealth and real political power. This represents a deep paradox, a fundamental and perhaps irreconcilable contradiction between capitalism, on the one hand, and its political formula and moral principle, on the other – a contradiction which is intensifying exponentially under the global economy.

The ideology of "liberal democracy" emerged in Europe from the seventeenth to the twentieth century as an instrument in the struggle of an emergent capitalist class against two adversaries: the feudal aristocracy, and lower-class masses newly freed from manorial ties but not yet incorporated into a hegemonic capitalist order.[43] It developed first to counter the ideology of the old feudal order, and later to legitimize the new capitalist order and incorporate subordinate groups. It involved resurrecting the doctrine of "natural law" of antiquity to substitute the "divine right" of the feudal aristocracy, and then to transform "natural right" into the social contract. The social contract replaced divine right at the level of ideology in parallel with the replacement of fixed economic exchanges of feudalism with market relations of exchange. From divine law or equality before God, natural law and the social contract brought equality before the law, or juridical equality, and transformed the state from divine authority to the protector of juridical equality and guarantor of private property. The ideology of individualism and doctrines of individual liberties countered the feudal corporate ideologies and restrictions on the activities of emergent merchants and industrialists.

The philosophical notion of isolated individuals as the possessors of innate rights and the ideal of free individual development bequeathed by the "Enlightenment" was a powerful ideological weapon against the constraints placed on economic and social life by the feudal aristocracy. The notion of self-contained individuals stemming from the empirical philosophers of the seventeenth and eighteenth centuries formed the philosophical basis of the juridical equality and individual rights under polyarchic capitalism, and as well, the philosophical basis for the structural-functionalist meta-theory that would later girder the twentieth century theories of modernization and of a "more realistic" definition of democracy. Hobbes's worldview was of a universe made up of atoms having only external relations with one another, which in social theory became isolated individuals externally linked via market exchange and whose behavior is regulated by the state as a sovereign and coercive authority preventing the "war of all against all" and sanctifying the "natural right" of private property.

But this same "Enlightenment," culminating in the ideals of the French Revolution, inspired not just the emergent capitalists but also the lower classes newly freed from feudal bonds. A careful study of the thought of Hobbes, Locke, Burke, J. S. Mill, Tocqueville, Voltaire, Rousseau, and other great "democratic thinkers" of the modern order reveals a central preoccupation not with mass, popular democracy, but with the construction of political systems that would be most propitious to simultaneously containing subordinate classes and achieving working consensus among dominant groups on the basis of the organizing principle of the most "fundamental liberty" of property rights and the freedom of the market. It should be recalled that when Locke spoke of "majority rule" his definition of this majority was limited strictly to property-owners. Locke, like Hobbes, did not advocate political rights for the propertyless. John Adams had noted a decade after the US Revolution that "it is essential to liberty that the rights of the rich be secured; if they are not, they will soon be robbed and become poor, and in turn rob the robbers, and thus neither the liberty or property of any will be regarded."[44] According to Adams, "the rich, the well-born and the able" should be manifestly in charge of government.[45] James Madison argued that the assumption of rule by and for the propertied and the theory of popular sovereignty would become more and more impossible to reconcile. He predicted quite prophetically that capitalism would face a major crisis in the mid-thirties of the twentieth century.

350

Once the emergent capitalist class had triumphed over the feudal aristocracy, the new challenge became the threat from below. Unlike their predecessors such as Hobbes and Locke, the next generation, among them Jeremy Bentham, James Mill, and John Stuart Mill, turned to the problem of the inherent contradiction in a mass of propertyless and a minority of propertied under a capitalist system whose ideology proclaimed equality and individual liberty. The tension and ambivalence evident in their thought stemmed from the formal equality of exchange relations which masked the real, living inequalities of classes and groups under capitalism. The dilemma for these thinkers in the eighteenth and nineteenth centuries was remarkably similar to the problem Samuel Huntington pointed to in the Trilateral Commission's report, *The Crisis of Democracy*, of how democracy legitimizes capitalism yet "too much" democracy becomes a "threat" to the capitalist social order. Their social thought centered on how to extend formal political rights, including the vote, to the mass of the propertyless, without destabilizing the system of private property itself, or in the words of political scientist George Novack, "how can wealth persuade poverty to use its political freedom to keep wealth in power."[46] The intrinsically contradictory nature of democratic thought under capitalism, in which one side stresses the sanctity of private property (from which flows inequalities in the "social rewards" of wealth, status, and power) and the other popular sovereignty, has bedeviled theorists of "democratic capitalism" who followed the classical thinkers. As analyzed in chapter 1, the third generation of "democratic thinkers," from Joseph Schumpeter and on, clustered in US academia, constructed the new "realistic" definition of democracy in an effort to resolve the inherent tension between capitalism and democracy.

The Machiavellis of the modern order churned out social theories that served as the intellectual and ideological midwife of modern capitalism and yet expressed in themselves the tension between democracy and capitalism. The contradiction has not been reconciled, despite the new "realistic" definition. Every demand for deeper democratization, for popular democracy, touches upon the nerve center of the social order, the material (socioeconomic) distinctions and systematic inequalities among classes and groups. Absolute abstraction of ideal equality is at variance with the fundamental facts of capitalist life, a phenomenon which is becoming patently manifest in the emergent global society. There is a glaring discrepancy between the dominant democratic ideology, with its pretensions of equality, and the persistence and dramatic deepening under global capitalism of inequalities at all levels of social life. A precise identification of this contradiction requires a brief theoretical excursion.

The relationship in theoretical perspective

In chapter 1 it was demonstrated that the organic separation of the political from the social and the economic in the discussion on democracy – rooted theoretically in the structural-functionalist disaggregation of spheres in the social totality and rooted politically in the interests of those who benefit from unjust social and economic structures in an asymmetric world system – is an illusion whose antinomy was exposed through a cursory analysis of the very discourse and premises of those who posit such a separation. The separation of the political and the economic is *formal* but not *organic* – illusory in the last instance. However, this separation does find a certain theoretical validity in the nature of capitalism itself, and provides the key to identifying the contradictory nature of democracy under capitalism. The relations between economic and political power can be quite complex and difficult to decipher. As is well known, there is no simple correspondence between economic and political power, and governing political elites may rule politically without necessarily forming the dominant class, or the class which holds economic power. However, this was not the case in pre-capitalist societies, where political and economic power were much more transparent by virtue of their fusion. Through historical analysis which transcends the particular conditions of capitalism and inquires into the nature of the relation between the political and the economic in social formations, we are able to pinpoint the objective contradiction between capitalism and democracy.

Karl Polanyi, Nicos Poulantzas, and Antonio Gramsci have analyzed the *formal* separation of the economic from the political under the capitalist mode of production. Polanyi, in his classic work *The Great Transformation*, showed how the transition from pre-capitalist systems to capitalism involves the emergence and extension of markets as the underlying dynamic in the making of the modern order. In pre-capitalist societies, for Polanyi, economic relations are "embedded" in the social structure, and thus there is a "natural economy" which fuses the economic and the social (including the political). With the spread of capitalism, the central social dynamic is the separation of the economic (market, or exchange) relations from the social fabric, so that the economy is no longer "embedded" in the social order. The market, for

Polanyi, becomes determinative of all aspects of social and political life, including a new type of state, in which public (the state) and private (producers for the market) become fused, the former in function of the market, yet remain separated at the formal level.[47]

Poulantzas extended this analysis in order to arrive at his central tenet: the relative autonomy of the state, and, by extension, the formal and relative autonomy of the political sphere under capitalism. In pre-capitalist societies, there was a direct correspondence between the economic and the political, e.g. the feudal lord was at once the political authority and the economic authority. The production relations which brought lord and serf together were at once political and economic relations fused in the lord–serf social relation. Recall that the term "state" is derived precisely from "estate", in which the pre-capitalist estate was at once the fused economic and political domain. Under capitalism, the political and economic are completely separate. Capitalist production relations are strictly economic relations between individual agents of production (this is the private, non-political sphere), whereas the state (and the political system) is the site of political relations (political society). The economic domain of the "estate" becomes the "economy," and remains private, although commodified, while the political domain of the "estate" becomes public, that is, the "state." However, to elevate this formal separation into an organic and theoretical severance of the "estate" from the "state," or to sever the "political" in the state and the socioeconomic in society (and, by extension, to posit democracy as a purely political phenomenon, as merely a "system of government") is to fall into an illusion.[48]

Gramsci developed his theory of the rise of civil society and of hegemony as a form of class domination (consensual domination) exercised from within civil society precisely on the theoretical basis of the separation of the political and the economic (political and civil society) under capitalism. Because their hegemony is firmly entrenched in civil society (the "private" sphere in which economic relations unfold), the dominant classes do not necessarily need to run the state themselves (this explains, for instance, the seventeenth- and nineteenth-century states in England and Germany which were run by landlords and Junkers even as capitalist production relations were unequivocally taking hold in the economy). The state in the Gramscian construct is an enlarged state, encompassing both political society, which is the *formal* political/public sphere, or what mainstream social science refers to as the state proper (the government and its executive, administrative, and coercive apparatus, and the site of "democracy"), and civil society, which is the private sphere. Thus the political and the economic are separable spheres in a *formal* (methodological) sense but not in any *organic* conceptualization.

This separation of the economic from the political for the first time in history under capitalism – that is, the *apparent* condensation of class domination from a fused economic-political sphere into a more exclusively economic sphere – explains *both* the emergence of democracy under capitalism and its contradictory status under capitalism. In pre-capitalist societies or "natural economies," owing to the fusion of the economic and the political, any economic demand of dominated classes was by definition also a political demand, and vice versa. In the capitalist mode of production, economic demands of dominated classes are not necessarily political demands, and so long as consensual mechanisms of domination are at play such demands do not transgress the private sphere. Economic demands are raised in the private sphere, as private affairs, and political demands in the public sphere, as public affairs. Yet formal juridical equality and political liberties, or formal democracy, under capitalism specifically sanctions the placing of demands in both the economic and the political spheres. Under these conditions, democracy in the political realm tends to "overflow" into demands for democratization of social life (the social order), which means questioning the legitimacy of capitalism. The paradoxical situation of formal democracy side by side with systematic social inequalities runs up against the legitimizing ideology of capitalism, which is democracy and its ideals of "liberty, equality, fraternity." The process of capitalist production, allowed to operate unfettered, generates both wealth and social polarity. In turn, systematic socioeconomic inequalities generate political demands and social conflict that can rarely be contained without repression. Yet such repression transgresses the norms and the legitimizing ideology of democracy. This repression – however much it is more low-key, selective, and secondary than consensual mechanisms of domination – remains a subterranean but permanent feature of "capitalist democracies" around the world, in both the North and the South, as annual reports of international human-rights monitoring groups make clear year after year. This includes the United States, as sociologist Alan Wolfe, among others, documents and analyzes in his study *The Seamy Side of Democracy*.[49]

The fundamental theoretical conclusion is the following: *the relation-*

ship between capitalism and democracy is contradictory because democracy implies placing demands on the political sphere transposed from the economic sphere, which the political sphere cannot manage without transgressing capitalism. The argument that democracy – and, by extension, democratization movements, which were the object of this study – is more a matter of methods than of objectives becomes theoretically unintelligible. Achieving "liberty, equality, fraternity" can only fully be realized with the democratization of social and economic life. The contradiction can ultimately be resolved only in the transformation of the social order itself. Thus democracy is an historical process which began under capitalism but can only be consummated with the supersession of capitalism.

Examining the paradoxical situation in which it was capitalism which first ushered democracy into the world, and yet it is capitalism that blocks the consummation of democracy, was the concern of sociologist Goran Therborn in his pathbreaking article, "The Rule of Capital and the Rise of Democracy." He argued that the relationship between capitalism and democracy "contains two paradoxes – one Marxist and one bourgeois... How has it come about that, in the major and most advanced capitalist countries, a tiny minority class – the bourgeoisie – rules by means of democratic forms."[50] Political scientist George Novack emphasizes the same paradox of political democracy on the basis of "socioeconomic dictatorship."[51] As both note, to point to this contradiction is not to exhibit "skepticism about democracy" but to acknowledge theoretically that capitalism and democracy become a contradiction in terms when one moves from a democratic form of political life to a democratic content in social life (in which political life is subsumed), that is, when pondering the elimination of actual rule by an exploiting minority. Democracy is thus real, but limited, under capitalism ("restricted democracy," "limited democracy," "partial democracy," "low-intensity democracy").

The historical emergence of capitalism as a new social system brought with it new political forms distinct from earlier forms of class domination. The requirements for the emergence and development of capitalism were also conducive to polyarchy, e.g., a free labor market, a Weberian rationalization and bureaucratization process, juridical equality, legal social contract, and so on. There is therefore a certain historical "elective affinity" between capitalism and democracy, *under certain conditions* (to be explored below). What is required is a reexamination of the relationship between capitalism and polyarchy.

The relation between capitalism and polyarchy: elements of a Gramscian model for a research agenda

Much social science investigation into polyarchy in recent decades has been concerned with examining the interrelationships through time between capitalism and "democracy." Ever since Barrington Moore's classic study *The Social Origins of Dictatorship and Democracy*, a central concern in this regard has been to explore the "preconditions" for the emergence of "democracy," and more recently, the conditions under which "democracy" breaks down and is restored.[52] Moore managed in his study to link "structural" and "process-oriented" analysis, in which structure informed historical outcomes but issues of process conditioned those outcomes. Subsequent research has generally split into two separate tracks: structural or process-oriented. However, what has been referred to in general as "democracy" should more properly be called polyarchy, since the concept associated with the term polyarchy more accurately describes the new political system which emerged under capitalism: elite minority rule and socioeconomic inequalities alongside formal political freedom and elections involving universal suffrage.

Using the comparative historical method first developed by Weber, Moore investigated different patterns in which the struggle between social classes (in particular, peasantries and aristocracies) interfaced with socioeconomic structures in producing different outcomes or "paths to the modern world." His essential conclusion is that the emergence of a strong and independent bourgeoisie is essential to polyarchy ("no bourgeoisie, no democracy"). His study is masterful, but from beginning to end Moore fuses what are two distinct variables. He is concerned with two outcomes: what accounts for "democracy" versus an outcome of authoritarianism (either its fascist or "totalitarian/communist" variants); and what accounts for the outcome of economic development, or "modernization." But how historical class struggles lead to specific political systems and how these struggles lead to economic development are two very distinct variables. The failure to make this distinction leads to two related flaws.

First, the underlying process which informs Moore's study is how different classes respond to what he calls the process of "commercialization," or the development of capitalism. Yet this process is taken as a given; there is no attempt to explain the development of capitalism itself. It simply "appears" in history. Since Moore gives commercializa-

356

tion a pivotal causality in the entire process, he would need to incorporate into the analysis an explanation of how and why capitalism emerged and developed. In turn, an analysis of the process of capitalist development is crucial to analyzing the relationship between capitalism and polyarchy. Second, Moore does not incorporate a broader historical-international or world-system perspective into his study. In his chapter on India, for instance, there is scant understanding of colonialism, much less any notion that what brought industrialization to England and backwardness to India are part of the same historical process. The development of some regions of the world and the underdevelopment of others are not separate dynamics which can be treated and compared as autonomous and externally related phenomena, but are tied into the same world-historical dynamic – the emergence of capitalism as a world system.

In their 1992 work *Capitalist Development and Democracy*, sociologist Dietrich Rueschemeyer and political scientists Evelyne Stephens and John Stephens summarize much of the accumulated research since Moore's 1966 study and offer several new elements.[53] Their essential conclusion is that as capitalist development changes the class structure, new working and middle classes, to the extent that they are able to, do away with the landlord class and usher in polyarchy (like Moore, they define "democracy" as a political system meeting three conditions – universal suffrage, free elections, and civil liberties). In this "working class thesis" – first developed by Goran Therborn in his article "The Rule of Capital and the Rise of Democracy" – the working class is the key to polyarchy ("no working class, no democracy"). The two studies combined underscore one essential element (almost tautological) of a Gramscian model: the two classes germane to capitalism, the bourgeoisie and the working class, constitute the essential class base of polyarchy, and the struggle between classes is determinative in political outcomes.[54]

However, the model established by Rueschemeyer and the Stephens exhibits an underlying flaw similar to Moore's. The triad construct which they say will inform their analysis – the intersection of "class power," "state power," and "transnational structures of power" – leaves out the underlying factor which is determinative in shaping the triad and which would operationalize and make intelligible their model: capital accumulation and capitalist development in the context of the world system. "Transnational power structures," as they define them, do not refer to capital accumulation and class formation on a global scale, but to geo-political competition between European coun-tries and to "dependency" in Latin America, which they reduce to "outside domination." This omission means that the model is unable in the first place to explain what accounts for the development of bourgeois and working classes and for "class power" and "state power." Their essential explanation for the strength of "democracy" in Europe and its weakness in Latin America is the following: the working class plays the key role in "democratization" and is larger and stronger in the advanced European countries than in Latin America, and thus "democracy" is better established in the advanced countries and weaker in Latin America. But, in turn, how are they to explain the existence of a mass-majority working class in Europe and a small-minority working class in Latin America? This is to be explained precisely in analysis of a process of global capital accumulation in which accumulation (and thus wage labor) is concentrated in the core. It is the development of capitalism that generates classes and their size, structure, and so on.

In contrast, a Gramscian model of the interrelationship over time between capitalism and polyarchy takes as its basis Therborn's essen-tial argument: polyarchy has been the outcome of multiple classes in struggle in the context of the emergence and consolidation of capit-alism as a mode of production. "Democracy" (polyarchy) has also shown to be the best mechanism of assuring compromise and stability in situations of disunited ruling classes and competing capitalist fractions and groups. It is thus concerned with relations between dominant and subordinate classes as well as within dominant classes and groups, and is grounded structurally and historically in the process of capitalist production.[55] However, the Gramscian model I propose, as a working hypothesis to be developed, goes further in two crucial respects. First, it incorporates the world system and capitalism in its global setting. It posits that the stable exercise of polyarchy as a political form of class domination requires particular conditions of capital accumulation, and those conditions are to be identified through international political economy and world-system analysis. Second, it is absolutely essential to be precise on the terminology used for *concepts* which form the raw materials of social science. Therefore, the more precise and clearly defined concept of *polyarchy* must substitute in any analysis the essentially contested concept of *democracy*. This is not semantics; it is of crucial import to any theoretical discussion and to establishing the validity of empirical relations between variables. The consequences of uncritically using an essentially contested concept is that key political and ideological notions, meanings and assumptions embedded in language, as well as underlying theoretical discourse and levels of analysis, remain implicit and, at times, even unrecognized by social scientists. Implicit assumptions and meanings often guide, and circumscribe, the types of questions and testable hypotheses to be raised and the interpretation given to empirical data, even beyond the conscious intent of the researcher. Using the most precise language possible regarding a concept under study helps make explicit under-lying meanings, expose assumptions, and uncover key political and ideological notions. It can even change the entire frame of inquiry. In short, it allows social science to move beyond self-constructed impasses and quandaries such as the debate on the "preconditions" of democracy or the causes of its breakdown and restoration.

Gramsci's concept of hegemony has remarkable explanatory and predictive powers in analyzing the relationship between capitalism and polyarchy. When hegemony by dominant classes has been achieved, coercive mechanisms of social control remain latent, in the background, and instead, consensual mechanisms of social control are at play. Consensual mechanisms of social control correspond roughly to a polyarchic political system. When these consensual mechanisms break down, coercive mechanisms pass from latent to active, under a coercive, or authoritarian, political system. These same consensual mechanisms for the reproduction of a given dominant constellation of social forces ("historical bloc"), involve mechanisms for consensus among dominant groups themselves (e.g., the competing elites of polyarchy), as well as between dominant and subordinate groups. On the surface, Gramsci's notion of hegemonic social order under capit-alism is not too different from Dahl's polyarchy, yet for Gramsci, the political structure is grounded, ultimately, in exploitative social rela-tions of production and conflicting class and group interests therein (whereas Dahl sees elites as responsive to the interests of masses and separates the political from the social and economic). Alterations in the structure of production or of power may lead to breakdowns in the mechanisms of social control. Historical periods in which the structure of production undergoes alterations or experiences endemic instability or crises generally involve concomitant shifts in the mechanisms of social control – indeed, this goes far in explaining the "pendular swings" between authoritarianism and polyarchy in Latin America.

"Transitions to democracy" and "democratic breakdowns" in the capitalist epoch of world history, whether seen in the "long historical" perspective or in shorter conjunctural circumstances, should be seen as constructions, breakdowns, and reconstructions of consensual mechanisms of class domination within a given social structure. The research agenda poses the problem as the interrelationship over time between capitalism and the distinct patterns of social control under which it functions. The key question is: under what conditions do consensual mechanisms of class domination become viable and stable, and under what conditions do they exhibit instability and a tendency for breakdown? What are the factors associated with the emergence and maintenance of polyarchy? The conditions in which consensual versus coercive domination may prevail are determined by a complex array of historical and conjunctural factors, and there is a risk of simplification. However, the viability of polyarchy under capitalism has been, above all, a function of three interrelated factors.

The first factor is consensual mechanisms among dominant groups. Political mechanisms must be in place for the resolution of intra-elite disputes. The "breakdown" of polyarchy may result from the inability of these mechanisms to achieve consensual relations among the dominant groups themselves ("breakdown of consensus among elites"). In turn, this "breakdown" is closely tied to the second and third factors. The second factor is demands for popular democratization by subordinate groups. When demands from subordinate groups do not threaten the social order (class domination itself), these demands for democratization help facilitate transitions to, or the consolidation of, polyarchy. This is what took place in the United States and much of Western Europe with the gradual enfranchisement and incorporation of the working classes into the political system. When these demands challenge class domination itself, such as in Spain under the Republic, Chile under Allende, and Haiti under Aristide, the "outcome" is not polyarchy, or relations of consensual domination, but coercive domination or authoritarian political forms (or its opposite, popular revolution). The third factor is the stabilization of a given pattern of capital accumulation. The viability of a given "social structure of accumulation" conditions, and may be determinative of, the first and second factors. Polyarchy is an historical outcome of class struggles that took place around the emergence of capitalism and the formal separation under capitalism of the economic and the political. Specific historical outcomes to the combination of class struggle and the accumulation process, in the context of the emergence of capitalism, produce different forms of state (e.g., republic, constitutional monarchy, etc.) and different political forms (authoritarianism, polyarchy, "Bonapartism," etc.). Polyarchy is one specific political form of the capitalist state, and that form which tends to emerge and/or stabilize under conditions of stable capital accumulation and/or in the absence of subordinate class challenges which threaten the social order itself.

Polyarchy and the world system

Above I have shown that the contradiction between democracy and capitalism lies theoretically in placing demands in the political sphere transposed from the economic sphere which the political sphere cannot manage without transgressing capitalism. Therefore, polyarchy is maintained so long as the political sphere has the capacity to meet (through a myriad of methods) the demands placed on it transposed from the economic sphere. But this capacity is, in turn, a variable relying on a process of capital accumulation sufficient to offset the social contradictions that capitalism generates. An assessment of the prospects for the stability of polyarchy therefore rests on an assessment for the prospects of capitalism.

Polyarchy is a political system which corresponds more organically to the capitalist economic organization of society at the centers of world accumulation, where production and social relations are "concentric." It should be recalled that the historical emergence of polyarchy in the advanced capitalist core involved a dual transition: in the social order itself from feudalism to capitalism, and in the political sphere from pre-polyarchic political forms (absolute monarchies, etc.) to polyarchy, whereas the recent "transitions" in the Third World have involved no change in the social order, but only in the political structure. Polyarchy as the political system based on consensual domination under the social system of capitalism requires that the process of capital accumulation and the generation of wealth be sufficient to sustain or contain the demands from subordinate groups placed on the system. Therefore, polyarchy exhibits greater stability precisely in the centers of the world system, where wealth is concentrated and the process of capital accumulation most dynamic.

The transplant of polyarchy into peripheral regions, through what I have analyzed as the new political intervention, is an attempt to artificially implant a political "organ." This does not mean that polyarchy will not take hold in the periphery, or that there are no exceptions. But it does mean that polyarchy is considerably more fragile in peripheral countries. It is more vulnerable and less stable precisely because of the much more tenuous nature of capital accumulation in peripheral regions of the world system. Social struggles unfolded in core regions in the context of "endogenous" or "autocentric" patterns of accumulation particular to the centers of world capitalism, whereas the pattern of accumulation tends to be "extraverted" in peripheral regions. The material basis for polyarchic stability is more propitious in the center than in the periphery of the world system.

Perhaps unintentionally, Samuel Huntington stumbled across the relation between polyarchy and location in the world system when he argued that "probably the most striking relationship between economics and politics in world affairs is the correlation between political democracy and economic wealth... Rich countries are democratic countries and with only a few exceptions democratic countries are rich countries."[56] Huntington has in fact identified a causal relation, although he has confused the lines of causation. Polyarchy is not the causal factor for the accumulation of wealth. Polyarchy emerged as a political requisite of the emergent capitalist system in Europe, and it was the emergence of capitalism in Europe that provides causal explanation for the current unequal distribution of wealth among center and periphery in the world system. Countries are rich in the world because of their privileged location in a world system based on asymmetries and surplus flows out of some regions and into others, and because capital accumulates and capitalism develops unevenly, with the dynamic centers of accumulation concentrated in the "core" of the world system. The process of capitalist development, shaped by the intersection of local class and social struggles with international political economy and the dynamics of the world system, is the causal variable in the relation between capitalism and polyarchy.

It is precisely when given patterns of capital accumulation in the center countries have broken down that these countries have experienced dramatic jolts in their political systems. These jolts have resulted either in the replacement of consensual by coercive domination (fascism in Germany, Italy, and Japan), or in the sweeping reorganization of the terms of consensual domination – the Keynesian welfare state in most other countries. Those countries which turned to welfare capitalism and thus preserved consensual domination did so on the basis of the successful defense of their position in the world system from the "latecomer" challengers – Germany, Italy, and Japan. The challengers could not fully penetrate the center stage of world capitalism. Meanwhile, those states which have been unable in critical moments of modern world history to remain within the center of the world economy, which have moved outward from the center toward the peripheral zones or into what Immanuel Wallerstein calls the semi-periphery, such as the Mediterranean countries, have also tended to lapse into coercive systems of domination.

As a general rule, those countries which have always been in the periphery, the "Third World proper," have been largely pre-capitalist, or only partially capitalist, in their economic systems and authoritarian in their political systems until the current period of globalization. What I have referred to as "low-intensity democracy" should more aptly be called *peripheral polyarchy*, a particular regime of political domination corresponding to peripheral capitalism. The tendency towards peripheral polyarchy, corresponding to the emergence of a global economy, appears as a variant of polyarchy which tends to take hold as capitalist production relations fully penetrate and become consolidated in the peripheral, semi-peripheral, and underdeveloped regions of global society. The penetration by transnational capital of the most remote regions of the world is expanding, and generalizing the existence of, the two classes which form the class base of polyarchy – the bourgeoisie and the working class. Yet the balance between consensual and coercive mechanisms in peripheral polyarchy tends to weigh more heavily toward the coercive side, such as in most Latin American nations, or the Philippines, where systematic human rights violations remain a permanent feature of the political landscape, notwithstanding formal polyarchies which include elections, intra-elite competition, and formal constitutional rights.

Globalization as system change: the need for reconceptualizations

The promotion of polyarchy as a transnational project reflecting globalization

I have discussed the promotion of polyarchy as a *US* policy and simultaneously a policy response to an agenda of a *transnational* elite. My reasoning is that the United States, or more precisely, dominant groups in the United States, on the eve of the twenty-first century, are assuming a leadership role on behalf of a transnational hegemonic configuration. If my reasoning is correct, the promotion of polyarchy should increasingly become a policy practiced by the transnational elite. This policy initiative *was* being adopted in the 1990s by other Northern states and by the supranational institutions. In effect, the promotion of polyarchy is a policy initiative which is becoming transnationalized under US leadership.

This process is taking place through the development at two distinct levels of transnational mechanisms for promoting and institutionalizing a polyarchic global political system.[57] The first level is that of other Northern countries. These countries have set up their own government-linked "democracy promotion" agencies and launched programs to intervene in the political systems and civil societies of the Third World, in coordination with US programs. By the early 1990s: the British government had established a quasi-private foundation similar to the NED, the Westminster Foundation; the Canadian government had established a similar International Center for Human Rights and Democratic Development; Sweden, Japan, and France were expected to develop their own foundations; and several German foundations which had been active in limited "political aid" programs overseas since the 1970s, began to expand these programs and to coordinate them with the NED.[58] In 1993, the NED sponsored a "democracy summit" in Washington of officials from "the world's government funded democracy foundations to explore how our work might be coordinated."[59] The NED also proposed ongoing "coordinating meetings" and that "the Endowment will develop a database of democracy grant-making that could be accessed by all of the participating foundations, thereby further enhancing possibilities for coordination."[60]

The second level is that of international forums and of multilateral lending agencies. The UN, the OAS, the Conference on Security and Cooperation in Europe, and the European Community had all established diverse "democracy units" whose functions ranged from electoral observation, technical assistance programs for elections and for "civic groups" in Third World countries, to mechanisms for the application of coordinated international diplomatic pressures against states which threatened to relapse from polyarchic to authoritarian governments.[61] In 1991, the UNDP initiated "political institution building activities" and set up an electoral monitoring unit, and the

OAS set up a "Unit For Democracy," among other such developments within international organizations.[62] Similarly, the multilateral lending agencies such as the IMF and the World Bank proposed making multilateral aid, bilateral aid, and access to international financial markets in general, conditional upon a polyarchic system in the recipient country.[63] The importance of the multilateral and supranational institutions in reflecting of the internationalization of the state is discussed below. We can hypothesize a gradual shift in political aid and "democracy promotion" in the twenty-first century away from autonomous agencies such as the NED or the AID and toward centralized core-state organs such as departments of state and foreign ministries, and a concomitant transfer of these activities from core states to supranational organs. Future research should investigate the coordination of the promotion and defense of polyarchy among Northern states and of the use of multilateral and supranational institutions for this purpose, reflective of the transnationalization of policy.

Towards a transnational hegemony and an internationalized state

The notion of promoting polyarchy as a policy initiated by the United States on behalf of a transnational elite is closely tied to the issue of an emergent transnational configuration. Contrary to predominant views, I believe that the historical pattern of successive "hegemons" has come to an end, and that the hegemonic baton will not be passed from the United States to a new hegemonic nation-state. *Pax Americana* was the "final frontier" of the old nation-state system and "hegemons" therein. Instead, the baton will be passed in the twenty-first century to a transnational configuration. Precisely because it was the last "hegemon" among the core countries – that is, because the globalization process emerged in the period of worldwide US empire – the United States has taken the lead in developing policies and strategies on behalf of the agenda of the transnational elite. The effort to bring about a transition to global polyarchy is being conducted under the aegis of the United States as the twentieth-century "hegemon" and as the world's only post-Cold War "superpower." Examining the foreign policy of the United States as the last "hegemon" gives us an indication of where things are going globally and what types of initiatives respond to the transnational agenda. Put in other words, the "US contingent" of the transnational elite was the first to become thoroughly transnationalized, and is the most transnationalized. What was the monopoly capitalist class fraction in the United States became, through the post-World War II process of internationalization and reconstruction of world order, the first "national contingent" of the transnational elite, and the leadership fraction among that elite. Osvaldo Sunkel and Edmundo F. Fuenzalida capture this dynamic:

> Although the immediate origin of transnational capitalism is the oligopolistic corporate sector of the American economy, and the techno-scientific establishment of American society, as well as parts of its government apparatus, its American "national" character has been gradually eroded as similar dynamic cores of business, science, technology and government have emerged in the revitalized industrial centres of Europe and Japan, and as their subsidiaries expand and penetrate the underdeveloped countries and even, to a more limited extent, the socialist countries. The original American drive to reorganize capitalism has therefore been transformed, becoming a transnational drive, which is in turn penetrating and affecting American society itself, as well as others.[64]

When this passage was written in 1979, US and European capital had long since thoroughly interpenetrated. The 1980s saw the massive penetration of the US and, to a lesser extent, the European economy by Japan-based capital.[65] Gill argues that the 1990s and onward should see the counterpenetration of Japan by United States and Europe-based capitals, thus completing the Northern transnational fusion. As I argued in chapter 1, globalization is also integrating Southern-based elites into the transnational configuration, and US political intervention programs are facilitating that integration by linking civil society and political systems in the South to each other and to Northern counterparts.

My notion of a transnational configuration is quite distinct from that found in much international relations, world systems, and related social science literature. The three paradigms in international relations – liberalism/pluralism, realism, and the class model – have all sustained an internal logic and consistency on the basis of the nation-state and on the international state system as the unit of analysis. With the rise of the global economy and globalization processes, the nation-state is increasingly becoming obsolete as the unit of analysis. The very term "international" is revealing: it means, literally, inter-national, or between nations. The forefathers of liberalism (Smith and Ricardo in particular), the class model (Marx), and realism (Weber and Morgenthau, among others), all analyzed a world in which labor and capital were nation-based and international relations were based on national products. But globalization is undermining the logic of viewing worldwide intercourse as exchanges between nations. Trade between nations is no longer the exchange between individual nations of goods that each has produced; it is merely formal linkage as the surface reflection of integrated participation in a singular global production process. The notion that the nation-state system is an immutable or timeless phenomenon is ahistorical and undialectic. The nation-state is an historically bound phenomenon which emerged in the past 500 years or so, in conjunction with the consolidation of national markets, productive structures, and concomitant states and polities. In the age of the nation-state, these units incubated and circumscribed class formation. Dominant groups and their subordinate adversaries (or allies) exhibited a certain congruence with nation-states and governments, and international arenas involved intersections of territorially organized groups whose social protagonism became expressed in the policies of nation-states.

The global economy is eroding the very material basis for the nation-state, yet social scientists, for the most part, stubbornly cling to outdated notions of international relations as a phenomenon in the social universe whose principal dynamic is interaction between nation-states. This outdated nation-state framework conceives of states and their agencies as the most important actors in the global system and fetishizes inter-state relations. I concur with Sklair's critique of "state-centric approaches": "state-centrists, transnational relations advocates and Marxists of several persuasions, while acknowledging the growing importance of the global system in one form or another, all continue to prioritize the system of nation-states, they all fall back on it to describe what happens in the world, and to explain how and why it happens."[66] But I part ways with Sklair in his conceptualization of the state as a territory-bound unit, in contrast to social classes that have become transnational. States should appropriately be conceived as sets of social relations with no theoretical requirement that these sets correspond to a territorial unit. These sets of social relations unfolded within territorial coordinates in an historical period now being superseded by the material and social processes bound up with globalization. Gramsci's concept of the extended state shows the way forward

367

by placing the emphasis fully on to social classes acting in and out of formal state institutions in political societies which need not necessarily be territorially conceived. Political societies are becoming transnationalized as arenas of institutionalized social (class) relations even though governments as territorially bound juridical units remain in place as transmission belts, filtering devices, and targets of "condensation" for dominant and subordinate social classes whose objective identities are not determined by relations to any specific government or to nationally bound material processes.

Utilizing the concepts of nation-state analysis can be highly misleading and illusory. For instance, the old units of analysis such as national trade deficits and current account balances acquire an entirely different meaning once it is pointed out that the vast majority of world trade is currently conducted as "intra-firm trade," that is, as trade between different branches of a few hundred oligopolistic transnational corporations. What is meant by intra-firm trade is when a single global corporation operates numerous branches and subsidiaries across the globe, each with specialized operations and output. Therefore, what *appears* as trade between "nations" is actually movements between different branches and units of global corporations that have no single national headquarters. Robert Gilpin has estimated that such intra-firm trade now accounts for some 60 percent of US imports.[67] The World Bank estimated that by the early 1980s, intra-firm trade within the largest 350 transnational corporations contributed about 40 percent of global trade.[68] Seen through the lenses of the nation-state system, the much talked about "US trade deficit" is characterized as a situation in which the United States imports more goods from other countries than it exports to other countries. But this is a meaningless construct. In reality the trade deficit has nothing to do with nation-state exchanges, but is a consequence of the operation of totally mobile transnational capital between the ever more porous borders of nation-states across the globe. This intra-firm trade belies liberal notions that a world market is operating in which price and market mechanisms allocate resources and regulate output. When the same agent – the global corporation – acts as buyer and seller, there is no market and there is no price mechanism, as Adam Smith himself would argue. What we have is a centrally planned global economy, or what Barnet and Muller refer to as a "post-market global economy," in which neither markets nor states are the agents of planning. Planning is done by transnational capital which has taken the institutional form of an oligopolist cluster of global corporations. To be sure, trade and current account deficits are not irrelevant, but they must be seen in a different light, not as indicators of national economies competing with each other but as factors which upset macro-economic indicators in individual national territories and therefore impede the cross-border operations of transnational capital. The point is that a correct understanding of intra-firm trade and a centrally planned global economy demonstrates how inappropriate and misleading the old nation-state framework of analysis can be.

On the basis of the logic of a competitive nation-state system, much international relations, world-system, and Marxist literature has searched for signs of a "new hegemon," for a continuation of the historical succession of "hegemons," from the United Provinces to the United Kingdom and the United States. Among the predictions are the emergence of a Japanese- or Chinese-centered Asian hegemony; a Pacific Basin hegemonic bloc incorporating the United States and Japan (the "Nichibie economy"); a split in the centers of world capitalism into three rival blocs and their respective peripheral and semi-peripheral spheres (North America and its Western Hemispheric sphere, Western Europe and its Eastern European and African spheres, and Japan and its Asian sphere), and so on. These different scenarios of a new "hegemon" or "hegemonic bloc" among regional rivals are all predicated on important phenomena in the global economy. The problem lies in how to interpret empirical data, and the pitfall is in looking for a new "hegemon" based on the outdated notion that a competitive nation-state system is the backdrop to international relations. For instance, the "three competing blocs" prognosis correctly notes that each bloc is developing its own trade, investment, and currency patterns. It makes reference in this regard to widely circulated *World Investment* reports for 1991 and 1992 by the United Nations' Centre on transnational corporations.[69] Those reports concluded that investment patterns by transnational corporations (TNCs) were driving the evolution of the world economy, and that three "clusters" based in the United States, Japan, and the European community had each developed as a "pole" around which a handful of "developing" countries were grouped. But what the "three competing blocs" prognosis fails to note is that, in turn, each "cluster" is thoroughly interpenetrated by the other two. The United Nations' reports, in fact, stressed that the three regional structures formed an integrated global "Triad." This in turn is based on the thorough interpenetration of capital among the world's top TNCs, such that countries in the South tend to become integrated vertically into one of three regional poles, while in turn the Triad members themselves exhibit horizontal integration In effect, therefore, regional accumulation patterns do not signify conflicts between regions or core-country "blocs" but rather certain spatial distinctions complementary to increasingly integrated transnational capital which is managed by a thoroughly transnationalized and now-hegemonic elite.

For both realists and world system analysts, hegemony is inextricably tied up with state power, and state power is conceived in terms of the nation-state. Clinging to the logic of a competing nation-state system as the basis for international relations leads analysts to search for hegemony in some type of *nation-state configuration* in the new world order. I propose that class power and state power (conceived of in terms of nation-states), while still related, needs to be entirely redefined, and that the emergence of a new historical bloc, global in scope and based on the hegemony of transnational capital, constitutes a new formulation of class hegemony in which the relation between political and civil society needs to be reconceived in a cross- or transnational setting. From a Gramscian viewpoint, this is logical: the *extended state* which incorporates civil and political society and upon which hegemony is constructed needs in no way to be correlated, theoretically, with territory, or with the nation-state. (Even Weber's definition of the state as that institution which holds a monopoly on the legitimate use of force within a given territory loses its logic under globalization, since global economic and social forces may exercise veto power or superimpose their power over any "direct" state power exercised in the Weberian sense – see below.) Stephen Gill's views come closest to my own. On the basis of the leadership role played by the United States in the emergent transnational configuration, Gill argues that "American hegemony" is not coming to an end but is undergoing redefinition. In my view, Gill has correctly identified the leadership role of the United States for the transnational elite, but is confusing "US" hegemony with the hegemony of a transnational class configuration, on the basis of his realist retention of the notion that, even in the age of global society, analysis in international relations is still centered around nation-states and their roles.

I submit the following as a theoretical proposition for future exploration. A transnational hegemonic configuration is conceptualized on the basis of the transcendence of the competitive nation-state framework, yet not on the transcendence of capitalism as a world system. This emergent configuration may be conceived in social (class), institutional, and spatial terms. The social composition of the configuration is of class fractions drawn from the different countries and regions of the three clusters and increasingly fused into a transnational elite and a privileged stratum underneath this elite comprising 20 percent of the world's population. The institutional embodiment of this configuration is the TNCs which are driving the global economy and society, taken together with emergent supranational institutions, which incorporate junior managers in the South and senior managers in the North. Spatially, the configuration takes shape as vertical and horizontal integration around the Triad identified by the United Nations' Centre on Transnational Corporations. A "transnational managerial class" at the apex of the global class structure provides leadership and direction to such a new "historical bloc." The reason why such a configuration is conceived as hegemonic, in the Gramscian sense, is because it exercises structural dominance *and also* its ideology of neo-liberalism and polyarchy has become internalized as legitimate and "natural" at the level of international discourse and among broad sectors of the global population.

To be sure, the organic unification of a transnational elite which leaves behind any national identity or consciousness should not be exaggerated. There are tensions and contradictory impulses which checker all historical processes. The view that a transnational elite has become hegemonic, is consolidating its class domination under the global economy, and is constructing a new "historical bloc" needs to be tempered. There are well-known arguments regarding competition between nationally based capitalist fractions in countries of the North whose interests remain tied to the nation-state, as well as national economic and political elites in the South whose interests lie in local accumulation and development. State managers or "proximate policymakers" in center countries are often drawn from the ranks of the transnational elite (members of the Trilateral Commission have occupied the key posts in every US administration since the Carter presidency). As state managers, they respond to the agenda of the transnational elite. But they must simultaneously sustain legitimacy among nation-based electorates in fulfillment of the state's legitimacy function. This can produce confusing and contradictory behavior on the part of policymakers.[70] What is unfolding is a gradual process which requires a long-historical view. The supersession of the nation-

371

state system will be drawn out over a lengthy period and checkered by all kinds of social conflicts played out along national lines and as clashes between nation-states. However, social science should be less concerned with static snapshots than with the dialect of historical *movement*, with capturing the central *dynamics* and *tendencies* in historical processes. The central dynamic of our epoch is globalization, and the central tendency is the *ascendance* of transnational capital, which brings with it the transnationalization of classes in general. In the long-historical view, the nation-state system, and all the frames of reference therein, is in its *descendance*.

One key disjuncture in the transnationalization process which has caused confusion in this regard is the internationalization of productive forces within an institutional system still centered around the nation-state. A full capitalist global society would mean the integration of all national markets into a single international market and division of labor, and the disappearance of all national affiliations of capital. These economic tendencies are already well underway. What is lagging behind are the political and institutional concomitants – the globalization of the entire superstructure of legal, political, and other national institutions, and the internationalization of social consciousness and cultural patterns. Ultimately, a world state would come to supersede nation-states. The globalization process is leading to such an outcome. Whether capitalism breaks down before it becomes a single global system is not known; there are no predetermined outcomes. More important are the following two points: first, predictions or discussion of a world state should be seen in the long-historical context; and, second, the emergence at some point in the future of a world state could come about through a lengthy, tension-ridden, and exceedingly complex process of the internationalization of the state.

This internationalization of the state, lagging behind the globalization of production, has involved the emergence of truly *supranational* institutions. These supranational institutions of the late twentieth century are gradually supplanting national institutions in policy development and global management. The IMF, the World Bank, and GATT (now supplanted by the World Trade Organization) are assuming management of the global economy and owe their allegiance not to any one state but to the transnational elite.[71] Within these powerful supranational economic institutions, technical economic criteria corresponding to the objective needs of capital replace, as Robert Gilpin observes, "parochial political and national inter-

372

ests."[72] This phenomenon expresses transnational capital's unity of political interests and lack of any national interests. The shift from national to supranational institutions is also evident in supranational political institutions. Such political forums as the Trilateral Commission, the UN, OAS, and the Conference on Security and Cooperation in Europe have acquired new-found and increased importance as political organs responsive to the agenda of the transnational elite, although their functions as components of an "internationalized state" are considerably less developed than those of the supranational economic institutions.

These emergent supranational institutions are representative of new forms of state power in the context of an internationalized state, in which state apparatuses and functions (coercive and administrative mechanisms, etc.) do not necessarily correspond to nation-states. These supranational institutions are incipient reflections of the political integration of core states and their Southern "clusters." It is not that the nation-state will disappear. Rather, important functions of the nation-state are gradually being transferred to supranational economic, social, and political institutions. In the mid-1990s, for instance, US and core-state bilateral foreign aid levels began to drop simultaneously with an increase in financial flows through supranational institutions. Viewing things through the nation-state framework, some interpreted plans to downsize the AID and other autonomous foreign-policy organs, and to centralize them in the State Department, as signs of a "new isolationism" or as consequences of budgetary constraints.[73] To the contrary, the decrease in core-state foreign aid reflects the declining importance of "aid" in imposing policy conditionality on the periphery given the structural power of transnational capital to do so. More importantly, such plans reflected an accelerated transnationalization and externalization of states, in which the tendency is for increased core-state centralization and a shift in the functions of core states to supranational institutions. The function of the nation-state is shifting from the formulation of national policies to the administration of policies formulated by the transnational elite acting through supranational institutions. However, hegemony is exercised in these transnational institutions under relations of international asymmetry. These organizations impose their rules on every "national" society in the context of structural inequality in the world system. The more subordinate each nation-state is in the world system, the less ability it has to resist external impositions. Therefore, the emergent internationalized state plays a dual role: reproduction of the relations of transnational class domination, and reproduction of asymmetries in the world system. This raises the issue of world order and its prospects, and puts in a new light the contradictions internal to the project of the transnational elite.

Polyarchy and world order

Globalization presents a contradictory situation. The prospects for world order are *enhanced* on the basis of a greater worldwide unity of interests, and therefore consensus, among elites, and on the diminished threat that social conflict poses. At the same time, the prospects for world order are *threatened* by the maturation under globalization of contradictions internal to capitalism.

Because of the very nature of globalization – the new international division of labor and global class structure it is bringing about – there is less tension between senior Northern elites and junior Southern elites than in earlier periods. Globalization has redefined both the relationship between Northern and Southern elites and between elites and popular classes in the South. There is no longer a solid class base among Third World elites for the old populist projects, for calls for a New International Economic Order, and so on. Instead, elites in the South, as local contingents of the transnational elite, are increasingly concerned with creating the best local conditions for transnational capital within the new North–South international division of labor, in which the South provides cheap labor for the labor-intensive phases of transnational production. Fulfilling this function requires, in essence, prostituting a population. Making a national labor force attractive, and thereby "marketable," means assuring the lowest possible wages and the highest level of docility on the part of labor. State administrators therefore increasingly act as the pimps of global capitalism. As David Mulford, Undersecretary of the Treasury for International Affairs in the Bush administration, put it: "The countries that do not make themselves more attractive will not get investors' attention. This is like a girl trying to get a boyfriend. She has to go out, have her hair done up, wear makeup..."[74] The impulse to prostitute popular majorities, besides positing competition instead of cooperation as the basis of human interaction, is conducive to highly authoritarian and antidemocratic social relations even under formal polyarchic systems.

Meanwhile, elected offices and public institutions under polyarchic

374

systems are not controlled by mass constituencies. But they are subject to minimal public pressure and scrutiny. However, international agencies are secretive, anti-democratic, and dictatorial in the imposition of their policies, with absolutely no accountability to the mass publics to which under polyarchic systems states are ostensibly accountable. New institutions required for the management of globalized production have come into being, conceived here as components of an internationalized state, but they are even less democratic and less accountable than nation-states. These institutions have usurped the functions of economic management from the public sphere (governments) and transferred them to their own private, and almost secretive, spheres. This means that individual states, not the supranational institutions of transnational capital, must bear the problems of legitimacy crises and social protest generated by the processes of neo-liberal adjustment and integration into the world economy. This phenomenon is, in turn, linked to the general decline in the legitimacy of the nation-state. Both states and political parties not only face mounting crises of legitimacy but are increasingly unable to deal with problems of social decay, cultural alienation, and political crises that accompany the rise of global "poverty amidst plenty."

I noted above the contradiction between growing socioeconomic inequalities on a world scale and stability. The relation between a global polyarchic political system and world order, which is not synonymous with social stability, needs to be reexamined. By world order I do not mean the absence of conflict, but stable patterns of social relations around a global production process. Do the large-scale upheavals and political turmoil around the world of the 1980s and the 1990s point to a period of protracted worldwide conflict that could threaten global accumulation, or rather to the rough bumps and instability associated with an uncertain period of transition toward a consolidated global social structure of accumulation which manages to achieve a certain world order? History has shown that it would be foolish to underestimate the resilience of capitalism as a social system or its ability to develop mechanisms which attenuate the contradictions internal to it. For instance, will some form of "global Keynesianism" come to stabilize global capitalism in the same way as national Keynesianism stabilized national capitalism half a century ago? A more pertinent and pointed issue is not whether capitalism itself will survive in the foreseeable future, but whether polyarchy will remain tenable as a political system of capitalism. The question is equally pertinent for polyarchy in the periphery as it is for the center regions of the world system.

The dramatic worldwide increase in poverty and in inequalities within and between nations makes clear that polyarchy as the legitimizing political system of global capitalism is not matched by any material basis to sustain relations of consensual domination in global society. A generalized reversion to such authoritarian systems as dictatorship and fascism, in the North or the South, should certainly not be ruled out. However, for a number of reasons, the more likely scenario in the emergent global society is a situation of increasingly hierarchical and authoritarian social relations permeating every aspect of life, from public institutions such as school systems and government bureaucracies, to workplaces in office and administrative headquarters and direct sites of material production. We can expect an ever-widening gap between the maintenance of the formal structures of polyarchy, such as regular elections and a functioning constitution, and authoritarianism in everyday life deriving from the increasing powerlessness of people to control or even exert any influence over the conditions of social life.

We are already witnessing such "social authoritarianism." The brand of polyarchy which is becoming universalized is not the more "liberal" version traditionally associated with the developed capitalist nations but the more "authoritarian" and exclusionary version associated with "peripheral polyarchy." A situation of *anomie* is becoming endemic in life around the world on the eve of the twenty-first century: pandemics of crime and drugs, crises of "governability," the disintegration of family and community bonds, widespread personal alienation and despondence, and so on. The type of hegemonic order we are witnessing in this "brave new world" of global capitalism is, without doubt, what some Gramscians might refer to as "hegemony based on fraud," in which a rapacious global elite is thrusting humanity into deeper levels of material degradation and cultural decadence.[75] Under such conditions, there are no guarantees for the personal security of any member of society, even that 20 percent of the world's population that forms the privileged stratum under the global economy. The United States seems to be the model, not the exception. While the United States "promotes democracy" around the world, Amnesty International released annual reports in the early 1990s documenting a growing pattern of systematic human rights violations inside the United States.[76] The US prison population doubled between 1960 and

1980, and then tripled between 1980 and 1990.[77] Robert Reich reports that private security guards constituted a full 2.6 percent of the US workforce in 1990, double the percentage in 1970, and outnumbered public police officers.[78] He describes a situation of "fortress cities" and "social class apartheid" which is nearly identical to patterns found in most Third World countries. In Latin America, meanwhile, the number of those living below the poverty line increased 44 percent between 1980 and 1990, from 136 million to 196 million, representing nearly one-half of Latin America's population.[79] In that same period, 90,000 people were "disappeared" by government and security forces. A frightening new phenomenon appeared in the capitals of nearly every Latin American country: "social cleansing," or the systematic killing, sometimes by official security forces but mostly by shadowy private paramilitary groups and security guards tied to the wealthy, of indigent people pushed by economic forces beyond their control to the margins of society.[80] And this was the decade of "transitions to democracy" in Latin America. Will "social cleansing" become a standard feature of the new world order?

The historical relation between nation-states and capital is being transformed through globalization. But transnational capital still requires the state (a neo-liberal state) for the three functions of macroeconomic stability, the provision of infrastructure, and assuring an environment of political stability and social peace. It is this last function which threatens polyarchy. As social tensions and political polarization mount in the face of global inequalities, states are likely to turn to diverse forms of repression. However, we are more likely to see new types of repression under "peripheral polyarchy" than a reversion to outright dictatorship or fascism. This is to be explained in part by the very nature of the global economy, which redefines spatial and social organization and human settlement. The disaggregation and atomization of individuals brought about by the fragmentation of the production process means that subordinate groups are no longer aggregated into large production units. Intersubjectivities tend to be linked via communications (symbols) rather than by physical association. The nature of repression is thus modified. The isolation of individuals and groups tends to impede traditional forms of collective action and make unnecessary the old forms of mass repression. For instance, in the "social apartheid" which is now found in much of the United States, those who are excluded from the benefits of global capitalism are segregated into urban zones. The social control of those locked into these socially and economically depressed zones involves *containment* rather than repressive incorporation. This containment function is conducted more easily by small-scale police units and sophisticated technologies of control rather than by crude weapons of repression.[81]

There is a huge pool of humanity that has become alienated from the means of production but not incorporated as wage labor into the capitalist production process, encompassing hundreds of millions, if not billions, of supernumeraries on a global scale. These "supernumeraries" appear to be of no *direct* use to capital, and pose a potential massive threat to the stability of global capitalist society. How to prevent poverty and marginalization from fueling revolt, particularly organized revolt, is a major challenge for the transnational elite, made easier, but certainly not resolved, by two intertwined factors. One is the existence of solid polyarchic structures of incorporation, which lead to political disaggregation and apathy, rather than authoritarianism, which can lead to political aggregation and mobilization against visible targets such as dictatorships. The other is the dominant culture imposed by the transnational elite, what Sklair calls the "culture-ideology of consumerism," or the cultural component in his model of transnational practices, which "proclaims, literally, that the meaning of life is to be found in the things that we possess."[82] Escalating global inequalities mean that only a shrinking minority of humanity can actually consume. But the "culture-ideology of consumerism," disseminated through omnipresent symbols and images made possible by advanced communications technologies, is a powerful message that imbues mass consciousness at the global level. Its manifest function is to market goods and make profits, but its latent political function is to channel mass aspirations into individualist consumer desires and to psychologically disaggregate intersubjectivities. Induced wants, even though they will never be met for the vast majority, serve the purpose of social control by depoliticizing social behavior and preempting collective action aimed at social change, through fixation on the search for individual consumption. Personal survival, and whatever is required to achieve it, is legitimized over collective well-being. Social bonds of pre-alienation (pre-capitalist bonds) dissolve but new bonds are not forged among marginalized supernumeraries. Social disaggregation makes control of these teeming masses easier since the prospects of development of a counter-hegemonic alternative are more difficult on the basis of marginalization (see below). One outcome of the social polarization and other contradictions of global capitalism that should not be ruled out is general mass apathy and random violence within marginalized communities which do not pose any fundamental threat, in the foreseeable future, to the stability of the new world capitalist order.

Another outcome might be local and regional conflicts which bring prolonged suffering to millions of people yet, paradoxically, do not undermine world order itself. This is because capital and its circuits are so mobile that productive phases can shift almost instantaneously from one geographic location to another without interrupting the global accumulation process. (The exception is conflict located in regions which contain indispensable natural resources, such as the Middle East. In these areas, transnational capital can apply massive direct coercive power to attain its interests, as was seen in the 1991 Gulf War.) Side by side with a tendency toward a transition from authoritarianism to polyarchy is a generalized pattern of political instability in diverse locations around the world. Such instability ranges from civil wars in the former Yugoslavia and in numerous African countries, to simmering social conflict in Latin America and Asia, endemic civil disturbances, sometimes low-key and sometimes high profile, in Los Angeles, Paris, Bonn and most metropolises of the Northern countries, and diverse forms of fundamentalism, localism, nationalism, and racial and ethnic conflict. The disproportionate concentration of people of color among supernumeraries in the North, and the turn to religious and ethnic loyalties in the North and South in the face of uncertain survival and insecurities posed by global capitalism bodes a period of heightened racial and ethnic conflict in global society. However, the question is whether such local and regional conflicts pose any threat to global order. In many respects, the world has become "safer" for local and regional conflicts as a result of the end of the Cold War and the reduction of the nuclear threat to a minimum. I would submit that one major structural phenomenon, theoretically conceived, that accounted for a good part of the conflicts in the early 1990s (although certainly not the only one) was the disjuncture mentioned above, and that it was rooted in the nature of the globalization process, the transition between the historic functions of the nation-state in maintaining the internal unity, cohesion and reproduction of each social formation, and the emergence of supranational structures, still in the process of consolidation, conceived as internationalized state apparatuses. The decline of the capacity of individual nation-states to control processes within their own borders and to maintain the unity of national formations left major social, political, economic, cultural, and ideological vacuums which were not filled by the emergent transnational elite and its international state apparatuses.

Another consequence of globalization is the possible heightened conflict between nation-states and transnational capital, in instances where these states become arenas disputed by different classes, class fractions, and groups. But as the case studies made clear, and Gill and Law argue, the structural power of capital is such that it is super-imposed on the "direct power" of states. Even states that attempt to respond to the needs of popular majorities, such as the Sandinista government in Nicaragua and the Aristide government in Haiti, are deeply constrained in what they can actually do. Transnational capital controls global resources and gateways to world markets.

Prospects of popular democracy and a counter-hegemonic bloc

> Since it is not for us to create a plan for the future that will hold for all time, all the more surely what we contemporaries have to do is the uncompromising critical evaluation of all that exists, uncompromising in the sense that our criticism fears neither its own results nor the conflict with the powers that be.
>
> Karl Marx

There are many contradictions internal to the agenda of the transnational elite. But the existence of these contradictions does not mean that this elite will not succeed in implementing its project and consolidating its hegemony. Contradictions always exist within a given set of historical social arrangements. This is the law of dialectics as applied to the social universe. It is not the mere existence of contradictions which determines whether or not these social arrangements are sustained. Global capitalism may result in worldwide "poverty amidst plenty," in a predatory degeneration of civilization. However, there are no automatic resolutions to such a crisis. Human misery and world order are not necessarily incompatible. That global capitalism is generating social crises for billions of people does not at all mean that capitalism will automatically be superseded. A popular resolution to the social

380

crises of global capitalism does not lie in discovering any "laws" of social development. Historical outcomes are not predetermined. The social evolutionary overtones of Marxist and other "meta-theories" are useful insofar as they help identify general tendencies in historical processes, indicate *possible* outcomes, and provide analytical constructs for making sense out of reality. There is nothing to indicate, for instance, that the crisis of global capitalism, rather than leading to its supersession by socialism, will not end up in the breakdown of civilization and the destruction of our species, or indeed, of our planet. The "subject" side in the relation between subject and object is not predetermined in any way and authoritative predictions for the future are of little value.

In fact, much of Antonio Gramsci's thought and political activity was aimed at countering economistic and deterministic notions of an inevitable breakdown and supersession of capitalism. Gramsci's polemic with the political and intellectual colleagues of his day, including those in the Second International, was that the supersession of capitalism by socialism involves the dialectic between social structure and human agency (or between "structure and superstructure"). His concept of hegemony weighed heavily on the human agency side, on subjective factors, and the role of subjectivities. For the supersession of capitalism, the social order has to experience an "organic crisis," not just a structural crisis of capitalism but a correlating "superstructural" crisis, or political-ideological crisis predicated on the breakdown of the dominant classes' hegemony and the development of "counter-hegemony" among subordinate classes and groups. A counter-hegemonic bloc would have to articulate a viable alternative for organizing society. This alternative would have to achieve ideological hegemony, that is, it would have to be seen by popular majorities as both viable and necessary. The form and emergence of a popular counter-hegemonic bloc in global society is entirely unclear at this time, but we can advance several observations.

A counter-hegemonic bloc requires the development of concrete programmatic alternatives to neo-liberalism. But these alternatives must go beyond national projects. The global economy places enormous constraints on popular democratic transformations in any one country. Governments in the new global society may be captured by national coalitions in which popular sectors are heavily represented. The contradictions of neo-liberalism open up new possibilities as well as enormous challenges for a popular alternative. Without their own viable socioeconomic model, popular sectors run the risk of political stagnation under the hegemony of the transnational elite, or even worse, being reduced, if they come to occupy governments, to administering the social crises of neo-liberalism with a consequent loss of legitimacy. Under such a scenario, the hegemonic view that there is no popular alternative to unbridled global capitalism becomes reinforced. But a popular project as a viable alternative for each country inserted into global society is far from elaborated.

These issues and a host of questions they raise are best left for future research. However, there is a theoretical point to be made here. In the age of the global economy into which all nations are inexorably drawn, the notion developed by Nicos Poulantzas of the distinction between legal or formal ownership and "economic ownership" of the means of production becomes crucial in conceptualizing power. Poulantzas referred to economic ownership as "the power to assign the means of production to given uses and so to dispose of the products obtained," in distinction to formal legal ownership or possession of the means of production.[83] In this regard, we have seen that even if peasants in Nicaragua have formal ownership of their land, transnational capital operating at the level of the global economy has the structural power to decide how and under what terms those means of production are actually put to use. Similarly, the debt crisis, as analyzed in the chapter on Chile, plays the same role in assigning to transnational capital "economic ownership" of the means of production in debtor countries, in the sense meant by Poulantzas, even when formal, legal ownership remains in the hands of local groups. The challenge, therefore, is how to counter the structural power, *at the transnational level*, of transnational capital.

Any counter-hegemonic bloc would, of necessity, have to be a transnational bloc linking popular majorities across national borders and advancing a concrete, viable program for the organization of global society. One of the consequences of globalization is a redefinition of the relations between nations and classes. The frame of reference for classes is no longer the nation-state. Global class structures tend to become superimposed on national class structures, and both dominant and subordinate classes are involved in global class formation.[84] The "race to the bottom" – the worldwide downward leveling of living conditions and the gradual equalization of life conditions in North and South – creates fertile objective conditions for the development of transnational intersubjectivies, solidarities, and political projects. The communications revolution has facilitated global elite coordination but it can also assist global coordination among popular classes. A class-conscious transnational elite is already a political actor on the world stage – a "class-for-itself." Will subordinate classes become "transnationalized," not only structurally, but in developing a consciousness of transnationality and a global political protagonism? Will they become global popular "classes-for-themselves"? There were some signs in the early 1990s that this was beginning to occur. Popular political parties and social movements in the South began to establish diverse cross-national linkages and a general awareness of the need for concerted transnational action. Discussions were not limited to exchanging national experiences, but addressed developing forms of transnational coordination of national strategies, actions, and programs.[85] Ironically, the new forms of US intervention act as "integrative mechanisms" for both dominant and subordinate groups in the South. However, this nascent tendency should not be exaggerated. National identities and nationalisms as ideologies will persist for generations to come, as will the nation-state as the concrete and practical arena of social struggle. Transnational political protagonism among subordinate classes means developing transnational consciousness and protagonism at the mass, grassroots level – a transnationalized participatory democracy – well beyond the old "internationalism" of political leaders and bureaucrats.

A counter-hegemonic project would not entail resisting globalization – alas, we cannot simply demand that historical processes be halted to conform to our wishes, and we would do better to understand how we may influence and redirect those processes – but rather trying to convert it into a *globalization from below*. Such a process from the bottom up would have to address the deep racial/ethnic dimensions of global inequality, resting on the premise that, although racism and ethnic and religious conflicts rest on real material fears among groups that survival is under threat, they take on cultural, ideological and political dynamics of their own which must be challenged and countered in the programs and the practice of counter-hegemony. A counter-hegemonic project would have to be thoroughly imbued with a gender equality approach, in practice and in content. It would also require alternative forms of democratic practice within popular organizations (trade unions, the "new social movements", etc.), within political parties, and – wherever the formal state apparatus is captured, through elections or other means – within state institutions. These new egalitarian practices

383

must eschew traditional hierarchial and authoritarian forms of social intercourse and bureaucratic authority relations, and must overcome personality cults, centralized decision-making, and other such traditional practices. The flow of authority and decision-making in new social and political practices within any counter-hegemonic bloc must be from the bottom up, not from the top down, as alluded to in the model of popular democracy.

A counter-hegemonic bloc would have to counterpose the legitimizing discourse of polyarchy to that of popular democracy. As we have seen with particular clarity in the cases of Haiti and Nicaragua, and also in Chile and the Philippines, the struggle between dominant and subordinate groups is played out, in part, around the issue of what is legitimate and what is illegitimate in a polyarchic political system. Capitalism and democracy are ultimately contradictory and theoretically incompatible. But to what extent any popular democratization can take place within the constraints of polyarchic political systems is not clear. Robert Barros poses this dilemma as one of a "Gordian knot: How can institutions designed to minimize the extent of post-authoritarian transformations both be strengthened and at the same time subverted? In other words, how can a popular movement strengthen democracy so as to avoid another collapse into military rule, while simultaneously challenging the exclusionary mechanisms of specific democratic institutions?"[86] As we saw with crystal clarity in the case of Haiti, there is no easy undoing of this Gordian knot. However, the construction of counter-hegemony would include challenging the conceptual status polyarchy currently enjoys as the *hegemonic* definition of democracy. In this regard, a counter-hegemonic bloc would require the full development of a *theory* of popular democracy.

Polyarchy in the emergent global society has as little to do with democracy as "socialism" in the former Soviet bloc had to do with socialism. V. I. Lenin argued that "the victory of socialism is impossible without the realization of democracy."[87] The reverse is equally true: the victory of democracy is impossible without the realization of socialism. A democratic socialism founded on a popular democracy may be humanity's "last, best," and perhaps only, hope. Under the global economy the world's productive resources are controlled by an ever smaller circle of human beings. It is estimated that by the year 2000, some 400 transnational corporations will own about two-thirds of the fixed assets of the planet.[88] This makes transnational corporations, the institutional agents of transnational capital, more powerful than any government in the world. With the world's resources controlled by a few hundred such global corporations, the life-blood and the very fate of humanity is in the hands of transnational capital, which holds the power to make life and death decisions for millions of human beings. Such tremendous concentrations of economic power lead to tremendous concentrations of political power at a global level. Any discussion of "democracy" under such conditions becomes meaningless. It should be recalled that capital organizes production not in order to meet human needs (create use values) but in order to generate profit (realize exchange values). The way in which the overwhelming majority of humanity's resources is used is decided not on the basis of humanity's needs but on the basis of the drive for profit by transnational corporations. The burning challenge of our time is how to wrest such enormous power away from transnational capital and its agent, the transnational elite. This challenge amounts to no more or less than how to democratize global society.

It is fitting by way of conclusion to point to another element any counter-hegemonic popular bloc would require: its own organic intellectuals. Social phenomena are always, and inevitably, many times more complex than our explanations. Analytical constructs (such as the present study) are simplifications of reality that facilitate our understanding and also guide our social action. Yet erecting analytical constructs is very much a form of social action. It is social action in the world that makes history and constantly transforms reality, thus providing social science with the raw material of its trade. Social scientists, in order to truly understand reality, must participate in its transformation. And participate we do. The question is: for *whom* are we doing the thinking? We who claim the mantle of social science run the risk of becoming the new mandarins of an anti-democratic global society founded on injustice and inequality. Truth, in Gramsci's view, is always revolutionary. This is because to arrive at the truth we must act; truth compels actions.

Notes

Introduction. From East–West to North–South: US intervention in the "new world order"

1 Barrington Moore, *Social Origins of Dictatorship and Democracy: Lord and Peasant in the Making of the Modern World* (Boston: Beacon, 1966), p. 523.
2 Department of State, Policy Planning Study (PPS) 23 *Foreign Relations of the United States (FRUS)*, 1948, vol. I (part 2), February 24, 1948, p. 23.
3 Carl Gershman, "Fostering Democracy Abroad: The Role of the National Endowment for Democracy," speech delivered to the American Political Science Foundation Convention, August 29, 1986.
4 A summary of the book's argument may be found in William I. Robinson, "Globalization, the World System, and 'Democracy Promotion' in U.S. Foreign Policy," *Theory and Society* 25 (1996).
5 William I. Robinson, *A Faustian Bargain: U.S. Intervention in the Nicaraguan Elections and American Foreign Policy in the Post-Cold War Era* (Boulder: Westview, 1992).
6 See, e.g., Joshua Mavavchik, *Exporting Democracy: Fulfilling America's Destiny* (Washington, D.C.: The AEI Press, 1992); Ralph M. Goldman and William A. Douglas, *Promoting Democracy: Opportunities and Issues* (New York: Praeger, 1988); Brad Roberts (ed.), *The New Democracies: Global Change and U.S. Policy* (Cambridge, Mass./Washington D.C.: MIT Press/Washington Quarterly, 1990); Commission on Behavioral and Social Sciences and Education, National Research Council, *The Transition to Democracy: Proceedings of a Workshop* (Washington, D.C.: National Academy Press, 1991).
7 See, e.g., Abraham Lowenthal (ed.), *Exporting Democracy: The United States and Latin America, Themes and Issues* (Baltimore: Johns Hopkins University Press, 1991); Howard J. Wiarda, *The Democratic Revolution in Latin America: History, Politics and U.S. Policy* (New York: Holmes and Meier, 1990); Tony Smith, *America's Mission: The United States and the Worldwide Struggle for Democracy in the 20th Century* (Princeton: Princeton University Press, 1994).
8 Francis Fukuyama, "The End of History?," *The National Interest*, no. 16 (Summer 1989), 3–18.

1 From "straight power concepts" to "persuasion" in US foreign policy

1   Gaetano Mosca, *The Ruling Class* (New York: McGraw-Hill, 1965), p. 51.

2   Michael Crozier, Samuel P. Huntington, and Joji Watanuki, *The Crisis of Democracy: Report on the Governability of Democracies to the Trilateral Commission* (New York: New York University Press, 1975), pp. 20, 21.

3   Literature on the makings of the post-World War II order is extensive. See, among others, Laurence H. Shoup and William Minter, *Imperial Brain Trust: The Council on Foreign Relations and United States Foreign Policy* (New York: Monthly Review, 1977); Stephen E. Ambrose, *Rise to Globalism: American Foreign Policy, 1938–1980*, 7th edn. (New York: Penguin, 1993); Thomas J. McCormick, *America's Half Century: United States Foreign Policy in the Cold War* (Baltimore: Johns Hopkins University Press, 1989); William Appleman Williams, *America Confronts a Revolutionary World* (New York: Morrow, 1976).

4   National Security Council, Memorandum NSC-68 (April 7, 1950), *Foreign Relations of the United States* (*FRUS*), 1950, vol. I, pp. 252, 263, 272.

5   Some of the symptoms were the Cuban revolution, the fall of the South Vietnamese regime, mass protests against the authoritarian states in the Philippines, South Korea, and elsewhere in Asia, the collapse of Portuguese colonialism in Africa, a surge of mass popular movements in South America and elsewhere, and the Iranian, Grenadian, and Nicaraguan revolutions.

6   For example, Lars Schoultz asserts that US policy towards Latin America seeks *stability*, a condition required for the satisfaction of geopolitical, economic and military concerns (the three "national security" concerns): "This basic causal linkage – instability in Latin America causes a threat to United States security – is the cognitive bedrock of United States policy toward Latin America." *National Security and United States Policy toward Latin America* (Princeton: Princeton University Press, 1987), p. 38.

7   The "communist threat," it could be convincingly argued, has, until the end of the Cold War, merely been the term employed to brand those regimes which attempted to alter existing arrangements. Many destabilization campaigns, such as that against Panama or Jamaica, did not target communism. And US intervention in Latin America predates the birth of communist movements internationally.

8   Lloyd C. Gardner, "The Evolution of the Interventionist Impulse," in Peter J. Schraeder (ed.), *Intervention in the 1980s: U.S. Foreign Policy in the Third World* (Boulder: Lynne Rienner, 1989).

9   Most importantly, see Immanuel Wallerstein's *The Modern World System* (New York: Academic Press, 1970) and *The Capitalist World Economy* (Cambridge: Cambridge University Press, 1979). Samir Amin, *Accumulation on a World Scale: A Critique of the Theory of Underdevelopment* (New York: Monthly Review, 1974), is a classic statement from this framework as seen from the South. L. S. Stavrianos, *Global Rift: The Third World Comes*

of Age (New York: William Morrow, 1981), provides an encyclopedic world historical account from the world system framework. A summary of the literature is provided in Anthony Brewer, *Marxist Theories of Imperialism: A Critical Survey* (London: Routledge and Kegan Paul, 1980).

10 Throughout this book, the term *fraction* is used to denote segments within classes determined by their relation to social production and the class as a whole, whereas I occasionally use the term *faction* in an entirely different sense, to denote clusters that are drawn together in pursuit of shared political objectives within diverse specific settings (e.g., factions within a political party, a social movement, a cabinet, or ministry) and may involve people from various social classes, strata, and groups.

11 Antonio Gramsci, *Selections From Prison Notebooks* (New York: International Publishers, 1971), p. 12.

12 Robert W. Cox is perhaps the pathbreaker in a Gramscian model of international relations. See his "Social Forces, States and World Orders: Beyond International Relations Theory," *Millennium: Journal of International Studies*, 10 (1981), no. 2, 126–155; "Gramsci, Hegemony and International Relations: An Essay in Method," *Millennium*, 12 (1983), no. 2, 162–175; and *Production, Power, and World Order: Social Forces in the Making of History* (New York: Columbia University Press, 1987).

An important exception to the focus on intra-core rather than core–periphery and/or global relations is Enrico Augelli and Craig Murphy, *America's Quest for Supremacy and the Third World, A Gramscian Analysis* (London: Pinter, 1988), although they, along with Cox, retain a primary emphasis on global intra-elite relations.

See also, Ker Van der Pijl, *The Making of an Atlantic Ruling Class* (London: Verso, 1984); Stephen R. Gill and David Law, "Global Hegemony and the Structural Power of Capital," *International Studies Quarterly*, 33 (1989), no. 4, 475–499; Stephen R. Gill, *American Hegemony and the Trilateral Commission* (New York: Cambridge University Press, 1990); Stephen R. Gill (ed.), *Gramsci, Historical Materialism, and International Relations* (New York: Cambridge University Press, 1993). This latter volume launched an interdisciplinary research agenda into a Gramscian model of international relations.

13 Thomas R. Dye, *Who's Running America?*, 4th edn. (Englewood Cliffs, Prentice Hall, 1986), p. 1.

14 An exhaustive review of relevant political sociology literature is to be found in Robert R. Alford and Roger Friedland, *Powers of Theory: Capitalism, the State, and Democracy* (Cambridge: Cambridge University Press, 1985). Robert Gilpin, *The Political Economy of International Relations* (Princeton: Princeton University Press, 1987) provides a good comparative overview of the liberal, realist, and Marxist perspectives in international relations. Roughly speaking, pluralism in political sociology corresponds to liberalism in international relations, the elitist/managerial model to realism, and the class model to Marxism.

15 In international relations, Steven Krasner's *Defending the National Interest: Raw Materials Investments and U.S. Foreign Policy* (Princeton: Princeton University Press, 1978) is a basic statement in this regard. Sociologist Theda Skocpol, in her classic *States and Social Revolutions: A Comparative Analysis of France, Russia and China* (Cambridge: Cambridge University Press, 1979), also develops this view of the state, and elaborates a "state-centered" theory which shares much with realists as regards international relations.

16 Very briefly, the "instrumentalist" approach focuses on how the capitalist class or other classes with capitalist interests dominate and utilize the state directly via occupying key policy posts in government, lobbying state managers, etc. The "structuralist" approach focuses on underlying structural constraints on state behavior. For a discussion and critique, see, e.g., Eric Nordlinger, *On the Autonomy of the Democratic State* (Cambridge: Cambridge University Press, 1981).

17 C. Wright Mills, *The Power Elite* (New York: Oxford University Press, 1959); Ralph Miliband, *The State in Capitalist Society* (New York: Basic Books, 1969); G. William Domhoff, *Who Rules America?* (Englewood Cliffs: Prentice Hall, 1967; 2nd edn., 1986); G. William Domhoff, *The Higher Circles* (New York: Random House, 1970); G. William Domhoff, *The Powers that Be* (New York: Random House, 1978); Dye, *Who's Running America?*.

There are important differences between these writers, particularly in debate over whether power is deposited in institutions, in social classes, or in elite groupings. However, all these views converge in their distinction to the pluralist theories, according to which no one group dominates in society and the political systems allow all groups to share in the exercise of power. Similarly, they all thoroughly document and analyze the nexus between economic power, hegemony in civil society, and governmental power and policies, i.e., the symbiosis of wealth and power in the United States. My own view is that power is *embodied* in wealth (the means of production and the social product), and *exercised* through institutions.

18 Dye borrows the term "proximate policymaker" from Charles E. Lindblom, *The Policy-Making Process* (Englewood Cliffs: Prentice Hall, 1968) and then builds on it. See Dye, *Who's Running America?*, pp. 260–262.

19 See Domhoff, *Who Rules America Now?*, pp. 82–115.

20 Karl Marx, Preface to "A Contribution to the Critique of Political Economy", in Robert C. Tucker (ed.), *The Marx–Engels Reader*, 2nd edn. (New York: W. W. Norton and Company, 1978), p. 4.

21 The state is "the entire complex of theoretical and practical activities with which the ruling class not only maintains its dominance, but manages to win the consent of those over whom it rules... [The state is] political society plus civil society, hegemony armored by coercion." Gramsci, *Prison Notebooks*, p. 262.

22 *Ibid.*, p. 244.

23 A concrete example is the following: slavery in pre-Civil War US society

was maintained by direct coercion. Slaves did not actually believe that they were sub-human or destined by God to slavery. When not rebelling, they gave their consent to slavery because the lash and lynching met rebellion. In turn, once hegemony was achieved in US society under modern industrial capitalism, workers gave not just their consent to, but also consensus on, the social relations of capitalist production. As US labor history reveals, workers demanded wage increases not because surplus value is a relation of exploitation which domination sustains, or because higher wages would increase the relative power of the working class *vis-à-vis* its class antagonist, but because workers are entitled to a better life which capitalism promises or because higher wages benefit "business" (the capitalist class) by increasing market demand.

24 For a particularly crisp analysis of Gramsci on ideology, see Augelli and Murphy, *America's Quest*, ch. 1.

25 Works on the global economy are numerous. This section draws on, among others, the following: Joyce Kolko, *Restructuring the World Economy* (New York: Pantheon, 1988); J. Caporaso (ed.), *Changing International Division of Labor* (Boulder: Lynne Rienner, 1987); Richard J. Barnet and Ronald E. Muller, *Global Reach: The Power of the Multinational Corporation* (New York: Simon and Schuster, 1974); Arthur MacEwan and William K. Tabb, *Instability and Change in the World Economy* (New York: Monthly Review, 1989); Tamás Szentes, *The Transformation of the World Economy: New Directions and New Interests* (London: Zed, 1988); David Gordon, "The Global Economy: New Edifice or Crumbling Foundations?," *New Left Review*, no. 168 (March/April 1988), 24–64.

26 Gill, *American Hegemony*.

27 Barnet and Muller, *Global Reach*, pp. 91–92.

28 Cox, "Social Forces," 147.

29 Osvaldo Sunkel and Edmundo F. Fuenzalida, "Transnationalization and its National Consequences," in Jose J. Villamil (ed.), *Transnational Capitalism and National Development: New Perspectives on Dependence* (Brighton: Harvester, 1979), p. 75.

30 See works by Domhoff cited in note 17.

31 Gill, *American Hegemony*.

32 Peter Evans, *Dependent Development: The Alliance of Multinational, State, and Local Capital in Brazil* (Princeton: Princeton University Press, 1979).

33 James O'Connor, *The Fiscal Crisis of the State* (New York: St. Martin's Press, 1973). This chronic crisis of legitimacy under globalization also explains the growing significance in the new world order of highly visible charismatic figures who substitute concrete political projects or "social pacts" in the legitimization process.

34 Gill and Law, "Global Hegemony," point out that there is a complementary and contradictory relationship between powers of state and powers of transnational capital. The point, however, needs further theoretical treatment.

35 See, e.g., the articles in "A Market Solution for the Americas?: The Rise of Wealth and Hunger," *NACLA Report on the Americas*, 26 (1993), no. 4, which document the sharp rise in Chile, Costa Rica, and Mexico of poverty, income inequality, the concentration of productive assets, and social polarization in direct correlation to adjustment programs. The example of these three countries is instructive because of the high degree of differentiation among the three and because they are touted as neo-liberal "success stories."

36 Stephen R. Gill, "Epistemology, ontology, and the 'Italian school'," in Gill, (ed.), *Gramsci*, p. 48.

37 Crozier, *et al.*, *Crisis of Democracy*, p. 13.

38 Cox, "Gramsci," p. 171.

39 Karl Polanyi, *The Great Transformation* (Boston: Beacon Press, 1957; first published in 1944); Nicos Poulantzas, *Political Power and Social Classes* (London: New Left Books, 1975; first published in 1968).

40 Cox, "Gramsci," pp. 170–172.

41 While space constraints prohibit a discussion, Cox, Augelli and Murphy, and others discuss the failure of the New International Economic Order (NIEO) but do not link this "failure" to globalization, which countered "national logics" in the South and unified North–South elite interests by *absorbing* Southern elites into the emergent global transnational elite. The NIEO was less a "failure" than a project which became outdated by globalization. In any event, even if it had resulted in a shift in relative power to the Third World, the NIEO, as articulated by Third World elites, would not have represented a global hegemony because neither elites in the South nor those in the North with whom they negotiated proposed a shift to consensual domination over subordinate groups in the periphery.

42 Leslie Sklair, *Sociology of the Global System: Social Change in Global Perspective* (Baltimore: Johns Hopkins University Press, 1991), p. 2.

43 Cited in Irving M. Zeitlin, *Ideology and the Development of Sociological Theory* (Englewood Cliffs: Prentice Hall, 1990; first published in 1968), p. 312.

44 Gill and Law, "Global Hegemony," p. 488.

45 Dye, *Who's Running America?*, p. 246.

46 Robert W. Cox, "Ideologies and the New International Economic Order: Reflections on Some Recent Literature," *International Organization*, 33 (1979), 257–302 at p. 260.

47 The literature on democratization that sprang up in the 1980s and early 1990s is too vast to attempt even a selected bibliography here. Two of the most widely circulated works which my analysis focuses on are: Guillermo O'Donnell, Philip C. Schmitter, and Laurence Whitehead (eds.), *Transitions from Authoritarian Rule*, 4 vols. (Baltimore: Johns Hopkins University Press, 1988); Larry Diamond, Juan J. Linz, and Seymour Martin Lipset, *Democracy in Developing Countries*, 4 vols. (Boulder: Lynne Rienner and the National Endowment for Democracy, 1989).

48 This blurring of power-holder and scholar is not just in the abstract. Many

people who become prominent in the scholarly community become government officials, and many government officials become members of the scholarly community. See, e.g., discussion by McCormick, *America's Half Century*, pp. 12–16.

49 The Diamond, *et al.* volumes were commissioned by the NED (see Annual Reports, 1984–1987). Diamond is co-editor of the NED's quarterly publication, *Journal of Democracy*. Linz and Lipset are members of the journal's editorial board. Lipset is also an Advisory Board member of the American Initiatives Project, set up by the World Without War Council. This council was founded as part of the White House's Office of Public Diplomacy in the early 1980s to disseminate propaganda in the United States and abroad in favor of US foreign policy (see chapter 2). Regarding Lipset's participation, see Sara Diamond, "The World Without War Council," *Covert Action Information Bulletin*, no. 31 (Winter 1989), p. 61. The O'Donnell, *et al.* volumes were sponsored by the Woodrow Wilson Center, which was established by Congress, and were funded through congressional appropriations. The point is not that the Woodrow Wilson Center (or any of these scholars) is fraudulent, but that it is one of many think-tanks linked formally and informally to the US state that are crucial components of the policy planning process. These policy planning institutes constitute institutional gateways between academia and the state apparatus.

50 The concrete links, including funding, institutional overlaps, and so forth, between universities, the government, and the literature, are well documented. On the close relation between the US government and universities in modernization and political culture/development theories, see, e.g., Alvin So, *Social Change and Development: Modernization, Dependency and World-System Theories* (Newbury Park: Sage Publications, 1990), pp. 17–19. As noted above, the government has funded the research, publication, and dissemination of seminal "democratization" studies. The AID has sponsored many workshops and conferences on "democratization" and "democracy promotion" and brought together scholars and policymakers into overlapping networks out of which flow numerous published works. There are other types of linkage: for example, scholars who publish works that become authoritative were themselves policymakers, or later return to policymaking posts – one such scholar is Abraham Lowenthal (former ambassador to the OAS), editor of *Exporting Democracy* and other works. Other studies are published and disseminated with funding from the government or from policy planning institutes; an example is Goldman and Douglas's, *Promoting Democracy*, funded by the Center for the Study of Democratic Institutions, funded in turn by the AID. And so on.

51 Cited in Ronald H. Chilcote and Joel C. Edelstein, *Latin America: Capitalist and Socialist Perspectives of Development and Underdevelopment* (Boulder: Westview, 1986), p. 67.

52 Works on modernization and political culture/political development

theories are vast. Some of the most prominent are: W. W. Rostow, *The Stages of Economic Growth: A Non-Communist Manifesto* (Cambridge: Cambridge University Press, 1960); Gabriel Almond and Sidney Verba, *The Civic Culture* (Boston: Little Brown, 1963); Lucien W. Pye and Sidney Verba (eds.), *Political Culture and Political Development* (Princeton: Princeton University Press, 1965); Samuel P. Huntington, *Political Order in Changing Societies* (New Haven: Yale University Press, 1968). See bibliographies in So, *Social Change and Development*, and Chilcote and Edelstein, *Latin America* for a fuller listing.

53 Almond and Verba, *Civic Culture*, p. 67.

54 David Easton, *The Political System: An Inquiry Into the State of Political Science* (New York: Knopf, 1953); David Easton, *A Systems Analysis of Political Life* (New York: Wiley, 1965).

55 For an excellent critique, see Mark Kesselman, "Order or Movement? The Literature of Political Development as Ideology," *World Politics*, October 1973, 139–154.

56 *Ibid.*

57 As cited in *ibid.*, 139.

58 Alford and Friedland, *Powers of Theory*, pp. 394–395.

59 Joseph A. Schumpeter, *Capitalism, Socialism and Democracy*, 2nd edn., (New York: Harper and Row, 1947), p. 285.

60 W. B. Gallie, "Essentially Contested Concepts," *Aristotelian Society*, no. 56 (1956), 167–198.

61 Robert A. Dahl, *Polyarchy: Participation and Opposition* (New Haven: Yale University Press, 1971). Despite its limitations and irrespective of my own disagreement with the pluralist model and the structural-functionalist meta-theoretical framework he employs, Dahl's is an excellent study. Dahl, it should be noted, does not argue, normatively, that polyarchy is "ideal" democracy but the only "realistic" democracy possible in complex modern societies.

62 Samuel P. Huntington, "The Modest Meaning of Democracy," in Robert A. Pastor, *Democracy in the Americas: Stopping the Pendulum* (New York: Holmes and Meier, 1989), pp. 12–13.

63 See, for instance, Philip Schmitter and Terry Karl, "What Democracy Is... And Is Not," *Journal of Democracy*, 2 (1991), no. 3, 75–88. Similarly, Diamond, *et al.*, *Democracy*, state that by democracy they are referring specifically to polyarchy (IV, p. xvi).

64 Peter Bachrach, *The Theory of Democratic Elitism: A Critique* (Lanham, Md.: University of America Press, 1980), p. 17.

65 Schumpeter, *Capitalism, Socialism and Democracy*, p. 269.

66 Huntington, "Modest Meaning," p. 24.

67 Cited in Alford and Friedland, *Powers of Theory*, p. 27.

68 *Ibid.*, p. 29.

69 Adam Przeworski, "Some Problems in the Study of Transition to Democracy," in O'Donnell, *et al.*, *Transitions*, pp. 56–57.

70   Diamond, *et al., Democracy,* VI, p. xvi.
71   Huntington, "Modest Meaning," p. 18.
72   See Diamond, *et al., Democracy,* IV, pp. 44–47.
73   "The Democratcy Initiative," Agency for International Development, Department of State, Washington, D.C., December 1990.
74   A full listing of literature referring to popular democracy is impossible here. Moreover, this literature is highly heterogeneous and exhibits distinct theoretical discourses. Antonio Gramsci and Rosa Luxemburg would be the classical thinkers in the Marxist tradition on democracy. For works discussing theoretical and historical issues of liberal capitalist and Marxist concepts, see, among others: Alan Hunt (ed.), *Marxism and Democracy* (London: Lawrence and Wishart, 1980); George Novack, *Democracy and Revolution* (New York: Pathfinder Press, 1971); David Held, *Political Theory and the Modern State: Essays on State, Power, and Democracy* (Stanford: Stanford University Press, 1989); L. Earl Shaw (ed.), *Modern Competing Ideologies* (Lexington, Mass.: D. C. Heath, 1973). For discussion on some contemporary attempts to elaborate a theory and model of popular democracy (referred to as such, or as "participatory democracy," "strong democracy," "direct democracy," etc.), see, among others: David Held and Christopher Pollitt (eds.), *New Forms of Democracy* (London: Sage Publications, 1986); Daniel C. Kramer, *Participatory Democracy: Developing Ideals of the Political Left* (Cambridge, Mass.: Schenkman, 1972); Benjamin Barber, *Strong Democracy: Participatory Politics for a New Age* (Berkeley: University of California Press, 1984); Carl Cohen, *Democracy* (New York: The Free Press, 1971).
75   *Ibid.*
76   For instance, see Schmitter and Karl, "What Democracy Is," pp. 81, 84.
77   Miliband, *State in Capitalist Society,* p. 194.
78   Gramsci, *Prison Notebooks,* p. 176. Cox, in "Gramsci," first drew attention to the particular passage and explored its significance as regards international relations.
79   Max Weber, "Value Judgements in Social Science," in W. G. Runciman (ed.), *Weber: Selections in Translation* (Cambridge: Cambridge University Press, 1978), p. 89.
80   Mosca, *Ruling Class,* p. 154.
81   On anti-systemic movements, see Immanuel Wallerstein, "Antisystemic Movements: History and Dilemmas," in Samir Amin, *et al., Transforming the Revolution: Social Movements and the World-system* (New York: Monthly Review, 1990).
82   Gramsci, *Prison Notebooks,* p. 210.
83   These arguments are detailed in volume IV of O'Donnell, *et al., Transitions,* co-authored by O'Donnell and Schmitter.
84   *Ibid.,* IV, pp. 62–63.
85   For analysis, see William I. Robinson, "Demilitarization in Central America: Beginning of a New Era?," (2 parts), *Central American Update*

(Albuquerque: Latin American Data Base, University of New Mexico), January 17 and 24, 1992.

86 Carl Gershman, "The United States and the World Democratic Revolution," *Washington Quarterly*, Winter 1989, 127–139.

87 *Ibid.*

88 James F. Petras and Morris H. Morley, "The U.S. Imperial State," in James F. Petras, *et al.* (eds.), *Class, State and Power in the Third World* (Montclair, N.J.: Allanheld, Osmun, 1981).

89 *Ibid.*, pp. 6–7.

90 *Ibid.*, p. 115.

91 Henry Kissinger, *The White House Years* (Boston: Little, Brown, 1979), p. 654.

92 See *ibid.* and also Gill, *American Hegemony*. It should be noted that the Trilateral Commission's report focused in particular on the "crisis in democracy" in the developed, industrialized countries.

93 Kissinger, *White House Years*, pp. 53, 55.

94 Gill, *American Hegemony*, p. 163.

95 Schmitter and Karl, "What Democracy Is," p. 80.

96 Samuel Huntington, "Will More Countries Become Democratic?" *Political Science Quarterly*, 99 (1984), no. 2, 206. Huntington's article is basic reading for "democratization" courses in US universities. It involves two propositions which combine vulgar ideology with more empirically testable propositions. The first is that democracy in the Third World declined in the 1960s and 1970s because "Anglo-American influence" had declined, and it should spread again in the 1980s because that influence was then increasing. The proposition does not hold up empirically: in the post-World War II heyday of US influence abroad, authoritarianism flourished in the Third World because the United States ("Anglo-American influence") actively promoted it and not democracy. Neither does the second proposition, a direct three-way correlation between democracy, free markets, and economic development, hold up to empirical scrutiny. In Huntington's two "premier democracies," the United States and Britain, for example, polyarchy evolved side by side with active states that intervened and regulated capital accumulation, *not* under free-market conditions. And in the Third World the correlation has been between high growth/development and authoritarian regimes (such as the Asian Tigers, Brazil, Argentina, Mexico, etc.), not polyarchies, and these regimes all turned to heavy state intervention, not free markets. Huntington also distorts historical *facts*. Democracy, for him, is defined by near-universal adult suffrage, and the United States is "a 200-year-old democracy." Yet at the time of the founding of the US republic, neither women, nor blacks, nor Indians, nor other non-white peoples could vote. Nor could propertyless or illiterate white males vote. In "The Rule of Capital and the Rise of Democracy" (*New Left Review*, no. 103, 1977, 3–41), sociologist Goran Therborn uses the same measurement as Huntington – near-universal

adult suffrage – to place the establishment of democracy in the United States at *c*. 1970. Given such blatant inconsistencies and false propositions, it is remarkable that Huntington's article is taken with any seriousness by the academic community.

97 This type of "consensual" power is what Steven Lukes referred to as the third of three dimensions of power in *Power: A Radical View* (London: Macmillan, 1974). The first is the formal decision-making process, in which there is pluralist distribution of power. The second, a hidden dimension, is what Bachrach and Baratz refer to as "non-decision making," or the confining of the scope of decision-making such that alternative choices are suppressed (Peter Bachrach and Morton S. Baratz, *Power and Poverty: Theory and Practice*, New York: Oxford University Press, 1970). Both these dimensions locate power within the behavioral realm and involve manifest conflict. The third combines the behavioral and the structural realms, based on real interests, whether subjectively perceived or not. Power is exercised by keeping potential manifest conflicts over real interests latent. This third dimension of power functions under conditions of consensual, not coercive, domination.

2 Political operations in US foreign policy

1 Howard Wiarda, *The Democratic Revolution in Latin America: History, Politics, and U.S. Policy* (New York: Holmes and Meier, 1990), p. 270.

2 Department of State, "Democracy in Latin America and the Caribbean: The Promise and the Challenge," Bureau of Public Affairs, Special Report no. 158, Washington, D.C., March 1987, p. 13.

3 For the distinction between dominant groups and governing groups, see Domhoff *Who Rules America?* and Poulantzas *Political Power*.

4 Council on Foreign Relations, 1980s Project: Albert Fishlow, Carlos F. Diaz-Alejandro, Richard R., Fagen, and Roger D. Hansen, *Rich and Poor Nations in the World Economy* (New York: McGraw-Hill, 1978); Trilateral Commission: Richard N. Cooper, Karl Kaiser, and Masataka Kosaka, *Towards a Renovated International System*, Triangle Papers 14 (New York: The Trilateral Commission, 1977), as cited and discussed in Cox, "Ideologies and the New International Economic Order." See also Domhoff, *Who Rules America?*, pp. 88, 112 n8; Lawrence Shoup, *The Carter Presidency and Beyond*, (Palo Alto: Ramparts Press, 1980); Dye, *Who Runs America?*, pp. 244–252.

5 See, e.g., Peter J. Schraeder (ed.), *Intervention in the 1980s: U.S. Foreign Policy in the Third World* (Boulder: Lynne Rienner, 1989).

6 The Committee of Santa Fe, *A New Inter-American Policy for the Eighties*, (Santa Fe: Council for Inter-American Security, 1980), p. 5.

7 Jeanne J. Kirkpatrick, "Dictators and Double Standards," *Commentary* no. 68 (November 1979), p. 36.

8 Augelli and Murphy, *America's Quest for Supremacy*.

9   Wiarda, *Democratic Revolution*, p. 145.

10 See Carnes Lord, "The Psychological Dimension in National Strategy," in Carnes Lord and Frank R. Barnett (eds.), *Political Warfare and Psychological Operations: Rethinking the U.S. Approach* (Washington, D.C.: National Defense University Press, 1988), p. 18. Lord was Director of International Communications and Information Policy on the NSC in the first Reagan administration.

11 Alfred H. Paddock, Jr., "Military Psychological Operations", in Lord and Barnett (eds.), *Political Warfare*, p. 45. Paddock is the former Director of Psychological Operations in the Office of the Secretary of Defense.

12 Angelo M. Codevilla, "Political Warfare," in Lord and Barnett (eds.), *Political Wafare*, pp. 77–79. Codevilla was a senior staff member of the Senate Select Committee on Intelligence.

13 Lord and Barnett (eds.), *Political Warfare*, introduction, p. xiii.

14 See Doug Bandow, "Economic and Military Aid," in Schraeder (ed.), *Intervention in the 1980s*, p. 63. Note that if US aid channeled through multilateral agencies is included, the figure nearly doubles.

15 NSC-68 described economic aid as "a major instrument in the conduct of United States foreign relations. It is an instrument which can powerfully influence the world environment in ways favorable" to US interests. National Security Council, NSC-68, p. 258. See Augelli and Murphy, *America's Quest for Supremacy*, ch. 4, for a Gramscian focus on ideology and foreign aid.

16 For more on low-intensity warfare and its doctrinal emergence, see William I. Robinson and Kent Norsworthy, *David and Goliath: the U.S. War Against Nicaragua* (New York: Monthly Review, 1987), particularly ch. 1; Michael T. Klare and Peter Kornbluh (eds.), *Low Intensity Warfare, Counter-insurgency, Proinsurgency, and Antiterrorism in the Eighties* (New York: Pantheon, 1988); Frank R. Barnett, B. Hugh Tovar and Richard H. Shultz (eds.), *Special Operations in U.S. Strategy* (Washington, D.C.: National Defense University Press, 1984); Lord and Barnett (eds.), *Political Warfare*.

17 Richard H. Shultz, Jr., "Low Intensity Conflict, Future Challenges and Lessons From the Reagan Years," *Survival* (International Institute for Strategic Studies), 31 (1989), no. 2; Paddock, "Military Psychological Operations," p. 50.

18 See the report commissioned by the NSC, *Discriminate Deterrence: Report of the Commission on Integrated Long-Term Strategy* (Washington, D.C.: US Government Printing Office, 1988), which calls for a shift in primary emphasis towards engagement in the Third World. See also four-part series in *New York Times*, May 20–23, 1990.

19 Lord, "Psychological Dimension," p. 20.

20 Princeton Lyman, "An Introduction to Title IX," *Foreign Service Journal*, March 1970, 6–48, pp. 6–8 in particular.

21 Susan George, *A Fate Worse Than Debt* (London: Penguin Books, 1988), p. 232.

22 Michael A. Samuels and William A. Douglas, "Promoting Democracy," *Washington Quarterly*, 4 (1981), no. 3, 52–65, at pp. 52–53.
23 American Political Foundation, "A Commitment to Democracy: A Bipartisan Approach," Washington, D.C., November 30, 1983. The report was commissioned by the NSC to draft recommendations for developing "democracy promotion" in foreign policy.
24 William A. Douglas, *Developing Democracy* (Washington, D.C.: Heldref, 1972). Douglas drew heavily on Huntington's *Political Order in Changing Societies* and the other political development literature cited in chapter one.
25 *Ibid.*, pp. 16–22.
26 *Ibid.*, pp. xiii, 43.
27 Gershman, "Fostering Democracy Abroad."
28 Ralph M. Goldman, "The Democratic Mission: A Brief History," in Goldman and Douglas (eds.), *Promoting Democracy*; Ralph M. Goldman, "Assessing Political Aid for the Endless Campaign," *ibid.*, p. 253.
29 Goldman, "Democratic Mission," p. 16.
30 The US Senate's Church Committee estimated that the CIA carried out at least 900 covert operations between 1960 and 1975, but former CIA officer John Stockwell estimated the total number since its founding at up to 20,000 (interview with the authors in Managua, 1985, cited in Robinson and Norsworthy, *David and Goliath*, p. 15). Another former CIA officer, Philip Agee, pointed out that in Indonesia alone, between 500,000 and one million people were killed in the wake of the CIA-orchestrated coup against Sukarno. See Philip Agee, *Inside the Company* (London: Bantam 1976), p. ix.
31 These defectors included Philip Agee, John Stockwell, Ralph McGehee, and David MacMichael, among others. The most well known is Agee (see *ibid.*). See also Victor Marchetti and John D. Marks, *The CIA and the Cult of Intelligence*, (New York: Dell, 1974). An excellent summary is William Blum, *The CIA, A Forgotten History*, (London: Zed, 1986).
32 Samuels and Douglas, "Promoting Democracy," p. 53.
33 *New York Times*, June 1, 1986.
34 William E. Colby, "Political Action – In the Open," *Washington Post*, March 14, 1982, D-8.
35 See John Pike, "Uncloaking Daggers: CIA Spending for Covert Operations," *Covert Action Quarterly*, no. 48 (Winter 1994–5), 48–55.
36 Charles W. Kegley, Jr. and Eugene R. Wittkopf, *American Foreign Policy: Pattern and Process*, 4th edn (New York: St. Martin's Press, 1991), pp. 252–253.
37 For background on these early efforts, see Douglas, *Developing Democracy*, pp. 172–177.
38 White House press release, March 29, 1967, cited in Holly Sklar and Chip Berlet, "NED, CIA, and the Orwellian Democracy Project," in *Covert Action Information Bulletin*, no. 39 (Winter 1991–2), 10–13 at p. 11.
39 Wiarda, *Democratic Revolution*, p. 148.

40   General Accounting Office, *Events Leading to the Establishment of the National Endowment for Democracy*, GAO/NSIAD-84–121, July 6, 1984; Goldman, "Democratic Mission," pp. 18–22; Wiarda, *Democratic Revolution*, pp. 148–149.

41   See Lord, "Psychological Dimension," p. 14.

42   National Security Action Memo No. 1224, January 18, 1962, as reported by Worth Cooley-Prost, *Democracy Intervention in Haiti: The U.S. AID Democracy Enhancement Project* (Washington, D.C.: Washington Office on Haiti, 1994), p. 19.

43   By 1989, its budget had climbed to some one billion dollars annually. Intelligence and national security officials continue to rotate in and out of the USIA, the NED and other agencies. For discussion, see Council on Hemispheric Affairs/Inter-Hemispheric Education Resource Center *National Endowment for Democracy (NED): A Foreign Policy Branch Gone Awry* (Washington, D.C./Albuquerque: 1990), which provides an excellent account of the creation and *modus operandi* of the NED.

44   See Robert Parry and Peter Kornbluh, "Iran–Contra's Untold Story," *Foreign Policy*, no. 72 (Fall 1988), pp. 5, 9, for background on Raymond. For his relation to North, see *Report of the Congressional Committees' Investigation of the Iran–Contra Affair* (Washington, D.C.: Govt. Printing Office, 1988), and in particular Raymond's deposition before the Congressional Committees, in Appendix B of the report (vol. XXII, pp. 1–520). See John Spicer Nichols, "La Prensa: The CIA Connection," *Columbia Journalism Review*, 27 (1988), no. 2, p. 13, for mention of Raymond's NSC role as liaison with NED.

45   Cited in Council on Hemispheric Affairs/Resource Center, *National Endowment for Democracy*, pp. 12–13.

46   *Ibid.*; Parry and Kornbluh, "Iran–Contra's".

47   Goldman, "Democratic Mission...," p. 21, and Council on Hemispheric Affairs/Resource Center, *National Endowment for Democracy*.

48   Ronald Reagan, "Promoting Democracy and Peace" (June 8, 1982 speech before the British parliament), *Current Policy*, no. 399, Department of State, Bureau of Public Affairs, Washington, D.C.

49   *New York Times*, February 15, 1987.

50   This figure is mentioned by former Secretary of State George Shultz. See "Project Democracy," statement by Shultz before the Subcommittee on International Operations of the House Foreign Affairs Committee, February 23, 1983, reprinted as *Current Policy*, no. 456, Department of State, Bureau of Public Affairs, Washington, D.C.

51   Richard F. Staar (ed.), *Public Diplomacy: USA versus USSR* (Stanford: Hoover Institute, 1986), pp. 297–299. Staar published the unclassified three–page directive, but did not indicate if this version was the full text of the original classified version. The directive contains four aspects, but two, an International Information Committee and an International Broadcasting Committee, would appear to overlap. See also, *New York Times*, February 15, 1987.

52 See Peter Kornbluh, *Nicaragua: The Price of Intervention* (Washington, D.C.: Institute for Policy Studies, 1987).

53 *New York Times*, February 15, 1987.

54 *Ibid.*

55 *Ibid.*

56 Raymond D. Gastil, "Aspects of a U.S. Campaign for Democracy," in Goldman and Douglas (eds.), *Promoting Democracy*, p. 49.

57 *Ibid.*, pp. 28–29.

58 This figure is arrived at by totalling the amounts of annual Congressional appropriations for the NED, as reported in the NED Annual Reports, 1984–1992.

59 For these details, see Council on Hemispheric Affairs/Resource Center, *National Endowment for Democracy*, particularly, pp. 23–39.

60 *New York Times*, February 15, 1987.

61 Wiarda, *Democratic Revolution*, pp. 277–278.

62 The boards of directors and principal officers of the NED itself, the core groups, and numerous other pass-throughs, can best be described as diverse groups of "proximate policymakers" and seasoned political operatives. For a detailed breakdown of the structure of interlocking boards of directors see, among others, Council on Hemispheric Affairs/Resource Center, *National Endowment for Democracy*; Inter-Hemispheric Education Resource Center, *The Democracy Offensive* (Albuquerque, 1989). Both these publications provide diagrams and flow charts.

63 American Political Foundation, "A Commitment to Democracy."

64 John W. Sewell and Christine E. Contee, "U.S. Foreign Aid in the 1980s: Reordering Priorities," in Kendall W. Stiles and Tsuneo Akaha (eds.), *International Political Economy: A Reader* (New York: HarperCollins, 1991), particularly p. 318.

65 See Agency for International Development, Department of State, "The Democracy Initiative," Washington, D.C., December 1990.

66 For details, see "U.S. Electoral Assistance and Democratic Development," proceedings of a conference sponsored by the Washington Office on Latin America, January 19, 1990, Washington, D.C.

67 Agency for International Development, Department of State, "FY 1990 Democratic Initiatives and Human Rights Program Summary," Washington, D.C., 1990.

68 Lord, "Psychological Dimension," pp. 19–20.

69 See "Reagan's Global Reach," *Columbia Journalism Review*, 24 (1985), no. 1, 10–11.

70 Phone interview with *Journal of Democracy* editorial assistant Susan Brown, May 27, 1994, and letter from Brown, dated May 27, 1994, who described the journal as "really a magazine of the NED."

71 General Accounting Office, *Promoting Democracy: Foreign Affairs and Defense Agencies Funds and Activities – 1991 to 1993 GAO/NSIAD–94–83,*

January 1994, p. 3. The report specifies that these figures do not include US contributions to the UN and its peacekeeping activities.

72 These policy outlines were scattered throughout all of Clinton's speeches in his first few months in office. For a summary analysis, see "Clinton y America Latina; Un Nuevo Govierno y Antiguas Crisis," *Enlace*, 2 (1993), no. 1, pp. 1–3, 5.

73 The quote is from Resource Center, "Democratization: U.S. Governmental Actors," *Democracy Backgrounder* (1995), no. 1, 4. The $296 million figure is from General Accounting Office, *Promoting Democracy*, p. 2. For the increase to $48 million, see "Better Dead Than N.E.D.," *The Nation*, July 12, 1993, 6. For the administration's long-term proposals, see Larry Diamond, "An American Foreign Policy for Democracy," *Policy Report* (Progressive Policy Institute, Washington, D.C.), no. 11 (July 1991), 3.

74 Resource Center, "Democratization," 4–5.

75 Morton H. Halperin, "Guaranteeing Democracy," *Foreign Policy*, no. 91 (Summer 1993), 105–106.

76 For a discussion on "party-building" in intervened countries, see Ralph M. Goldman, "Transnational Parties as Multilateral Civic Educators," in Goldman and Douglas (eds.), *Promoting Democracy*.

77 Douglas, *Developing Democracy*, pp. 128–129.

78 Miliband, *State in Capitalist Society*, p. 187.

79 Talcott Parsons, "'Voting' and the Equilibrium of the American Political System," in Parsons (ed.), *Sociological Theory and Modern Society* (New York: Free Press, 1967), p. 244.

80 For a summary of labor's role see Roy Godson, "Labor's Role in Building Democracy," in Goldman and Douglas (eds.), *Promoting Democracy*.

81 Cited in Tom Barry and Deb Preusch, *AIFLD in Central America: Agents as Organizers* (Albuquerque: Inter-Hemispheric Education Resource Center, 1987), p. 31.

82 For a summary of this sectoral approach to political intervention, see Samuels and Douglas, "Promoting Democracy."

83 CIA Directorate of Intelligence, "CIA Views on the Third World Population Issues," June 11, 1984 (declassified January 1995), 5, reproduced in part in Information Project for Africa, *Excessive Force: Power, Politics, and Population Control* (Washington, D.C., 1995), pp. 33–34; Neil W. Chamberlain, *Beyond Malthus: Population and Power* (New York: Basic Books, 1970), pp. 54–55.

84 Women in Development (WID) literature is prolific. A succinct introduction is Annette Fuentes and Barbara Enrenreich, *Women in the Global Factory* (Boston: South End, 1983).

85 Samuels and Douglas, "Promoting Democracy," p. 56.

86 See respective chapters and sections for Nicaragua, Chile, and South Africa. For Cuba, see William I. Robinson, "Pushing Polyarchy: The U.S.– Cuba Case and the Third World," *Third World Quarterly: Journal of Emerging Areas*, 16 (1995), no. 4, 631–647.

87 This "multiplier effect" method of political organization developed by U.S. foreign-policy experts in political warfare is recommended in CIA, AID, and Department of Defense political operations manuals. See Robinson, *A Faustian Bargain*, pp. 74, 210 n44.

88 Cited in Barry and Preusch, *AIFLD in Central America*, p. 61.

89 Shultz, "Project Democracy." The following citations are all from Shultz.

90 Gershman, "United States."

91 Blum, *The CIA*, provides a concise documentation of these post-World War II US electoral interventions.

92 For an account of these types of elections put together in Washington and exported to the target countries as part of war policy, see Edward S. Herman and Frank Brodhead, *Demonstration Elections: U.S.-Staged Elections in the Dominican Republic, Vietnam, and El Salvador* (Boston: South End, 1984).

93 Ralph M. Goldman, "The Donor–Recipient Relation in Political Aid Programs," in Goldman and Douglas (eds.), *Promoting Democracy*, pp. 59, 66–68.

94 See, e.g., Sharon Beaulaurier, "Profiteers Fuel War in Angola," *Covert Action Quarterly*, no. 45 (Summer 1993), 61–65.

95 Colby, "Political Action – In The Open."

96 Wiarda, *Democratic Revolution*, p. 207. Wiarda was for most of the 1980s a resident scholar of the American Enterprise Institute (AEI), a policy planning group that worked closely with the US government in Project Democracy and in formulating "democracy promotion" strategies.

3   The Philippines: "Molded in the image of American democracy"

1 Cited in Daniel B. Schirmer and Stephen Rosskamm Shalom, *The Philippines Reader: A History of Colonialism, Neocolonialism, Dictatorship, and Resistance* (Boston: South End, 1987), p. 22. I have made extensive use of this excellent 400-page compendium of official documents, newspaper and magazine articles, excerpts from books on the Philippines and United States–Philippine relations, and original essays by the editors.

2 Cited in Laurence Whitehead, "International Aspects of Democratization," in Guillermo O'Donnell, Philip C. Schmitter, and Laurence Whitehead (eds.), *Transitions from Authoritarian Rule* (Baltimore: Johns Hopkins University Press, 1988), p. 7.

3 For a definitive history of the U.S. colonial conquest of the Philippines, see Luzviminda Francisco, "The First Vietnam: The Philippine–American War, 1899–1902," in *The Philippines: End of an Illusion* (London: AREAS, 1973), reprinted, in part, in Schirmer and Shalom, *Philippines Reader*, pp. 8–20.

4 *Ibid.*, p. 11.

5 CIA, *Philippines: General Survey* (National Intelligence Survey, NS 99), July 1965, reprinted in Schirmer and Shalom, *Philippines Reader*. See p. 128 for citation.

6   William J. Pomeroy, *The Philippines: Colonialism, Collaboration, and Resistance* (New York: International Publishers, 1992), although an American citizen, gives a good insider's account of the "Huk" movement.

7   "A Report to the President by the National Security Council on the Position of the United States with Respect to the Philippines" (November 9, 1950), *Foreign Relations of the United States, 1950* (Washington, D.C.: US Government Printing Office, 1976), declassified in 1975, reprinted in part in Schirmer and Shalom, *Philippines Reader*, pp. 109–110.

8   As cited in Schirmer and Shalom, *Philippines Reader*, p. 119.

9   For a summary of CIA activities in the Philippines, see Blum, *The CIA*, pp. 37–43, and numerous entries in Schirmer and Shalom, *Philippines Reader*.

10 International Labor Office, *Sharing in Development: A Programme of Employment, Equity and Growth for the Philippines* (Geneva: International Labor Organization, 1974), reprinted in *ibid.*, citation on p. 135.

11 Richard J. Kessler, "Marcos and the Americans," *Foreign Policy*, no. 63 (Summer 1986), p. 52.

12 US Senate Committee on Foreign Relations, *Korea and the Philippines: November 1972*, Committee Print, 93rd Congress, 1st session, February 18, 1973, reprinted in part in Schirmer and Shalom, *Philippines Reader*, citation on p. 168.

13 As cited in *ibid.*, p. 229.

14 For these details, see *ibid.*, p. 226.

15 *Ibid.*, pp. 226–227.

16 See, e.g., Pomeroy, *Philippines*; James Putzel, *A Captive Land: The Politics of Agrarian Reform in the Philippines* (New York: Monthly Review, 1992); Gary Hawes, "Theories of Peasant Revolution: A Critique and Contribution from the Philippines," *World Politics*, 42 (1990), no. 2, 215–229.

17 A detailed account of this debate and an excellent journalistic record of US policy and US–Philippine relations is Raymond Bonner, *Waltzing With a Dictator* (New York: Times Books, 1987).

18 Stephen W. Bosworth, October 25, 1984 speech before the Rotary Club of Makati West, Manila, Philippines, reprinted as *Current Policy*, no. 630, Bureau of Public Affairs, Department of State, Washington, D.C.

19 The NSC directive is reprinted in Schirmer and Shalom, *Philippines Reader*, pp. 322–323.

20 Paul Laxalt, "My Conversation with Ferdinand Marcos," *Policy Review*, no. 37 (Summer 1986), 2–5.

21 The $9 million figure is based on NED annual reports from 1984 to 1990, but the actual amount is probably much higher, since millions more were sent to the Philippines circuitously via such organizations as the AAFLI and via the CIA and other "national security" related spending, which is classified.

22 The Convenors' Statement is reprinted in Schirmer and Shalom, *Philippines Reader*, pp. 306–308.

23 Cited in Walden Bello, "Counterinsurgency's Proving Ground: Low Intensity Warfare in the Philippines," in Klare and Kornbluh (eds.), *Low Intensity Warfare*, p. 169.

24 *Far Eastern Economic Review*, March 6, 1986.

25 NED Annual Report, 1987, Washington D.C., pp. 9–10.

26 For this background, see Stephen R. Shalom, "Counterinsurgency in the Philippines," *Journal of Contemporary Asia*, 7 (1977), no. 2, 153–172. See also Bonner, *Waltzing*, pp. 40, 368, 376.

27 NED Annual Report, 1986, Washington, D.C., p. 14.

28 Schirmer and Shalom, *Philippines Reader*, p. 309.

29 The KABATID worked in coordination with the Asia Foundation, reportedly a CIA front organization. See Marchetti and Marks, *The CIA*, pp. 150–151.

30 "KABATID," NED internal funding proposal for the 1990 fiscal year, undated, obtained through the FOIA.

31 Letter from KABATID chairperson Dette Pascual to NED program officer Marc Plattner, August 15, 1989, obtained through the FOIA.

32 For instance, KABATID's vice-chair, Pacita Almario, was a regional chair of NAMFREL, and owns and manages a chain of restaurants in Manila; Secretary-General Frances Gloria runs her family's export firm and was a Manila coordinator of NAMFREL; Assistant Secretary-General Sony Sison is General Manager of Manila Exports, a major exporting firm; Treasurer Rose Yenko, a former NAMFREL leader, is Executive Vice-President of Y Engineering Cooperation and a managing partner in Development Consultants' Network, a major consulting firm for transnational corporations. Trustee member Carmencita Abella is also Executive Vice-President of the Development Academy of the Philippines, a association of national and foreign big-business interests; trustee Lourdes Baua is Services Chief of the Human Resources Division of the government's Department of Trade and Industry; trustee May Fernandez was Director of the Presidential Staff, Office of the Cabinet Secretary, under President Aquino; and so on. For this biographical data, see "One Page Summary of Proposal," KABATID funding proposal submitted to the NED for fiscal year 1991, dated February 22, 1990, obtained through the FOIA.

33 See "Program Proposal," 8, attached to letter from Tony and Tita Dumagsa, Coordinators of Friends of NAMFREL, to Marc Plattner, NED program officer, dated March 31, 1988, obtained through the FOIA.

34 Through a NED-organized program for "government monitoring and public outreach," KABATID board members set up a "speakers bureau" and became regular featured commentators on television news and radio talk shows, effectively utilizing in this way the mass media. All "these activities have been made possible through grants provided by ... the US National Endowment for Democracy," noted the KABATID report, "One Page Summary of Proposal," dated February 22, 1990, obtained through the FOIA.

35 See letter from KABATID Projects Director Gina Pascual to Friends ,of NAMFREL, dated February 5, 1989, Annex I, "KABATID Foundation, Inc., Policies and Procedures," obtained through the FOIA, and "One Page Summary of Proposal."

36 NED Annual Reports, 1986–88, Washington, D.C.

37 NED Annual Report, 1987, Washington, D.C.

38 Enid Eckstein, "What is the AFL-CIO Doing in the Philippines?," *Labor Notes* (Detroit), July 1986, p. 1.

39 For a detailed description of the KMU composition, program, and organizational structure, see Kim Scipes, "Aquino's Total War and the KMU," *Z Magazine*, January 1990, 116–121. See also Beth Sims, *Workers of the World Undermined: American Labor and the Pursuit of U.S. Foreign Policy* (Boston, South End, 1993).

40 NED Annual Reports, 1984–91, Washington, D.C.

41 NED Annual Report, 1984, Washington, D.C., 19.

42 Tim Shorrock and Kathy Selvaggio, "Which Side Are You On, AAFLI?," *The Nation*, February 15, 1986, p. 170.

43 See minutes of the March 17, 1989 meeting of the Board of Directors of the National Endowment for Democracy, Washington, D.C., obtained through the FOIA.

44 Phil Bronstein and David Johnston, "U.S. Funding Anti-Left Fight in Philippines," *San Francisco Examiner*, July 21, 1985.

45 "Proposal from the FTUI to the NED for 1989 Programs," December 1988, Section B, Asia, 29, obtained through the FOIA.

46 Shorrock and Selvaggio, "Which Side Are You On, AAFLI?," p. 171.

47 "Proposal for 1989 Programs," Section B, Asia, 30, obtained through the FOIA.

48 "Request to the National Endowment for Democracy for Funds for the Free Trade Union Institute for FY 1988 Programs," December 16, 1987, Section B, Asia, 31–32, obtained through the FOIA.

49 *Ibid.*, 30.

50 "Proposal for 1989 programs," p. 29.

51 Scipes, "Aquino's Total War," pp. 116–121; Adele Oltman and Dennis Bernstein, "Counterinsurgency in the Philippines," *Covert Action Information Bulletin*, no. 29 (Winter 1988), 18–20.

52 See, e.g., Kay Eisenhower, "AFL-CIO Agency Offers Cash to Filipino Union Leader for Vote on U.S. Bases Treaty," *Labor Notes*, no. 152 (November 1991), 1–6.

53 For excellent analyses of the complex post-Marcos situation, see Walden Bello and John Gershman, "Democratization and Stabilization in the Philippines," *Critical Sociology*, 17 (1990), no. 1, 35–56; James B. Goodno, *The Philippines: Land of Broken Promises* (London: Zed, 1991).

54 Benedict J. Kerkvliet and Resil B. Mojares (eds.), *From Marcos to Aquino: Local Perspectives on Political Transition in the Philippines* (Honolulu: University of Hawaii Press, 1991), p. 5.

55 Cited in Bello and Gershman, "Democratization and Stabilization," p. 37.

56 Assistance for Democracy Act of 1986, House of Representatives, 99th Congress, 2nd session, Report 99–722, July 30, 1986, Washington, D.C. The package provided balance-of-payments support, budget support, and funds for the dismantling of "crony capitalism," the introduction of neo-liberal economic reform programs, payments on Manila's foreign debt, and other assistance.

57 Sandra Burton, "Aquino's Philippines: The Center Holds," *Foreign Affairs*, 65 (1987), no. 3, 525–537 at p. 533.

58 Agency for International Development, "Philippine Assistance Strategy: U.S. Fiscal Years 1991–1995", Washington D.C., July 1990, p. 1.

59 Bello and Gershman, "Democratization and Stabilization," p. 45. The two note the example of the January 1988 local elections, when "electoral competition between the traditional elite parties was feverish, but candidates of the leftist Partido ng Bayan, fearing for their lives, dared not run in areas dominated by military-backed vigilante groups," and that "dissent is indeed possible, but within sharply circumscribed limits. Those who breach the limits become fair game for death squads and right-wing vigilantes."

60 Carl H. Landé, "Manila's Malaise," *Journal of Democracy*, 2 (1991), no. 1, 51.

61 For analyses of low-intensity warfare in the Philippines in the 1980s and the US role, see Bello, "Counterinsurgency's Proving Ground"; Arnel de Guzman and Tito Craige, "Counterinsurgency War in the Philippines and the Role of the United States," *Bulletin of Concerned Asian Scholars*, 23 (1991), no. 1, 38–47; Oltman and Bernstein, "Counterinsurgency in the Philippines," pp. 18–21. Washington reportedly authorized stepped-up clandestine CIA operations against the left in the Philippines, including a $10 million allocation to the NAFP for enhanced intelligence-gathering operations, and an increase in the number of CIA personnel, from 115 to 127, attached to the US embassy in Manila. See Bello, "Counterinsurgency's Proving Ground," p. 177; Oltman and Bernstein, "Counterinsurgency in the Philippines," p. 20.

62 For a discussion of these pressures on Aquino, see Bello, "Counterinsurgency's Proving Ground," pp. 171–174. See chapter 5 on Nicaragua for similar pressures placed on Chamorro.

63 Cited in Bello, "Counterinsurgency's Proving Ground," p. 174.

64 Putzel, *A Captive Land*.

65 For these specific statistics, see Michele Douglas, "Unfulfilled Dreams: Philippine Land Reform," *Asia-Pacific Backgrounder* (Third World Reports, Boston), 3 (1990), no. 4, p. 1.

66 NED Annual Report, 1984, Washington, D.C., p. 20.

67 Oltman and Bernstein, "Counterinsurgency in the Philippines," p. 19.

68 See, e.g., Rigoberta Tiglao, "Agrarian Reform Program Fails in Its Objectives: Repeat Offenders," *Far Eastern Economic Review*, September 5, 1991, 16–20.

69 See, for example, *Philippines – The Killing Goes On* (London/New York: Amnesty International, 1992); *Bad Blood – Militia Abuses in Mindanao* (New York: Asia Watch, 1992).

70 For instance, see David Timberman, "The Philippines at the Polls," *Journal of Democracy*, 3 (1992), no. 4, 119–124.

71 For details, see Agency for International Development, "Philippine Assistance Strategy," citation on p. 76; Doug Cunningham, "U.S. Philippine Relations: Taking a New Turn," Philippine International Forum, Occasional Article No. 5, Cebu City, Philippines, August 1992.

72 For a discussion on the dilemmas of the Filipino left in the post-Marcos period, see Bello and Gershman, "Democratization and Stabilization," pp. 48–50.

73 Timberman, "The Philippines at the Polls," pp. 119, 121.

74 Agency for International Development,, "Philippine Assistance Strategy," p. 76.

75 Cited in *Manila Chronicle*, April 8, 1992. For more details, see Cunningham, "U.S. Philippine Relations."

4 Chile: Ironing out "a fluke of the political system"

1 Cited in Seymour M. Hersh, "The Price of Power: Kissinger, Nixon, and Chile," *Atlantic Monthly*, December 1982, 21–58, at p. 35.

2 *Ibid.*, 27.

3 Henry Kissinger, *The White House Years* (Boston: Little, Brown, 1979), p. 654.

4 United States Senate, Select Committee to Study Governmental Operations with Respect to Intelligence Activities. *Covert Action in Chile, 1963–1973* (Washington, D.C., 1975).

5 Michael T. Klare, *War Without End* (New York: Vintage Books, 1972), p. 280.

6 David Horowitz, "The Alliance for Progress," in Robert I. Rhodes (ed.), *Imperialism and Underdevelopment: A Reader* (New York: Monthly Review, 1970).

7 Nelson Rockefeller, *The Rockefeller Report of a United States Presidential Mission for the Western Hemisphere* (Chicago: Quadrangle Books, 1969).

8 Crozier, *et al.*, *Crisis of Democracy*.

9 Commission on United States–Latin American Relations, *The Americas in a Changing World* (New York: Quadrangle Books, 1973).

10 National Bipartisan Commission, *The Report of the National Bipartisan Commission on Central America* (New York: Macmillan, 1984). The report was in specific reference to Central America, but was seen as a general policy statement for Latin America.

11 For such arguments, see, e.g., Karen Remmer, *Military Rule in Latin America* (Boulder: Westview, 1989); Alfred Stepan, *Rethinking Military Politics* (Princeton: Princeton University Press, 1988).

12 There is abundant literature on dependency and on the specific ISI model.

See, among others, Fernando Cardoso and Enzo Faletto, *Dependency and Development in Latin America* (Los Angeles: University of California Press, 1979); Guillermo O'Donnell, *Modernization and Bureaucratic Authoritarianism* (Berkeley: University of California Press, 1973). A good overview is Ronald H. Chilcote and Joel C. Edelstein, *Latin America: Capitalist and Socialist Perspectives of Development and Underdevelopment* (Boulder: Westview, 1986).

13 The debt crisis dates back to the 1970s' "global shocks" triggered by the OPEC oil crisis. Behind this crisis was the unprecedented transfer of resources and economic power to international finance capital. OPEC governments and oil company deposits in Western banks led to huge investible bank surpluses that were "recycled" as loans to Latin America. Beneath the surface, the transnationalized fraction of capital, and particularly finance capital, became hegemonic, as money capital became the regulator of the international circuit of production rather than investment capital. On the relation between the 1970s shocks and global restructuring, see Kolko, *Restructuring the World Economy*. On the debt crisis, among others, see Arthur MacEwan, *Debt and Disorder: International Economic Instability and U.S. Imperial Decline* (New York: Monthly Review, 1990); Jackie Roddick (ed.), *The Dance of the Millions: Latin America and the Debt Crisis* (London: Latin America Bureau, 1988).

14 There was a definite element of intentionality on the part of transnational capital concerning the accumulation of debt and its consequences. Jerome I. Levinson, a former IDB official explained: "The debt crisis afforded an unparalleled opportunity to achieve, in the debtor countries, structural reforms... The core of these reforms was a commitment on the part of the debtor countries to reduce the role of the public sector as a vehicle for economic and social development and rely more on market forces and private enterprise, domestic and foreign." World Bank official Sir William Ryrie described the debt crisis as "a blessing in disguise." Citations in Doug Henwood, "Impeccable Logic: Trade, Development and Free Markets in the Clinton Era," *NACLA Report on the Americas*, 26 (1993), no. 5, p. 25.

15 Rolando Munck, *Latin America: The Transition to Democracy* (London: Zed, 1989), pp. 49–52.

16 Eduardo Silva, "Capitalist Coalitions, the State, and Neo-Liberal Economic Restructuring," *World Politics*, 45 (1993), no. 4, 526–559; Alex E. Fernandez Jilberto, "Chile: The Laboratory Experiment in International Neo-Liberalism," in Henk Overbeek, *Restructuring Hegemony in the Global Political Economy* (Routledge: London and New York, 1993).

17 Gramsci, *Prison Notebooks*, p. 208. In *Dependent Development*, Evans shows how states legitimize themselves when they serve the needs of general accumulation and lose legitimacy when they begin to act as "states-for-themselves," whether military or civilian. Thus in Brazil, new elite fractions closely tied to multinational capital began to push in the 1970s

for "democratization and de-statization," meaning polyarchy and neo-liberalism. Peter Evans, *Dependent Development: The Alliance of Multinational, State and Local Capital in Brazil* (Princeton: Princeton University Press, 1979), pp. 266, 269, 272, 279.

18 See, e.g., Maurice Zeitlin and Richard Earl Ratcliff, *Landlords and Capitalists: The Dominant Class of Chile* (Princeton: Princeton University Press, 1990).

19 For these franchise details see William F. Sater, *Chile and the United States: Empires in Conflict* (Athens: University of Georgia Press, 1990), pp. 129–130, 139. The strength of the polyarchic system led to a relatively non-political military – another factor often mentioned by these observers. But its "constitutional character" should not be confused with its repressive capacity. The Chilean armed forces, like their Latin American counter-parts, have a long tradition of repressing popular sectors, including massacres in 1907, 1921, 1925, 1953, and 1967.

20 Cited in Wiarda, *Democratic Revolution*, p. 98.

21 Thomas E. Skidmore and Peter H. Smith, *Modern Latin America*, 2nd edn. (New York: Oxford University Press, 1989), p. 112.

22 US Senate, *Covert Action*, p. 8.

23 Sater, *Chile and the United States*, p. 131.

24 US Senate, *Covert Action*, p. 16

25 *Ibid.*, 14, 18.

26 Sater, *Chile and the United States*, p. 140.

27 Hersh, "The Price of Power," p. 32.

28 Cited in Alonso Aguilar, *Pan-Americanism from Monroe to the Present: A View from the Other Side* (New York, Monthly Review, 1986), p. 119.

29 These are AID figures, cited in Cole Blasier, *The Hovering Giant: U.S. Responses to Revolutionary Change in Latin America, 1910–1985* (Pittsburgh: University of Pittsburg Press, 1985), pp. 263–264.

30 US Senate, *Covert Action*, p. 9.

31 Sater, *Chile and the United States*, p. 132.

32 James Petras and Morris Morley, *The United States and Chile: Imperialism and the Overthrow of the Allende Government* (New York, Monthly Review, 1975), pp. 8–9.

33 Hersh, "The Price of Power," p. 32.

34 The best source for the UP program is the published official program itself, *Programa de la Unidad Popular* (Santiago, 1969), reproduced in English as *The Popular Unity Program* (New York: North American Congress on Latin America, 1972).

35 Documentation is voluminous. For US government reports, see US Senate, *Covert Action*, and US Congress, Select Committee to Study Governmental Operations with Respect to Intelligence Activities, *Interim Report: Alleged Assassination Plots Involving Foreign Leaders*, 94th Congress, 1st Session, November 10, 1975, hereafter referred to as *Assassination Report*. For an extensively footnoted summary, see Blum, *The CIA*, particularly pp. 232–243. See also: Petras and Morley, *United States and Chile*; Hersh, "The Price

of Power." Poul Jensen, *The Garotte: The United States and Chile, 1970–1973*, 2 vols. (Aarhus, Denmark: Aarhus University Press, 1988), is probably the single most comprehensive source of information and analysis of US intervention in the Allende period, and includes a critical review of existing literature.

36 US Congress, *Assassination Report*, p. 23.

37 Hersh, "The Price of Power"; Petras and Morley, *United States and Chile*, pp. 40–41.

38 Hersh, "The Price of Power," p. 57.

39 US Senate, *Covert Action*, p. 33.

40 For details on Aylwin's "white *coup d'état*" strategy, see Sobel, *Chile and Allende*, pp. 135, 138; Gabriel Smirnow, *The Revolution Disarmed: Chile 1970–1973* (New York: Monthly Review, 1979), pp. 111–113, 127–128, 152.

41 US Congress, *Assassination Report*, p. 140.

42 Petras and Morley, *United States and Chile*, p. 82.

43 AID figures cited in Blasier, *Hovering Giant*, p. 264.

44 US Senate, *Covert Action*, p. 38.

45 Petras and Morley, *United States and Chile*, p. 6.

46 This estimate was officially accepted by the US State Department in February 1974. See Sobel, *Chile and Allende*, p. 168.

47 *New York Times*, September 17, 1974, as reproduced in Sobel, *Chile and Allende*, p. 170.

48 US Senate, *Covert Action*, p. 47; Blum, *The CIA*, p. 242.

49 US Congress, *Assassination Report*, p. 229.

50 Petras and Morley, *United States and Chile*, p. 14.

51 *Ibid.*, p. 76.

52 A critical analysis of how three distinct variables came together in the Chilean counterrevolution is Smirnow, *Revolution Disarmed*.

53 Smirnow, *Revolution Disarmed*, p. 68. A day after the coup, Frei released a PDC communique welcoming the coup in unambiguous terms. For a summary of the PDC post-coup positions, see John Dinges, "The Rise of the Opposition," *NACLA Report on the Americas*, 17 (1983), no. 5, 16, 26. Even before the coup, key PDC leaders, including Frei and Aylwin, had made discreet contact with the military to lobby for a coup. Pamela Constable and Arturo Valenzuela, *A Nation of Enemies: Chile Under Pinochet* (New York: W. W. Norton, 1991), pp. 281, 352 n. 28.

54 See, for instance, Sobel, *Chile and Allende*, p. 170. Constable and Valenzuela, *Nation of Enemies*, pp. 281, 352 n. 28; Dinges, "Rise of the Opposition," p. 26.

55 Nora Hamilton, *The Limits of State Autonomy: Post-Revolutionary Mexico* (Princeton: Princeton University Press, 1982). In contrast to Mexico, the UP government never controlled the state *per se*, only the executive branch within the state (the presidency). The UP coalition was unable to capture a controlling proportion of the legislature, which remained an instrument of the dominant classes, and was never able to control the judicial system,

which also operated as a potent weapon of the elite – particularly since the UP government was committed to abiding by the constitutional framework which authorized the judicial system to rule on what it could and could not do "constitutionally."

56 The *Le Monde* report is reproduced in Sobel, *Chile and Allende*, p. 169.
57 Lance Compa, "Laboring for Unity," *NACLA Report on the Americas*, 22 (1988), no. 2.
58 For details of the recruitment by the AID of the "Chicago Boys," see Constable and Valenzuela, *Nation of Enemies*, pp. 166–168.
59 Arturo Valenzuela, "Chile: Origins, Consolidation, and Breakdown of a Democratic Regime," in Larry Diamond, Juan J. Linz, and Seymour Martin Lipset, *Democracy in Developing Countries*, 4 vols. (Boulder: Lynne Rienner, 1989), IV, p. 200.
60 Constable and Valenzuela, *Nation of Enemies*, pp. 166–168.
61 For these statistics, see Sobel, *Chile and Allende*, p. 190. Regarding CIA technical assistance to DINA, see Constable and Valenzuela, *Nation of Enemies*, p. 91.
62 Petras and Morley, *United States and Chile*, p. ix.
63 Sater, *Chile and the United States*, p. 191; Constable and Valenzuela, *Nation of Enemies*, p. 172.
64 Sater, *Chile and the United States*, pp. 191, 195.
65 *Ibid.*, p. 194.
66 *Congressional Record*, Senate, 99th Congress, 1st Session, vol. 131, no. 141, October 25, 1985, p. 13763.
67 An excellent summary of the 1985–1988 shift is Martha Lyn Doggett, "Washington's Not-So-Quiet Diplomacy," *NACLA Report on the Americas*, 22 (1988), no. 2, 29–38.
68 For details, see *ibid.*; Constable and Valenzuela, *Nation of Enemies*, p. 290. They point out that Barnes, in addition, visibly kept at arm's length from the leftist and popular opposition.
69 Sater, *Chile and the United States*, p. 201.
70 Elliot Abrams, "Latin America and the Caribbean: The Paths to Democracy," June 30, 1987 address before the Washington World Affairs Council, Washington, D.C., reprinted by the Department of State, Bureau of Public Affairs, *Current Policy*, no. 982 (July 1987).
71 Sater, *Chile and the United States*, p. 200.
72 This strategy is outlined, among other places, in a slew of "working papers" and policy proposals funded by the NED (see below for details on this NED involvement), among them: Genaro Arriagada, *Negociacion politica y movilizacion social: la critica de las protestas* (Santiago: Centro del Estudios de Desarrollo, 1987); Ignacio Balbontín, *Movilizacion social, control social de los conflictos y negociacion politica* (Santiago: Centro del Estudios de Desarrollo, 1987); Hernán Pozo, *Partidos politicos y organizaciones poblacionales: una relacion problematica* (Santiago: FLACSO, 1986); Philip Oxhorn, *Democracia y participacion popular: organizaciones poblacionales en la futura*

democratica chilena (Santiago: FLACSO, 1986). The strategy is also discussed by one of its architects and activists, Genaro Arriagada, *Pinochet: The Politics of Power* (Boston: Unwin Hyman, 1988), esp. pp. 70–78. Arriagada was a top PDC leader.

73 *New York Times,* December 2, 1984.

74 Sater, *Chile and the United States,* p. 200.

75 *Ibid.,* p. 201.

76 *Ibid.,* p. 203.

77 For these details, see Fernando Villagran, "Me or Chaos," *NACLA Report on the Americas,* 22 (1988), no. 2, 14–20; Arriagada, *Pinochet,* pp. 69–70.

78 A useful review of the origins, strategies, leadership and thinking of twenty-two of the Chilean political parties is the compendium edited by Patricio Tupper, *88/89: Opciones politicas en Chile: La voz de los partidos politicos, movimientos y corrientes de opinion. Lideres, ideas y programs* (Santiago: Ediciones Colchagua, 1987).

79 Washington condemned the FPMR's "terrorism" and assisted in counter-insurgency efforts by providing the junta with intelligence information. See Arriagada, *Pinochet,* p. 77.

80 See, e.g., Department of State, Office of Democratic Initiatives, Latin American Caribbean Bureau, "Evaluation of Voter Education Program in Chile Inter-American Institute of Human Rights – CIVITAS," final report, LAC grant number 0591-G-SS-8005-00, Agency for International Development, Washington, D.C., February 1989, p. iii.

81 Doggett, "Washington's Not-So-Quiet Diplomacy," p. 36.

82 Arriagada, *Pinochet,* p. 69; Dinges, "Rise of the Opposition," pp. 18–20; *Congressional Record,* Senate, 99th Congress, 1st Session, vol. 131, no. 141, October 22, 1985, p. 13763.

83 Arriagada, *Pinochet,* pp. 75–78. The specific citation is on p. 78.

84 See Villagran, "Me or Chaos," for details on the polls. See NED Annual Report, 1988, for details on the NRI funding.

85 Arriagada, *Pinochet,* p. 68.

86 For these NED spending figures, see Annual Reports, 1984–1991. For ODI funding, see Doggett, "Washington's Not-So-Quiet Diplomacy," pp. 34–35.

87 Sobel, *Chile and Allende,* pp. 43, 47–48. Boeninger was rector of the University of Chile during the Allende years.

88 Regarding this strategy, and PDC leaders' roles, see Paul H. Ooeker, *Lost Ilusions: Latin America's Struggle for Democracy, as Recounted by its Leaders* (La Jolla/New York: Institute of the Americas/Markus Wiener Publishers, 1990), pp. 21–23, 35–36, 39, 44; Constable and Valenzuela, *Nation of Enemies,* p. 284.

89 NED Annual Reports, 1986–1991. Two of the studies to come out of the FLACSO-NED programs were: Heraldo Muñoz and Carlos Portales, *Una amistad esquiva: Las relaciones de Estados Unidos y Chile* (Santiago: FLACSO/ PROSPEL-CERC, 1987); Eduardo Boeninger, *et al., Estados Unidos y Chile hacia 1987* (Santiago: FLACSO, 1987). Muñoz, Portales, Boeninger, and

other contributors to these studies were all closely associated with the PDC, with one or another NED, or AID-funded programs and/or with the elite transition strategy in general. Portales went on to become Deputy Minister of Foreign Relations in the Aylwin government. Boeninger went on to become Aylwin's chief advisor.

90 The study group published a subsequent report, by Mark Falcoff, Arturo Valenzuela, and Susan Kaufman Purcell, *Chile: Prospects for Democracy* (New York: Council on Foreign Relations, 1988). See p. 79 for a list of the study group members. Domhoff, *Who Rules America Now?*, pp. 85–88, notes that Council "study groups" are central components of the US foreign policymaking process, the creation of a study group signals that some new policy initiative is underway, and the results of these study groups generally guide policymakers.

91 NED Summary, "Development of Democracy Project," dated February 19, 1985, obtained through the FOIA.

92 NED Annual Report, 1986, pp. 31–32. Constable and Valenzuela noted that "the emerging opposition parties and press were relying on them [the US-funded think-tanks] for expertise. Under Edgardo Boeninger, the Centro de Estudios para el Desarrollo (CED) became a meeting ground" and clearing-house for the opposition. *Nation of Enemies*, p. 253.

93 Sobel, *Chile and Allende*, pp. 47–48; Smirnow, *Revolution Disarmed*, p. 142; Constable and Valenzuela, *Nation of Enemies*, p. 255.

94 NED Annual Report, 1986, 31.

95 For summaries on Freedom House, see Council on Hemispheric Affairs/ Resource Center, *National Endowment for Democracy*, pp. 67–69; *Freedom House*, Groupwatch series (Albuquerque: The Resource Center, 1989).

96 NED Annual Reports, 1986–1991. For the specific citations, see 1987 report, p. 50.

97 The five parties were the right-wing National Unity Movement and the centrist Christian Democratic, Social Democrat, Christian Humanist, and Radical parties. See NED Summary, "Editorial Fund for the Dissemination of Democratic Thought in Chile," one-page project summary (undated), obtained through the FOIA.

98 See, e.g., NED Annual Reports, 1988 and 1989.

99 Valenzuela, "Chile: Origins, Consolidation, and Breakdown," particularly pp. 186–187.

100 See, e.g., Hernán Larrain F., *Governabilidad en Chile luego del regimen militar* (Santiago: Centro de Estudios del Desarrollo, August 1987); Manuel Antonio Garreton M., *En busca de la democracia perdida* (Santiago: Centro de Estudios del Desarrollo, August 1985); Arriagada, *Negociacion politica*; Balbontin, *Movilizacion social*; Pozo, *Partidos politicos*; Oxhorn, *Democracia y participacion*.

101 NED Annual Reports, 1989, p. 31; 1990, p. 38. See also Edgardo Boeninger, "Lessons from the Past: Hopes for the Future," *Journal of Democracy*, 1 (1990), no. 2, 13–17.

102 "Delphi International Services, National Endowment for Democracy, Grant with Delphi for the Implementation of the Project with Participa," final activities report, grant number 89–50.1, April–December, 1989, dated February 28, 1990, obtained through the FOIA.

103 NED Annual Reports, 1984–1990.

104 For details on the CIA Institute and its revival by the NED, see Wiarda, *Democratic Revolution*, p. 106. For the founding of the School in Venezuela, see NED Annual Report, 1984, p. 32.

105 See National Democratic Institute, *Chile's Democratic Transition* (Washington D.C., 1988); NED Annual Report, 1985, pp. 5, 16.

106 *New York Times*, January 27, 1986; Doggett, "Washington's Not-So-Quiet Diplomacy."

107 Constable and Valenzuela, *Nation of Enemies*, p. 289.

108 See, for example, Mark Falcoff, "Chile: A Cognitive Map," in Falcoff, *et al.*, *Chile: Prospects for Democracy*.

109 NED Annual Report, 1984, p. 34.

110 NED Annual Report, 1986, p. 33.

111 NED Annual Report, 1986, p. 32.

112 See, e.g., NED Annual Report, 1989, p. 30.

113 See, e.g., NED Annual Report, 1987, pp. 50–51.

114 NDI, *Chile's Transition*, pp. 5–6.

115 NED Annual Report, 1987, p. 50; NDI, *Chile's Transition*, p. 6.

116 *Ibid.*, p. 7.

117 NED Summary, "Committee for Free Elections (Chile)," undated, obtained through the FOIA.

118 NED Annual Reports, 1987–1989.

119 NED Summary, "Committee for Free Elections: FY 1987 Evaluation," obtained through the FOIA.

120 *New York Times*, November 18, 1988. Frank Hartwig was the NDI-contracted polling analyst.

121 For these details, see the following NED Summaries: "Supplement for Participa (Chile)," undated; "Candidate Forums in Chile: A Nonpartisan Voter Education Service"; "Delphi International Services, National Endowment for Democracy, Grant with Delphi for the Implementation of the Project with Participa, final activities report, grant number 89–50.1, April–December, 1989," dated February 28, 1990, all obtained through the FOIA.

122 See Fred Landis, "C.I.A. Psychological Warfare Operations: Case Studies in Chile, Jamaica, and Nicaragua," *Science for the People*, January–February 1982, 6–37.

123 See NED Annual Reports, 1988–1990; NED Summary "*La Epoca* Newspaper," undated, apparently 1989, obtained through the FOIA.

124 For an overview, see Peter Winn, "U.S. Electoral Aid in Chile: Reflections on a Success Story," paper presented at the Washington Office on Latin America (WOLA) conference, *U.S. Electoral Assistance and Democratic Development*, Washington, D.C., January 19, 1990. The precise figures are

$2.7 million provided by the NED (NED Annual Report, 1988), and $1.2 million provided by the AID through the Democratic Initiatives Office. See Agency for International Development, *FY 1990 Democratic Initiatives and Human Rights Program Summary* (Washington, D.C., 1989), p. 12.

125 For background on CAPEL, see Robinson, *Faustian Bargain*, pp. 98–99.

126 For these details, see NED Annual Reports, 1987–1990; NED Summary, "Candidate Forums in Chile: A Nonpartisan Voter Education Service," 1989, obtained through the FOIA.

127 This was said by Frank Greer, "Media Consultant" for NDI, in testimony before the Bipartisan Commission for Free and Fair Elections in Nicaragua," May 9, 1989, Washington, D.C. I attended the Commission's hearings.

128 Ooeker, *Lost Illusions*, p. 48.

129 For documentation and analysis of the electoral results see Cesar N. Caviedes, *Elections in Chile: The Road Toward Redemocratization* (Boulder: Lynne Rienner, 1991).

130 For self-congratulatory discussion on the success of the elite strategy see Joseph S. Tulchin and Augusto Varas (eds.), *From Dictatorship to Democracy: Rebuilding Political Consensus in Chile* (Washington, D.C./Boulder: Woodrow Wilson Center/Lynne Rienner, 1991).

131 *New York Times*, October 16, 1973, reprinted in Sobel, *Chile and Allende*, p. 153.

132 NED Summary, "Democratic Action in Slum Areas ('Poblaciones')", May 1985, obtained through the FOIA.

133 "Center for Youth Development (FY 1987) Evaluation," NED summary document on its youth program in Chile, September 9, 1988, obtained through the FOIA.

134 For Quintero's background, see Robinson, *Faustian Bargain*, p. 51.

135 Constable and Valenzuela, *Nation of Enemies*, p. 226.

136 "National Endowment for Democracy: Grant with Delphi For the Implementation of the Project with Accion Vecinal y Comunitaria," final report, grant number 88-513-E-039-22.0, March 1988–February 1989, dated August 31, 1989, obtained through the FOIA.

137 "Proyecto de Apoyo, Formacion y Asistencia Tecnica a Dirigentes y Organizaciones Poblacionales de Inspiracion Democratica (Renovacion)," document submitted on AVEC letterhead to the NED along with a cover letter from Sergio Wilson Petit to NED official Katty Kauffman, dated February 8, 1988, obtained through the FOIA.

138 "National Endowment for Democracy: Grant with Delphi," 31 August 1989.

139 *Ibid.*

140 "The Delphi International Group, National Endowment for Democracy, Grant with Delphi for Accion Vecinal Y Comunitaria (AVEC)," quarterly report, grant no. 88-513-E-039-22.0, October 1988–December 1988, dated March 15, 1989, obtained through the FOIA.

141 The FTUI received some $1 million between 1984 and 1990 for its Chile programs. NED Annual Reports, 1984–1990. To this must be added several million dollars more in regional Latin American FTUI programs in which Chilean trade unions were involved, as well as millions of dollars more which the Chilean unions received, not through the FTUI, but through other AFL-CIO channels.

142 Villagran, "Me or Chaos," p. 17.

143 See, e.g., Compa, "Laboring for Unity," pp. 21–28; Smirnow, *Revolution Disarmed*, pp. 28–29, 82–85.

144 See, e.g., Compa, "Laboring for Unity," pp. 24, 25; Smirnow, *Revolution Disarmed*, pp. 82–85.

145 See, e.g., Compa, "Laboring for Unity," p. 27. Constable and Valenzuela, *Nation of Enemies*, pp. 228–229, report that the AFL-CIO's AIFLD sent a delegation to Chile in 1978 to meet with Pinochet. The delegation told Pinochet that radical unionism would get the upper hand if the regime did not allow the Group of Ten to operate freely. Pinochet obliged.

146 See, e.g., Dinges, "Rise of the Opposition," pp. 21–23.

147 NED Annual Report, 1984, p. 16.

148 NED Annual Report, 1984, p. 16; 1985, p. 14.

149 Compa, "Laboring for Unity," p. 27.

150 For these NED-FTUI funding cycles, see NED Annual Reports, 1984–1992.

151 See, e.g., "Quarterly Report to the National Endowment for Democracy from the Free Trade Union Institute, AFL-CIO," 1st, 2nd, 3rd, and 4th quarters, 1988 and 1989; NED Summary "Democratic Labor and the Chilean Transition to Democracy," undated (contents indicate it was drafted after the October 1988 plebiscite and before the December 1989 national elections), obtained through the FOIA.

152 Free Trade Union Institute, "Request to the National Endowment for Democracy for Funds for the Free Trade Union Institute, FY 1990," March 5, 1990, obtained through the FOIA.

153 "Quarterly Report to the National Endowment for Democracy from the Free Trade Union Institute, AFL-CIO, Regarding Activities and Expenditures Undertaken Pursuant to Grants Made in FY '88, FY '89 and FY '90, First Quarter 1990 (January 1, 1990 through March 31, 1990)," dated April 30, 1990, p. 26, obtained through the FOIA.

154 "Center for Youth Development (FY 1987) Evaluation," September 9, 1988.

155 NED Summary, "Formation of Youth Leaders for Democracy," July 12, 1984, obtained through the FOIA.

156 NED Summary, "Center for Youth Development," undated (contents indicate it was drafted in early 1988), obtained through the FOIA.

157 Letter from Miguel Salazar to Katty Kauffman of the National Endowment for Democracy, on CDJ letterhead, March 29, 1988, obtained through the FOIA.

158 NED Annual Report, 1986, p. 33.

159 *Ibid.*, p. 33.

160 "Funcionamiento de la Nueva Institucionalidad Democratica, Proyecto 'CEL'," summary document by Sergio Molina on CEL activities and future plans, submitted to the NED with a cover letter on Delphi letterhead, November 30, 1989, obtained through the FOIA.

161 See, e.g., NED Annual Reports, 1990–1992.

162 Cathy Schneider, "The Underside of the Miracle," *NACLA Report on the Americas*, 26 (1993), no. 4, 18–19.

163 See, e.g., Paul E. Sigmund, *The United States and Democracy in Chile* (Baltimore: Johns Hopkins University Press, 1993).

164 Boeninger, "Lessons from the Past," p. 13. Boeninger asserts that, in the seventeen years of dictatorship, "The Chilean Left learned the hard way – through exile, torture, and proscription – to appreciate political freedoms... Never again will democracy be threatened from the left of our political spectrum" (p. 14). Given Boeninger's apparent historical amnesia, it should be recalled that it was *not* the Chilean left that departed from the "democratic" rules, but the Chilean center, including his own PDC, the right and the United States.

165 Cited in James Petras and Steve Vieux, "The Chilean 'Economic Miracle': An Empirical Critique," *Critical Sociology*, 17 (1990), no. 2, 56–72, quote from p. 70. I draw on this excellent article in the following section. For succinct critique of the "miracle," see also Duncan Green, "Chile: The First Latin American Tiger?," *NACLA Report on the Americas*, 28 (1994), no. 1, 12–16.

166 See, e.g., Thomas Klubock, "And Justice When?," *NACLA Report on the Americas*, 24 (1991), no. 5, 6–7.

167 Petras and Vieux, "Chilean 'Economic Miracle'," p. 66.

168 *Ibid.*

169 ECLAC report released in Santiago, Chile, on October 23, 1990, reported in *Agence France Presse* news dispatch from Santiago, October 13, 1990.

170 Skidmore and Smith, *Modern Latin America*, p. 138.

171 Petras and Vieux, "Chilean 'Economic Miracle'," p. 64.

172 *Ibid.*, pp. 58–59.

173 *Ibid.*

174 Pedro Vuskovic Bravo, "Chile: Mito y Realidad de un Milagro," *Pensamiento Propio*, no. 85 (October 1991), 7–11.

175 Petras and Vieux, "Chilean 'Economic Miracle'," pp. 60–61.

176 *Ibid.*, pp. 62–63.

177 Green, "Chile: The First Latin American Tiger?"

178 Arturo Valenzuela and Pamela Constable, "Chile after Pinochet: Democracy Restored," *Journal of Democracy*, 1 (1990), no. 2, p. 6.

179 Petras and Vieux, "Chilean 'Economic Miracle'," p. 59.

180 See Vuskovic Bravo, "Chile: Mito y Realidad," p. 9.

181 Boeninger, "Lessons from the Past," p. 15.

182 Petras and Vieux, "Chilean 'Economic Miracle'," p. 70.

417

5 Nicaragua: From low-intensity warfare to low-intensity democracy

1 Henry Kissinger and Cyrus Vance, "Bipartisan Objectives for American Foreign Policy," *Foreign Affairs*, 66 (1988), no. 5, p. 919.

2 Cited in Penny Lernoux, "The Struggle for Nicaragua's Soul: A Church in Revolution and War," *Sojourners*, May 14, 1989, p. 23. Neuhaus was a founding member of the conservative Institute on Religion and Democracy (IRD), which helped promote US policy toward Nicaragua in the 1980s.

3 Peter Rodman, Special Assistant to the President on National Security Affairs. Cited in Robinson, *A Faustian Bargain*, p. 25. This work will be referred to simply as *AFB* in subsequent notes for this chapter.

4 Robert Pastor, *Condemned to Repetition: The United States and Nicaragua* (Princeton: Princeton University Press, 1987), p. 16.

5 A penetrating overview of this period is Bradford E. Burns, *Patriarch and Folk: The Emergence of Nicaragua, 1798–1858* (Cambridge, Mass.: Harvard University Press, 1991).

6 Karl Bermann, *Under the Big Stick: Nicaragua and the United States since 1848* (Boston: South End, 1986), p. 16. This is an excellent analysis of US–Nicaragua relations in historical perspective.

7 For an in-depth study of the Zelaya period, see Oscar René Vargas, *La Revolucion que Inicio el Progreso: Nicaragua 1893–1909* (Managua: Ecotextura/Consa, 1990).

8 Bermann, *Big Stick*, p. 141.

9 For an account of this spate of elections, see Oscar René Vargas, *Elecciones en Nicaragua, 1912–1932: (Analisis socio-politico)* (Managua: Fundacion Manolo Morales, 1989).

10 The definitive biography of Sandino and his movement is Gregorio Selser, *Sandino* (New York: Monthly Review, 1981).

11 Cited in Bermann, *Big Stick*, p. 213.

12 Richard Millett, *Guardians of the Dynasty* (New York: Maryknoll, 1977), is the classic work on the National Guard.

13 There is no direct evidence of such involvement. However, the circumstantial evidence suggests the historical record is still undetermined. For discussions on the possible US role, see Bermann, *Big Stick*, pp. 221–222, and Selser, *Sandino*, pp. 174–179.

14 There are many works on the Somoza dynasty. See, e.g., Bernard Diederich, *Somoza and the Legacy of U.S. Involvement in Central America* (New York: E. P. Dutton, 1981).

15 Cited in Bermann, *Big Stick*, p. 219.

16 *Ibid.*, p. 247. See also Thomas Walker, *Nicaragua: The Land of Sandino* (Boulder: Westview, 1981), p. 89.

17 For these details, see Millett, *Guardians*, pp. 200, 252; Tom Barry, Debrah Preusch, and Beth Wood, *Dollars and Dictators* (New York: Grove, 1983), pp. 66–73; George Black, *Triumph of the People: The Sandinista Revolution in Nicaragua* (London: Zed, 1981), pp. 47–48.

18 See, e.g., Victor Blumer Thomas, *The Political Economy of Central America since 1920* (Cambridge: Cambridge University Press, 1987); Jaime Wheelock, *Imperialismo y Dictadura* (Mexico City: Siglo Veintiuno, 1975).

19 See Kent Norsworthy, *Nicaragua: A Country Guide* (Albuquerque: The Resource Center, 1990), pp. 78, 193 n. 18; See also Black, *Triumph*, pp. 28–41, 68–70; Thomas, *Political Economy*, pp. 150–225.

20 Cited in Pastor, *Condemned to Repetition*, p. 162.

21 For discussion, see William I. Robinson and Kent Norsworthy, *David and Goliath: The US War Against Nicaragua* (New York: Monthly Review, 1987), ch. 7.

22 Jaime Wheelock, *El Gran Desafio* (Managua: Editorial Nueva Nicaragua, 1983), p. 26.

23 A detailed chronicle of events leading to the 1979 Sandinista revolution is Black, *Triumph*. For an insider's account of the elite opposition, see Pedro Joaquin Chamorro, *Diario Politico* (Managua: Editorial Nueva Nicaragua, 1990), posthumous.

24 Pastor, *Condemned to Repetition*, pp. 79, 86.

25 For details, see Bermann, *Big Stick*, pp. 261–272.

26 Pastor, *Condemned to Repetition*, pp. 93, 107.

27 See *ibid.*, pp. 151–159, for these details.

28 Cited in *Chronicle of Latin American Economic Affairs*, Latin America Data Base, Latin American Institute, University of New Mexico, Albuquerque, March 24, 1994.

29 Literature on the revolution's economic and social programs is vast. On agrarian reform, see, e.g., Joseph Collins, *et al.*, *Nicaragua: What Difference Could a Revolution Make: Food and Farming in the New Nicaragua* (San Francisco: Institute for Food and Development Policy, 1985); *La reforma agraria en Nicaragua 1979–1989: cifras y referencias documentales* (Managua: CIERA, 1989). On the world-recognized Sandinista literacy crusade, see Valerie Miller, *Between Struggle and Hope: The Nicaraguan Literacy Crusade* (Boulder: Westview, 1985). For an account of the revolution's health programs, see Richard Garfield and Glen Williams, *Health and Revolution: The Nicaraguan Experience* (London: Oxfam, 1989). For general description of post-1979 economic democratization, and social and cultural achievements, see Norsworthy, *Nicaragua*; Thomas Walker (ed.), *Nicaragua: The First Five Years* (New York: Praeger, 1985).

30 For discussion on democracy in Nicaragua between 1979 and 1990, see, e.g., Jose Luis Coraggio, *Nicaragua: Revolucion y Democracia* (Mexico: Editorial Linea, 1985); Gary Ruchwarger, *People in Power: Forging a Grassroots Democracy in Nicaragua* (South Hadley, Mass.: Bergin and Garvey, 1987); Harry E. Vanden and Gary Prevost, *Democracy and Socialism in Sandinista Nicaragua* (Boulder: Lynne Rienner, 1993).

31 On the 1984 elections and US strategy toward them, see, among others, William I. Robinson and Kent Norsworthy, "Elections and U.S. Intervention in Nicaragua," *Latin American Perspectives*, 12 (1985), no. 2, 22–24;

John A. Booth and Mitchell A. Seligson (eds.), *Elections and Democracy in Central America* (Chapel Hill: University of North Carolina Press, 1989); Roy Gutman, *Banana Diplomacy* (New York: Simon and Schuster, 1988), pp. 232–257.

32 Vanden and Prevost, *Democracy and Socialism*, p. 19.
33 *Ibid.* See also Dennis Gilbert, *Sandinistas*, Oxford: Basil Blackwell, 1988; Ruchwarger, *People in Power*.
34 For this type of critique, see Carlos Vilas, *La Revolucion Sandinista: Liberacion nacional y transformaciones sociales en Centroamerica* (Buenos Aires: Editorial Legasa, 1984). Vilas's is a brilliant study; I differ with him on the "scope conditions" under which the revolutionary project should be assessed.
35 Works on the US war against Nicaragua are numerous. See, e.g., Robinson and Norsworthy, *David and Goliath*; Thomas Walker (ed.), *Reagan Versus the Sandinistas: The Undeclared War on Nicaragua* (Boulder: Westview, 1987); Holly Sklar, *Washington's War on Nicaragua* (Boston: South End, 1988); Kornbluh, *Nicaragua*.
36 The $447.69 million figure is from US congressional reports reproduced in Norsworthy, *Nicaragua*, p. 176. For breakdown on the $2 billion figure, see Robinson and Norsworthy, *David and Goliath*, pp. 86–94.
37 For these details, see *ibid.*, pp. 100–102, 123–124, 161–163.
38 *AFB*, p. 36.
39 For more details, see *AFB* and Robinson and Norsworthy, *David and Goliath*, ch. 7.
40 This section draws heavily from *AFB*. Readers interested in original sources are referred to that volume, which contains a hundred pages of notes and reproduced US government documentation.
41 *Ibid.*, p. 28.
42 *Ibid.*, pp. 28, 195 n. 6.
43 *Ibid.*, pp. 29–30, 196, nn. 11–15.
44 These figures are drawn from the National Endowment for Democracy's Annual Reports, 1984 through 1992. The 1984–1991 spending is described and analyzed, item by item, in *AFB*.
45 For these citations, see *ibid*, p. 48.
46 *Ibid.*, p. 49.
47 For the detailed account of the formation by US officials of the UNO coalition, see *ibid.*, pp. 47–65.
48 *Ibid.*, pp. 50–51.
49 Ibid.
50 For these citations and more details, see *ibid.*, pp. 52–53.
51 *Ibid.*, p. 52
52 For these details, see *ibid.*, p. 53.
53 See *ibid.*, pp. 58–60.
54 For summaries of Obando y Bravo's US ties, and on his role in the anti-

Sandinista campaign, see Irene Selser, *Cardenal Obando* (Managua: Centro de Estudios Ecumenicos, 1989); Robinson and Norsworthy, *David and Goliath*, pp. 208–219, 241–248.

55 Status Report on the Task Force on Humanitarian Assistance in Central America, *Report on Phase III*, May 1–August 31, 1989, Agency for International Development, September 17, 1989, Washington, D.C. This money was used for establishing a national logistical network of communications and transportation for his archdiocese.

56 For these details, see *AFB*, pp. 59–60.

57 For details and analysis, see *ibid.*, pp. 60–65, 67–89.

58 *Ibid*, pp. 114–115.

59 *Ibid*, p. 62.

60 According to Peter Montgomery, "1980–1990: The Reagan Years," *Common Cause Magazine*, November 1990, p. 12, Bush spent a total of $70 million in public and private funds.

61 For these details, see *AFB*, pp. 63–65.

62 *Ibid.*, pp. 67–68.

63 For details, see *ibid.*, pp. 69–70.

64 Ibid., p. 70.

65 Ibid.

66 Ibid.

67 See *ibid.*, p. 71.

68 For example, see Orlando Nunez, "La ideologia como Fuerza Material, y La Juventud como Fuerza Ideologica," in *Estado y Clases Sociales en Nicaragua* (Managua: CIERA, 1982).

69 *AFB*, p. 72.

70 *Ibid*.

71 *Ibid.*, p. 74.

72 *Ibid*.

73 "Political and Social Action Project, Nicaragua," Delphi International Group, undated document obtained through the FOIA.

74 *AFB*, p. 75

75 Ibid.

76 See Holly Sklar, "US Wants to Buy Nicaragua's Elections – Again," *Zeta*, November 1989, 39–40.

77 *AFB*, p. 76.

78 *Ibid*.

79 For discussion on propaganda and the communications media in US policy towards Nicaragua, see sources listed in *ibid.*, p. 211, n. 61.

80 *Ibid*, p. 78.

81 See *ibid.*, p. 78, and discussion and sources listed in pp. 211–212, n. 61, 63–65.

82 For details, see sources in *ibid.*, p. 212, n. 65.

83 *Ibid.*, p. 79.

84 For details, see *ibid.*
85 For documentation on the CIA connection, see sources listed in *ibid.*, p. 212, n. 70.
86 *Ibid.*, pp. 81–82.
87 *Ibid.*, p. 87.
88 The most exhaustive analysis of pre-electoral polls is William A. Barnes, "Rereading the Nicaraguan Pre-Election Polls," in Vanessa Castro and Gary Prevost (eds.), *The 1990 Elections in Nicaragua and Their Aftermath* (Lanham, Md.: Rowman and Littlefield, 1992). See also *AFB*, pp. 87–89.
89 See, e.g., *ibid.*, p. 104.
90 *Ibid.*, p. 105.
91 For details on this aid package, and Contra activity during the electoral process, see *ibid.*, pp. 134–140.
92 *Ibid.*, p. 137.
93 *Ibid.*
94 *Ibid.*
95 *Ibid.*
96 For these statistics, and for an overall analysis of the rural aspects of the electoral process, see Vanessa Castro, *Resultados Electorales en el Sector Rural* (Managua: Instituto para el Desarrollo de la Democracia, 1990).
97 Alvin H. Bernstein, "Political Strategies in Coercive Diplomacy and Limited War," in Lord and Barnett (eds.), *Political Warfare*, p. 146.
98 Norsworthy, *Nicaragua*, p. 67.
99 Cited in *AFB*, p. 141.
100 See White House statement, November 8, 1989, released by the Office of the Press Secretary.
101 *AFB*, pp. 143–144.
102 For details, see *ibid.*, p. 144.
103 See Vanden and Prevost, *Democracy and Socialism*, pp. 142–143.
104 Paul Oquist, "The Sociopolitical Dynamics of the 1990 Elections" in Castro and Prevost (eds.), *1990 Elections*, p. 29.
105 "Recibí al Pais en un Profundo Abismo," *La Jornada* (Mexico), June 25, 1993, 1.
106 On post-revolutionary Nicaragua and US activities therein, see, among others, Oscar René Vargas, *A donde va Nicaragua: perspectivas de una revolucion latinoamericana* (Managua: Ediciones Nicarao, 1991); William I. Robinson and Kent Norsworthy, "The Nicaraguan Revolution Since the Elections," *CrossRoads*, no. 6 (January 1991), 21–27; Midge Quandt, "U.S. Aid to Nicaragua: Funding the Right," *Z Magazine*, November 1991, 47–51; George R. Vickers and Jack Spence, "Two Years After the Fall," *World Policy Journal*, Summer 1992, 533–562.
107 For discussion on the FSLN and the popular organizations after the elections, see Midge Quandt, *Unbinding the Ties: The Popular Organizations and the FSLN in Nicaragua* (Washington, D.C.: Nicaragua Network Education Fund, 1992).

108 Remark made during an April 5, 1990 press conference, cited in "Family Frictions," *Barricada Internacional,* no. 320 (April 12, 1990), p. 3.
109 Agency for International Development, "Country Development Strategy Statement: U.S.AID/Nicaragua 1991–1996," Washington, D.C. June 14, 1991, pp. 62–63.
110 For the $541 million figure, see AID, "Strategy Statement," resource table, appearing on an unnumbered page following the last numbered page (63). See also: AID, "Nicaragua: A Commitment to Democracy, Reconciliation, and Reconstruction" ("Fact Sheet" prepared for reporters and the public, March 1990); AID, "Economic Assistance Strategy for Central America, 1991–2000," Washington, D.C. January 1991. For detailed analysis, see the excellent studies by two Nicaraguan economists: Angel Saldomando, *El retorno de la AID, caso de Nicaragua: condicionalidad y reestructuracion conservadora* (Managua, Ediciones CRIES, 1992); Adolfo Acevedo Vogl, *Nicaragua y el FMI: el pozo sin fondo del ajuste* (Managua: Ediciones CRIES, 1993). Also see interview with Saldomando, "U.S.AID's Strategy in Nicaragua," *Envio,* no. 142 (May 1993), 23–31.
111 *AFB,* p. 164.
112 For details, see *ibid.,* pp. 164, 237 nn. 7–10.
113 Vargas, *A donde va Nicaragua.*
114 *AFB,* p. 163.
115 AID, "Strategy Statement," pp. 47–48.
116 AID, "Strategy Statement," pp. 15–16, 45.
117 For details on the AID textbooks, see Quandt, "U.S. Aid to Nicaragua."
118 *AFB,* pp. 165–166.
119 AID, "Strategy Statement," p. 46.
120 *AFB,* p. 166.
121 See NED Annual Reports, 1990–1992. For the television program, see 1992 Report, 75.
122 *AFB,* p. 166.
123 Quandt, "U.S. Aid to Nicaragua."
124 *Ibid.*
125 Saldomando interview, "U.S.AID's Strategy in Nicaragua," pp. 26–27.
126 William I. Robinson, "AID to Nicaragua: Some Things Aren't What They Seem," *In These Times,* October 24–30, 1990.
127 See Roberto Larios, "Bowing Before Financial Organizations," *Barricada Internacional,* nos. 367–8 (Nov.–Dec. 1993), pp. 8–9.
128 Anne Larson, "Foreign Debt: Where Have All the Dollars Gone?," *Envio,* no. 143 (June 1993), 4–10.
129 For these details and statistics, see Larson, "Foreign Debt."
130 AID, "Strategy Statement," p. 39.
131 See *ibid.,* resource table; Saldomando, *El retorno,* p. 97, and pp. 88–89 for a listing of the new private banks and their principal board members.
132 *Ibid.,* p. 92.
133 Larios, "Bowing Before Financial Organizations."

134 "Why Social Conflict," *Envio*, no. 138 (Jan.–Mar. 1993), p. 18.

135 Larios, "Bowing Before Financial Organizations."

136 See, e.g., AID, "Strategy Statement"; AID, "Economic Assistance Strategy." For further discussion of this general model for the Caribbean Basin, see, e.g., H. Rodrigo Jauberth Rojas *et al.*, *La triangulacion Centroamerica–Mexico–EUA: una oportunidad para el desarrollo y la paz?* (Managua: Ediciones CRIES, 1991).

137 See "Welcome to the Free Trade Zone," *Envio*, no. 150, 27–33.

138 AID, "Strategy Statement," p. 25.

139 Saldomando, *El retorno*, pp. 74–78.

140 See, e.g., *ibid.*, p. 80.

141 AID, "Strategy Statement," p. 20.

142 See, e.g., Department of State, Office of the Assistant Secretary Spokesman, "Statement by Richard Boucher, Spokesman," press release, April 2, 1993, which outlines strict conditions imposed by the Clinton administration for the release of frozen US funds, including a purging of Sandinistas from the government, the dismissal of army chief Humberto Ortega (a Sandinista) and other high-level EPS officials.

143 For an explanation of this doctrine, as described by Humberto Ortega, see interview with Ortega in *Barricada* [Managua], December 29, 1992, 1.

144 AID, "Strategy Statement," p. 63.

145 There is considerable literature on these measures and debate on whether they were necessary or in the popular interests. See, e.g., Richard Stahler-Sholk, "Stabilization, Destabilization., and the Popular Classes in Nicaragua, 1979–1988," *Latin American Research Review*, 25 (1990), no. 3, 55–88. For a summary, see *AFB*, pp. 141–144.

146 "Why Social Conflict," 18.

147 *Ibid.*

148 Susanne Andersson, "New National Health Care Policy: Undercover Privatization," *Barricada Internacional*, no. 367–8, (Nov.–Dec. 1993), 12–13.

149 For discussion on the debate in the FSLN and in the left in Latin America, see, e.g., Gary Prevost, "The FSLN in Opposition," in Castro and Prevost (eds.), *1990 Elections*; Vargas, *A donde va Nicaragua*; William I. Robinson, "The Sao Paulo Forum: Is There a New Latin American Left?," *Monthly Review* (1992), no. 7, 1–12.

150 AID, "Strategy Statement," p. 8.

6 Haiti: The "practically insolvable problem" of establishing consensual domination

1 Cited in Hans Schmidt, *The United States Occupation of Haiti, 1915–1934* (New Brunswick, N.J.: Rutgers University Press, 1971), pp. 62–63.

2 Steve Meacham, "Popular Power in Haiti," *Forward Motion* (1991), no. 3, p. 23.

3 General works in English on which I draw include: Elizabeth Abbott, *Haiti: The Duvaliers and their Legacy* (New York: Simon and Schuster, 1988);

Patrick Bellegarde-Smith, *Haiti: The Breached Citadel* (Boulder: Westview, 1989); Paul Farmer, *The Uses of Haiti* (Monroe, Me.: Common Courage, 1994); James Ferguson, *Papa Doc, Baby Doc: Haiti and the Duvaliers* (New York: Blackwell, 1987); Mats Lundahl, *Peasants and Poverty: A Study of Haiti* (London: Croom Helm, 1979); Rod Prince, *Haiti: Family Business* (London: Latin American Bureau, 1985); Michel-Rolph Trouillot, *Haiti, State against Nation: The Origins and Legacy of Duvalierism* (New York: Monthly Review, 1990); Amy Wilentz, *The Rainy Season: Haiti since Duvalier* (New York: Simon and Schuster, 1989).

4 See, e.g., the classic study in English on the Haitian revolution, C. L. R. James, *The Black Jacobins: Toussaint L'Ouverture and the San Domingo Revolution* (New York: Random House, 1963), p. ix.

5 Robert Debs Heinl, Jr. and Nancy Gordon Heinl, *Written in Blood: The Story of the Haitian People, 1492–1971* (Boston: Houghton Mifflin, 1978), p. 33. The Heinls' exhaustive historical account, like earlier colonial historical logs, is steeped in racism and ethnocentric assumptions. The Haitians are not only "primitive" and exhibit some mystical "psyche," but are a people inexplicably incapable of resolving their own problems since they do not fit the Eurocentric logic of the observers.

6 For analysis, see James, *Black Jacobins*.

7 Cited in Prince, *Family Business*, p. 32.

8 Prince, *Family Business*, pp. 13–14.

9 Although space constraints preclude discussion, in reality a "pure" peasant economy never existed in Haiti, and has rarely existed in human history. The peasant economy was highly stratified, an amalgamation of subsistence production and semi-feudal rural production relations, in which large holders were in turn "articulated" to capitalist production relations via marketing in the world economy through a commercial bourgeoisie and a state bureaucracy. See, e.g., Trouillot, *State against Nation*.

10 See, e.g., Ferguson, *Papa Doc, Baby Doc*, pp. 17, 21.

11 Abbott, *The Duvaliers*, p. 18; Bellegarde-Smith, *Breached Citadel*, pp. 48–55.

12 André Gunder Frank, *Capitalism and Underdevelopment in Latin America: Historical Studies of Chile and Brazil* (New York: Monthly Review, 1967).

13 These statistics are summarized in Prince, *Family Business*, pp. 1–4, 43, 53–55.

14 For details, see Abbott, *The Duvaliers*, p. 172.

15 Cited in Schmidt, *United States Occupation*, p. 48.

16 Fritz Longchamp and Worth Cooley-Prost, "Breaking with Dependency and Dictatorship: Hope for Haiti," *Covert Action Information Bulletin*, no. 36 (Spring 1991), 54–58, at p. 55.

17 Schmidt, *The United States Occupation*, p. 31.

18 *Ibid.*, p. 103, Emily Greene Balch, *Occupied Haiti* (New York: The Writers Publishing Co., 1927).

19 As cited in Paul W. Drake, "From Good Men to Good Neighbors: 1912–1932," in Lowenthal (ed.) *Exporting Democracy*, p. 25.

20 Schmidt, *United States Occupation*, p. 145.
21 *Ibid.*, pp. 108–112.
22 For these details, see *ibid.*, pp. 37–40, 48–52; Paul H. Douglas, "Political History of the Occupation," in Balch, *Occupied Haiti*, pp. 18–21 and Douglas, "Economic and Financial Aspects," in *ibid.*, pp. 44–46, 54–56.
23 E. G. Balch, "Public Order," in *ibid.*, p. 130.
24 E. G. Balch, "Charges of Abuses in Haiti," in *ibid.*, p. 125.
25 *Ibid.*, pp. 123–127; Schmidt, *United States Occupation*, pp. 86–91, 100–102.
26 *Ibid.*, pp. 86–91; Trouillot, *State against Nation*, pp. 104–108.
27 Noirism was in turn a Haitian version of Negritude, an anti-colonial ideology of the disenfranchised African middle class in French colonies who took over the reins of direct government from departing white administrators in new neo-colonial states.
28 On US support for Duvalier's electoral bid, see Bellegarde-Smith, *Breached Citadel*, pp. 94–95.
29 Wilentz, *Rainy Season*, p. 42.
30 See Abbott, *The Duvaliers*, for graphic descriptions of Duvalierist terror, and pp. 184 and 234, respectively, for the specific statistics.
31 Note that *vodoun* is alternatively spelled *vodun, voudou*, and *voodoo*. *Vodoun*, a blend of African animist religions and Catholicism, developed during the colonial period as a means of uniting people and organizing resistance, both spiritual and worldly. The US occupation force, mulatto governments, and the conservative Catholic Church hierarchy had long tried forcibly to suppress it. The Machiavellian Duvalier, on the other hand, won support by encouraging *voudoun* as a source of black pride and practiced the religion himself, and was able to incorporate many *houngans* into the Macoute network. For discussion, see Bellegarde-Smith, *Breached Citadel*, pp. 9–22.
32 Abbott, *The Duvaliers*, p. 87.
33 *Ibid.*, pp. 108–111.
34 *Ibid.*, pp. 93, 105, 114; Prince, *Family Business*, pp. 26–27, 36, 38; Ferguson, *Papa Doc, Baby Doc*, pp. 62, 78.
35 *Ibid.*, p. 42.
36 Abbott, *The Duvaliers*, p. 163; Prince, *Family Business*, p. 31; Ferguson, *Papa Doc, Baby Doc*, pp. 55, 57.
37 See *ibid.*, pp. 68–69. Bellegarde-Smith, *Breached Citadel*, p. 100, estimates that total U.S. economic aid to the Duvalier regime between 1957 and 1986 was about $900 million.
38 See, e.g., Prince, *Family Business*, pp. 43–46; Lundahl, *Peasants and Poverty*, various chapters; Tom Barry, Beth Woods, and Deb Preusch, *The Other Side of Paradise: Foreign Control in the Caribbean* (New York: Grove Press, 1984), pp. 330–341.
39 For analyses of the CBI and the arrival of the global economy in the Caribbean, see Kathy McAfee, *Storm Signals: Structural Adjustment and*

Development Alternatives in the Caribbean (Boston: South End 1991); Barry, *et al., Other Side of Paradise*..

40   Prince, *Family Business*, pp. 47–51.
41   Cited in Barry, *et al., Other Side of Paradise*, p. 336.
42   See Prince, *Family Business*, pp. 48, 72. Prince notes that Haitian workers in the free-trade zone showed to be just as productive as those working in core countries, which belies the argument that lower wages in the Third World are a result of lower productivity.
43   Abbott, *The Duvaliers*, p. 176.
44   The World Bank report is cited in Noam Chomsky, *Year 501* (Boston, South End, 1993), pp. 206–207; the AID report in Bellegarde-Smith, *Breached Citadel*, p. 127.
45   For instance, Duvalier official Clemard Joseph Charles, who had established the local Commercial Bank and also served as Jean-Claude's "bagman," in charge of managing the Duvaliers' Swiss bank accounts, was also on the boards of fourteen major transnational corporations operating in Haiti, among them General Electric, Siemens, Schuckerwerke, and Toyota Motors. See Abbott, *The Duvaliers*, p. 182.
46   Longchamp and Cooley-Prost, "Breaking with Dependency," pp. 56–57.
47   Truillot, *State against Nation*, pp. 218–219.
48   While the old-style dictatorships of the Philippines, Nicaragua, and Haiti demonstrate both these flaws of authoritarianism, Chile, with its "bureaucratic-authoritarian regime" under Pinochet, provided technical and administrative efficiency but demonstrated the second failing, generating mass resistance to dictatorship that threatens the social order.
49   Prince, *Family Business*, p. 71.
50   Abbott, *The Duvaliers*, p. 305; Wilentz, *Rainy Season*, p. 39. The US Embassy–Namphy conspiracy to remove Duvalier is detailed in Abbott, *The Duvaliers*, pp. 285–293, 302–314, 321–333.
51   *Ibid.*, pp. 287, 292–293.
52   *Ibid.*, pp. 299–300.
53   Ferguson, *Papa Doc, Baby Doc*, p. 112.
54   Abbott, *The Duvaliers*, p. 306.
55   *Ibid.*, p. 308; Ferguson, *Papa Doc, Baby Doc*, p. 119.
56   *Ibid.*, p. 121.
57   *Ibid.*, p. 176.
58   Americas Watch/National Coalition for Haitian Refugees, *Silencing a People: The Destruction of Civil Society in Haiti* (New York/Washington, February 1993), pp. 3–4.
59   Abbott, *The Duvaliers*, p. 305.
60   *Ibid.*, p. 335; Ferguson, *Papa Doc, Baby Doc*, pp. 123, 128, 140–142.
61   See Thomas Carothers, "The Reagan Years: The 1980s," in Lowenthal, *Exporting Democracy*, p. 113.
62   Longchamp and Cooley-Prost, "Breaking With Dependency," p. 57.

63 "Assistance for Democracy Act of 1986," Report 99–722, House of Representatives, 99th Congress, 2nd Session, July 30, 1986, p. 21. Of the $4 million, $2.8 million was disbursed before a November 1987 suspension of military aid, according to Trouillot, *State against Nation*, p. 222.

64 Ferguson, *Papa Doc, Baby Doc*, p. 161; Bellegarde-Smith, *Breached Citadel*, p. 123.

65 See, e.g., Tim Weiner, "Key Haitian Leaders Said to Have Been in CIA's Pay," *New York Times*, November 1, 1993, A-1; Tim Weiner, "CIA Formed Haitian Unit Later Tied to Narcotics Trade," *New York Times*, November 14, 1993, A-1.

66 *Ibid.*

67 See, e.g., eyewitness accounts by Abbott in *The Duvaliers*, esp. p. 320. See also Ferguson, *Papa Doc, Baby Doc*, p. 125.

68 For a discussion of these parties, see Bellegarde-Smith, *Breached Citadel*, pp. 154–157.

69 See Weiner, "CIA Formed Haitian Unit."

70 Longchamp and Cooley-Prost, "Breaking with Dependency," p. 57. For details and eyewitness descriptions of the repression under the National Government Council, see Wilentz, *Rainy Season*, and Abbott, *The Duvaliers*, esp. pp. 331–367.

71 Wilentz, *Rainy Season*, p. 358.

72 For details on Adams and his activities, see Longchamp and Cooley-Prost, "Breaking with Dependency," p. 54.

73 *Ibid.*

74 On the formation of these and other broad democratic coalitions, see Michael S. Hooper, "The Monkey's Tail Still Strong," *NACLA Report on the Americas*, 21 (1987), no. 3, 24–31; Wilentz, *Rainy Season*, esp. pp. 209–211, 233; Mark V. Aristide and Laurie Richardson, "Profiles of the Popular Currents," *NACLA Report on the Americas*, 27 (1994), no. 4, 32–33; Mark V. Aristide and Laurie Richardson, "Haiti's Popular Resistance," *NACLA Report on the Americas*, 27 (1994), no. 4, 30–36.

75 For descriptions of these peasant federations, see *Silencing a People*, pp. 9–26. See also Robert E. Maguire, "The Peasantry and Political Change in Haiti," *Caribbean Affairs*, 4 (1991), no. 2, 1–18.

76 Eric R. Wolf, *Peasant Wars of the Twentieth Century* (New York: Harper and Row, 1969).

77 In *The Rainy Season*, Wilentz, who as a reporter in Port-au-Prince held numerous interviews with U.S. Embassy officials, amply documents this distrust and hostility. See, e.g., pp. 11, 114–115, 120, 128, 129, 220–221, 390.

78 For summaries, see NED Annual Reports, 1985–1990; Resource Center, "Populism, Conservatism, and Civil Society in Haiti," *The NED Backgrounder*, 1 (1992), no. 2; Cooley-Prost, *Democracy Intervention in Haiti*. This booklet contains summaries and reprints of sections of several AID documents released to the Washington Office on Haiti through the FOIA.

79 AID, "Democracy Enhancement Project (521–0236) Project Paper," Wa-

shington, D.C., June 20, 1991, reproduced in part in Cooley-Prost, *Democracy Intervention in Haiti*, p. 7.

80 See, e.g., letter from Berlanger to NED officer Marc F. Plattner, December 2, 1985, obtained through the FOIA.

81 See "Haitian International Institute for Research and Development (IHRED), Proposal to Conduct Forums for the Promotion and Development of Democracy in Haiti," January 1989, released through the FOIA.

82 See NED Annual Reports, 1987–1990.

83 NED Annual Report, 1987, p. 57.

84 Memo from US Embassy in Port-au-Prince to NDI regarding party-building workshops, August 1986, obtained through the FOIA.

85 See, e.g., Ferguson, *Papa Doc, Baby Doc*, p. 139.

86 "The 1990 Elections in Haiti," report of the electoral observation mission sponsored by the National Republican Institute for International Affairs, undated, p. 30.

87 See the following four documents obtained through the FOIA: "NRIIA Final Program Report: NED Grant #90–132.0 Haiti, AID Funds, Project Title: Democratic Institution Development and Election Observation," undated; "Grant Agreement Between the National Endowment for Democracy, Incorporated, and the National Republican Institute for International Affairs, NED Grant No. 90–132.0," undated; "National Democratic Institute for International Affairs, Quarterly Report to the National Endowment for Democracy (July 1 – September 30, 1991)," October 31, 1991; "Haiti Aid, Grant Number: 90–132.0, Program Title: Political Party Development." Regarding the 1990 electoral results, see Washington Office on Haiti, "Report on the Elections of December 16, 1990," Washington, D.C. March 1991; "The 1990 Elections in Haiti."

88 See Abbott, *The Duvaliers*, pp. 254–255; Ferguson, *Papa Doc, Baby Doc*, p. 127.

89 *Ibid.*

90 The businessman was Vernon Gentry, cited in a commentary he published, "State Department Rebuffed in Haiti," *Times of the Americas* (Washington, D.C.), December 26, 1990, 25.

91 Cited in Americas Watch, National Coalition for Haitian Refugees, and Physicians for Human Rights, *Return to the Darkest Days: Human Rights in Haiti Since the Coup* (New York: Americas Watch, December, 1991), pp. 16–17.

92 See "Toward a New Future: Emerging Democracy in Haiti," *Haiti Backgrounder* (1991), no. 1 (published by Third World Reports, Cambridge, Mass.)

93 Resource Center, "Populism"; Cooley-Prost, *Democracy Intervention in Haiti*, p. 7.

94 See Cooley-Prost, *Democracy Intervention in Haiti*, p. 7, and the following documents obtained through the FOIA: America's Development Foundation (ADF) summary of proposal to NED, February 13, 1991; "National

Endowment for Democracy/Haiti Election, America's Development Foundation Civic Education Proposals," undated; "Quarterly Program Report, National Endowment for Democracy Haiti Elections, Grants # 90–121.0, 90–122.0, 90–123.0, 90–124.0, 90–129.1, October 1, 1990 – December 31, 1990."

95 See Resource Center, "Populism,"; Allan Ebert, "Haiti and the AIFLD: A Burden Removed... A Burden Renewed," *National Reporter*, Summer 1986, 19–21. Ebert documents how, in the wake of Duvalier's departure, the AIFLD dispatched a delegation to Haiti to set up a full-time office and work closely with the FOS.

96 Weiner, "Key Haitian Leaders."

97 See "FY 1990 Democratic Initiatives and Human Rights Program Summary," Agency for International Development, Department of State, Washington, D.C.

98 Meacham, "Popular Power in Haiti," p. 24.

99 See Washington Office on Haiti, "Report on the Elections"; "The 1990 Elections in Haiti."

100 See, e.g., Xavier Gorostiaga, "La avalancha haitiana," *Pensamiento Propio*, March 1991, 1–3.

101 Cited in William I. Robinson, "The Tragic History of the Haitian Republic," *Notisur*, Latin America Data Base, Latin America Institute, University of New Mexico, Albuquerque, vol. 2, no. 2 (January 22, 1992).

102 See Washington Office on Haiti, "Update on Haiti," Washington, D.C., April 18, 1991.

103 *Ibid.*; Barbara Briggs and Charles Kernaghan, "The U.S. Economic Agenda: A Sweatshop Model of Development," *NACLA Report on the Americas*, 27 (1994), no. 4, 37–40.

104 Amy Wilentz, "Haiti: The September Coup," *Reconstruction* (1992), no. 4, p. 103.

105 See Kim Ives, "The Unmaking of a President," *NACLA Report on the Americas*, 27 (1994), no. 4, p. 17.

106 The list is cited and discussed in Niki Joseph, "Haiti: The Long March to Popular Democracy," *CrossRoads*, no. 15 (November 1991); Also, the *New York Times*, October 13, 1991, A-1 reported that individual enlisted soldiers and policemen were paid as much as $5,000 each to support the coup.

107 Prince, *Family Business*, pp. 51, 57.

108 However, there might well have been covert involvement which has not – and may never – become public knowledge.

109 See, e.g., Allan Nairn, "Our Man in FRAPH: Behind Haiti's Paramilitaries," *The Nation*, 259 (1994), 458–461.

110 E.g., U.S. ambassador Alvin Adams, in the days prior to the coup, had presented a number of Haitian army demands to Aristide officials in a coercive diplomacy tactic to place pressure on Aristide to cede a greater quota of power to adversaries in and out of the armed forces and to take measures that would strengthen the state's coercive apparatus. See

Notimex news dispatch, datelined Mexico City, February 3, 1992, "Aristide Adviser Charges U.S. Involved in Coup," reproduced in FBIS-LAT-92–023, Washington, D.C., February 4, 1992.

111 See "Mobilizing Resources for Development," *International Policy Report* (Center for International Policy, Washington, D.C.), May 1992; Briggs and Kernaghan, "The U.S. Economic Agenda."

112 See Ferguson, *Papa Doc, Baby Doc*, p. 146; Bellegarde-Smith, *Breached Citadel*, p. 135; Trouillot, *State against Nation*.

113 AID, "Democracy Enhancement Project (521–0236), Project Paper, Project Summary," 1–8, reprinted in Cooley-Prost, *Democracy Intervention in Haiti*, appendix.

114 For these citations and details, see Cooley-Prost, *Democracy Intervention in Haiti*, pp. 8–9.

115 *Ibid.*, p. 12.

116 On US policy between 1991 and 1994, see, among others, John Canham-Clyne, "U.S. Policy on Haiti: Selling Out Democracy," *Covert Action Quarterly*, no. 48 (Spring 1994), 4–9, 52–56; Ives, "Unmaking of a President"; Farmer, *Uses of Haiti*; James Ridgewood (ed.), *The Haiti Files: Decoding the Crisis* (Washington D.C.: Essential Books/Azul Editions, 1994).

117 *New York Times*, October 7, 1991, A-1.

118 See, among others, Lawyers Committee for Human Rights, *Haiti: A Human Rights Nightmare* (Washington, D.C./New York, 1992); Amnesty International, *Haiti – The Human Rights Tragedy: Human Rights Violations since the Coup* (New York, January 1992). The Washington Office on Haiti ("Human Rights in Haiti," Washington, D.C., January 1992) documented that the military committed an average of twenty-four rights violations per month under Aristide. Under the regime of Gen. Prosper Avril (September 1988–March 1990), the average was seventy-three per month, and under former provisional president Ertha Pascal Truillot (March 1990–February 1991), fifty-nine per month. Independent reports, while praising his government's record, also criticized Aristide for failing to condemn, and for speeches which seemed to encourage, mass mobilizations and sometimes direct violent attacks against former Duvalierists, Macoutes, and representatives of the wealthy elite. Although space constraints preclude discussion, at play was the contradiction between the formal structures of representative democracy (dysfunctional as they were) – i.e., a government structure that could constitutionally block basic social change in Haiti – and popular democracy. Whether *unarmed* "intimidation," via mass mobilization, of a privileged minority, such as took place under Aristide, or the blocking by that historically privileged minority of social change to the benefit of an historically oppressed and exploited majority, is the greater "human rights violation," is a matter of dispute. Besides, the documentation indicates that Aristide's "inflammatory speeches" were themselves taken out of context and distorted by US officials for the

purpose of discrediting him and justifying US policy. See, e.g., Wilentz, 'The September Coup," p. 102; Anne-Christine D'Adesky, "Haiti, Père Lebrun in Context," *NACLA Report on the Americas*, 25 (1991), no. 3, 7–9.

119 "CIA Report on Aristide False, Newspaper Says," *Washington Post*, December 2, 1993, A-18; James Carroll, "The CIA Can be a Poor Judge of Character," *Boston Globe*, October 26, 1993, A-1.

120 Ives, "'Unmaking of a President," p. 38.

121 The document, titled "Memo from Consultant to the U.S. Embassy in Port-au-Prince," was reproduced in Ridgewood (ed.), *Haiti Files*, pp. 104–107.

122 See Howard French, "U.S. Presses Ousted Haitian Chief to Negotiate a Return from Exile," *New York Times*, June 27, 1992, A-1.

123 Ives, "'Unmaking of a President," p. 29. Also see, e.g., Haitian Information Bureau, "Subverting Democracy," *Multinational Monitor*, March 1994, 13–15.

124 See, e.g., Lawyers Committee, *Human Rights Nightmare*, Amnesty International, *Human Rights Tragedy*; Human Rights Watch/Americas, National Coalition of Haitian Refugees, *Terror Prevails in Haiti*, reproduced in Ridgewood (ed.), *Haiti Files*.

125 Americas Watch, *et al.*, *Return to the Darkest Days*, as cited in Chomsky, *Year 501*, p. 212.

126 See, e.g., Paul Quinn-Judge,"Haitians Trained After Coup," *Boston Globe*, December 6, 1993, A-1.

127 *New York Times*, September 27, 1992, A-1.

128 See, e.g., Americas Watch/National Coalition for Haitian Refugees, *Half the Story: The Skewed U.S. Monitoring of Repatriated Haitian Refugees* (New York: Americas Watch, June 1992); Emma D. Navajas, "Haitian Interdiction: An Overview of U.S. Policy and Practice," *Migration World*, 20 (1991/2), no. 1, 38–41; Bill Frelick, "Haitians at Sea: Asylum Denied," *NACLA Report on the Americas*, 26 (1992), no. 1, 34–39.

129 Nairn, "Our Man in FRAPH," p. 458.

130 See, e.g., *ibid.*

131 General Accounting Office, "Summary of Shipments to Haiti After November 20, 1991, Compliance with the OAS Recommended Embargo," report no. B-248828, 1994; Charles Kernaghan, "Skirting the Embargo," *Multinational Monitor*, March 1994, pp. 16–17.

132 These figures are cited in "Haiti: U.S. Trade With Haiti Increases, Despite Embargo," *Chronicle of Latin American Economic Affairs*, Latin America Data Base, Latin American Institute, University of New Mexico, March 10, 1994, and also in Kernaghan, "Skirting the Embargo," pp. 16–17. U.S. officials justified these exemptions by arguing that the embargo had brought great suffering to the poor. These same officials rejected similar arguments that poor, innocent civilians were the victims of embargoes against Cuba, Iraq, and other countries.

133 "U.S.AID/Haiti Democracy Factsheet," September 2, 1993, reprinted in Cooley-Prost, *Democracy Intervention in Haiti*, pp. 14–15. For analysis of

post-coup political aid programs, see also Haitian Information Bureau, "Subverting Democracy," *Multinational Monitor*, March 1994, pp. 13–15; Canham-Clyne, "U.S. Policy on Haiti."

134 See, e.g., Haitian Information Bureau, "Subverting Democracy," pp. 13–15; Cooley-Prost, *Democracy Intervention in Haiti*, pp. 14–15; Canham-Clyne, "US Policy on Haiti."

135 For analysis of the invasion and its relation to "democracy promotion" intervention, see, among others, William I. Robinson, "Haiti: Behind the Occupation is Washington's Elusive Goal of Stabilizing Elite Rule," *Notisur*, Latin America Data Base, Latin American Institute, University of New Mexico, vol. 4, no. 37 (October 7, 1994); Jane Regan, "A.I.D.ing U.S. Interests in Haiti," *Covert Action Quarterly*, no. 51 (Winter 1994–95); Kim Ives, "The Second U.S. Occupation," *NACLA Report on the Americas*, 28 (1995), no. 4, 6–10.

136 Ernest H. Preeg, "The Haitian Challenge in Perspective," in Georges Fauriol (ed.), *The Haitian Challenge: U.S. Policy Considerations* (Washington D.C.: Center for Strategic and International Studies, 1993), p. 2. Preeg was U.S. ambassador to Haiti from 1981 to 1983, and was then transferred to Manila, where he partook in the "transition" in that country.

137 The company official was Charles McKay, as quoted in "Massive Foreign Assistance Expected to Pour Into Haiti," *Chronicle of Latin American Economic Affairs*, Latin America Data Base, Latin American Institute, University of New Mexico vol. 9, no. 39 (October 20, 1994).

138 Cited in Allan Nairn, "Occupation Haiti: The Eagle is Landing," *The Nation*, 259 (1994), no. 7, 344.

139 Ibid.

140 Cited in *ibid*.

141 AID, "U.S.AID/Haiti Briefing Book," Washington, D.C., November 1994.

142 See, e.g., "Massive Foreign Assistance Expected to Pour into Haiti"; "Haiti: U.S. Plan for Economic Recovery Depends Heavily on Private Sector Reactivation," *Chronicle of Latin American Economic Affairs*, Latin America Data Base, Latin American Institute, University of New Mexico vol. 10, no. 18 (May 4, 1995); Douglas Farah, "$1.2 billion to Build Haiti from Scratch," *Washington Post*, October 21, 1994, A-1. On the details of the neo-liberal program, see "République d'Haiti Strategy for Social and Economic Reconstruction," and "Statement by Hon. Mark Schneider, World Bank Informal Donors Meeting, August 26, 1994," reproduced as Annexes B and A, respectively, in AID, "U.S.AID/Haiti Briefing Book."

143 Regan, "A.I.D.ing U.S. Interests," p. 12.

144 Cited in Ives, 'Second U.S. Occupation," p. 10.

145 Regan, "A.I.D.ing U.S. Interests," p. 13.

146 See, e.g., "Haiti: New Prime Minister Names Cabinet as First Step in Socioeconomic Reconstruction," *Chronicle of Latin American Economic Affairs*, Latin America Data Base, Latin American Institute, University of New Mexico, vol. 9, no. 42 (November 10, 1994).

147 Catherine S. Manegold, "Aristide Picks a Prime Minister with Free-Market Ideas," *New York Times,* October 25, 1994, A-1.
148 For details, see Regan, "A.I.D.ing U.S. Interests," p. 11; Nairn, "Occupation Haiti."
149 Establishing precise figures for these programs is difficult because they were so extensive, overlapping and handled by numerous public and quasi-private agencies, and budgets were constantly being redrawn. The $85 million figure is cited in "Statement by Hon. Mark Schneider," p. 4. See also AID, "U.S.AID/Haiti Elections Factsheet, March 10, 1995"; Voices for Haiti, "A Report on U.S. Elections Assistance to Haiti," Washington, D.C., June 1995; AID, Bureau of Legislative and Public Affairs, "Fact Sheet: Haiti Recovery Program," Washington D.C, undated, distributed to journalists in mid-October 1994. Apart from overt but nearly-impossible-to-track political aid, the Clinton administration approved a $5 million CIA covert program for unspecified "political activities." See Elaine Sciolino, "C.I.A. Reportedly Taking a Role in Haiti," *New York Times,* September 28, 1994, A-7.
150 Cited in Regan, "A.I.D.ing U.S. Interests," p. 12.
151 Cited in "A Democracy Made of Cardboard," *Briefing* (Haiti Support Group), no. 12 (April 1995), p. 1, reprinted in *Haitian News and Resource Service*, Washington Office on Haiti, Washington, D.C., April–June 1995.
152 Cited in Nairn, "Occupation Haiti," p. 348.
153 Ives, "'Unmaking of a President," pp. 17, 23.
154 Amilcar Cabral, *Revolution in Guinea* (New York, Monthly Review, 1969).
155 Jean Casimir (interview), "Haiti After the Coup," *World Policy Journal*, 9 (1992), 354, 357.
156 J. P. Slavin, "Haiti: The Elite's Revenge," *NACLA Report on the Americas*, 25 (1991), no. 3, 4.
157 Casimir, "Haiti After the Coup," p. 354.
158 *Ibid.*, p. 352.
159 Further discussion is not possible here, but note that this fact poses a challenge to both the transnational elite project and to popular leaders and leftist intellectuals who have argued that formal state power in the new world order is no longer necessary.

7 Conclusions: The future of polyarchy and global society

1 Barnet and Muller, *Global Reach*, p. 190.
2 Eric Wolf, *Europe and the People Without History* (Berkeley: University of California Press, 1982), p. 3.
3 Carl Bernstein, "The Holy Alliance," *Time*, February 24, 1992, 28–35, at p. 30.
4 For a review of the Eastern European revolutions of 1989 and their aftermath, see John Feffer, *Shock Waves: Eastern Europe After the Revolutions* (Boston: South End, 1992). Feffer interviewed hundreds of grassroots leaders, politicians, and intellectuals who led the revolutions. The predo-

minant vision among them was not an emulation of Western capitalism but the construction of an authentically democratic socialism.

5 Among other sources, the following section is based on: "Support for Eastern European Democracy, National Endowment for Democracy: Proposal for Program to Support East European Democracy," January 1990, obtained through the FOIA; NED Annual Bulletins, 1984–1992; *Covert Action Information Bulletin*, no. 35 (Fall 1990), special issue, "Friendly Enemies: The CIA in Eastern Europe"; Sean Gervasi, "Western Intervention in the Soviet Union," *Covert Action Information Bulletin*, no. 39 (Winter 1991–2), 4–9; Kevin Coogan and Katrina Vanden Huevel, "U.S. Funds for Soviet Dissidents," *The Nation*, March 19, 1988, 377–381; Council on Hemispheric Affairs/Resource Center, *National Endowment for Democracy*.

6 Bernstein, "The Holy Alliance," pp. 28–29.

7 *Ibid.*, 34. For a detailed analysis of the destabilization strategy, see Gervasi, "Western Intervention."

8 NED Annual Reports, 1984–1992.

9 Gershman, "United States," pp. 131–132.

10 David Ignatius, "Spyless Coups," *Washington Post*, September 22, 1991, C-1.

11 The "strategy paper" is cited and discussed in Gervasi, "Western Intervention," pp. 5–6.

12 For CFD programs, see NED Annual Reports, 1984–1992. For the specific citations, see 1988 Report, p. 27.

13 For NED funding to the IRG, see NED Annual Reports, 1989–1991. For general discussion, see Russ Bellant and Louis Wolf, "The Free Congress Foundation Goes East," *Covert Action Information Bulletin*, no. 35 (Fall 1990), 29–32; Sara Diamond, "Contra Funders Aid Soviet Right," *Guardian*, September 26, 1990, 16. For analyses (among many) of different factions that emerged following the demise of the USSR and the inklings of transnationalized fractions, see: Fred Weir, "An Interview with Roy Medvedev," *Monthly Review* 44 (1993), no. 9, 1–10; Roger Burbach, "Russia's Upheaval," *ibid.*, 11–24.

14 Yeltsin sent a fax from Moscow to CFD president Allen Weinstein four days after the failure of the attempted *coup d'état* on August 19, 1991: "I thank you for the sincere congratulations you sent me in connection with the victory of the democratic forces and the failure of the attempted August 19, 1991 coup. We know and appreciate the fact that you contributed to this victory." Translation from the Russian of the fax from "B. Yeltsin" to "Allen Weinstein, President, National Endowment for Democracy, Washington, D.C., U.S.A.," August 23, 1991, as reported in Gervasi, "Western Intervention," p. 4.

15 See NED Annual Reports and Bellant and Wolf, "Free Congress Foundation," pp. 30–31.

16 For strategic discussion from within the extended policymaking community on how to proceed with the transnational project, see Charles Wolf, Jr.

(ed.), *Promoting Democracy and Free Markets in Eastern Europe: A Sequoia Seminar* (San Francisco: Institute for Contemporary Studies, 1992); Shafiqul Islam and Michael Mandelbaum (eds.), *Making Markets: Economic Transformation in Eastern Europe and the Post-Soviet States* (New York: Council on Foreign Relations, 1993).

17 NED Annual Report, 1987, p. 15.

18 Mohamed A. El-Khawas and Barry Cohen (eds.), *National Security Study Memorandum 39: The Kissinger Study of Southern Africa* (Westport: Lawrence Hill, 1976).

19 Works on US policy toward South Africa are voluminous. See, e.g., Kevin Danaher, *The Political Economy of U.S. Policy Towards South Africa* (Boulder: Westview, 1985). On the relation between transnational capital, South Africa, and the southern and central African political economy, see Ann Seidman and Neva Seidman Makgetla, *Outposts of Monopoly Capitalism: Southern Africa in the Changing Global Economy* (Westport: Lawrence Hill, 1980). The strategic thinking in the extended policymaking community and the transnational elite on South Africa is summarized in a series of studies commissioned by the Council on Foreign Relations (CFR), funded by the Ford Foundation, and published by the CFR-affiliated Foreign Policy Association (New York) in the late 1980s and early 1990s under the heading "South Africa Update Series." Among others, volumes included Pauline Baker, *The United States and South Africa: The Reagan Years* (1989); Robert Schrire, *Adapt or Die: The End of White Politics in South Africa* (1991); Tom Lodge, *et al.*, *All, Here, and Now: Black Politics in South Africa in the 1980s* (1991).

20 See Study Commission on US Policy Toward South Africa, *South Africa: Time Running Out* (Berkeley: University of California Press, 1981).

21 The Act was passed in the House by a 317–83 margin, and in the Senate by a 78–21 margin. For a summary discussion, see R. Hunt Davis and Peter J. Schraeder, "South Africa," in Schraeder (ed.) *Intervention In the 1980s*.

22 *Ibid.*, p. 265.

23 *Ibid.*, p. 266.

24 *Ibid.* The "Inkathagate" scandal of 1991 revealed that Buthelezi and Inkatha had been built up by the South African government as a rival to the ANC and led to a loss of Inkatha credibility as an alternative to the ANC.

25 NED Annual Report, 1985, p. 26.

26 See NED Annual Bulletins, 1985–1992.

27 AID, as cited in Davis and Schraeder, "South Africa," p. 265.

28 For a breakdown of these programs, see NED Annual Reports, 1986–1992. For discussions, see Council on Hemispheric Affairs/Resource Center, *National Endowment for Democracy*, pp. 52, 63, 65–67; Beth Sims, *Workers of the World Undermined: American Labor and the Pursuit of U.S. Foreign Policy* (Albuquerque: Resource Center, 1991), pp. 15–16, 45, 58, 64, 69; Davis and Schraeder, "South Africa," pp. 264–266.

29 These figures are obtained from the NED Annual Reports for 1984–1992. Regarding the European category, five of the countries were not specifically Eastern or Central Europe. They were Northern Ireland, Portugal, Spain, Greece, and France.

30 NED, Minutes of the Annual Meeting of the Board of Directors of the National Endowment for Democracy Washongton. D.C., January 22, 1993 3, obtained through the FOIA.

31 There are hundreds of concrete examples as documented in the NED Annual Reports. For instance, the 1991 Report includes a program "for international participants representing organizations engaged in educational reform to review civic education and methodologies and materials that promote an understanding of democracy in the formal and informal educational system" (p. 68). A program such as this, which links the curricula of educational systems of different countries – and injects into those curricula the ideology and outlook of the transnational elite agenda – should be seen as movement towards organic linkage of the institutions of the Gramscian extended state across nations (in this case educational systems), indicating transnationalization of the extended state.

32 United Nations Development Program (UNDP), *Human Development Report 1992* (New York: UNDP/Oxford University Press, 1992), pp. 35–36.

33 *Ibid.*, p. 34.

34 For data and analysis on income polarization, see Denny Braun, *The Rich Get Richer: The Rise of Income Inequality in the United States and the World* (Chicago: Nelson-Hall, 1991). See also Robert B. Reich, *The Work of Nations*, 2nd edn. (New York: Vintage Books, 1992), although Reich's solution is utopian: a call for that 20 percent of the population advancing under the global economy to resolve the crisis of polarization by being more sharing and concerned about the plight of the other 80 percent.

35 US Bureau of the Census, as cited in Jerry S. Kloby, "Increasing Class Polarization in the United States," in Berch Berberoglu (ed.), *Critical Perspectives in Sociology*, 2nd edn. (Dubuque, Ia.: Kendal/Hunt, 1993) pp. 27–43. The following data are from the Bureau, as cited by Kloby, unless otherwise indicated.

36 See, e.g., William I. Robinson, "The Global Economy and Latino Populations in the United States: A World Systems Approach," *Critical Sociology*, 19 (1993), no. 2, 29–59.

37 Edward A. Muller, "Democracy, Economic Development, and Income Inequality," *American Sociological Review*, 53 (1988), 50–68, at p. 56. Muller also published an earlier study indicating a direct correlation between socioeconomic inequalities and political instability: "Income Inequality, Regime Repressiveness, and Political Violence," *American Sociological Review*, 50 (1985), 47–61.

38 Agency for International Development, Department of State, "The Democracy Initiative," Washington, D.C., December 1990, p. 3.

39 Quoted in V. I. Lenin, *Imperialism, the Highest Stage of Capitalism* (Moscow: Progress Publishers, 1978 [1917]), p. 75.
40 The 1900 figure is cited in Barnet and Muller, *Global Reach*, p. 190; the 1960 figure is from the UNDP report.
41 Mosca, *Ruling Class*, p. 62.
42 *Ibid.*, p. 71.
43 Literature on the philosophical and ideological roots and evolution of classical "democratic" thought is vast. See, e.g., C. B. MacPherson, *The Political Theory of Possessive Individualism* (London: Oxford University Press, 1962), and "Politics: Post-Liberal-Democracy?," in Robin Blackburn (ed.), *Ideology in Social Science: Readings in Critical Social Theory* (London: Fontana/Collins, 1972); George Novack, *Democracy and Revolution* (New York: Pathfinder, 1971); Herbert Aptheker, *The Nature of Democracy, Freedom and Revolution* (New York: International Publishers, 1967); David Held, *Political Theory and the Modern State: Essays on State, Power, and Democracy* (Stanford: Stanford University Press, 1989).
44 Cited in Novack, *Democracy and Revolution*, p. 181.
45 Cited in Aptheker, *Nature of Democracy*, p. 27.
46 Novack, *Democracy and Revolution*, p. 144.
47 Polanyi, *Great Transformation*.
48 Poulantzas, *Political Power and Social Classes*.
49 Alan Wolfe, *The Seamy Side of Democracy: Repression in America* (New York: David McKay, 1973).
50 Therborn, "Rule of Capital", p. 3. More explicitly, the "Marxist paradox" is how a tiny minority rules through democratic means, and the "bourgeois paradox" is how to assure private property and minority rule under democracy.
51 Novack, *Democracy and Revolution*.
52 Moore, *Social Origins*.
53 Dietrich Rueschemeyer, Evelyne Huber Stephens, and John D. Stephens, *Capitalist Development and Democracy* (Chicago: Chicago University Press, 1992).
54 This point is important, since it often escapes the process-oriented approaches, such as that advanced by Reinhard Bendix in *Nation-Building and Citizenship: Studies of our Changing Social Order* (New York: Wiley, 1964), as well as much of the more recent "transitions" and "democratization" literature which stresses "democratization" as a strictly intra-elite affair.
55 Therborn, "Rule of Capital."
56 Huntington, "Modest Meaning," p. 19.
57 That promoting polyarchy would increasingly be accompanied by other types of transnational intervention, such as military action, was suggested by Morton Halperin, US Assistant Secretary of Defense for Democracy and Peacekeeping: "The United States, the United Nations, and regional organizations should insist on a guarantee clause by which they ensure

the maintenance of constitutional democracy. An international guarantee clause will be credible only if key countries, including the United States, commit to using force if necessary to restore or establish constitutional democracy" ("Guaranteeing Democracy," in *Foreign Policy*, no. 91 [Summer 1993], 121). If US marines intervened unilaterally in the past to shore up pro-US authoritarian regimes, now US and other international forces would intervene, through multilateral umbrellas under the pretext of "peacekeeping," "humanitarian missions," and "defense of democracy," to install, defend from threats (particularly from popular sectors transgressing the "legitimate" rules of polyarchy) and/or bolster elites around the world organized politically in polyarchic regimes.

58 See, among other sources, NED Annual Report, 1992, p. 9.

59 See Minutes of the Annual Meeting of the Board of Directors of the National Endowment of Democracy, Washington, D.C., January 22, 1993, p. 3, obtained through the FOIA.

60 NED Annual Report, 1992, p. 9.

61 These developments are discussed in a special issue of the *Journal of Democracy* (4 (1993), no. 3), "International Organizations and Democracy."

62 These are discussed in various articles in *ibid*.

63 For discussion, see Joan M. Nelson and Stephanie J. Eglinton, *Encouraging Democracy: What Role for Conditional Aid?* (Washington, D.C.: Overseas Development Council, 1993).

64 Sunkel and Fuenzalida, "Transnationalization," p. 82.

65 See Gilpin, *Political Economy*; Gill, *American Hegemony*.

66 Sklair, *Sociology of the Global System*, p. 5.

67 Gilpin, *Political Economy*, p. 254.

68 World Bank, *Global Economic Prospects and the Developing Countries*, World Bank Annual Report, 1992 (Washington D.C.: World Bank, 1992), p. 33, as cited in Doug Henwood, "Impeccable Logic: Trade, Development and Free Markets in the Clinton Era," *NACLA Report on the Americas*, 26 (1993), no. 5, p. 26.

69 United Nations Centre on Transnational Corporations, *World Investment Report 1991* (New York: United Nations, 1991). In 1992, the Centre changed its name to the Transnational Corporations and Management Division, but its report retained the same title (*World Investment Report 1992*).

70 This was the case, e.g., regarding the Pentagon's classified "Defense Planning Guidance – 1994–99," leaked to the *New York Times*, March 8, 1992 ("U.S. Strategy Plan Calls for Insuring No Rivals Develop, A-1), which called for a military policy to ward off "competitor" nation-states and preserve US state domination. The point is that the emergence of a transnationalized elite is an exceedingly complex process that should be seen in longer historical terms than just from one US administration to the next, and states remain highly complex institutions involving intricate,

multifarious processes, fractions, pulls and tugs at play, and so forth. The social scientist must be able to extract from day-to-day and year-to-year events, and from policymakers' own perceptions and statements on those events.

71 For instance, the Uruguay round of the GATT gave the World Trade Organization powers to oversee compliance with the agreement over any one nation-state.

72 Gilpin, *Political Economy*, p. 153.

73 See, e.g., John M. Goshko, " 'Super State Department' May Absorb Other Agencies," *Washington Post*, January 11, 1995, A-1.

74 Cited in Henwood, "Impeccable Logic," p. 28.

75 Space constraints preclude discussion. This distinction between "hegemony based on fraud" and "ethical hegemony" was brought to my attention in personal correspondence with Craig Murphy, and is discussed in Augelli and Murphy, *America's Quest for Supremacy*.

76 See, for instance, Dean E. Murphy, "Amnesty International Blasts U.S. on Refugee Treatment," *Los Angeles Times*, June 27, 1992.

77 The 1960–1980 doubling figure is cited in Reich, *Work of Nations*, p. 269. The 1980–1990 figure is from a US Department of Justice report released in June 1994 and reported by an Associated Press dispatch, datelined Washington, June 1, 1994.

78 *Ibid.*, p. 269.

79 Economic Commission for Latin America and the Caribbean, as reported in *Chronicle of Latin American Economic Affairs*, Latin America Data Base, Latin American Institute, University of New Mexico, December 3, 1992.

80 See, for instance, Leslie Wirpsa, " 'Social Cleansing' Haunts Bogota's Indigent," *Latinamerica Press*, 26 (1994), no. 1, 4. The article reported at least 505 such documented killings in Bogota alone in 1993. The systematic rounding up and mass killing of "street children" in Guatemala, Brazil, and other countries became major scandals in the early 1990s. The 90,000 figure was reported by the Latin American Human Rights Association. See "Human rights suffer in 1993" (unsigned), in *ibid.*, 4.

81 For chilling analysis of such new forms of social control, see Mike Davis's two-part article in *New Left Review*: "Who Killed Los Angeles: A Political Autopsy," no. 198 (March/April 1993), 3–28; "Who Killed Los Angeles? Part II: The Verdict is Given," no. 199 (May/June 1993), 29–54; Mike Davis, *City of Quartz: Excavating the Future in Los Angeles* (London: Verso, 1990).

82 Sklair, *Sociology of the Global System*, p. 41.

83 Nicos Poulantzas, *Classes in Contemporary Capitalism* (London: New Left Books, 1975), p. 18.

84 Karl Marx referred to a "class-in-itself" as the objective status of a class defined by its relation to the production process, and a "class-for-itself" as a class as class protagonist, dependent on the extent to which a class (or classes) becomes conscious of itself. Only a "class-for-itself" becomes a political actor. Wallerstein has argued that there is an antinomy in the

capitalist world system between "class-in-itself" defined by relations to a world economy, and "class-for-itself" defined by classes as political actors located in particular nation-states – an antinomy between "class-in-itself" in the world system and "class-for-itself" in the nation-state. Wallerstein, *The Capitalist World Economy*, p. 196. However, it seems fairly logical that globalization is dissolving this antinomy.

85 See, for instance, discussion of this process in Latin America in Robinson, "The São Paulo Forum."

86 Robert Barros, "The Left and Democracy: Recent Debates in Latin America," *Telos*, no. 68 (Summer 1986), 49–70, at pp. 64–65.

87 Cited in Vanden and Prevost, *Democracy and Socialism*, p. 17.

88 Andrew Webster, *Introduction to the Sociology of Development*, 2nd edn. (London: Macmillan, 1990), p. 5.

Select bibliography

Books

Abbott, Elizabeth. *Haiti: The Duvaliers and their Legacy*. New York: Simon and Schuster, 1988.

Alford, Robert R., and Friedland, Roger. *Powers of Theory: Capitalism, the State, and Democracy*. Cambridge: Cambridge University Press, 1985.

Ambrose, Stephen E. *Rise to Globalism: American Foreign Policy Since 1938*, 7th edn. New York: Penguin, 1993.

Arriagada, Genaro. *Pinochet: The Politics of Power*. Boston: Unwin Hyman, 1988.

Augelli, Enrico, and Murphy, Craig. *America's Quest for Supremacy and the Third World: A Gramscian Analysis*. London: Pinter, 1988.

Bachrach, Peter. *The Theory of Democratic Elitism: A Critique*. Lanham, Md.: University of America Press, 1980.

Barnet, Richard J., and Muller, Ronald E. *Global Reach: The Power of the Multinational Corporation*. New York: Simon and Schuster, 1974.

Bellegarde-Smith, Patrick. *Haiti: The Breached Citadel*. Boulder: Westview, 1989.

Bermann, Karl. *Nicaragua and the United States since 1848*. Boston: South End, 1986.

Black, George. *Triumph of the People: The Sandinista Revolution in Nicaragua*. London: Zed, 1981.

Blum, William. *The CIA: A Forgotten History*. London: Zed, 1986.

Bonner, Raymond. *Waltzing with a Dictator*. New York: Times Books, 1987.

Braun, Denny. *The Rich Get Richer: The Rise of Income Inequality in the United States and the World*. Chicago: Nelson Hall, 1991.

Castro, Vanessa, and Prevost, Gary (eds.). *The 1990 Elections in Nicaragua and their Aftermath*. Lanham, Md.: Rowman and Littlefield, 1992.

Cohen, Carl. *Democracy*. New York: The Free Press, 1971.

Constable, Pamela, and Valenzuela, Arturo. *A Nation of Enemies: Chile Under Pinochet*. New York: W. W. Norton, 1991.

Cooley-Prost, Worth. *Democracy Intervention in Haiti: The USAID Democracy Enhancement Project*. Washington, D.C.: Washington Office on Haiti, 1994.

Cox, Robert W. *Production, Power, and World Order: Social Forces in the Making of History*. New York: Columbia University Press, 1987.

Crozier, Michel, Huntington, Samuel P., and Watanuki, Joji. *The Crisis of Democracy: Report on the Governability of Democracies to the Trilateral Commission*. New York: New York University Press, 1975.

Dahl, Robert A. *Polyarchy: Participation and Opposition*. New Haven: Yale University Press, 1971.

Danaher, Kevin. *The Political Economy of U.S. Policy Towards South Africa*. Boulder: Westview, 1985.

Diamond, Larry, Linz, Juan J., and Lipset, Seymour Martin. *Democracy in Developing Countries*, 4 vols. Boulder: Lynne Rienner and the National Endowment for Democracy, 1989.

Domhoff, G. William. *Who Rules America Now?* 2nd edn. Englewood Cliffs: Prentice Hall, 1986.
  The Powers that Be. New York: Random House, 1978.
  The Higher Circles. New York: Random House, 1970.

Douglas, William. *Developing Democracy*. Washington, D.C.: Heldref, 1972.

Dye, T. R. *Who's Running America?*, 4th edn. Englewood Cliffs: Prentice Hall, 1986.

Easton, David. *A Systems Analysis of Political Life*. New York: Wiley, 1965.
  The Political System: An Inquiry into the State of Political Science. New York: Knopf, 1953.

El-Khawas, Mohamed A., and Cohen, Barry (eds.). *National Security Study Memorandum 39: The Kissinger Study of Southern Africa*. Westport, Conn.: Lawrence Hill, 1976.

Evans, Peter. *Dependent Development: The Alliance of Multinational, State, and Local Capital in Brazil*. Princeton: Princeton University Press, 1979.

Falcoff, Mark, Valenzuela, Arturo, and Purcell, Susan Kaufman. *Chile: Prospects for Democracy*. New York: Council on Foreign Relations, 1988.

Farmer, Paul. *The Uses of Haiti*. Monroe, Me.: Common Courage, 1994.

Fauriol, Georges A. (ed.). *The Haitian Challenge: U.S. Policy Considerations*. Washington, D.C.: Center for Strategic and International Studies, 1993.

Feffer, John. *Shock Waves: Eastern Europe After the Revolutions*. Boston: South End, 1992.

Ferguson, James. *Papa Doc, Baby Doc: Haiti and the Duvaliers*. New York: Blackwell, 1987.

Fishlow, Albert, Díaz-Alejandro, Carlos F., Fagen, Richard R., and Hansen, Roger, D. *Rich and Poor Nations in the World Economy*. New York: McGraw-Hill, 1978.

Gill, Stephen. *American Hegemony and the Trilateral Commission*. New York: Cambridge University Press, 1990.
  (ed.). *Gramsci, Historical Materialism, and International Relations*. New York: Cambridge University Press, 1993.

Gilpin, Robert. *The Political Economy of International Relations*. Princeton: Princeton University Press, 1987.

Select bibliography

Goldman, Ralph M., and Douglas, William A. (eds.). *Promoting Democracy: Opportunities and Issues.* New York: Praeger, 1988.

Goodno, James B. *The Philippines: Land of Broken Promises.* London: Zed, 1991.

Gramsci, Antonio. *Selections from Prison Notebooks.* New York: International Publishers, 1971.

Hamilton, Nora. *The Limits of State Autonomy: Post-Revolutionary Mexico.* Princeton: Princeton University Press, 1982.

Held, David. *Political Theory and the Modern State: Essays on State, Power, and Democracy.* Stanford: Stanford University Press, 1989.

Held, David, and Pollitt, Christopher (eds.). *New Forms of Democracy.* London: Sage, 1986.

Hunt, Alan (ed.). *Marxism and Democracy.* London: Lawrence and Wishart, 1980.

Huntington, Samuel, P. *Political Order in Changing Societies.* New Haven: Yale University Press, 1968.

Jensen, Paol. *The Garotte: The United States and Chile, 1970–1973,* 2 vols. Aarhus, Denmark: Aarhus University Press, 1988.

Kerkvliet, Benedict J., and Mojares, Resil B. (eds.). *From Marcos to Aquino: Local Perspectives on Political Transition in the Philippines.* Honolulu: University of Hawaii Press, 1991.

Klare, Michael T., and Kornbluh, Peter (eds.). *Low Intensity Warfare, Counterinsurgency, Proinsurgency, and Antiterrorism in the Eighties.* New York: Pantheon, 1988.

Kolko, Joyce. *Restructuring the World Economy.* New York: Pantheon, 1988.

Kornbluh, Peter. *Nicaragua, The Price of Intervention.* Washington, D.C.: Institute for Policy Studies, 1987.

Kramer, Daniel C. *Participatory Democracy: Developing Ideals of the Political Left.* Cambridge, Mass.: Schenkman, 1972.

Lenin, V. I. *Imperialism, the Highest Stage of Capitalism.* Moscow: Progress Publishers, 1978 (first published in 1917).

Lord, Carnes, and Barnett, Frank R. (eds.). *Political Warfare and Psychological Operations: Rethinking the U.S. Approach.* Washington, D.C.: National Defense University Press, 1988.

Lowenthal, Abraham (ed.). *Exporting Democracy: The United States and Latin America, Themes and Issues.* Baltimore: Johns Hopkins University Press, 1991.

Lukes, Steven. *Power: A Radical View.* London: Macmillan, 1974.

Lundahl, Mats. *Peasants and Poverty: A Study of Haiti.* London: Croom Helm, 1979.

McCormick, Thomas J. *America's Half Century: United States Foreign Policy in the Cold War.* Baltimore: Johns Hopkins University Press, 1989.

MacEwan, Arthur. *Debt and Disorder: International Economic Instability and U.S. Imperial Decline.* New York: Monthly Review, 1990.

MacEwan, Arthur, and Tabb, William K. *Instability and Change in the World Economy.* New York: Monthly Review, 1989.

Marchetti, Victor, and Marks, John D. *The CIA and the Cult of Intelligence.* New York: Dell, 1974.

Miliband, Ralph. *The State in Capitalist Society.* New York: Basic Books, 1969.

Millett, Richard. *Guardians of the Dynasty.* New York: Maryknoll, 1977.

Mills, C. Wright. *The Power Elite.* New York: Oxford University Press, 1959.

Moore, Barrington, *Social Origins of Dictatorship and Democracy: Lord and Peasant in the Making of the Modern World.* Boston: Beacon, 1966.

Mosca, Gaetano. *The Ruling Class.* New York: McGraw-Hill, 1965.

Munck, Ronaldo. *Latin America: The Transition to Democracy.* London: Zed, 1989.

Nelson, Joan M. and Eglinton, Stephanie J. *Encouraging Democracy: What Role for Conditional Aid?* Washington, D.C.: Overseas Development Council, 1993.

Norsworthy, Kent. *Nicaragua: A Country Guide.* Albuquerque: Inter-Hemi-spheric Education Resource Center, 1990.

Novack, George. *Democracy and Revolution.* New York: Pathfinder, 1971.

O'Connor, James. *The Fiscal Crisis of the State.* New York: St. Martin's Press, 1973.

Pastor, Robert. *Condemned to Repetition.* Princeton: Princeton University Press, 1987.

Petras, James, and Morley, Morris. *The United States and Chile: Imperialism and the Overthrow of the Allende Government.* New York: Monthly Review, 1975.

Polanyi, Karl. *The Great Transformation.* Boston: Beacon Press, 1957 (first published in 1944).

Poulantzas, Nicos. *Political Power and Social Classes.* London: New Left Books, 1975 (first published in 1968).

Classes in Contemporary Capitalism. London: New Left Books, 1975.

Prince, Rod. *Haiti: Family Business.* London: Latin American Bureau, 1985.

Putzel, James. *A Captive Land: The Politics of Agrarian Reform in the Philippines.* New York: Monthly Review, 1992.

Reich, Robert B. *The Work of Nations.* New York: Vintage Books, 1991.

Ridgewood, James. *The Haiti Files: Decoding The Crisis.* Washington, D.C.: Essential Books/Azul Editions, 1994.

Robinson, William, I. *A Faustian Bargain: U.S. Intervention in the Nicaraguan Elections and American Foreign Policy in the Post-Cold War World.* Boulder: Westview, 1992.

Robinson, William I., and Norsworthy, Kent. *David and Goliath: The U.S. War Against Nicaragua.* New York: Monthly Review, 1987.

Rueschemeyer, Dietrich, Stephens, Evelyne Huber, and Stephens, John D. *Capitalist Development and Democracy.* Chicago: Chicago University Press, 1992.

Saldomando, Angel, *El Retorno de la AID, Caso de Nicaragua: Condicionalidad y Reestructuracion Conservadora.* Managua: Ediciones CRIES, 1992.

Sater, William F. *Chile and the United States: Empires in Conflict.* Athens: University of Georgia Press, 1990.

Schirmer, Daniel B., and Shalom, Stephen Rosskamm. *The Philippines Reader: A History of Colonialism, Neocolonialism, Dictatorship, and Resistance.* Boston: South End, 1987.

Schoultz, Lars. *National Security and United States Policy toward Latin America.* Princeton: Princeton University Press, 1987.

Schraeder, Peter J. (ed.). *Intervention in the 1980s: U.S. Foreign Policy in the Third World.* Boulder: Lynne Rienner, 1989.

Schumpeter, Joseph A. *Capitalism, Socialism and Democracy,* 2nd edn. New York: Harper and Row, 1947.

Seidman, Ann, and Seidman, Neva Makgetla. *Outposts of Monopoly Capitalism: Southern Africa in the Changing Global Economy.* Westport, Conn.: Lawrence Hill, 1980.

Shaw, Earl L. (ed.). *Modern Competing Ideologies.* Lexington, Mass.: D. C. Heath, 1973.

Shoup, Laurence H. and Minter, William. *Imperial Brain Trust: The Council on Foreign Relations and United States Foreign Policy.* New York: Monthly Review, 1977.

Sims, Beth. *Workers of the World Undermined.* Boston: South End, 1993.

Sklair, Leslie. *Sociology of the Global System.* Baltimore: Johns Hopkins University Press, 1991.

Smirnow, Gabriel. *The Revolution Disarmed: Chile 1970–1973.* New York: Monthly Review, 1979.

Sobel, Lester A. (ed.). *Chile and Allende.* New York: Facts on File, 1974.

Study Commission on US Policy Toward South Africa. *South Africa: Time Running Out.* Berkeley: University of California Press, 1981.

Trouillot, Michel-Rolph. *Haiti, State against Nation: The Origins and Legacy of Duvalierism.* New York: Monthly Review, 1990.

Vanden, Harry E., and Prevost, Gary. *Democracy and Socialism in Sandinista Nicaragua.* Boulder: Lynne Rienner, 1993.

Van der Pijl, Kees. *The Making of an Atlantic Ruling Class,* London: Verso, 1984.

Vargas, Oscar René. *A Donde Va Nicaragua?: Perspectivas de una Revolucion Latinoamericana.* Managua: Ediciones Nicarao, 1991.

Walker, Thomas (ed.). *Reagan Versus the Sandinistas: The Undeclared War on Nicaragua.* Boulder: Westview, 1987.

Nicaragua: The First Five Years. New York: Praeger, 1985.

Wallerstein, Immanuel. *The Capitalist World Economy.* Cambridge: Cambridge University Press, 1979.

The Modern World System. New York: Academic Press, 1970.

Wiarda, Howard J. *The Democratic Revolution in Latin America: History, Politics and U.S. Policy.* New York: Holmes and Meier, 1990.

Wilentz, Amy. *The Rainy Season: Haiti Since Duvalier.* New York: Simon and Schuster, 1989.

Williams, William Appleman. *America Confronts a Revolutionary World.* New York: Morrow, 1976.

Zeitlin, Irving M. *Ideology and the Development of Sociological Theory*. Englewood Cliffs: Prentice Hall, 1990.

Articles, reports, and speeches

Agency for International Development, Department of State. "USAID/Haiti Briefing Book." Washington, D.C., November 1994.

"Country Development Strategy Statement: US AID/Nicaragua 1991–1996." Washington, D.C., June 14, 1991.

"The Democracy Initiative." Washington, D.C., December 1990.

"Philippine Assistance Strategy: US Fiscal Years 1991–1995." Washington, D.C., July 1990.

American Political Foundation. "A Commitment to Democracy: A Bipartisan Approach." Washington, D.C., November 30, 1983.

Americas Watch/National Coalition for Haitian Refugees. *Silencing a People: The Destruction of Civil Society in Haiti*. New York/Washington, D.C., February 1993.

Barros, Robert. "The Left and Democracy: Recent Debates in Latin America," *Telos*, no. 68 (Summer 1986), 49–70.

Bellant, Russ, and Wolf, Louis. "The Free Congress Foundation Goes East," *Covert Action Information Quarterly*, no. 35 (Fall 1990), 29–32.

Bello, Walden, and Gershman, John. "Democratization and Stabilization in the Philippines," *Critical Sociology*, 17 (1990), no. 1, 35–56.

Bernstein, Carl. "The Holy Alliance," *Time*, February 24, 1992, 28–35.

Burton, Sandra. "Aquino's Philippines: The Center Holds," *Foreign Affairs*, 65 (1987), no. 3, 525–537.

Canham-Clyne, John. "US Policy on Haiti: Selling Out Democracy," *Covert Action Quarterly*, no. 48 (Spring 1994), 4–9, 52–56.

Casimir, Jean. "Haiti After the Coup" (interview by John Canham-Clyne), *World Policy Journal*, 9 (1992), no. 2, 349–364.

Colby, William E. "Political Action – In the Open," *Washington Post*, March 14, 1982, D-8.

Committee of Santa Fe. *A New Inter-American Policy for the Eighties*. Santa Fe: Council for Inter-American Security, 1980.

Coogan, Kevin, and Huevel, Katrina Vanden. "US Funds for Soviet Dissidents," *The Nation*, March 19, 1988, 377–381.

Council on Hemispheric Affairs/Inter-Hemispheric Education Resource Center. *National Endowment for Democracy (NED): A Foreign Policy Branch Gone Awry*. Washington, D.C./Albuquerque, 1990.

Cox, Robert, W. "Gramsci, Hegemony and International Relations: An Essay in Method," *Millennium: Journal of International Relations*, 12 (1983), no. 2, 162–175.

"Social Forces, States and World Orders: Beyond International Relations Theory," *Millennium: Journal of International Studies*, 10 (1981), no. 2, 126–155.

"Ideologies and the New International Economic Order: Reflections on Some Recent Literature," *International Organization*, 33 (1979), no. 2, 257–302.

Department of State. "Democracy in Latin America and the Caribbean: The Promise and the Challenge." Bureau of Public Affairs, Special Report no. 158. Washington, D.C., March 1987.

Dinges, John. "The Rise of the Opposition," *NACLA Report on the Americas*, 17 (1983), no. 5, 16–26.

Gallie, W. B. "Essentially Contested Concepts," *Aristotelian Society*, no. 56 (1956), 167–198.

General Accounting Office. *Events Leading to the Establishment of the National Endowment for Democracy*. GAO/NSIAD-84-121, July 6, 1984.

Promoting Democracy: Foreign Affairs and Defense Agencies' Funds and Activities – 1991 to 1993. GAO/NSIAD-94-83, January 1994.

Gershman, Carl. "The United States and the World Democratic Revolution," *Washington Quarterly*, Winter 1989, 127–139.

"Fostering Democracy Abroad: The Role of the National Endowment for Democracy," speech delivered to the American Political Science Foundation Convention, August 29, 1986.

Gervasi, Sean. "Western Intervention in the Soviet Union," *Covert Action Information Bulletin*, no. 39 (Winter 1991–2), 4–9.

Gill, Stephen, and Law, David. "Global Hegemony and the Structural Power of Capital," *International Studies Quarterly*, 33 (1989), no. 4, 475–499.

Gordon, David. "The Global Economy: New Edifice or Crumbling Foundations?" *New Left Review*, no. 168 (March/April 1988), 24–64.

Halperin, Morton H. "Guaranteeing Democracy," *Foreign Policy*, no. 91 (Summer 1993), 105–106.

Hersh, Seymour M. "The Price of Power: Kissinger, Nixon, and Chile," *Atlantic Monthly*, 250 (1982), no. 6, 21–58.

Huntington, Samuel, P. "The Modest Meaning of Democracy," in Robert A. Pastor (ed.), *Democracy in the Americas: Stopping the Pendulum*. New York: Holmes and Meier, 1989.

"Will More Countries Become Democratic?" *Political Science Quarterly*, 99 (1984), no. 2, 193–218.

Inter-Hemispheric Education Resource Center. "Populism, Conservatism, and Civil Society in Haiti," *The NED Backgrounder* (Albuquerque), 1 (1992), no. 2.

Ives, Kim. "The Unmaking of a President," *NACLA Report on the Americas*, 27 (1994), no. 4, 16–29.

Kesselman, Mark. "Order or Movement? The Literature of Political Development as Ideology," *World Politics*, 26 (1973), no. 1, 139–154.

Landis, Fred. "C.I.A. Psychological Warfare Operations: Case Studies in Chile, Jamaica, and Nicaragua," *Science for the People* January/February, 1982, 6–37.

Longchamp, Fritz, and Cooley-Prost, Worth. "Breaking with Dependency and Dictatorship: Hope for Haiti," *Covert Action Information Bulletin*, no. 36 (Spring 1991), 54–58.

Muller, Edward. A. "Democracy, Economic Development, and Income Inequality," *American Sociological Review*, 53 (1988), 50–68.

"Inequality, Regime Repressiveness, and Political Violence," *American Sociological Review*, 50 (1985), 47–61.

National Endowment for Democracy. "International Organizations and Democracy," special issue, *Journal of Democracy*, 4 (1993), no. 3.

Annual Reports, 1984–1992. Washington D.C.

National Security Council, Memorandum NSC-68 (April 7, 1950). *Foreign Relations of the United States* (*FRUS*), 1950, vol. I, pp. 235–292.

North American Congress on Latin America. "A Market Solution for the Americas?: The Rise of Wealth and Hunger," *NACLA Report on the Americas*, 26 (1993), no. 4.

Petras, James, and Morley, Morris H. "The US Imperial State," in James F. Petras (ed.), *Class, State and Power in the Third World*. Montclair, N.J.: Allanheld, Osmun, 1981.

Petras, James, and Vieux, Steve. "The Chilean 'Economic Miracle': An Empirical Critique," *Critical Sociology*, 17 (1990), no. 2, 56–72.

Reagan, Ronald. "Promoting Democracy and Peace," speech before the British parliament, June 8, 1982, *Current Policy*, no. 399 (June 1982), Department of State, Bureau of Public Affairs, Washington, D.C.

Regan, Jane. "A.I.D.ing US Interests in Haiti," *Covert Action Quarterly*, no. 51 (Winter 1994–5), 7–13, 56–58.

Robinson, William, I. "Pushing Polyarchy: The US–Cuba Case and the Third World," *Third World Review: Journal of Emerging Areas*, 16 (1995), 631–647.

"The São Paulo Forum: Is There a New Latin American Left?," *Monthly Review*, 44 (1992), no. 7, 1–12.

Robinson, William I., and Norsworthy, Kent. "Elections and US Intervention in Nicaragua," *Latin American Perspectives*, 12 (1985), no. 2, 83–110.

Samuels, Michael A., and Douglas, William A. "Promoting Democracy," *Washington Quarterly*, 4 (1981), no. 3, 52–65.

Schneider, Cathy. "The Underside of the Miracle," *NACLA Report on the Americas*, 26 (1993), no. 4, 18–19.

Scipes, Kim. "Aquino's Total War and the KMU," *Z Magazine*, 3 (1990), no. 1, 116–121.

Shorrock, Tim, and Selvaggio, Kathy. "Which Side Are You On, AAFLI?" *The Nation*, February 15, 1986.

Shultz, George. "Project Democracy," *Current Policy*, no. 456, Department of State, Bureau of Public Affairs, Washington, D.C., February 1983.

Sklar, Holly, and Berlet, Chip. "NED, CIA, and the Orwellian Democracy Project," *Covert Action Information Bulletin*, no. 39 (Winter 1991–2), 10–13, 59–62.

Sunkel, Osvaldo, and Fuenzalida, Edmundo F. "Transnationalization and its National Consequences," in Jose J. Villamil (ed.), *Transnational Capitalism and National Development: New Perspectives on Dependence*. Brighton: Harvester Press, 1979.

Therborn, Goran. "The Rule of Capital and the Rise of Democracy," *New Left Review*, no. 103 (May–June 1977), 3–41.

Select bibliography

United Nations Centre on Transnational Corporations. *World Investment Report 1991, World Investment Report 1992.* New York: United Nations. (In 1992, the Centre changed its name to the Transnational Corporations and Management Division.)

United Nations Development Program. *Human Development Report 1992.* New York: UNDP/Oxford University Press, 1992.

United States Congress, Select Committee to Study Governmental Operations with Respect to Intelligence Activities. *Interim Report: Alleged Assassination Plots Involving Foreign Leaders*, 94th Congress, 1st Session, November 10, 1975.

United States Senate, Select Committee to Study Governmental Operations with Respect to Intelligence Activities. *Covert Action in Chile, 1963–1973.* Washington, D.C., 1975.

Index

"1980s Project" (Council on Foreign Relations) 75, 76

AAFLI (Asian-American Free Labor Institute) 135, 137
Abrams, Elliot 168, 170, 180
Acheson, Dean 120
active consent
  and hegemony 21
Adams, Alvin P. 281–2
Adams, John 350
ADIH (Haitian Industrialists Association) 274–5, 277, 285
Adrien, Father Antoine 309
Afghanistan 92
AFL-CIO (American Federation of Labor-Congress of Industrial Organizations) 90, 95, 96
  and the Soviet bloc 322
Africa
  democracy promotion operations 332, 333
  US interventionism in 14
agrarian reform
  in Chile 165
  in Nicaragua 246–7
  in the Philippines 137–8, 142–4
AID (Agency for International Development) 48, 55–6, 82, 89, 93, 96, 98, 100, 365
  and Chile 184–5
  and Haiti 270, 271, 272, 279, 286, 287, 288–9, 292, 295, 296, 297, 309
  and Nicaragua 225, 226, 241, 242, 243, 244–5, 246–7; Strategy Statement 250, 251, 254
  and the Philippines 140, 143
  and South Africa 330–1

AIFLD (American Institute for Free Labor Development)
  and Haiti 288–9
  and Nicaragua 227, 234
Alessandri, Arturo 186
Alessandri, Jorge 157, 159
Alford, Robert 48, 52, 53
Algeria 113
Allen, Richard 90
Allende, Salvador 69, 87, 146, 156, 157, 159–63, 167, 218, 232
Alliance for Progress 48, 157–8, 269
Almond, Gabriel 46
Amnesty International 376
ANC (African National Congress) 327, 328, 329, 331
Angola 111, 328
APF (American Political Foundation) 89–91
APN (National Popular Assembly, Haiti) 282
Aquino, Benigno 123, 126
Aquino, Corazon 126, 127, 128–9, 130, 138–9, 140, 141, 142, 143, 225
Arbenz, Jacobo 87
Aristide, Father Jean-Bertrand 108, 257, 273, 280, 281, 284, 287, 288
  government 290–2, 293, 295–6, 314
  ousted by coup 297–302, 304
  return to power 305–11
Armitage, Richard 142
Arriagada, Genaro 174, 176, 183
Arrocha, Plutarco 224
associations
  and the CIA 86
asymmetry in international relations 18
  and hegemony 23–5
Augelli, Enrico 30, 77

451

Index

Schmitter, Philip 45, 64, 69
Schneider, Cathy 193
School for Democracy (Chile) 180
Schumpeter, Joseph 49, 51, 351
Senat, Joseph 289
Shafter, General 118
Shlauderman, Harry 242
Shultz, George 107, 170
Silva, Eduardo 152
Sklair, Leslie 40–1, 367, 378
slavery
    in Haiti 258–9, 260, 262
Smith, Adam 368
social apartheid
    in the United States 377–8
social control
    and polyarchy 71
    and reconstituting democracy 68–9
social instability
    causes of 339–45
social structure of accumulation 32
socialism
    and democracy 384
socioeconomic inequalities
    between rich and poor nations 339–41
    in Chile 196–7
    and globalization 339–44
    and labor structure 342
    in Nicaragua 211
    and social stability 375–6
    in the United States 341
socioeconomic system
    separation of politics from 53, 55
sociological imagination 14
SOFA (Haitian Women's Solidarity) 283
Somoza dictatorship (Nicaragua) 66, 76,
    122, 202, 209–15, 228
Sorel, George 348
South Africa 10, 16, 114, 319–20, 326–32
    apartheid 320, 328–30
    Assistance for Disadvantaged South
        Africans 330–1
    comparative perspective 333–9
    political parties 106
sovereignty
    and popular democracy 61–2
Soviet Union/Soviet bloc countries 3, 10
    and Chile 162
    collapse of 5, 93, 320, 326
    comparative perspective 333–9
    IRG (Inter-Regional Deputies Group)
        324–5
    and US foreign policy 78, 80–1, 113–14
    US intervention and globalization
        319–26

stability
    and the CIA 87
    and US foreign policy 17
state
    and civil society 27, 28, 39, 58, 152
    extended 21, 22–3, 28, 367–8, 370
    Gramscian concept of the 353–4
    "imperial state" 68
    imperialism and democracy 346–8
    managerial dilemma/fiscal crisis of the
        36
    and society, politics and power 26, 27
Stephens, Evelyne 357
Stephens, John 357
Stimpson, Henry 208
STR (scientific and technological
    revolution) 31–2
structural adjustment
    and Nicaragua 254
structural analysis 6, 10, 20–1, 318
    of capitalism and polyarchy 356
    and the Gramscian construct of
        hegemony 24, 25
    of the Philippines 123–4
structural autonomy 164
structural determinism 10
structural-conjunctural analysis 10, 21, 318
structural-functionalism
    and democratization 149
    and modernization theory 46
    politics and power 26
    and polyarchy 49
Sunkel, Osvaldo 33, 366
supranational institutions 372–4
SWAPO (South-West African People's
    Organization) 327

Taft, William 207
Talbott, Strobe 311
Thatcher, Margaret 225
Theberge, James 168
Therborn, Goran 355, 357, 358
Third World
    and the global economy 37
    and low-intensity warfare 80–1
    and modernization theory 46
    nationalist revolutions 74
    political and civic institutions 70
    and political development theory 47, 48
    prospects of democratization 344–5
    and US foreign policy 81–2; neo-
        conservative 76
TNCs (transnational corporations) 369,
    371, 384–5
TNPs (transnational practices) 40–1

CAMBRIDGE STUDIES IN INTERNATIONAL RELATIONS